THE OXFORD HIS

General I

The Oxford History of Anglicanism, Volume I
Reformation and Identity, c.1520–1662
Edited by Anthony Milton

The Oxford History of Anglicanism, Volume II
Establishment and Empire, 1662–1829
Edited by Jeremy Gregory

The Oxford History of Anglicanism, Volume III
Partisan Anglicanism and its Global Expansion, 1829–c.1914
Edited by Rowan Strong

The Oxford History of Anglicanism, Volume IV
Global Western Anglicanism, c.1910–present
Edited by Jeremy Morris

The Oxford History of Anglicanism, Volume V
Global Anglicanism, c.1910–2000
Edited by William L. Sachs

The Oxford History of Anglicanism, Volume III

Partisan Anglicanism and its Global Expansion, 1829–c.1914

Edited by
ROWAN STRONG

OXFORD
UNIVERSITY PRESS

OXFORD
UNIVERSITY PRESS

Great Clarendon Street, Oxford, OX2 6DP,
United Kingdom

Oxford University Press is a department of the University of Oxford. It furthers the University's objective of excellence in research, scholarship, and education by publishing worldwide. Oxford is a registered trade mark of Oxford University Press in the UK and in certain other countries

First published 2017
First published in paperback 2019

Published in the United States of America by Oxford University Press
198 Madison Avenue, New York, NY 10016, United States of America

British Library Cataloguing in Publication Data
Data available

Library of Congress Cataloging in Publication Data
Data available

ISBN 978–0–19–969970–4 (Hbk.)
ISBN 978–0–19–882230–1 (Pbk.)

Acknowledgements

The Oxford History of Anglicanism has been nearly a decade in the making, so it is important to acknowledge here people and institutions that would otherwise go unnoticed by you the reader. The first of these is Oxford University Press itself, which, in the person of its Commissioning Editor for Religion, Tom Perridge, responded so positively to the unprecedented concept of an extensive five-volume series on the history of one Christian denomination when I first presented it to him in 2007. The normal careful and critical review process of the Press for any publication proposal brought to the original proposal the insights of its anonymous readers, which resulted in a more international authorship and significantly improved the original concept. At every stage of its production, from writing, copy-editing, and final publication, the supportive and attentive work of the Tom Perridge and his team in the Religion department of the Press has proved to be a boon to the series's editorial team.

However, my idea for an historical series on Anglicanism, even with the endorsement of a world-class academic publisher, could only be realized by the hard work of many historians over a number of years. So this series could not have happened without an editorial team of world-class experts in their respective historical periods. Initially, editors Anthony Milton, Jeremy Gregory, and Jeremy Morris worked with me to frame and revise the successful publication proposal to OUP. Then, with the addition of William Sachs, they undertook the long years and onerous minute burdens of editors. I will greatly miss our annual meetings in Cambridge where the Anglican ball was tossed around, but I rejoice in the continued friendship of such significant scholars who managed to squeeze things Anglican into lives already crowded with the pressures of modern academic life. The quality of the series is a tribute to their prolonged commitment. But editors need something to edit. The positive response by an international variety of historians, some well-established scholars, others more new to our trade, was a gratifying endorsement of the importance of the project. It has also been a sign of their continued good will that they have borne with patience the constant requests for revisions that have come from their editors, and the general editor, who were not always experts in their various fields. The critical quality of the series, encompassing not just recent published work but also some fine original research, owes a great deal to the contributors' commitment to a high standard of historical analysis of Anglicanism. Their work, presented to the reader here, suggests that the turn to religion in the discipline of history has not at all sacrificed any of the usual rigorous critical standards demanded of historians.

Unlike some other historical series, this one has been researched, written, and published without any particular financial assistance, other than the usual employment provided by the institutions in which the contributors work. It is an indication of the difficulties faced by the Humanities in garnering support for research or substantial projects in most modern universities. For myself, I have to thank my own institution, Murdoch University, for its generous provision of a semester's research leave every three years, two periods of which were instrumental in the development and editing of the series. Colleagues in the Theology department of the School of Arts, Nancy Ault, Suzanne Boorer, Mark Jennings, Jeremy Hultin, Alex Jensen, and James Trotter, have been patient of my time spent on the series when the administrative demands on them have increased, as they have for academics in all universities. Conversations with some of my research students, particularly Robert Andrews, Peter Elliot, and John Cardell-Oliver were important avenues for academic debate around some of the historiographical ideas in the series, which were also floated in my classes at Murdoch University as well as at the Anglican theological college in Perth. As a financial partner in the Theology department at Murdoch University, the Anglican diocese of Perth has also assisted in funding aspects of my research leave. I was particularly aided by my time spent as a Visiting Fellow at Clare Hall, Cambridge, during research leave in 2012. That small and hospitable college of a great university has become a second home for myself, and Jill, my wife; and my ongoing Life Membership of the college, and the friendships made there, are the greatest boons I treasure from my work on the series.

Nevertheless, if I had realized quite what I was letting myself in for, and for how long, I might have been more aware of how time-consuming it would be, and how much it would devour of my time away from Jill and our family, especially during what became a period of major loss and grief. Yet throughout the project Jill has remained my greatest support, never doubting my abilities to complete the task, and giving of her own managerial skills to the editorial team as project manager for a period.

All good history is a communal endeavour, building on the work of scholars past and present. I have always been fascinated by the periods of history when scholarship was at its most creative, which were usually periods of unprecedented interchange such as the Republic of Letters of the eighteenth century, the European networks around Erasmus and the Protestant Reformers, and the inter-religious creativity of the twelfth century that prompted the West to create universities as sites of universal learning. This past decade, due to the rapid communication made possible by modern technology, I have been enabled from Perth, Australia, to be at the heart of a similar creative network. This series is the consequence of an international scholarly exchange in our contemporary world where the age-old scholarly pursuit of knowledge and truth for its own sake gets swamped in universities by the pressures of funding and bureaucratic demands of all kinds. So I am grateful to all those mentioned here who by their good will, hard work, support, and historical abilities have made such an outcome possible with respect to the history of Anglicanism.

Contents

List of Contributors

Robert M. Andrews is Honorary Research Associate at Murdoch University and Lecturer in Church History at the Catholic Institute of Sydney for Theology and Ministry. His main research interests focus on High Church Anglicanism in the eighteenth and nineteenth centuries. He is the author of *Lay Activism and the High Church Movement of the Late Eighteenth Century: The Life and Thought of William Stevens, 1732–1807* (2015).

Andrew Atherstone is Tutor in History and Doctrine, and Latimer Research Fellow at Wycliffe Hall, Oxford, and a member of Oxford University's Faculty of Theology and Religion. His books include *Oxford's Protestant Spy: The Controversial Career of Charles Golightly* (2007); *Archbishop Justin Welby: Risk-taker and Reconciler* (2014); *Evangelicalism and the Church of England in the Twentieth Century* (co-editor, 2014); and *The Journal of Bishop Daniel Wilson of Calcutta, 1845–1857* (2015).

Stewart J. Brown is Professor of Ecclesiastical History at the University of Edinburgh. He has published widely on the religious and social history of modern Britain and the empire. His books include *The National Churches in England, Ireland and Scotland 1801–46* (2001); *Providence and Empire: Religion, Politics and Society in the United Kingdom 1815–1914* (2008); and *The Oxford Movement: Europe and the Wider World* (co-edited with Peter Nockles) (2012).

Hilary M. Carey is a historian of religion. Since 2014 she has been Professor of Imperial and Religious History and Head of the School of Humanities at the University of Bristol. She has published widely on the history of religion in the British world, including *God's Empire* (2011) and *Religion and Greater Ireland* (co-edited with Colin Barr) (2015). She is currently working on a history of religion and convict transportation.

Mark D. Chapman is Professor of the History of Modern Theology at the University of Oxford and Vice-Principal of Ripon College, Cuddesdon. His books include *The Fantasy of Reunion: Anglicans, Catholics and Ecumenism, 1833–1882* (2014); *Anglican Theology* (2012); and *Anglicanism: A Very Short Introduction* (2006). He is also editor (with Martyn Percy and Sathianathan Clarke) of the *Oxford Handbook of Anglican Studies* (2015).

Allan K. Davidson taught Church history at St John's College, Auckland, and the University of Auckland. He has written extensively on New Zealand and Pacific religious history, and in retirement has edited: *Living Legacy: A History* *of the Anglican Diocese of Auckland* (2011); *A Controversial Churchman, essays on Bishop George and Sarah Selwyn* (2011); and (with Stuart Lange, Peter J. Lineham, and Adrienne Millar) *Te Rongopai 1814, essays marking the bicentenary of Christianity in New Zealand* (2014). He was appointed an Officer of the New Zealand Order of Merit for services to history in 2010.

Jeremy Dibble is Professor of Music at Durham University where, as part of his wider specialism in British music of the nineteenth and twentieth centuries, he has a particular interest in English Church music and hymnody. He has published monographs on Huber Parry (1992; rev. 1998), Charles Villiers Stanford (2002), and John Stainer (2007). His most recent monographs, *Michele Esposito* (2010) and *Hamilton Harty: Musical Polymath* (2013) reflect an interest in Irish music of the same period. He is presently working on a study of the music of Frederick Delius and an edition of essays on British musical criticism.

Diarmid A. Finnegan is Senior Lecturer in Human Geography in the School of Geography, Archaeology and Palaeoecology, Queen's University, Belfast. He is the author of *Natural History Societies and Civic Culture in Victorian Scotland* (2009) as well as several articles on the relations between science and religion in the nineteenth century.

Robert Eric Frykenberg, born and reared in India by missionaries, is Professor Emeritus of History and South Asian Studies, University of Wisconsin, Madison. An authority on local influence and central authority under the Raj, he is the author of numerous books and articles including *Christianity in India: Beginnings to the Present* (2008, 2010) and the editor of numerous other works, including *Christians and Missionaries in India: Cross-Cultural Communication since 1500* (2003) and *Pandita Ramabai's America: Conditions of Life in the United States* (2003).

Jane Garnett is Fellow and Tutor in History at Wadham College, Oxford. She has published widely on religious, intellectual, and cultural history, principally of the nineteenth to twenty-first centuries, and on themes of gender and visual culture over longer periods. Her book (co-authored with Gervase Rosser), *Spectacular Miracles: Transforming Images in Italy from the Renaissance to the Present* (2013) was jointly awarded the 2014 ACE/Mercers' International Book Award 'for a book which makes an outstanding contribution to the dialogue between religious faith and the visual arts'.

Carol Engelhardt Herringer is Professor of History at Wright State University. She is the author of *Victorians and the Virgin Mary: Religion and Gender in England, 1830–85* (2008) as well as a number of articles and book reviews on religious and cultural history in Victorian Britain. She is the co-editor (with Rowan Strong) of *Edward Bouverie Pusey and the Oxford Movement* (2012).

Ayla Lepine is a Visiting Fellow in the School of Philosophy and Art History at the University of Essex. Following a PhD on the Gothic Revival and theological architecture at the Courtauld Institute of Art, she has held postdoctoral fellowships at the Courtauld Research Forum and Yale's Institute of Sacred Music. An editor for *Marginalia Review of Books* and for Routledge's series on Religion, Architecture and Visual Culture, her recent publications include essays on modern medievalism (*Visual Representations*, 2016; *Architectural History*, 2014), the book *Revival: Memories, Identities, Utopias* (2015), and studies of Anglican visual culture for Yale's MAVCOR project.

Duane Alexander Miller is Adjunct Professor of Theology at St Mary's University in San Antonio, Texas, and Lecturer in Church History and Theology at Nazareth Evangelical Theological Seminary in Nazareth, Israel. Forthcoming publications are *Living among the Breakage: Contextual Theology-Making and ex-Muslim Christians* (Pickwick); *Two Stories of Everything: The Competing Metanarratives of Islam and Christianity* (Whitchurch); and he has co-authored with Azar Ajaj and Philip Sumpter, *Arab Evangelicals in Israel* (Pickwick). His main areas of interest are Anglican mission in the Ottoman Empire, contextual theologies, and religious conversion from Islam to Christianity.

Susan Mumm is Dean of Arts and Science at Queen's University and Principal Designate of Brescia University College. She has published two books on Anglican sisterhoods, *All Saints Sisters of the Poor: An Anglican Community in the Nineteenth Century* (2001), and *Stolen Daughters, Virgin Mothers: Anglican Sisterhoods in Victorian Britain* (1999).

James Pereiro is a Research Fellow in the University of Navarra. He has been a member of Oxford University History Faculty and published extensively on nineteenth-century ecclesiastical history. His latest book is *Theories of Development in the Oxford Movement* (2015).

David Rock is Research Professor at the University of California, Santa Barbara, and a specialist in the history of Latin America, principally Argentina. His works include *Argentina, 1516–1987* (1985); *Authoritarian Argentina: The Nationalist Movement, Its History and Its Impact* (1993); and chapters in *The Cambridge History of Latin America*. He is currently completing *Empire without Dominion: Britain and the British in the Rio de la Plata, 1800–2000.*

Brian Stanley is Professor of World Christianity, and Director of the Centre for the Study of World Christianity, in the University of Edinburgh. He has published widely on the history of the missionary movement and world Christianity, including *The World Missionary Conference, Edinburgh 1910* (2009). He is currently writing a world history of Christianity in the twentieth century for Princeton University Press.

Rowan Strong is Professor of Church History at Murdoch University, Perth, Australia. His publications on religion and Anglicanism in the nineteenth century and in the history of the British Empire include *Alexander Penrose Forbes: The First Tractarian Bishop* (1995); *Episcopalianism in the Nineteenth-Century: Religious Responses to a Modernizing Society* (2002); and *Anglicanism and the British Empire c.1700–1850* (2007). He is now working on religion and British migration into the British Empire in the nineteenth century; and the influence of the High Church party on early nineteenth-century Anglican imperial expansion.

Philip L. Wickeri is Advisor to the Archbishop on Theological and Historical Studies, Hong Kong Sheng Kung Hui, and teaches at Ming Hua Theological College. He is Adjunct Professor at the Graduate Theological Union, Berkeley, California (USA), and Visiting Professor in the Department of History, Shanghai University, China. His most recent book is *Christian Encounters with Chinese Culture: Essays on Anglican and Episcopal History in China* (2015), and he is author of the award winning *Reconstructing Christianity in China: K. H. Ting and the Chinese Church* (2007).

Emma Wild-Wood is Lecturer in World Christianities at the University of Cambridge and was previously Director of the Cambridge Centre for Christianity Worldwide. She is researching a book on religious encounter in colonial Uganda. She has written *Migration and Christian Identity in Congo (DRC)* (2008).

Peter W. Williams is Distinguished Professor Emeritus of Comparative Religion and American Studies at Miami University in Oxford, Ohio, USA. He is the author of *Popular Religion in America* (1980, 1989); *America's Religions* (1989, 2001, 2008, 2015); *Houses of God: Region, Religion and Architecture in the United States* (1997, 2000); and *Religion, Art, and Money: Episcopalians and American Culture from the Civil War to the Great Depression* (2016). He is also editor of four multi-volume reference sets and the nine-volume series *Studies in Anglican History* (1995–2004), sponsored by the Historical Society of the Episcopal Church.

John Wolffe is Professor of Religious History at the Open University and was recently an RCUK Global Uncertainties Leadership Fellow and President of the Ecclesiastical History Society. His publications include *A Short History of Global Evangelicalism* (with Mark Hutchinson) (2012); *Protestant–Catholic Conflict from the Reformation to the 21st Century* (2013); and *Irish Religious Conflict in Comparative Perspective* (2014).

Series Introduction

Rowan Strong

Even Henry VIII at his autocratic best could hardly have imagined that his Church of England would, nearly five centuries after he had replaced papal authority with his own, become a global Christian communion encompassing people and languages far beyond the English. Formally, Henry asserted his royal power over the national Church on a more global scale—on the imperial theory that 'this realm of England is an empire' asserted the Act in Restraint of Appeals (to Rome) in 1533. Yet this was sixteenth-century imperial theory serving a national end. England was an empire and therefore King Henry was an emperor, that is, a ruler who was the paramount earthly authority and consequently superior to the papacy. So Henry's Church of England was always a national project, meant first and foremost to be the Church of the English—all the English—who would, if necessary, be compelled to come in. That national politico-religious agenda—a Church of all the English with the monarchy as its supreme head—formed the thrust of the policy of all but one of the succeeding Tudor monarchs. However, that royal agenda of the inclusion of all the English lay at the heart of the problem of this national ecclesiastical project.

At no time since Henry VIII ushered in his religious revolution did all the English wish to be part of this Church of England, though for over two centuries the monarchy and the English ruling classes attempted to encourage, cajole, or compel everyone in England to at least attend their parish church on Sunday. In Henry's reign, religious dissent from this monarchical Church was disparate and small, partly because Henry ensured it was dangerous. So some advanced Evangelicals (as early Protestants were called), such as Robert Barnes and William Tyndale, were executed by the regime in the early years of the religious revolution. Later, some prominent conservatives influenced by Catholic reform, such as Bishop John Fisher, Sir Thomas More, and some members of particular observant religious orders, followed their Evangelical enemies to the scaffold or the block. As the Protestant Reformation unfolded, and Catholic reform began to gather definition, from the reign of Edward VI onwards, those among the English who dissented from, or who were dissatisfied with, this national Church began to increase in numbers. Even those within it argued among themselves as to what the Church of England stood for.

Consequently, the Church of England, and its later global Anglican expansion, was always a contested identity throughout its history. It was contested both by its own adherents and by its leadership. This series looks at the history of that contestation and how it contributed to an evolving religious identity eventually known as Anglican. The major question it seeks to address is: what were the characteristics, carriers, shapers, and expressions of an Anglican identity in the various historical periods and geographic locations investigated by the volumes in the series? The series proposes that Anglicanism was not a version of Christianity that emerged entire and distinct by the end of the so-called Elizabethan Settlement. Rather, the disputed and developing identity of the Church developed from Henry VIII's religious revolution began to be worked out in the various countries of the British Isles from the early sixteenth century, went into a transatlantic environment in the seventeenth century, and then evolved in an increasing global context from the eighteenth century onwards. The series proposes that the answer to 'what is an Anglican?' was always debated. Moreover, Anglican identity over time experienced change and contradiction as well as continuities. Carriers of this developing identity included formal ecclesiastical dimensions such as clergy, Prayer Books, theology, universities, and theological colleges. Also among such formal carriers of Anglican identity was the English (then the British) state, so this series also investigates ways in which that state connection influenced Anglicanism. But the evolution of Anglicanism was also maintained, changed, and expressed in various cultural dimensions, such as architecture, art, and music. In addition, the series pays attention to how Anglicanism interacted with national identities, helping to form some, and being shaped itself by others. Each volume in the series devotes some explicit attention to these formal dimensions, by setting out the various Anglican identities expressed in their historical periods by theology, liturgy, architecture, religious experience and the practice of piety, and its interactions with wider society and politics.

A word needs to be said about the use of the term 'Anglicanism' to cover a religious identity whose origins lie in the sixteenth century when the name was not known. While recognizing the anachronism of the term Anglicanism, it is the 'least-worst' appellation to describe this religious phenomenon throughout the centuries of its existence. It is a fallacy that there was no use of the term Anglicanism to describe the Church of England and its global offshoots before John Henry Newman and the Oxford Movement in the 1830s. Newman and his Tractarian *confreres* certainly gave wider publicity to the name by using it to describe the separate Catholic culture of their Church. However, its usage predates the Tractarians because French Catholic writers were using it in the eighteenth century. It has become acceptable scholarly usage to describe this version of Christianity for the centuries prior to the nineteenth, notwithstanding its admittedly anachronistic nature.[1] Into the nineteenth century

[1] John Spurr, *The Restoration Church of England* (New Haven, CT, 1991), pp. xiii–xiv; John Walsh, Colin Haydon, and Stephen Taylor (eds.), *The Church of England c.1689–c.1833*

contemporaries used the terms 'Church of England' or 'Churchmen' to encompass their Church, even in countries and colonies beyond England. However, these names are not acceptable or understood today with their formerly inclusive meaning. The latter is objectionable on gender terms; and the former, while used by Anglicans in a variety of different lands and cultures, only leads to confusion when addressing the Church of England beyond England itself. Consequently, it has long been recognized in the scholarly literature that there is a need for some term that enshrines both the Church of England in England, its presence beyond that nation, and for that denomination over its entire historical existence. The most commonly adopted term is Anglicanism, and has been used by a number of recent scholars for periods prior to the nineteenth century.[2] A less Anglo-centric term—'Episcopal' or 'Episcopalianism'—is widely used in some parts of world for the same ecclesiastical phenomenon—Scotland, North America, and Brazil. However, that term does not figure as widely as Anglican or Anglicanism in the historical literature, so it is the predominant usage in this series.

Consequently, Anglicanism is understood in this series as originating as a mixed and ambiguous ecclesiastical identity, largely as a result of its foundation by the Tudor monarchs of the sixteenth century who were determined to embrace the whole of the English nation within their national Church. It is, consequently, a religious community that brings together aspects of ecclesiastical identity that other Western Churches have separated. From an English Church that was predominantly Reformed Protestant in the sixteenth century, emerging Anglicanism developed a liturgical and episcopal identity alongside its Protestant emphasis on the Bible as the sole criterion for religious truth. The series therefore views Anglicanism as a Church in tension. Developing within Anglicanism over centuries was a creative but also divisive tension between Protestantism and Catholicism, between the Bible and tradition, between the Christian past and contemporary thought and society, that has meant Anglicanism has not only been a contested, but also at times an inconsistent Christian identity.

Within England itself, the Tudor project of a Church for the English nation became increasingly unrealistic as that Church encompassed people who were not English, or people who thought of themselves less as English than as different nationalities. But it has proved to have a surprisingly long life for the English themselves. The series demonstrates various ways in which the

(Cambridge, 1993), ch. 1; J. C. D. Clark, *English Society 1660–1832* (Cambridge, 2000 edn.), p. 256; Nigel Voak, *Richard Hooker, and Reformed Theology: A Study of Reason, Will, and Grace* (Oxford, 2003), pp. 1–5; Patricia U. Bonomi, *Under the Cope of Heaven: Religion, Society, and Politics in Colonial America* (Oxford, 2003 edn.), pp. 40–61.

[2] John Frederick Woolverton, *Colonial Anglicanism in North America* (Detroit, 1984); Thomas Bartlett, 'Ireland and the British Empire', in P. J. Marshall (ed.), *The Oxford History of the British Empire: The Eighteenth Century* (Oxford, 1998), p. 270.

Church over the centuries attempted to enforce, encourage, or cling to its national identity in England, with some degree of success, not least in retaining an enduring cultural appeal for some English who were only loosely connected to its institutional life, or barely to its theological or religious claims. Even today English cathedrals often attract audiences to daily Evensong that otherwise would not be there.

But for those in England and beyond for whom their Church was more central, contestation, and the evolution of identity it prompted, was probably inevitable in a Church that, after its first two supreme heads, was deliberately re-founded by Elizabeth I to be ambiguous enough in certain key areas to give a Church for all the English a pragmatic chance of being accomplished. But this was a loaded gun. A basically Protestant Church, aligned with the Swiss Reformation, but with sufficient traditional aspects to irritate convinced Protestants at home (though less so major European Reformers); but insufficiently Catholic to pull in reformed Catholics for whom papal authority was non-negotiable, simply pleased no one for quite a while. It was neither Catholic fish nor properly Protestant fowl, at least according to those English that wanted the Church of England to conform completely to the worship and polity of Geneva, by the later sixteenth century the pre-eminent centre of international Protestantism. Even Elizabeth's bishops were not entirely comfortable with the Church they led, and some of them tried to push the boundaries towards a properly Reformed Church modelled on that of the New Testament. Until, that is, they realized Elizabeth was having none of it, and made it clear she would not deviate beyond the Church and worship enacted by Parliament in 1558–9. In her mind, though probably in no one else's, those years constituted 'the settlement' of religion. When her archbishop of Canterbury, Edmund Grindal, refused to suppress the so-called 'prophesyings' of local clergy meeting for what would now be termed professional development, the queen simply suspended him for the rest of his life and put his functions into the hands of an appointed committee. Royal Supremacy was an undoubted component of the Church of England's identity, and Elizabeth and her successors for many years were not about to let anyone forget it, be they bishops or religiously interfering Members of Parliament.

The fact that Elizabeth emulated the long reigns of her father and grandfather, and not the short ones of her half brother and half sister, meant that her Church of England had time to put down local roots, notwithstanding the 'Anglican' puritans who sought to remake it in Geneva's image; or the zealous Catholic mission priests who hoped to dismantle it by taking Catholics out of it completely.

Where the English went their Church was bound to follow, though this intensified the unhappy situation of Ireland where the English had for centuries sought political domination undergirded by settlement. The consequence of legally establishing a Protestant Church of Ireland was to add religious difference to the centuries-old colonial condition of that island, whose Gaelic-speaking population remained stubbornly Catholic, in part because the Catholic Church was not English. Generally, the Irish wanted no part of this Church, aside from a small percentage of Irish who stood to gain from alliance with the prevailing Protestant power.

The following century saw the contest for the Church of England become more militant and polarized, until the English went to war to settle the issue among themselves. Perhaps the most surprising development was the emergence of a group of Anglicans who began to publicly advocate for the conservative aspects of the Church of England, a group that coalesced and became another sort of Anglican to the usual sort of Calvinist. This new variety of Anglican was particularly encouraged by specific royal patronage under the first two Stuart kings, James I and Charles I. These new contestants for the identity of the Church have been called by various names—Arminians, Laudians, avant-garde conformists—partly because they were not tightly defined but represented various agendas. Some sought, with the support of Charles I (the first Supreme Governor to be raised in a settled Church of England), to bolster the independence and wealth of the Church; others, to oppose the Church's Calvinist theology and particularly the doctrine of predestination; others, to redress the lack of attention given to the sacraments and sacramental grace compared with the fervour for preaching among the more devout. But all were more or less agreed that the worship of the Church and the performance of the liturgy were woeful and needed to be better ordered, and churches should be more beautiful as aids to devotion and the fundamental significance of the sacraments.

But whether their agenda was liturgical, theological, or sacramental, to their puritan opponents this new Anglicanism looked like Catholicism, and that was the Antichrist from whose idolatrous and superstitious clutches the Protestant Reformation had released the English into true Christianity. They were not prepared to hand over the Church of England to a Catholic fifth-column. But while James I was cautious in his support for these avant-garde Anglicans, liking their support for divine-right monarchy but not their anti-Calvinism, his aesthetic, devout, and imperious son was markedly less so. The religious ball was in the royal court, particularly when Charles pulled off, in the 1630s, a decade of ruling without calling a Parliament, thereby silencing that body's uncomfortable and intolerable demands for royal accountability and religious reform.

The export in 1637 of Charles's particular version of the Church of England to his other kingdom of Scotland, in the form of a Scottish Prayer Book, not only stoked the fires of Scottish Presbyterian nationalism, but also released the pent-up energies of those within the Church of England who wanted an end to what they saw as royal absolutism and religious renovation by would-be papists. The rapid result of this intensification of political and religious contestation was the outbreak in 1642 of years of civil war in the royal Supreme Governor's three kingdoms. The internal Anglican quarrel, part of wider political differences, ended with the demise of the revolution begun by Henry VIII—the legal abolition of the Church of England, sealed in 1645 in the blood of the beheaded archbishop of Canterbury, William Laud; and followed by that of his Church's head, Charles I, in 1649. For the first time in its legal existence the Church of England (and the Church of Ireland) no longer officially existed.

Then an unexpected thing happened—some people continued to worship and practise their devotional lives according to the use of the defunct Church of England, demonstrating that its identity, though contested, was by this time a genuine reality in the lives of at least some of the English. They did this despite it being illegal, though the republican regime under Oliver Cromwell was not particularly zealous in its proscription of such activities. However, the diarist John Evelyn was present one Christmas Day when a covert congregation in London was dispersed by soldiers while keeping the holy day (proscribed by the regime) by gathering for Holy Communion according to the Book of Common Prayer.[3] Evelyn and others worshipped this way, and numbers of clergy used as much of the Prayer Book as they could in the parishes, notwithstanding that their leaders, the bishops, did little to set an example or to ensure the continuation of their illegal order. Anglican identity through worship and the ordering of the week and the year according to the Prayer Book and the Calendar of the Church of England was now being maintained, not by the state, but at the clerical and lay grassroots.

When Charles II landed in Dover in 1660 as the recognized king of England, after the rapid demise of the republican regime with its non-episcopal quasi-congregationalist Church following the death in 1658 of Lord Protector Oliver Cromwell, one outcome was the restoration of the legal monopoly of the Church of England. What that legal restoration did not do was to restore the spirituality, devotion, practice, and belief of the Church of England, because these had been ongoing in the period of the Church's official demise. Nevertheless, the legislation that brought back the establishment of the Church of England did newly define some ingredients of Anglican identity.

Before the Commonwealth the Church of England had not made ordination by bishops a non-negotiable aspect of Anglicanism. While it was certainly normal, there were exceptions made for some ministers who had been ordained in non-episcopal Churches elsewhere to minister in the Church of England without re-ordination. Now all clergy in the Church had to be episcopally ordained, with the sole exception of those clergy who came from Churches with a long historic tradition of episcopacy—the Roman Catholic,

[3] William Bray (ed.), *Diary and Correspondence of John Evelyn FRS* (1878, 4 vols.), I, p. 341 (25 Dec. 1657).

Orthodox, and the Church of Sweden. So from 1662 episcopacy became a basic characteristic of Anglicanism. The result was the expulsion of hundreds of clergy who would not conform to the requirement and to that of using only the Book of Common Prayer in worship. These dissenting clergy and laity, most of whom came from the previous Calvinist and puritan groups, now became permanent Nonconformists outside the Church of England. In 1662 a slightly revised Book of Common Prayer was passed by Parliament as the only authorized liturgy for the Church therefore reinforcing liturgical worship as a fundamental criterion of Anglican identity. Parliament again passed an Act of Uniformity and various other acts against Nonconformist worship. Uniformity was restored as an aspect of Anglicanism. So also was the royal supremacy.

However, while episcopacy has remained virtually unquestioned, and liturgical worship remained uncontested within Anglicanism until the late twentieth century, the same could not be said for the other dimensions of the 1662 resettlement of Anglicanism—legal establishment, the royal supremacy, and uniformity. These identifiers were to be victims of the global success of Anglicanism from the eighteenth century, as the Church of England expanded; first across the Atlantic into North American colonies, and then globally within and beyond the British Empire. The first to go was legal establishment when the Americans successfully ushered in their republic after their War of Independence with Britain and some Anglicans remained in the new state. No longer could these Anglicans be subject to the British crown, or be legally privileged in a country in which they were a decided minority, when the Americans had gone to so much trouble to jettison these things. So an Anglicanism—known after the Scottish precedent as Episcopalianism—came into existence for the first time in history without monarchical headship, but rather as a voluntary association. Even within the British Empire these legal and political aspects of Anglicanism, so much a part of its foundation in the sixteenth century, were in trouble by the 1840s. It was then that the bishop of a very new colony, almost as far away from England as you could get, started acting as though the monarchy and establishment were Anglican optional extras. Inspired by the United States precedent, Bishop Augustus Selwyn began unilaterally calling synods of his clergy just four years after New Zealand had been annexed in 1840 as a crown colony, and a few years later he was leading his Church into a constitution which made authoritative synods of laymen, clergy, and bishops. Voluntaryism was catching on in international Anglicanism.

Contestation and evolution continued to be a part of Anglicanism. One of its most enduring characteristics, the sole use of an authorized liturgical form for public worship, began to be challenged by two mutually hostile internal parties—Evangelicals and Anglo-Catholics. In some dioceses the latter succumbed to the temptation to use the Roman missal with the permission of sympathetic diocesan bishops. In contrast, encouraged by the global ambitions of the wealthy diocese of Sydney, some of the former had *de facto* abandoned the use of an authorized Prayer Book entirely. Into this recent Anglican contest has been thrown issues of human sexuality which have conflicted wider society, particularly in the West, but which have been accentuated for Anglicans by questions of how varieties of human sexuality conform or do not conform to the authority of Scripture. So these historical forces have not ceased to play their part within the dynamic of Anglican identity. The post-colonial era following the retraction of the British Empire has brought further criticism, from Anglicans themselves, about the extent to which their denomination was complicit in British imperialism, and that therefore their identity suffers from being an imperial construct. For such Anglican critics, necessary deconstruction has to occur which allows English markers of identity, even as basic as liturgical worship or episcopacy, to be questioned or even relinquished.

Since the nineteenth century and the effective end of the royal supremacy—whether that was exercised by the monarch or the British Parliament—emerging global Anglicanism was increasingly beset into the twenty-first century by the issue of authority. There has been no effective replacement for the royal supremacy, in part because of Anglicanism's historical origins in anti-papal national royalism. Beyond the purely diocesan level, the Anglican Communion struggled to find an operative replacement for the authority of the royal supremacy. Various attempts at authority by moral consensus, all bedevilled by anxiety that something akin to a centralized (i.e. papal) authority was being constructed, were tried. But all such central organizations of an emerging international communion were saddled with the original limitations imposed by Archbishop Longley when he agreed to call the first Lambeth Conference of diocesan bishops in 1867. By repudiating any real global authority, and opting for the consultative label of 'conference' rather than 'synod', Longley found a way to bring opposing parties of Anglicans together. But the emerging Anglican Communion, with its so-called 'Instruments of Unity'—be they the Anglican Consultative Council, or Primates' Meeting—tried to emulate Longley and both avoid the devil—papal centralism—and the deep blue sea—myriad manifestations that belied the claim to unity. True to its origins, Anglicanism perhaps remained more comfortable with its various national existences, than with its international one.

However, the history of Anglicanism is not merely the tracing of the evolution of a now global form of Western Christianity, important though that may be to tens of millions of contemporary Anglican adherents. As part of the historical turn to religion in recent academic interest, in the past two decades there has been a great increase of interest in the history and development of both the Church of England and its global offshoots. Scholars have investigated a plethora of facets of these religious phenomena, from the institutional to the popular, from formal theological belief and worship to informal, more diffusive faith. Other historians have looked at seminal

Anglican figures and movements. As well as specifically religious history, other historians have been recapturing the pivotal importance of Anglicanism in wider social and political contexts.

There has been a general historiographical revision which might broadly be described as moving the Church of England (and religion generally) from the margins to the centre of major economic social, political, and cultural development in English, British, imperial, and global history from the sixteenth to the twentieth centuries. The Church of England, Anglicanism, and religion more generally are now seen to be seminal dimensions of these various historical periods. So, for example, the significance of religion in the British Empire has now been recognized by a number of important scholars.[4] However, the major religious denomination in that empire, the Church of England, has been only sparsely studied compared to Nonconformity and is just now beginning to be critically examined.[5] Belatedly religion is moving up the scale of historical importance in British, imperial, and global history, but it still lags behind the significance and attention that it has received from historians of England. There have been various studies of the Church of England in its national context, but these have not always been integrated into wider British and global studies.[6]

A number of studies of historical Anglicanism have focused on the narrative of the institutional and theological history of Anglicanism, either as the Church of England or as an Anglican Communion. These include Stephen Neil's now very dated *Anglicanism*, originally published in 1958. More recently, there have been William L. Sachs's *The Transformation of Anglicanism: From State Church to Global Communion* (1993), and Kevin Ward's *A History of Global Anglicanism* (2006). However, these scholarly histories are single-volume histories that inevitably provide insufficient depth to do justice to the breadth of scholarship on their subject. Anglicanism is now a subject of such complexity as both an institutional Church and a religious culture that sufficient justice cannot be done to it in a single-volume historical treatment.

But there is now sufficient international historical interest and extant scholarship to make an extensive, analytical investigation into the history of Anglicanism a feasible intellectual project. In undertaking such a challenge the

[4] Andrew Porter, *Religion versus Empire? British Protestant Missionaries and Overseas Expansion, 1700–1914* (Manchester, 2004); Catherine Hall, *Civilising Subjects: Metropole and Colony in the English Imagination 1830–1867* (Chicago, 2002); Jeffrey Cox, *The British Missionary Enterprise since 1700* (Abingdon, 2008).

[5] Rowan Strong, *Anglicanism and the British Empire 1700–c.1850* (Oxford, 2007); Steven S. Maughan, *Mighty England Do Good: Culture, Faith, Empire, and World in the Foreign Missions of the Church of England, 1850–1915* (Grand Rapids, MI, 2014).

[6] Nancy L. Rhoden, *Revolutionary Anglicanism: The Colonial Church of England Clergy during the American Revolution* (Basingstoke, 2007); Rowan Strong, *Episcopalianism in Nineteenth-Century Scotland: Religious Responses to a Modernizing Society* (Oxford, 2000); Bruce Kaye (ed.), *Anglicanism in Australia* (Melbourne, 2002).

scholars who embarked on the project back in 2012 understand that not only was Anglicanism a religious identity shaped by theological and ecclesiastical understandings, but Anglicans were also formed by non-religious forces such as social class, politics, gender, and economics. Anglicanism has, therefore, been an expression of the Christianity of diverse social groups situated in the differing contexts of the past five centuries—monarchs, political elites, and lower orders; landowners and landless; slave-owners and slaves; missionaries, settlers, and indigenous peoples; colonizers and colonized—and by their enemies and opponents, both within and without their Church.

1

Introduction

Rowan Strong

The nineteenth century began for Anglicans not in 1800 when their constitutional situation in Britain was the same as it had been since the sixteenth century. Rather, it began in the late 1820s with major constitutional change in Britain when the political and legal monopoly they had enjoyed was quite suddenly removed by Parliament. Both domestically and imperially Anglicanism was permanently affected by unprecedented changes to the legislative position of the Church of England in Britain in respect to other denominations. Thereafter, for the rest of the nineteenth century both in England, Wales, later in Ireland, and in the empire the Church of England was increasingly just one denomination among others. So, for Anglicanism, the nineteenth century began in 1829 after the constitutional changes that brought an end to its privileged legal position that had been foundational to Anglicanism since the sixteenth-century Reformation. The constitutional revolution enacted by Parliament in 1828–9 meant Anglicans ceased to be the only enfranchised population in England, Wales, and Ireland, and Parliament was no longer legally solely an Anglican body, though it could still legislate for the Church of England. The repeal of the Test and Corporation Acts in 1828 brought Nonconformists officially within the political nation. While this had not previously prevented Protestant dissenters from taking the political test of the eucharistic sacrament in an Anglican church and entering Parliament or local government, it now made them enfranchised citizens in their own right without the notional cover of pretending to be Anglicans. In 1829 a much more radical departure from the Anglican state happened when the Catholic Emancipation Act enfranchised Roman Catholics, the theological and political foes of the Established Church, opposition to which was a substantial part of the *raison d'être* of Anglicanism coming into existence in the sixteenth century. Catholic emancipation was the political response of the Tory government of Lord Wellington to defuse the political strategy of Daniel O'Connell's Catholic Association in Ireland. That strategy had Catholic candidates elected to Westminster, but unable to take their seats. It spelt the political end to the claim of the Church of England to be the national Church, even if that reality continued to be resisted by English Anglicans for some time to come. In addition, it undercut the Protestant Ascendancy in Ireland and would lead directly to the disestablishment of the minority Church of Ireland by William Gladstone's Liberal government in 1869.

In 1800 Anglicanism in its ecclesiastical format consisted overwhelmingly of the United Church of England and Ireland (which included Wales). Beyond that there were small, emerging Churches catering for British settlers, convicts, or temporary expatriate communities such as soldiers and traders in overseas colonies in British North America (later Canada), the Caribbean, India, and Australia. The only Anglican Churches existing independently of the Church of England were in the United States, and the tiny Scottish Episcopal Church which had suffered decades-long diminution due to its illegal association with Jacobitism. But by the end of the century Anglicanism was a global entity with millions of adherents in every settled continent on earth, with institutional structures from diocesan to international levels. However, the ambiguous nature of Anglicanism that was a marked feature of its sixteenth-century origins would see this nineteenth-century expansion develop an unprecedented divisive partisan culture within the new global Anglicanism. So the contestation for Anglican identity would expand and intensify in this watershed century.

Scholarship on Anglicanism has rarely tended to focus on that denominational identity, historians preferring to tackle it as part of area or thematic studies. Consequently, much historical writing on this subject is to be found scattered throughout nationally focused histories, or topics such as poverty and philanthropy, or on particular Anglican Churches, especially the Church of England. This scholarship can be found informing the various chapters that follow in this volume. Historiographical attention to the few histories that in the last few decades have dealt with Anglicanism as a world-wide phenomenon can be found in the series introduction at the beginning of this volume. But some remarks can be made about the interpretations of these few scholars on global Anglicanism about their subject in the nineteenth century. Stephen Neill, writing in the 1950s, saw this period as one in which Anglicanism escaped the restricting state connection in colonies and missions where it grew in independent self-government, a requirement necessary to its world-wide expansion.[1] William Sachs saw this period as heralding the birth of the concept of Anglicanism, i.e. as one in which Anglican Christianity began to understand itself as something more than 'merely English'. This is a view that this series on an 'Anglicanism' traceable from the sixteenth century obviously

[1] Stephen Neill, *Anglicanism* (London, 1977 edn.), pp. 278, 357.

questions.[2] Kevin Ward, writing in 2006, while understanding the nineteenth century as the period of globalizing *par excellence* in the history of Anglicanism, sees it nevertheless as one in which the emerging Anglican Communion was still in thrall to the 'Anglo-Saxon captivity' of its metropolitan centre and English bishops in most overseas sees.[3] The chapters in this volume raise questions about this view of nineteenth-century Anglicanism as an English 'captivity'. Many of the English leaders of global Anglicanism were at the forefront of independence movements from the Church of England for their Churches. Neither was global Anglican leadership, formal and informal, quite as homogeneously English as this phrase stipulates.

In my own work into the connection between international Anglicanism and the British Empire, Anglican expansion in this period was driven by three constituent parts of a revising Anglican identity that was basically theologically constructed. The imperative of missionary and colonial expansion derived from an Anglican self-confidence in the quality of their Church; by the need to respond to the universal imperative of the gospel; and by a long-standing conviction that the British Empire was a divine gift conditional upon it being used to spread the gospel. These ingredients of nineteenth-century imperial Anglican identity resulted in the rapid development early in this period of a new paradigm of autonomous episcopally based expansion that increasingly distanced itself from the English state connection. Joseph Hardwick, one of the most recent scholars on global nineteenth-century Anglicanism, investigates the imperial expansion of the institutional Church of England and its provision for colonial settlers. Hardwick sees a shift from an earlier colonial Anglicanism which looked to metropolitan England, to one that developed largely distinctive colonial Churches. These colonial Churches had a number of salient features, including lay involvement in new synodical government, a varied clerical workforce, and they played a key role in the development of settler societies.[4]

Notwithstanding its development into a world-wide Christian body, in this period for much of that global growth Anglicanism was led by the Church of England, and propelled by changes and issues within British society and politics. There were some exceptions to this Anglo-centric nature of nineteenth-century Anglicanism, particularly in the machinery of denominational identity within the settler colonies which in the mid-Victorian decades were in advance of the metropolitan centre, building on the example of the independent Episcopal Church of the USA. In Britain, John Wolffe in his

[2] William Sachs, *The Transformation of Anglicanism: From State Church to Global Communion* (Cambridge, 1993), pp. 2–3.

[3] Kevin Ward, *A History of Global Anglicanism* (Cambridge, 2006), p. 300.

[4] Joseph Hardwick, *An Anglican British World: The Church of England and the Expansion of the Settler Empire c.1790–1860* (Manchester, 2014).

chapter on Anglicanism in Britain and Europe sees it as adapting successfully to the various political and cultural challenges it encountered. In this adaptation Anglicanism was assisted particularly by disestablishment in Ireland (and later in Wales), which removed a centuries-old grievance of unjustified privilege. In addition, Anglicans eventually came to an acceptance of the greater diversity within their Church produced in this century.

Britain entered the chronological nineteenth century still an agrarian and rural society. In its first decades over two-thirds of the population lived in the countryside and worked on the land or in domestic service. The new mill towns created by industrial technology and burgeoning factories only began to expand during the 1780s, but widespread industrialization was beginning to change British society from the 1830s. By 1851 about 54 per cent of the population of England and Wales lived in towns of more than 2,500 people.[5] In Scotland a decade later in 1861, 39 per cent of the population lived in settlements of more than 5,000, and this compared with 31 per cent in 1831.[6] Clearly by the mid-century the move from a rural and agricultural society to an urban one was already well underway. But not all urban growth was as a result of industrialization. Brighton, for example, grew rapidly during the 1820s as a result of increasing leisure time and the need for organized recreation. Nor was all industry urbanized, with many industries being sited outside towns near coalfields. But where industrialization and urbanization went together such large towns were in the forefront of the change towards an urbanized, industrialized, populous society. For the first half of the century this was particularly true of the spinning mills of the textile industry. These have been described as 'the advance guard of the factory system' and therefore as 'the birthplace of the industrial proletariat'.[7] However, not all industries were large-scale factory enterprises. Even in the textile industry, in 1841 only a third of all operatives in Lancashire worked in firms employing more than 500 people, while a fifth worked in 714 firms of less than 150.[8] Most people in urban areas continued to work in small-scale firms. Yet, large or small, these industrial employers were absorbing most of the British workforce by the mid-nineteenth century, as compared with agriculture at the beginning of the period.

By 1900, from a largely agricultural and rural nation, Britain had become an overwhelmingly industrial and urban-dwelling society. A hierarchical society dominated by the landowning gentry and aristocracy had experienced the rise of the middle classes to increasing political power and representation,

[5] K. Theodore Hoppen, *The Mid-Victorian Generation 1846–1886* (Oxford, 1998), p. 56.

[6] R. J. Morris, 'Urbanisation and Scotland', in W. Hamish Fraser and R. J. Morris (eds.), *People and Society in Scotland*, vol. II: *1830–1914* (Edinburgh, 1990), p. 74.

[7] F. M. L. Thompson, *The Rise of Respectable Society: A Social History of Victorian Britain, 1830–1900* (London, 1988), pp. 22–3.

[8] Hoppen, *Mid-Victorian Generation*, p. 59.

beginning with the Reform Act of 1832. Towards the end of the century the enfranchisement of working men was also beginning to be felt in Parliament and women were pushing for the vote.

Linked to these internal changes within Britain were those in her empire. In this century Britain continued the imperial expansion that had begun to take off following her victories in the Seven Years War when she eclipsed France as the major European imperial power. But for Anglicanism the revived Church–state partnership that had developed after the loss of the British North American colonies in 1783 broke down after 1830. It was eroded by a growing political liberalism in Britain which favoured religious toleration, and by a radical political response to the political circumstances of the 1820s. The growth of free trade as a commercial and cultural ideal of the rising middle classes also promoted a free trade in religion in contrast to the formerly protected Anglicanism. Stewart Brown in his chapter demonstrates how Anglicans configured their engagement with the British Empire in theological terms, persistently understanding it as providential gift for the spread of the gospel, and viewing their Christianity as providing a particular unifying force for the empire's disparate dimensions, and the empire was also a challenge to mission for the Church of England and even colonial Anglican Churches. However, while many Anglicans of varying theological persuasions saw a fundamental difference between empire and Church, there were some who conflated the two, and by the end of the century increasing numbers of Anglicans were beginning to understand an emerging imperative for a separation between Englishness and Anglicanism.

The fundamental constitutional change to the Anglican monopoly in the British state forced the Church of England to adjust to the *de facto* loss of its legislative and political monopoly that had undergirded its claim as the national Church. It did this in two ways. First, by reinventing its claim to be the national Church away from its previous legal basis to a more cultural and moral position based upon its majority adherence among the English population. Second, by developing the structures and capabilities of a denomination in distinction from the state. Compared with other denominations in Britain, the Church of England had virtually no institutional structures as an autonomous Church in 1830. Until then it had no need for independent fabric as it had enjoyed a legal monopoly in England and Wales and Ireland almost continuously since the 1530s. But prompted by the changes to its constitutional status in the late 1820s, by the end of the century the Church of England had generated a denominational structure with diocesan synods, a national general synod, and at a more local level, effective archdeaconries and rural deaneries.

But alongside these burgeoning denominational forms, English Anglicans were reluctant to relinquish their status as the national Church and attempted to find alternative ways to give that old identity renewed substance, especially after the religious census of 1851 shocked the Church of England into realizing that its adherents were only about 50 per cent of the population of England and Wales. One of the most effective reinventions of the Church of England's national character came from Broad Churchmen in the second half of the nineteenth century, where they promoted the concept of the Church of England as having a special mission to direct the nation's moral and spiritual life because of its comprehensive composition. This thinking had its origin in Samuel Taylor Coleridge, and was taken up by Thomas Arnold, the famous headmaster and reformer of Rugby School. Accordingly, Broad Churchmen, unlike their Evangelical and Anglo-Catholic counterparts, opposed any attempts to impose tighter doctrinal tests or restrictions upon the clergy. In his chapter Mark Chapman draws attention to the ways in which these liberal Anglicans in the nineteenth century strove to engage Christian truths with other intellectual discoveries because they believed that the Church was not the sole repository of truth in this world. Inevitably, with their focus on the intellect, the universities were a major context for their struggle, with liberal churchmen predominating in this environment and in ecclesiastical contexts, such as cathedrals, that supported scholarly clergy. As liberal Anglicans generally contended for widening the boundaries of Christian doctrine and ecclesiastical formularies, their nineteenth-century battles were fought to support opening the historic universities of Oxford and Cambridge to non-Anglicans. But their emphasis on the moral dimension of Christianity often saw liberal Anglicans in influential positions in English public schools, epitomized by Thomas Arnold's campaign for a manly moral culture at Rugby School.

Traditional High Churchmen also worked to reinvent the national character of their Church, by building on organizations they had developed before the constitutional revolution. Most of all, this was the purpose they conceived for the National Society for Promoting the Education of the Poor in the Principles of the Church of England. In pursuit of a goal of controlling national elementary education, and in competition with the Nonconformist-supported British and Foreign Schools Society, parochial clergy made valiant efforts to establish parish schools. In such schools basic literacy was taught in association with the catechism of the Church of England, an effort which was often varied in quality and ultimately beyond the Church's resources. As Robert Andrews demonstrates, High Churchmen were successors to a tradition emphasizing sacramental grace, prayer, and the importance of the Church in divine Providence that traced its roots back to the early seventeenth century. They were distinct from Tractarian and Anglo-Catholic Anglicans in their reverence for the English Reformation, holding a more positive view of the Church of England's Protestant and established character. Their ongoing existence and influence in the nineteenth century has been blurred in the historiographical literature by the tendency of scholars to use the term 'High Church' as a catch-all phrase for all three Anglican strands which placed a high value on the Catholic nature of their Church—High Churchmen, Tractarians, and Anglo-Catholics. However, recent research has begun to rescue traditional High Churchmen from their undeserved obscurity in the nineteenth century, as they were often at the forefront of efforts to uphold the importance of the Established Church for a Christian Britain, and in the diocesan revival of effective Church government.

However useful for a continuing national role for Anglicanism in England, these various justifications for some sort of continuing Anglican establishment made use of the concept of nationalism, a concept prevalent in the nineteenth century, centred around a connection between Englishness and Anglicanism. But this link could constitute a barrier to the expansion of Anglicanism beyond the English at home and in the colonies in the nineteenth century when Britain acquired a maritime empire unequalled in size which constituted another, imperial, British state. My chapter on Church and state points to the ways in which the constitutional changes to Anglicanism in the metropolitan centre of this imperial state consequently impacted on its colonial peripheries. There too Anglicanism lost its privileged position in the wake of the growing religious neutrality of the home government and its colonial offshoots. From a period of increased support for Anglican establishment following the loss of the thirteen North American colonies in 1783, colonial governments moved quite quickly from the 1830s to a similar position to the metropolitan government of denominational even-handedness in respect to financial and legal support for colonial Churches. Prompted in part by this shift in the official position of their local administrations, colonial Anglican Churches in settler colonies were in the vanguard of the development of an Anglican denominational identity. Beginning in New Zealand in the 1840s, and followed quite quickly in the Australian colonies and in Canada, colonial Anglican Churches began to develop their own diocesan synodical government. Emulating the practice of Anglicanism in the newly independent United States these colonial synods also moved at different times and speeds to incorporate male laity as one of the three voting houses of such synods. This lay involvement in Church government took longer to initiate in Britain where there was greater episcopal and clerical resistance to involving laity in doctrinal deliberations.

White British settlement and the consequent export of British denominations was not just occurring within the British Empire, but also beyond the empire as British and Irish migrants left their homelands for other shores either permanently or as temporary expatriates. These migrating populations of the British and Irish Isles took their Anglicanism with them not just to America, but also to Latin America, British India, Egypt, and numerous other places where generations of schoolchildren could trace the expansion of the pink-coloured territories on maps that revealed an increasingly British globe. In Carol Herringer's narrative chapter on developments beyond the British

Empire she finds steady but not spectacular growth, with the United States as the country where Anglicanism had the most impact, an outcome which came not from its relatively small numbers, but from its elite cultural and political influence.

In the following chapters the expansion of global Anglicanism can be seen to be varied in its growth, which was largely dependent on significant leaders or groups negotiating the local contexts of their environment to bring about permanent establishment for their Church in a recognizable Anglican form. Some of these local contexts were those where an eighteenth-century establishment or quasi-establishment Anglicanism had to give way to the new official neutrality, while others were formed entirely in that new nineteenth-century reality. Other new Anglican Churches grew in places where there was no British flag and Anglican founders were left more to their own devices to go about the business of creating their Church. By the start of the Anglican nineteenth century in 1830 the near-establishment status of the Churches in the Caribbean, Australian, and Canadian colonies was crumbling, while the independent Church in the new United States was recovering its self-confidence after erosion caused by the British loyalism of many of its clergy and laity. As the chapters by Peter Williams and Hilary Carey demonstrate, while the US Church largely depended on its own resources to expand into the American West and even overseas into US-controlled territories such as the Philippines, the Australian Church remained remarkably in thrall in this century to the English Church for its identity and all of its bishops. The Canadians, however, moved more quickly to develop their own native episcopal leadership. However, all three Churches, the US most of all, struggled to expand their membership beyond the middle and upper classes of society. They also largely failed in missionary endeavours to their respective indigenous peoples, the Australian Church almost completely. In contrast, Allan Davidson describes how the New Zealand Anglican Church began as an indigenous mission and only nearly three decades later commenced to be a settler Church, a development that moved remarkably quickly into developing its own governing synods, though that often involved Anglicans in double-jeopardy when settler and Māori fought over land in the 1840s and again in the 1860s.

Outside the white settler colonies, Emma Wild-Wood on Anglicanism in sub-Saharan Africa finds that amidst the frequent continuities with English Anglicanism there was also a surprising local shaping of this imported European Christianity, largely as a consequence of those missional areas where it grew due to local African agency. Anglicanism was present in Africa due to two major forces—British imperialism and missions—with two major foci—British settlers and expatriates, and non-Christian Africans—and once there it could hardly escape imperial cultural and political forces. However, Anglican hierarchy and modernity was attractive to Africans who found their own ways to adhere to and use this Christian import.

In North Africa and the Middle East Anglicanism encountered monotheistic Islam and also ancient Monophysite Christian Churches. Also, with the exception of Egypt where Britain from the 1880s developed a *de facto* rule under notional Ottoman sovereignty, it was a region that had a prevailing imperial power in Ottoman Turkey. Duane Miller's exploration of new intentional mission work by Anglicans in this ancient area of Christianity and Islam illustrates how various Anglican missions involved different conceptions of Anglicanism, which were at times in conflict with one another. Some Anglicans, largely Evangelicals, saw their mission here as connected to the advent of the *Parousia* and therefore as involving converting Jews, which spilled over into converting Christians from ancient communities. Others believed their mission was to establish relations with these historic Middle Eastern Churches and help them to become stronger in the modern world.

In Latin America, according to David Rock's exploration, Anglicanism also encountered another Christianity, this time Roman Catholicism, long the bitter foe of the Church of England. It also began its life there among nations newly independent from the Spanish Empire. Consequently, Anglicanism generally followed British commercial developments, and became extended as British investment widened in these new countries. It also was largely an Evangelical Anglican enterprise and had no qualms about converting Roman Catholics. However, despite efforts from particular individuals and mission societies such as the South American Missionary Society, Anglicanism in Latin America remained throughout the nineteenth century almost completely an Anglophone enterprise with little contact or conversions among Latin American people.

Such cultural and linguistic isolation was certainly not true of Anglicanism in East Asia. In China, Anglicanism, like other forms of Christianity, had to overcome the barrier of its foreignness, and a major means of doing so was for missions to use Chinese and to have the Scriptures translated into the local language. However, Philip Wickeri's chapter shows how the Anglican missions differed in their wider commitment to indigenization, with the American Episcopalian missions more committed to developing Chinese leadership than were the Church of England missions. In Japan, the smaller homogeneous nature of the country meant the Anglican Church was established much more quickly than in China, though by the end the century it was still dependent upon foreign resources and leadership. In all these East Asian countries, including Korea, missionaries contributed to modernization and Westernization by their very presence, though the liturgical nature of Anglican worship demanded a great deal of the literacy of converts.

In these global locations the engagement and status of local Anglican Churches and missions could vary enormously, and also change over time. At one extreme was the Anglican Church in British India, which in this period came to encompass what today is Pakistan, India, Bangladesh, Sri Lanka, and

Burma. Anglicanism here remained an established Church, begun with the first bishopric in Calcutta in 1813 and maintained as a financially supported establishment by the Indian government throughout the nineteenth century. This connection with the imperial raj, as Robert Frykenberg's chapter evinces, impeded the mission of the Anglican Church to indigenous peoples in India, and, along with a persistent aim of indirect conversion of Indian social elites through hospitals and schools, was a major contributory cause of Anglicanism in India missing out on mass conversion movements among Dalit and tribal peoples. At another end of the scale were those Anglican endeavours which took place entirely outside British imperial territory. In between there were various degrees of cooperation and hostility between local officialdom and Anglican Churches and missions. In some instances there was active cooperation with imperial authorities, as in the annexed territory of the Xhosa people in South Africa which in 1866 became British Kaffraria where a British mission and subsequent Anglican diocese (Natal) followed the flag. In contrast, the Anglo-Catholic Universities Mission to Central Africa became remarkably hostile to British imperial or colonial contacts, seeing these presences as carriers of a Western settlement and urban civilization that degraded Africans.

Gradually a global Anglicanism evolved throughout the nineteenth century, not just through the export from Britain of Britons into their empire, to the United States, and beyond, but also through the activism of old and new mission societies. Evangelicalism brought a new vigour and voluntarism to the older Anglican mission associated with the Society for the Propagation of the Gospel (SPG). This new missionary activism was slow to take off, the Evangelical Church Missionary Society (CMS) having to rely on German missionaries for some years after its foundation in 1799. However, by the 1830s it was well on the way to becoming the largest of all Protestant mission societies in the nineteenth century, and was the first Anglican missionary society to send missionaries to the indigenous populations of Africa and Asia. Revitalized by this new Evangelical missionary organization and effort, and initially advised and assisted by the CMS, the SPG also began to move towards developing local lay voluntary groups and to target not just settlers overseas but also indigenous non-Christian populations. In this way, the expansion of Anglicanism in the nineteenth century was two-pronged. One fork, known as colonial missions, supported the extension and development of Anglican ecclesiastical infrastructure and clergy for British populations in overseas colonies. The other fork was foreign missions which moved to make new Anglicans from evangelistic missions among non-Christian peoples both within and beyond the British Empire. Brian Stanley's chapter on these mission societies points to the predominant model of the voluntary society, whose aims and methods could at times be in tension with those of its parent denomination, a reality that was certainly found in Anglicanism. The history of nineteenth-century Anglican missions is one where various attempts, not always successful, were made to reconcile this tension.

During the nineteenth century, as a consequence of its foreign missions, Anglicanism became an increasingly non-white Church in many regions of the world, making it a major player in the development of a global Anglophone world as it grew a substantial but subordinate non-Caucasian adherence for the first time in its history. The only previous Anglicans of colour had come from the sporadic missions of the eighteenth century in the North American and Caribbean colonies to Indian peoples, and to some black slaves, which had meant negotiating a very restricted missionary access because entry to plantations was tightly controlled by the slave-owning oligarchies in such colonies.

But it was not all sweetness and light in this brave new global Anglican world. This international Anglicanism was very much in the control of white male clergy, though by the end of the century that hegemonic control was beginning to be challenged. Of course, clergy had in some sense always had to share their ecclesiastical authority in the Church of England with laymen in Parliament; and with a layperson, either male and female, if they happened to be the monarch and the supreme governor of the Church of England and the Church of Ireland. However, in the nineteenth century this gendered white clerical control was both challenged and reinforced, sometimes by the same group of Anglicans over time. So Brian Stanley analyses the story of the freed slave, Samuel Ajayi Crowther, who in 1864 became the first African bishop, in charge of African missionaries in West Africa. This unprecedented initiative was the outcome of the policy of the innovative secretary of the CMS, Henry Venn, who advocated 'a native Church'. Venn believed his society's missions should be making Churches which depended upon the resources and leadership of the converted local peoples, and consequently European missionaries would become redundant. It was a common policy among many Evangelical missions in the mid-Victorian period. However, by the end of the century white domination came to be reasserted by a new generation of Anglican CMS missionaries which undercut and destroyed Crowther's leadership and reputation.

While non-white indigenous leadership in this period was rare amidst increasing British racism in the nineteenth century, another challenge to traditional leadership in Anglicanism was coming from women, as Susan Mumm describes in the growing feminization of Anglicanism in the nineteenth century. Women in this century became not just the larger proportion of Sunday worshippers compared with men, but began to develop their own organizations. Initially these were explicitly auxiliary to male-run societies, particularly in missions. But by the end of the century women were beginning to assert greater control over their own affairs in various philanthropic organizations. In some areas of Anglican life they exercised a disturbing autonomy, and took advantage of career openings for single women in missions that came to alter the perceptions and roles of women back in metropolitan Britain. The most unsettling aspect for Victorian culture of Anglican women's choices came in the form of the revival from the 1840s of the vowed religious life in Anglicanism, as a consequence of the catholicizing agenda of the Oxford Movement. The advent of monks and nuns in the Church of England three centuries after they were extinguished as part of the unfolding English Reformation shocked fundamental aspects of Anglican and Victorian culture. Anglican nuns were a particular challenge to Victorian paternalism which saw them as single women dangerously outside the proper authority of family males. Bishops often came to feel the same way about these communities of women which were not always reassuringly submissive to their ecclesiastical authority, and which had an unsettling tendency to make their own community decisions. But these women's communities, which far outnumbered their male religious counterparts, played an important part in the outreach of Anglicanism to the new urban masses of the industrial cities that were, to a great extent, unchurched; and also in foreign and colonial missions where they brought with them an explicit Anglo-Catholic culture.

Anglican sisterhoods were one aspect of the nineteenth-century Catholic revival within Anglicanism. The forum for this catholicizing initiative was initially Oxford University between 1833 and 1845. This was an ideal place as the university, along with Cambridge, functioned as the nearest thing to a seminary for clergy of the Church of England. In addition to intending clergymen, the university's other students came from the ranks of the landed gentry and aristocracy, plus the sons of professional men. Therefore, any intellectual or religious movement in the two English universities was well-placed to influence the future elites of English society. The Oxford Movement certainly excited the adherence of a number of young men at Oxford with the feeling of doing something different, and challenging established authorities of the university, the Church, and possibly paternal authority as well. Distressed by the departure of Parliament from the Anglican confessional state, the Oxford Movement leaders began to assert the independent Catholic authority of the Church of England. They attempted to do this by encouraging the clergy to assert the spiritual authority of their office by virtue of the Church's foundation by Christ. For over a decade after 1833, the Oxford Movement held sway at Oxford University until the secession of John Henry Newman to Roman Catholicism in 1845.

Newman's theological preoccupations formed much of the theology of the Oxford Movement. The importance of dogmatic truth as an adequate symbol of revelation; the need to uphold this against a relativistic theological liberalism supported by the need of the state for comprehension of religious pluralism; the necessary connection between doctrine, morality, and worship; the Church as the authorized teacher and interpreter of divine truth; and the

Church of England as part of the Catholic Church and therefore having an existence and authority independent of the state. The prominent place of Athanasius in Newman's thinking also pointed to the Movement's sacerdotalism, an exalting of the priestly office as a guarantee of the Church's independent authority. James Pereiro's chapter on the Oxford Movement details how the catholicizing movement spread from beyond the confines of Oxford University to be transformed by parish clergy and influential and wealthy men and women, and to be caught up in the Victorian push to evangelize the urban masses and the foreign heathen.

Central to the wider attraction of the movement was its facet as a holiness movement. The ideal of sanctity attracted undergraduates to Newman's afternoon sermons and early morning eucharists, and caused them to emulate his mannerisms. Many of the characteristic publications of the movement, the ninety *Tracts for the Times*, were devoted to devotional subjects such as the daily office, and to the ascetic element which was such a feature of Tractarian spirituality. This spirituality was fundamentally a response prompted by the Romantic Movement working on imaginations awakened by the history of Catholic piety at a time when Victorian Britain was beginning to appreciate its medieval past, as, for example, in the novels of Sir Walter Scott. But while followers of the Oxford Movement were influenced by the Romantic Movement (especially evident in Keble's poetry), their spirituality was fundamentally opposed to the individualism and subjectivism of Romanticism.

This avant-garde catholicizing movement came up against the embedded anti-Catholicism of the Protestant British which had been such a predominant aspect of Anglicanism in all its previous centuries. At the time of the Oxford Movement in the 1830s the Protestantism of the Church of England had been invigorated by the long-lasting effects of the eighteenth-century Evangelical Revival. Evangelicals rightly detected the fundamental agenda of the Oxford Movement, which, negatively put, was the de-Protestantizing of the Church of England; or, positively, the reclaiming of the Catholic nature of Anglicanism. Its catholicizing and holiness aims came together to make the movement more positive towards Roman Catholicism than had been traditional in Anglicanism, or was acceptable to the contemporary parties of Evangelical and High Churchmen. The latter supported the movement during the 1830s, but by the 1840s, as the younger adherents of the movement began to ape the more explicit liturgical Catholicism of Rome, the High Church began to see this as the error of their ways.

Evangelicals in the Church of England, as a consequence of the French Revolution and the fear of social unrest spreading to Britain, adopted a greater respect for the Church and began to loosen their dissenting connections. But Anglican Evangelicals retained characteristics common to dissenting Evangelicals. Preaching was primarily a method for conversion which was identified with justification by faith; that is, an acceptance by God through faith alone.

Such a conversion was understood as the sole mark of becoming a Christian. Evangelical activism was the transformation of the level of work in ministers and particularly their focus on wider social issues beyond the parish, plus a high degree of lay religious involvement. All spiritual truth was found solely in the Bible, and consequently there was a deep Evangelical reverence for Scripture which was regarded as divinely inspired and literally infallible, although Evangelicals held no common theory about how this was so. Gratitude for salvation by Christ was the Evangelical motive for holiness, although they were divided over questions about just who it was that Christ died for. These were the common aspects of an Evangelical religious culture which dominated the middle classes of nineteenth-century Britain.

Evangelical activism endeavoured to come to grips with some of the most appalling conditions of industrial and urban society without challenging the social order. Nor was this philanthropy an end in itself, but a recognition that you could not save a person's soul until you had relieved him or her from the oppression of physical misery or exploitation. Evangelical involvement in social amelioration had been evident since its leadership of the anti-slavery campaign during the 1790s. But as Evangelical influence grew in the British Churches and society so did the impact of their social conscience, particularly in the decades of Evangelical ascendancy during the 1850s and 1860s. However, Evangelicals' failure to transform social relief into structural social change derived in part from their espousing the principles of political economy with its emphasis on helping the deserving rather than the undeserving poor; and also from their theology which emphasized the salvation of the individual rather than society. Andrew Atherstone's chapter delineates the ways in which Anglican Evangelicals thrashed out an Anglican Evangelical identity emphasizing loyalty to bishops and the historic Reformation formularies. This identity came under stress but it remained one that was increasingly important during the nineteenth century.

Evangelicalism, with its busy multitude of voluntary associations, did most to set the tone of the prevailing British moral culture. Government social regulation and legislation, though growing in complexity and scope through the collectivism of the liberal state, were only just developing in the second half of the nineteenth century. It was the Churches which still exercised the most immediate social control and influence on the population, especially in respect of sex and drink which the Victorians believed would lead to social anarchy if not rigorously controlled. Most of these controls were aimed at the working classes but it was the middle classes which mainly observed them as part of the emerging Victorian cult of respectability, reflecting the growth in numbers and influence of the middle classes during the nineteenth century.

By the mid-Victorian decades explicit and rival parties began to coalesce within the Church of England that formed around national organizations to create a more divided, antagonistic, partisan Anglicanism than had existed at the beginning of the nineteenth century. Then, notwithstanding their differences, Evangelicals in the CMS were perfectly willing to help modernize the largely High Church SPG, and both groups cooperated to lobby successfully for India to be opened to missions at the renewal of the East India Company's charter by Parliament in 1813. Catalyzed by the Oxford Movement, in 1846 like-minded Anglicans joined with their Evangelical counterparts in other denominations to form the Evangelical Alliance specifically to combat popery and Puseyism. There was also the more specifically Anglican organization, the Evangelical Church Society, founded in 1865 precisely to protect the Church of England from those who would 'assimilate her services to those of the Church of Rome'. Oxford Movement followers, by then beginning to call themselves Anglo-Catholics, formed the English Church Union in 1859 in pursuit of making their catholicizing eucharistic liturgical innovations canonically acceptable. Late in the century liberal Anglicans also formed a looser alliance when, in the Church of England, they formed in 1898 the Churchman's Union for the Advancement of Liberal Religious Thought. They thought to cry a plague on both Evangelicals and Anglo-Catholics in the name of a theological alliance with modern thought. The High Churchmen tended to stay aloof from this partisan Anglicanism, as they agreed with the Anglo-Catholics about the Catholic nature of their Church; but also with the Evangelicals about the absolute necessity of the English Reformation sweeping away accretions of medieval superstition and the consequent need of the Roman Church for reform.

Evangelical Anglicans disliked the Catholic revivalists because they feared for the Protestant heritage of Anglicanism. Anglo-Catholics disliked Evangelicals because they feared the threat of Protestantism to their Church's Catholic nature. These were the two largest groups in Anglicanism by the late nineteenth century and between them they organized Anglicanism into a partisan Church. These groups began to take on the nature of a party with their own organizations and sets of principles, and equivalents of these two parties could also be found in many overseas Anglican Churches, and in the various Anglican mission societies. Thus each alliance, seeking exclusivity for its own particular brand of Anglicanism, assisted the division of their Church into antagonistic parties.

It has been customary to denigrate this partisan Anglicanism of the Victorian period, but recent research has demonstrated that it helped engender a culture of internal competition that invigorated Anglicans and provided much of the motivation and energy for missions, and for its Church extension into the new urban areas of industrializing Britain and in British settler colonies. Anglican diversity was much more than just the broad divisions of High Church, Evangelical, Broad Church, and Anglo-Catholic. Within these customary divisions there was even greater diversity as these partisan Anglican groupings developed internal shadings in responding to various contemporary pressures and developments. So while Evangelicals upheld the work of the CMS, pre-millennialist Evangelicals particularly contributed to missions such as the Church's Ministry among the Jews. High Church and Anglo-Catholic Anglicans were generally the principal supporters of the SPG, but Anglo-Catholics also liked their own, more ritualist missions often centred around the work of religious orders, such as the Community of the Resurrection in South Africa. Denominational extension in settler colonies, the work of colonial mission societies, also reflected this partisan competitive Anglicanism. In addition to missionary societies that also engaged in colonial mission, such as the SPG, there was the (Evangelical) Colonial and Continental Church Society, and various overseas educational foundations of religious orders.

By the late nineteenth century the various forces and agencies outlined above had created a global Anglican world, albeit somewhat strained by issues of ecclesiology and authority which it was ill-equipped to deal with on such a large scale. One development within globalizing Anglicanism brought together two major strands of its nineteenth-century history—partisanship and expansion—when traditional ecclesiastical authority wielded by the Tractarian-influenced High Church bishop of Cape Town was used to attempt to smother the biblical criticism of a missionary bishop in South Africa. The outcome was something new for Anglicanism. Robert Grey as metropolitan bishop attempted to depose Bishop Colenso of Natal for his book on the Pentateuch because Colenso had adopted some moderate findings of German biblical criticism, including repudiating that Moses wrote the first five books of the Old Testament. Grey, and some like-minded colonial bishops, wanted a means to exercise authority in an international way over what they saw as heretical developments in their new global communion. Accordingly, they proposed to Archbishop Longley of Canterbury that he initiate an international pan-Anglican council of bishops, as the traditional central figures of Anglicanism. Longley did so, but avoided the juridical nature of such a council, aware that such an institution would be unacceptable to Broad Churchmen and Evangelicals, even if the latter group largely agreed with Grey's assessment of Colenso. The result was the Lambeth Conference of 1867, the first of what became the Instruments of Unity of the Anglican Communion. This was followed two decades later by the Lambeth Quadrilateral, which originated in the General Convention of the Episcopal Church of the USA in 1886 as markers of Anglican identity prompted by unity initiatives from the nascent ecumenical movement. They were the Old and New Testaments containing all matters essential to salvation; the Apostles' and Nicene Creeds as sufficient summaries of Christian faith; two sacraments of baptism and eucharist as instituted by Christ; and 'the Historic Episcopate'. Anglican identity, as well as being contested, was also coalescing.

But while Anglicans were exceedingly busy developing, adapting, exporting, and innovating the old shape and certainties of their Church through missions and colonial settlements, they were also at the forefront of responding to the challenges of modern thought to orthodox Christianity. Such a role for Anglicanism was nothing new in British Christianity. In the previous century orthodox Anglicans had used contemporary thought to oppose the radical Enlightenment when it came to them in the form of Deism—a theism that upheld a creator God, but one who ceased to have any providential role in the universe. It could also be said that the origins of sixteenth-century Anglicanism were to be found in reformers who were versed in the modern biblical and textual humanism of their day.

Two aspects of modern thought that increasingly troubled Christian orthodoxy in the nineteenth century were biblical criticism and physical science—the latter after previous decades of largely untroubled interaction between science and Christianity as Diarmid Finnegan's chapter reveals. During the earlier decades of the century geological science raised questions about the account of creation in Genesis, but its findings were largely able to be explained within that biblical framework. Indeed Anglican clergy and orthodox laymen were prominent among the natural philosophers whose work had not yet evolved into that of scientists—full-time professional investigators of the natural world.

In contrast, Charles Darwin's work, *The Origin of Species*, published in 1859, brought a new tension between the scientific and religious explanations for the physical world into sharp focus, by opening the debate up to the general public. This was a surprise to Darwin himself as his book was a substantial piece of scientific work and not easy reading. But it became popularized by the efforts of various educated agnostics such as T. H. Huxley. Darwin's work was so explosive not because he was the first to postulate a theory of biological evolution, but because he offered massive and overwhelming evidence to support his theory, the result of twenty years of scientific labour. According to Darwin, all species multiplied and developed through time according to their potential to survive, or to fit, in a given environment. This survival of the most appropriate species over an immense past time contradicted the standard religious claims of a six-day creation in which God created and fixed all species in their present form. It also offended against traditional belief because Darwin's theory presupposed no place for any external divine purpose, but argued that evolution was a natural mechanism. The survival of the fittest also suggested to the Victorians a nature 'red in tooth and claw' in which the strongest triumphed over the weakest. What then could be said about a creation by a good and loving God?

Darwin performed a minor ecclesiastical miracle. In a British Christianity increasingly divided into warring factions, he succeeded in uniting Evangelicals and Anglo-Catholics, Anglicans and Nonconformists in common hostility to this impious absurdity. In the 1860s religious men went onto the attack out of pure reaction.

But not only science seriously questioned the literal truth of the Bible. In 1860 an attack on this divine source of Christian authority came from within the ranks of Anglican churchmen themselves. In that year a group of liberal Anglican scholars published a collection of chapters under the title of *Essays and Reviews*. They were attempting to address the implications of unrestricted theological enquiry for Scripture and Christian belief. The essayists' use of biblical criticism was cautious compared to their contemporaries in Germany, but for most British churchmen and the wider reading public *Essays and Reviews* was their first introduction to biblical criticism. Consequently, the book initiated one of the fiercest religious controversies of Victorian Britain. It had not been thoroughly prepared by its contributors and their haste in assembling their chapters led to some unconsidered statements which the authors later regretted or wished to modify. But there was a basic theological presupposition among the authors that religious belief should be defended by an appeal to morality, rather than to doctrine as objective, God-given truth. It was a liberal Anglican agenda—that Christianity was important as a moral religion and as an ethical force rather than as the revelation of supernatural truth encapsulated either in the doctrines of the Church or in the literal veracity of Scripture. In line with the commonly accepted presuppositions of German biblical criticism the essayists saw both of these things—the Church's doctrine and the words of Scripture—as historically conditioned rather than as timeless truths. But Victorian religion generally accepted that the Bible was authoritative for Christians because it was inspired literally; that is, the text itself was the inspiration of God and therefore the Bible was textually infallible.

It would not be until the end of the 1880s in the publication of another set of theological chapters in a book entitled *Lux Mundi* (1889), this time by young Anglo-Catholic scholars, that a more constructive approach than mere reaction to the authority of Scripture in relation to modern science and biblical criticism would be found by the orthodox. Along with the work of biblical scholars at Cambridge—B. F. Westcott, R. H. Lightfoot, and F. J. A. Hort—it was the *Lux Mundi* group which provided the theology enabling believing men and women, clerical and lay, to appropriate biblical criticism without jettisoning most of the fundamental tenets of the old orthodoxy. The contributors to the book accepted that the revelation of God was a progressive unfolding through history which provided the basis for their acceptance of biblical criticism. The chapterists' aim was to 'put the Catholic faith into its right relation to modern intellectual and moral problems', and the principal contributor, Charles Gore, later bishop of Oxford, argued for the acceptance of critical views of the Old Testament by proposing that its myths were best understood not as contradictory of modern historical and scientific discoveries, but rather as the apprehension of faith by primitive people. *Lux Mundi* brought relief to many educated Christians who found in it a way to bring together their religion and their learning, and it went through ten editions in a year.

Undoubtedly, the older pre-critical teaching, writing, and preaching continued among clergy. But increasingly, so did the newer critical outlook. While the rural parish pulpit may have taken longer to experience biblical criticism (though even here we should remind ourselves that many Oxbridge graduates became country parsons), clergy, theological students, and some laity were enabled by *Lux Mundi* to become less defensive towards modern thinking and biblical criticism. This may have meant that theology and devotion were becoming more separated at the end of the century compared with its beginning. In 1800 theologian and parishioner shared a common outlook—the historical accuracy of the Bible, its literal veracity, the timelessness of doctrine, and a culture largely permeated by Christianity. By 1900 Christian clergy and many educated laity were more aware than their forebears that these beliefs were difficult to sustain. But while theology and educated belief was being based on newer, critical, and historical perspectives which resonated with the nineteenth century's confidence about progress and development, the Christian devotion of the church-going may have very well remained in a pre-critical culture.

But the spread of Anglicanism in the nineteenth century was not only a matter of church extension, missions, and theological and denominational developments. Anglicanism also formed a substantial dimension of the global spread of an Anglophone culture. Churches, art, and music probably formed one of the most common ways in which the Church of England touched the lives of most people, as this was a period of unprecedented church building, and music was played in cathedrals and churches to a population that was still predominantly church-going (even if the Victorians remained anxious about those who did not go to church). In addition, in this period church music, and other music inspired by Christianity, was being played in the new large-scale concert halls to mass, albeit middle-class, audiences. Congregations in churches and cathedrals were increasingly exposed to an unprecedented variety and style of music. This could range from rousing hymnody that owed much to Methodism, to Latin mass settings in Anglo-Catholic churches. It was in the context of this plethora and diversity of music in Anglican churches that the styles, professionalism, and standards of Anglican music were formed, as Jeremy Dibble recounts in his chapter. Important in this process was not just the tensions between the various theological strands of nineteenth-century Anglicanism, and between the range of cooperation and tensions between clergy, choirs, and choirmaster; but also the cross-fertilization between the cathedral and the parish church. Similarly, the demands of nineteenth-century Anglicanism for new churches, including cathedrals, were a major agent in spreading not just a variety of church music throughout the Anglophone world and beyond, but also the culture of the Gothic Revival. While other denominations also built Gothic churches in this century, considered to be the proper form of church building, the large scale of international Anglicanism, and its need for an internal space centred around an altar similar to that of medieval churches, made Anglicanism a primary vehicle in the dispersion of this fundamental aspect of nineteenth-century culture. Ayla Lepine's chapter on art and architecture shows how Anglicanism was a significant component of various cultural movements in this century, including the Pre-Raphaelites, which allowed a distinctive Anglican aesthetic to emerge in the Victorian era centred around theological themes, particularly Christology. This aesthetic was epitomized in Holman Hunt's painting of Christ as 'The Light of the World', endlessly reproduced in the new mass printing processes of the Victorian age.

In contrast, Jane Garnett's chapter focuses on the things of earth and Anglican participation in social and economic life. She draws attention to the cosmopolitan nature of Anglican intellectual thought, which covered a wide spectrum from conservative to radical, though it has been typically portrayed as only the former. It involved a debate both within Anglican circles and between Anglicans and those beyond, but this occurred within a long-established tradition of moral theological criticism within Anglicanism. Anglican engagement was not limited to intellectual and moral debate, but also developed significant practical engagement with all the major social and economic movements of its day in Britain, the United States, and the British Empire.

In the century following the demise of the Anglican confessional state in the constitutional revolution of 1828 and 1829 Anglicans began to show signs of a greater religious radicalism. Whether prompted by their greater distance from the state, or their greater distance in the mission field from the Church of England, Anglicans explored the possibilities of their new legal or geographical positions, notwithstanding that in England at least they continued to seek for ways to maintain a sense of being the Church for the nation. In Britain, there was a surprising embracing of a cautious Socialism in the Christian Social Union begun in 1889, a development that had some earlier roots in the 1840s Christian Socialists, and the idiosyncratic Guild of St Matthew founded in 1877 by the Anglo-Catholic priest Stewart Headlam to reach out to the working class of London and particularly its actors. In global Anglicanism the mission field was beginning to insert itself into Anglican theologies. As much as most upheld the traditional view that the sole divine truth was deposited in Christianity, some clergy were beginning to see good in the religion of others. Of course individual Anglican laity had come to this conclusion in the previous century, particularly among some of the leading officials of the East India Company, though some of these officials who embraced Indian culture and its religions left their Christianity behind them. In the twentieth century C. F. Andrews would renounce his priesthood to follow Mahatma Ghandi. There were more clergy who retained their Anglicanism but adopted radical appreciations of other religions, albeit seeing them as fulfilled in their partial truth by Christianity. Such theological extremists included Fr Geoffrey Calloway and Bishop Colenso in Africa, unable to deny all truth to the religion of the Zulus they worked amongst. Others sought a more indigenized, less foreign-dominated mission, such as Henry Venn or, later, Roland Allen, whose writings were more influential in the twentieth century but were based on his missionary work in China in the 1900s. But radical Anglicanism did not always come from theological or religious extremists. It was present in the first Anglican bishop of New Zealand who in the 1840s devised a way for his new colonial and missionary Church to be free of the royal supremacy, which had until then been an indispensible mark of Anglicanism. As much as Anglicanism continued in this period to be a contested identity, extremely so as Anglican tendencies organized into mutually hostile parties to uphold their version of it, Anglicanism was also capable of surprising adaptations to an increasing variety of global places and contexts.

In many ways this development of a global Anglicanism is astonishing. A Church which began as a purely national entity deliberately separating itself from the predominant international Christian community then existing—the Western Catholic Church—and which was formed to uphold the supremacy of monarchical power over its adherents, ended the nineteenth century shaking itself increasingly loose from both that nationalism and monarchalism. It did so in order to become a global Christian entity—not quite a global Church because its nationalism morphed into independent national Churches, regions called provinces, or dioceses. With the important exception of the United States, the relinquishing of its monarchalism was a process not quite completed in the nineteenth century, when even independent Churches like New Zealand existed in colonial states that were subjects of the British crown, and where their settler populations were more than happy to be so. At the end of the nineteenth century, the Anglican Communion was still largely the English at prayer, colonial and missionary Anglicans having been exported or remade to a large extent in an English image—their Church led by English bishops, an English Prayer Book, and formularies derived from the Church of England. However, by then there were also indications that this would not always be the case, including initiatives overseas which influenced not just local variations of an English Anglicanism but also those, like the Lambeth Conference and the Lambeth Quadrilateral, that shaped the entire Anglican Communion. As Anglicanism began to evolve beyond its English roots in the nineteenth century, the question would arise in the twentieth century as to what then would keep this surprising global communion together?

Readers of this volume will note that its chapters are grouped in four sections. The first section comprises chapters that provide a narrative spine to the entire volume. Here the authors concentrate on what happened in nineteenth-century global Anglicanism, in chapters that have as their subjects Anglicanism in Britain and Europe, the British Empire, and developments beyond the British Empire. The next section comprises chapters on major internal developments within Anglicanism, so that readers will have an early exposure to the intra-Anglican parties which so coloured and shaped the domestic cultures and divisions of Anglicanism before embarking on chapters that cover global Anglicanism in more analytical detail. The following section provides chapters with distinct regional foci, going into more detail and analysis of world-wide developments that were covered broadly in the initial narrative chapters. The final section covers themes which were broadly influential throughout the Anglican world at this time. Readers may of course not follow this pattern by reading the volume consecutively, so the chapters are designed to also make sense as stand-alone works, though further detail can be followed up in other chapters. At the end of each chapter is a select bibliography. This bibliography is not intended to be exhaustive on the subject of the chapter, but to provide a selection of works chosen by the author as the principal ones related to the chapter's subject. These are predominantly recent and in English as they are designed to facilitate the unfolding of the subject to a wider than academic readership, though some further bibliographic information can be gleaned from each chapter's footnotes.

SELECT BIBLIOGRAPHY

Best, Geoffrey, 'The Constitutional Revolution, 1828–1832, and it Consequences for the Established Church', *Theology*, 52 (1959): 226–34.

Bremner, G. A., *Imperial Gothic: Religious Architecture and High Anglican Culture in the British Empire c.1840–1870* (New Haven, CT, 2013).

Brown, Stewart J., 'The Broad Church Movement, National Culture, and the Established Churches of Great Britain, c.1850–c.1900', in Hilary M. Carey and John Gascoigne (eds.), *Church and State in Old and New Worlds* (Leiden, 2011), pp. 99–128.

Brown, Stewart J., *The Oxford Movement: Europe and the Wider World 1830–1930* (Cambridge, 2012).

Burns, Arthur, *The Diocesan Revival of the Church of England c.1800–1870* (Oxford, 1999).

Hardwick, Joseph, *An Anglican British World: The Church of England and the Expansion of the Settler Empire c.1790–1860* (Manchester, 2014).

Maughan, Steven S., *Mighty England Do Good: Culture, Faith, Empire, and the World in the Foreign Missions of the Church of England, 1850–1915* (Grand Rapids, MI, 2014).

Reardon, Bernard M. G., *Religious Thought in the Victorian Age: A Survey from Coleridge to Gore* (London, 1980 edn.).

Sachs, William, *The Transformation of Anglicanism: From State Church to Global Communion* (Cambridge, 1993).

Stephenson, Alan M. G., *Anglicanism and the Lambeth Conferences* (London, 1978).

Strong, Rowan, *Anglicanism and the British Empire c.1700–1850* (Oxford, 2007), chs. 4 and 5.

Strong, Rowan, 'The Church of England and the British Imperial State: Anglican Metropolitan Sermons of the 1850s', in Hilary M. Carey and John Gascoigne (eds.), *Church and State in Old and New Worlds* (Leiden, 2011), pp. 183–205.

Ward, Kevin, *A History of Global Anglicanism* (Cambridge, 2006).

2

British and European Anglicanism

John Wolffe

In 1847, the Revd Richard Thomas Lowe, then the Anglican chaplain on Madeira but best known to posterity as a naturalist, became the subject of a heated exchange between two of the most redoubtable public figures of the early Victorian age, the bishop of London, Charles James Blomfield, and the Foreign Secretary Lord Palmerston. Lowe was a supporter of the Oxford Movement, which sought to renew Catholic tradition within the Church of England. Although Lowe's consequent changes to worship at the English church on the island were quite modest, they were implemented in a self-important and tactless manner that antagonized the majority of the congregation.[1] Palmerston was initially slow to become involved, but when he did take an interest his approach was characteristically decisive. He wrote to the bishop on 8 June 1847, who was responsible for licensing Anglican chaplains abroad, telling him that Lowe's removal was a matter of 'urgent necessity' as he was alienating British residents in Madeira from the Church of England and bringing 'discredit upon our National Church in the opinion of the people of Madeira, by publicly exhibiting to their view differences and disputes which ill befit the members of a Christian community'. Blomfield responded that he did not feel justified in dismissing Lowe, but would ask him to resign.[2] The latter, however, refused to go quietly, while Blomfield refused to force the issue by withdrawing his licence. Faced with a continuing impasse, in December 1847 Palmerston himself wrote to Lowe, informing him that he was dismissed 'for the purpose of restoring peace, and of avoiding further scandal to the English Church'. When Blomfield pointed out that Lowe still held his licence which he was not prepared to revoke, Palmerston directed his fury at the bishop, claiming that licences were not legally required by chaplains abroad and, moreover,

1 Roy Nash, *Scandal in Madeira: The Story of Richard Thomas Lowe* (Lewes, 1990), pp. 34–87.

2 National Archives (NA), Palmerston to Blomfield, 8 June 1847; Blomfield to Palmerston, 21 June 1847, FO 425/12, p. 115.

> that which has happened in the case of Mr Lowe shows that the practice is calculated to create misconceptions both at home and abroad, as to powers and authorities, to the inconvenience of the public service. It is my intention to alter the existing regulations in this respect, and to abstain in future from troubling your Lordship to grant licences to clergymen officiating abroad.[3]

In the event, Palmerston did not carry out this threat, but the incident serves effectively to introduce the three central themes of this chapter. First, it illustrates the intensity of internal divisions in Victorian Anglicanism, which, while indicative of its vitality and creativity, divided congregations and communities, not only in distant Madeira but also in England itself. Second, it was symptomatic of major tensions in the relationship between Church and state, which, after a long period of substantive stability between 1688 and 1829, was a matter for almost continual change and controversy between 1829 and 1914. Third, it highlights the ambiguities in the situation of Anglicanism outside England, which were apparent not only in Madeira, but also in continental Europe and, closer to home, in Ireland, Scotland, and Wales. The remainder of this chapter explores these three issues in turn.

CHURCH CRISIS AND PARTY CONFLICT

Although the late Hanoverian Church of England was by no means an internally harmonious institution, with sometimes considerable hostility between High Churchmen and Evangelicals, the early Victorian period saw the emergence of much sharper internal polarities than had previously existed. Victorian Church party divisions had their roots in the past—in the long-term legacy of the Elizabethan Settlement that sought to maintain a Church that was at once Reformed and comprehensive; and in the more recent 'new wine' of the Evangelical Revival—but their particular form and intensity derived from more immediate circumstances. The 1820s saw a growing sense of Anglican insecurity in the face of the rapid growth of religious dissent and especially of Methodism, and the looming sense of constitutional crisis that was to result in Catholic Emancipation in 1829 and the Great Reform Act in 1832. A further source of alarm was Roman Catholic resurgence, both on the continent and in Ireland.

Evangelicals were the first to respond with the re-emergence of pronounced Calvinism and the development at the influential Albury conferences of the late 1820s of a polemical anti-Catholicism associated with a premillenialist

[3] Palmerston to Lowe, 22 Dec. 1847; Blomfield to Palmerston, 28 Dec. 1847; Palmerston to Blomfield, 21 Jan. 1848, NA, FO 425/12, pp. 122–5.

eschatology. This new harsher mood in Anglican Evangelicalism was both focused and propagated by the influential *Record* newspaper, which began publication in 1828. Meanwhile the building of Exeter Hall in central London between 1829 and 1831 provided Evangelicals with a physical hub and meeting place, especially for the sequence of May gatherings of their numerous societies, thus strengthening a sense of party identity. A parallel trend among High Churchmen is conventionally dated to the beginning of the Oxford Movement in 1833, immediately stimulated by the Whig government's reforms of the Church of Ireland condemned by John Keble as 'national apostasy', but rooted in an impulse to reassert the Catholic identity of the Church of England as its best security against dissent and Erastianism. Despite their radical theological divergences, the 'Recordites' and the 'Tractarians'—as they became known after their respective trademark publications—were thus responding to the same circumstances, driven by the absolute conviction that only their own prescriptions could save the Church from potentially fatal maladies. Moreover the pronounced anti-Catholicism of the Recordites preconditioned them to deep suspicion of the Tractarians who, for their part, viewed hardline Evangelicalism as inimical to essential Anglican identity.

The situation was further complicated by a third set of proposed remedies issuing from the liberal Anglican or Broad Church school, led by Thomas Arnold, who wrote in 1833 that insistence on a unity based on narrow doctrinal agreement was 'the great mischief, both of the Christian church in general, and of the Church of England in particular, and has brought about in the latter that monstrous state of things in which a total Reform can alone save it from complete destruction'.[4] For Arnold, the salvation of Anglicanism lay not in the assertion of a narrow identity, but rather in moving to a comprehensiveness that would enable it to reconcile the great majority of mainstream Christians. The resulting theological imprecision was anathema to Recordite and Tractarian alike.

Church party divisions were further polarized by the events of the 1830s and 1840s—notably the conversion to Roman Catholicism of John Henry Newman and some other leading Tractarians in 1845 and a protracted legal battle between 1847 and 1850 in which the High Church (but not Tractarian) bishop of Exeter, Henry Phillpotts, attempted to exclude a well-connected Evangelical clergyman, George Gorham, from a living in his diocese. Lowe's ritual innovations at the Madeira chapel were, by all accounts, quite modest ones, but his difficulties at this same period illustrate how in this context of heightened party tensions, minor differences could escalate into serious conflicts.

In 1853 William John Conybeare, then vicar of Axminster, published in the *Edinburgh Review* an incisive and witty analysis of the current make-up of the

[4] Thomas Arnold, *Principles of Church Reform* (London, 1833), p. 40.

Church of England. He estimated that among the 18,000 clergy, there were 7,000 High Churchmen, 6,500 Low Churchmen, and 3,500 Broad Churchmen, as well as 1,000 'peasant clergy in the mountain districts, who must be classed apart'. Conybeare further subdivided the High Church and Low Church categories into what he termed normal, exaggerated, and stagnant varieties, respectively Anglican, Tractarian, and 'High and Dry', and Evangelical, Recordite, and 'Low and Slow'. He calculated that the exaggerated variants were still in the minority, especially on the High Church side, but as they were more numerous among younger clergy, and also made conspicuous by their actions and opinions, they were increasingly setting the tone of the Church as a whole. Conybeare's 'Low and Slow' and 'High and Dry' categories encompassed those clergy, usually older men, who had lapsed into inertia. He thought they had much in common with each other: 'Their professed doctrines, indeed, are dissimilar, but these are only accidentally adopted, and make no essential distinction. In sluggish mediocrity, in hatred of zeal, in dread of innovation, in abuse of Dissent, they are in perfect harmony.'[5]

In 1860 the publication of *Essays and Reviews* by seven leading Broad Churchmen brought that school of thought into greater and controversial prominence. The essay by Henry Wilson restated Thomas Arnold's vision of a comprehensive Church of England, while other contributors, notably Benjamin Jowett and Rowland Williams, advocated a rationalist critical approach to the text of the Bible and the accommodation of Christian teaching to contemporary thought, such as Charles Darwin's recently-published *On the Origin of Species*. Williams and Wilson were prosecuted for heresy, and the appointment in 1869 of another contributor, Frederick Temple, as bishop of Exeter stirred major controversy. Meanwhile another liberal bishop, John William Colenso of Natal, whose publications questioned the historicity of the Pentateuch and the book of Joshua, also excited hostility and alarm among conservatives in England as well as in southern Africa.

The second half of the nineteenth century saw substantial continuing intra-Anglican tensions over the ritual and devotional practices stimulated by the Oxford Movement. There were disturbances at churches—for example in London at St Barnabas Pimlico in 1850 and at St George's in the East in 1859—and prosecutions of leading ritualists, such as Alexander Mackonochie in 1867, Arthur Tooth who was imprisoned for contempt of court in 1877, and most high profile of all, the bishop of Lincoln, Edward King, from 1888 to 1892. Party alignments were further institutionalized, with the formation on the Anglo-Catholic side of the Society of the Holy Cross in 1855 and the English Church Union in 1860, and on the Evangelical side of the Church

[5] W. J. Conybeare, 'Church Parties', ed. Arthur Burns, in Stephen Taylor (ed.), *From Cranmer to Davidson: A Miscellany* (Church of England Record Society 7, Woodbridge, 1999), pp. 213–385, especially p. 335.

Association in 1866, with the primary purpose of prosecuting ritualists. In 1897 the Protestant agitator Walter Walsh could still secure a wide readership for his *Secret History of the Oxford Movement* which effectively restated earlier Evangelical polemics.

Nevertheless, by the turn of the twentieth century, Victorian Church party conflicts were losing some of their earlier intensity. All groups were obliged tacitly to accept that none of them would be able to claim a monopoly of the Church of England and that internal diversity was inevitable in the future. This recognition was symbolized by the appointment as archbishop of Canterbury in 1896 of the aged Frederick Temple, erstwhile contributor to *Essays and Reviews*, who in his closing years thus came to embody the fulfilment of a comprehensive vision of the Church of England.

CHURCH, STATE, AND REFORM

The divisions within the Church of England were inextricably bound up with its problematic and rapidly changing relationship with the state, which was itself a reflection of its increasingly contested situation on the ground. Whereas in the eighteenth century Dissenters and Roman Catholics had been small minorities who challenged Anglican monopoly but not Anglican dominance, during the first half of the nineteenth century their numbers increased rapidly. Methodist growth was especially spectacular: reported membership in England was still only 56,605 when John Wesley died in 1791, but in 1831 it was 288,182 and in 1861 513,628.[6] Moreover, during this period Methodist links to the Church of England weakened: whereas John Wesley had always perceived his movement as a society *within* the Church rather than as a new denomination, in his later years momentum was building towards separation. After his death Methodism divided, with the New Connexion and the Primitives more hostile to the Church of England than the original Wesleyan strand. And although in 1834 Bishop Phillpotts could still regard Wesleyans as 'sincere friends of the Church' and, even in the 1860s some of them were still attending parish churches as well as their own chapels, for them too the trend towards a distinct denominational identity was inexorable.[7] When the one and only systematic religious census was taken in 1851 it revealed that only 48.57 per cent of recorded church attendances were Anglicans ones, and that they were almost

[6] A. D. Gilbert, *Religion and Society in Industrial England: Church, Chapel and Society Change 1740–1914* (London, 1976), p. 31.

[7] Exeter Cathedral Library, Phillpotts to C. Cooke, 15 Jan. 1834, ED/11/76; Edward Royle, 'When did Methodists Stop Attending their Parish Churches?' *Proceedings of the Wesley Historical Society*, 56 (2008): 275–96.

equalled by the combined forces of Protestant Dissent and Methodism, with 47.43 per cent. Roman Catholics accounted for most of the balance. Locally, and even regionally, notably in Wales and in Yorkshire, the Church of England was shown to be very much in a numerical minority.[8] From an Anglican point of view these figures were deeply disturbing, even if they only confirmed the impressions of informed observers such as W. F. Hook, the vicar of Leeds, who in 1837 described Methodism as the '*de facto* established religion of the town'.[9] If the Church no longer retained the loyalties of the majority of the population its privileged relationship with the state was open to redefinition or even abolition.

The repeal of the Test and Corporation Acts in 1828 followed by Catholic Emancipation in 1829 had already ended the exclusively Anglican (and Scottish Presbyterian) character of the institutions of government, and thereby gave rise to the diverse and divisive reassertions of Anglican identity surveyed in the previous section. In the early 1830s the unequally distributed wealth of the Church of England became a prime target for radicals, but in 1835 Sir Robert Peel's establishment of the Ecclesiastical Commission to recommend reforms headed off the attacks of more hostile critics. The commission nevertheless proposed substantial changes which were carried into legislation in the late 1830s, including the creation of new bishoprics at Ripon and Manchester to serve the industrializing north, the equalization of episcopal revenues, the stripping of excessive endowments from cathedrals to support poorer parishes, and strict controls on pluralism to prevent clergy holding more than one living unless these were contiguous and poorly endowed. Reasonable though these changes were, such state intervention was nevertheless offensive to many High Churchmen and stimulated sympathy for the leaders of the Oxford Movement and their endeavours to reassert the spiritual and historic integrity of the English Church.

In 1845 it was the turn of Evangelicals to be outraged when Peel's government proposed permanent state support for the Roman Catholic seminary at Maynooth near Dublin. While Maynooth had long been receiving annual grants, its permanent endowment appeared fundamentally to compromise the Protestant nature of the British state, a concern that Evangelicals shared with conservative High Churchmen. The extra-parliamentary agitation against the measure was, however, spearheaded by the Anti-Maynooth Committee, an uneasy alliance of Anglican Evangelicals with Protestant Dissenters, which broke down when some of the latter insisted on grounding antagonism to the Maynooth grant on the principle of opposing all state endowment of

[8] *Census of Great Britain, 1851: Religious Worship, England and Wales—Report and Tables*, House of Commons Sessional Papers, 1852–3, LXXXIX.

[9] Quoted in W. R. W. Stephens, *The Life and Letters of Walter Farquhar Hook*, 2 vols. (London, 1879), I, p. 404.

religion. Vociferous though the government's critics were, they were too divided to prevent the measure being enacted.

From the perspective of committed Anglicans, the rub was that the state seemed to be having things both ways, by curtailing the constitutionally privileged status of the Church of England *and* seeking to exercise a greater degree of control over its affairs. Parallel tensions had exploded in 1843 in the Church of Scotland which, although Presbyterian in polity, was the counterpart of the Church of England in respect of its established status. The Church of Scotland was embroiled in long-running disputes with the civil courts over both the right of congregations to reject a patron's nominee and the status of new parishes created in response to urban growth. When the government failed to act to uphold that Church's position, over a third of its ministers and laity seceded to set up the competing Free Church of Scotland. Hence as Church party tensions intensified in the mid-to-late 1840s, the prospect of a parallel substantial schism south of the border seemed a very real one. The state was actively implicated in these controversies, as was illustrated by Palmerston's intervention in the Madeira chaplaincy affair, and above all in the Gorham case. This long-running legal saga reached its climax in March 1850 when the Judicial Committee of Privy Council, the final court of appeal in the matter, found in Gorham's favour, ruling that his Evangelical beliefs on baptism were consistent with Anglican doctrine. He was accordingly instituted to his benefice over the head of his diocesan bishop. For High Churchmen and Tractarians the appearance that a civil court, only set up in its present form in 1833, was defining the boundaries of Church doctrine was, if anything, even more offensive than the outcome itself. Consequently a few prominent Tractarians, notably Henry Manning, the future second archbishop of Westminster, converted to Roman Catholicism, but had the judgement gone the other way it is likely that there would have been a more substantial secession of Evangelicals who would have felt that their position within the Church of England was rendered untenable. As it was, Evangelical secessions, like Tractarian conversions, never became a large-scale movement. They did, however, include a few prominent individuals, notably Baptist Noel, a leading London clergyman who in 1848 published an *Essay on the Union of Church and State* justifying his decision to become a Baptist, and James Shore, whose own dispute with Bishop Phillpotts of Exeter culminated with his departure in 1844 to found the small Free Church of England.

In the late Georgian period the Church of England was still able to obtain substantial additional support from the state, notably the total of £1.5 million provided in 1818 and 1824 for the so-called Waterloo churches, which were an initial response to rapid population growth. This provision did not, however, come close to meeting the needs of the Church, which was struggling to manage enormous unwieldy parishes in expanding towns like Leeds. Here, as in the numerous populous settlements remote from medieval parish churches that were developing in rural or semi-rural areas, Methodists and other Dissenters stepped in to fill some of the gaps in Anglican provision, although a substantial minority—perhaps even a majority—of the population lacked a regular association with organized Christianity. After 1830, however, despite the obvious insufficiencies of existing church provision, the political climate turned decisively against making further state grants for building churches, as was apparent in 1840 in the defeat of a parliamentary motion by Sir Robert Inglis calling for grants to be made for this purpose. Accordingly the Church was forced back on voluntary donations, which proved to be forthcoming on an impressive scale, enabling the building or rebuilding of many thousands of churches, and the provision of endowments for their clergy. In 1831 there were 11,883 churches and 14,993 clergy; in 1901 there were 17,368 churches and 23,670 clergy.[10] The state facilitated this process insofar as it reduced the legal obstacles to the creation of new parishes and eventually enabled the creation of further new bishoprics at St Albans (1877), Truro (1877), Newcastle (1882), Southwell (1884), Wakefield (1888), Birmingham (1905), and Southwark (1905) but it did not support it financially.

The financing of extensive church building by voluntary donations was a key aspect of a wider movement for internal reform and renewal in a Church that increasingly recognized that it could no longer depend on state support. The need to raise funds itself necessitated new organizational structures, such as the Metropolis Churches Fund in 1836 and its successor, the Bishop of London's Fund in 1863. The need for increased human resources as well as new churches was recognized by the formation of the Church Pastoral Aid Society (CPAS) in 1836 and its High Church equivalent, the Additional Curates Society (ACS) in 1837. Unlike the CPAS, the ACS would only support clergy and not lay agents. The period also saw a revival in the diocesan structures, led by energetic bishops, who differed in party outlook, but shared a common commitment to the efficient functioning of the Church on the ground. Leading figures in this movement included the Evangelical Sumner brothers, Charles Richard (Winchester 1827–69), and John Bird (Chester 1828–48; Canterbury 1848–62); conservative High Churchmen such as John Kaye (Lincoln 1827–53), Henry Phillpotts (Exeter 1830–69), and Samuel Wilberforce (Oxford 1845–69; Winchester 1869–73), the Tractarian Walter Kerr Hamilton (Salisbury 1854–69), and the Broad Church Archibald Campbell Tait (London 1856–68; Canterbury 1868–82). Such bishops oversaw their clergy more closely than their predecessors, preventing unjustified pluralism and non-residence, and encouraging them to see their pastoral responsibilities as extending well beyond the conduct of Sunday worship, to include notably the provision and support of Church schools. They also encouraged a revival

[10] Gilbert, *Religion and Society*, p. 28.

of activity by intermediate officers, rural deans, and archdeacons. Clergy began to meet together more regularly to discuss common concerns and share good practice. Some such gatherings, such as the (Evangelical) Islington Clerical Conference, dating from the 1820s, developed on party rather than geographical lines, but rural deanery chapters, gathering momentum in the 1840s and 1850s, increasingly brought together clergy of diverse views from a particular locality. In 1851 Bishop Phillpotts convened the first modern diocesan synod in England at Exeter Cathedral: although this had the primary partisan aim of repudiating the Gorham Judgment it also proved to be an opportunity for more wide-ranging discussion. Other bishops began to hold diocesan assemblies in the 1860s and 1870s. Such activity helped to ensure that 'High and Dry' and 'Low and Slow' clergy were dying breeds.

The culminating element in the Church's revival of internal structures was the convocations, gatherings of representatives of the clergy from across the two ecclesiastical provinces of Canterbury and York. The Canterbury Convocation began to meet in the 1850s for the first time since the early eighteenth century, to be followed by York a few years later. They gradually moved from merely formal business to active discussion of current concerns. In the 1880s and 1890s lay representatives were added, providing the basis for the institution that evolved into the Church Assembly in 1919 and, eventually, the General Synod in 1970. In parallel the later nineteenth century saw an annual series of Church Congresses in different towns and cities: unlike the convocations these lacked formal legal status but were well-supported forums for discussion of shared Anglican concerns.

The development of increasingly robust and active internal structures helped to ensure the institutional stability of the Church of England in the face of significant political challenges. From 1844, the Anti-State Church Association, later known as the Liberation Society, waged a sustained campaign to curtail the privileges of the Church of England. It was unsuccessful in its long-term objective of disestablishment, but secured notable victories, especially the abolition in 1868 of compulsory church rates. This controversial levy had hitherto been imposed on all property owners—even non-Anglicans—to support the maintenance of local church fabric and worship. Thus, although the Church of England has retained its residual links to the state down to the present time, the actual significance of establishment was much altered between 1828 and the end of the nineteenth century.

IRELAND, WALES, AND SCOTLAND

The situation of Anglicanism was different in each of the non-English nations of the United Kingdom. The position of the Church of Ireland had always seemed particularly anomalous. Although it was the state Church, in 1834 it commanded the loyalty of only 10.7 per cent of the population, with 8.1 per cent of the remainder being Presbyterian and 80.9 per cent Roman Catholic.[11] Moreover in much of the country, especially in the south and west, the Catholic predominance was even greater. The Church of Ireland was strongest in and around Dublin, and in Ulster, but as Presbyterians were heavily concentrated in the north-east they outnumbered Anglicans in counties Antrim and Down and in the rapidly growing town of Belfast. The Church of Ireland's continuing established status was thus a by-product of the long-standing political and social ascendancy of English-speaking landlords and grounds for resentment among the majority of the population. Its more visionary supporters, however, still viewed it as the potential providential instrument for the eventual conversion of Ireland to Protestantism. Hopes that such a vision might become a reality were briefly rekindled in the so-called 'Second Reformation' movement of the 1820s. However, there was never any realistic prospect that the great majority of the Irish population would change its religious allegiance, and the sharpening of political and religious polarities that accompanied Catholic Emancipation in 1829 made even small-scale conversions much less likely.

Hence the reforming Whig government, in power in London from 1830, saw the current position of the Church of Ireland as even more indefensible than that of the Church of England. In 1833 they brought forward legislation that substantially reduced its top-heavy structures, by amalgamating its twenty-two dioceses into twelve, and reducing two of its four archbishoprics to bishoprics. Appointments to parishes where no services had been held for three years were suspended, and the money saved by these and other measures placed under the control of an Ecclesiastical Commission. As we have seen, these measures had substantial repercussions in England where they were the immediate stimulus for the Oxford Movement, while in the Church of Ireland itself it reinforced a sense of crisis also stemming from Catholic Emancipation and from the refusal of many Catholics to pay tithes. Despite these challenges, or perhaps in some respects because of them, the middle decades of the nineteenth century saw significant renewal in the Church of Ireland, especially on its Evangelical wing. The Irish Church Missions to Roman Catholics, founded in 1849, spearheaded further proselytizing endeavours: its positive achievements were limited but it reinforced Catholic resentments.

Nevertheless, although the political onslaught on the Church of Ireland receded in the 1840s and 1850s, even in its reduced state its established status was untenable in the long term and in 1869 another reforming Liberal government enacted its disestablishment. For many Irish Anglicans this

[11] Sean Connolly, *Religion and Society in Nineteenth-Century Ireland* (Dundalk, 1985), p. 3.

initially seemed a disaster, a mood evoked by hymn-writer Cecil Frances Alexander, in a verse sung when the act came into force on 1 January 1871:

> Look down, Lord of heaven, on our desolation!
> Fallen, fallen, fallen is now our Country's crown,
> Dimly dawns the New Year on a churchless nation,
> Ammon and Amalek tread our borders down.[12]

In the event, however, the Church of Ireland was to adapt quite successfully to its changed circumstances, making good use of the financial compensation its clergy had received and developing its own effective organizational structures. It was now free to concentrate on ministering to its own minority constituency, without being burdened by an unrealistic sense of responsibility to the Catholic majority who were more likely to be provoked than edified by its attentions. Despite the increasing tendency of the non-Roman Catholic population to gravitate towards Ulster, it retained a sense of itself as an all-Ireland institution.

The four Welsh dioceses—Bangor, Llandaff, St Asaph, and St Davids—were, unlike the Church of Ireland, historically structurally integrated into the Church of England, as part of the province of Canterbury. They were relatively poorly endowed, meaning that prior to the reforms of the 1830s they were liable to be career staging posts for rising ecclesiastics, who would rapidly move on to a richer English see, or worse still hold a Welsh bishopric alongside a preferment elsewhere and seldom visit their diocese. This neglect at the top was paralleled by inadequate resources at the parochial level, which to a greater extent even than in England left the door wide open to the growth of religious dissent in order to meet the resulting pastoral deficiencies. The religious census of 1851 showed Wales to have a high level of religious observance, but with Anglicans very much in the minority. It was true attitudes in the Church were already changing, with nineteenth-century bishops such as Thomas Burgess (St Davids 1803–25), Connop Thirlwall (St Davids 1840–74), and Alfred Ollivant (Llandaff 1849–82) noticeably more conscientious that their predecessors. Like their counterparts in England they presided over substantial church building and pastoral and spiritual renewal. Nevertheless insofar as such efforts were an endeavour to maintain Anglicanism's claim to a privileged status in Wales, there was a sense of shutting the stable door after the horse had bolted. Although the Welsh Church was not to be disestablished until 1920, its political vulnerability was clear.

Anglicanism in Scotland developed in a very different religious context from that in Ireland and Wales. The dominance of Presbyterianism in Scotland had been decisively established in 1689, and between that date and the mid-nineteenth century Episcopalians became reduced to a small

[12] Quoted in P. M. H. Bell, *Disestablishment in Ireland and Wales* (London, 1969), p. 158.

minority, most of whom were subject until 1792 to penal laws because of their Jacobite loyalties. A significant minority, who were prepared to take an oath of obedience to the Hanoverian dynasty, worshipped in so-called 'qualified chapels' but were disowned by other Episcopalians. Episcopalians were more numerous in the north, where they developed distinctive traditions and liturgy, the Scottish Communion Office. Although most of their clergy had a natural affinity with High Churchmen on the other side of the border, links to the Church of England were stronger among the handful of more Anglicized congregations in the south.

The party divisions of the Church of England were strongly echoed in Scotland. Although Evangelicals were a minority within a minority, they were an active one. In 1842, an Edinburgh clergyman, D. T. K. Drummond, following a clash with his bishop over the holding of non-liturgical evangelistic meetings, left the Scottish Episcopal Church to initiate a small movement of independent Episcopal churches in Scotland which sought oversight from Church of England and colonial bishops. Most of them rejoined the Scottish Episcopal Church after 1890.

The spiritual independence of the Scottish Episcopal Church made it attractive to the Oxford Movement, which had a significant early impact in Scotland. When Alexander Forbes became bishop of Brechin in 1847, he was the first Tractarian to be elevated to the episcopate in any part of the United Kingdom. Impressive new churches, such as St John's Jedburgh (1844) and St Ninian's Cathedral Perth (1850), expressed both the liturgical principles of the Oxford Movement and the enhanced confidence and visibility of Scottish Episcopalians.[13] Tractarianism, however, proved controversial and divisive in Scotland as well as in England: for example in 1857 Forbes's views on the real presence of Christ in the eucharist gave rise to major controversy, and led in 1860 to his trial by his fellow bishops who reached an equivocal conclusion clearly designed to avoid schism.[14]

Nevertheless, despite such internal divisions, the nineteenth century was a period of substantial growth for the Scottish Episcopal Church, which had an estimated 15,000 adherents (including the qualified chapels) in 1800 but increased to over 116,000 in 1900,[15] an increase that was nearly eight-fold against a three-fold increase in the overall population of Scotland during the course of the nineteenth century. This disproportionate growth was in part a consequence of English and Irish migration to Scotland, but also attributable

[13] Stewart J. Brown, 'Scotland and the Oxford Movement', in Stewart J. Brown and Peter Nockles (eds.), *The Oxford Movement: Europe and the Wider World* (Cambridge, 2012), pp. 61–5.

[14] Rowan Strong, *Alexander Penrose Forbes of Brechin: The First Tractarian Bishop* (Oxford, 1995), ch. 4.

[15] Rowan Strong, *Episcopalianism in Nineteenth-Century Scotland: Religious Responses to a Modernizing Society* (Oxford, 2002), pp. 19, 29.

to the increasing appeal of the Episcopal Church to socially aspiring Scots. Although a minority within the Church sought to maintain distinctively Scottish traditions, the dominant trend was towards Anglicization, which was both symbolized and facilitated by the removal in 1864 of the legal obstacle to clergy ordained in Scotland transferring to benefices in England or Wales (whereas such movement had always been open to Church of Ireland clergy).

At the end of the period, in 1911, Anglican communicants made up 6.5 per cent of the population of Wales and Episcopalian members 3.0 per cent of that of Scotland. In Ireland, 13.1 per cent of the population identified themselves as Anglicans. These statistics are not equivalent, as the Irish figure represents minimal identification, whereas the Welsh and Scottish ones represent active practice and committed membership respectively. Moreover the comparable figure for communicants in Scotland was only 1.15 per cent of the population, indicating that despite the advances of the previous century Anglicanism there was still much weaker numerically than in Wales.[16] Nevertheless by the early twentieth century the situations of the three Churches were broadly similar, with destinies independent of the state and the Church of England (but with close links to it), and ministering to significant minority populations.

ANGLICANS IN EUROPE

Anglicanism in continental and Mediterranean Europe was a scattered but growing presence in increasingly numerous expatriate communities. Some chaplaincies, such as Hamburg and Constantinople, had a history dating back to the early seventeenth century, and in 1633 the Privy Council placed them under the jurisdiction of the bishop of London.[17] Until the early nineteenth century, however, such provision was limited to embassies and merchant factories, notably those supported by the Levant Company in the eastern Mediterranean. Following the restoration of peace in 1815 English communities on the continent grew rapidly, accompanied by the formation of new Anglican congregations, for example in Tours in 1815, Boulogne and Rome in 1816, and Brussels, Florence, and Lausanne in 1819.[18] The Consular Advances Act of 1825 provided for the appointment and payment of chaplains in cities

[16] Robert Currie, Alan Gilbert, and Lee Horsley, *Churches and Churchgoers: Patterns of Church Growth in the British Isles since 1700* (Oxford, 1977), pp. 128, 220–2.

[17] Henry J. C. Knight, *The Diocese of Gibraltar: A Sketch of its History, Work and Tasks* (London, 1917), pp. 4, 25; Paul W. Schniewind, *Anglicans in Germany: A History of Anglican Chaplaincies in Germany until 1945* (Umkirch, 1988), p. 112.

[18] Knight, *Diocese of Gibraltar*, p. 34; George E. Biber, *The English Church on the Continent* (London, 1846), pp. 29, 32, 46, 70.

where there was a British consulate. However, the situation of chaplains was inconsistent and unstable. Those in locations without a consulate were entirely dependent on support from their congregations and from voluntary societies; the Foreign Office stipend that came with a consular presence still needed to be matched by congregational contributions, and gave the consul himself a controlling influence comparable to that of a village squire at home. This was the situation in Madeira, where the long-standing and wealthy British consul, Henry Veitch, was an amateur architect who had himself designed the English church. Such appointments were also subject to licensing and oversight by the bishop of London, who was inevitably poorly informed regarding individuals and local circumstances. Non-consular chaplains, on the other hand, could in practice operate without any episcopal licence.

The consequent confusions of governmental and Church responsibility were well illustrated by the clash between Blomfield and Palmerston over the Madeira chaplaincy. A further example was the case of the Revd Thomas Harvey who, between 1831 and 1845, served chaplaincies in four different cities—Leghorn, Genoa, Frankfurt-am-Main, and Antwerp—where he found himself repeatedly at odds both with dissident groups in successive congregations and with Bishop Blomfield of London. Harvey's troubles culminated in 1845, when after the British consul in Antwerp had attempted to exclude him from his own church, Blomfield advised the Foreign Secretary, Lord Aberdeen, to dismiss him from the Antwerp chaplaincy 'in order to prevent continued scandal to the church'. It seems that the specific root of the problem was that Harvey's staunch churchmanship offended dissenting elements among eclectic expatriate English-speaking congregations, who thus echoed attacks on the Church of England at home, but his case also pointed up significant unresolved confusions in the organization of the chaplaincies.[19]

In 1845 the Revd George Biber, with the sanction of Bishop Blomfield, carried out a survey of the continental chaplaincies. His report gave striking evidence of the growth of such provision since 1815: he listed twenty-five permanent congregations in France, eighteen in Germany, eleven in Italy, nine in Belgium, seven in Russia (including Poland), four in Switzerland, three in the Netherlands, two apiece in the Ionian Islands, Portugal, and Turkey, and one in Greece, as well as churches in the British colonies of Gibraltar and Malta. There were also some transient and seasonal congregations. In his introduction Biber highlighted the obstacles they faced, particularly the inadequate pay of the chaplains and widespread dependence on borrowed or shared church buildings or on rented rooms in hotels and other secular buildings.[20]

[19] Thomas Harvey, *An Appeal to the Right Hon. Lord John Russell, MP Against the Proceedings of the Bishop of London* (London, 1847), pp. 5–6, 12–14, 18–19.

[20] Biber, *English Church*, pp. 3–8.

Awareness of the need for closer oversight of the chaplains had already, in 1824, prompted the consecration as a bishop of Matthew Luscombe by the Scottish Episcopal Church, but with the tacit approval of the government, the archbishop of Canterbury, and the bishop of London. Luscombe's letters of collation made it clear that his jurisdiction was limited to professed Anglicans and Scottish Episcopalians, and that there was no intention 'to disturb the peace of any Christian Society established as a National Church'.[21] He was based in Paris, where he financed the building of his own church. However, his authority was seldom recognized outside France, and the majority of chaplains in northern and central Europe continued to be licensed by Blomfield, or to operate independently without any licence. The presence of two bishops claiming jurisdiction in the region led to divided loyalties and when Luscombe died in 1846 he was not replaced.[22]

Meanwhile, in 1842, the see of Gibraltar was established to exercise jurisdiction over 'the Clergy and Laity of the communion of the United Church of England and Ireland resident within Gibraltar and Malta and diverse places within the islands and countries situated in and around the Mediterranean'. As with Luscombe's appointment, there was thus an anxiety to avoid any appearance of establishing a territorial episcopal jurisdiction that would conflict with that of Roman Catholic and Orthodox bishops. Indeed the very choice of Gibraltar for the see, rather than Valetta, which would have been more geographically central, was due in large part to the prior existence of a Roman Catholic bishopric of Malta.[23] Although the bishop of Gibraltar's responsibilities were eventually to extend from the shores of the Atlantic to those of the Caspian Sea, they did not include countries north of the Alps or France apart from the Mediterranean coast. These regions remained the responsibility of the bishop of London.

The first two bishops of Gibraltar, George Tomlinson (1842–63) and Walter Trower (1863–8), struggled to exercise effective pastoral oversight over their dispersed flocks, in part because of their own reluctance to travel continuously, but also because their authority was open to contestation by independent-minded chaplains and congregations. In 1850, Archbishop Sumner of Canterbury was obliged to issue a pastoral letter declaring that the bishop of Gibraltar was entitled to the same obedience as a diocesan bishop in England.[24] The diocese was consolidated under Charles Harris (1868–73) and Charles Sandford (1874–1903) who more readily adapted to an itinerant lifestyle. Sandford in particular promoted a collective identity through his own

[21] Knight, *Diocese of Gibraltar*, p. 40.

[22] John Pinnington, 'Bishop Luscombe and Anglican Order in Continental Europe', *Historical Magazine of the Protestant Episcopal Church*, 38 (1969), pp. 381–92; Edward Luscombe, *Matthew Luscombe* (Dundee, 1992).

[23] Knight, *Diocese of Gibraltar*, pp. 42–3.

[24] Knight, *Diocese of Gibraltar*, pp. 52–3.

regular pastoral letters, and in 1894, the convening of the first diocesan conference.[25]

The bishops of Gibraltar remained very concerned to avoid any appearance of proselytizing among indigenous Roman Catholic or Orthodox populations. They were indeed instrumental in promoting better communication and understanding between the Anglican and Eastern Churches. During this period, however, no such dialogue was possible with the Roman Catholic Church, and relations were further complicated by the tendency of reforming movements within the Catholic Church, notably in Italy and Spain, to look to the Anglicans for support and even alternative episcopal oversight. In particular Bishop Sandford refused requests to take charge of the small Spanish and Portuguese Reformed Episcopal Church, realizing that to do so would both exceed his brief and appear provocative towards the Catholic Church. Irish Anglican bishops, however, eventually in 1894 consecrated Juan Bautista Cabrera as an indigenous bishop to serve the new Church.[26]

In 1873, following the disestablishment of the Church of Ireland, the British government, seeking to apply the principle of religious equality elsewhere, discontinued its grants to consular chaplaincies. Anglicans in Europe were thus left entirely dependent on their own resources, albeit sometimes supplemented by the (Evangelical) Colonial and Continental Church Society or the (High Church) Society for the Propagation of the Gospel. Nevertheless the late nineteenth century was a period of substantial growth, with many new chaplaincies established, and existing ones moving from temporary accommodation into purpose-built churches. This expansion mirrored the extensive building of new churches in expanding middle-class suburbs in England. In 1884, oversight of regions outside the jurisdiction of the bishop of Gibraltar was strengthened through the appointment of Jonathan Holt Titcomb as first 'Bishop Co-adjutor of London for Northern and Central Europe'. In 1885 Titcomb reported that there were now eighty-three permanent chaplaincies under his charge, as well as seasonal chaplaincies in holiday resorts and provision for British sailors visiting European ports, and fifty-three of the permanent chaplaincies now had their own churches.[27] In 1914 the diocese of Gibraltar had ninety-eight chaplaincies of which fifty-six were permanent. Additionally there were the chaplaincies in Madeira and the Canary Islands, which remained under the direct jurisdiction of the Bishop of London.[28] Royal patronage played a significant role in developing the numerous chaplaincies in Germany, following the marriages of Queen Victoria's eldest daughter to

[25] Knight, *Diocese of Gibraltar*, pp. 126–8.

[26] Knight, *Diocese of Gibraltar*, pp. 161–75.

[27] J. H. Titcomb, *The Church of England in Northern and Central Europe: A Pastoral Addressed to the Chaplaincies* (London, 1885), pp. 13–14.

[28] Knight, *Diocese of Gibraltar*, pp. 258–61.

Crown Prince Frederick of Prussia in 1858, and that of two of her sisters to other German princes.[29] In 1886, following the building of the Berlin church to mark his silver wedding, the Crown Prince told Titcomb's successor Bishop Wilkinson that 'the more English churches you build in Germany the better I shall like it'.[30]

Bishops Titcomb and Wilkinson were assiduous travellers who took seriously responsibilities that extended from Archangel to Biarritz. They also instituted clerical conferences that promoted solidarity among the chaplains, thus replicating the increased coherence and stronger episcopal oversight that developed in the diocese of Gibraltar during the final quarter of the nineteenth century. Some of the topics chosen for discussion at conferences give suggestive hints of the continuing organizational and pastoral challenges facing Anglicans on the continent: 'The instability of the present financial arrangements for the Continental bishopric' (1885); 'English children in continental schools: our duties and difficulties in respect to them' (1889); 'Elasticity of public worship in reference to Continental requirements' (1889); 'Our Relations and Responsibilities to Religious Bodies and Movements on the Continent' (1893).[31] In 1906, in his preface to Wilkinson's memoirs, Sir Edmund Monson, a former British ambassador to Vienna and Paris, assessed the current state of the chaplaincies. He noted that whereas in the 1840s provision had been ad hoc and scanty there were now resident chaplains in many continental towns and cities, with substantial purpose-built churches. However these were sustained by the sacrificial giving of small resident expatriate communities, with transient visitors reluctant to make meaningful contributions. Chaplains themselves were often poorly paid and had uncertain future prospects.[32]

In most places in Europe, American Episcopalian travellers and residents attended the English chaplaincies,[33] but in a few key locations they founded their own churches. The earliest of these was in Paris, where services were held in various locations, notably at the home of a wealthy American resident, Colonel Herman Thorn, until Holy Trinity church was consecrated in 1864.[34] It moved to a larger building in 1886, which eventually in 1922 became the pro-cathedral for American Episcopalians in Europe. Meanwhile, William

[29] Schniewind, *Anglicans in Germany*, p. 17.

[30] Thomas Wilkinson, *Twenty Years of Continental Work and Travel* (London, 1906), p. 27.

[31] *The XV Anglican Church Conference of British Chaplains and Laity from Northern and Central Europe* (Vienna, 1896).

[32] Edmund Monson, 'Preface' to Wilkinson, *Twenty Years of Continental Work and Travel*, pp. viii–x.

[33] Wilkinson, *Twenty Years of Continental Work and Travel*, p. xiv.

[34] W. S. Scott, *A Crusading Dean: An Era in the Life of the American Colony in Paris* (Langham, 1967), pp. 34–6; <http://americancathedral.org/History.html>, accessed 8 Jan. 2015. Scott states that the services at Thorn's home began in 1847, whereas the American Cathedral's website dates their commencement to the 1830s.

Chauncey Langdon, an ecumenical enthusiast who sought to promote the reform of the Roman Catholic Church, in 1859 organized an Episcopalian congregation in Rome. Services were initially held at the American legation, and subsequently in various temporary rented premises, until the building of a permanent church, which was consecrated in 1886. Meanwhile in October 1860 Langdon also began American services in Florence, but these were initially only continued for a few months. In 1867 the Florence church was revived and established on a permanent footing, led by the maverick Pierce Connolly, a former convert to Roman Catholicism, who had subsequently reverted to Episcopalianism. Langdon also settled in Florence in 1867, with a view to advancing his Italian reform vision, but finding his efforts frustrated by Connolly, he eventually moved to Geneva, where in 1873 he was the founding rector of Emmanuel Episcopal church. American congregations were also established in Dresden in 1869 and Munich in 1896.[35]

In a sermon in Florence in 1868 Langdon had articulated his expansive vision for Anglicans in Europe as the future agents for reforming both corrupt Roman Catholicism and decaying Protestantism:

> Over the European Continent . . . English and American Churchmen are sojourning and travelling by . . . tens of thousands. As in the age of the first preaching of Christianity, God provided Himself in the Jewish dispersion, instruments in every land of the propagation of the glad tidings of a Redeemer: so, now, in the age when that faith is to be rescued, and the unity of the Church of Christ and the purity of Christianity is to be restored, He has provided Himself with a like instrument in the *Anglican dispersion* . . . Her Churches . . . are, or at least *ought to be*, centers of a religious and spiritual power and influence which bear witness against the destroying heresies which assault the faith on either side.[36]

Realities were rather more prosaic. Anglican churches in continental Europe were only grudgingly tolerated by Catholic authorities on the understanding that their ministrations were limited to their own expatriate communities and that they did not engage in proselytism. Anglican hopes of significant reform in the Roman Catholic Church were dashed in 1870 by the conservative affirmations of the First Vatican Council and any hopes of collaboration destroyed by the papal condemnation of Anglican orders in 1896. Serious attempts were made to establish intercommunion with the Old Catholic Churches of the Netherlands, Germany, Austria, and Switzerland, which had left the Roman Church because of their dissent from the Vatican Council, but this was not to be fully achieved until 1932. On the Protestant front, the

[35] Clement W. Walsh, 'The Episcopal Church in Florence: A Tale of Two Beginnings', *Anglican and Episcopal History*, 56 (1987): 423–43; Schniewind, *Anglicans in Germany*, pp. 92, 145.

[36] Wm Chaunchy Langdon, *Anglican Responsibility: Practical Considerations for English and American Churchmen on the European Continent* (Florence, 1868), 17–18.

creation in 1841 of a bishopric for Jerusalem jointly with the Prussian state Church had initially seemed a promising initiative, but the project proved highly controversial in Germany as well as among Oxford Movement Anglicans, and the Prussians eventually withdrew from it. Other contacts with continental Protestant Churches were very limited until after the First World War. It was against this background of ecumenical frustration that Henry Knight, bishop of Gibraltar from 1911, reiterated denials that the Anglican chaplaincies in Europe were an intrusion into other ecclesiastical jurisdictions and defended the right of the Church of England 'to commission a Bishop and clergy to minister to her own sons and daughters who would otherwise be sheep not having a shepherd'.[37] Nevertheless, despite these limited ambitions, the development of European chaplaincies was a significant and hitherto largely neglected aspect of nineteenth-century Anglican history. They reflected the growth of tourism and the expansion of English and American expatriate communities, in which they provided an important cultural and social focus as well as religious services.[38]

CONCLUSION

It is very possible to narrate the history of British Anglicanism in the nineteenth and early twentieth centuries as one of decline, of the loss of state connection in Ireland, and of its weakening and loss of numerical dominance even in its English heartland. That decline moreover was punctuated and, arguably, accelerated by the bitter internal divisions arising from the growth of ritualism inspired by the Oxford Movement and from the development of liberal theological ideas. This chapter, however, suggests a counter-narrative of renewed organizational and spiritual vitality, which enabled Anglicanism to adapt creatively to the loss of much of its historic constitutional privilege, to recover some lost ground in English cities, and build a significant presence on previously slender foundations, notably in Scotland and in continental Europe. Moreover the capacity of Anglicanism to gain ground in locations where it had hitherto been marginal or non-existent, depending entirely on the financial resources of its own congregations and supporters, demonstrated that state connection and endowment were by no means indispensable.

The Anglican Church of the early twentieth century was also substantially more professional and participatory than it had been in pre-Victorian times. The development of diocesan structures and clerical conferences was paralleled by improvement in the training of clergy in theological colleges such as

[37] Knight, *Diocese of Gibraltar*, p. xiv.

[38] Archives at Lambeth Palace Library and the London Metropolitan Archives.

St David's Lampeter (1822), Cuddesdon (1854), Wycliffe Hall Oxford (1877), Ridley Hall Cambridge (1881), and Mirfield (1903). The laity began to secure a voice in the formal governance of the Church, building on the contribution they had long been making through voluntary societies. Although the ordination of women lay long in the future, many of them found active alternative roles as parish visitors and teachers. The development of Anglican sisterhoods inspired by the Oxford Movement, and the revival of the order of deaconesses in the 1860s offered opportunities for women committed to full-time ministry. A small number of devout Anglican women achieved considerable prominence as poets and hymn-writers (for example Cecil Frances Alexander, Frances Ridley Havergal, Christina Rossetti), as novelists (Charlotte Elizabeth Tonna, Charlotte Mary Yonge), or as social activists (Josephine Butler, Henrietta Barnett). Much larger numbers of women were mobilized and supported by Church-based organizations, notably the Girls Friendly Society (founded in 1875) and the Mothers Union (1876).

The early twentieth century also saw British and European Anglicanism more at ease with its environment than in the past. Disestablishment in Ireland and, eventually, Wales removed a perception of unjustified privilege, and allowed Anglicanism there to adjust to cultural and political realities. Meanwhile, following a last major outbreak of political controversy over the pro-Anglican provisions of the 1902 Education Act, English Nonconformists seemed prepared tacitly to accept the continuance of the residual privileges of the Church of England. Internally, all but the most doctrinaire came to accept that diversity of theology and ritual practice within the Church was inevitable. Anglicanism had indeed averted the 'total destruction' that Thomas Arnold had feared in 1833, and demonstrated its capacity to adapt and flourish in a wide variety of contexts.

SELECT BIBLIOGRAPHY

Akenson, Donald Harman, *The Church of Ireland: Ecclesiastical Reform and Revolution, 1800–1885* (New Haven, CT, 1971).

Bebbington, David, *Evangelicalism in Modern Britain: A History from the 1730s to the 1980s* (London, 1989).

Bell, P. M. H., *Disestablishment in Ireland and Wales* (London, 1969).

Brown, Stewart J., *The National Churches of England, Ireland, and Scotland 1801–46* (Oxford, 2001).

Brown, Stewart J. and Peter Nockles (eds.), *The Oxford Movement: Europe and the Wider World 1830–1930* (Cambridge, 2012).

Burns, Arthur, *The Diocesan Revival in the Church of England c.1800–1870* (Oxford, 1999).

Chadwick, Owen, *The Victorian Church*, 2 vols. (London, 1966, 1970).

Flew, Sarah, *Philanthropy and the Funding of the Church of England, 1856–1914* (London, 2015).
Heeney, Brian, *The Women's Movement in the Church of England 1850–1930* (Oxford, 1988).
Knight, Henry J. C., *The Diocese of Gibraltar: A Sketch of its History, Work and Tasks* (London, 1917).
Machin, G. I. T., *Politics and the Churches in Great Britain 1832 to 1868* (Oxford, 1977).
Marsh, P. T., *The Victorian Church in Decline: Archbishop Tait and the Church of England 1868–1882* (London, 1969).
Meldrum, Patricia, *Conscience and Compromise: Forgotten Evangelicals of Nineteenth-Century Scotland* (Carlisle, 2006).
Rowell, Geoffrey, *The Vision Glorious: Themes and Personalities of the Catholic Revival in Anglicanism* (Oxford, 1991).
Strong, Rowan, *Episcopalianism in Nineteenth-Century Scotland: Religious Responses to a Modernizing Society* (Oxford, 2002).
Wolffe, John, *God and Greater Britain: Religion and National Life in Britain and Ireland, 1843–1945* (London, 1994).
Yates, Nigel, *Anglican Ritualism in Victorian Britain 1830–1910* (Oxford, 1999).

3

Anglicanism in the British Empire, 1829–1910

Stewart J. Brown

In 1849, Daniel Wilson, the Evangelical bishop of Calcutta and metropolitan of India, published a charge to his clergy. He began by observing how God had preserved Britain from violent upheaval during the revolutionary year of 1848, and indeed, from the successive waves of revolution that had swept Europe since 1789. However, he continued, there was still greater evidence of the providential purpose for Britain. This was the extraordinary expansion of the British Empire over the past sixty years. Not only had Britain been spared revolution, but it had been '*raised during this very period to the possession of the most wonderful empire, and the widest influence which the world has ever seen, either in ancient or modern times*'. 'And for what purpose?' he continued, 'Why has India been given to us, as it were by miracle? Why are our Colonies extended over the universe?' There could be but one answer: 'that it may be seen whether we will communicate to India and the world the immense blessings of the Gospel which have been committed to our trust'. And it was the Anglican Church establishment in India, he further maintained, that was the only sure way of fulfilling this trust. The Anglican Church, moreover, would help consolidate the political empire in India. Through its ministry, 'the Native population would be permanently gained over to our Empire; and, instead of our being in danger from half-educated, babbling Metaphysicians . . . we should have intelligent, attached and obedient Christian subjects'.[1]

Wilson's charge reflected a prevalent mid-nineteenth-century Anglican discourse. For many Anglicans, as Rowan Strong has shown, the expansion of the British Empire from the 1780s, and especially the conquest of much of

[1] Daniel Wilson, *A Charge Delivered to the Clergy of the Four Dioceses of Calcutta, Madras, Bombay, and Colombo* (London, 1849), pp. 10, 16, 21.

India, was inexplicable in worldly terms.[2] For them, the empire was clearly destined by God to be for the wider world what the ancient Roman Empire had been for the Mediterranean world—the means by which Christianity would be spread. The real strength of Britain's empire, they believed, lay in its Christianity, especially its Anglicanism, which united Church and state for a higher aim. The expanding empire provided the social and political framework for the wider mission of the Anglican Church. The empire, moreover, gave Anglicanism a renewed sense of purpose, particularly in the aftermath of the 'constitutional revolution' of 1828–32, which had largely ended the confessional state in the United Kingdom and weakened the influence and authority of the Established Church of England.

THE CONSTITUTIONAL REVOLUTION OF 1828–32 AND IMPERIAL ANGLICANISM

Our period opens with the Church of England under serious threat at home. The constitutional revolution of 1828–32, which is explored in another chapter, undermined the old alliance of Church and state. The repeal of the Test and Corporation Acts in 1828, Catholic Emancipation in 1829, and the parliamentary Reform Act of 1832, brought a legal end to the confessional state, and its principle that positions of trust in the state must be reserved for members of the Established Church. The constitutional changes were followed in the 1830s by popular calls to abolish the tithes and church rates which maintained the Church of England, while the reformed Parliament soon decided that it would provide no additional grants of public money for the Church.

Leaders of the Church of England responded vigorously to the new political order. During the 1830s, the Church adopted a series of reforms, aimed at strengthening its pastoral ministry, eliminating pluralism and sinecures, and building new churches and schools. A key figure in the reform movement was Charles James Blomfield, the High Church bishop of London, who initiated a church building programme in the capital that was soon emulated across the country, with hundreds of new Anglican churches erected by voluntary donations. The 1830s also witnessed the beginnings of what Arthur Burns has termed the 'diocesan revival', by which a new breed of energetic and talented bishops, among them Blomfield and Samuel Wilberforce of Oxford, became more regular in their visitations, improved discipline and pastoral care

[2] Rowan Strong, 'The Church of England and the British Imperial State: Anglican Metropolitan Sermons of the 1850s', in Hilary M. Carey and John Gascoigne (eds.), *Church and State in Old and New Worlds* (Leiden, 2011), pp. 183–205.

among their diocesan clergy, revived rural deaneries, and established diocesan societies for church building, school building, and support of overseas missions.[3] Another expression of Anglican renewal was the Oxford, or Tractarian Movement, which aimed at recovering a sense of the Church of England as a branch of the ancient catholic and apostolic Church. The Oxford divines emphasized the authority of the bishops, the disciplined Christian life, and the spiritual independence of the Church of England from state control. There was also a new zeal among Anglican Evangelicals, with many embracing millenarianism and the study of biblical prophecy, alongside the older Evangelical emphases on the atonement, conversion, and social activism.

The spirit of Anglican renewal found expression in 1841 in three initiatives linked to the expanding British Empire. First, there was the Niger expedition, intended to provide a new beginning for the anti-slavery campaign. In 1807, largely as a result of the political campaign led by the Evangelical Anglican William Wilberforce, Parliament had abolished the slave trade, and in 1833 Parliament enacted the end of slavery within the British Empire. Beginning in 1808, Britain had stationed a West African Squadron of warships to intercept slave ships from Africa and liberate their human cargoes. Although it numbered about thirty warships by the later 1830s, the squadron was largely ineffective against the faster slave ships and managed to intercept only about 10 per cent of the human cargoes. The slaves that British warships did recapture were landed at the British colony of Sierra Leone, where many found their way into one of the colony's Anglican churches. But there was consternation among British Christians over the continuing slave trade and the small numbers being rescued.

The Evangelical Anglican Thomas Fowell Buxton was successor to Wilberforce as parliamentary leader of the anti-slavery movement. During the 1830s, Buxton developed a plan to eradicate the slave trade at its source, by ending the tribal warfare and anarchic conditions in the African interior that led to the capture of slaves. Buxton's plan involved developing settled agriculture in the African interior, including palm oil and cotton farms, which would provide alternative occupations to tribal warfare and human trafficking. The Niger River and its tributaries would form a great artery for peaceful trade. Along its banks there would be farming villages, with churches and schools for the spread of Christianity and civilization. 'It is', Buxton famously asserted, 'the Bible and the plough that must regenerate Africa.'[4] He enlisted the support of leading public figures, including Prince Albert, and funds were raised for an expedition up the Niger River, to map its course and set up model farms.

[3] Arthur Burns, *The Diocesan Revival in the Church of England c.1800–1870* (Oxford, 1999).

[4] Quoted in C. P. Groves, *The Planting of Christianity in Africa*, 4 vols. (London, 1948–58), II, p. 6.

In April 1841, the expedition, including missionaries, scientists, and agricultural experts, began its journey up the Niger in three specially designed iron steamships. The expedition, however, failed disastrously. The Europeans were devastated by illness; of the 145 Europeans on the expedition, 130 fell ill of fever, and 40 died. After establishing only one model farming village, the expedition had to be withdrawn. Nonetheless, despite the failure, a new Christian imperial ideal was defined—that Africa could be redeemed and slavery ended through commerce and Christianity. There would be further expeditions to the Niger in the 1850s, and for many Anglicans a vital purpose of the empire would be to end slavery.

The second event of 1841 expressing the spirit of imperial Anglicanism was the establishment of the Jerusalem bishopric. This was a joint venture of the Church of England and the Protestant Church in Prussia. The stated aim of the joint bishopric was to offer protection and support to Protestants residing in Palestine and the Near East. However, there were scarcely any Protestants in the region, and in truth the Jerusalem bishopric was entangled with the 'Eastern Question' and European efforts to carve out spheres of influence within the weakening Ottoman Empire. Britain and Prussia jointly endowed the bishopric, and the two monarchs agreed to alternate in nominating the bishop. Most Tractarians opposed the joint bishopric, believing that the Prussian state Church had been corrupted in doctrine and that no good would come of such cooperation. Anglican Evangelicals, however, warmly supported the venture. For many, Scripture foretold that the restoration of the Jews to the Holy Land would be a sign of Christ's imminent return in glory. The Jerusalem bishopric, they believed, would promote the return of the Jews to the Holy Land, and open them to Christian influence and conversion, in preparation for the Second Advent. Here was further evidence of the providential purpose of the British Empire. 'It is surely', observed the Evangelical Lord Ashley in 1839, 'a high privilege reserved to our Church and nation to plant the true cross on the Holy Hill of Zion; to carry back the faith we thence received from the apostles; and... "light such a candle in Jerusalem, as by God's blessing shall never be put out" .'[5]

A third major event of 1841 was the establishment of the Colonial Bishoprics Fund.[6] This was largely the initiative of Bishop Blomfield, who in 1840 published a letter to the archbishop of Canterbury, William Howley, pleading for the provision of settled episcopal government in all Britain's colonies of settlement. At this time, there were only ten overseas Anglican bishoprics in the empire, and Blomfield insisted that the Anglican Church was failing to

[5] Quoted in Donald M. Lewis, *The Origins of Christian Zionism: Lord Shaftesbury and Evangelical Support for a Jewish Homeland* (Cambridge, 2010), p. 165.

[6] Rowan Strong, *Anglicanism and the British Empire c.1700–1850* (Oxford, 2007), pp. 198–221.

meet its imperial responsibilities.[7] In response to Blomfield's appeal, the archbishop convened a large public meeting in April 1841 in London. In his opening address to the meeting, Howley emphasized the value of colonial bishoprics, including 'the improved condition of society in every Colony where Episcopal authority has been established within the last twenty years'. Blomfield gave the second address, highlighting the prospect of episcopal government in uniting the empire on the basis of 'Apostolic order and discipline'. For another speaker, Charles Sumner, the Evangelical bishop of Winchester, 'we have been too regardless of Christianising our colonies on any plan'. 'We have sent our ships', he asserted, 'but we have not sent our religion.'[8] The meeting agreed to establish a Colonial Bishoprics Fund as a voluntary Church of England association, under the direction of the bishops and with the aim of raising money to endow new colonial bishoprics. The High Church politician William Ewart Gladstone was appointed one of the three treasurers, a position he would hold for the next fifty years. A little over a month after the creation of the Fund, the Church of England bishops met at Lambeth and decided on the first six colonial bishoprics to be created.

The Colonial Bishoprics Fund proved highly successful at fundraising, and within fifty years, the number of colonial dioceses grew from ten to eighty-two.[9] The consecrations of colonial bishops now became major public events, held in Westminster Abbey, St Paul's Cathedral, or Canterbury Cathedral. The consecration in 1847 in Westminster Abbey of a new bishop of Cape Town, along with three new Australian bishops, was the first in the new style and it generated great public interest. The colonial bishops were closely identified with the imperial state. Not only did they carry royal letters patent, but they normally sailed for their colonial responsibilities as guests of the Royal Navy. In 1849, a Council for Colonial Bishoprics was created, made up of all the bishops and archbishops of the United Church of England and Ireland. The Anglican commitment to the British Empire found further expression in 1848 with the foundation of the College of St Augustine's, Canterbury, for the training of colonial clergy and missionaries.[10] The college was a High Church initiative, and was supported by voluntary donations. It was built on the site of the former monastery of St Augustine, which one of the college founders, Edward Coleridge, described as the 'Site of Sites', reflecting both the sixth-century mission of St Augustine to England and the nineteenth-century

[7] Charles James Blomfield, *A Letter to his Grace the Lord Archbishop of Canterbury, upon the Formation of a Fund for Endowing Additional Bishoprics in the Colonies* (London, 1840).

[8] *Proceedings of a Meeting of the Clergy and Laity...for the Purpose of Raising a Fund towards the Endowment of Additional Colonial Bishoprics* (London, 1841), pp. 4, 6, 7, 18.

[9] W. F. France, *The Oversea Episcopate: Centenary History of the Colonial Bishoprics Fund 1841–1941* (London, 1941).

[10] Hilary M. Carey, *God's Empire: Religion and Colonialism in the British World, c.1801–1908* (Cambridge, 2011), pp. 271–86.

British mission to the world.[11] There was some opposition to the college. The Church Missionary Society (CMS) had since 1826 maintained a missionary training college in Islington, and could not see the need for another college. Many suspected that the real aim of St Augustine's was to spread Tractarian teachings to the empire. However, St Augustine's gained influential support, especially from the Society for the Propagation of the Gospel (SPG). Over the next century, St Augustine's College sent some 1,000 Anglican workers to the colonies and mission fields, as well as educating a large number of Africans, Asians, and Americans.

The decade of the 1840s was, according to the historian Hans Cnattingius, one of 'epoch-making importance in the evolution of Anglicanism into a World Church'. 'The heads of the Church of England', he added, 'had shown that, as builders of a spiritual empire, they were worthy to take their place beside the builders of the political empire.'[12] After the constitutional revolution of 1828–32 and the weakening of the Church–state alliance, the Church of England now found a new confidence, which was closely linked to the expanding empire. In the Niger expedition, Jerusalem bishopric, and Colonial Bishoprics Fund, the Anglican Church renewed its sense of mission, amid visions of a providential purpose behind imperial expansion. Voluntary giving to the two main Anglican missionary societies, the SPG and the CMS, increased dramatically, from a total of £63,248 in 1830, to £184,756 in 1846, to £224,330 in 1852.[13] By 1851, there were 1,183 Anglican clergymen serving in the British colonies and dependencies, representing some 15 per cent of the total number of Anglican clergy.[14] The Anglican imperial commitments reflected the Evangelical passion for souls and millenarian beliefs, as well as High Church and Tractarian emphases on the bishops as the successors to the apostles and the Anglican Church as the repository of divine truth.

ANGLICANISM IN THE SETTLEMENT COLONIES

During the nineteenth century, the world was transformed by what the historian James Belich has described as the 'Settler Revolution', a movement comparable in its global impact to the Industrial Revolution or the Democratic

[11] Quoted in G. A. Bremner, *Imperial Gothic: Religious Architecture and High Anglican Culture in the British Empire, c.1840–1870* (New Haven, CT, 2013), p. 332.

[12] Hans Cnattingius, *Bishops and Societies: A Study of Anglican Colonial and Missionary Expansion 1698–1850* (London, 1952), pp. 204–5.

[13] Bob Tennant, *Corporate Holiness: Pulpit Preaching and the Church of England Missionary Societies, 1760–1870* (Oxford, 2013), p. 214.

[14] Michael Gladwin, *Anglican Clergy in Australia 1788–1850: Building a British World* (Woodbridge, 2015), pp. 3–4, 15–16.

Revolution. Between 1815 and 1930, an estimated twelve million people emigrated permanently from the British Isles to North America, Australasia, and South Africa. They formed an English-speaking population in the world which grew sixteen-fold between 1790 and 1930, from about 12 million to some 200 million.[15] A large proportion of these English-speaking migrants went to the British settlement colonies in Canada, Australia, New Zealand, and South Africa. They formed what in 1868 the English politician and author Charles Dilke famously called the 'Greater Britain'.

From the beginnings of British colonialism in the seventeenth century, the Church of England endeavoured to provide colonists with clergy, churches, and schools—and this continued into the nineteenth century. The first Anglican clergy in the colonies were chaplains (so designated as they were outside the ordinary jurisdictions of parish clergy), and by the late eighteenth century chaplains were normally appointed by the Colonial Office, and were under the jurisdiction of the governor. A chaplain, Richard Johnson, accompanied the first fleet of convicts and settlers to Australia in 1788, and from 1788 to 1820, fourteen chaplains served the new Australian colonies; they were paid by the crown, which also paid for new churches. Colonial chaplains accompanied the first British settlers in the Cape Colony in South Africa after it was taken from the Dutch in 1806. There were army chaplains accompanying the regiments and military garrisons in the colonies; the military chaplains often took on additional roles as schoolmasters and preachers to the colonists. By a parliamentary act of 1825, British consuls serving overseas were empowered to appoint chaplains, provided they had been duly licensed by the bishop of London. The Anglican missionary societies, the SPG, the CMS, and the Society for Promoting Christian Knowledge (SPCK), also sent chaplains to work among the settler populations.

There were, however, concerns over such a loose and unsystematic provision of clergy in the settlement colonies, and a belief that a scattering of chaplains could not meet the long-term spiritual needs of the settlers. For many Anglicans, it was imperative to bring to the colonies the full benefits of the Established Church of England—including endowments, episcopal government, diocesan and parish structures, schools and colleges, and a close alliance of Church and state. This, some claimed, had been the lesson of the American Revolution and the loss of the North American colonies in 1783, which they argued would not have happened had the colonists been instructed under a proper Anglican establishment with colonial bishops. The aim, as Samuel Wilberforce had expressed it in 1838, should be 'to send out *The Church*, and not merely *instructions about religion*'.[16] But planting Established

[15] James Belich, *Replenishing the Earth: The Settler Revolution and the Rise of the Anglo-World, 1783–1939* (Oxford, 2009), pp. 58, 4.

[16] A. R. Ashwell, *Life of the Right Reverend Samuel Wilberforce*, 2 vols. (London, 1880), I, pp. 128–9.

Churches proved difficult in the colonies—where there were no ecclesiastical courts, no tithes or historic endowments to support an ecclesiastical establishment, and few colonial bishops before the 1840s.

Nonetheless, efforts were made. In Canada, there was an established Anglican Church from 1787, when in the aftermath of the American Revolution Charles Inglis was consecrated bishop of Nova Scotia, with episcopal authority extending over the whole of British North America. In 1791, with the Constitution Act for British North America, the British Parliament set aside one-seventh of the land in Upper and Lower Canada (the so-called 'clergy reserves') as an endowment for the new Anglican establishment. It was a significant expression of state commitment. From 1814, moreover, the imperial state provided a grant to the SPG for the support of additional Anglican clergy in Canada.

By the early 1820s, however, many Canadian colonists, including the large Catholic majority in Lower Canada and the large number of Methodists and Presbyterians in Upper Canada, were opposing the Anglican establishment in a religiously diverse Canada, where Anglicans were a minority. They objected to the exclusive grant of the 'clergy reserves' to the Anglican Church. In response to the widespread popular opposition to the idea of an Established Church, the imperial state began withdrawing its financial support from the Canadian Anglican Church. In 1831, the government announced that over the next four years it would end its grant to the SPG for the support of Anglican clergy. And in 1840, the imperial Parliament passed an act which divided the clergy reserves among the different denominations in Canada, with half the land to be divided between the Anglicans and the Presbyterians, and the rest distributed among the other denominations according to their numbers. But by now the idea of land grants to any Church had become highly unpopular in Canada; indeed, the clergy reserves had formed one of the grievances behind the Rebellion of 1837–8 in Upper Canada. Following the Union of Upper and Lower Canada in 1840, and the granting of responsible government to Canada from 1849, the imperial Parliament left the question of the clergy reserves to the Canadian legislature. In 1854, the Canadian legislature secularized the clergy reserves, effectively disestablishing the Anglican Church in Canada.[17]

There was a similar story in Australia. In 1826, the British government, acting on the Canadian model, endowed the Anglican Church with one-seventh of all crown lands in New South Wales for the provision of parish churches, clergy, and schools. By 1829, nearly 420,000 acres had been granted to the Anglican establishment in Australia. However, there was also growing opposition to these land grants among the colonists, and in 1829 the governor suspended any new land grants. A few years later, in 1833, it was agreed that

[17] Alan Wilson, *The Clergy Reserves of Upper Canada* (Ottawa, 1969).

the lands previously given to the Anglican Church would now be divided among the main denominations in the colony, including the Catholic Church. The governor of New South Wales, Sir Richard Bourke, observed in 1833 that in rejecting the idea of an Established Church 'the inclination of these Colonists ... keeps pace with the Spirit of the Age'.[18] In 1836, the New South Wales colonial legislature passed a Church Act, by which the state provided financial subsidies to all Christian denominations, according to how much they could raise themselves. Similar Church Acts were passed by the colonial legislatures in the other three Australian colonies by 1847. 'The Church Acts', Michael Gladwin has observed, 'enshrined religious pluralism and ended Anglican pretensions to establishment'.[19]

As the imperial and colonial governments moved away from policies of endowing Anglican establishments in the settlement colonies, the colonial Anglican Churches had to develop their own forms of support and governance. The colonial clergy were often more than willing to do so, being at great distances from the metropole, dependent on local communities, and working in very different environments. Some colonial Church leaders, moreover, were attracted to Tractarian ecclesiology, with its high views of episcopacy, its commitment to the practices of the early Church, and its emphasis on the Church's spiritual independence. From the 1840s, the colonial Churches began developing forms of synodical Church government, by which they would largely govern themselves through their bishops, supported by diocesan and provincial synods (with lay representation), and by which they would frame their own constitutions, elect their bishops, and enforce ecclesiastical discipline.

The Church in New Zealand was the first to develop independent synodical government. The Anglican mission to New Zealand began in 1814. Following the establishment of British sovereignty in 1840, the first Anglican bishop of New Zealand, George Augustus Selwyn—young, confident, and athletic, with High Church convictions—was consecrated in 1841. Three years later, in 1844, Selwyn summoned his small group of clergy to meet as a synod, in order to frame a set of rules for the Church. In England, there were complaints that Selwyn's synod was an infringement on the royal supremacy and thus illegal, but he persevered. 'My desire is', he wrote to friends in England in May 1845, 'in this country ... to try what the actual system of the Church of England can do, when disencumbered of its earthly load of seats in Parliament, Erastian compromises, corruptions of patronage, confusion of orders, synodless bishops, and an unorganized clergy.'[20] Selwyn held a second synod in

[18] Quoted in G. P. Shaw, *Patriarch and Patriot: William Grant Broughton 1788–1853* (Melbourne, 1978), p. 79.

[19] Gladwin, *Anglican Clergy in Australia*, pp. 7–20, quotation on p. 16.

[20] W. P. Morrell, *The Anglican Church in New Zealand* (Dunedin, 1973), p. 48.

1847, and ten years later, he held a conference of clergy, which prepared a new constitution, including provisions for a general synod and diocesan synods, for the Anglican Church in New Zealand. By 1858, the Anglican Church in New Zealand comprised four dioceses, with Selwyn as metropolitan.

Similar developments followed in the colonies in Australia. William Grant Broughton, a High Church Anglican, had in 1829 been appointed archdeacon of New South Wales, under the authority of the bishop of Calcutta. In early 1836, he was consecrated the first bishop of Australia, with an income provided by the SPG and the crown. By 1847, largely through the work of the Colonial Bishoprics Fund, the number of bishops in Australia had increased to five, and the archbishop of Canterbury designated Broughton, who was now bishop of Sydney, as metropolitan. Of the five bishops, four were High Churchmen, who were attracted to Tractarian views of bishops as successors of the apostles and the Church as spiritually independent from the state. Late in 1850, Broughton convened a conference of the five Australian bishops, along with Bishop Selwyn of New Zealand, in Sydney. The conference discussed the potential benefits of regular diocesan and provincial synods, with representation of the clergy and laity. They also discussed a doctrinal issue, baptismal regeneration, which was then, as a result of the Gorham case, bitterly dividing the Church of England. Although technically not a synod, the Sydney conference of 1850 laid the foundation for future independent synodical government in Australia.[21] The first formal diocesan synod was convened by the bishop of Adelaide in 1855, and the first general synod of the Church of England in Australia met in Sydney in 1872.

There were also movements towards synodical government in Canada and South Africa. In 1851, a year after the Sydney conference, George Mountain, bishop of Quebec, chaired a conference of the bishops of Canada; five of the eight bishops attended, and they recommended the formation of diocesan synods, the holding of regular provincial synods, and the appointment of a metropolitan. In 1853, the first diocesan synod was convened by John Strachan, bishop of Toronto. Although regular synodical government was rendered difficult by the vast distances to be travelled in Canada, a first provincial synod for Eastern Canada was held in 1861, and the first general synod for the Church in Canada was held in 1893. The Church in South Africa developed independent synodical government under the forceful leadership of the High Churchman with Tractarian sympathies Robert Gray, who was consecrated the first bishop of Cape Town in 1847. Gray convened his first diocesan synod (which included representatives of the laity) in 1856. Then, in his capacity as

[21] E. D. Daw, 'Church and State in the Empire: The Conference of Australian Bishops 1850', *Journal of Imperial and Commonwealth History*, 5(3) (1977): 251–69; A. Cooper, 'The Australian Bishops and the Oxford Movement', in Stewart J. Brown and Peter B. Nockles (eds.), *The Oxford Movement: Europe and the Wider World 1830–1930* (Cambridge, 2012), pp. 99–113.

metropolitan, he famously convened the first provincial synod of South African bishops in 1863 in order to try one of their number, John William Colenso, bishop of Natal, for heresy—over his critical writings on the Pentateuch. The provincial synod ruled against Colenso and deposed him from his bishopric. Colenso, however, appealed to the British courts, which in 1864 decided that as Colenso had been appointed by the crown, the provincial synod convened by Gray did not have jurisdiction over him. Undeterred by this judgement, the South African provincial synod proceeded to consecrate another bishop for Colenso's diocese, a diocese which then had two competing bishops until Colenso's death in 1883. Despite the tensions over the Colenso affair, Gray managed to consolidate the Church of the Province of South Africa, with five dioceses and regular synodical government, before his death in 1872.

By the later nineteenth century, then, independent Anglican Churches had emerged in the settlement colonies in Australia, New Zealand, Canada, and South Africa. While these Churches saw themselves as part of a world-wide Anglican Communion, they were not Established Churches; apart from a few remaining chaplaincies and subsidies, they had no legal connections to the imperial state. They came to value their independence from the state, and looked to the Protestant Episcopal Church of the United States as a model. In 1874, the imperial Parliament formally recognized their independence with the Colonial Clergy Act, which allowed the archbishops of Canterbury and of York to consecrate colonial bishops without requiring 'the oath of due obedience to the archbishop [of Canterbury]'. The connections of the colonial Churches to the mother Church of England were henceforth based—not on law—but on sentiment, doctrine, ecclesiology, and loyalty to the empire. 'It is given to the Church of England', observed G. R. Wynne in 1901, 'at once to minister to the souls of the colonists, and also to rivet, in the best of bonds, his affections to the old land of his fathers.'[22] 'It is the desire of the Church of England', wrote Alfred Barry, former bishop of Sydney, in 1895, 'true to her ancient spirit and traditions, to sit, not as a queen over spiritual dependencies, but as a mother among her daughter Churches.'[23] The colonial Churches shared a commitment to promoting order, hierarchy, harmony, and cultivation among the settler populations. The colonial Anglican clergyman, observed the English Broad Church jurist and legal scholar John Westlake in 1868, is 'the representative of civilization'. 'And he is so', Westlake added, 'by virtue of his connexion with the Church at home, not through any legal status accorded to him in the colony.'[24] As Howard le Couteur has observed, the

[22] G. Robert Wynne, *The Church in Greater Britain* (London, 1901), p. 66.

[23] Alfred Barry, *The Ecclesiastical Expansion of England in the Growth of the Anglican Communion* (London, 1895), p. 27.

[24] J. Westlake, 'The Church in the Colonies', in W. L. Clay (ed.), *Essays on Church Policy* (London, 1868), p. 234.

discourse relating to Anglicanism and the settlement colonies was 'not about conversion and civilisation, but "cultivation"; how to transmit more fully to such colonies the benefits of... English/Anglican culture'.[25] The majority of the nineteenth-century colonial bishops were High Church, often Tractarian in their theology, with high views of the bishops as successors of the apostles and vital to Church life. The growing confidence of the colonial Churches was reflected in their cathedrals, often majestic neo-Gothic buildings, such as Christ Church Cathedral in Christchurch, New Zealand (built between 1862 and 1904), St James's Cathedral in Toronto (built between 1850 and 1874), or the cathedral of St Michael and St George in Grahamstown, South Africa.

THE ANGLICAN CHURCH IN INDIA

For many nineteenth-century Anglicans, Britain's rule in India could only be explained in providential terms. The rapid conquest of the vast subcontinent, located thousands of miles away from the British Isles, and with a huge and varied population, otherwise seemed inexplicable. When Anglican commentators referred to India, they generally spoke of Britain's responsibilities, under God, to the peoples of India. And for many Anglicans, especially before 1857, the highest of these responsibilities was to Christianize India. 'Why should it be thought incredible', asked the Evangelical Anglican and former East India Company chaplain Claudius Buchanan in 1812, 'that Providence hath been pleased, in a course of years to subjugate this Eastern empire to the most civilised nation in the world, for *this very purpose*?'[26] In 1813, with the renewal of the East India Company charter to govern India, Parliament responded to an Evangelical popular agitation by requiring the Company not only to open India to Christian missionary activity, but also to endow an established Anglican Church for India, including a bishopric in Calcutta, and archdeaconries in Bombay and Madras. The new Anglican establishment in India was controversial, with many believing Britain should not interfere with the beliefs of Hindus, Muslims, and other faith communities in India. The first bishop of Calcutta, Thomas Middleton, was consecrated very quietly in Lambeth Palace Chapel in 1814.

However, the Anglican Church in India steadily grew, with the CMS and SPG providing an increasing number of missionaries. Anglican schools were especially valued by the Indian elite. In 1820, Middleton, together with the

25 Howard le Couteur, 'Anglican High Churchmen and the Expansion of Empire', *Journal of Religious History*, 32 (2008): 193–215 (p. 196).

26 C. Buchanan, *Memoir of the Expediency of an Ecclesiastical Establishment for British India* (London, 1812 edn.), p. 48.

SPG, established Bishop's College in Calcutta, which trained Indian converts for missionary work and produced Christian literature in the Indian languages. The arrival of an Evangelical Anglican governor-general, Lord William Bentinck, in 1829 brought a new level of cooperation between the state and the Anglican establishment, and a new willingness to impose Christian morals on Indian society. Bentinck's administration outlawed *sati*, or the ritual burning alive of widows, in 1829, and began a campaign that same year to suppress *thuggee*, or the ritualized murder and robbery of travellers by devotees of the Hindu goddess Kali. In 1833, at the renewal of the British East India Company Charter, Parliament enlarged the Anglican establishment, elevating the archdeaconries of Madras and Bombay into bishoprics, and making the bishop of Calcutta the metropolitan. By the later 1850s, the CMS was supporting 124 ordained missionaries and the SPG 53 ordained missionaries in India.[27] Anglican missions had particular success in South India, where the CMS and SPG missionaries worked effectively together, in part through the leadership of the gifted Irish linguist and SPG missionary Robert Caldwell. With its many schools and colleges, including schools for girls and women, Tirunelvēli would become known as the 'Oxford of South India'.

There were, however, major tensions between the Evangelical CMS missionaries and the bishops in India, especially after the arrival of the forceful Daniel Wilson as bishop of Calcutta in 1832. Although himself an Evangelical, Wilson was also a strong churchman with high views of episcopal authority. For Wilson and his fellow bishops, the priority was to create a settled Anglican Church in India, with episcopal authority and a disciplined parish clergy, to ensure the nurture of the faithful in the Christian life. The bishops insisted on exercising authority over the CMS missionaries, including the authority to supervise missionaries and assign them to mission stations. The CMS missionaries, however, believed that they were accountable primarily to their local CMS committees, which were often led by laymen, and to the CMS parent committee in London. The CMS missionaries held that their committees, which provided the financial support for the missionaries, should have the authority to assign the missionaries to mission stations and to supervise them. Behind the CMS missionaries' desire for autonomy was a distrust of the bishops, with their often High Church ecclesiology, and, more important, a long-term commitment to forming an independent Indian Church, which they recognized might take a different form from the Church of England.

The tensions were largely resolved following the appointment in 1841 of the able ecclesiastical statesman Henry Venn as the London-based secretary of the CMS, a position he would hold for over thirty years. Venn believed that the goal of the missionary movement should be to help develop self-supporting,

[27] Edward Storrow, *India and Christian Missions* (London, 1859), p. 43.

self-governing, and self-propagating 'native' Churches in Asia and Africa. However, Venn was also a loyal Anglican churchman and pragmatist, and he managed to convince the CMS local committees and missionaries in India to accept the authority of the Anglican bishops.[28] Under Bishop Wilson's leadership, meanwhile, the Anglican Church expanded its pastoral care, and had some 300 clergy and 200 churches in India and Ceylon by 1849. In 1847, the majestic Gothic St Paul's Cathedral was consecrated in Calcutta, as a symbol of an Anglican India.

In May 1857, north-central India was swept by a series of mutinies among Indian sepoy soldiers, which quickly developed into a general uprising aimed at ending British rule and achieving Indian independence. The rising was accompanied by large-scale killings of European civilians, including missionaries and their families, as well as Indian Christian converts, before it was brutally suppressed by British and loyal Indian troops. The Indian 'Mutiny', as it was called in Britain, came as a profound shock to the British public, which was horrified by the killings of European women and children, and the intensity of hatred. Many Anglicans viewed the Mutiny as a divine summons to Britain to redouble its efforts to Christianize the subcontinent.[29] 'Who can doubt', proclaimed Samuel Wilberforce, bishop of Oxford, in an address in November 1857, 'that God has so dealt with us, in order that we may . . . act, as we never yet have acted, with true Christian zeal and courage in the administration of our Eastern Empire?'[30] For many others, however, the major cause of the Mutiny had been not divine disfavour, but rather Hindu and Muslim resentment against the Christian missionaries. After the Mutiny, the imperial state adopted a policy of strict religious neutrality in governing India. In the Royal Proclamation of 1858, while the Queen affirmed her own Christian faith, she disclaimed 'alike the right and desire to impose our convictions on any of our subjects'. The state also made it clear that it would provide no additional grants to the Anglican establishment in India.[31] Many British residents, moreover, became convinced that the Anglican Church should restrict its ministry to the Europeans and cease its missions to the Indian population, as these only created resentments and stoked communal violence. It should be a Church for Europeans. This view of the Anglican establishment was reflected in the exclusive European composition of many of its churches in India. Arriving as bishop of Calcutta in 1900, James Welldon had expected to

[28] Timothy Yates, *Venn and Victorian Bishops Abroad* (Uppsala, 1978), pp. 30–42; C. P. Williams, *The Ideal of the Self-Governing Church: A Study in Victorian Missionary Strategy* (Leiden, 1990); Cnattingius, *Bishops and Societies*, pp. 159–85.

[29] Brian Stanley, 'Christian Responses to the Indian Mutiny of 1857', *Studies in Church History*, 20 (1983): 277–89.

[30] Samuel Wilberforce, *Speeches on Missions*, ed. H. Rowley (London, 1874), p. 106.

[31] G. Cotton, bishop of Calcutta, to S. Wilberforce, 8 July 1858, Wilberforce Papers, Bodleian Library, Oxford, *c.*20, fos. 53–6.

see many Indians in the cathedral congregation. However, 'except on rare occasions, he saw few or none at all'.[32]

Despite the waning state support, the Anglican Church continued its missions and experienced modest growth in the later nineteenth century, with assistance from the Colonial Bishoprics Fund, the SPG, and the CMS. After the Mutiny, the SPG and CMS had rushed to rebuild their mission stations. New Anglican bishoprics were formed at Lahore (1877), Rangoon (1877), Tavancore and Cochin (1879), Chota-Nagpur (1890), Lucknow (1893), Tirunelvēli and Madura (1896), and Nagpur (1903). The Church established schools and hospitals, including a hospital at Quetta, founded in 1885, which under the skilled eye surgeon Henry Holland became celebrated for its innovative work in cataract surgery. However, all the nineteenth-century Anglican bishops in India were British or Irish and the Church leadership remained closely identified with the British Empire and a paternalistic, civilizing mission idea. There was little movement towards developing an independent Indian Anglican Church. And for believers in the providential nature of Britain's dominion in India, the numbers of Indian converts to Christianity, in proportion to India's immense population, remained disappointingly small.

A bishopric of Colombo was established in 1845 in Ceylon, where the CMS had been conducting a mission since 1818 and the SPG was active from about 1840. Ceylon was a crown colony, and the bishopric of Colombo was not part of the established Anglican Church in India, although it was under the metropolitan authority of the bishop of Calcutta. The CMS dominated the mission in Ceylon, and had a leading role in the multi-denominational Tamil Coolie Mission, established in 1854 with support from local planters for mission work among the migrant labourers in the coffee plantations. Ceylon was a difficult mission field. There was a popular belief, wrote one CMS missionary in 1868, that 'Christianity is an upstart religion, which has no vitality, and which, if unsupported by the ruling powers, cannot stand'.[33] The consecration of a young Oxford High Churchman, Reginald Copleston, as bishop of Colombo in late 1875 led to a serious conflict, as the 'Boy Bishop' attempted to regularize ecclesiastical government by placing the CMS missionaries, including those of the Tamil Coolie Mission, under the authority of chaplains ministering to European planters. The predominantly Evangelical CMS missionaries resisted Copleston's plans for them, while they also opposed his ritualism and sacramental piety. Some CMS missionaries formed separatist churches and a major schism was only averted by the mediation of a committee of English bishops convened by the archbishop of Canterbury.

[32] Bernard Palmer, *Imperial Vineyard: The Anglican Church in India under the Raj from the Mutiny to Partition* (Lewes, Sussex, 1999), p. 35.

[33] Eugene Stock, *The History of the Church Missionary Society*, 3 vols. (London, 1899), I, p. 218.

In 1881, the government of Ceylon decided to disestablish the Anglican Church and end further subsidies. Further east, British control of the Malacca Straits, including Singapore and parts of Malaysia, led in 1855 to the creation of the bishopric of Labuan, which from 1868 became the bishopric of Singapore, Labuan, and Sarawak. The Anglican chaplains ministered mainly to the European soldiers, officials, and merchants in Singapore and Penang, although the SPG conducted missions, mainly among Tamil and Chinese migrants, from about 1860.

In India, the CMS and SPG were by the 1870s experiencing difficulties in recruiting male ordained missionaries for the India mission; however, this was more than offset by an influx of single women missionaries, many of them trained at the Evangelical Mildmay Deaconesses Centre, or at the High Church SPG deaconess training house in south London. There was a growing recognition that the seclusion of women in Muslim and Hindu homes meant that women missionaries, especially medical missionaries, were vital in bringing Christian teachings to the female population. In 1880, the Church of England Zenana Missionary Society was formed, with close links to the CMS, to evangelize among Indian women in their homes. As Jeffrey Cox has shown, the SPG sent over 300 unmarried women missionaries to Delhi and Lahore in the century after 1850, more than six times the number of male missionaries. Many became members of Anglican sisterhood communities, such as St Stephens in Delhi or St Hilda's in Lahore, where the women lived communal lives in compounds and went out for household visiting, teaching, or medical service.[34] Edith Langridge ('Mother Edith'), an accomplished Oxford-educated classicist, linguist, and skilled nurse, arrived in India in 1903 and for forty years served, with impressive strength and versatility, the Anglican Sisterhood of the Epiphany.

In the 1870s, in response to the relatively small numbers of converts in India, some liberal, or Broad Church thinkers within the Church of England began exploring fresh approaches to the Anglican mission in India. Among them was the Cambridge professor Brooke Foss Westcott, who argued in an address in late 1872 that God's purpose for the Anglican Church in India might not be to Christianize India, but to nurture dialogue and understanding between the faiths of the East and West. 'God', Westcott argued, 'has fitted us as a people and as a church . . . to be the interpreters of the East to the West, and of the West to the East, to be the witnesses and heralds of truth recognised as manifold.'[35] Westcott envisaged the creation of a new community in India, in connection with Cambridge University, to promote inter-religious understanding; it would be a 'new Alexandria' and a melting pot of theologies. The

[34] Jeffrey Cox, *The British Missionary Enterprise since 1700* (New York, 2008), pp. 188–95.

[35] B. F. Westcott, 'The Universities in Relation to Missionary Work', in B. F. Westcott, *On Some Points in the Religious Office of the Universities* (London, 1873), p. 68.

following year, in 1873, the Oxford professor of comparative philology F. Max Müller gave a public lecture on missions at Westminster Abbey. He offered a similar vision of mission, in which the aim would not be to convert the peoples of India from Hinduism or Islam to Christianity; rather, missionaries should seek to live out their faith through selfless service among the poor, and engage in inter-faith dialogue. The results, Müller suggested, might not be individual conversions, but rather the encouragement of ethical movements in Hinduism and Islam, so that through shared service to humanity all faiths might be elevated.[36] In 1876, inspired by such ideas, some members of Cambridge University formed the Cambridge University Missionary Brotherhood in Delhi, which combined educational work and social service in the slums of Delhi with theological dialogue with Hindus and Muslims. In 1879, members of Oxford University, including several Anglo-Catholics, formed an Oxford University Missionary Brotherhood for work in Calcutta, which also combined educational work, social service, and inter-religious dialogue. Among the members of the Cambridge University Missionary Brotherhood was C. F. Andrews, an Anglican priest who arrived in Delhi in 1904, immersed himself in inter-faith dialogue, became a confidant of M. K. Gandhi, and later renounced his Anglican orders. The missionary brotherhoods, however, were but one element in the work of the Anglican Church in India, and some were critical of their approach. 'It may suggest the idea', observed Alfred Barry in 1895, 'only too congenial to the Hindu mind, that Christianity is only a philosophy to be intellectually learnt, or a morality which can be disassociated from its doctrines.'[37] For many Anglicans, the ideal remained a Christian India, although there were, according to the 1911 census, only 492,752 Indian Anglicans, out of an Indian population of over 300 million.[38] The Anglican establishment was clearly failing in its goal of converting the Indian peoples, but it would leave a legacy of social service idealism, as well as schools, colleges, and hospitals.

MISSIONS AND MISSIONARY BISHOPS

In 1854, Bishop Selwyn of New Zealand gave an emotive series of four sermons at Cambridge University on 'The Work of Christ in the World', appealing to university students to offer themselves for service as missionaries or colonial clergy. There could be no higher calling, he proclaimed, than to be

[36] F. Max Müller, 'Westminster Lecture on Missions', in F. Max Müller, *Selected Essays on Language, Mythology and Religion*, 2 vols. (London, 1881), II, pp. 46–86.

[37] Barry, *Ecclesiastical Expansion of England*, pp. 137–8.

[38] Palmer, *Imperial Vineyard*, pp. 84–5.

a 'soldier of the Cross' and 'to fight manfully under his Lord's banner, and to bear it to the utmost bounds of the habitable globe'.[39] Selwyn's appeal had a particular impact because of his remarkable story. A formidable 'muscular Christian', he carried on an active mission to the Māori of New Zealand, travelling extensively and defending Māori rights. In one six-month period in 1842, Selwyn travelled 2,277 miles around New Zealand, by foot, horseback, and boat. From 1847, moreover, he began making regular missionary voyages in a schooner among the Pacific islands. For Selwyn, who was a High Churchman, bishops should lead missions, as they had in the early Church, and he personally led missionary expeditions far beyond the formal borders of the British Empire. Later, in 1856, Selwyn was joined by John Coleridge Patteson, another High Churchman, who served with great courage first as Selwyn's missionary chaplain and then, from 1861, as missionary bishop of Melanesia—until he was martyred by Nukapu islanders in 1871.

A few years after Selwyn's Cambridge sermons, another missionary hero delivered a memorable set of lectures at Cambridge University. This was the African missionary David Livingstone, who had recently returned from an epic journey in which he traversed Africa from east to west, and explored the course of the Zambezi River. For his Cambridge audience, he revived the ideal of the Niger expedition of 1841, and its vision of ending the slave trade by bringing the Bible and the plough to Africa. He begged his hearers to direct their attention to Africa. 'I go back to Africa', he proclaimed, 'to make an open path for commerce and Christianity; do you carry out the work which I have begun. I LEAVE IT WITH YOU.'[40] In response to these appeals, members of both Cambridge and Oxford Universities now undertook to support a mission up the Zambezi, to regions which were then outside the crown's dominions. They were joined by members of Durham University and Trinity College, Dublin, to form an Anglican Universities' Mission to Central Africa (UMCA). The Convocation of Canterbury agreed that the Central African Mission should be headed by a missionary bishop, and in early 1861, Charles Frederick Mackenzie, an Anglican missionary serving in Natal, was consecrated bishop of Central Africa by the South African bishops at a service in Cape Town.

A few weeks later, Mackenzie and his party of UMCA missionaries met up with Livingstone and a state-supported expedition of explorers at the Kongone mouth of the Zambezi, and together they moved inland to end the slave trade by bringing commerce and Christianity into Central Africa. But both the mission and the expedition were soon enveloped in tragedy. The Zambezi proved largely inaccessible to Livingstone's steamboats, and the expedition

[39] George Augustus Selwyn, *The Work of Christ in the World: Four Sermons Preached before the University of Cambridge* (Cambridge, 1855), p. 46.

[40] David Livingstone, *Dr Livingstone's Cambridge Lectures*, ed. W. Monk (London, 1860 edn.), p. 168.

was weakened by illness and infighting. Livingstone left the missionaries, who established a mission station in the Shire uplands. There the missionaries used armed force to liberate slaves being driven to the coast; it seemed to them immoral not to free slaves when they had the opportunity. However, by liberating slaves, who had been captured by local warlords, the missionaries became parties in the local warfare, which undermined their mission to bring the gospel to all. In January 1862, Mackenzie died of malaria, and the mission was left leaderless and adrift. A new bishop, William George Tozer, was consecrated in Westminster Abbey to replace Mackenzie, and in 1864 Tozer withdrew the mission from the Zambezi to Zanzibar. The Zambezi expedition, like the Niger expedition twenty years before, had been a costly failure. Many blamed the failure on Livingstone, whose wife, Mary, had died of malaria while accompanying the expedition; Livingstone soon disappeared into the African interior. But the Universities Central African Mission continued, building a cathedral in Zanzibar on the site of a former slave market, sending missionaries into the interior of East Africa, establishing mission stations, and providing support and schools for freed slaves. It became Anglo-Catholic in ethos, with emphasis on episcopal authority.[41]

In 1864, soon after Bishop Mackenzie's death by the Zambezi, another missionary bishop was consecrated to lead an Anglican mission to regions of West Africa that were then outside the crown's dominions. This was Samuel Ajayi Crowther, the first African Anglican bishop. While Mackenzie's missionary bishopric owed its inspiration to the UMCA, Crowther's missionary bishopric had its origin in the Evangelical CMS, and the vision of its secretary, Henry Venn. Crowther had been liberated from slave traders as a child and landed in Sierra Leone, where he was baptized. After accompanying the ill-fated Niger expedition of 1841 as an interpreter, Crowther attended the CMS training college at Islington, and was ordained in 1843. He accompanied further exploratory expeditions up the Niger in 1854, 1857, and 1859, and translated the Book of Common Prayer and the Bible into the Yoruba language. One reason for consecrating Crowther as a missionary bishop was that it meant he would not have authority over European missionaries, most of whom would have refused to serve under an African bishop. More important, Henry Venn of the CMS hoped that Crowther's missionary bishopric would lead to an independent West African Anglican Church.

Crowther presided over an exclusively African clergy. He established a number of mission stations, where there were some mass conversions, and he nurtured good relations with local rulers. Scholarly, devout, and gentle, Crowther was blameless in his personal life. However, by the late 1870s, there were reports of scandals and irregularities in the Niger region under

[41] F. Winspear, 'A Short History of the Universities Mission to Central Africa', *Nyasaland Journal*, 9 (1956): 11–50.

Crowther's authority, including immorality among some African clergy and agents, involvement of the clergy in private trading, especially the trade in gin, and heterodox theology among the convert congregations. While many of the reports were false or exaggerated, some were not. In 1890, following an investigation by the CMS Finance Committee, there was a purge of leading African clergy, including Crowther's son, which led to a schism in the West African Church. Crowther, now in his mid-eighties, was devastated by the purge, seeing it as a condemnation of his life's work; he suffered a stroke and died in late 1891. The CMS became convinced by the Niger scandal that British supervision was necessary—because of African 'weakness'—and an Englishman was consecrated as Crowther's successor.[42]

As Andrew Porter has shown, a major factor in the CMS purge of the African Church in Yorubaland was a new spirit in Anglican Evangelicalism from the mid-1870s, associated with the Keswick conferences, and their 'holiness teachings' concerning the prospects of a 'higher life' for the converted Christian—a life characterized by a complete trust in God and freedom from any desire to sin. In the mission fields, this higher life included belief that God would provide for the missionary's every need, both spiritual and material. There was an emphasis on personal character and the potential of the individual Christian, when filled with God's Spirit, to achieve momentous change. Keswick influences spread to the universities, especially Cambridge, where they inspired a new generation of missionaries, many of them members of the Cambridge Inter-Collegiate Christian Union, formed in 1877, or educated at Cambridge's Ridley Hall, an Evangelical training college established in 1881. The new-style missionaries were confident, uncompromising, and vocal critics of what they perceived as a worldly spirit in existing missions. They embraced a commitment to the empire, including paternalistic attitudes towards what were termed the 'child' races, which needed to be protected from traders and nurtured under imperial tutelage. Keswick Evangelicalism contributed to an increase in the numbers of missionaries and a late Victorian missionary boom. The CMS, as Brian Stanley has observed, sent out 50 per cent more missionaries between 1880 and 1904 than it had during the first eighty years of its history. This included a significant increase in female CMS missionaries, many drawn to the African mission. By 1899, the CMS had 1,134 missionaries, of whom 281 were single women and 323 were missionary wives—which meant that women made up 53 per cent of the total.[43]

42 Adrian Hastings, *The Church in Africa 1450–1950* (Oxford, 1994), pp. 338–93; Williams, *Ideal of the Self-Governing Church*, pp. 90–101, 125–97.

43 Brian Stanley, *The Bible and the Flag* (Leicester, 1990), p. 80; J. Murray, 'The Role of Women in the Church Missionary Society, 1799–1917', in Kevin Ward and Brian Stanley (eds.), *The Church Mission Society and World Christianity, 1799–1999* (Grand Rapids, MI, 2000), pp. 82, 89.

Many Keswick Evangelicals were drawn to the faith mission ideal, with its pre-millennialist belief in the imminent return of Christ, and its commitment to communicate the gospel to as many people as possible before that event. The faith missions relied on small teams of itinerant missionaries, who would adopt the clothing, diet, and customs of the people among whom they evangelized. Their aim was to evangelize the world in their generation, or in other words to preach, with a sense of urgency, the gospel to every inhabitant. Among the new-style Evangelicals was the CMS missionary Graham Wilmot Brooke, who went to the Niger in 1889, and took a leading role in criticisms of the Niger Church.[44] In 1890, Brooke convinced the CMS to support a faith mission, the Sudan Mission Party, which he proposed to lead to the upper reaches to the Niger and then into the Sudan, evangelizing among the largely Muslim population. He renounced the ideal of bringing Christianity and commerce to the African interior; his aim was simply to bring the gospel to as many as possible. But Brooke died of fever in 1892 before reaching the Sudan.

Britain's occupation of Egypt in 1882, and its conquest of the Sudan in 1899, opened new mission fields in predominantly Islamic lands. Indeed, by the 1890s, the British Empire ruled over more Muslims than any other state, including the Ottoman Empire. For some, this meant that the Anglican Church now had a special mission to Islam. Many Anglicans were attracted to the story of General Charles Gordon, an Evangelical and anti-slavery activist, who had been killed in 1885 at the fall of Khartoum, where he had been sent to evacuate Egyptians from the Sudan following a Muslim rising. For his admirers, Gordon had died a martyr's death while endeavouring to rescue Muslims, and his example inspired Anglican engagement with Islam. The CMS had supported a small mission in Egypt, mainly proselytizing among Coptic Christians, from 1824 to 1862. The first Anglican church in Egypt was consecrated in 1855 in Alexandria. The CMS returned to Egypt in 1887, following the British occupation, with a new confidence—to establish schools and hospitals and to evangelize among Muslims. In the later 1890s, two admirers of Gordon, Douglas Thornton and William Temple Gairdner, went to Cairo as CMS missionaries to evangelize among students and educated Muslims. Thornton died in 1907, but Gairdner continued working in Cairo, producing a steady stream of publications which were aimed at both communicating Christianity to Muslims and promoting Anglican understanding of Islam.[45] Following the British occupation of the Sudan, the CMS

[44] Andrew Porter, 'Cambridge, Keswick, and Late-Nineteenth-Century Attitudes to Africa', *Journal of Imperial and Commonwealth History*, 5 (1976): 5–34; Andrew Porter, 'Evangelical Enthusiasm, Missionary Motivation and West African in the Late Nineteenth Century: The Career of G. W. Brooke', *Journal of Imperial and Commonwealth History*, 6 (1977): 23–46.

[45] Michel T. Shelley, 'Temple Gairdner of Cairo Revisited', *Islam and Christian-Muslim Relations*, 10 (1999): 261–78.

established a Gordon Memorial Mission, while a large Anglican church, which later became a cathedral, was built in Khartoum in Gordon's memory between 1904 and 1912. The missions in Egypt and the Sudan were under the authority of the Anglican bishop in Jerusalem. The joint British–Prussian Jerusalem bishopric, established in 1841, had dissolved in 1881. But an exclusively Anglican bishopric in Jerusalem was established in 1887, with Francis Blyth serving as bishop from 1887 to 1914. The Anglican St George's college and church complex, with schools, hospital, library, and clergy house, was built in an English style between 1895 and 1912. Many Anglican Evangelicals, including those influenced by Keswick, continued to believe that the Jerusalem bishopric was destined by Providence for a special role in the return of the Jews to the Holy Land, the conversion of Jews and Muslims, and the Second Coming of Christ. There were, however, very few Anglican converts from either Islam or Judaism.

FROM IMPERIAL TO WORLD ANGLICANISM

The language of imperial Christianity and the providential mission of the British Empire remained strong in the last years of the nineteenth and first years of the twentieth century. There was a sense that the empire promoted the spread of Anglicanism, and that Anglicanism elevated the empire with a higher mission. 'As a rule', wrote Alfred Barry in 1895, 'the mission of the [Anglican] Church has been to interpenetrate with a diviner life and unity the ever-widening sphere of English power and responsibility.'[46] For some observers, the Anglican Church was a vital bond of empire. 'Our empire', noted Bernard Wilson in 1900, 'is composed of absolutely diverse peoples spread over the five continents of the world. No natural bond of union exists which can cement these heterogeneous elements into one.' 'Only the inspiring force of religion', he continued, 'and the sound moral code which flows from it, can weld into one great whole so composite a State.' For Wilson, the Anglican Church should be the 'Church of the British Empire'.[47] The vision of an imperial Anglicanism uniting the settlement colonies, triumphing over Hinduism and Islam, and 'civilizing' the 'child races' had a powerful appeal. Henry Montgomery, former bishop of Tasmania and from 1901 secretary of the SPG, was an ardent supporter of imperial Christianity. His professed aim, he informed the SPG standing committee, was 'to revolutionise Church ideals

[46] Barry, *Ecclesiastical Expansion of England*, p. 9.

[47] B. Wilson, 'The Church and the Empire', in H. Hensley Henson (ed.), *Church Problems: A View of Modern Anglicanism* (London, 1900), pp. 372, 393.

and make the ancient Church of England more completely an Imperial Church'.[48]

However, many other early twentieth-century Anglicans perceived the British Empire and the Church as fundamentally different, with the one based on trade, national interest, and temporal power, and the other on spiritual truths, sacrifice, and eternal prospects. As Brian Stanley and Andrew Porter have shown, Christians, including Anglicans, could be among the most vocal critics of imperialism.[49] Missionaries often witnessed at first-hand the cruelties and injustices perpetrated by traders, settlers, colonial legislatures, and imperial governors upon the peoples of Australasia, South Asia, and the Americas. They saw the effects of imperial economic policies in impoverishing millions, or in forcing the mass migrations of peoples to work in plantations or mines—and they also observed closely the emerging movements for independence in India and Africa. They understood that the use of providentialist language linking British imperial expansion and the spread of Christianity was presumptuous. 'I believe', wrote G. A. Lefroy of the Cambridge Mission to Delhi (and later bishop of Calcutta) in 1879, 'that our position as the ruling power puts a dead weight on the missionary enterprise which nothing but the direct grace of God can possibly enable us to lift.'[50] By the early years of the twentieth century, the darker side of imperialism, including a pervasive racism, was becoming all too evident—for example, in the revelations of atrocities in the Congo associated with the collection of rubber. For many Anglicans, there was an imperative now to disentangle Anglicanism from Englishness, and the Church from the empire, and to work instead for a truly global Anglican Communion.

SELECT BIBLIOGRAPHY

Bremner, G. A., *Imperial Gothic: Religious Architecture and High Anglican Culture in the British Empire, c.1840–1870* (New Haven, CT, 2013).

Brown, Stewart J., *Providence and Empire: Religion, Politics and Society in the United Kingdom, 1815–1914* (Harlow, 2008).

Carey, Hilary M., *God's Empire: Religion and Colonialism in the British World, c.1801–1908* (Cambridge, 2011).

[48] Stephen Maughan, 'An Archbishop for Greater Britain: Bishop Montgomery, Missionary Imperialism and the SPG, 1897–1915', in Daniel O'Connor (ed.), *Three Centuries of Mission: The United Society for the Propagation of the Gospel 1701–2000* (London, 2000), p. 362.

[49] Stanley, *The Bible and the Flag*; Andrew Porter, *Religion versus Empire? British Protestant Missionaries and Overseas Expansion, 1700–1914* (Manchester, 2004).

[50] Quoted in Jeffrey Cox, *Imperial Fault Lines: Christianity and Colonial Power in India, 1818–1940* (Stanford, CA, 2002), p. 221.

Cnattingius, Hans, *Bishops and Societies: A Study of Anglican Colonial and Missionary Expansion 1698–1850* (London, 1952).

Cox, Jeffrey, *The British Missionary Enterprise since 1700* (New York, 2008).

Cox, Jeffrey, *Imperial Fault Lines: Christianity and Colonial Power in India, 1818–1940* (Stanford, CA, 2002).

Gibbs, M. E., *The Anglican Church in India 1600–1970* (Delhi, 1972).

Gladwin, Michael, *Anglican Clergy in Australia 1788–1852: Building a British World* (Woodbridge, 2015).

Hastings, Adrian, *The Church in Africa 1450–1950* (Oxford, 1994).

Hinchliff, Peter, *The Anglican Church in South Africa* (London, 1963).

Jacob, W. M., *The Making of the Anglican Church Worldwide* (London, 1997).

Kaye, Bruce N., T. R. Frame, Colin Holden, and Geoffrey R. Treloar (eds.), *Anglicanism in Australia: A History* (Melbourne, 2002).

Maughan, Steven S., *Mighty England do Good: Culture, Faith, Empire, and World in the Foreign Missions of the Church of England, 1850–1915* (Grand Rapids, MI, 2014).

Morrell, W. P., *The Anglican Church in New Zealand: A History* (Dunedin, 1973).

O'Connor, Daniel (ed.), *Three Centuries of Mission: The United Society for the Propagation of the Gospel 1701–2000* (London, 2000).

Palmer, Bernard, *Imperial Vineyard: The Anglican Church in India under the Raj from the Mutiny to Partition* (Lewes, Sussex, 1999).

Porter, Andrew (ed.), *The Oxford History of the British Empire*, vol. III: *The Nineteenth Century* (Oxford, 1999).

Porter, Andrew, *Religion versus Empire? British Protestant Missionaries and Overseas Expansion, 1700–1914* (Manchester, 2004).

Sachs, W. L., *The Transformation of Anglicanism: From State Church to Global Communion* (Cambridge, 1993).

Stanley, Brian, *The Bible and the Flag: Protestant Missions and British Imperialism in the Nineteenth and Twentieth Centuries* (Leicester, 1990).

Strong, Rowan, *Anglicanism and the British Empire c.1700–1850* (Oxford, 2007).

Tennant, Bob, *Corporate Holiness: Pulpit Preaching and the Church of England Missionary Societies, 1760–1870* (Oxford, 2013).

Ward, Kevin, *A History of Global Anglicanism* (Cambridge, 2006).

Williams, C. P., *The Ideal of the Self-Governing Church: A Guide to Victorian Missionary Strategy* (Leiden, 1990).

Yates, Timothy E., *Venn and Victorian Bishops Abroad: The Missionary Policies of Henry Venn and their Repercussions upon the Anglican Episcopate of the Colonial Period 1841–1872* (Uppsala, 1978).

4

Anglicanism beyond the British Empire, 1829–1910

Carol Engelhardt Herringer

INTRODUCTION

In the period from 1829 to 1910, the history of Anglicanism outside the British Empire reflected in many ways the history of Anglicanism within the empire, in that it was most successful in the white-dominated former colony of the United States of America and struggled to gain a foothold in Africa, Latin America, and Asia. Even the success in the United States was relative: the Protestant Episcopal Church of the United States, as it was formally known after the American Revolution, remained a small denomination dominated by white elites, with far fewer adherents than the Methodists, Baptists, or Roman Catholics. In 1830 Episcopalians were about 0.25 per cent of the US population; in 1860, about 0.5 per cent of the population; and in 1900, about 1 per cent of the population. However, their political, cultural, and social influence was far greater than their numbers would suggest. For example, five of the twenty US presidents and fourteen of the US Supreme Court justices (about one-third of the total number of justices) in this period were Episcopalian. In other parts of the world and notwithstanding dedicated missionaries who put their health and even lives at risk, Anglicanism attracted few converts but had a significant impact on education and health, thanks to the educational institutions, hospitals, orphanages, and similar institutions established by missionaries and converts.

Scholarship, most if not all by members of the Anglican Communion, has followed this history in its focus on the Protestant Episcopal Church of the United States, especially the white majority. While recent surveys provide useful overviews of the Church's development, scholarly monographs present a picture of a Church divided between Evangelicals and High Church, and Anglo-Catholic Episcopalians for much of the period until the decline of

Episcopalian Evangelicals and the rise of the Broad Church party at the end of the nineteenth century. If scholarship on the Protestant Episcopal Church of the United States in this period is relatively slim, there are very few recent scholarly monographs on Anglicanism in areas outside the British Empire beyond the United States.

THE DEVELOPMENT OF THE PROTESTANT EPISCOPAL CHURCH OF THE UNITED STATES

By 1829, the Protestant Episcopal Church had made the transition from the partly Established Church of the colonial period to an independent denomination, and had largely overcome its association with the British government during the colonial period as well as low attendance and sloppy church services. Over the course of the nineteenth century, it was briefly divided by the Civil War, expanded its organizational structure to all parts of the continental United States as well as Hawai'i and Alaska, and even sent missionaries abroad. Throughout, its history remained closely tied to that of the Church of England. In addition to personal relationships between Episcopalian and Anglican clergymen, movements that began in England—including the Oxford Movement, ritualism, and the Broad Church movement—also impacted the Episcopal Church. Yet even as it grew in numbers (partly thanks to conversions from other Protestant denominations), it remained a minority Church that was strongest in the North and in urban areas, and was dominated by a white elite. A handful of African-American congregations that were served by African-American clergy were established in large cities such as New York and Philadelphia; only St James's church in Baltimore, Maryland, was south of the Mason–Dixon line (the traditional dividing line between North and South in the eastern part of the United States). Until the end of the nineteenth century, the growth of the Episcopal Church was hampered by a lack of funds and clergymen, and an inability to appeal to immigrants other than those from Britain and Ireland.

Over the course of the nineteenth century, dioceses were established and divided, usually to reflect state boundaries, as the Episcopal Church matured administratively. In New England, for example, between 1832 and 1847 the states of Vermont, Rhode Island, New Hampshire, and Maine withdrew from the Eastern Diocese, leaving only Massachusetts, so that each state became its own diocese. Connecticut, where the Episcopal Church was stronger, already comprised a separate diocese. By the last third of the century, dioceses were regularly created within states in the eastern and Midwestern parts of the United States.

The establishment of dioceses west of the Mississippi River occurred more slowly. While Ian T. Douglas ascribes the Church's slow progress in its missionary endeavours to its 'schizophrenic understanding of mission', which was a result of its 'inability to reconcile successfully a catholic theology of missiology with an American Protestant mission strategy',[1] there were also practical problems, including a lack of funds and clergymen, as well as a lingering suspicion that the Episcopal Church was too formal for the frontier. In recognition of these challenges, in the early 1830s the Domestic and Foreign Missionary Society became the responsibility of the entire Church and administration of the society was taken over by the General Convention. One consequence of this change was the creation of missionary bishops, the first of whom was the energetic and successful Jackson Kemper, who was appointed Missionary Bishop to Missouri and Indiana in 1835. By 1859 there were missionary bishops in all areas of the United States that did not already have an established bishop. As the Church organization spread throughout the United States, it became increasingly under direct control of the bishops. Canons in the 1870s placed the Domestic and Foreign Missionary Society under episcopal control, and in 1877 the General Convention made itself the Board of Missions, with a Board of Managers in charge of the practical details of running the missions, which had previously been handled by the committees of the Domestic and Foreign Missionary Society. The American Church Missionary Society, which had been strongly Evangelical, became first an auxiliary member of the Board of Missions before being absorbed by it. Especially after 1870, when the Commission on Indian Affairs was created within the Board of Missions, westward expansion included missions to Native Americans.

In the western part of the United States, the same pattern of eventually establishing smaller dioceses was followed. Many western dioceses began as geographically unwieldy combinations of states and territories, but by 1880 the diocesan boundaries were beginning to reflect state boundaries. Missouri became a diocese in 1840, Nebraska in 1868, Colorado in 1887, and Oregon in 1874. The twenty-two dioceses in 1835 had become forty-eight dioceses by 1883. Throughout, the work was slow, because the Episcopal Church was more a Church of settled areas, not the frontier. In 1880 these eight western states and territories had sixty-seven clergymen and about 3,800 communicants; at the end of the nineteenth century, there were 174 clergymen and about 17,000 communicants in these areas. This growth was part of growth in the Church overall: in 1832 there were about 120,000 people attending the Protestant Episcopal Church, about a quarter of whom were communicants. In comparison, the Methodist Church had 638,784 communicants and about

[1] Ian T. Douglas, *Fling out the Banner! The National Church Ideal and the Foreign Mission of the Episcopal Church* (New York, 1996), p. 23.

2,000,000 people attending services. By 1890 there were 484,020 Episcopalian communicants, of whom 10 per cent lived west of the Mississippi. This growth in communicants was thirteen times in a period when the national population had quadrupled: in 1830 one in every 416 residents of the United States was an Episcopalian communicant, a ratio that was 1:102 by the end of the nineteenth century.

Throughout this period, the Episcopal Church established educational institutions to support its growth. Most Episcopal churches had a Sunday school by the 1820s, and in the second half of the nineteenth century, thanks largely to local initiatives, these Sunday schools grew markedly, although not enough to keep pace with population growth. Between 1866 and 1900, the number of Sunday school students almost tripled, from 158,000 to 430,000, while the 18,000 teachers in 1866 had become 46,000 by the turn of the century. Some of this growth was the result of an adult education programme, begun in the 1880s. National administration of the Sunday schools was shared by the American Church Sunday School, founded in 1884, and the Sunday Schools Commissions. In addition, many boarding schools affiliated with the Episcopal Church were founded after the Civil War. These schools, many of which remain prestigious, included St Mark's (1865), Groton (1884), Chatham Hall (1894), and National Cathedral School (1900). These were in addition to Episcopalian universities, including Trinity University, Hobart University, and the University of the South, although in the nineteenth century the education offered at these institutions was generally not of a very high calibre. More impressive were the seminaries. The first two were founded in the 1820s: the General Theological Seminary, founded in New York City by the High Church bishop John Henry Hobart in 1822; and the Virginia Theological Seminary, founded in 1823 by Evangelicals. Like these two, seminaries founded later were typically aligned with either the High Church or Evangelical branches of the Episcopal Church: Nashotah House, in Wisconsin, with Anglo-Catholics; while the Philadelphia Divinity School and the Episcopal Theology School in Boston (1867) were founded by Evangelicals.

Robert W. Pritchard is one of the few scholars who emphasize unity in the nineteenth-century Episcopal Church; most scholars pay more attention to the divisions.[2] Like their British counterparts, Evangelical Episcopalians emphasized the importance of a conversion experience and subsequent holy living, were more open to cooperation with other Protestant denominations, placed less importance on the sacraments, and were more accepting of the role of emotions in religion. Evangelical Episcopalians were often linked with Presbyterians, partly because both groups tended to be wealthy, white, conservative, and influential. Like other Evangelicals, they emphasized the

[2] Robert W. Prichard, *The Nature of Salvation: Theological Consensus in the Episcopal Church, 1801–73* (Urbana, IL, 1997).

atonement and a personal relationship with Christ, were scriptural literalists, and promoted extemporaneous preaching, informal mid-week services, and revival meetings. The Evangelical Episcopalians' paper was the *Washington Theological Repertory*, founded in 1819 and published throughout the nineteenth century. Evangelical Episcopalians were in a difficult position, as they defied High Church Episcopalians by aligning with other denominations (particularly the Congregational and Presbyterian Churches) but also had to defend the episcopacy that most other Evangelicals rejected. The centre of Episcopalian Evangelicalism was in the mid-Atlantic states, especially Virginia, and New England outside of Connecticut.

The leading Evangelical Episcopalian in this period was Charles Pettit McIlvaine, who in 1832 became the second bishop of Ohio and head of what became Kenyon College. He became famous at a young age for the success of his revivals, first in New York and then in Ohio, in attracting new converts, and later as a defender of Evangelical principles. But like most of his fellow Evangelical Episcopalians, McIlvaine valued his Episcopalian identity over his Evangelical one, choosing, for example, to support the Domestic and Foreign Missionary Service rather than to cooperate with other Protestant denominations' missionary efforts.[3] Such was his status that in 1865 the House of Bishops authorized McIlvaine to write a letter condemning Bishop John Colenso and *Essays and Reviews*.

THE EPISCOPAL CHURCH IN THE CIVIL WAR

The position of Evangelical Episcopalians was weakened by their being at the centre of two schisms in the Episcopal Church, the first of which occurred during the American Civil War (1861–5). At the beginning of the nineteenth century, Evangelical Episcopalians had begun to look for the gradual abolition of slavery; but by the 1840s many of them, as well as many High Church Episcopalians, avoided the issue, because many southern slaveholders were Episcopalian. Two of the largest slaveholders were Bishop Leonidas Polk of Louisiana and Bishop Stephen Elliott of Georgia. Polk, a graduate of West Point and, like many Episcopalians in the South, a supporter of the Confederacy, became a general in the Confederate army and was killed while on a reconnoitring mission during the war. (General Robert E. Lee and Jefferson Davis, president of the Confederate States of America, were also Episcopalian.) Geography alone did not divide the Church, for some northerners also supported slavery. Samuel Seabury, a grandson of the first American bishop

[3] Diana Hochstedt Butler, *Standing Against the Whirlwind: Evangelical Episcopalians in Nineteenth-Century America* (New York, 1995), ch. 3.

and editor of the High Church publication *The Churchman*, and Bishop John Henry Hopkins of Vermont, were vocal northern supporters of slavery. One popular Episcopalian justification for slavery in the decades before the Civil War was that it was a biblical institution that could lead to the conversion of slaves. However, Episcopalians had little success in converting African-Americans in the South; on the eve of the Civil War there were only about 35,000 African-American Episcopalians in the South (out of a total slave population of almost 4 million). They were more successful in the North and West, where there were large African-American congregations served by African-American clergy, although there was continued marginalization of black Episcopalians by the white majority.[4]

The coming of the Civil War convinced some Evangelical Episcopalians to become abolitionists. Stephen Tyng, a leading Evangelical clergyman, became a prominent abolitionist after the tragic death of his son Dudley, who had lost his pulpit as a result of his opposition to slavery. McIlvaine gradually became an abolitionist, although he was initially reluctant to make public statements on the issue.

In 1861, many southern dioceses left the Episcopal Church and established the Protestant Episcopal Church in the Confederate States of America. This Church was not entirely unified, as it did not initially include Florida (which joined in 1863), Louisiana, or Tennessee. Given the distances and military conflicts that made communication difficult, the nine dioceses often operated independently. Because this new Church never considered that it had officially split from the northern Church, in 1865, at the conclusion of the Civil War, the southern bishops took their seats in the House of Bishops at the General Convention, where they were welcomed without condemnation by their fellow bishops.

AFRICAN-AMERICAN EPISCOPALIANISM

Recognizing the challenge of attracting African-Americans to the Church, at the end of the Civil War the white members of the Episcopal Church established the Freedman's Commission (1865), which was renamed the Commission on Home Missions to Colored People in 1868. Under both names, this body focused on education, establishing Sunday schools, industrial schools, and parochial schools. While these initiatives showed an awareness of the need to keep African-Americans in the Episcopal Church, these efforts were hampered by the continuing treatment of African-Americans as a separate group.

[4] Harold T. Lewis, *Yet With a Steady Beat: The African American Struggle for Recognition in the Episcopal Church* (Valley Forge, PA, 1996), ch. 1.

One of the most egregious examples of this treatment was the 1883 proposal by southern bishops that a separate missionary organization be established to minister to black Episcopalians.[5] Therefore, it was not surprising that most freed slaves left the Episcopal Church of their previous owners for more congenial, and non-white-sponsored, denominations in which formal education was not always required for ordination. In recognition of this failure, the Freedman's Commission was disbanded in 1878. However, the Episcopal Church continued its missionary efforts to African-Americans. In 1887 instruction began at the Bishop Payne Divinity School, chartered by the trustees of the Virginia Theological Seminary to educate African-Americans for the priesthood and for missionary service abroad. After the Civil War, congregations of African-American Episcopalians were established in northern and Midwestern cities, including Newark, New Jersey; Buffalo, New York; Detroit; Chicago; and St. Louis. The question of whether congregations should be racially segregated was discussed throughout the remainder of the nineteenth century, as black Episcopalian leaders, including George Freeman Bragg, Jr., continued to ask for equality within the Church and white bishops resisted, preferring a paternalistic model. It was not until 1910 that the General Convention approved in principle suffragan bishops for the African-American community and not until 1918 that Edward Thomas Denby was consecrated suffragan bishop of Arkansas. By this point, the numbers of black Episcopalians were slowly increasing, thanks in part to immigration from the West Indies.

EPISCOPALIAN DIVISIONS

The second Episcopalian schism had its origins in the 1871 trial and deposition of Charles Edward Cheney, the rector of Christ Church, Chicago, for omitting the words 'regenerate' and 'regeneration' from the baptismal office. In response to this and other defeats, in 1873 George D. Cummins, the assistant bishop of Kentucky, along with eight ministers and nineteen laymen who saw in Tractarianism a threat to their Church, established the Reformed Episcopal Church. Among this number was Cheney, whom Cummins consecrated a bishop. Contrary to Cummins's expectations of being joined by more Evangelical Episcopalians, most of them condemned his actions and chose their Episcopalian over their Evangelical identity. The Reformed Episcopal Church kept the Prayer Book and episcopacy but remained a very small denomination.

[5] Lewis, *Yet with a Steady Beat*, pp. 67–9.

Evangelicals' influence peaked in the 1830s, but by the end of the nineteenth century, there were very few of them left in the Episcopal Church. Their decline in influence and numbers was the result of several factors besides the schisms of the 1860s and 1870s. The growing appeal of Tractarianism and of ritualism, a post-Civil War shift to Broad Church sympathies by many old-style Evangelical leaders, the defence of conservative biblical views by a small group and the consequent development of proto-fundamentalist positions, the emphasis on pre-millennial views, and their position against infant baptism all contributed to their declining influence. But while Evangelicalism declined in the Protestant Episcopal Church, it flourished elsewhere and often developed into fundamentalism by the beginning of the twentieth century.

In contrast to the declining numbers and influence of Evangelical Episcopalians, the High Church party grew in strength. For much of the nineteenth century, until the Civil War, the High Church wing was dominated by the 'Hobartian synthesis', the legacy of John Henry Hobart, bishop of New York from 1816 until his death in 1830. Hobart's view of the Episcopal Church as descended from the Church of the first Christian centuries, or the 'Primitive Church', strengthened his opposition to ecumenical cooperation and Church involvement in secular matters. Like other High Churchmen, he believed in free will, the consistent operation of grace over a violent conversion experience, the efficacy of the sacraments, and a high valuation of the ordained role. However, the Hobartian synthesis failed in the face of the growing challenge posed by slavery, and its inability to deal with new challenges such as rationalism and science.

There were several reasons for the ascendancy of High Church Episcopalians over the course of the nineteenth century. Their greater tolerance for amusements such as dancing, card-playing, and horse-racing made them more appealing than Evangelical Episcopalians;[6] and an informal agreement had given them control over domestic missions, which meant that they dominated the expanding dioceses within the United States and Alaska.

As they did in the Church of England, the *Tracts* divided the Episcopal Church. Evangelical Episcopalians, including Bishops McIlvaine, Manton Eastburn, and William Meade, perceived the *Tracts*, as did their counterparts in Britain, as dangerously Roman Catholic and even a harbinger of the Antichrist. The *Tracts* were supported by Bishop Doane of New Jersey, Bishop William DeLancey of Western New York, Bishop Benjamin T. Onderdonk of New York, and Samuel Seabury. Other bishops cautiously supported the Tractarian movement while worrying about 'Romanism' and the potential for schism.

The introduction of Tractarianism and ritualism led to some conversions to Roman Catholicism. Approximately forty Episcopal clergymen converted in

[6] Richard Rankin, *Ambivalent Churchmen and Evangelical Churchwomen: The Religion of the Episcopal Elite in North Carolina, 1800–1860* (Columbia, SC, 1993), p. 81.

the 1840s and 1850s. The most prominent convert was Levi Silliman Ives (1797–1867), bishop of North Carolina and son-in-law of Bishop Hobart.

These movements also led to controversies over ritual and belief. The most significant Tractarian-inspired controversy was over the ordination of Arthur Carey, who had been trained at the General Theological Seminary. He was investigated in 1843, prior to his ordination, for a pamphlet in which he had, like John Henry Newman in Tract 90, minimized the theological differences between the Episcopalian and Roman Catholic Churches. Carey was finally ordained in 1843 and served briefly as Seabury's assistant at the Church of the Annunciation before dying at age 21 in 1844, an event that led some Episcopalians to compare him to Richard Hurrell Froude.[7] Twice in 1844 the General Theological Seminary was investigated for its promotion of Tractarianism, with the result that some faculty resigned and some were admonished. In 1844–5, Evangelical hostility was one incentive for the trial of Bishop Benjamin T. Onderdonk for irregularities involving women (although not adultery). Onderdonk was suspended rather than deposed, and he lived in retirement until he died in 1861. Shortly thereafter another *bête noire* of the Evangelicals, Onderdonk's brother Bishop Henry U. Onderdonk of Pennsylvania, was investigated for his drinking, which had become problematic after he was told to drink alcohol to compensate for a digestive problem. The Evangelicals in his diocese refused to accept his resignation but suspended him until 1856, by which time Alonzo Potter had been elected bishop. In 1874 the House of Deputies at the General Convention refused to confirm George F. Seymour as bishop of Illinois because the doctrine of the corporeal (Real) Presence had been popular with students at the General Theological Seminary when he was dean there. The next choice of the diocese of Illinois, James deKoven, also was not confirmed on the grounds that his Marian devotion marked him as too 'high'.

However, by the end of the nineteenth century, ritualistic practices—including the wearing of surplices, surpliced choirs, saints' days, and the use of stone altars, candles, and crosses—had become the norm in many of the neo-Gothic churches that were built beginning in the 1830s. All these changes made the Episcopal Church more appealing to converts in the decades after the Civil War.

BROAD CHURCH EPISCOPALIANS

The third major party within the Episcopal Church, the Broad Church party, had its roots in the Muhlenberg Memorial, which was championed by

[7] Peter B. Nockles, 'The Oxford Movement and the United States', in Stewart J. Brown and Peter B. Nockles (eds.), *The Oxford Movement: Europe and the Wider World 1830–1930* (Cambridge, 2012), pp. 133–50.

William Augustus Muhlenberg, a leading Episcopal clergyman noted especially for his commitment to liturgical reform and parish involvement in urban life. Muhlenberg identified himself as an Evangelical Catholic, indicating that he did not side with either Evangelicals or supporters of the Oxford Movement. The Muhlenberg Memorial sought to achieve unity within the Church by allowing more latitude in the ordination of non-Episcopalian Protestants and in liturgical practices. It was presented to the General Convention on 18 October 1853 and signed by a number of clergymen, many of whom were well-known Evangelicals who wanted to work more closely with other Protestant denominations; some High Churchmen signed with reservations. However, its lack of specifics and the general opposition to it by High Church Episcopalians meant that it was much discussed but never enacted.

However, the principles the Muhlenberg Memorial advocated were to rise in the next decades, in spite of the opposition of both Evangelical and High Church Episcopalians to rationalism. As in the Church of England, a major controversy erupted with the publication of *Essays and Reviews* in 1860. The collection was condemned by the American House of Bishops, but a generational shift was obvious in the fact that most who voted to condemn the book had been born in the late eighteenth or early nineteenth century. In fact, the Broad Church movement was key to the growth of the Episcopal Church after the Civil War. Broad Church Episcopalians were committed to social causes, to consensus and unity within the Church and ecumenism outside it, and to an acceptance of contemporary culture. They were leaders in the social gospel movement, which was also supported by High Church and Anglo-Catholic Episcopalians, especially deaconesses and sisters. In the late nineteenth century the influence of Frederick Denison Maurice (1805–72) and the shock of the violence in the nationwide railroad workers' strike of 1877 and the industrial and railroad workers' strikes of 1886 (both of which were related to workers' attempts to unionize) led men like Washington Gladden and Lyman Abbot to champion social justice in the Episcopal Church.[8] Three organizations were founded to further this cause: the Church Association for the Advancement of the Interests of Labor (1887–1928); the Society for Christian Socialists (founded 1889); and the Christian Social Union (1891–1912).

The Broad Church movement owed much to Phillips Brooks, who was one of the most popular American preachers in the nineteenth century. He sought unity within the Episcopal Church and with other Protestant denominations, a trait that may have been a legacy of his family's Unitarian heritage. His optimistic, passionate sermons generally avoided controversial topics, including slavery, to stress God's love for sinners and appeal to the

[8] See Jacob Henry Dorn, *Washington Gladden: Prophet of the Social Gospel* (Columbus, OH, 1967).

congregation's sense of duty, self-respect, and individuality.[9] Consecrated bishop of Massachusetts in 1891, he died suddenly of an infection in 1893. Although he was often opposed by High Church and Evangelical Anglicans, his compelling sermons brought many people into the Episcopal Church.

WOMEN IN THE EPISCOPAL CHURCH

As in the Church of England and most Christian denominations, women were typically involved in unpaid volunteer work that was traditionally deemed feminine, including teaching, nursing, and furnishing and maintaining church textiles. Occasionally some women rose to public prominence. One notable example was Lydia Sigourney, an Anglican convert who published fifty-six books—some of which advocated her pacifist beliefs—between 1815 and her death in 1865.[10] After the Civil War, women could become teachers of freed slaves under the auspices of the short-lived Freedman's Commission, or join the Women's Auxiliary to the Board of Missions of the Episcopal Church (previously the Ladies Domestic Missionary Relief Association), which was formally organized by the Board of Missions in 1871 to recruit missionaries, train teachers, and raise money for the missions. As Ian T. Douglas notes, their contributions to foreign and domestic missionary work are often overlooked by those who concentrate on men's work.[11] As part of this work, women also served as nurses, teachers, and school principals to Native Americans. The Women's Auxiliary was dominated by the four Emery sisters—Mary Abbot Emery (general secretary 1872 until her marriage in 1876), Julia Chester Emery (head 1876–1906), Susan Lavinia Emery, and Margaret Theresa Emery. By 1874 it had moved beyond gathering boxes of clothes and funds for the missionaries to having long-range goals, including organizing women in every parish. This goal was reached by 1910, by which point its work was also promoted by the periodical *The Spirit of the Missions*.

One of the most organized options for women was the religious sisterhood, an outgrowth of the Tractarian movement. The first sisterhood established in the United States was the Sisterhood of the Holy Communion in New York City, which was founded by Anne Ayres in Muhlenberg's parish in 1853, a year after Muhlenberg had expressed his support for such orders in *Two Letters on Protestant Sisterhoods*. The sisters first operated a small infirmary

[9] David B. Chesebrough, *Phillips Brooks: Pulpit Eloquence* (Westport, CT, 2001), pp. 49, 84, 86–8.

[10] Patrick G. Blythe, 'Visions of a Peaceful World: Locating Peace in Early Nineteenth-Century New England, 1805–1850', PhD thesis, University of Connecticut, 2012.

[11] Douglas, *Fling out the Banner!*, pp. 53–4.

and then became the head nurses when St Luke's Hospital, New York City, opened in 1858. This order, which was suspended in 1863 as a result of personality clashes and resistance to Anne Ayres's leadership, was in some ways more like a deaconess order, as the sisters did not take perpetual vows or do work outside the parish or hospital. The first permanently vowed sisterhood was the Sisterhood of St Mary, founded in New York in 1865 by Harriet Starr Cannon, who was one of the sisters to leave the Sisterhood of the Holy Communion in the winter of 1862–3. Within seven years of its founding the sisterhood had opened many institutions, including a home for abandoned girls, a hospital, a school, a convent and novitiate. The sisterhood later expanded, at the invitation of bishops, to Tennessee and Wisconsin. Over the next several decades, at least eight other orders were established on the east coast and in the Midwest, including the Society of the Transfiguration, which was the first to send sisters as foreign missionaries. Deaconess orders were also established beginning in 1871 and were formally approved in 1889, and schools to train the deaconesses were quickly established on the east and west coasts. Two orders for men, the Brotherhood of St Andrew (1883; St James's church, Chicago), and the Order of the Holy Cross (1884) were also established. The Society of St John the Evangelist, popularly known as the Cowley Fathers, established in the Church of England in 1866 by Richard M. Benson, became independent in its American branch in 1914. Notwithstanding the energy evident in these orders, the General Convention responded even more slowly than did the Church of England hierarchy; it was not until 1913 that the General Convention approved orders for men and women.

CHINA

As the Episcopal Church grew, it was able to devote more attention to overseas missions. By the end of the nineteenth century, there were Episcopalian missions in Brazil, China, Cuba, the Dominican Republic, Haiti, Hawai'i, Japan, Liberia, Mexico, Panama, the Philippines, and Puerto Rico. Most American clerical missionaries were trained at the more Evangelical Virginia Theological Seminary.

However, Episcopalians' early attempts at overseas mission work were unimpressive. What turned out to be a short-lived mission was established in Greece in 1830 by several Americans. Even less successful was the attempt by the Revd Horatio Southgate to set up missionary work in Persia beginning in 1835. He returned to the United States in 1849 and resigned the following year, which marked the end of any Episcopalian attempt to convert people in the Ottoman Empire.

Episcopalians had somewhat more success in Asia. Anglican missionaries from Britain, the United States, and (later) Canada went to China, as did missionaries of other Christian denominations, especially after the Second Opium War (1856–60) which forcibly opened China to Western missionaries. The Church of England, working primarily through the CMS and the SPG, and the Episcopal Church, working through the American Church Mission (ACM), were competitors in China for much of the nineteenth century. The real founder of the Episcopalian mission in China was William J. Boone, a graduate of both medical school and the Virginia Theological Seminary, who in 1844 became the first Episcopalian bishop for foreign missionary service when he was appointed bishop for Xiamen and other parts of China. He moved the mission back to China from Java in 1842, and in 1845 he and eight new missionaries from the Virginia Theological Seminary opened a mission in Shanghai. Within a year they had a school for boys (taught in English) and were preaching and distributing tracts.

At about the same time, in 1844, the CMS sent Thomas McClatchie and George Smith to visit Hong Kong and the five treaty ports (Guangzhou, Xiamen, Fuzhou, Ningbo, Shanghai). McClatchie settled in Shanghai and was preaching and translating the Book of Common Prayer by 1845. In 1850, the CMS began work in Fuzhou thanks to Dr William Welton and Robert David Jackson. Also in 1850, the CMS and the ACM opened their first churches in China, and the following year the first two baptisms were held in China, in Zheijang. However, progress was slow in the 1850s; most years few or no Chinese were baptized. Until 1861, most Anglican work in Hong Kong was directed at Europeans, not Chinese. These Anglican missionaries faced Chinese hostility; but both Episcopalians and Anglicans persisted, establishing churches and schools, mostly in the dioceses associated with the port cities. Women were an integral part of this missionary work. One of them, the Episcopalian Mary Elizabeth Wood arrived in China in 1899 to join her brother Robert, an Episcopalian missionary; working in China for the next several decades, she became known as the founder of the Chinese library system.[12] These missionaries had some small successes: for example, in 1871 there were 150 ACM communicants in Shanghai and central China. However, it was not until 1882 that the first diocesan conference was held in the North China diocese. By the end of the nineteenth century, Fujian was the focus for CMS work, where by 1900 the missionaries had established over 600 institutions in the region, including primary schools, schools for the blind, hospitals, and homes for lepers. The Boxer Rebellion (1900) briefly disrupted this work, as missionaries and their buildings were attacked, and some missionaries were

[12] George W. Huang, 'Miss Mary Elizabeth Wood: Pioneer of the Library Movement in China' (1975; <http://140.122.104.2/ojs../index.php/jlis/article/viewFile/6/6>, accessed 4 Dec. 2014).

killed. However, in 1900 three young doctors set up a Chinese branch of the CMS, to be funded entirely by the Chinese; in 1902 work began in Hunan province and the first Chinese priest was ordained by Anglicans in Sichuan. By 1915 there were almost 3,500 communicants.

JAPAN

In Japan, missionaries were allowed to enter unofficially as English teachers beginning in 1859. Notwithstanding renewed persecutions between 1867 and 1872, Christianity was tolerated. However, until 1890, all foreigners had to stay within twenty-five miles of the treaty ports unless they had a special passport. Among the first Christian missionaries were two American Episcopal priests who arrived in 1859: John Liggins and Channing Moore Williams, who were associated with the Episcopal Mission in China. Liggins contracted malaria and returned to the United States in 1860, but Williams stayed for fifty years, and in 1866 became bishop with authority over both China and Japan. In 1874 his territory was limited to Japan as he became bishop of Tokyo. At first he evangelized quietly, learning the language, translating key texts like the Lord's Prayer, and serving as a teacher. Although the Episcopal missionaries were hampered by the Civil War, by 1890 they were the fourth-largest Protestant group in Japan. Anglican missionaries arrived later, partly because their government, attuned to geopolitical interests, was less supportive of their work. The first Anglican missionary, George Ensor of the CMS, arrived in Nagasaki in 1869; he was followed in 1873 by two other SPG priests. By 1875 there were eight more men associated with the CMS.

Unlike in China, the Episcopal and Anglican missionaries in Japan agreed to work together to produce a common Japanese Prayer Book and a united Japanese Church, which was established in 1887 by a convention of Anglicans and Episcopalians in Osaka. The Church was named the Nippon Seikokwai, or Japan Holy Catholic Church, and became, in terms of support from the population, the most successful Anglican Church in Asia: while its membership remained small (0.5 per cent of the population), its leadership was gradually taken over, beginning at the end of the nineteenth century, by Japanese Anglicans. The first Japanese man ordained was Masakazu Tai, in 1889, and the following year Holy Communion was celebrated for the first time in Japan by a Japanese priest and deacon. In 1900 Sidney Catlin Partridge was consecrated the first bishop of Kyoto, which was the first time a bishop had been consecrated in Japan.

A major accomplishment of the missionaries in Japan was establishing schools, especially for girls, whose educational needs were largely ignored by the government. Although the schools faced challenges, including a lack of teachers, buildings destroyed by fire and earthquakes, and irregular attendance by students, they persevered. The missionaries also opened two hospitals, St Barnabas's in Osaka (1874) and St Luke's (1902). A nursing school, opened in 1902, became the first College of Nursing in Japan in 1928. Other charitable institutions included a lepers' hospital; the Hospital of the Resurrection of Hope in Kumamoto, founded in 1895 by Hannah Riddell, an Anglican who was not formally associated with the Church of England missionary work; and homes for orphans. An entirely Japanese-run project was the Widely Loving Society in Osaka, a home and school established for poor children by the Kobashi brothers and entirely funded by the Japanese Church. The Widely Loving Society exemplifies the degree to which Japanese Anglicans shared the work of the Church with Anglican and Episcopalian missionaries. The Church in Japan relied on Japanese who ran Bible classes, taught Sunday school, and ran societies like the Women's Auxiliary, and the Young Men's Society. In contrast to China, the Church in Japan was established as a separate Church relatively quickly and benefited from the cooperation rather than competition of Anglicans and Episcopalians. The success of the Church in Japan may be attributed in part to its appeal to the elite, thanks to its emphasis on philanthropic work and its disinterest in political activity.[13] Nonetheless, although Christianity was officially recognized as a religion in 1911, the Church in Japan remained a tiny proportion of the Japanese population.

KOREA AND THE PACIFIC

Anglican bishops from Japan and China visited Korea and sent Japanese missionaries in 1880, but initially had no success. In 1889 Edward Benson, archbishop of Canterbury, consecrated the Anglo-Catholic Charles John Corfe, as bishop of Korea. His public appeal for funds and men generated little response, but one of the two priests who did volunteer, Herbert Kelly, founded the Korean Missionary Brotherhood (later the Society of the Sacred Mission), which worked in Korea for some years until moving to the Orange Free State in Africa. Bishop Corfe, accompanied by Eli Landis, an American medical doctor, arrived in Korea in 1890. Within two years they had established St Michael's church at Inchon and a church in Seoul, as well as a hospital in Seoul that was run with the help of nuns from the Community of St Peter in England. The first converts were Japanese; the first Korean baptisms did not occur until 1897. The first Korean to be baptized, Mark Kim, later became the first Korean ordained, in 1914. Corfe, exhausted, resigned in

[13] Cyril Hamilton Powles, *Victorian Missionaries in Meiji, Japan: The Shiba Sect, 1873–1900* (Toronto, 1987), p. 9.

1904 and was succeeded by Bishop Arthur Turner (1904–9). He died of overwork in 1910, by which point the Church had spread throughout much of what is now South Korea.

Missionary work in the Philippines began as a result of the Spanish–American war in 1898, when several American Episcopalian chaplains who had accompanied the invading troops began holding services for American soldiers and other English speakers. One of them, Charles B. Pierce, served briefly as a spy for the American forces in 1899 and also performed official military duties, from identifying the dead to burying them. In response to the overwhelming work, these chaplains devised a Chaplain's Conference to organize their work so that they could devote more time to the spiritual care of the soldiers. These chaplains also began providing health care and burial services to Filipinos in Manila. Suffering from overwork, Pierce returned to the United States in 1900, where he promptly began a lecture tour to raise funds for a Philippine mission.

Although Episcopalianism was brought to the Philippines by military chaplains, and notwithstanding President McKinley's belief that the United States should 'civilize and Christianize' the Filipinos,[14] in the Philippines as elsewhere missionary work was not supported officially or otherwise by the United States government, which was constitutionally forbidden to establish a state Church. Even some representatives to the General Convention of 1898 were wary of Church involvement in the Philippines, and so any action had to wait until the next triennial Convention in 1901, at which date the Episcopal Church constituted the Philippines a missionary district and consecrated Charles Henry Brent, a Canadian who was an enthusiastic supporter of American imperialist adventures and trained by the Cowley Fathers, as the first missionary bishop. Bishop Brent and the early missionaries directed their efforts to converting the 20 per cent of the population that was not Roman Catholic, focusing on the Igorot population in north Luzon who eventually made up the majority of the Philippines Episcopal Church.[15] They also worked to combat the narcotics trade and build schools and hospitals as well as churches to serve the Filipino population. During this time, Bishop Brent became internationally known as an expert on opium. His largely unsuccessful attempts at ecumenism in the Philippines convinced him to work for Church unity there and throughout his career.[16]

[14] Quoted in Mark Douglas Norbeck, 'False Start: The First Three Years of Episcopal Missionary Endeavor in the Philippine Islands, 1898–1901', *Anglican and Episcopal History*, 62 (1993): 215–36 (p. 227).

[15] See Arun W. Jones, 'A View from the Mountains: Episcopal Missionary Depictions of the Igorot of Northern Luzon, The Philippines, 1903–1916', *Anglican and Episcopal History*, 71 (2002): 380–410.

[16] Frank E. Sugeno, 'Charles Henry Brent, Apostle for Unity', *Anglican and Episcopal History*, 70 (2001): 75–9 (pp. 76–8).

In Hawai'i cooperation between Episcopalians and Anglicans in missionary work was initially postponed as a result of the American Civil War. The first Anglican missionary, the Revd John Diel, went to Honolulu in 1833, but his departure in 1840 left Anglicans without a regular clergyman until 1862, when the new bishop for Honolulu, Thomas Nettleship Staley, arrived along with his family and two other clergymen. After their arrival, King Kamehameha IV and Queen Emma were received into the Church, but few Hawai'ians followed their example or that of Kamehameha V, who became king after his brother's early death in 1863. In spite of the lack of success at winning converts, the Church persisted in establishing schools, an effort that received English support after Queen Emma's 1865 visit to England. Another direct result of Queen Emma's trip was the 1867 visit of Priscilla Lydia Sellon, founder of the Anglican Society of the Most Holy Trinity (SMHT), and three sisters of the order, who joined the three SMHT sisters who had arrived in 1865. Thanks to a sizeable donation by Sellon, St Andrew's Priory, a girls' school, was established in 1867. By the time Bishop Staley, facing internal disputes, resigned as bishop in 1870, three Anglican schools provided education to day and boarding students in Hawai'i. After an unsuccessful attempt to replace Bishop Staley with an American bishop, an Englishman, Alfred Willis, was consecrated bishop of Honolulu in 1872. Throughout his tenure and partly as a consequence of his rigid personality, Bishop Willis faced financial difficulties, an unwieldy administrative system, and a schism within the cathedral between three congregations, two English-speaking and one Hawai'ian.[17] These problems were solved when the annexation of the territory by the United States in 1898 allowed the long-delayed plan to work more closely with the Episcopal Church to be enacted, as the mission was transferred to the Episcopal Church. The Missionary District of Honolulu was established in 1901, with the first American bishop, Henry B. Restarick, elected in 1902. At this point, there were six priests, two deacons, and 720 communicants in Hawai'i, with the majority being in the capital city of Honolulu.

LATIN AMERICA AND THE CARIBBEAN

Missionaries, mostly from the Protestant Episcopal Church of the United States but also some from the Church of England, began establishing a presence in Latin America in the last third of the nineteenth century. In Mexico, which shared a lengthy border with the United States, the Anglican

[17] Henry Bond Restarick, *Hawaii 1778–1920 from the Viewpoint of a Bishop: Being the Story of English and American Churchmen in Hawaii with Historical Sidelights* (Honolulu, 1924), chs. 15–18.

presence was the result of two related developments, one indigenous and one foreign. In the last third of the nineteenth century, Anglican missions were established for English speakers who had come to Mexico to work; as a result, Christ Church was established in Mexico City in 1882. At about the same time, former Roman Catholics began the work of establishing what became the Mexican Episcopal Church, which was also known as the Church of Jesus and the Mexican Catholic Apostolic Society. This Church was one legacy of the Mexican Civil War, which ended in 1860, and the resulting nationalization of church property and extension of religious tolerance. It was begun in 1861 by Mexican Roman Catholic priests who sought reform of the existing Church and were consequently excommunicated; they emphasized the primacy of the early Church, held services in Spanish, and allowed priests to marry. To establish a hierarchy, they turned to the Episcopal Church but their request for a bishop was initially refused on canonical grounds and as a result of Episcopalians' concern that the break from the Roman Catholic Church had been too recent. However, the Episcopal Church maintained an interest in the welfare of the Mexican Church, sending in 1865 a priest, E. C. Nicholson, to investigate it. In 1869 the American and Foreign Christian Union, an interdenominational society formed to convert Latin American Roman Catholics, sent the Revd Dr Henry Chauncey Riley to Mexico City. He provided the funds for the Mexican Church to purchase two of the churches being sold by the anti-clerical Mexican government, one of which—the Church of San José de Gracia—became the cathedral of the Mexican Episcopal Church, or Church of Jesus. While still reluctant to ally formally with the Church of Jesus, first the American Church Missionary Society, and then the Episcopal Church, continued to support it financially.

By 1879 the Mexican Church had fifty congregations and 3,500 communicants, and in 1885 the Church asked to become a regular mission of the Episcopal Church. Short of funds, the Episcopal Church leadership agreed only to send a clergyman, William B. Gordon, who was in Mexico from 1887 to 1892. Gordon was succeeded by Henry Forrester, who as Resident Commissioner—or Episcopal Delegate—from 1893 to 1904 helped shape the Church as a blend of Hispanic and American influences and restore order. Yet official progress remained slow as membership rose and fell; in 1896 there were just eight clergy, two of whom were deacons, and still no bishop. Finally, in 1904, as a result of increasing American immigration to Mexico, the Episcopal Church organized the Missionary District of Mexico, which encompassed both English- and Spanish-speaking churches. This new status meant that the Church lost its autonomy and that tension between English speakers and the majority Mexican congregation continued, as the Missionary District was primarily concerned with Americans living in Mexico. The Church was also consistently hampered by ongoing Roman Catholic hostility, financial difficulties, and a lack of leadership. At this point there were sixty-one

American congregations with about 600 communicants and thirty-four Mexican congregations with about 1,400 communicants; eight of Bishop Riley's schismatic clergy and their followers also joined. The development of the Church was further hampered by the Revolution of 1910, after which many Americans and British left Mexico permanently.

The introduction of Anglicanism in South America was the work of individual Anglican missionaries. After two failed attempts in 1826 and 1850, sustained conversion efforts in Patagonia began in 1856 when the Revd George Despard, the secretary of the Patagonian Missionary Society, took his family to live on Keppel Island, but he and most of the later arrivals left after many of their number were massacred in 1859. One who stayed was Thomas Bridges, the adopted son of Despard, who was 'not only a well-read man with a keen mind but also an adventurer and explorer'.[18] After being ordained and married, Bridges moved in 1871 to Ushuaia, on the mainland of Argentina. Here he succeeded the Revd Waite Hockin Stirling, who was the Superintendent of the Patagonian Missionary Society, now renamed the South American Missionary Society, when he became the Anglican bishop for the Falkland Islands. Bridges, an intellectual who loved the outdoors, became a leader among the Yaghan Indians, many of whom he converted. Concerned for the future of the Yaghan Indians, whose numbers were already declining as a result of disease and competition for resources with Europeans, in 1887 Bridges resigned from the mission and established a farm at Haberton, where he employed about sixty Yaghans. He died in 1898.

Bridges was succeeded by Dr Edwin Aspinall, who also realized that the station at Ushuaia was not well-placed. In 1888–9 Aspinall went to England on a speaking trip; having been ordained, he returned to England to be married in 1892 before arriving in Port Stanley in the Falkland Islands to become missionary to the English community at the end of 1892. Aspinall negotiated with the Chilean government to move the mission to the Bayly Islands, in the Cape Horn group. Here, in the southernmost mission of the Anglican Church, much of the work was done by Leonard and Nellie Burleigh. After three years, they, along with their children and another missionary family, were transferred to a mission at Tekenika Bay on Hoste Island, but conditions there were equally difficult. After Burleigh drowned in 1893, the mission moved to Punta Arenas, where in 1896 the Revd John Williams went with his wife and children to minister to the British colony, which numbered about 1,000 in the town and about 3,000 in the countryside. However, thanks to poor roads and competition from the Presbyterians, church attendance was always low during the six years Williams was at Punta Arenas. Williams's work with Spanish speakers ended after he was transferred to Mission Tekemika in 1902; he was replaced

[18] Elizabeth Dooley, *Streams in the Wasteland: A Portrait of the British in Patagonia* (Puntas Arenas, 1993), p. 14.

by Aspinall, who preferred to concentrate his work on British Protestants, and so the missionary efforts to Spanish speakers ended.

Anglican chapels, hospitals, and cemeteries were established in Rio de Janeiro and other major Brazilian port cities beginning in the 1820s to minister to British subjects, a concession granted by a Treaty of Navigation and Commerce between Britain and Portugal (1810). Indicative of the focus on the spiritual lives of British Anglicans rather than potential Brazilian converts is the fact that these parishes reported to the bishop of London until 1869, when the bishop of the Falkland Islands assumed responsibility for them. Missionary efforts to Brazilians were the work of American seminarians from the Virginia Theological Seminary who arrived in the 1890s. In 1899 one of those original missionaries, L. L. Kinsolving, was consecrated bishop and sent to Brazil by the Episcopal Church; his successes included building twenty-five churches, baptizing almost 14,000 people, and confirming almost 5,000 people.

Missionary work in islands of the Caribbean outside the British Empire was equally small and haphazard and often the result of American efforts. In 1861 an African-American priest, James T. Holly, led a group of African-Americans to Haiti where they established the Church of the Holy Trinity at Port-au-Prince. Holly became the first Episcopalian bishop of Haiti and served until his death in 1911. In 1900 he presided over a diocese of four clergy ministering to six congregations. In 1871, Edward Kenney arrived in Cuba as a missionary in Cuba. After the United States took Cuba as a protectorate in 1898, Cuba was established as a Missionary District in 1904 before receiving Albion W. Knight as its first bishop. James H. Van Buren became the first missionary bishop for Puerto Rico in 1902. By the late nineteenth century, emigration from the West Indies helped to increase the number of black clergymen and parishioners in the United States.

AFRICA

In Africa, the only Anglican mission other than those in the British colonies was in Liberia. This mission was, fittingly for the colony founded as a refuge for freed African-American slaves, the joint project of white and black Episcopalians. It was initially based in the Maryland colony at Cape Palmas, where four black missionaries—Gustavus V. and Elizabeth Caesar, and William and Elizabeth Johnson—arrived in 1831 and 1832 respectively. Only Elizabeth Johnson survived past 1834, but she continued to serve the mission, along with her second husband, James M. Thomson, an Episcopalian teacher and lay reader, until her death in 1864. In 1836 and 1837 three white recruits from the Virginia Theological Seminary—Thomas S. Savage, John

Payne, and Launcelot B. Minor—arrived in Liberia, but their work was also hampered by ill health. Only Payne had a long tenure: after returning to the United States for health reasons in 1841 he served as the first missionary bishop of Cape Palmas from 1851 to 1871.

From the beginning the mission was hampered by racial conflicts between white and black Americans as well as with the native Grebo. The missionary work of the Caesars and the Johnsons was not supported by the Foreign Committee; Thomson faced unsubstantiated accusations of adultery that were dismissed; and Bishop Payne, the son of a wealthy slave-owner, resisted accepting black leadership and frequently clashed with African-American clergymen.[19] The Grebo, who along with American settlers were the focus of missionary activity, were torn between their identities as Western-educated and as native Africans, and they periodically came into armed conflict with the American settlers. One of the most destructive of these conflicts began when, in 1841, Minor asked the US Secretary of the Navy to punish those responsible for the massacre of the white crew of the ship the *Mary Carver*. When Commodore Matthew Perry arrived at Cape Palmas with three ships in December 1843, he and his crew razed six coastal towns, killing twelve men and impairing relations with the Grebo.

Nevertheless, the mission slowly grew with support from Liberians. By the early 1850s, the Episcopal Church had moved beyond the Maryland colony and coastal towns and was established in Monrovia and surrounding areas and was building churches, hospitals, schools, and orphanages. Johann Gottlieb Auer, a German Lutheran convert who became the second missionary bishop of Cape Palmas and Parts Adjacent in 1872, encouraged black leadership, educational reform, and preaching in Grebo. His influence was significant in spite of his short tenure; he died ten months after his election.[20] His successor, Charles Clifton Penick, had served in the Confederate army and did little to stabilize the Liberian Mission during his tenure, which lasted from 1877 to 1884.

Penick was succeeded by Samuel David Ferguson, a black clergyman who had immigrated to Liberia from the United States with his family at the age of six. As bishop, Ferguson focused on education, evangelism, and self-sufficiency, and under his leadership the mission prospered. The 408 communicants in 1883 had become 2,450 at his death in 1916, and all but two of the twenty-six clergymen were Liberian by this date. Additionally, annual contributions, which had suffered thanks to the American Civil War and the shift in focus to Asian missions, had increased from $414 in 1886 to $4,000. Although a legacy of inter-racial misunderstanding continued, the Church in Liberia was well established by the early twentieth century.

[19] D. Elwood Dunn, *A History of the Episcopal Church in Liberia 1821–1900* (Metuchen, NJ, 1992), pp. 38–9, 49, 79–81, 85–93.

[20] Dunn, *Episcopal Church in Liberia*, pp. 106–13.

CONCLUSION

In those countries outside the British Empire the Church grew steadily but unspectacularly throughout the period 1829–1910. Although relatively few people chose to join the Church in these countries, the numbers of communicants and church-goers alone do not tell the entire story. Anglicanism had its most significant impact in the United States, where it had been nurtured during the colonial period. Although the American Revolution led to a backlash against Anglicanism, by the 1830s the Church had improved its worship services and had begun to organize the missionary and educational institutions that shaped a culture. Although they were proportionately a small Church, the cultural and political influence of Episcopalians was significant, as indicated by their disproportionately high representation in the highest government offices and elite educational institutions. Some Episcopalians were at the forefront of social change movements like the social gospel movements, although the legacy of the Civil War-era schism remained into the twentieth century. In other countries, such as Japan, Anglicanism was also especially attractive to the elite. This appeal, as well as the educational and health-care institutions established by missionaries, ensured that Anglicanism would have a significant and continuing impact on local populations whether or not they attended the Church. An unquantifiable but significant result of the spread of Anglicanism was the missionaries who provided a model of a committed life of faith even in the face of personal danger. Their legacy was the foundation of a Church that would continue to grow in the twentieth century.

SELECT BIBLIOGRAPHY

Austin, Alvyn, *China's Millions: The China Inland Mission and Late Qing Society, 1832–1905* (Grand Rapids, MI, 2007).

Butler, Diana Hochstedt, *Standing Against the Whirlwind: Evangelical Episcopalians in Nineteenth-Century America* (New York, 1995).

Chesebrough, David B., *Phillips Brooks: Pulpit Eloquence* (Westport, CT, 2001).

Douglas, Ian T., *Fling out the Banner! The National Church Ideal and the Foreign Mission of the Episcopal Church* (New York, 1996).

Dunn, D. Elwood, *A History of the Episcopal Church in Liberia, 1821–1980* (Metuchen, NJ, 1992).

Hein, David and Gardiner H. Shattuck, Jr., *The Episcopalians* (Westport, CT, 2004).

Holmes, David, *A Brief History of the Episcopal Church* (Valley Forge, PA, 1993).

Lewis, Harold T., *Yet with a Steady Beat: The African American Struggle for Recognition in the Episcopal Church* (Valley Forge, PA, 1996).

Mullin, Robert Bruce, *Episcopal Vision/American Reality: High Church Theology and Social Thought in Evangelical America* (New Haven, CT, 1986).

Norbeck, Mark Douglas, 'False Start: The First Three Years of Episcopal Missionary Endeavor in the Philippine Islands, 1898–1901', *Anglican and Episcopal History*, 62 (1993): 215–36.

Prichard, Robert W., *The Nature of Salvation: Theological Consensus in the Episcopal Church, 1801–73* (Urbana, IL, 1997).

Rankin, Richard, *Ambivalent Churchmen and Evangelical Churchwomen: The Religion of the Episcopal Elite in North Carolina, 1800–1860* (Columbia, SC, 1993).

Shattuck, Gardiner H. Jr., *Episcopalians and Race: Civil War to Civil Rights* (Lexington, KY, 2000).

5

Anglicanism and the State in the Nineteenth Century

Rowan Strong

There were three principal states that Anglicanism came into extensive contact with in this period. There was the old relationship with the Westminster government within which the United Church of England and Ireland still formed a constitutional part as a consequence of the royal supremacy over the Church of England formulated and effected from the reign of Henry VIII. Then there was the British imperial state. The imperial government in London and diverse colonial governments formed a variable relationship for emerging colonial Anglican Churches across the burgeoning British Empire. The third substantial Church–state relationship for nineteenth-century Anglicanism was in the United States of America, with its commitment to the separation between the two, an arrangement that was an entirely new ball-game for Anglicanism. This chapter will deal with each of these Church–state relationships in turn.

However, before doing so it is useful to remind ourselves of Anglican thinking on Church and state at the close of the eighteenth century. This is found in the concept of the 'Protestant constitution', by which Anglicanism, monarchy, and an aristocratic social order provided the ideological framework of English, Welsh, and Irish political, cultural, and social life throughout the long eighteenth century.[1] In 1713 Bishop Gibson of London had encapsulated it in an understanding that was echoed by other Anglicans throughout the long eighteenth century.

> That the Spiritual Body was independent of and equal to the Temporal, that the Temporal Courts ought to be restrained from interference with the Ecclesiastical, that the clergy were the proper judges of the degree of assistance which the

[1] J. C. D. Clark, *English Society, 1660–1832: Religion, Ideology and Politics during the Ancien Regime* (Cambridge, 2000 edn.), ch. 6.

> Church required from the State, and of the means by which that support should be rendered, and that the suppression of vice was the proper function of the Spirituality not of the laity.[2]

According to this classic view of Church and state both entities were of divine creation and were interdependent in a society that was explicitly Christian. However, the French Revolution caused Anglican upholders of establishment to climb down from these lofty theological heights and defend the state connection on the utilitarian grounds of the Church being a defender and promoter of social order and morality, as instanced by the most known of their writers, William Paley.[3]

CHURCH AND STATE IN BRITAIN

At the end of the long eighteenth century the Anglican Church found itself in an unprecedented situation with respect to its centuries-old partnership with the state as a consequence of constitutional changes between 1828 and 1832. These changes were revolutionary for the Church and the British state.[4] While they were perhaps caused most directly by the need to take more notice of Ireland since that country had been taken into closer political union in 1801, they were also forced upon the conservative ministry of Lord Wellington by the European forces of democratization and fears about political revolution released by the French Revolution. Ever since the overthrow of the Catholic Church as the state Church in revolutionary France in the early 1790s, confessional regimes throughout Europe found their alliances of state and Church increasingly difficult in the face of liberal agitation for change. As a result of enfranchising Nonconformists in 1828, then Roman Catholics in 1829, and the Reform Act of 1832 that enfranchised the propertied middle-class where Nonconformity in 1832 was strong, the Church of England, and its established status, came under severe attack in the following decades.

After 1832, for the first time in English history the political nation legally embraced substantial numbers of non-Anglicans, and this process continued throughout the nineteenth century as first Jews, then atheists, were constitutionally able to sit in Parliament. As a consequence, the state moved quickly from the 1830s to a pragmatic position of increasing denominational

[2] Clark, *English Society*, p. 101.

[3] Robert Hole, *Pulpits, Politics and Public Order in England, 1760–1832* (Cambridge, 1989), pp. 73–82.

[4] Geoffrey Best, 'The Constitutional Revolution, 1828–1832, and its Consequences for the Established Church', *Theology*, 52 (1959): 226–34; Boyd Hilton, *A Mad, Bad and Dangerous People: England 1783–1846* (Oxford, 2006), pp. 379–83.

neutrality. The last parliamentary grant for church extension for the Church of England was in 1824, after which it became impossible politics because the electorate in England, Wales, and Ireland was no longer solely Anglican and in many areas Nonconformity was influential. The relationship between Church and state in Britain during the nineteenth century can be summed up as the Church of England reluctantly adjusting to this move from an Anglican confessional state to the modern Western religiously neutral one. Probably a majority of clergy maintained a rearguard defence of the establishment principle, together with some significant laity, such as the young William Gladstone in his book *The State in its Relations with the Church* (1836). Gladstone's defence of an effective Anglican establishment, however, soon became evidently impractical politics in the next decade.[5] Gladstone himself began to shift under the influence of John Keble's Tractarian criticism of his book in the *British Critic*, which pointed out the transcendent importance of the Church over the state as God's kingdom, and the state's essential subordination to serve that purpose.[6] But Gladstone's position was also reflected in the Association of the Friends of the Church, formed to support establishment, which submitted a petition that had not just 7,000 clergy signatures, but close to a quarter of a million signatures from heads of families.[7]

The last major partnership between Church and state in Britain in support of the Church of England alone was in 1834 with the advent of the government's Ecclesiastical Commission, appointed by Parliament with the support of Sir Robert Peel's minority ministry. Established to reform the revenues and organization of the Church in order to strengthen its domestic mission, the Commission was composed of clergy and MPs who were members of the Church of England. Against a growing climate of support for voluntaryism, the Commission was driven particularly by the pragmatic bishop of London, Charles Blomfield, to push through important readjustments to the medieval structures of the Church and head off growing criticism of its wealth. On the basis of four reports between March 1835 and the summer of 1836, the Commission prepared three bills for Parliament. The first, the Established Church Act 1836, redistributed the incomes of the English bishops to make them more equitable, redrew diocesan boundaries into more manageable entities, created two new dioceses—Ripon and Manchester—and turned the Ecclesiastical Commission into a permanent body to advise on the finances of the Church. After the second bill, passed as the Plurality Act in 1838, it was illegal to hold more than one benefice, except with special dispensation from

[5] H. C. G. Matthew, *Gladstone 1809–1874* (Oxford, 1988), pp. 68–9.

[6] Perry Butler, *Gladstone: Church, State, and Tractarianism: A Study in his Religious Ideas and Attitudes, 1809–1859* (Oxford, 1982), pp. 77–92.

[7] Stewart J. Brown, *The National Churches of England, Ireland, and Scotland 1801–46* (Oxford, 2001), p. 272.

the archbishop of Canterbury, and even then only two could be held together. The Dean and Chapter Act 1840 shrank the inflated numbers and wealth of cathedral clergy, and redistributed the saved monies into new parochial ministries among the new urban masses of the burgeoning Victorian cities. But Parliament did not just legislate in support of the Church of England; it also enacted legislation in the 1830s to reduce the legal privileges of the Church with respect to its traditional denominational opponents. The tithe system in England and Wales was reformed in 1836 to allow a simple cash charge on rent instead of the tithe. As tithes only affected landowners, it was the church rate set by parish vestries for the upkeep of the parish church, imposed on all parishioners, including non-Anglicans, that was the more explosive issue, until the compulsory church rate was abolished in 1868. In 1836 also, the Civil Marriage Act legalized marriages outside the parish church, including by a civil registrar, as well as Nonconformist and Roman Catholic chapels. The following year the Civil Registration Act removed the registration of birth, deaths, and marriages from the parish clergy to the civil registration offices.[8]

The most substantial ongoing dimension left to the Established Church by the emerging collectivization of the state was education. The Church's competition with Nonconformity in this area was fierce, and directly contributed to the failure of England to devise a national system of elementary education until 1870. Nonconformists, whose numbers collectively by mid-century were roughly equivalent to the Church of England, supported the British and Foreign Schools Society and the Anglicans their National Society for Promoting the Education of the Poor in the Principles of the Church of England. However, for some decades the government simply funded both societies, beginning with an annual grant of £20,000 in 1833 for England and Wales. This reluctance of the government to become directly involved in education was partly a result of the rivalry between the Church and Nonconformity, and partly the continuation of an older view which saw education as the responsibility of the Church rather than the state. Until the Education Act of 1870, and the establishment of state board schools, the energy of the Church of England in this area, and its larger size, saw it accumulate the great majority of state funding by meeting the criterion of half the money coming from private sources.[9]

But there remained a real bias towards Anglican schools in England and Wales in successive Education Acts of the nineteenth century, demonstrating that the ongoing movement of the state from its Anglican partnership remained at the ebb and flow of successive governments during that century. Even in the 1902 Act, which sought to address the disorganized diversity of

[8] Stewart J. Brown, *Providence and the Empire 1815–1914* (Harlow, 2008), pp. 92–6.

[9] G. Paz, *The Politics of Working-Class Education in Britain, 1830–50* (Manchester, 1980), p. 61.

state education by giving local authorities control over schools in their area, this Anglican bias can be seen. In this legislation, for the first time, denominational schools were brought into the system and, in return, received rate aid. This move benefited the Church of England (as well as the small number of Roman Catholic schools) because it had by far the largest number of schools in England and Wales, and was something that Church had long been seeking. Nonconformists organized substantive protests against the Act, partly because it was seen as another example of Anglican privilege enacted by the state, and partly because their rates were also funding Roman Catholic schools, or 'Rome on the rates'. The issue was particularly acute in Nonconformist Wales where it led to numbers of local councils refusing to provide rate aid to denominational schools unless they were given control of them, and directly contributed to the move towards Anglican disestablishment.[10]

Much of the legislation supportive of the reform of the Church of England occurred during the ministry of the Tories, and that drew the Church of England closer to that party. Whigs and Liberals became increasingly identified with Dissent, so that ecclesiastical sympathies became part of the mix of party identity in the emerging political environment of Westminster. There were votes in religious connections. However, notwithstanding the religious sympathies of the Tories towards Anglicanism its establishment became further diminished because support for this cause became more a matter of party politics and less and less one of national significance.

The slow demise of a genuine religious establishment increasingly pushed the Church of England to develop the characteristics of a denomination. After centuries of a monopolistic, though fluctuating, Church–state partnership the Church of England found itself having to act autonomously in pursuit of its goals, and depend on voluntarism in support of them. One early indication of a new autonomous paradigm for the Church was in church extension, both domestic and imperial. The latter dimension will be discussed more fully in the section on the Church and the imperial state. But within Britain, this new autonomous way of acting was evident in the foundation by Bishop Blomfiel of the Metropolis Churches' Fund in 1836 that, within a year, had already raised over £100,000 for church extension in London. This initiative was soon followed by other dioceses, so that by 1839 similar societies had been founded in fifteen of the twenty-six dioceses in England and Wales, and over 600 churches built.[11] Developing acceptance of its own responsibility for domestic church extension in the later 1830s was followed by a growing call for the revival of provincial

[10] Gerald Parsons, 'Liberation and Church Defence: Victorian Church and Victorian Chapel', in Gerald Parsons (ed.), *Religion in Victorian Britain*, vol. II: *Controversies* (Manchester, 1988), pp. 158–9; E. J. Feuchtwanger, *Democracy and Empire: Britain 1865–1914* (London, 1985), p. 246.

[11] Brown, *Providence and Empire*, p. 96.

church government, now that Parliament was no longer a purely Anglican body and could not be relied upon to legislate for the advantage of the Church of England.

Moves towards some domestic denominational autonomy by the Church of England had begun from the start of the nineteenth century through the efforts of High Churchmen. This 'diocesan revival' identified by Arthur Burns revitalized the diocesan structure of that Church so that it rivalled the organizational capacity of the state for much of the nineteenth century in England and Wales.[12] But a more intentional distancing of the Church from the state was promoted by the mindset of clergy and laity influenced by the Oxford Movement, because the initial Tractarian leadership was spurred to action by the changing Church–state paradigm of the early 1830s. As is well known, the beginning of the movement was identified by John Henry Newman as John Keble's 1833 Assize sermon, where he lambasted as 'National Apostasy' the decision of Parliament to reduce the number of Irish bishoprics and use the money saved for educational purposes. To Keble this was an Erastian measure illegitimately invading the superior sphere of the Church. Keble's anti-Erastian theme carried into the early numbers of the *Tracts for the Times* in 1833 where Newman forthrightly upheld the foundation of the Church of England as divine from Christ, and not the creation of the state. In upholding this distinction of the Church from the state he could be belligerent.

> Should the Government and Country so far forget their GOD as to cast off the Church, to deprive it of its temporal honours and substance, *on what* will you rest the claim of respect and attention which you make upon your flocks? . . . Is it not our very office to *oppose* the world? can we then allow ourselves to *court* it? to preach smooth things and prophesy deceits? to make the way of life easy to the rich and indolent, and to bribe the humbler classes by excitements and strong intoxicating doctrine? Surely it must not be so;—and the question recurs, on *what* are we to rest our authority, when the State deserts us? CHRIST has not left His Church without claim of its own upon the attention of men. . . . I fear we have neglected the real ground on which our authority is built,—OUR APOSTOLICAL DESCENT.[13]

In his first book, *Arians of the Fourth Century* (1833), published the same year as the *Tracts for the Times* began, Newman used the Church of the fourth century as a prism for the contemporary situation of the Church of England and amidst a number of jeremiads upon it, he railed against an Erastian view of the Church. 'Then as now, there was the prospect, and partly the presence in

[12] Arthur Burns, *The Diocesan Revival in the Church of England c.1800–1870* (Oxford, 1999).

[13] John Henry Newman, 'Thoughts on the Ministerial Ministry, Respectfully Addressed to the Clergy': *Tracts for the Times*, no. 1 (1833), Project Canterbury, <http://anglicanhistory.org/tracts/tract1.html>, accessed 1 Apr. 2014.

the Church, of an Heretical Power enthralling it, exerting a varied influence and a usurped claim in the appointment of her functionaries, and interfering with the management of her internal duties.'[14] Newman was echoed that same year by the *enfant terrible* of the Oxford Movement, Richard Hurrell Froude; when commenting on the constitutional changes to Parliament he maintained 'by the operation of recent changes, *the CONDITIONS on which Parliament has been allowed to interfere in matters spiritual are CANCELLED*'.[15] That Parliament 'interfered' in the Church, with its militant suggestion of Erastianism, had never occurred to anyone in the eighteenth century where a Church–state partnership was axiomatic. This stream of Tractarian anti-establishment invective continued throughout the century whenever their anxieties were raised by political moves deemed to be Erastian. However, Simon Skinner has pointed out that anti-Erastianism did not necessarily equate to anti-establishmentarianism in Tractarian thinking. In their more measured moments the Tractarians upheld establishment as the ideal (as opposed to the actual situation under the reformed Parliament) based on the grounds of the Church's spiritual superiority. The connection of the state to the Church enabled the state to be an agency for divine grace to combat the pernicious forces of secular liberalism. Disestablishment would, in other words, be detrimental to the state rather than the Church.[16] Nevertheless, that their anti-Erastian rhetoric had an influence is hard to dismiss when the actions of the Tractarians' ritualist successors are considered.

The ritualists exhibited growing impatience with the legal constraints of a state they believed was increasingly deserting its Christian commitments. Defining Christianity in terms of a belligerent catholicity enshrined in episcopacy, sacramental grace, and catholic traditions, Tractarians and Anglo-Catholics looked aghast at a state that was more accommodating to Nonconformity when they were anxious to de-Protestantize the Church of England. Their view of an Erastian state seemed to them fulfilled by the Gorham Judgment. When the High Church bishop refused to license Gorham to a living in 1847 on the grounds that he found the Calvinist clergyman unsound on the doctrine of baptismal regeneration, the consequent appeal went through the Church courts which found for the bishop, and eventually ended in the Judicial Committee of the Privy Council which found for the clergyman. This ruling by a secular court seemed to many High Churchmen, Tractarians, and Anglo-Catholics as an outrageous instance of the state intruding into the doctrine of the Church and famously caused the conversion

[14] John Henry Newman, *Arians of the Fourth Century* (London, 1871 edn.), p. 406.

[15] Quoted in Simon Skinner, *Tractarians and the 'Condition of England': The Social and Political Thought of the Oxford Movement* (Oxford, 2004), p. 88.

[16] Skinner, *Tractarians*, pp. 90–3.

of Henry Manning to Roman Catholicism, among others.[17] Driven by their understanding of Anglican catholicity, Anglo-Catholic ritualists began to uphold their ecclesiastical right to liturgical rituals even if that should be found to be against the law. This could cause uproar, as in the infamous example of St George's in the East, one of the poorest parishes in London, when the ritualism of the clergy provoked mobs, sometimes in their thousands, to disrupt services over many years from the late 1840s and into the 1850s, resulting in substantial police numbers at services, and questions in Parliament.[18] This conflict became acute following the passing of the Public Worship Regulation Act of 1874 sponsored by Archbishop Tait with the support of Disraeli's new Conservative government, the queen, and the great majority of the bishops. It was an attempt to use parliamentary legislation to curb ritualism and to clarify the ambiguities of the Prayer Book in this area. However, it became a rather damp squib. Ritualist clergy prosecuted under the Act were prepared even to go to prison for their cause, an intransigence they had already given notice of in previous decades. Their unyielding stance not only gave encouragement to supporters, but also created uncertainty among moderates about the possible Erastianism of the Act. One historian of the Act believes that the controversy surrounding the passing and implementation of the Act was a watershed in bringing to the fore the issue of the Church of England's authority over its own affairs. It ushered in decades of agonizing over liturgical reform in the twentieth century and highlighted the fact that the Church was still subordinated to Parliament in revising its own worship.[19] It was a case of the leadership of the Church harnessing the power of the state and its courts to act against another section of the Church, a recourse that was used by both parties, high and low, in the increasingly partisan and contested Anglicanism of the nineteenth century.

Many within the older High Church tradition, however, desired the state connection to continue, not out of mere reaction, though this is how Simon Skinner has viewed it;[20] and certainly not for the liberal reasons advocated by Broad Church Anglicans. Notwithstanding the continual examples of the retreat from the confessional state throughout the nineteenth century, High Church Anglicans largely maintained a rearguard belief in the old political theology which saw Church and state as two aspects of the same organism, providentially brought together by God as equally divinely constituted partners. For them, the retreat of the state from the Church in the nineteenth century was a resiling not just from its Christian basis but also of its

[17] J. C. S. Nias, *Gorham and the Bishop of Exeter* (London, 1951).

[18] Phillip T. Smith, 'The London Police and the Holy War: Ritualism and St George's-in-the-East, London, 1859–1860', *Journal of Church and State*, 28 (1986): 107–19.

[19] James Bentley, *Ritualism and Politics in Victorian Britain: The Attempt to Legislate for Belief* (Oxford, 1978), pp. 37–8, 40–4, 81, 97–114, 123, 126.

[20] Skinner, *Tractarians*, pp. 134–5.

providential purpose to uphold and extend Christianity. Within the Church of England one of the most prominent upholders in the nineteenth century of the maintenance of what was understood as the old Constitution was Archdeacon George Anthony Denison. Denison was not the belligerent ritualist he has been portrayed as, but an authentic High Church representative of this older form of Anglicanism among the parochial clergy of the Church of England.[21] Although in the end the effective demise of the old Constitution defeated him and other supporters of a substantive Anglican establishment, their energetic defence of it did mean that such High Churchmen were prominent in strategies to assert the role of the Church in national society. Most prominent among such efforts was the push to make the Church of England the educator of the nation through the elementary schools of the National Society.

The attitudes and actions of Anglican Evangelicals with regard to the Church–state connection have not been as well explored by historians as their Anglican High Church and Broad Church counterparts. This lack of analysis is an important oversight given the famous readiness of Evangelicals to use parliamentary legislation to promote a more godly society that facilitated the collectivization of the Victorian state. The defence of establishment divided them from Nonconformists, with whom, otherwise, they were largely in sympathy. Nonconformists' increasing opposition to the Established Church coalesced first in the Anti-State Church Association organized in 1844, and then in the Liberation Society from 1853. This militant anti-establishment Nonconformist crusade in support of voluntaryism prompted Anglican Evangelicals to public support for establishment in the 1830s on a similar basis to that of the older High Churchmen: that Church and state were complementary realities under the providential rule of God. Societies were formed to promote this, such as the Established Church Society in 1834, and alliances made with Presbyterians of the equally Established Church of Scotland. Similar societies also got off the ground in the 1850s specifically to combat the Liberation Society, such as the Church Defence Institution in 1859.[22] The importance of the state connection to English Evangelical Anglicans has been underlined in an important study of British anti-Catholicism. Paz believes that it was the Evangelical Anglicans who upheld the state connection because they saw in it a defence against the growth of Anglo-Catholicism, understood as crypto-popery, within the Church. For this reason they formed the strongest component of defence against the disestablishment of the Church of Ireland.[23]

21 John Cardell-Oliver, 'George Anthony Denison (1805–1896): A Georgian High Churchman in Victorian Times', PhD thesis, Murdoch University, 2015.

22 David Bebbington, *Evangelicalism in Modern Britain: A History from the 1730s to the 1980s* (London, 1989), pp. 98, 136–7.

23 D. G. Paz, *Popular Anti-Catholicism in Mid-Victorian England* (Stanford, CA, 1992), pp. 106–7.

In contrast, Stewart Brown believes that finding a meaningful place for a reduced establishment within the Church of England was the particular achievement of the Broad Church party in the second half of the nineteenth century. This took place against the backdrop of the disestablishment campaign which included Irish Catholics and a mixture of liberals and secularists. During this period Broad Churchmen promoted various bases for the state connection of the Church of England, largely grounded on the idea of that Church as a comprehensive establishment epitomizing a national religion with a mission to shape the moral and spiritual life of the nation. This thinking had its origins in the progenitor of Broad Church Anglicanism, Samuel Taylor Coleridge. Coleridge helped to free nineteenth-century Anglicans from thinking of their Church only as an establishment by making an important distinction between the Church as founded by Christ and the National Church, and the Church in that national conception being responsible for the moral life of the nation.[24] But this distinction, which in the National Church under the term 'clerisy' Coleridge conceived of as embracing all the cultivated professional elite of the nation, lacked sufficient specificity to justify the national establishment of the Church of England. But there were a number of Broad Church thinkers in the mid-Victorian period, influenced by Coleridge, who were keen to provide that justification, including Thomas Arnold. Probably the most sophisticated was F. D. Maurice, who argued that both Church and nation were providential realities used by God to foster divine order and overcome human selfishness; consequently they belonged together.[25] In the same vein, the Cambridge academic F. J. A. Hort could defend the establishment of the Church of England as the 'primary spiritual organ of the nation', representing the 'sense of the intimate relations between the Christian faith and character on the one hand and all human interests and social duties on the other'.[26] For Broad Churchmen the Church of England was uniquely placed to carry out this national mission because of its internal diversity, and they accordingly opposed any attempts to impose tighter confessional or doctrinal tests or restrictions upon the clergy. As most of these justifications for Anglican establishment made use of the concept of nationalism, a concept prevalent in the nineteenth century, and consequently made an integral connection between Englishness and Anglicanism, they could have little relevance for the identity of the Church of England beyond England itself.

[24] Henry Nelson Coleridge, Preface to Samuel Taylor Coleridge, *Church and State* (1839) in John Colmer (ed.), *On the Constitution of the Church and State* (Princeton, NJ, 1976), p. 193.

[25] Jeremy Morris, *F. D. Maurice and the Crisis of Christian Authority* (Oxford, 2005), pp. 102–5.

[26] Stewart J. Brown, 'The Broad Church Movement, National Culture, and the Established Churches of Great Britain, c.1850–c.1900', in Hilary M. Carey and John Gascoigne (eds.), *Church and State in Old and New Worlds* (Leiden, 2011), p. 117.

Indeed, it could constitute a barrier to the expansion of the Church beyond the English and English colonists as it developed into the Anglican Communion.

So various parties within the Church of England attempted to uphold establishment, or at least prevent disestablishment, which contributed to the process of the state retreating from confessionalization being slowed in England. Slowed, but not stopped. The retreat of the state from confessionalism under the impetus of religious pluralism was marked by the admission of Dissenters to Oxford and Cambridge, divorce reform, Jewish emancipation, and the eventual admission of the atheist Charles Bradlaugh as an MP. Accordingly, disestablishment did occur in one part of British Anglicanism—in Ireland in 1869. Politically, the drive for this measure was led by the Liberal Party headed by William Gladstone as prime minister. Gladstone had shifted far from his ultra-Tory politics as a young man in support of Church establishment to lead a party whose constituency was substantially grounded in middle-class Nonconformity. Allied to this was the Whig tradition of antagonism towards the privileges of the Established Church in Ireland, which they saw as the bloated Church of a minority Irish Ascendancy. It was an issue that Liberals, at the time divided in opposition after their loss of government in 1866, could agree on, and which would assist Gladstone in cementing his leadership of the party. Lacking a genuine claim to be representative of that nation, the Church of Ireland, for Gladstone, had no alternative to embracing voluntaryism.[27] Gladstone, as treasurer and trustee of the Colonial Bishoprics Fund, was encouraged by his support for independent colonial Anglican Churches as to what could be done by an Anglicanism freed from the shackles of the state connection.[28] He had also been a long-standing supporter of the Scottish Episcopal Church that, conspicuously among British Anglican Churches, lacked the state connection.[29] The measure passed in Parliament with little dissent among Anglicans who largely accepted that an establishment whose adherents were only a small fraction of the Irish population was no longer supportable.

Despite the fact that the issue of Church and state remained a major concern during the nineteenth century in Britain, the Church of England continued to be the Established Church in England and Wales in part because the major opponent of its established status, the Nonconformists, while organized against it, were insufficiently united in their opposition. In addition, Gladstone, as the major political figure instrumental in achieving the disestablishment of the Church of Ireland, was implacably opposed to the same

[27] Theodore Hoppen, *The Mid-Victorian Generation: England 1846–1886* (Oxford, 1998), pp. 229, 595.

[28] Hilary Carey, 'Gladstone, the Colonial Church, and Imperial State', in Carey and Gascoigne (eds.), *Church and State*, pp. 178–9.

[29] Rowan Strong, 'High Churchmen and Anglo-Catholics: William Gladstone and the Eucharistic Controversy in the Scottish Episcopal Church, 1856–60', *Journal of Religious History*, 20 (1996): 175–84 (pp. 177–8).

cause in England. He regarded the status of the Church of England as genuinely more representative of the nation than it was in Ireland. These views seemed to have some genuine grounds when the slogan of the 'Church in danger' was capable of generating political and social heat in the last decades of the century. But probably most significant of all was that the disestablishment of the Church in England became overtaken as a political issue by more pressing concerns, particularly Home Rule for Ireland and the growth of the Labour movement which redirected working-class attention away from the disestablishment issue.[30]

A DISESTABLISHED CHURCH IN THE UNITED STATES

The disestablishment of Anglicanism occurred in one part of the world long before it came about in Ireland. In the United States of America Anglicanism lost its connection with the state as a consequence of the ideals that coalesced to form the American Revolution. In the British colonies before independence Anglicanism had been legally established in a partial form in Virginia, New York, North and South Carolina, Maryland, and Georgia. But religious establishment in the North American colonies was not peculiar to Anglicanism. Congregationalism was established in three of the New England colonies. However, after the successful end of the American War of Independence the Church of England had ceased to be the Established Church in these colonies, beginning with Virginia whose colonial assembly had, in 1785, passed the Statue for Religious Freedom. However, colonial established Anglicanism in North America had been a seriously deficient institution, as it had little in the way of organization beyond the local congregation and its minister. British government policy had prevented the foundation of a colonial episcopate; there were no church courts to impose sanctions on immoral laity or contumacious clergy as in England; nor, in the religious pluralism of the colonies, any prospect of imposing the sort of society-wide adherence that was traditionally associated with Established Churches in Europe. Many of the diverse Churches that had expanded under the impetus of the Evangelical Revival had their own history of experience of state coercion and were strongly opposed to giving the government any possibility of power over religion.

After independence, the Virginia experiment of the separation of Church and state (initiated by state legislature in the Statute for Religious Freedom passed in 1785), or, more negatively, the refusal to countenance the establishment of any one Church, proved influential in the drafting of the first

30 Noel J. Richards, 'Disestablishment of the Anglican Church in England in the Late Nineteenth Century: Reasons for Failure', *Journal of Church and State*, 12 (1970): 193–211.

amendment of the US constitution which forbade the state to make any laws for such establishment or to prevent the exercise of religious freedom. Episcopalians, as United States Anglicans were known, had been largely opposed to this, as it contradicted everything they and their Church had known since its legal foundation by Parliament in the sixteenth century. The disestablished world of United States Episcopalianism was uncharted territory for Anglicans, and most were reluctant to enter it.

However, by the nineteenth century United States Episcopalians began to find their way in this disestablished world of religious pluralism and had accommodated themselves to it with some expeditiousness, considering Anglicanism's almost complete lack of experience in doing without the state connection. By the end of the 1780s American Episcopalians had established state and national conventions, which included laymen, and bishops whose dioceses were coterminous with their states. It was a remarkably rapid reconstitution of the Church on a voluntarist basis, though their repudiation of the emotional religion of the Evangelical Revival contributed to the Episcopal Church becoming predominantly middle and upper class, albeit influential among the social and political elites. One of its most prominent bishops, John Henry Hobart, bishop of New York from 1811, was inspired by the writing of the High Church Hackney Phalanx to stress the nature of the Church as an alternative visible society to the nation, rather than idealizing the Christian state as the English writers did. This also led him to promote the Episcopal Church's distinctiveness from other denominations as a society which drew inspiration from the pre-Constantinian early Church. This stress on the corporate nature of the Church ran counter, to some extent, to the prevailing Evangelicalism and individualism of American society.[31] However, a disposition to see itself as personifying the national conscience, perhaps a cultural hangover of Anglicanism's long centuries as a national Church, also gave the Episcopal Church a disposition to work with the state that could have unfortunate results. Notwithstanding an early nineteenth-century commitment to Indian mission, the Church came, at times, to be seen as a government agency in its handling of government grants. This meant collusion to an extent with government policies that were principally aimed at clearing Indian peoples from their lands, and subjecting them to official control. The close, though informal, connection between Episcopalians and the political and planter elite of southern Confederacy during the American Civil War demonstrated the commitment of most Episcopalians in the South to racial segregation, which furthered the exodus of Black Americans from the Episcopal Church.[32] By the later nineteenth century, Anglicanism, even in its disestablished United States

[31] William L. Sachs, *The Transformation of Anglicanism: From State Church to Global Communion* (Cambridge, 1993), pp. 60–9.

[32] Kevin Ward, *A History of Global Anglicanism* (Cambridge, 2006), pp. 55–8.

form, was still disposed to look generously at the state, and generally lacked the ability to maintain a critical distance from it.

THE CHURCH AND THE BRITISH IMPERIAL STATE

If the nineteenth century witnessed the effective end of the confessional state in Britain, that demise spread with remarkable rapidity to the British Empire as well. Following the American and French Revolutions, there had been a revival of state support for the establishment of the Church of England in the British Empire caused by political anxieties over ways to foster loyalism in the colonies. This had resulted in state-supported ecclesiastical establishments in Canada, Australia, West Indies, and India. There was also a short-lived Ecclesiastical Department in the Colonial Office, established in 1825.[33] However, that comparatively well-resourced imperial extension of established Anglicanism came to an end for the same reason it had in Britain—the enfranchisement of non-Anglicans in the constitutional revolution of the late 1820s and the growth of a religiously-pluralistic society. The British state abandoned the centuries-old Anglican hegemony in favour of increasing political neutrality towards British and colonial Churches. The example of one colony—Western Australia—demonstrates just how quickly the imperial state shadowed its metropolitan counterpart in moving from a confessional to a denominationally neutral position.

Western Australia, proclaimed and settled as a British colony in 1829, initially had a colonial chaplain on its civil establishment with an official salary of £250 plus allowances who was also appointed a Justice of the Peace in the early years of the colony. But this was as far as official preference for the Church of England was to go in that colony, and by 1842 the clergy were petitioning their bishop, the remote and nominal figure of Bishop Broughton in Sydney, that the government was not treating them as '*the* Church' but rather just like any other denomination. That outcome was a result of the local Churches Act, modelled on that of Governor Richard Bourke's similar Act in New South Wales passed in 1836. This provided government funding for churches, schools, and clergy stipends to all denominations in the colony that had sufficient numbers of adherents to qualify. While the Anglicans, who massively outnumbered all other denominations in Western Australia, benefited most from the legislation, prompting contemporary non-Anglicans and later historians to berate the colonial government for bias, it is clear that

[33] D. M. Young, *The Colonial Office in the Early Nineteenth Century* (London, 1961), pp. 76–7.

government funding followed impartially the numerical strengths and fundraising of each denomination.[34]

If that was true for a colony that was among Britain's most remote and least desirable for settlers, it was certainly true for more populous and denominationally diverse older colonies also. In Canada and New South Wales there were crown lands set aside for the use of the Church of England for schools, glebes, and churches, an initiative that went back to 1791 and 1824 respectively. From the late 1820s the colonial legislature of Upper Canada had attempted to sell these lands and use the proceeds for general educational purposes, though it was blocked by the Westminster Parliament until 1854. In New South Wales colonial government retreat from the Anglican hegemony was effected with Governor Bourke's 1836 Church Act.

The major exception to this withdrawal from a substantive Anglican establishment by the imperial state was India. Both Evangelicals and High Churchmen had been active in the promotion of an Indian Church establishment as part of the parliamentary review of the East India Company's charter in 1813, and were successful in having a bishop of Calcutta and three archdeacons appointed the following year. This officially supported ecclesiastical establishment was one dimension of the increasing push, particularly by Charles Grant and other leading Evangelicals in the Company, for the 'civilization', or Europeanizing of India, and its Christian conversion. By the formation of the diocese of Dornkal in 1912 there were twelve dioceses in British India, which also encompassed Ceylon and Burma, paid for by the government of India's Ecclesiastical Establishment. However, this support was predicated on the basis that the Establishment existed for ministry to the expatriate English. As Robert Frykenberg has made clear, any attempt to impose an Anglican hegemony on India was doomed to failure in the face of Hindu and Muslim resistance, which could threaten the stability and existence of British rule. Consequently, an ecclesiastical establishment could only be tolerated because it did not entail any excessive favouritism for Anglicanism by the Indian government, and also that government supported Islam and, more particularly, Hindu civic religion. It was *de facto* a 'Hindu Raj'.[35] The payment of bishops and chaplains from the Indian civil list turned them into civil servants and their Church into a colonialist entity for the rest of the nineteenth century. Bishops remained English expatriates appointed by the British government, and though Indian clergy were ordained, the Anglican dioceses in India remained essentially part of the imperial system there.[36] This undoubtedly

[34] Rowan Strong, 'Church and State in Western Australia: Implementing New Imperial Paradigms in the Swan River Colony 1827–1857', *Journal of Ecclesiastical History*, 61 (2010): 517–40.

[35] Robert E. Frykenberg, *Christianity in India from Beginnings to the Present* (Oxford, 2008), pp. 266–7, 285.

[36] Stephen Neill, *A History of Christianity in India 1707–1858* (Cambridge, 1985), pp. 266, 275.

hampered the growth of an indigenous Anglican Church, and also resulted in Anglican missions having comparatively little success measured against Nonconformist missions which were not connected to the imperial establishment.

However, the early decades of the Western Australia colony demonstrate that what did persist for longer within the British imperial state during the nineteenth century than the official preferencing of the colonial Church of England, was an Erastian culture among colonial officials towards that Church. This official attitude subordinating the colonial Church of England was facilitated by the perpetuation of government funding, albeit now on a religiously neutral cross-denominational basis. In poor colonies such as Western Australia where the state provided virtually the only funding for the Churches, the maintenance of government stipends over many decades made the governor, rather than a remote bishop, the effective head of the Church. It demonstrated that while the relationship of Church and state had changed from an Anglican hegemony, albeit imperfectly realized either at home or overseas, that political revolution did not of itself bring about a concomitant change in the Erastian mindset that came all too readily for government officials used to interpreting the royal supremacy in this way. So, in 1841, following the marriage of Queen Victoria to Prince Albert, it was the colonial government in Western Australia that published the decision of the Privy Council to insert Prince Albert's name into the prayers of the Book of Common Prayer. The official instruction to the clergy justified it on the basis that the governor was acting as the Church of England's Supreme Governor's local embodiment.[37] In 1844 when Governor Hutt issued instructions regarding the solemnization of marriages by the Anglican clergy, it was also on the basis that he was, in the absence of a bishop, acting 'as the representative of Her Majesty'.[38] The first four governors, from 1829 to 1855, were quite at ease determining the placement of clergy, setting regulations about marriage and the reading of banns in church, and chastising them for various inadequacies in their religious duties.

That Erastian bureaucratic mindset of interpreting the royal supremacy as privileging the government over the Church of England stretched all the way from the colonial peripheries to the imperial centre. Lord Grey in 1847 rejected the nomination of the archbishop of Canterbury for the new see of Newcastle in New South Wales, notwithstanding the see was founded and endowed entirely by the Church of England through its newly founded Colonial Bishoprics Fund. For Grey, such a nomination by the archbishop was an unacceptable flouting of his exercise of the royal prerogative.[39]

[37] State Record Office of Western Australia [henceforth SROWA], Govt. Notice 173, 21 Dec. 1841, ACC 49/14, fo. 104.

[38] Col. Sec. to Colonial Chaplain, 8 June 1844, SROWA, ACC 49/18, fos. 231–3.

[39] G. P. Shaw, *Patriarch and Prophet: William Grant Broughton 1788–1835: Colonial Statesman and Ecclesiastic* (Melbourne, 1978), p. 205.

It is clear that both in the metropolitan centre of empire and in the colonies a fundamentally Erastian viewpoint persisted towards the Church of England in the minds and attitudes of many government officials. The legal acts enfranchising non-Anglicans in Britain and its colonial counterparts created a conscious turn away from Anglican hegemony in a format these officials were familiar with. These cultural legal forms central to this official world barred Anglican officials favouring their own Church, at least too explicitly. But, even earlier Acts of Parliament enshrined a much older official *mentalité*—the Act of Supremacy and the Act of Uniformity of 1559 which set forth the royal supremacy in the Church of England—and these continued to support the Erastianism of officialdom. Consequently, a *mentalité* which was both old and not legally altered by the constitutional changes of 1828–32 persisted. This framework made it more difficult for officials to adapt to the constitutional changes which logically permitted the Church of England greater freedom than it previously had when it owed obligations to the state as a consequence of a substantive establishment. Its Erastian persistence was also encouraged by Anglican clergy in the colonies who complained of a lack of special treatment being awarded to them as ministers of the Established Church.

A NEW ANGLICAN PARADIGM

As we have seen, a number of colonial and metropolitan clergy and leading laity bemoaned the retreat from the Anglican hegemony by the state, because they saw the state as a Christian one with a duty to uphold Christian truth, which they equated with their own Church. However, a long-term and more constructive Anglican response to this severing of the centuries-old partnership with the state, both at home and abroad, was developing from the mid-1830s. This was the shift by the Church to a new autonomous paradigm of church extension, and, in the colonies, to associate this new Anglican autonomy with an episcopal paradigm of Anglican development.

Autonomous domestic church extension began by the Church of England in 1835 with the foundation of Bishop Blomfield's widely copied initiative of the Metropolis Churches' Fund. By 1841 this autonomous action by the Church had spread to the empire with the inauguration in that year of the Colonial Bishoprics Fund. This fund also was the initiative of Bishop Blomfield. However, at the London public meeting to launch it, the colonial church extension centred around colonial bishoprics created by the independent action of the Church clearly had widespread support, not just from leading ecclesiastics but also from laymen and women, including Anglican politicians such as William Gladstone and Henry Labouchere. Present at the launch of the Fund were also aristocrats, Whigs, Tories, Evangelicals, and High

Churchmen both old and of the newer variety, such as Archdeacon Henry Manning. Later contributors to the fund were overshadowed by the generosity of Angela Burdett Coutts, the incredibly wealthy heiress of a banking fortune. Between 1845 and 1858 she gave at least £85,000 to endow three dioceses in Australia, South Africa, and Canada.[40]

In establishing the fund most of the speakers made it clear that they would have preferred to have still acted in partnership with the state; however, they reluctantly bowed to the realities of a changed situation for the empire as well as the home country. The tenor of this reluctant shift from the Church–state partnership to the brave new world of going it alone can be seen in the speech of Gladstone, still at this time an ultra-Tory MP committed to preserving the old Anglican polity.

> And therefore much as has been said of the duty of the State with regard to this matter,—a duty up to this moment so partially fulfilled, and ardently as I long to see the day when that duty shall be more adequately recognised, yet I do not scruple to utter a sentiment in which I am sure I shall carry with me universal concurrence, that we should lament to see the State in such sort charging itself with the fulfilment of these sacred obligations, as to make the provision for the religious wants of the Colonies altogether a mechanical, or altogether a legal matter, and thus depriving the members of the Church amongst us of the opportunity of bringing their free-will offerings into the treasury of God.[41]

This was more of the same establishmentarianism that had undergirded the Anglican political theology of the Church–state partnership for centuries, albeit with a new *realpolitik* than previously. Bishop Blomfield, the instigator of the colonial initiative was more forthright.

> Let us leave the State to consider its duty; let us be diligent and faithful in performing ours. That it is, indeed, the duty of the State, of every Christian State, as administering one province of God's universal empire, to provide that all its subjects should have the full enjoyment of their Christian privileges and means of performing their Christian duties,—and in order thereto, to send out from time to time an adequate supply of labourers into the Lord's harvest,—I shall ever be forward to contend. We have only to look at the fruits which have been gathered from that harvest-field, where it has been duly cultivated, and at the briars and noxious weeds which overspread its surface where it has been neglected, to convince us, that, if the full and complete discharge of this duty on the part of the State would have drawn largely upon the country's resources, the non-performance of that duty has occasioned it an expenditure of tenfold the amount.[42]

[40] Diana Orton, *Made of Gold: A Biography of Angela Burdett Coutts* (London, 1980), pp. 105, 185.

[41] *Proceedings at a Meeting of the Clergy and Laity Officially Called by His Grace, the Lord Archbishop of Canterbury, and Held at Willis's Rooms, 27th April, 1841, for the Purpose of Raising a Fund towards the Endowment of Additional Colonial Bishoprics* (London, 1841), p. 29.

[42] *Proceedings*, p. 7.

Archdeacon Henry Manning delivered an imperial theology that tied the fortunes of the empire to that of the Church. To the Church alone was given a divine guarantee of endurance, and only insofar as the state supported the Church would the state share in the permanency of the Church. Otherwise, the British Empire would suffer the same ephemeral condition as empires before it and eventually vanish into history.

> Surely, as citizens, the only hope we can have for the perpetuity of this great Christian empire, is that . . . its unity of organization shall be identified with the unity and organization of the church of Christ, and so be made partaker of her perpetuity. If we look back, as every Christian man will look back, to the history of past empires—not regarding the history of the world as a turbulent rolling sea, in which empires rise and fall by chance, driven about by some blind destiny, but recognising some moral law, guided by an unerring Governor, determining the rise and fall of empires, as of men . . . when we behold these things, and see that it has pleased the providence of the same Supreme Governor to raise us up now to stand where they stood, and to commit to us the same deposit—to make us carriers of the light, we surely have the choice to make, whether we will be the mere beast of burthen for all nations, or the evangelizer of the world. Whether it may please the same Ruler who has raised us up to continue us as we are, to make us an empire which shall last with the perpetuity of his Church.[43]

The meeting, of course, passed the resolution that based future Anglican colonial extension upon episcopacy: 'That the Church of England, in endeavouring to discharge her unquestionable duty of providing for the religious wants of her members in foreign lands, is bound to proceed upon her own principles of Apostolical order and discipline'.[44] The new Anglican paradigm of acting autonomously as a Church for episcopal extension around the world was cemented after the formation of the Colonial Bishoprics Fund by a declaration a month later by the bishops of the United Church of England and Ireland of their responsibility for administering the fund. Then followed the same year the passing of the Colonial Bishoprics Act (5 Vict., c. 6) giving legislative authority to the Church to create in British imperial territories the colonial sees envisaged by the Fund.[45]

The parliamentary legislation demonstrates that the Church of England was, in England, Wales, and Ireland, still formally the legally Established Church and therefore required laws to enable it to adapt to new situations. However, the contrast with the previous century over the issue of colonial bishoprics is pointed. During the eighteenth century the government repeatedly blocked moves by the Church to establish bishops in colonial North America, concerned that the opposition of the powerful Dissenting Churches in those colonies could undermine its control. From 1841 the Colonial

[43] *Proceedings*, p. 25. [44] *Proceedings*, p. 7.

[45] Rowan Strong, *Anglicanism and the British Empire c.1700–c.1850* (Oxford, 2007), p. 210.

Bishoprics Fund indicated that the Church of England would no longer acquiesce in state constraints upon its global expansion, but was prepared to develop its own means to do so; that such extension would be in an episcopal form; and that it now questioned the reality of the state's commitment to Christianity.

Although, as we have seen, Erastian attitudes did still prevail within the government and its officials, the dissolving of the Church–state partnership into a formalist shell inevitably began to erode the efficacy of the royal supremacy within Anglicanism. Just as that supremacy began to pass from the prerogative of the crown to the ruling ministry during the eighteenth century, so the constitutional revolution of the 1820s caused it effectively to begin to wither, prompted both by the state treating the Established Church as one among a number of denominations, and by the Church claiming more of its own autonomy. This latter dimension would accelerate in the nineteenth century as the Church of England moved to revive existing internal government structures, and also to create new ones. The ancient Convocations of York and Canterbury were reconstituted in 1852 and 1861 respectively, though still as exclusively clerical institutions. Diocesan assemblies involving laymen began to be summoned in the 1860s, and these two developments came together in the 1880s when the Convocations began to meet together with a 'House of Laymen' elected by the diocesan assemblies. A legal authority for central autonomous government by the Church of England, however, had to wait until 1920.[46]

This gradual development of autonomy in England was less hampered by the state connection in the empire, which began to provide examples and models of how an independent Anglicanism could be governed. The imperial connection was not one-way within the development of a global autonomous Anglicanism in the nineteenth century; and it was colonial Anglicanism that was in advance of its older British progenitor, though this often depended on the outlook of local Anglican leaders, usually in form of colonial bishops. We can see this clearly in the parallel initiatives of adjacent colonial bishops: William Grant Broughton, bishop of Australia, and his younger contemporary, George Augustus Selwyn, bishop of New Zealand.

Broughton was the older man, formed in a High Church establishment Anglicanism and seeking to uphold that in the colonial Australian context when he arrived there as archdeacon of New South Wales in 1829. When Anglican monopolistic support from the state began to dissolve in 1829 after the Secretary of State for the Colonies suspended the Church and Schools Corporation which set aside one-seventh of crown lands in New South Wales for the Church of England, Broughton continued to lobby for an informal

[46] Burns, *Diocesan Revival*, ch. 9.

superiority for his Church by opposing the cross-denominationalism of Governor Bourke's Church Act. This colonial context alerted Broughton more quickly to the state's retreat from Anglican confessionalism than his High Church colleagues at home, and by the late 1830s he was showing definite signs of adopting the new autonomous episcopal paradigm, by visiting the CMS mission in New Zealand which was outside his legal jurisdiction, but claiming to do so on the basis of his spiritual authority as a bishop. By 1850 Broughton had reached a position of unequivocal attachment to an episcopal authority derived from the Church and not the state, and his consequent empowerment to act independently of the state, when he called a meeting of all the Australian bishops, plus Selwyn of New Zealand, to what he wished to call a 'synod'.[47]

Across the Tasman Sea the implementation of that autonomous episcopal paradigm had proceeded apace almost immediately following the arrival of Broughton's younger colleague. Selwyn landed in his new see bearing, like Broughton, letters patent from the crown; in his case enacting him as bishop of New Zealand. But Selwyn, born in 1809, and ordained in 1832, had grown to maturity during the years when the state was enfranchising non-Anglicans. Just two years after arriving he called a synod of his clergy together on the basis of his episcopal authority explicitly to discuss the rules and shape of a New Zealand Church. In doing so Selwyn had been influenced by the example of the Episcopal Church in the United States. In 1846 Selwyn wrote to Gladstone suggesting that a polity like that of the Episcopal Church would release the energies of his Church for evangelism. 'If we had a constitution in many respects similar to the American Church, we might soon hope to fill up our waste places, and exhibit the powers of a a [*sic*] Episcopal Church as practical realities before mankind, aggressive upon the ranks of heathenism & infidelity: and not merely keeping its own.'[48]

When criticized by English friends for acting contrary to the royal supremacy over the Church of England, his response was an unequivocal defence of a Church unshackled from an Erastian state and free to conduct its own affairs on its own authority, criticizing in return the lack of these things in England.

> My desire is, in this country, so far as God may give me light and strength, to try what the actual system of the Church of England can do, when disencumbered of its earthly load of seats in parliament, Erastian compromises, corruption of patronage, confusion of orders, synodless bishops, and an unorganised clergy. None of these things are inherent in our system, and therefore not to be imposed as faults.[49]

[47] Strong, *Anglicanism and the British Empire*, pp. 230–53.

[48] Selwyn to Gladstone, 15 September 1846, Alexander Turnball Library, New Zealand, Selwyn Papers, Micro MS 426.

[49] John H. Evans, *Churchman Militant: George Augustus Selwyn, Bishop of New Zealand and Lichfield* (London, 1964), pp. 136–7.

He called a further synod in 1847, giving a charge to the assembly which maintained that in the colonial context the Church of England was freed from establishment, but needed to avoid two pitfalls—on the one hand avoiding excessive claims to superiority in a British colony, and on the other the 'no less fatal error of servility to the ruling powers of the State'.[50] In a pastoral letter to all the Anglicans in his diocese in April 1852 Selwyn proposed to extend the synodical government to include not just the clergy and their bishop but also laymen.

> The necessity of this measure arises mainly from two causes: First, that the Church in this colony is not established by law, and consequently that a large portion of the ecclesiastical law of England is inapplicable to us; Secondly, that the Church in this colony is dependent mainly upon the voluntary contributions of its members... We can scarcely expect that such a revision of the ecclesiastical law as would meet our wants will be undertaken in England, because the Convocation of the clergy is no longer allowed to meet for deliberation, and the British parliament is no longer composed only of members of the Church... It follows, therefore, that we must either be content to have no laws to guide us, or that we must apply for the usual power granted to all incorporated bodies—to frame by-laws for ourselves in all such matters as relate to our own peculiar position, reserving to Her Majesty and to the heads of the Church in England such rights and powers as may be necessary to maintain the Queen's supremacy, and the unity and integrity of our Church.[51]

It might be thought that in maintaining the royal supremacy Selwyn was not fully committed to relinquishing the state connection. But he clearly saw no role in the colonial Anglican Church for a British Parliament or government that was no longer exclusively Anglican. His reference is to the monarch alone. This is in the manner of traditional High Church theology, which viewed the crown as a sacred and separate entity from Parliament and the crown's ministers; as a genuinely Anglican monarchy exercising, by virtue of the royal coronation oath, a lay but genuinely Anglican supremacy over the Church. Selwyn was willing to give a share in the government of the colonial Church of England to the ecclesiastical heads of the Church in England, including the archbishop of Canterbury, and the monarch in its ecclesiastical person as the Supreme Governor of the Church of England, but no longer to Parliament and politicians. In addition, the legal position of the Church in New Zealand needed to be secure, and that required an act of the imperial Parliament, though it was clear that Parliament would only legally enable what the Church was in process of realizing anyway. At a meeting of the clergy and

[50] George Augustus Selwyn, *A Charge Delivered to the Clergy of the Diocese of New Zealand at the Diocesan Synod, in the Chapel of St John's College, on Thursday, September 23, 1847* (London, 1849), pp. 8–10.

[51] Evans, *Churchman Militant*, pp. 139–40.

laity of New Zealand Anglicans in Auckland, in May 1857, a draft constitution for an Anglican Church in New Zealand independent of the state and autonomous was agreed.[52]

The increasing separation of the Church of England from its state connection, even with respect to the royal supremacy, was messily demonstrated in the colonial Anglican Church as a consequence of the Colenso controversy in 1863. John William Colenso was the first bishop of Natal in southern Africa and, as a consequence of his concern to indigenize Christianity among the Zulus, produced volumes of biblical criticism on the Old Testament dedicated to proving that those Scriptures were not dictated verbatim by God and so they could be interpreted to permit greater adaptation to Zulu custom. Bishop Robert Gray of Cape Town, as Colenso's metropolitan according to Gray's letters patent, tried Colenso for heresy in 1863 and deposed him, though Colenso refused to accept Gray's authority. The authority that both bishops claimed for their differing understandings of Colenso's episcopal independence was their letters patent from the crown, notwithstanding that in reality the constitution had evolved to remove the royal supremacy from the monarch's prerogative to that of the governing ministry. That supremacy had already been limited in law in 1857 when, in the Eton case, the courts found that in colonies with an independent legislature the Church of England could not simply be an extension of the Church in England and thereby also be treated as established. When Colenso sought a ruling on Gray's claim from the Judicial Committee of the Privy Council it was held that both bishops' letters patent were void because the Cape Colony and Natal both had their own legislatures. The legal documents encapsulating the royal supremacy with respect to Anglican sees, were now, by that same system, shown to have no validity outside England. As the historian of the confused case comments, the vestigial royal supremacy 'had become an impersonal legal abstraction. Most of those who wished to maintain the constitutional links with the crown did so because they thought of the queen, personally, as one of their most treasured links with England. They wished to think of themselves as *her* people. But the law had created an impenetrable system which no one could operate.'[53] In fact, if not transparently in law, the royal supremacy, insofar as it did apply, did so only to the Church of England in England and Wales after the disestablishment of the Church of Ireland.

[52] Strong, *Anglicanism and the British Empire*, pp. 278–9.

[53] Peter Hinchliffe, 'Colonial Church Establishment in the Aftermath of the Colenso Controversy', in Nigel Aston (ed.), *Religious Change in Europe 1650–1914: Essays for John McManners* (Oxford, 1997), pp. 345–63 (p. 363).

SELECT BIBLIOGRAPHY

Bentley, James, *Ritualism and Politics in Victorian Britain: The Attempt to Legislate for Belief* (Oxford, 1978).

Best, Geoffrey, 'The Constitutional Revolution, 1828–1832, and its Consequences for the Established Church', *Theology*, 52 (1959): 226–34.

Brown, Stewart J., 'The Broad Church Movement, National Culture, and the Established Churches of Great Britain, c.1850–c.1900', in Hilary M. Carey and John Gascoigne (eds.), *Church and State in Old and New Worlds* (Leiden, 2011), pp. 99–128.

Brown, Stewart J., *The National Churches of England, Ireland, and Scotland 1801–46* (Oxford, 2001).

Brown, Stewart J., *Providence and the Empire 1815–1914* (Harlow, 2008).

Burns, Arthur, *The Diocesan Revival in the Church of England c.1800–1870* (Oxford, 1999).

Carey, Hilary M. and John Gascoigne (eds.), *Church and State in Old and New Worlds* (Leiden, 2011).

Clark, J. C. D., *English Society, 1660–1832: Religion, Ideology and Politics during the Ancien Regime* (Cambridge, 2000 edn.).

Hinchliffe, Peter, 'Colonial Church Establishment in the Aftermath of the Colenso Controversy', in Nigel Aston (ed.), *Religious Change in Europe 1650–1914: Essays for John McManners* (Oxford, 1997), pp. 345–63.

Sachs, William L., *The Transformation of Anglicanism: From State Church to Global Communion* (Cambridge, 1993).

Skinner, Simon, *Tractarians and the 'Condition of England': The Social and Political Thought of the Oxford Movement* (Oxford, 2004).

Strong, Rowan, *Anglicanism and the British Empire c.1700–c.1850* (Oxford, 2007).

Strong, Rowan, 'Church and State in Western Australia: Implementing New Imperial Paradigms in the Swan River Colony 1827–1857', *Journal of Ecclesiastical History*, 61 (2010): 517–40.

6

Anglican Missionary Societies and Agencies in the Nineteenth Century

Brian Stanley

The dominant model of organization for Protestant foreign missions in the nineteenth century was that of a voluntary society, controlled by a committee of predominantly lay directors and responsible to a constituency of mainly lay subscribers, whose support had to be cultivated by a constant stream of attractive missionary 'intelligence' that was supplied both in print and by itinerant deputation speakers. A missionary society was not an ecclesial body and quite frequently drew its missionaries and members from more than one denomination. The model reflected the animating ethos of eighteenth-century Pietism, with its conviction that true spirituality resided in, and effective mission flowed from, informal bands or societies, quite distinct from Church structures, and made up of those who had been regenerated from 'formal' Christian adherence by the power of the Spirit. In Britain the model was enthusiastically adopted by Evangelical Nonconformists, and in the United States, that Mecca of voluntary Christianity, by almost all Protestants. However, for many Anglicans and others of pronounced Church principles, such as Presbyterians of the Moderate party in the Church of Scotland or the higher sort of Wesleyan Methodists, the voluntary society approach to the dissemination of the Church overseas could pose difficulties. How could such voluntary lay bodies maintain due Church order and authority? How could they avoid the excesses of popular control? The Church of England had its own long and honourable tradition of religious societies dedicated to the advancement of the faith at home or abroad, most notably the Society for Promoting Christian Knowledge (SPCK; 1698) and the Society for the Propagation of the Gospel in Foreign Parts (SPG; 1701). Whilst the SPCK was a voluntary society rather than a chartered body, it always remained firmly submissive to episcopal and clerical authority. The two societies between them represented the missionary arm of the Church of England, and in the eighteenth century did not face any significant challenge to their monopolistic status. The story of Anglican missionary societies in the nineteenth century is one of divergent and sometimes unsatisfactory solutions to the problem of how to reconcile the added and potentially ecclesiastically subversive dynamic that voluntary religious organizations acquired in the wake of the eighteenth-century Evangelical Revival with the heightened sensitivity to Anglican episcopal order produced by the Oxford Movement.

VOLUNTARIZING THE SOCIETY FOR THE PROPAGATION OF THE GOSPEL

The SPG, founded by royal charter in 1701, possessed the apparently large advantages of official approval by both Church and state. The society received public financial aid in the form of occasional Royal Letters and parliamentary grants for the support of the colonial clergy. Despite such advantages—or rather because of them—the SPG prior to the mid-1820s possessed no network of local associations, held no public meetings, and issued no literature for public consumption. It sensed no need to do so. However, during the 1820s the society began to stir into new life under the stimulus of the opening up of a new field of operations in India. Bishop Thomas Middleton's project for the foundation of Bishop's College in Calcutta led to the formation of the first SPG parochial associations, and in 1825 the society took over the south Indian missions of the SPCK. Yet as late as 1833 the voluntary income of the SPG amounted to only £8,747, compared with an equivalent figure for its Evangelical Anglican counterpart, the Church Missionary Society (CMS), of £45,707.[1]

The transformation of the SPG into a major missionary society with a popular base was the product of two coincidental historical developments in the 1830s. One was a steep increase in the annual rate of emigration from the British Isles—especially to Canada, where the total number of emigrants rose from 12,084 in 1828 to 66,339 in 1832.[2] The other was the application to the colonial Church of the sustained crisis in Church–state relations provoked by the repeal of the Test and Corporation Acts in 1828. In 1832 the new Whig government informed the SPG that the parliamentary grant towards the maintenance of the clergy in Upper and Lower Canada, entrusted to the society in 1813, would be discontinued in 1833. The Church in the Canadian colonies thus found itself deprived of state support at the very time that the influx of settlers from Britain reached unprecedented levels. The SPG

[1] *SPG Report* for 1866, p. 198; Church Missionary Society, *The Centenary Volume of the Church Missionary Society 1799–1899* (London, 1902).

[2] W. A. Carrothers, *Emigration from the British Isles* (London, 1965 edn.), p. 305.

responded by making a public appeal in 1832: new local committees were formed, public meetings held, and the society offered to make available for general distribution copies of its annual report and extracts from missionary correspondence.[3] A new secretary, the Revd A. M. Campbell, was appointed, and income increased substantially for 1834, only to fall back over the next three years. Many doubted whether it was seemly for 'the Venerable Society' to employ deputation agents and indulge in rousing platform oratory in a shameless bid to compete with the CMS for lay support. As Archbishop Beresford of Armagh confessed to an SPG public meeting in 1838: 'It has happened to this Society, that what constitutes its merits in the eyes of the wise and judicious part of the community has been one cause of the failure, to a certain extent, of its popularity.'[4]

After some vacillation, the SPG made its decisive choice in the early summer of 1838, summoning a large public meeting at Willis's Rooms in London on 22 June to launch a national propaganda campaign on behalf of the society. The speakers, Bishop John Inglis of Nova Scotia among them, deplored the culpable neglect by the government of its duty to make provision for the spiritual needs of the flood of emigrants to British North America, but urged the Anglican faithful to awaken the government to its responsibilities by the scale of their voluntary exertions.[5] Over the next twelve months public meetings in support of the SPG were convened in 144 venues throughout the country. Inglis himself was indefatigable in his advocacy: by the time of his return to Nova Scotia in early 1840, he had preached eighty sermons and spoken at nearly one hundred meetings on behalf of the society.[6] Another powerful advocate was Samuel Wilberforce, then rector of Brighstone in the Isle of Wight, who conducted a deputation tour of Exeter diocese between 8 October and 19 October 1839, travelling nearly 1,500 miles and speaking up to three times a day.[7] This tour proved to be not simply the turning point in Wilberforce's ecclesiastical career, but also a decided stimulus to the gradually reviving fortunes of the SPG. Income from subscriptions, donations, and collections had shown a steep increase in 1838–9 in response to the campaign initiated in June 1838, but the increase from 1839 to 1840 was more dramatic still—from £22,821 to £38,730.[8] Despite the grave initial doubts of traditional High Churchmen such as Joshua Watson of the Hackney Phalanx about the wisdom of advocating the cause of the colonial Church 'at public meetings and on platforms',[9] the success of Inglis and Wilberforce was unanswerable. By 1840 voluntary effort on behalf of the colonial Church had become a priority

[3] *SPG Report* for 1833, pp. 64–5. [4] *SPG Report* for 1838, p. 29.
[5] *SPG Report* for 1838, pp. 29–66.
[6] Edward Churton (ed.), *Memoir of Joshua Watson* (London, 1861), II, p. 102.
[7] Bodleian Library, MS Wilberforce e.7, fos. 171–95.
[8] *SPG Report* for 1866, p. 198.
[9] Churton (ed.), *Memoir of Joshua Watson*, II, p. 100.

for all those committed to what Wilberforce termed 'the sound Church principle'.[10] Moreover, the lay enthusiasm which Inglis and Wilberforce had kindled was soon extended to Anglican activity in new colonial dioceses in India and South Africa where the dominant mode of SPG work was that of a missionary society working among the indigenous population, in contrast to North America, where the society's function as a colonial agency providing ministry to British settlers had been predominant, though it had never ignored the missionary responsibility to the surrounding indigenous population laid upon it by its founding charter. 'A large experience shows that nothing more kindles the church feelings of any flock than thus interesting them in the spread of the church in foreign parts', mused Wilberforce.[11] By 1853 Africa accounted for 28.8 per cent and India 25.5 per cent of SPG expenditure.[12] The society was no longer so closely identified with the support of the clergy in Britain's American colonies. SPG work grew rapidly in size and geographical extent during the second half of the nineteenth century. By the date of its bicentenary in 1901, the society supported no less than 753 clergy overseas, in addition to 186 women missionaries supported by the SPG Women's Association. Donations, subscriptions, and collections to its general fund amounted to £88,453, and over 11,000 churches supported the society.[13] It was now much more difficult than before for Evangelicals to claim a monopoly on missionary zeal in the Church of England.

REGULARIZING THE CHURCH MISSIONARY SOCIETY

If the story of the SPG in the 1830s and 1840s is one of a traditional Church body having under political necessity to 'learn the ways of voluntaryism',[14] the CMS in the same period was obliged to follow an opposite trajectory, attempting to combine its voluntary ethos with a more transparent submission to episcopal authority than it had displayed hitherto. Again, the crisis in Church–state relations supplied the motive power driving the realignment: in the polarized ecclesiastical politics of the 1830s, the CMS could no longer afford

[10] Wilberforce to Manning, 4 Oct. 1839, cited in David Newsome, *The Parting of Friends: The Wilberforces and Henry Manning* (Grand Rapids, MI, 1993 edn.), p. 255.

[11] [Samuel Wilberforce] draft letter to parochial clergy, n.d. [1839], Bodleian Library Oxford, USPG archives, CH. 25.

[12] Hilary M. Carey, *God's Empire: Religion and Colonialism in the British World, c.1801–1908* (Cambridge, 2011), pp. 86, 111.

[13] H. P. Thompson, *Into all Lands: The History of the Society for the Propagation of the Gospel in Foreign Parts 1701–1950* (London, 1951), p. 241.

[14] R. T. Handy, *A History of the Churches in the United States and Canada* (Oxford, 1976), p. 236.

to appear as less than a fully Church society. Established in 1799 as 'the Society for missions to Africa and the East', the CMS did not adopt the formal title of 'The Church Missionary Society for Africa and the East' until 1812. It was a voluntary agency formed in imitation of its Nonconformist predecessors (the Baptist and London Missionary Societies, founded in 1792 and 1795 respectively). Its first president, Admiral Lord Gambier, was a layman, and its relationship to the bishops of the Church of England was tenuous: no bishop was prepared to be publicly identified with the CMS until 1815, when Henry Ryder, the Evangelical bishop of Gloucester, and Henry Bathurst, bishop of Norwich, agreed to become vice-presidents of the society. Between 1824 and 1840 the number of English bishops lending their official patronage to the society rose from two to eight, but the CMS remained acutely conscious of its slender base of episcopal approval, in contrast to the SPG, of which all bishops were *ex officio* patrons. High Church criticisms of the constitution and ecclesiastical practice of the CMS multiplied during the turbulent decade of the 1830s. The CMS, under the direction of its combative lay secretary, Dandeson Coates, became embroiled in a series of disputes over the powers of licensing, stationing, and superintendence of missionaries with the bishops of Jamaica, Barbados, and even Calcutta—where the bishop from 1832, Daniel Wilson, was a notable Evangelical and former CMS committee member.

However, the uneasy and often fractious relationship between the CMS and the bishops gradually improved between 1836 and 1841. The first sign of the new mood was an agreement between Bishop Wilson and the CMS which was embodied in a series of rules proposed by Wilson in June 1836 and subsequently adopted by the society. The central principle of the agreement was that the society did not claim spiritual authority over its ordained missionaries—that was the sole prerogative of the bishop—but exercised the role of a lay patron, presenting candidates to the bishop for ordination and approval to serve in a certain location.[15] Henry Venn (1796–1873), vicar of St John's, Holloway, a member of the CMS Committee and a personal friend of Wilson, expanded on these points in a document entitled 'Remarks on the Constitution and Practice of the Church Missionary Society, with reference to its Ecclesiastical Relations', which was published as an appendix to the society's annual report in 1839, and reproduced in every CMS annual report until 1877.[16] Thus Venn repeated Wilson's argument that the society was 'strictly a Lay Institution' with a role analogous to a lay patron of a beneficed clergyman.

15 'Regulations of the Parent Society as to the Relation of the Bishop to the Corr. Committee & Missionaries' (1836), cited in Hans Cnattingius, *Bishops and Societies: A Study of Anglican Colonial and Missionary Expansion, 1698–1850* (London, 1952), p. 176.

16 'Remarks on the Constitution and Practice of the Church Missionary Society, with Reference to its Ecclesiastical Relations', in *Proceedings of the Church Missionary Society*, 15 (1838–9): 135–9; Eugene Stock, *The History of the Church Missionary Society: Its Environment, Its Men and Its Work*, 4 vols. (London, 1899–1916), I, p. 387.

Even Venn's insistence that the CMS went further than a lay patron in providing the funds to pay a missionary's stipend, and hence possessed the rights of a trustee, was based on Wilson's words in a letter to the Calcutta Corresponding Committee of the CMS in May 1837.[17] Whilst Venn's paper was a robust defence of that society's rights in its own 'temporal' sphere, it skilfully deployed Wilson to make the case for ecclesiastical respectability. CMS operations, Venn astutely concluded, 'may be regarded as the acts of the Church of England, putting forth its energy for the Conversion of the Heathen World'.[18]

Such affirmations provided Bishop Blomfield of London, addressing the launch meeting of the Colonial Bishoprics Fund on 27 April 1841, with the assurance he needed that means could now be devised whereby the SPG and (more especially) the CMS 'might be induced to carry on their operations under the same superintendence and control'. The present moment, 'when we are preparing to extend the full benefits of our ecclesiastical polity, in all its completeness, to all the dependencies of the empire', was in his view 'peculiarly appropriate' for such a step.[19] Blomfield then secured agreement at the CMS general meeting in July 1841 for the adoption of a new law in its constitution which specified that on all matters of ecclesiastical order and discipline, where a difference should arise between any colonial bishop and any committee of the society, the matter should be referred to the archbishops and bishops of the United Church of England and Ireland, whose decision thereon shall be final. The immediate consequence of the constitutional alteration was that the archbishops of Canterbury and York, Bishop Blomfield, and six other English bishops joined the CMS (the archbishop of Canterbury as vice-patron, and the other as vice-presidents). In October 1841 Henry Venn was appointed honorary clerical secretary of the CMS (initially on a temporary and part-time basis), a role he was to occupy until his retirement in 1872.

Some provincial CMS supporters greeted the change in constitution with a measure of hesitation: 'Sad indeed would be the day', warned the Birmingham CMS committee in 1841, 'in which individuals would join the Society not from hearty and affectionate attachment to its evangelical principles, but merely or even primarily, from regard to its being officially patronized and acknowledged as a Church Society.' Nevertheless, the Birmingham committee grasped the point of the changes clearly enough, expressing the hope that Blomfield's words of commendation of the CMS in his speech of 27 April 1841 'will be sufficient... to silence once for all those who have characterised the Propagation Society, and not *this*, as peculiarly "THE Church Missionary Society to

[17] 'Remarks on the Constitution and Practice of the Church Missionary Society', pp. 135, 137.
[18] 'Remarks on the Constitution and Practice of the Church Missionary Society', p. 138.
[19] Stock, *History of the CMS*, I, p. 390.

the Heathen"'.[20] Neither such hopes that episcopal sanction would afford the CMS a decisive advantage in its competition with a revived SPG for Anglican generosity, nor the parallel fears that the Evangelical identity of the CMS would be swamped by the adhesion of High Church supporters, proved well grounded. Nevertheless, the initiatives taken by Venn and Blomfield from 1839 to 1841 established the ecclesiastical framework that would enable the CMS over the next century to become the most influential instrument for the transmission of the Anglican tradition to the tropical world, thereby ensuring that large sections of global Anglicanism—particularly in West and East Africa—would exhibit a markedly Evangelical character.

By the end of our period the CMS had grown into one of the largest and most administratively complex voluntary bodies in Britain. In 1906 the society had an annual income of about £300,000 (equivalent to about £30 million today). It employed 975 missionaries, 8,850 native agents, and operated 37 theological and training colleges, 92 boarding schools, 12 industrial institutions, 2,400 elementary schools, 40 hospitals, 73 dispensaries, 21 leprosaria, 6 homes for the blind, 18 orphanages, 6 other homes and refuges, and 17 presses and publishing offices. At the high-point of the British Empire, the CMS was, as Peter Williams, its most accomplished modern historian, observes, itself 'a mini-empire'.[21]

MISSIONARY BISHOPS AND NATIVE BISHOPS: THE CONTRASTING IDEALS OF EPISCOPACY OF SAMUEL WILBERFORCE AND HENRY VENN

Both Samuel Wilberforce and his friend Henry Edward Manning welcomed the rapprochement between the CMS and the bishops in the forlorn hope that it would prove a first step towards a union of the CMS and the SPG, and bind the CMS irrevocably to the principle that episcopacy would constitute the invariable basis of all its future work. The conviction that, in J. H. Newman's words, 'the only right way of missionary-izing is by bishops'[22] was common to both traditional High Churchmen and Tractarians in this period, but Newman and his closest supporters had other priorities than the Church overseas. The most ardent advocates of the idea of 'missionary bishops' were Manning,

[20] University of Birmingham Cadbury Research Library, CMS archives, Birmingham Church Missionary Society, Minutes of Committee (Soc. 4 C1/1), printed annual report for 1840. The annual report for 1840 was not adopted till June 1841.

[21] C. Peter Williams, *The Ideal of the Self-Governing Church: A Guide to Victorian Missionary Strategy* (Leiden, 1990), p. 262.

[22] Cited in Newsome, *Parting of Friends*, p. 217.

W. E. Gladstone, Bishop Blomfield of London, Bishop Gray of Cape Town, and, perhaps more than any other, Samuel Wilberforce. Wilberforce's *History of the Protestant Episcopal Church in America* (first published in 1844) reveals him to have been much impressed by reading the sermon preached in Norwalk, Connecticut, on 25 September 1835 by Dr George Washington Doane, bishop of New Jersey. The occasion of the sermon was the consecration of Dr Jackson Kemper as the Episcopal Church's first 'missionary bishop', sent to the frontier territories of Missouri and Indiana. The conception of a bishop as one '*sent forth* by the Church, not *sought for of* the Church; going *before* to organize the Church, not waiting till the Church has been partially organized',[23] was not peculiar to Doane, but was rather the central principle of a new constitution which the Protestant Episcopal Church had just adopted at its Convention in Philadelphia at the end of August 1835 with a view to making that Church more responsive to the missionary demands on the extending American frontier. Doane's sermon appealed strongly to Wilberforce as a confirmation of the apostolic principle that mission must be conducted on the basis of the logical priority of the episcopate: he believed that 'the Presbytery and the Diaconate were evolved out of the Episcopate, and not the Presbytery and the Diaconate run up into the Episcopate'.[24] A later section of this chapter will trace the lines of descent whereby this distinctively catholic version of Anglican missiology was adopted by a variety of High Church or Anglo-Catholic agencies in the second half of the nineteenth century. George Augustus Selwyn's sense of calling to New Zealand owed much to Manning's passionate oral and written advocacy of the idea of missionary bishops. By means of Wilberforce and Gray, the idea was taken up by the founders of the Universities' Mission to Central Africa (UMCA), and embodied in the first bishop of Central Africa, Charles F. Mackenzie.

Missionary bishops appealed to theological idealists who were determined to preserve the Church in its apostolic purity, unencumbered by ties to the colonial state. Those who thought more in terms of the realities of church-planting on the mission fields were not always so convinced. Paramount among them was Henry Venn. Venn relied on the British colonial state to provide the necessary legal structures of episcopal authority as an interim framework for missionary operations. He raised much of the endowment for the new bishopric of Sierra Leone (1852), in the expectation that the arrival of a colonial bishop would 'hasten the day when a goodly body of native

[23] Samuel Wilberforce, *A History of the Protestant Episcopal Church in America* (London, 1856 edn.), pp. 375–94 (at p. 375).

[24] Samuel Wilberforce, 'Upon the Extension of the Episcopate in the Colonies' (1853), in Henry Rowley (ed.), *Speeches on Missions by the Right Reverend Samuel Wilberforce, D.D.* (London, 1874), p. 295.

missionaries will be "sent forth" from Sierra Leone into the regions beyond'.[25] But for Venn, this was a matter of convenience rather than theological principle. In a manner characteristic of nineteenth-century Evangelicalism, he believed that in the New Testament evangelism was the result of 'individual earnestness' rather than episcopal command.[26] The appointment of a bishop to a native Church should be the coping-stone of a truly indigenous Church. As such, the episcopal appointment would be the culmination of an extended process whereby in any one locality the missionary society accomplished its own 'euthanasia' by raising up a 'three-self' Church that would be self-governing, self-funding, and self-extending—with its own ordained ministry, financed out of the voluntary giving of its members, and engaging in its own mission. Venn looked wistfully over his shoulder at missions sent by Nonconformist Churches which exemplified these principles in their own domestic life and applied them accordingly in their overseas missions. However, 'in our Church', Venn lamented, 'the Clergy find everything relating to elementary organisation settled by the Law of the Land'—the apparatus of tithes, church rates, and the legal constitution of parishes meant that Anglican clergy were ill-equipped to think through questions of Church organization from first principles. The only remedy for this 'imperfection' in Anglican missions was for missionaries to maintain a clear distinction between their evangelistic work and their ministry to the native Church, where they should follow a set of principles aimed at developing a native ministry and indigenous episcopate.[27]

PLANTING A THREE-SELF ANGLICAN CHURCH: THE AMBIGUOUS LEGACY OF HENRY VENN

Alongside his American Congregationalist contemporary, Rufus Anderson (Foreign Secretary of the American Board of Commissioners for Foreign Missions from 1832 to 1866), Venn is remembered today as one of the two architects of the three-self theory of missions. This defined the goal of missionary work as the establishment of indigenous churches that would be self-governing, self-supporting, and self-propagating. In point of fact, Venn and Anderson simply refined and formalized a theory of missions whose essential features were shared by other Evangelical mission strategists in the

[25] Jehu Hanciles, *Euthanasia of a Mission: African Church Autonomy in a Colonial Context* (Westport, CT, 2002), p. 45.

[26] *Church Missionary Intelligencer* (1858), p. 152, cited in Williams, *Ideal of the Self-Governing Church*, p. 17.

[27] 'The Organization of Native Churches' (1861), minute published in Max Warren (ed.), *To Apply the Gospel: Selections from the Writings of Henry Venn* (Grand Rapids, MI, 1971), pp. 67–8.

mid-nineteenth century. The interdenominational Liverpool missionary conference of 1860, for example, affirmed that the supreme object of the missionary enterprise was the establishment of Churches which should depend, 'not upon distant and foreign Churches, but upon their own exertions and their own spiritual graces'.[28] It is also widely said that the theory ceased to command general assent in the late Victorian period, being undermined by 'scientific' racism and the high imperial mood of those years. In fact, the theory still retained its status of missionary orthodoxy in 1910, as the report of Commission II on 'The Church in the Mission Field' presented to the World Missionary Conference held in Edinburgh revealed. Indeed, the idea was still in general circulation as late as the mid-twentieth century: the 'Christian Manifesto' drawn up in 1950 by nineteen Chinese Protestant leaders as a basis for negotiation with Zhou Enlai and the new Communist regime conceded that 'The movement for autonomy, self-support, and self-propagation hitherto promoted in the Chinese church has already attained a measure of success.'[29] The selection in 1954 of the title 'Three-Self Patriotic Movement Church' for the government-regulated Protestant church in China suggests both that the *theory* still retained its currency and that Western missions were seen to have failed to put their theory sufficiently into practice. The story of CMS policy in the second half of the nineteenth century provides ample illustration of this hypothesis.

In his later years Venn became convinced that the distinctive needs and characteristics of different races (we would use the term 'cultures') dictated the goal of planting native Churches which should be entirely independent of the Church of England. In areas such as India or New Zealand where there were English Anglicans this implied the creation of territorially overlapping episcopates—one for indigenous people and another for English settlers. This idea was anathema to High Churchmen. Bishop Selwyn, for example, insisted on a gradual 'Euthanasia of the Mission' in New Zealand whereby the missionary Church would be progressively absorbed into the colonial Church, which, inevitably, would be under European leadership.[30] Venn's principle also attracted the censure of the first Lambeth Conference in 1867, which pointed out the 'manifest objections to the appointment of a Bishop to minister to certain congregations within the diocese of another Bishop, and wholly independent of him'.[31] Venn's ecclesiastical apartheid—which was what it was—looked increasingly out of place in the later Victorian period,

[28] *Conference on Missions Held in 1860 at Liverpool... edited by the Secretaries to the Conference* (London, 1860), p. 310, also pp. 192–231, 309–13.

[29] Printed in V. E. W. Hayward, *Christians and China* (Belfast, 1974), p. 50.

[30] Cited in Allan K. Davidson, 'Culture and Ecclesiology: The Church Missionary Society and New Zealand', in Kevin Ward and Brian Stanley (eds.), *The Church Mission Society and World Christianity, 1799–1999* (Grand Rapids, MI, 2000), p. 216.

[31] Cited in Williams, *Ideal of the Self-Governing Church*, p. 85.

with its developing consciousness of the unity of both the British Empire and the Anglican Communion. Ironically, the Anglican Church of Aotearoa, New Zealand, and Polynesia would in 1992 return to Venn's principles by adopting a tripartite structure for Māori, Pākehā (European), and Polynesian. What was tragically lost in the 1880s and 1890s was Venn's firm commitment to make an indigenous Church led by indigenous bishops a realistic prospect in the immediate future. Whilst all Protestant missions succumbed during this period to this sceptical lengthening of the timescale of devolution of power to indigenous Christian leadership, the problem for the Churches planted by the CMS was accentuated by the growth of a more 'catholic' understanding of episcopacy within Anglicanism which made Venn's concept of territorially overlapping episcopates unacceptable.

Graphic evidence of the yawning gap that had developed between the theory of a three-self Church and its practice was provided by the Niger crisis of 1891. The Yoruba freed slave Samuel Ajayi Crowther had been consecrated in 1864 with the expansive if vague title of 'Bishop of the countries of Western Africa beyond the limits of the Queen's dominions'. He was the first non-white bishop anywhere in the Anglican Communion. However, in 1891 he was humiliated by seeing his episcopal authority openly usurped by younger and spiritually zealous CMS missionaries who had grown sceptical of the capacity of Africans to exercise godly leadership—a marked reversal of Venn's confidence in African Christian capabilities. In the light of the Niger affair, Eugene Stock, the dominating influence on CMS policy at the end of the century (as well as its historian), had by 1901 turned his back on Venn's notion of racially separate Churches, adopting instead the optimistic view that Europeans and native could work harmoniously together in a single ecclesiastical structure in which Europeans would gradually cede control to indigenous clergy. In point of fact, there would not be another African diocesan Anglican bishop until 1951, when the Nigerian A. B. Akinyele was consecrated as the bishop of the new diocese of Ibadan.

ANGLO-CATHOLICISM AND APOSTOLIC PATTERNS OF MISSION

The SPG was representative of the 'Orthodox' High Church tradition within the Church of England, although it was affected to a limited extent by the Tractarian and ritualist movements. The society received considerable criticism from Evangelicals after its appointment of an avowed Tractarian, A. W. Street, to a professorship at Bishop's College, Calcutta, in 1839. From October 1842 the *Record* newspaper (the organ of the most decided Evangelical opinion) called on its readers to withdraw all support from the SPG, and accused Ernest Hawkins, its secretary from 1843 to 1864, of 'Romanizing' tendencies.[32] However, the society was too committed to presenting itself as *the* authorized missionary organ of the Church of England to risk too close an identification with a movement that was publicly identified as un-Protestant and therefore un-English. 'Orthodox' High Churchmen were still wary of many Tractarian emphases. George Selwyn, the first bishop to be appointed through the Colonial Bishoprics Fund, favoured some 'catholic' practices such as the use of altar candles, but was one of those bishops who lent his patronage to the CMS following the constitutional change of 1841; indeed, John Keble, an admirer of Selwyn, felt obliged to confess that 'he makes me *shiver* now and then with his Protestantisms, crying up the Ch. Miss. Society'.[33] Selwyn maintained good relationships with CMS missionaries in New Zealand until 1847, when he sided with Governor Grey in his attacks on them for excessive land-holding. Insofar as Selwyn was subject to the general ecclesiological influence of the Oxford Movement, the effect was to make him more prepared to develop in New Zealand a synodical pattern of church government free of the Erastian control of a British Parliament which could no longer be regarded as representative of lay Anglican opinion. Selwyn returned to Britain in 1854. His accounts of his pioneering labours in the Solomon Islands and New Hebrides for the Melanesian Mission, which he had established in 1849, conducted with an apostolic simplicity of lifestyle, appealed strongly to Anglicans of Catholic sympathies.

As the Victorian age proceeded, a new style of High Church Anglican missions became apparent. It was not at first explicitly Anglo-Catholic in flavour, but the idea of the missionary bishop was its governing principle. Paradoxically, the first example of this new pattern was a mission that owed its origins to the pioneering exploits of a Scottish Congregationalist and Evangelical missionary. The UMCA was formed in 1859 as a response by the Anglican universities of Oxford and Cambridge (and for a period also by the University of Durham and Trinity College, Dublin) to the stirring appeals issued by David Livingstone in Oxford and Cambridge in December 1857 for a missionary venture up the Zambezi valley. Livingstone had urged his hearers to join him in bringing civilization, commerce, and Christianity to a region which his recent trans-African journey had shown to be grievously afflicted by the East African slave trade. The prime movers in Cambridge, where Livingstone's oratory had its greatest impact, were Robert Gray, bishop of Cape Town, who visited Cambridge in October 1858, and William Monk, a Cambridge clergyman. Monk was a leading figure in the formation earlier that year of the Cambridge University Church Missionary Union—a body

[32] *The Record*, 20 Oct., 14 Nov., 1 Dec. 1842, 29 Apr. and 4 May 1843.

[33] J. T. Coleridge, *A Memoir of the Rev. John Keble, M.A., late Vicar of Hursley* (Oxford, 1869), II, p. 408, cited in Davidson, 'Culture and Ecclesiology', p. 212.

designed to encourage junior members of the university to devote themselves to missionary service, whether with the CMS or other Anglican missions. Monk secured Livingstone's agreement to edit his Cambridge lectures for publication on the understanding that 'an attempt should be made thereby to prepare the way for sending out a Cambridge Mission to Africa'.[34]

The surprising extent of Anglican enthusiasm for Livingstone's campaign owed much in Cambridge to the enduring impact on the university of a series of four Advent sermons preached by Bishop Selwyn in 1854 on the theme of the work of Christ in the world.[35] In Oxford and more generally it was indebted to the enthusiastic endorsement of Livingstone's appeal by the bishop of Oxford, Samuel Wilberforce, a close friend of Gray's. Wilberforce's parentage gave him enduring status as the unofficial voice of anti-slavery sentiment in Britain, whilst his unstinting advocacy of missionary bishops endeared him to High Churchmen. By May 1858 Wilberforce was publicly repeating Livingstone's argument that Zambezi-grown cotton would free the Lancashire cotton industry from its dependence on American slave-grown cotton, thus increasing English prosperity while at the same time striking a blow at American slavery.[36] In October 1859 he was back on his old stamping ground in the diocese of Exeter, informing an SPG audience that he had recently received a letter from 'that good and marvellous man Dr Livingstone' urging him to stir up support for the Zambezi expedition.[37] On All Saints' Day 1859 he was in Cambridge moving the resolution urging support of 'the Oxford and Cambridge Mission to Central Africa' both for evangelistic reasons and because of its potential for 'the civilisation of Africa by the extinction of the slave trade'.[38] In May 1860 he spoke in Manchester, Liverpool, and Leeds pleading the cause of the Universities' Mission, stressing that it was 'as little as it is possible to be a Society at all. It is more the Church acting without the instrumentality of a Society, than the creating [*sic*] any new association.'[39]

[34] Charles Gray (ed.), *Life of Robert Gray: Bishop of Cape Town and Metropolitan of Africa*, 2 vols. (London, 1876), p. 438; William Monk (ed.), *Dr Livingstone's Cambridge Lectures* (Cambridge, 1858 edn.), p. 327.

[35] G. A. Selwyn, *The Work of Christ in the World: Four Sermons Preached Before the University of Cambridge on the Four Sundays Preceding Advent in the Year of our Lord 1854* (Cambridge, 1855).

[36] S. Wilberforce, 'Upon the Evangelisation of the Native Tribes of Southern Africa', in Rowley (ed.), *Speeches on Missions*, pp. 157–8.

[37] S. Wilberforce, 'Upon the Standing-place, Work, and Prospects of the Society for the Propagation of the Gospel', in Rowley (ed.), *Speeches on Missions*, pp. 30–1.

[38] S. Wilberforce, 'Upon the Universities' Mission to Central Africa', in Rowley (ed.), *Speeches on Missions*, pp. 176–86.

[39] Wilberforce, 'Upon the Universities' Mission to Central Africa', pp. 187–229, quotation at p. 204.

The claim to be, not a voluntary society, but the Church of England acting corporately in a missionary capacity, had been characteristic of the SPG before its voluntaryization during the 1830s, and was now being advanced on behalf of the UMCA. Its Zambezi mission was to be led by Charles F. Mackenzie, formerly a Cambridge don and clergyman who owed his call to Africa in large part to Selwyn's Advent visit to Cambridge in 1854. Mackenzie was currently serving as archdeacon of Durban under Bishop Gray. He was consecrated in Cape Town in 1861 as the first purely missionary bishop of the Church of England, with no territory other than the unevangelized tribes of the Lake Nyasa and Shiré region, far beyond the boundaries of British colonial rule. But the Zambezi expedition was an ignominious failure and Mackenzie died in 1862. His successor, William Tozer, moved the base of the mission from the Zambezi valley to Zanzibar, but he broke down in health and resigned in 1873. The UMCA initially depended on the SPG for office space and administrative assistance, but from 1881 it became a mission agency in its own right. The parting of the ways with the SPG had the effect of giving the UMCA a more pronounced Anglo-Catholic flavour, as it began to cultivate a new constituency of support in ritualist parishes in London and the south-east of England. Under the third bishop, Edward Steere (1874–82), the UMCA began to follow a distinctive model of primitive apostolicity. Missionary priests were increasingly expected to be celibate, and lived in simplicity. In contrast to Livingstone's and Wilberforce's emphasis on the dissemination of commerce and civilisation, the UMCA began to argue that 'in some ways civilization is a positive hindrance to the missionary' and sought to protect its converts from the deleterious influence of urban society. Bishop Steere was strongly committed to developing an African ministry, believing, like Henry Venn, that European missionaries should never be allowed to assume pastoral charge of African congregations. From 1875 Steere appointed a number of the ex-slaves who made up much of the mission's Zanzibar congregation as Readers, with the eventual goal that they would be ordained. Sadly the momentum towards an African priesthood was not sustained under Steere's successors, not even under the episcopate of Frank Weston, bishop of Zanzibar from 1908 to his death in 1924. Nevertheless, it remains that case that leading UMCA missionaries, such as Chauncy Maples, made first bishop of Likoma in 1895 just before his death by drowning on Lake Nyasa, had begun to discover in Africans an innate religiosity lacking in increasingly secular Britain. Anglo-Catholic incarnational theology was enabling some Anglicans to revise their previously negative views of non-Western peoples and their religion.

The style of Anglo-Catholic mission increasingly represented by the UMCA was not original to the central African field. To some extent it was represented in the Pacific by the episcopate of John Coleridge Patteson, missionary bishop of Melanesia from 1861 until his tragic death at Nukapu in the Solomon Islands on 20 September 1871—an event which was widely depicted as a martyrdom; in Anglo-Catholic tradition the five stab wounds to his body became five sacred wounds, an imitation of the death of Christ.[40] In fact, even before the UMCA assumed its distinctively Anglo-Catholic character, a strongly primitivist model of Anglo-Catholic overseas mission had been pioneered by the Indian missions of the Society of St John the Evangelist (popularly known as the Cowley Fathers), a religious order founded by Fr Richard Benson in 1866.[41] The Cowley Fathers established two Indian missions in Indore and Pune near Bombay; the former mission particularly was characterized from its inception in 1874 by an emphasis on commending the gospel by the apostolic power of Christian communities living a life of prayer and poverty, rather than by any reliance on Western civilization or British imperial power. Although in the English context Benson's order looked to the appeal of ritual and elaborate church decoration to draw the working classes to the Church, in India an emphasis on asceticism—the beauty of holiness—was a more powerful magnet. Partly responsible for bringing the Cowley Fathers to India, and himself a notable member of the Pune community from 1877 to 1882, was the former CMS Brahman convert Nehemiah (Nilakanth) Goreh, who had come to see himself as a Christian *sannyasi* (ascetic).

Somewhat similar Anglo-Catholic approaches to mission in north India were taken by two affiliates of the SPG, the Cambridge Mission to Delhi (1877) and the Oxford Mission to Calcutta (1881), though both were primarily educational missions. The Cambridge Mission owed its origins to a joint initiative between a former CMS missionary, T. V. French, and Professor Brooke Foss Westcott of the University of Cambridge. Their scheme for a 'brotherhood' of Cambridge-educated clergy, selected in Cambridge for communal life in Delhi, could not be reconciled with the recruitment policies of the CMS. The Delhi brotherhood hence became attached to the SPG and derived its character more from Westcott than from French. Westcott hoped to make Delhi into a 'new Alexandria' in the East, where Christian faith could draw on the spiritual resources of Hindu devotional thought in the same way that in the second and third centuries Clement and Origen had once drawn on the philosophical resources of Greek Platonism. Although Westcott's rather romantic and orientalist vision proved impossible to sustain in Delhi, his emphasis on higher education remained, being expressed through the foundation of St Stephen's College, an institution which continues to this day to provide high-quality education in the city. Whilst he was less of an

[40] David Hilliard, 'The Making of an Anglican Martyr: Bishop John Coleridge Patteson of Melanesia', in Diana Wood (ed.), *Martyrs and Martyrologies*, Studies in Church History 30 (Oxford, 1993), pp. 333–45.

[41] Rowan Strong, 'Origins of Anglo-Catholic Missions: Fr Richard Benson and the Initial Missions of the Society of St John the Evangelist 1869–1882', *Journal of Ecclesiastical History*, 66 (2015): 90–115; also H. E. W. Slade, *A Work Begun: The Story of the Cowley Fathers in India 1874–1967* (London, 1970).

Anglo-Catholic than either Steere or Benson, Westcott shared the same incarnational emphasis in theology, and his mission displayed a similar reticence towards the British Empire. It is no accident that the most celebrated 'anti-colonial' missionary of twentieth-century India, C. F. Andrews, was a member of the Delhi brotherhood from his arrival in India in 1904 until 1914.

ANGLICAN WOMEN IN MISSION

Although the missionary enterprise depended heavily on the industry of women as fundraisers and local organizers in Britain, women were allowed to fulfil only a very limited role in the field for much of the nineteenth century. The CMS for long did not count missionary wives as missionaries in their own right, and until the mid-1880s did not encourage applications from single women. The society's printed register of missionaries contains a list of female missionaries from as early as 1820, but many of these women were sisters or widows of male missionaries who were 'taken up' by the CMS after the death in service of their brother or husband and allowed to remain in the field; others had been recruited as assistants to missionary wives to help them in their work with women and girls.[42] Most Anglican single women who sensed a calling to missionary service tended to be channelled into one of the societies which worked specifically among women and girls. The oldest of these, the Society for Promoting Female Education in the East (later known as the Female Education Society), was established in 1834. By 1848 it had about twenty missionaries working in China, India, Japan, Palestine, and South Africa.[43] A second society, the Indian Female Normal School and Instruction Society, was formalized in 1861, combining the work of the Calcutta Normal School (1851) with a programme of regular visitation of zenanas—the enclosed areas for high-caste Hindu women and girls; it subsequently extended its work to north-west and south India. Its constitution, framed by Henry Venn, was interdenominational, but in practice most of its links were to the CMS, and most of its supporters were Anglicans. When the Evangelical philanthropist Lady Mary Jane Kinnaird, a member of the Church of Scotland, led an attempt in 1879–80 to appoint a leading Scottish Presbyterian missionary to office in

[42] See Jocelyn Murray, 'The Role of Women in the CMS, 1799–1917', in Ward and Stanley (eds.), *The Church Missionary Society and World Christianity*, pp. 66–90; Church Missionary Society, *Register of Missionaries (Clerical, Lay, & Female) and Native Clergy, from 1804 to 1904* (London, n.d. [1905]), pp. 260–96.

[43] Stock, *History of the CMS*, I, p. 377; Margaret Donaldson, '"The Cultivation of the Heart and the Moulding of the Will . . .": The Missionary Contribution of the Society for Promoting Female Education in China, India, and the East', in W. J. Sheils and Diana Wood (eds.), *Women and the Church*, Studies in Church History 27 (Oxford 1990), pp. 429–42.

the Indian Female Normal School and Instruction Society in order to secure more support in Scotland, a specifically Church of England Zenana Missionary Society was formed in protest.[44] The new society, which remained formally autonomous of the CMS until as late as 1957, attracted the support of most of the Anglican members of the old society, and even extended its work to China.

CMS policy on the recruitment of women took a radically new turn in the mid-1880s. In part, this was a response to a number of offers of service from single women who were not simply gifted but had benefited from the widening educational opportunities opening to women with a view to entry to the teaching and the medical professions in particular. The first female graduate, Katherine Tristram, who had a degree in mathematics from London University, was accepted in 1888 for educational work in Japan. But even more important was the CMS desire to reap as large a share as possible of the harvest of missionary enthusiasm sown by the annual Keswick Conventions, established in 1875. The Keswick message of the need to consecrate oneself to the 'higher' or 'victorious' Christian life was gender-neutral, and, especially after the offer of the celebrated 'Cambridge Seven' to the China Inland Mission in 1885, became progressively linked to the challenge of the mission field: the most telling proof of full consecration to Christ was to volunteer for missionary service. In 1887, the Keswick audience received an unofficial appeal from a CMS missionary in Palestine, J. R. Longley Hall, for ten women to offer for that field; seventeen women volunteered in response, either for Palestine or other fields. From 1888 the organizers of the Convention instituted a missionary meeting as an official part of the programme. The numbers of women accepted by the CMS rose from seven in 1887 to eighteen in 1889 and forty-two in 1893. Whereas in the whole period from 1800 to 1879 the CMS had recruited only forty women missionaries (excluding missionary wives), a further forty were recruited in the 1880s alone, whilst in the 1890s the total soared to 315. In consequence by 1899, 53 per cent of all CMS women missionaries were single.[45] Between the mid-1880s and 1910 the gender composition of the CMS missionary force, as of the Protestant missionary movement as a whole, shifted markedly: by 1909, 824, or 59 per cent, of a total of 1,390 CMS missionary staff, were women.[46] The single woman, working as schoolteacher, nurse, or doctor, had become almost the archetype of the missionary.

[44] Stock, *History of the CMS*, III, p. 258; John C. Pollock, *Shadows Fall Apart: The History of the Zenana Bible and Medical Mission* (London, 1958), pp. 17, 45–55.

[45] Brian Stanley, *The Bible and the Flag: Protestant Missions and British Imperialism in the Nineteenth and Twentieth Centuries* (Leicester, 1990), p. 80; Murray, 'The Role of Women in the CMS, 1799–1917', pp. 81, 89.

[46] Sean Gill, *Women and the Church of England from the Eighteenth Century to the Present* (London, 1994), p. 173.

Although the spiritual impetus imparted by the Keswick movement was confined to the Evangelical wing of Anglicanism, the SPG also shared in some measure in the expansion of women's missionary work. As with missions of a more Protestant character, the distinctive requirements of women's work in India proved the thin end of the wedge. Hence 1866 saw the formation of 'The Ladies' Association for the Promotion of Female Education in India and other Heathen Countries, in connection with the Missions of the Society for the Propagation of the Gospel'. The activities of the Ladies' Association soon expanded to other fields than India, with the result that in 1895 the Association was given the new title of 'The Women's Mission Association for the Promotion of Female Education in the Missions of the SPG'. It appointed its first female medical missionary in 1897. By 1900 the Association had 186 missionaries in the field, six of them engaged in medical work.[47] However, the Association was slow to recruit women for medical work in comparison with other missions. In 1867 Priscilla Winter, a former zenana teacher in Calcutta, and the wife of an SPG missionary, had founded the Delhi Female Medical Mission to bring Christian medical care to women in the zenanas. In 1885 the Mission opened St Stephen's Hospital for Women and Children, which still flourishes today. The first woman doctor, Dr Jenny Muller, who had existing experience as a medical worker in the zenanas, was appointed in 1891. By 1904 there were twice as many female missionaries as male ones in the Delhi mission, though women's work accounted for only 37 per cent of the budget.[48]

The emphasis of the SPG and its affiliated missions on priestly ministry constrained to some extent the expansion of opportunities for the missionary service of women which so transformed the character of the Evangelical societies between the mid-1880s and the First World War. On the other hand, the catholic wing of the Church derived most of the benefit from the proliferation in Victorian Britain of Anglican religious communities for women. Some of these sisterhoods developed an overseas dimension to their work. Among the most important of these (and the first to commence mission work in India) was the Community of St Mary the Virgin, established in Berkshire by the vicar of Wantage, W. J. Butler, in 1848. From 1877 the community sent sisters to India to work in close association with the Cowley Fathers' mission in Pune. The Wantage sisters were a formative though not unproblematic influence on the early Christian life of Sarasvati Ramabai. Ramabai, an extremely learned Brahman woman (she was given the honorific title of 'Pandita'), owed her initial conversion to Nehemiah Goreh, and became

[47] Thompson, *Into all Lands*, pp. 235–6; Daniel O'Connor (ed.), *Three Centuries of Mission: The United Society for the Propagation of the Gospel 1701–2000* (London, 2000), pp. 343–5.

[48] Jeffrey Cox, 'Independent English Women in Delhi and Lahore', in R. W. Davis and R. J. Helmstadter (eds.), *Religion and Irreligion in Victorian Society: Essays in Honour of R. K. Webb* (London, 1992), p. 173.

perhaps the most renowned of all female converts to Christianity in nineteenth-century India. By 1886, however, Ramabai had repudiated her Anglo-Catholic tutelage as theologically unwarranted and personally restrictive; she later participated in one of the first Pentecostal movements in India. Other Anglican religious communities for women were established to serve a particular mission field. In 1874 Alan Becher Webb, second bishop of Bloemfontein, established the Community of St Michael and All Angels which would play a pioneering role in the development of both girls' education and nursing in South Africa; one of the six founding sisters of that community, Henrietta Stockdale, was instrumental in securing the state registration of nurses in the Cape of Good Hope Medical and Pharmacy Act of 1891—the first example of state registration of nurses anywhere in the world. She is remembered in the *Dictionary of South African Biography* as having 'laid the foundation of professional nursing and modern hospital organisation in Southern Africa'.[49] The sisterhoods undoubtedly opened new doors of opportunity for Anglican women who sensed a vocation to full-time service of the Church at home or overseas. Nevertheless, their activities in this period remained largely confined to those areas of work that conformed to Victorian notions of what were the proper spheres of female action—caring for the sick and education of the young, particularly of girls.

TWO ANGLICAN VISIONS OF IMPERIALISM: BISHOP TUCKER AND BISHOP MONTGOMERY

The period from 1880 to 1910 witnessed an enormous expansion in the territorial extent of the British Empire in Africa and other parts of the tropical world, and an attendant growth in popular enthusiasm for imperial ideals. It is tempting, but too simple, to suggest that the political context 'explains' the parallel expansion in the British missionary movement in the same period. There was undoubtedly a closer correspondence than earlier in the century between enthusiasm for overseas missions and enthusiasm for the spread of British imperial rule, but Christian devotion to empire was always subordinated to missionary priorities; it was neither blindly nationalistic nor uncritical in its support for European domination. Two episcopal examples from opposing ends of the ecclesiastical spectrum will illustrate the point. Alfred R. Tucker (1849–1914) was a CMS missionary to Uganda and third bishop of Eastern Equatorial Africa. The first bishop, James Hannington, had been

[49] W. J. De Kock, D. W. Krüger et al. (eds.), *Dictionary of South African Biography* (Pretoria, Cape Town, and Johannesburg, 1968–87), II, pp. 716–17; see also Dowr. Lady Loch and Miss Stockdale, *Sister Henrietta C.S.M. and A. A. Bloemfontein. Kimberley, 1874–1911* (London, 1914).

murdered in October 1885 on the instructions of Mwanga, the Kabaka (ruler) of Buganda, the ancient kingdom at the heart of what is now Uganda; the second bishop, Henry Parker, died en route to Uganda in March 1888. Alfred Tucker, curate of St Nicholas's Church in Durham, was consecrated as bishop in April 1890 soon after he had made an offer to go out to Uganda with the CMS. More than any other individual, he was responsible for orchestrating the public campaigns which led to Uganda being declared a British protectorate by Lord Rosebery's Liberal administration in August 1894. Tucker used the 1891 anniversary meeting of the CMS Gleaners' Union (a body of keen CMS supporters formed in 1886) to appeal for the funds to enable the Imperial British East Africa Company to continue its occupation of Uganda. £8,000 was promised within half an hour and another £8,000 came in within ten days. 'It may truly be said today', wrote Eugene Stock with untroubled pride in 1899, that 'England owes the great empire she now rules over in Central Africa to that memorable meeting of the Gleaners' Union in Exeter on October 30th 1891.'[50] The funds raised were, however, only an interim measure. Tucker also played a role in 1892–4 in the next and conclusive phase of the campaign—intended to 'save' Uganda from the hands of the Germans or (worse) the French, with all that implied for the revival of the East African slave trade and the delicate balance of power between Protestant and Catholic parties in the royal court of Buganda.

Alfred Tucker was, without doubt, a Christian imperialist, a 'muscular Christian' who saw his call to the unhealthy climate of Uganda as a discharge to God of the debt incurred by the unusual physical strength he had been given. Yet he also did his utmost to ensure that the constitution for the Church of Uganda should subject European missionaries to the full authority and structures of an indigenous Church. In double contrast to Venn, he believed that there should be no separate church structures for Europeans—yet also that the time was not ripe for an African bishop. It was a cause of great sadness to Tucker that when a constitution was finally drawn up in 1907, the CMS missionaries succeeded in excluding all their affairs from the authority of the Church of Uganda.

In the SPG the closest equivalent to Alfred Tucker was Bishop H. H. Montgomery, bishop of Tasmania from 1889 to 1901, and secretary of the SPG from 1901 to 1918. Montgomery was a fervent believer in imperial unity and in the role of Anglican Christianity as the only religious cement capable of binding the empire together. As secretary of the SPG, Montgomery hoped to revive the ailing fortunes of the society at a time when CMS finances were flourishing, and endeavoured to do so by hitching the SPG's mission to the cause of imperial duty. Nevertheless, for all his imperial zeal, Montgomery

[50] Stock, *History of the CMS*, III, pp. 439–40.

deserves to be remembered as one of those Christian thinkers of the Edwardian period who were beginning, albeit very imperfectly, to grasp the truth that the catholicity of the Church of God could never be adequately captured within a purely European understanding of the faith. He edited a series of essays written by various bishops and published in 1907 under the title *Mankind and the Church: Being an Attempt to Estimate the Contribution of Great Races to the Fullness of the Church of God*. Montgomery's extended introductory essay advanced the thesis that 'while the Church must be Catholic it must also be racially and nationally expressed . . . We shall never obtain the true contribution of any Church to the Body of Christ till the Church of that land is racy of the soil while it remains Catholic.' The Church of each race should reflect the peculiar characteristics of that race, and make those characteristics its distinctive contribution to the one Church Catholic. Although he believed that God had given a leadership role to the English race and its national Church, Montgomery found in the book of Revelation a vision of the final union of all races and, indeed, of the whole created order, joining together in worship of the one Creator.[51]

ANGLICANS AND THE WORLD MISSIONARY CONFERENCE, EDINBURGH 1910

At the World Missionary Conference in Edinburgh in 1910 Charles Gore, bishop of Oxford, developed Montgomery's theory of 'race Churches',[52] but purified it of some of its more overtly Anglo-Saxon features. Whilst Montgomery tended to see catholicity and the demands of racial authenticity as two poles that needed to be kept in tension, Gore's argument in presenting the report of Commission III on Christian education was that the essence of Christian universality lay precisely in the fact that the common message of the gospel is severally understood by various peoples in such diverse ways that 'each in receiving the one message brings out some different or special aspect of the universal truth or character which lies in the common religion'. In this way the vision of Revelation 21 of 'the glory and honour of all nations' being 'brought within the light and circle of the Holy City' was being fulfilled through the missionary endeavours of the Church.[53] The 1920 Lambeth

[51] H. H. Montgomery (ed.), *Mankind and the Church: Being an Attempt to Estimate the Contribution of Great Races to the Fullness of the Church of God By Seven Bishops* (London, 1907), pp. xxx, xlvii.

[52] Montgomery (ed.), *Mankind and the Church*, p. xxviii.

[53] World Missionary Conference, 1910, *Report of Commission III: Education in Relation to the Christianisation of National Life* (Edinburgh and London, n.d. [1910]), p. 406.

Conference in its encyclical letter took up Gore's theme by emphasizing that the Church, as the Body of Christ, is a community transcending race, in which the different nations are created by God so that each might bring 'their national way of walking in the fellowship of the Saints by the help of the One Spirit. Thus will the glory of the nations be brought into the Holy City.'[54]

Although there had been a series of interdenominational missionary conferences in Britain since the Liverpool conference in 1860, High Church Anglicans had always held aloof from events that were consistently Evangelical in tone and membership. That the acknowledged leader of the Anglo-Catholic party within the Church of England should in 1910 be present at a conference dominated by Evangelicals of various denominations and held in the Assembly Hall of a non-established dissenting Church (the United Free Church of Scotland), might seem remarkable. That Charles Gore should also have been given the prior responsibility of chairing one its commissions and writing its report on the subject of 'education in relation to the Christianisation of national life' may appear stranger still. Certainly it had required the protracted labours during 1909 of the conference secretary, J. H. Oldham, to convince Gore, Montgomery, Bishop Edward Talbot of Southwark, and Archbishop Randall Davidson himself that the conference was an event in which Catholic Anglicans could participate without injury to their ecclesial convictions. Under Montgomery's leadership the SPG eventually agreed to participate officially in the conference, despite the vocal opposition of many of its supporters and extreme reluctance of its standing committee. The full participation of the Church of England at Edinburgh would have been unthinkable without the precedent established by the Student Christian Movement (SCM) and its predecessors, whose meetings and conferences for university students in Britain since 1893 had been held on the 'interdenominational' principle that all participants agreed not to raise matters of Church order and doctrine; the same rule was applied at Edinburgh. According to Tissington Tatlow, the general secretary of the SCM, Edward Talbot and other leading Anglo-Catholics made no secret of the fact that it was the SCM which had converted them to the 'interdenominational' stance taken by the conference; the influence on Bishop Talbot of his son, Neville (later bishop of Pretoria), who from 1907 played a prominent leadership role in the SCM, cannot be discounted.[55]

Evangelicals had to pay a high price for the inclusion in the conference of the Church of England in all its theological diversity. The continent of Latin America had to be almost entirely excluded from the conference statistics of

[54] *Conference of Bishops of the Anglican Communion holden at Lambeth Palace, July 5 to August 7, 1920: Encyclical Letter from the Bishops, with the Resolutions and Reports* (London, 1920), p. 21.

[55] Tissington Tatlow, *The Story of the Student Christian Movement of Great Britain and Ireland* (London, 1933), pp. 155–6, 272, 392–4, 409–10.

missionary labour (and, by extension, from the agenda of the conference itself), since in the view of Anglo-Catholics it belonged in large part to Christendom due to the historic predominance of the Roman Catholic Church rather than to the 'the non-Christian world' which formed the object of the conference's attention. That was a heavy blow to most Evangelicals, including those Anglican Evangelicals involved in the South American Missionary Society (formerly the Patagonian Mission), which had worked, mainly in Argentina, Chile, and Paraguay since its formation by Captain Allen Gardiner in 1844. That society did have two representatives at the conference, since some of its work was among the unbaptized indigenous peoples of the continent, and was thus deemed eligible.[56]

In the long perspective, however, the full participation of the SPG in the World Missionary Conference could be said to mark the logical culmination of the bold decision that society took in 1838, when it finally opted to lay aside its chartered dignity and compete in the marketplace of religious philanthropy, alongside the CMS and other voluntary societies. Entry into the voluntaryist marketplace also ultimately propelled the SPG into the world of Evangelical ecumenism, and hence took the Church of England itself in the twentieth century into full participation in the global ecumenical movement. Not all Anglicans of High Church or Anglo-Catholic sympathies felt able to endorse the path taken by Gore, Talbot, and Montgomery in 1909–10. The UMCA as a body took no part in the conference, although its secretary, Duncan Travers, was appointed in a personal capacity to one of the commissions but was unable to serve owing to illness.[57] It could be plausibly suggested that those Anglicans who regarded participation in the conference as tantamount to heresy represented the most extreme ritualists. However, those who eventually joined the conference included some who owed much to the legacy of the Oxford Movement. F. J. Western of the Cambridge Mission to Delhi seemed to this Evangelical gathering 'a strange medieval apparition', in his brown habit, sandals, and huge silver crucifix.[58] Members of the eight commissions included Herbert H. Kelly of the Society of the Sacred Mission at Kelham, and Walter H. Frere of the Community of the Resurrection at Mirfield, later to become bishop of Truro and a renowned liturgist. Indeed Frere played a key role, together with John H. Ritson, a Methodist minister and secretary of the British and Foreign Bible Society, in devising the idea of a conference continuation committee—which led in 1921 to the formation of the International Missionary Council. The missionary movement was never free of the

[56] World Missionary Conference, 1910, *History, Records and Addresses of the Conference* (Edinburgh and London, n.d. [1910]), p. 48.

[57] World Missionary Conference, 1910, *Report of Commission II: The Church in the Mission Field* (Edinburgh and London, n.d. [1910]), p. viii.

[58] Brian Stanley, *The World Missionary Conference, Edinburgh 1910* (Grand Rapids, MI, 2009), p. 97.

complications brought by domestic Church politics, but it also brought new perspectives to the Church of England, softened old antagonisms, and even forged some surprising alliances.

SELECT BIBLIOGRAPHY

Carey, Hilary M., *God's Empire: Religion and Colonialism in the British World, c.1801–1908* (Cambridge, 2011).

Chadwick, Owen, *Mackenzie's Grave* (London, 1959).

Cnattingius, Hans, *Bishops and Societies: A Study of Anglican Colonial and Missionary Expansion, 1698–1850* (London, 1952).

Cox, Jeffrey, *The British Missionary Enterprise since 1700* (New York and London, 2008).

Cox, Jeffrey, 'Independent English Women in Delhi and Lahore, 1860–1947', in R. W. Davis and R. J. Helmstadter (eds.), *Religion and Irreligion in Victorian Society: Essays in Honour of R. K. Webb* (London, 1992), pp. 166–84.

Gill, Sean, *Women and the Church of England from the Eighteenth Century to the Present* (London, 1994).

Maughan, Steven, 'Imperial Christianity? Bishop Montgomery and the Foreign Missions of the Church of England, 1895–1915', in Andrew Porter (ed.), *The Imperial Horizons of British Protestant Missions, 1880–1914* (Grand Rapids, MI, 2003), pp. 32–57.

Newsome, David, *The Parting of Friends: The Wilberforces and Henry Manning* (Grand Rapids, MI, 1993 edn.).

O'Connor, Daniel (ed.), *Three Centuries of Mission: The United Society for the Propagation of the Gospel 1701–2000* (London, 2000).

Porter, Andrew, *Religion versus Empire? British Protestant Missionaries and Overseas Expansion, 1700–1914* (Manchester, 2004).

Stanley, Brian, *The Bible and the Flag: Protestant Missions and British Imperialism in the Nineteenth and Twentieth Centuries* (Leicester, 1990).

Stanley, Brian, *The World Missionary Conference, Edinburgh 1910* (Grand Rapids, MI, 2009).

Stock, Eugene, *The History of the Church Missionary Society: Its Environment, Its Men and Its Work*, 4 vols. (London, 1899–1916).

Strong, Rowan, *Anglicanism and the British Empire, c.1700–1850* (Oxford, 2007).

Strong, Rowan, 'Christianize but not Civilize: Fr Richard Benson and the Initial Missions of the Society of St John the Evangelist 1869–1882', *Journal of Ecclesiastical History*, 66 (2015): 90–115.

Strong, Rowan, 'The Oxford Movement and the British Empire: Newman, Manning and the 1841 Jerusalem Bishopric', in Stewart J. Brown and Peter B. Nockles (eds.), *The Oxford Movement: Europe and the Wider World* (Cambridge, 2012), pp. 78–98.

Thompson, H. P., *Into All Lands: The History of the Society for the Propagation of the Gospel in Foreign Parts 1701–1950* (London, 1951).

Ward, Kevin and Brian Stanley (eds.), *The Church Mission Society and World Christianity, 1799–1999* (Grand Rapids, MI, 2000).

Williams, Peter C., *The Ideal of the Self-Governing Church: A Guide to Victorian Missionary Strategy* (Leiden, 1990).

Yates, T. E., *Venn and Victorian Bishops Abroad: The Missionary Policies of Henry Venn and their Repercussions upon the Anglican Episcopate of the Colonial Period 1841–1872* (Uppsala and London, 1978).

7

High Church Anglicanism in the Nineteenth Century

Robert M. Andrews

> It becomes necessary for us . . . to speak of *Church of England Principles*, if we do not wish to be deceived or misunderstood, and to assert that, by Catholicism, we mean the doctrines of the Prayer Book.
>
> —Walter Farquhar Hook (1848)[1]

Arising as a distinct tradition in the seventeenth century, the High Church were those Anglicans who stressed their continuity with the pre-Reformation heritage of English and British Christianity—a continuity represented, most notably, by the retention of the apostolic succession, the three-fold order of bishops, priests, and deacons, with a liturgical standard that had retained elements of a patristic and medieval past—the Book of Common Prayer. However, as the opening quote illustrates, even in the decades following the Oxford Movement there was an altitudinal limit to how 'high' High Churchmen were willing to go in revering the past. 'All that is in antiquity is not good', Hugh James Rose wrote to John Henry Newman in 1836;[2] and Walter Farquhar Hook, reflecting upon the conversion of one of his curates to Roman Catholicism over a decade later, had come to the same conclusion.[3] Moored to the Protestantism of the Thirty-Nine Articles, for High Churchmen the authority of antiquity was measured against what was considered the scriptural standard recovered by the English Reformation.[4]

[1] Walter Farquhar Hook, *Our Holy and Our Beautiful House, The Church of England* (London, 1848), p. 22 (emphasis in original).

[2] Quoted in C. Brad Faught, *The Oxford Movement: A Thematic History of the Tractarians and Their Times* (University Park, PA, 2003), p. 36.

[3] Hook, *Our Holy and Our Beautiful House*, p. 22.

[4] Robert M. Andrews, *Lay Activism and the High Church Movement of the Late Eighteenth Century: The Life and Thought of William Stevens (1732–1807)* (Leiden, 2015), pp. 12–21.

High Church, however, was about more than simply delineating Anglican orthodoxy from other styles of churchmanship. To be High Church was to also embrace a particular approach to spirituality. For High Churchmen this meant an emphasis upon sacramental grace that was coupled with a practical piety that rejected overt introspection. They nurtured their faith within the official confines established by the Church, or at least as close as possible to that measure. Capable of mysticism in their spirituality, the practical piety of High Churchmanship has sometimes led to perceptions of a spirituality that was 'high and dry'. Though this was true in certain cases, one misreads High Church spirituality by mistaking conservatism for coldness.[5] Politically, High Churchmen were usually Tories, though it was entirely possible to be a Whig and possess a 'high' view of Church and sacraments. Nonetheless, there was a reason for the frequent High Church identification with Tory views: for most High Churchmen, Church and state were related parts of a divinely established order—ecclesiologically, in terms of the apostolic succession; politically, in terms of a belief that monarchs reigned by divine right.[6]

High Churchmen of the nineteenth century were aware that they had inherited a churchmanship that had not only survived and developed during the eighteenth century,[7] but had showed signs of revival and vitality, in addition to what Jeremy Gregory has referred to as a conservative 'reforming spirit'.[8] How many High Churchmen there were by the turn of the nineteenth century remains a matter of debate. Nancy Murray postulated there were no more than one hundred—a figure much too low; while F. C. Mather, citing the three thousand subscribers of the High Church *British Critic*, argued that the number was likely well into the thousands.[9] In terms of being a dedicated High Churchman, that is, one who was publicly engaged in theological activism, it is likely that late eighteenth-century High Churchmen were a vocal minority, making their presence more visible in British society following the accession of George III and the tumults of the American and French Revolutions—events they all interpreted negatively. Of course, High Churchmanship—and all forms of Anglican churchmanship in general—should never be too tightly defined. A mild High Churchmanship that emphasized the doctrines of apostolic succession, sacramental grace, fidelity to the Prayer Book, and a

[5] Robert M. Andrews, '"Master in the Art of Holy Living": The Sanctity of William Stevens', in Peter Clarke and Tony Claydon (eds.), *Saints and Sanctity* (Woodbridge, 2011), pp. 307–17.

[6] Andrews, *Lay Activism*, pp. 12–21.

[7] James Allan Park, *Memoirs of William Stevens* (London, 1825 edn.); Edward Churton, *Memoir of Joshua Watson* (London, 1863 edn.).

[8] Jeremy Gregory, *Restoration, Reformation, and Reform, 1660–1828: Archbishops of Canterbury and their Diocese* (Oxford, 2000), p. 68.

[9] Nancy Uhlar Murray, 'The Influence of the French Revolution on the Church of England and its Rivals, 1789–1802', DPhil thesis, Oxford University, 1975, p. 4; F. C. Mather, *High Church Prophet: Bishop Samuel Horsley (1733–1806) and the Caroline Tradition in the Later Georgian Church* (Oxford, 1992), p. 213.

sacral royalism, would have been more widespread. The popularity of conformist Anglican piety—much of which would have been High Church—has been established by a number of recent studies.[10] When in 1834 Joshua Watson boasted to Bishop Charles Blomfield that there were 'a good seven thousand' adherents of the doctrine of apostolic succession, it was this sort of generalized High Churchmanship that he was likely referring to.[11]

The most vocal High Churchmen within the late eighteenth-century Church of England were the Hutchinsonians, so named because of their advocacy of the intellectual system of John Hutchinson (1674–1737), a layman whose peculiar views on Scripture and science produced many High Church adherents.[12] They included George Horne (1730–92), the bishop of Norwich; William Jones of Nayland (1726–1800), perpetual curate of Nayland, Suffolk; Jonathan Boucher (1738–1804), the exiled North American Loyalist; and the layman William Stevens (1732–1807). Of course, not all of the late Georgian High Churchmen were Hutchinsonians. Two notable exceptions were Samuel Horsley (1733–1806), bishop of St Asaph, and Charles Daubeny (1744–1827), archdeacon of Salisbury.

In Ireland, Scotland, and the United States of America, High Church movements also existed, showing that High Churchmanship, though at home within a monarchical political constitution wherein Anglicanism was dominant, could also exist without such a connection. Of course, being a part of the establishment, High Churchmen within the Church of Ireland shared a particularly close relationship with English High Churchmen. The Church of Ireland, having been formally united with Church of England in 1801, ensured this. Though often seen as an ultra-Protestant body, High Churchmanship in the Church of Ireland has been shown to have undergone a modest revival by the turn of the nineteenth century.[13] Notable Irish High Churchmen included John Jebb (1775–1833), bishop of Limerick, and the enigmatic layman Alexander Knox (1757–1831). In Scotland, a strong and dominant High Church tradition could be found within the small Scottish Episcopal Church. Largely Hutchinsonian, this body would re-emerge in the nineteenth century after decades of obscurity.[14] It was to the non-established Scottish Church that English High Churchmen directed the Connecticut clergyman Samuel

[10] Frances Knight, *The Nineteenth-Century Church and English Society* (Cambridge, 1995); W. M. Jacob, *Lay People and Religion in the Early Eighteenth Century* (Cambridge, 1996).

[11] Quoted in A. B. Webster, *Joshua Watson: The Story of a Layman 1771–1855* (London, 1954), p. 19.

[12] Mather, *High Church Prophet*, pp. 12–13; Andrews, *Lay Activism*, pp. 113–18, 212–16.

[13] Peter B. Nockles, 'Church or Protestant Sect? The Church of Ireland, High Churchmanship, and the Oxford Movement, 1822–1869', *The Historical Journal*, 41 (1998): 457–93.

[14] Andrews, *Lay Activism*, pp. 241–60; Rowan Strong, *Alexander Forbes of Brechin: The First Tractarian Bishop* (Oxford, 1995); Rowan Strong, *Episcopalianism in Nineteenth-Century Scotland: Religious Responses to a Modernizing Society* (Oxford, 2002).

Seabury (1729–96) to receive episcopal consecration in 1784.[15] Seabury was already part of a well-established North American High Church tradition—a tradition carried on into the nineteenth century by individuals such as John Henry Hobart (1775–1830), bishop of New York.[16]

By the turn of the nineteenth century, it was arguably the layman William Stevens who produced the most memorable example of late eighteenth-century High Church piety and activism. A wealthy businessman who gave most of his spare time and money to ecclesiastical causes, for many nineteenth-century High Churchmen he symbolized the High Church ideal of a practical and orthodox faith that was rooted in the Church of England's doctrines and sacraments.[17] In 1800 a dining club, 'The Club of Nobody's Friends', was established in Stevens's honour ('Nobody' was Stevens's *nom de plume*). Most of the prominent High Churchmen of the nineteenth century can be found in this club's membership lists.[18] Included were the High Churchmen of the 'Hackney Phalanx', so named after the London parish of Hackney, of which John James Watson (1767–1839) was rector, and Henry Handley Norris (1771–1850), the perpetual curate of a chapel-of-ease in the parish St John of Jerusalem. Along with a number of powerful clergy and laity—most notably the wealthy wine merchant and lay protégé of Stevens, Joshua Watson (1771–1855)—the phalanx became the most important group of High Churchmen during the first four decades of the nineteenth century. Though one should not overstress the cohesion of the phalanx by thinking of it in terms of a formal body with a tightly defined membership, its core group nonetheless possessed a clear sense of identity as a group of like-minded churchmen who sought to use their influence to promote High Church principles.[19]

The Hackney Phalanx's influence was most evident in their revitalization of the old Church societies and the creation of new ones.[20] Ever since the founding of the Society for Promoting Christian Knowledge (SPCK) in 1698 and the Society for the Propagation of the Gospel in Foreign Parts (SPG) in 1701, High Churchmen—both clerics and lay—had sought involvement in societies that supported the Established Church's welfare.[21] As Robert Nelson set out in his influential manual of High Church piety, *A Companion for the*

[15] Mather, *High Church Prophet*, p. 121.

[16] Strong, *Episcopalianism in Nineteenth-Century Scotland*, pp. 11–21; E. Clowes Chorley, *Men and Movements in the American Episcopal Church* (New York, 1946), pp. 133–93.

[17] Andrews, *Lay Activism*.

[18] G. E. Cokayne, *Biographical List of the Members of 'The Club of Nobody's Friends'* (London, 1885).

[19] Churton, *Memoir*, pp. 54–5; Webster, *Joshua Watson*, ch. 2.

[20] Peter B. Nockles, *The Oxford Movement in Context: Anglican High Churchmanship 1760–1857* (Cambridge, 1994), p. 19.

[21] W. O. B. Allen and Edmund McClure, *Two Hundred Years: The History of The Society for Promoting Christian Knowledge 1698–1898* (London, 1898), p. 22.

Festivals and Fasts of the Church of England (1704), the Church societies represented an ideal method of ecclesial involvement for Anglicans.[22] Spurred on by competition presented by the Evangelical Church Missionary Society (est. 1799) and the British Foreign Bible Society (est. 1804), the early nineteenth century was a period of concentrated High Church involvement in various Church-related societies.[23] Thus the phalanx's members—especially Norris and Watson—played founding roles in the creation of the National Society for Promoting the Education of the Poor (est. 1811), the Incorporated Church Building Society (est. 1818), and the Church Building Commission (est. 1818), in addition to reforming and expanding the SPCK and the SPG.[24]

High Churchmen, especially the Hackney Phalanx, prospered during the Tory premiership of Lord Liverpool (1812–27) and while Charles Manners-Sutton (1755–1828) was archbishop of Canterbury. High Churchmen were close to Liverpool; his patronage in favour of the old and new Church societies being evident on numerous occasions.[25] Liverpool, however, was no patsy; he is known to have acted according to his own desire to see appropriate candidates elevated to the episcopal bench and he consulted accordingly.[26] A number of High Churchmen were given episcopal preferment under Liverpool, notably: George Pretyman Tomline (1750–1827), bishop of Winchester; Robert Grey (1762–1834), bishop of Bristol; William Van Mildert (1765–1836), bishop of Durham; William Howley (1766–1848), archbishop of Canterbury; William Carey (1769–1846), bishop of St Asaph; Thomas Fanshaw Middleton (1769–1822), bishop of Calcutta; Christopher Bethell (1773–1859), bishop of Gloucester (later transferred by the Duke of Wellington to the sees of Exeter then Bangor); Charles Lloyd (1784–1829), bishop of Oxford; and Charles James Blomfield (1786–1857), bishop of Chester and, later, bishop of London.[27]

In 1827 Liverpool suffered a stroke, sending his government into disarray. The following year, overseen by a succeeding Tory administration, the Test and Corporation Acts were repealed, admitting Nonconformists to officially share in an equal place in civil life. Similarly, in 1829 Roman Catholics were granted the same privilege. Parliament, which for centuries had been a sort of Anglican 'lay synod', was now officially a mixed body in terms of religious

[22] Robert Nelson, *A Companion for the Festivals and Fasts of the Church of England* (London, 1704), pp. ix–xii.

[23] Stewart J. Brown, *The National Churches of England, Ireland, and Scotland 1801–46* (Oxford, 2001), pp. 57–9; Gareth Atkins, 'Wilberforce and his Milieux: The Worlds of Anglican Evangelicalism, c.1780–1830', PhD thesis, University of Cambridge, 2009, pp. 73–96.

[24] Webster, *Joshua Watson*, chs. 3, 5, 9, 10.

[25] Churton, *Memoir*, pp. 77, 102, 112, 123; Webster, *Joshua Watson*, pp. 25–6, 52, 54, 61–6, 118.

[26] James Garrard, *Archbishop Howley, 1828–1848* (Farnham, 2015), pp. 9–11, 22–3, 35; Webster, *Joshua Watson*, p. 25; Atkins, 'Wilberforce and his Milieux', p. 85.

[27] Clive Dewey, *The Passing of Barchester* (London, 1991), pp. 151–66.

confessions. High Churchmen bitterly opposed these developments as betrayals of Britain's Protestant constitution.[28] Yet worse seemed on the horizon. Calls for widespread Church reform, which had gathered pace in the late 1820s, became a reality in 1830 when Tory rule was replaced by a reformist Whig government. If High Church opposition to the end of the confessional state now seems archaic—a defence of an outdated *ancien régime*—it needs to be kept in mind that the rapid pace of change, coupled with the possibility of far-reaching and expansive Church reform, only confirmed a genuine High Church fear of reform to be nothing more than, in the words of Edward Churton, 'a cloak for the designs of spoliation'.[29]

High Churchmen were not opposed to all reform, however. In 1831, in a pre-emptive move, Joshua Watson drew up his own draft proposal of what a 'Royal Commission of Enquiry' into the state of the Church could look like and achieve. His modest and conservative proposal for reform, to be undertaken exclusively by the clergy, was sent to the prime minister, but was rejected.[30] The new Whig government as a result of the 1832 Reform Act was not going to allow the clergy to reform the Church themselves. Nonetheless, Watson's proposal was a significant shift from one who, only a few years earlier, had enjoyed the patronage of the state. Now the state, once the friend of High Churchmen, was being kept at arm's length.

In the face of mounting attacks upon the established United Church of England and Ireland, seen most notably in John Wade's *Extraordinary Black Book* (1831), High Churchmen defended the Church in its existing state.[31] The fierceness of the attacks—some of which resulted in the physical intimidation of clergy—cornered them, to a large extent, into that position.[32] In 1832 the archbishop of Canterbury, William Howley, noted in his charge that the Church had already achieved substantial reforms on its own. Citing the recent revitalization of the old Church societies and the creation new ones, for which the Hackney Phalanx could claim much of the credit, Howley defended his Church as already possessing a reforming spirit, in addition to cautioning against drastic reforms.[33] There were, in his view, reasons to be positive.

> I am persuaded... that a general survey of the beneficial agency of the National Church, on the fair principle of comparison, not with models of ideal perfection, which have no existence in reality, but with the same Church at former periods,

[28] Brown, *The National Churches of England, Ireland, and Scotland*, pp. 140–5; G. F. A. Best, *Temporal Pillars: Queen Anne's Bounty, The Ecclesiastical Commissioners and the Church of England* (Cambridge, 1964), pp. 270–1.

[29] Churton, *Memoir*, p. 193; Best, *Temporal Pillars*, pp. 272–3; Garrard, *Archbishop Howley*, pp. 23–4, 45.

[30] The entire plan is reprinted in Churton, *Memoir*, pp. 191–2.

[31] See John Wade, *The Extraordinary Black Book* (London, 1831).

[32] Best, *Temporal Pillars*, p. 271; Garrard, *Archbishop Howley*, p. 45.

[33] *British Critic*, 13 (1833), pp. 214–22.

> when it was the pride and boast of the country, would produce a result very greatly in favour of the present Clergy.[34]

Howley's charge, as a historical source signifying High Church participation in the late Georgian 'impulse to reform', deserves to be taken seriously.[35] The Church of England, though far from perfect, had shown in the decades leading up to the 1830s that it could introduce reforms. Moreover, High Churchmen had taken a lead in this process. The reform of existing structures not only appealed to their innate conservatism, it played to the High Church strength of being able to work productively within the confines of the Established Churches of England and Ireland, especially in cooperation with the episcopate.[36]

Whatever the faults of the confessional state may have been, a majority of High Churchmen were committed to the defence of it whilst it existed. Added to this was a genuine fear of the consequences of reform, especially when fuelled by a recently enfranchised populace. It goes without saying that High Churchmen were, to say the least, deeply sceptical of the motives of liberal reformers, whom they thought represented a political philosophy one step away from revolution. The memory of what had happened in France only decades earlier lingered as they awaited what might happen at home.[37] Thus Howley, in the charge previously quoted, hinted at what he perceived to be the coming storm.

> I am far from insensible to the dangers which threaten our Establishment, nor can I view the position in which we are placed without serious concern and apprehension. In the Sister Island a plan has been organized for the subversion of the Irish branch of our Church by the general spoliation of its property; and, humanly speaking, nothing short of determined support on the part of the Government can preserve it from utter ruin.[38]

Thomas Arnold's oft-quoted statement, that 'The Church, as it now stands, no human power can save', had been made privately only a few months earlier.[39] Arnold's diagnosis and solution to the Church's problems was to seek reforms in the hope that it could emerge as a stronger institution. '[E]very year of delayed reform strengthens those who wish not to amend, but to destroy', he wrote in 1831.[40] Yet notwithstanding Joshua Watson's early attempt to allow

[34] *British Critic*, 13 (1833), p. 216.

[35] Gregory, *Restoration, Reformation, and Reform*, pp. 68, 285.

[36] Arthur Burns, *The Diocesan Revival in the Church of England c.1800–1870* (Oxford, 1999), pp. 18–19.

[37] Garrard, *Archbishop Howley*, pp. 23–4.

[38] *British Critic*, 13 (1833), p. 219.

[39] Thomas Arnold to J. E. Tyler, 10 June 1832, in Arthur Penrhyn Stanley, *The Life and Correspondence of Thomas Arnold, D.D.* (London, 1844 edn.), I, pp. 315–17.

[40] Arnold to Chevalier Hunsen, 20 March 1831, in Stanley, *The Life and Correspondence of Thomas Arnold*, p. 290.

the Church to direct its own reform, most High Churchmen, at least initially, bunkered down and opposed reform in the fear that the present danger to the Church was too great to do anything other than protect what already existed.[41]

On 1 March 1833 an article entitled 'Church Reform' appeared in the new High Church journal, the *British Magazine*.[42] Such was the writer's fears for the Church that the article contemplated the possibility of disestablishment, 'to excommunicate, as it were, the civil government' and to prepare the clergy and laity 'for a time when it may be necessary for them to chuse [*sic*] between separation and virtual apostasy, that they may not think all will be lost, when they are as Christians were in the time before Constantine'.[43] According to John William Burgon, the author of this article (who signed his name as 'K') was John Keble (1792–1866), the popular poet and fellow of Oriel College, Oxford.[44] The main issue prompting Keble's attention at that time—as it was for most High Churchmen—was the proposed reform being formulated for the Church of Ireland. Howley had already publicly warned about this the previous year. By 1833, however, High Church angst—one may even say, panic—had become frantic.[45] Keble would, more famously, make his views public on 14 July 1833 in a sermon—'National Apostasy'—that has since been mythologized in Anglican history.[46] Yet this sermon was only one of a number of voices articulating the fears of High Churchmen regarding ecclesiastical reform at the time.[47] What became the Irish Church Temporalities Act on 14 August 1833 reorganized the Church of Ireland by, among other things, reducing the number of bishops by almost half. The changes for High Churchmen had, in the words of Geoffrey Best, 'scared them stiff'.[48] With major reforms to the Church of England looming, the details of which they were not privy to, a new phase of High Church activism began to defend the Church of England.

The founding of the *British Magazine* can be interpreted as a shift in the history of the nineteenth-century High Church.[49] Up until this time, the ageing—albeit still influential and active—figures of the Hackney Phalanx, centred in London, had dominated High Church activism. Now a new and younger generation had emerged. Some of these had social and ideological connections with the traditional High Church movement, whilst others were of a different cast altogether. The *British Magazine* had been founded in 1832

[41] Dewey, *The Passing of Barchester*, pp. 31–2.

[42] *British Magazine*, 3 (1833), pp. 360–78.

[43] *British Magazine*, 3 (1833), p. 377.

[44] John William Burgon, *Lives of Twelve Good Men* (London, 1891), p. 86.

[45] Best, *Temporal Pillars*, pp. 278, 293–4.

[46] John Keble, *National Apostasy Considered in a Sermon Preached in St. Mary's, Oxford* (Oxford, 1833).

[47] Best, *Temporal Pillars*, pp. 273–4.

[48] Best, *Temporal Pillars*, p. 293.

[49] William Palmer, *A Narrative of Events Connected with the Publication of the Tracts for the Times* (Oxford, 1843), p. 5; Churton, *Memoir*, p. 193.

by Hugh James Rose (1795–1838), a young Cambridge graduate who, by the early 1830s, had established himself as a vocal High Church activist. Though a Cambridge man, Rose had come into alliance with a number of up-and-coming Oxford divines. These were, initially: Keble, William Palmer of Worcester College (1803–85), John Henry Newman (1801–90), Richard Hurrell Froude (1803–36), and Arthur Philip Perceval (1799–1853). Though they were all High Churchmen and, for the most part, ideologically united, this new group was nonetheless an eclectic body of men—its various factions already pointing to future divisions. Thus Rose, Palmer, and Perceval (later a Tractarian) were solidly at one with the ways and means of the Hackney Phalanx, whilst the likes of Newman (once an Evangelical) and Froude had already shown signs that they were going to be less willing to conform to the traditions of their elders in London, even if they would attempt to court their patronage. Keble may be said to have been somewhere in the middle. His background was solidly High Church, but he sided more with the radical camp of Newman and Froude than with the High Churchmanship of Rose, Palmer, and Perceval.[50]

Of these men, Rose stood out as a leader.[51] Had his health been more robust, it is highly likely he would have become one of the influential High Churchmen of the Victorian age.[52] As it was, he played a comparatively undervalued but significant role during the crisis years following 1828. Many years later, Newman painted an image of Rose as an intellectual powerhouse and commanding figure of influence. There was clearly something of the Romantic hero in Rose,[53] at least for Newman—someone to rally around in defence of the Established Church during a time of crisis.

> He [Rose] was the man above all others fitted by his cast of mind and literary powers to make a stand, if a stand could be made, against the calamity of the times. He was gifted with a high and large mind, and a true sensibility of what was great and beautiful; he wrote with warmth and energy; and he had a cool head and cautious judgment. He spent his strength and shortened his life, Pro Ecclesia Dei, as he understood that sovereign idea.[54]

[50] Simon A. Skinner, *Tractarians and the 'Condition of England': The Social and Political Thought of the Oxford Movement* (Oxford, 2004), p. 38 n. 40; Frank M. Turner, *John Henry Newman: The Challenge to Evangelical Religion* (New Haven, CT, 2002), p. 164.

[51] Churton, *Memoir*, p. 193; Burgon, *Lives of Twelve Good Men*, pp. 83–4; Jörg Manfred Gereon Mosig, 'The Birth Pangs of Neo-Protestantism: Hugh James Rose, Ernst Hengstenberg and the Conservative Response to German Rationalism', PhD thesis, Durham University, 2000, pp. 116–17.

[52] Churton, *Memoir*, p. 193; Mosig, 'The Birth Pangs of Neo-Protestantism', pp. 104–5, 108–9.

[53] Maurice Cranston, *The Romantic Movement* (Oxford, 1994), p. 17.

[54] John Henry Newman, *Apologia Pro Vita Sua & Six Sermons* (New Haven, CT, 2008 edn.), p. 164.

It was at Rose's rectory at Hadleigh, Suffolk, that Rose hosted Palmer, Perceval, and Froude, to confer on possible future activism in response to the Irish Church Temporalities Act and in view of looming reforms to their own Church.[55] The meeting occurred only a few weeks after Keble's sermon on 'National Apostasy'. It lasted almost a week, and though no firm plans were made two goals were agreed upon, namely: 'the necessity of some mode of combined action, and the expediency of circulating tracts or publications of ecclesiastical subjects'.[56] In making this joint decision, there was an almost immediate division among those who promoted the organizational course of action (Rose and Palmer), and those who promoted the publication of tracts authored by individuals (Froude). It was from here that the seeds of future division—already present but suppressed for the sake of outward unity—were sown.

Regarding 'combined action', an 'Association of Friends of the Church' was formed, though it was never established along anything more than informal lines. The aims of the society were briefly stated in a draft formulary that was privately circulated in the autumn of 1833:

1. To maintain pure and inviolate the doctrines, the services, and the discipline of the Church; that is, to withstand all change, which involves the denial or suppression of doctrine, a departure from primitive practice in religious offices, or innovation upon the Apostolical prerogative, order, and commission of bishops, priests, and deacons.
2. To afford Churchmen an opportunity of exchanging their sentiments, and co-operating together on a large scale.[57]

Though it was never a long-term success, the Association of Friends of the Church nonetheless produced a groundswell of High Church activism, both at national and local levels. In rapid time, informal subcommittees were created at London, Bath, Ripon, Cheltenham, and Winchester. Other places with groups of interested clergy and laity included Coventry and London, the latter being important because of its links to the Hackney Phalanx.[58]

It was the liturgical scholar Palmer of Worcester College who became the most active in organizing and promoting the aims of the association. Indeed, Palmer's leadership of the association signified the divisions previously mentioned. Newman's later critical assessment of Palmer's ability and preference for traditional High Church activism illustrates the difference between the two groups.

[55] Palmer, *A Narrative of Events*, p. 6; Burgon, *Lives of Twelve Good Men*, p. 93.
[56] Palmer, *A Narrative of Events*, p. 6.
[57] Quoted in Palmer, *A Narrative of Events*, p. 9.
[58] Palmer, *A Narrative of Events*, p. 10.

> Mr. Palmer had a certain connexion, as it may be called, in the Establishment, consisting of high Church dignitaries, Archdeacons, London Rectors, and the like, who belonged to what was commonly called the high-and-dry school. They were far more opposed than even he was to the irresponsible action of individuals. Of course their *beau idéal* in ecclesiastical action was a board of safe, sound, sensible men. Mr. Palmer was their organ and representative; and he wished for a Committee, an Association, with rules and meetings, to protect the interests of the Church in its existing peril.[59]

If, for Newman, the High Churchmen were 'high-and-dry', for Froude they were 'Z's' or 'pampered aristocrats', unprepared for the present tribulation—stuck as they were in the ways and means of a bygone age.[60] However, Newman's notion that 'Living movements do not come of committees',[61] may have sounded persuasive to his fellow idealists, as it continues to be for Newman's many contemporary hagiographers.[62] But on a practical level the more traditional High Churchmen had more than enough precedent for advocating the creation of an association, even if this one never formally established itself along the lines of the other High Church societies that arose in the 1810s and 1820s. Their processes and outcomes may have lacked the radical Romantic individuality and passion that drove Newman, Froude, and Keble, but the 'society model' was not only a natural High Church fit, a natural complement to their ecclesiology, it had been a very successful avenue for High Church activism in the recent past.

The activities of the Association of Friends of the Church illustrate a neglected side to the events of 1833, demonstrating not only the widespread diffusion of High Church principles, but also dispelling the false notion that traditional High Churchmen had been unable—unlike the Tractarians—to respond to the crisis of Church and state from 1828 to 1833. It has, for example, been claimed by a number of writers that the Hackney Phalanx had 'run out of steam' by the 1830s, thus passing the baton of activism to the Tractarians.[63] This mistaken notion not only results in an implicit underestimation of the divergent but influential High Church activism of Rose and Palmer (also a part of the Oxford Movement, if not the Tractarian Movement), it fails to take into account Palmer's frequent contact and cooperation with the Hackney Phalanx before, during, and after the crisis of 1833.[64] This

[59] Newman, *Apologia Pro Vita Sua & Six Sermons*, pp. 166–7 (emphasis in original).

[60] Nockles, *Oxford Movement in Context*, pp. 20, 186–7.

[61] Newman, *Apologia Pro Vita Sua & Six Sermons*, p. 166.

[62] See Simon A. Skinner, 'History versus Hagiography: The Reception of Turner's Newman', *Journal of Ecclesiastical History*, 61 (2010): 764–81.

[63] Webster, *Joshua Watson*, pp. 82–90; Nockles, *Oxford Movement in Context*, p. 325; James Pereiro, *'Ethos' and the Oxford Movement: At the Heart of Tractarianism* (Oxford, 2008), pp. 71–2.

[64] Palmer, *A Narrative of Events*, pp. 10–16; Churton, *Memoir*, pp. 203–4.

can be seen in one of the major achievements of the Association of Friends of the Church: namely, the clerical and lay declarations presented to the archbishop of Canterbury in 1834.

The clerical declaration, presented to Archbishop Howley on 6 February, contained the signatures of at least 6,530 clergy (perhaps as many as 7,000).[65] Its contents can be said to have been conciliatory and supportive in nature, mindful of the Church of England as it existed in its established state, but also declarative of the emphasis upon the apostolic nature of the Church that traditional High Churchmen shared with the Tractarians. It opposed any form of doctrinal and liturgical change but noted an openness to support and cooperate with prudent reform, if such reform was shown to be needed.[66] Similarly, the lay declaration—presented to the archbishop in May—defended the 'pure faith and worship, and . . . apostolic form of government' of the Church of England, but spent more time expressing support for preserving the Church as it existed in its established form.[67] The lay declaration was overseen by a London-based committee, which gathered and collated around 230,000 signatures.[68] Palmer of Worcester College was influential in the drafting and organization of both declarations, but the stalwart of the Hackney Phalanx, Joshua Watson, still one of the most powerful and influential laymen in England, also played an important role. Not only was he regarded as the main author of the lay declaration, Edward Churton, contrary to the claims of Palmer, argued that it was at Watson's home that the clerical address received its final form.[69] So this influential group of High Churchmen had not only acted to defend the Church, they had helped uncover a groundswell of latent High Churchmanship in England. Indeed, one can extend this claim beyond Britain by noting the similar declaration presented to the king by the Church of Ireland.[70]

John Henry Burgon's claim, made in 1888, that '*Church feeling was* EVOKED, *not* CREATED, *by the Movement of* 1833' can be argued as being a correct assessment of the period from 1833 to 1834.[71] But as Burgon additionally argued, the Oxford Movement contained a significant, if underappreciated, High Church element. There was indeed an Oxford Movement, but it did not only emerge from within the common room of Oriel College. Moreover, compared to High Church theology, the churchmanship of Newman, Froude, and Keble was idealistic and lacked grounding in the practicalities of the Church's position as a national and established entity.[72] Their spirituality may have possessed more of a radical Romantic and

[65] Palmer, *A Narrative of Events*, p. 96.
[66] Palmer, *A Narrative of Events*, p. 96.
[67] Palmer, *A Narrative of Events*, pp. 14–15.
[68] Palmer, *A Narrative of Events*, p. 15.
[69] Palmer, *A Narrative of Events*, p. 14; Churton, *Memoir*, pp. 206, 208.
[70] See Palmer, *A Narrative of Events*, pp. 110–12.
[71] Burgon, *Lives of Twelve Good Men*, pp. 153–4 (punctuation in original).
[72] Nockles, *Oxford Movement in Context*, pp. 86–90.

emotional character when compared to classical High Church piety, but even this aspect of Tractarianism has been exaggerated. The Romantic poets William Wordsworth (1770–1850) and Robert Southey (1774–1843) were an active part of the Hackney Phalanx—both adding a Romantic element to an already rich tradition of High Church lay piety.[73] Wordsworth's *Ecclesiastical Sketches* (1822) and Southey's *The Book of the Church* (1824) were notable examples of how these two devout laymen infused their Romantic ethos with the more restrained High Church piety of the phalanx. It is no accident that Keble's *The Christian Year* (1827) met with such a receptive and widespread audience when it was published in 1827, or that Edward Churton could declare Hugh James Rose to have been 'a devout disciple of... Wordsworth'.[74]

Differences aside, Palmer, Rose, and the Hackney Phalanx nonetheless began a genuine, if somewhat uncomfortable, cooperation with the Tractarians in the mid-1830s. There was doubtless much sympathy for the ideals of the Tractarians, even if their means of action was not seen as prudent. Newman and Keble, for example, were held in esteem. Joshua Watson, echoing the sentiments of many nineteenth-century observers, had a high degree of respect for Newman, recognizing his theological and homiletic talent. However, High Churchmen reacted to the *Tracts for the Times* 'with interest, with much sympathy, but with no little anxiety'.[75] While the Tractarians promoted High Church principles, the *Tracts for the Times* were publicly defended by High Churchmen, even if they privately expressed reservations about some of the theological ideas developing out of the movement. Of course, some High Churchmen were influenced by the theology of the *Tracts* more than others. Indeed, a generation of High Churchmen can be said to have imbued a Tractarian spirit, even if their own churchmanship remained traditionally High Church in identity. Thus the names of William Grant Broughton (1788–1853), Walter Farquhar Hook (1798–1875), Henry Edward Manning (1808–92), and George Augustus Selwyn (1809–78), all of whom have sometimes been regarded as Tractarians, should more accurately be labelled as High Churchmen influenced by Tractarianism.[76]

It would take a number of years before the controversies surrounding the constitutional revolution of 1828–32 and the crisis of 1833 settled down. Notwithstanding the events related to the growing radicalism of Tractarian theology—most notably, the 1837 publication of the late Hurrell Froude's *Remains* and Newman's secession to the Roman Catholic Church in 1845,

[73] Churton, *Memoir*, pp. 215–16, also 3, 178–9, 218–19; Brown, *The National Churches of England, Ireland, and Scotland*, pp. 83–5.

[74] Churton, *Memoir*, p. 173.

[75] W. R. W. Stephens, *The Life and Letters of Walter Farquhar Hook* (London, 1881 edn.), pp. 112–13.

[76] Rowan Strong, 'Review of James Pereiro, "*Ethos*" *and the Oxford Movement*', *Church History*, 78 (2009), p. 229.

High Churchmen adapted to the less eminent place of the national Church in the English constitution. Some did this with more willingness than others, and it took time for the realities of ecclesial life in the post-reform era to be fully accepted. In fairness, Peel's Ecclesiastical Commission of 1835 was, compared to the Irish Church Temporalities Act, a political process that was largely consultative and less traumatic than had been expected in the early 1830s.[77] Under the quiet and unassuming primacy of William Howley, whose commitment to reform during the mid-1830s has been recently shown to be far more effective than has previously been granted,[78] the success of the commission was also helped by a number of other High Church bishops who were conspicuous in supporting its reformist agenda. Aside from Howley were Charles James Blomfield of London (1786–1857), John Kaye of Lincoln (1783–1853), and James Henry Monk of Gloucester (1784–1856). Strengthened by the Pluralities Act of 1838, they represented a new interventionist episcopate. Furnished with greater powers of diocesan governance and discipline they cooperated with the reformist agenda of Peel's government.[79]

In adapting to the most significant legislative changes to the Church of England's governance and structure since the Reformation, one can discern a move by High Churchmen away from the highly ideological political theology that underpinned pre-reform apologies of the establishment, to a more pragmatic conception of the benefits of keeping the Church in connection with the state.[80] A few defining events marked the development of this post-reform evolution in High Church identity. The first was the so-called 'Maynooth Affair'. This was the opposition among English Protestants—including High Churchmen—to Peel's decision to increase the annual grant for the Roman Catholic seminary at Maynooth, Dublin, from £9,000—a sum first granted in 1795—to the much larger £26,360, in addition to making it a permanent endowment, rather than a grant to be renewed annually. Enacted on 4 February 1845, this move was seen by some High Churchmen—most notably Palmer of Worcester College and Christopher Wordsworth Jr (1807–85)—as the state officially encouraging an ecclesial system mired in theological error. However, other High Churchmen did not oppose the Maynooth reforms—evidence that they had begun to recognize that the old relationship between Church and state had changed. These included Hook, the energetic vicar of Leeds, and the younger phalanx loyalist, Edward Churton (1800–74), a former curate of Hackney, no less.[81] Though not disowning a sense of sacralism in the relationship between Church and state, a certain level of pragmatism and

[77] Best, *Temporal Pillars*, pp. 296–8.
[78] Garrard, *Archbishop Howley.*
[79] Knight, *The Nineteenth Century Church*, pp. 153–4.
[80] Simon A. Skinner, *Tractarians and the 'Condition of England': The Social and Political Thought of the Oxford Movement* (Oxford, 2004), pp. 93–6.
[81] Nockles, *Oxford Movement in Context*, pp. 90–3.

adjustment had become a part of how High Churchmen adapted to a post-reform England.

Following the Maynooth affair came the controversy surrounding the Evangelical clergyman, George Cornelius Gorham (1787–1857), who doubted the general High Church belief that regeneration always accompanied the baptism of an infant. Refused a living by the High Church bishop of Exeter, Henry Phillpotts (1778–1869), because of his sacramental view, Gorham took his case firstly to the Court of Arches (a Church court which found against him), and then to the (secular) Judicial Committee of the Privy Council, which declared that the Evangelical position could be held by clergy of the Church of England.[82] The results of what became known as the 'Gorham Judgment' were immense for both High Churchmen and Tractarians, and much controversy followed the decision. If it had been possible for High Churchmen to believe in a pre-1832 political theology up until this time, Gorham's case had made it almost impossible afterwards. The royal supremacy had gone too far, the result of which saw High Churchmen shifting towards an ecclesiological position that placed less emphasis on sacral royalism. Even Palmer of Worcester College admitted that the royal supremacy was no longer as it had been 'in the time of Elizabeth or James'.[83] This was not evidence of a latent Tractarianism, however, but a restatement of the High Church view that had a strong tradition of asserting that the Church had an identity independent of the state. So traditional High Churchmen had, by the middle of the nineteenth century, found some common ground with moderate Tractarians on this issue.[84]

In the words of Frances Knight, the nineteenth century witnessed the transition of the Church of England from 'national Church to denomination'.[85] Though this process was difficult for High Churchmen, it would be a mistake to view the history of High Churchmanship during the nineteenth century solely through the prism of its turbulent relationship with the political events previously discussed. Indeed, in England a largely High Church phenomenon of 'diocesan revival'—a phenomenon elucidated by the scholarship of Arthur Burns—has been shown to have been prominent within Church life from the 1820s through to the 1870s. By 'diocesan revival' Burns meant a renewal of the Church of England's existing diocesan structures, some of which had lain dormant. Importantly, the diocesan revival began as a pre-reform phenomenon, predating and transcending the parliamentary-led—and centralized—reforms that emanated from Westminster, such as the Ecclesiastical Commission. Characteristics of the diocesan revival included a reformed,

[82] John Wolffe, 'Gorham, George Cornelius', *ODNB*.

[83] Quoted in Nockles, *Oxford Movement in Context*, pp. 100–1.

[84] Nockles, *Oxford Movement in Context*, pp. 63–7, 101–3.

[85] Knight, *Nineteenth Century Church and English Society*, p. 201.

renewed, and expanded episcopate—exemplified by High Church bishops such as Phillpotts, Blomfield, and Kaye, whilst their episcopal office was supported by a similarly reformed and renewed archdiaconate. Other aspects of the diocesan revival included the reactivation of the office of rural dean and ruridecanal chapters, the revival of diocesan assemblies, and the incorporation of Church societies into a closer relationship with diocesan functions.[86] A key characteristic of the revival was the centrality and prominence of High Church participation which was fundamental to its effectiveness.[87] Not only does this development provide more evidence of the wide diffusion of High Churchmanship throughout England, but more often than not High Churchmen were able to show that their high view of the episcopal office translated into actual cooperation with diocesan ordinaries. The caricature of the Tractarian exaltation of episcopacy as meaning, in practice, that: 'I will do nothing without you; but mind this only holds as long as you and I agree',[88] was not a defining attribute of High Church activism.

The phenomenon of the diocesan revival and its High Church involvement highlights the fact that the Church of England continued, throughout the nineteenth century, to cater for a large proportion of the English population (one in four by the middle of the century). Moreover, even if the concept of churchmanship may have mattered less to the laity than it did to the clergy, the public received the benefits of numerous pastoral initiatives in which High Churchmen were involved.[89] The campaign for better theological training for ordinands, for example, though often attributed mainly to the influence of Tractarianism, also had significant High Church participation.[90] Additionally, the effectiveness of parochial ministry was boosted by the formation of the Additional Curates Society (ACS). Once again, the influence of Joshua Watson continued to make its mark upon the Church. The ACS was a High Church response to the Evangelical Church Pastoral Aid Society. The ACS constitution, drawn up by Watson, reflected its High Church principles. '[N]o application for aid can be received by the Committee but through the bishop of the diocese.'[91] It emphasized the need to cooperate with the episcopate and again illustrating how voluntary service in Anglican societies appealed to High Churchmen. By 1851, 323 curates were being aided by a society with an annual income of £19,000.[92]

One parochial ministry that the ACS assisted was that of Walter Farquhar Hook. Hook represents one of the outstanding examples of Anglican parochial

[86] Burns, *Diocesan Revival*, chs. 1–5.
[87] Burns, *Diocesan Revival*, pp. 18–22, 71–2, 261–2.
[88] Quoted in Burns, *Diocesan Revival*, p. 33.
[89] Knight, *Nineteenth Century Church and English Society*, pp. 209–10.
[90] Andrews, *Lay Activism*, p. 32.
[91] Quoted in Webster, *Joshua Watson*, p. 75.
[92] Webster, *Joshua Watson*, pp. 74–5.

ministry in the nineteenth century.[93] Though an early supporter of the Oxford Movement and the *Tracts for the Times*, Hook always remained a High Churchman. It was, however, the merging of his High Church views with a fervent dedication to parochial ministry—especially towards the working classes—that would distinguish Hook's contribution to nineteenth-century Anglicanism. Hook's vocation preceded the Oxford Movement, in his early ministries in Birmingham and Coventry during the 1820s. It was his appointment as vicar of Leeds—a post he held for over two decades from 1837 to 1859—that Hook made his mark, advancing the reputation of the Church of England in the growing urban centres, where Nonconformity was dominant. Hook worked tirelessly to overcome prejudice against both the Established Church and perceptions that his theology—with its Tractarian influences—had Roman Catholic tendencies. He succeeded, placing 'Church principles' at the forefront of his ministry, though combining this with a pastoral dedication that was mission-like in its dedication and intensity.[94] Though reputed to be a good preacher, it was the sacraments—especially the eucharist—that were central to Hook's ministry. 'I am most anxious', Hook wrote publicly in 1844, 'to secure for my poorer brethren the privileges of a free and unrestricted participation in the sacraments and ordinances of our holy Church.' Critical of the way in which he thought the national Church had too often privileged the 'wealthy and middle classes', Hook thought the parochial system needed to take in a wider social embrace, so that 'each poor man feels that he has as much right to take his place' within the Established Church.[95] When Hook left Leeds in 1859 to become dean of Chichester, he had doubled the number of churches and created twenty-nine schools. Moreover, such had been the growth of his parish that in 1844 it had been divided into four parishes by an act of parliamentary legislation.[96]

Hook's ministry is further evidence that traditional High Church principles could adapt to post-reform Anglicanism. Accepting the end of the confessional state, Hook nonetheless never wavered in his support for the Established Church and its place in English society. Though initially partial to Tractarianism, Hook—along with most High Churchmen—later perceived Tractarianism to have been overtaken by theological principles that could not be defended as being compatible with Anglicanism's Protestant character.[97] But Hook's High

[93] William L. Sachs, *The Transformation of Anglicanism: From State Church to Global Communion* (Cambridge, 1993), pp. 103–5; Harry W. Dalton, *Anglican Resurgence under W. F. Hook in Early Victorian Leeds: Church Life in a Nonconformist Town, 1836–1851* (Leeds, 2002), p. 1.

[94] 'Walter Farquhar Hook', *ODNB*; Sachs, *The Transformation of Anglicanism*, pp. 103–5.

[95] Quoted in Stephens, *The Life and Letters of Walter Farquhar Hook*, pp. 381–2.

[96] Dalton, *Anglican Resurgence*, pp. 102–3.

[97] Hook, *Our Holy and Our Beautiful House*, p. 22; Dalton, *Anglican Resurgence*, pp. 1–5, 114–16.

Churchmanship should not be viewed simply in its relationship to Tractrianism. It had its own internal vitality—in the words of William Sachs, a 'quixotic mixture of Evangelical and High Church piety'[98] that had a pioneering character in the development of Anglicanism into a religious tradition capable of adapting to the urban, demographic, social, and political changes of the nineteenth century.

As has been noted earlier, by the turn of the nineteenth century Anglicanism had a number of non-English High Church identities. Ireland was obviously one of these, even if their connections to the establishment meant that Irish High Churchmen shared to a large extent in the turbulent narrative related to the constitutional revolution and the Oxford Movement. There were other connections with English High Churchmanship, however. The previously discussed phenomenon of the diocesan revival had a similar—if smaller—corresponding movement in Ireland.[99] However, a major High Church influence within the Church of Ireland never materialized in the nineteenth century. By the middle of the century Irish High Churchmen were a clear minority, assailed within by Protestant Low Churchmanship and, to a lesser extent, Tractarianism. Combined with confident Roman Catholic critiques of High Church ecclesiology, Irish High Churchmanship, though still present among individuals such as Frederick Wynne (1827–96), bishop of Killaloe, or within the Irish Church Society (founded in 1866), had a declining influence within the Church of Ireland into the late nineteenth century. Disestablishment in 1869 only added to that decline.

The situation for High Churchmen in the Scottish Episcopal Church was very different. As has been noted, a dominant and renewed High Church tradition was present in the early nineteenth century, though by the middle of the century the High Church hegemony of Scottish Episcopalianism had been diluted by the presence of Tractarians and Evangelicals.[100] Though most Evangelicals existed as independent congregations outside of the native Scottish Church, the presence of Tractarians created tensions that were prominent during the second half of the nineteenth century. While the native Northern tradition of Scottish High Churchmanship continued into the nineteenth century, it was Southern Anglicized High Churchmanship, with its commitment to the English Book of Common Prayer and alliance with the Church of England, that played a more prominent role throughout the century. As Britain looked increasingly to England for inspiration and guidance, elements within Scottish Episcopalianism did as well. Conversely, English Anglicans of all types also looked to Scotland, seeing it as an area they could proselytize. In light of this, Scottish High Churchmanship had to

98 Sachs, *The Transformation of Anglicanism*, p. 104.
99 Brown, *The National Churches of England, Ireland, and Scotland*, pp. 77–8.
100 Strong, *Episcopalianism in Nineteenth-Century Scotland*, p. 29.

carefully delineate its history and theology from, on the one hand, Tractarians who romantically saw the Scottish Church as a sort of 'proto-Tractarian' entity, whilst similarly doing the same with Evangelicals, who saw High Churchmanship as nothing but a milder version of Tractarianism.[101] Nonetheless, though partisan debates and issues related to Anglican identity characterized nineteenth-century Scottish High Churchmanship, this small religious tradition, like its English counterpart, demonstrated an ability to adjust to the demographic changes, urbanization, and industrialization that, like England, had changed Scotland dramatically by the end of the nineteenth century.[102]

The context of nineteenth-century High Churchmanship is broadened further when its manifestation within the United States of America is taken into account. High Churchmanship within the Protestant Episcopal Church, along with Scotland, played an early role in the development of High Churchmanship as an ecclesial tradition that is not, fundamentally, English—or in the case of the United States, even British. The Episcopal Church shared a close history with the Scottish Episcopal Church and it is not surprising that High Churchmanship had become widespread and influential following the ministry of its first bishop, Samuel Seabury.[103] In addition to John Henry Hobart, already mentioned, other notable High Church figures were part of Hobart's milieu.[104] These included John Stark Ravenscroft (1772–1830), bishop of North Carolina, and Thomas Church Brownell (1779–1865), bishop of Connecticut and presiding bishop of the Episcopal Church from 1852 to his death.[105] As with Scotland, Tractarianism and the rise of Anglo-Catholicism created similar partisan disputes into the century.[106] Nonetheless, classical High Churchmanship continued as a movement into the late nineteenth century. John Henry Hopkins (1792–1868), for example, was prominent in delineating High Church principles from Tractarianism.[107] Additionally, as exemplified in the figure of John Williams (1817–99), bishop of Connecticut and presiding bishop in his final years, the Episcopal Church continued to produce adherents of what in the United States had become known as 'Connecticut Churchmanship' (after Seabury's first diocese), representing not only a classical High Church expression of Anglicanism, but like

[101] Peter B. Nockles, '"Our Brethren of the North": The Scottish Episcopal Church and the Oxford Movement', *Journal of Ecclesiastical History*, 47 (1996): 655–82; Strong, *Episcopalianism in Nineteenth-Century Scotland*, ch. 5.

[102] Strong, *Episcopalianism in Nineteenth-Century Scotland*, p. 311.

[103] Chorley, *Men and Movements in the American Episcopal Church*, pp. 137–40.

[104] Peter B. Nockles, 'The Oxford Movement and the United States', in Stewart J. Brown and Peter B. Nockles (eds.), *The Oxford Movement: Europe and the Wider World 1830–1930* (Cambridge, 2012), pp. 134–6.

[105] Chorley, *Men and Movements in the American Episcopal Church*, pp. 159–67.

[106] Nockles, 'The Oxford Movement and the United States', pp. 136–50.

[107] Nockles, 'The Oxford Movement and the United States', p. 146.

the Scottish tradition also showing the development of its own native identity.[108]

Within the British Empire, many of the first generation of colonial bishops consecrated by the Church of England for ministry in the colonies were High Churchmen with links to the Hackney Phalanx. For example, in Canada there was Charles Inglis (1734–1816) and later his son, John Inglis (1777–1850). It was in India, however, where High Churchmen most vigorously attempted to assert their vision of Anglicanism in the early nineteenth-century colonial sphere. There, the phalanx appointee, Thomas Fanshawe Middleton (1769–1822), the first bishop of Calcutta, with help from the SPG (which from 1814 had been in receipt of an annual parliamentary grant) and administrative help from High Churchmen in London—especially Joshua Watson—attempted to establish a High Church presence on the subcontinent.[109] Middleton's apparent initial success, which included the creation of a native seminary, Bishop's College, Calcutta (1820), was ineffective in terms of missionary outreach, mainly through cultural insensitivity on the part of the SPG missionaries.[110]

The High Church attempt to claim India ecclesiastically was one of the last gasps of the *ancien régime*, for the end of the confessional state by the 1830s obviously necessitated a change in imperial policy from all Anglicans. No longer could High Churchmen expect preferential treatment within Britain's colonies. Government grants to the SPG consequently quickly dried up, forcing the society to overspend its income into the late 1830s and to increasingly rely on voluntary donations.[111] Of course, the reformist governments of the 1830s did not immediately cease all support for colonial Anglican establishments and missions, but it did end the preferential treatment that the Church of England enjoyed abroad. Moreover, what official funding there was would be extended to all denominations.[112] Though another colonial bishopric, that of Australia, was created in 1836 with the consecration of the High Churchman, Broughton, it was clear the Church of England was going to have to adopt a more independent and vigorous campaign to address the pressing need for the spiritual care of Anglicans in the colonies. What was needed was a complete change in ecclesiastical policy—what Rowan Strong has termed a

[108] William Ford Nichols, *Memories Here and There of John Williams, D.D., L.L.D* (Hartford, CT, 1924), pp. 19–21.

[109] Hilary M. Carey, *God's Empire: Religion and the Colonialiam in the British World, c.1801–1908* (Cambridge, 2011), pp. 84–8; Robert M. Andrews, 'Joshua Watson and the Church Abroad: Lay Activism and the Administration of High Church Missions in the Early Nineteenth Century, 1814–1855', *International Bulletin of Missionary Research*, forthcoming.

[110] Robert Eric Frykenberg, *Christianity in India: From Beginnings to the Present* (Oxford, 2008), pp. 243–58.

[111] Webster, *Joshua Watson*, pp. 135–6; Andrew Porter, *Religion versus Empire? British Protestant Missionaries and Overseas Expansion, 1700–1914* (Manchester, 2004), p. 158.

[112] Carey, *God's Empire*, pp. 52–3.

'new Anglican imperial paradigm', which in practical terms meant a greater reliance on the Church of England's independence.[113] This received its embodiment in the establishment of the Colonial Bishoprics Fund (CBF) in 1841 and, in the same year, the enactment of the Colonial Bishoprics Act, which allowed for the creation of colonial sees. The CBF was a voluntary effort. Its future desire to fund the creation of a colonial episcopate was reliant upon the ability of Anglicans to draw upon their own resources. However, the motives behind the initiative did not appear out of nowhere. Voluntarism—clerical and lay—was a well-established phenomenon by the middle of the nineteenth century and, as the Church societies movement of the early nineteenth century attests, featured prominently within High Church activism. Led by the pragmatic High Church reformer Charles Blomfield, the CBF was due in part to High Church, Tractarian, and even Evangelical eagerness finally to make a lasting rectification of the Church's belated investment in the creation of colonial episcopal sees. This elevation in colonial awareness and activism, coupled with an increasing reliance upon the notion that Anglicanism had to sustain itself at a distance from the state, was in part a move foisted upon the Church by the political events of 1828–32; but it was, additionally, an attribute that had theological impetus from traditional High Church activism and theology.[114] A sense of independence from the state was, of course, encouraged by Tractarianism, but ecclesiological independence was also seen in High Church theology, and pragmatically given an emphasis in the high levels of voluntarism and charitable giving evident in High Churchmanship throughout the 1810s and 1820s.[115]

In his narrative of the creation of the worldwide Anglican Communion, William Sachs asserted that in the nineteenth century 'the Hackney concern to preserve a Church that was established and apostolic was eclipsed by the Oxford movement's contrast between apostolicity and establishment'.[116] Such a view—and views like it—remain ingrained in historical assumptions regarding the fortunes of the High Church movement in the nineteenth century. Even if the scholarship of historians such as F. C. Mather, Peter Nockles, and Arthur Burns has revised notions such as this by arguing for the persistence and vitality of High Churchmanship throughout the Georgian and Victorian periods, there remains an assumption that whatever vitality High Churchmanship may have shown in the first half of the nineteenth century, by the end the tradition had 'run out of steam',[117] or had been eclipsed

[113] Rowan Strong, *Anglicanism and the British Empire c.1700–1850* (Oxford, 2007), ch. 4.

[114] Strong, *Anglicanism and the British Empire*, pp. 216–17.

[115] Strong, *Anglicanism and the British Empire*, ch. 5.

[116] Sachs, *The Transformation of Anglicanism*, p. 147.

[117] See Nockles, *Oxford Movement in Context*, p. 325; Pereiro, *'Ethos' and the Oxford Movement*, pp. 71–2.

by Anglo-Catholicism, which appropriated the terminology of 'High Churchmanship' for itself. General histories of Anglicanism give the same impression.[118]

The narrative presented here questions such assumptions, at least up until the end of the nineteenth century. Throughout that century there were High Churchmen whose theological inheritance did not come from the *Tracts for the Times*, but who were heirs to a much older tradition—a tradition that was, of course, related in some theological principles, but which in other respects was an independent form of churchmanship that developed according to its own principles. Initially, these included a defence of what J. C. D. Clark has termed the 'confessional state'.[119] However, even within this paradigm, High Churchmen had shown they could both introduce new initiatives and reforms within the existing social and political framework. The renewal and creation of Anglican societies and High Church participation in the early diocesan revival were evidence of this. Of course, reform as enunciated by liberal political exponents scared them, sometimes in apocalyptic terms. Fearing the destruction of the Established Church they fought to preserve the status quo. Indeed, the centrality of the constitutional revolution to the direction of nineteenth-century High Church activism cannot be overstated. If, for the Tractarians, it created a rhetoric of disestablishment, for High Churchmen it prompted a defence of the Established Church and its place in the social welfare of the English nation. From the neglected attention to High Church participation in the Oxford Movement, to the renewed parochial ministry of Hook, High Churchmen were generally realists when it came to preserving the post-reform establishment and its place within English society, even if they were forced to adjust how their principles applied to the new order. In this sense the continuities in the face of change that was forced upon them from without deserve to be highlighted when considering the development of High Churchmanship after the 1830s.[120] If ideological adjustment and compromise was a part of this development, it demonstrated the adaptability of High Church principles rather than an obstinate adherence to an old paradigm. In this sense, the notion that the Oxford Movement and its 'contrast between apostolicity and establishment' represented a more appropriate theological paradigm to the post-1830s paradigm can be disputed. High Churchmen, with their ability to work within the existing system, rather than against it, were an important factor in the development of Anglicanism in the nineteenth century.

Yet even if the presence of High Churchmen up until the 1870s has been well established in a number of recent studies, after the 1870s the situation

[118] Aidan Nichols, *The Panther and the Hind: A Theological History of Anglicanism* (London, 1993), pp. 76–7, 174–5; Henry Chadwick (ed.), *Not Angels but Anglicans: A History of Christianity in the British Isles* (Norwich, 2000), chs. 22–30.

[119] J. C. D. Clark, *English Society: 1660–1832* (Cambridge, 2000 edn.), pp. 26–34.

[120] Strong, *Anglicanism and the British Empire*, pp. 216–18.

becomes patchy. Mostly this is due to a lack of studies that touch on the subject, but there is also the problem of changing terminology and the misunderstanding this produces. Given that the High Church label was overtaken by Anglo-Catholics, the meaning of High Churchmanship changed.[121] Some of the High Churchmen who lived after the 1870s included individuals already discussed in this chapter—notably, Palmer of Worcester College, George Anthony Denison,[122] the Church of Ireland bishop of Killaloe, Frederick Wynne, and the Episcopal bishop of Connecticut, John Williams. But there were others. John William Burgon (1813–88), author of the *Lives of Twelve Good Men* (1888), was an outspoken conservative advocate of High Church views.[123] Dean of Chichester from 1875 (succeeding Hook, no less), Burgon was especially scathing in his criticisms of the new 'High Churchmen', the Anglo-Catholics, especially those who attempted to revive medieval ceremonial, referring to that particular phenomenon as 'effete... of the earth, earthy, an unspiritual, an unwholesome, a mawkish, a wholly un-English thing'.[124] Another was the lay theologian and historian, John Wickham Legg (1843–1921), author of *English Church Life: From the Restoration to the Tractarian Movement* (1914), one of the first serious revisionist critiques of Anglo-Catholic historiography.[125] Yet notwithstanding these names, there is no question that even if High Churchmen continued to be present within Anglicanism up until the turn of the twentieth century, there is a sense that this generation was less visible than it had been. At the very least it had changed. For example, one can see within the rise of 'Central Churchmanship' figures who had many of the characteristics of High Churchmen, for example, Edward Harold Browne (1811–91), the successive bishop of Ely and Winchester.[126] Steering a middle course between Evangelicalism and Anglo-Catholicism, his example predates the rise of twentieth-century Central Churchmanship, whose exponents, having witnessed the nineteenth-century conflicts between Evangelicals and Anglo-Catholics, were more conscious of expressing a middle way between these two forms of churchmanship, rather than preserving the spirituality and theology of the Hackney Phalanx.[127] Yet even if by the turn of the twentieth century some High Churchmen felt a new label was needed to differentiate themselves from both Evangelicals

[121] Nockles, *Oxford Movement in Context*, pp. 34–5.

[122] Nockles, *Oxford Movement in Context*, pp. 39, 242; John Cardell Oliver, 'Archdeacon George Anthony Denison (1806–1896): A Georgian Churchman in Victorian Times', PhD thesis, Murdoch University, 2015.

[123] G. Martin Murphy, 'Burgon, John William', *ODNB*.

[124] Quoted in Francis Cruse, *A Few Facts and Testimonies Touching Ritualism* (London, 1874), p. 30.

[125] 'John Wickham Legg', *ODNB*.

[126] J. R. Garrard, 'Browne, Edward Harold', *ODNB*.

[127] Andrew Chandler and David Hein, *Archbishop Fisher, 1945–1961* (Farnham, 2012), p. 14.

and Anglo-Catholics,[128] High Churchmanship had nonetheless developed immensely from the late Georgian and Victorian periods. Not only had it become less easy to identify within a much more theologically diverse communion, its principles had changed. If at the beginning of the century High Churchmen had combined their theological and sacramental principles with a strong defence of the confessional state, by the Edwardian era their churchmanship no longer contained this element. To be a High Churchman in the early 1900s was to be a churchman who maintained a strong adherence to both the Reformed and Catholic elements of Anglicanism, holding both to be equal. It is to these individuals to whom the label 'High Church' has more of a historical resonance. The spirit of the Caroline Divines, if not the letter, continued to inspire Anglicans throughout Britain, the British Empire, and its former colonies.

SELECT BIBLIOGRAPHY

Andrews, Robert M., *Lay Activism and the High Church Movement of the Late Eighteenth Century: The Life and Thought of William Stevens* (Leiden, 2015).

Best, G. F. A., *Temporal Pillars: Queen Anne's Bounty, The Ecclesiastical Commissioners and the Church of England* (Cambridge, 1964).

Brown, Stewart J., *The National Churches of England, Ireland, and Scotland 1801–46* (Oxford, 2001).

Burns, Arthur, *The Diocesan Revival in the Church of England c.1800–1870* (Oxford, 1999).

Dalton, Harry W., *Anglican Resurgence under W. F. Hook in Early Victorian Leeds: Church Life in a Nonconformist Town, 1836–1851* (Leeds, 2002).

Dewey, Clive, *The Passing of Barchester* (London, 1991).

Garrard, James, *Archbishop Howley, 1828–1848* (Farnham, 2015).

Gregory, Jeremy, *Restoration, Reformation, and Reform, 1660–1828: Archbishops of Canterbury and Their Diocese* (Oxford, 2000).

Knight, Frances, *The Nineteenth-Century Church and English Society* (Cambridge, 1995).

Nockles, Peter B., *The Oxford Movement in Context: Anglican High Churchmanship 1760–1857* (Cambridge, 1994).

Sachs, William L., *The Transformation of Anglicanism: From State Church to Global Communion* (Cambridge, 1993).

Strong, Rowan, *Anglicanism and the British Empire c.1700–1850* (Oxford, 2007).

Strong, Rowan, *Episcopalianism in Nineteenth-Century Scotland: Religious Responses to a Modernizing Society* (Oxford, 2002).

Webster, A. B., *Joshua Watson: The Story of a Layman 1771–1855* (London, 1954).

[128] Owen Chadwick, *The Victorian Church*, Part II (London, 1972 edn.), p. 357.

8

Anglican Evangelicalism

Andrew Atherstone

Evangelicalism and Anglicanism are both contested global movements, with multiple identities which sometimes coalesce. This chapter examines the place of Evangelicals in the Church of England in the Victorian era. It does not narrate the plethora of their missional and philanthropic activities, nor their extensive and sometimes controversial impact upon culture and theology, but instead focuses on the debates about their relationship with the national Church and their attempts to construct an Evangelical brand of Anglicanism. Three particular aspects are analysed: the rhetoric and arguments concerning the perceived dominance and decline of the Evangelical party; the creation of Evangelical 'churchmanship' with its emphasis upon loyalty to bishops and to the historic Anglican formularies; and attitudes to cooperation with non-Evangelicals in the Church of England, for example in the Church Congress movement. The chapter demonstrates that Anglican Evangelical identities remained a fluid and contested construct with multiple expressions.

THE RHETORIC OF EVANGELICALISM: DOMINANCE AND DECLINE

Looking back upon the Wilberforce generation and the Claphamite fathers of the Anglican Evangelical movement, James Stephen encapsulated for the *Edinburgh Review* in 1844 the self-confident prophecies of his Evangelical contemporaries. What once was 'invidiously called a "Sect", is now spreading through the habitable globe', they claimed. 'The day is not distant when it will assume the form, and be hailed by the glorious title, of The Universal Church.'[1] From its small beginnings, Evangelicalism by the mid-nineteenth

[1] James Stephen, 'The Clapham Sect', *Edinburgh Review*, 80 (1844), p. 307.

century appeared to some observers to be entering upon a period of unprecedented 'dominance', not least in the Church of England.[2] Evangelical views were increasingly pervasive, as the *Christian Advocate* observed: 'The Clapham sect may no longer exist—the Simeonites may come to an end; but we firmly believe that year by year the numbers increase of those who give an Evangelical answer to the main question: What saith the Scripture?'[3]

If influence is to be measured by patronage and the weight of church dignitaries, the trends for Evangelicals were encouraging. Not only did they occupy significant colonial bishoprics, such as Daniel Wilson (metropolitan of India from 1835), but also seats on the episcopal bench at home, including John B. Sumner, first Evangelical archbishop of Canterbury from 1848. During Palmerston's premiership, the advocacy of Lord Shaftesbury ensured the appointment of a succession of Evangelical bishops and deans, which raised alarm in some quarters that the Church of England's dignitaries were becoming theologically monochrome.[4] The picture was more mixed under other prime ministers, but Evangelicals continued to receive the patronage of Downing Street.[5] The very popularity of Anglican Evangelicals became a subject of criticism. Lucy March Phillips reminded them in 1862 of Jesus' warning 'when all men speak well of thee'. She contrasted the movement unfavourably with the Anglican Evangelicals of fifty years earlier who were distinguished by their philanthropy and zeal for missions despite being excluded from preferment and widely ridiculed. Phillips observed: 'to be an Evangelical is, amongst clergymen, well-nigh the only way to praise of men; to be a popular Evangelical preacher is a sure road to preferment: religion walks abroad in her silver slippers'.[6] In 1800 the number of Anglican Evangelical churches in London and its environs could be counted on a child's fingers. Two generations later, E. H. Bickersteth announced, 'You could hardly count them now on the fingers of the hundred-handed Briareus.'[7]

Nevertheless, the multiplication of Evangelical clergymen and congregations was not necessarily evidence of increased strength. Francis Close (dean of Carlisle) told the Church Association in Liverpool in 1870 that at the start of the century Anglican Evangelicals had been a beleaguered minority, excluded

[2] David W. Bebbington, *The Dominance of Evangelicalism: The Age of Spurgeon and Moody* (Leicester, 2005).

[3] 'Evangelical Scholarship', *Christian Advocate*, n.s. 1 (1867), p. 676.

[4] Nigel Scotland, *'Good and Proper Men': Lord Palmerston and the Bench of Bishops* (Cambridge, 2000); *The Times*, 8 Apr. 1857, p. 8; 'The New Bishop', *Saturday Review*, 24 Nov. 1860, pp. 659–60.

[5] William T. Gibson, 'Disraeli's Church Patronage, 1868–1880', *Anglican and Episcopal History*, 61 (1992): 197–210.

[6] Lucy March Phillips, *Records of the Ministry of the Rev. E. T. March Phillips* (London, 1862), p. 26.

[7] E. H. Bickersteth, *Evangelical Churchmanship and Evangelical Eclecticism* (London, 1883), p. 13.

from influence, whereas now there were more Evangelicals in high office in the Church than ever before.[8] To this the *Church Times* retorted: 'One Cecil or Simeon is as much more than a thousand Closes, Barings, or McNeiles as one rifled cannon is to all the pea-shooters of schoolboys.'[9] The newspaper suggested that after the high days of the eighteenth-century revivals, Evangelicalism had 'subsided into the fashionable sloth of a proprietary chapel'.[10] It explained: 'The so-called "Evangelical" of the present day, with his narrow creed, and his cross-grained prejudices, has little affinity with the first fathers of his school. He hangs out the bare flag of their shibboleths, but their genuine earnestness awakens but a feeble response in his heart.'[11] Other Tractarian commentators likewise criticized contemporary Evangelicalism by comparing it unfavourably with the earlier Clapham Sect. One wrote: 'Personal religion declines among them, and a high standard of holiness can now only be found among Catholics—with perhaps a few exceptions, belonging to a generation fast dying out, and leaving no successors.'[12] Reviewing the history of the Eclectic Society in the early nineteenth century in the era of John Newton, Thomas Scott, Charles Simeon, and others, the *Contemporary Review* spoke of the subsequent 'declension and secularization' of the movement.[13] It was a charge which some Evangelicals acknowledged, and themselves lamented. For example, the Cornish clergyman H. A. Simcoe declared in 1862 that when compared with the Evangelical 'giants' of fifty years before, contemporary Evangelicals could match them for doctrine but not for spirituality: 'We are too worldly: our families are too worldly: the line of demarcation is too faint: our very charities have become worldly.'[14]

The standard historical narrative, which began to emerge by the end of the Victorian period, was of Evangelicalism's rise and fall, as its hegemony was undermined by theological rivals. Edward Lecky's magnum opus *History of England in the Eighteenth Century* (1878–90) claimed that Evangelicalism was the 'almost undisputed centre of religious life' and had transformed the character of the Church of England until its dominance was challenged by Tractarianism from the 1830s.[15] Yet William Gladstone denied that Evangelicalism had ever been dominant. He believed Evangelicals were by nature biased towards individualism, with little concept of churchmanship: 'They had

[8] 'The Church Association Conference in Liverpool', *The Record*, 28 Oct. 1870, p. 4.

[9] 'The Church Association', *Church Times*, 4 Nov. 1870, p. 467.

[10] 'Missionary Work', *Church Times*, 24 Oct. 1863, p. 300.

[11] 'Party Spirit', *Church Times*, 28 Mar. 1863, p. 61.

[12] 'The Last Thirty Years in the English Church: An Autobiography', in Orby Shipley (ed.), *The Church and the World: Essays on Questions of the Day* (London, 1866), pp. 216–17.

[13] 'Origines Evangelicae: "Eclectic Notes"', *Contemporary Review*, 1 (1866), p. 613.

[14] H. A. Simcoe, *The Distinctive Principles of Evangelicalism* (Cheltenham, 1862), p. 19.

[15] W. E. H. Lecky, *A History of England in the Eighteenth Century*, 8 vols. (London, 1878–90), II, p. 627.

in their congregations a zealous, liberal, and efficient following; but these congregations constituted a kind of sect within the Church of England: they were the *devôts*, the *bacchettoni*, the "saints", of the land.' Although Anglicanism was indebted to the Evangelical movement for having 'roused her from her slumbers', the Evangelical party was 'the very reverse of dominant. It was active, useful, respected, healthy, and thriving; but it was also repressed and struggling, and in some sense rebellious.' It would never be able to influence society at large, Gladstone argued, because it was out of step with literature and the arts.[16]

Anglican Evangelicalism's apparent dissociation from intellectual culture and higher learning was frequently alleged as reason for its decline in the last half of the nineteenth century. Thomas Arnold in 1829 famously parodied the typical Evangelical as 'a good Christian, with a low understanding, a bad education, and ignorance of the world'.[17] This accusation was picked up by others. Baron Bunsen mocked that they 'go on threshing the old straw'; while John Henry Newman wrote caustically in the 1865 revision of his *Apologia* that the Evangelical party 'at no time has been conspicuous . . . for talent or learning'.[18] Professor Döllinger from the University of Munich chimed in:

> the present race of Evangelicals may, in comparison with the former, be called a declining one. . . . The party is mostly deficient in university culture, and there is no question of theological science among its adherents . . . The Evangelicals are struck with sterility, and all the better intellects of the younger generation are turning with dislike and contempt from this degenerate school, whose average amount of culture does not attain to the degree of a good German schoolmaster.[19]

He reiterated that Anglican Evangelicals were 'wholly destitute of theological culture, and possess and produce only a popular, not a scientific literature. . . . They still exist on the credit of their greater and more active predecessors . . . they are not an advancing party, but the reverse'.[20] Likewise in his 1883 Hibbert Lectures the Unitarian scholar Charles Beard criticized the Evangelical movement as: 'not greatly in sympathy with learning, or science, or speculation of any kind . . . reading its own literature, absorbed in its own labours, content with its own life . . . it yields nothing to new knowledge that

[16] W. E. Gladstone, 'The Evangelical Movement; its Parentage, Progress, and Issue', *British Quarterly Review*, 70 (1879), pp. 7, 10, 13.

[17] A. P. Stanley, *The Life and Correspondence of Thomas Arnold* (London, 1846 edn.), p. 221.

[18] Christian von Bunsen to Julius Hare, 19 June 1842, in Frances von Bunsen, *A Memoir of Baron Bunsen*, 2 vols. (London 1868), II, p. 19; John Henry Newman, *History of My Religious Opinions* (London, 1865), p. 289.

[19] J. J. I. von Döllinger, *The Church and the Churches: or, The Papacy and the Temporal Power: An Historical and Political Review*, translated by W. B. MacCabe (London, 1862), pp. 161–2, 170.

[20] J. J. I. von Döllinger, *Lectures on the Reunion of the Churches*, translated by Henry N. Oxenham (London, 1872), p. 132.

it can by any artifice withhold, and when forced to give ground, gives it only slowly and grudgingly'.[21]

The *Church Times* agreed that Evangelicalism had produced no solid contribution to theology, since their publications were confined to tracts and sermons, pietistic biographies, and compilations of other people's writings,[22] leaving Evangelical tract-writer J. C. Ryle to comment ruefully: 'nobody, of course, being a theologian who does not agree with the *Church Times*!'[23] These were hostile caricatures in which most Anglican Evangelicals did not recognize themselves and which they readily dismissed.[24] Nevertheless they sometimes admitted their own weakness. For example, the *Christian Advocate* mourned that Evangelicalism had 'too little frequented the kingdom of ideas', and was 'an alienating influence in the seats of learning and the higher walks of literature'.[25] Evangelicals had 'never done themselves justice' in the realms of scholarship because they tended to view university prizes as a 'delusion and snare', subordinating their studies to the call of parochial ministry.[26] The education of clergy was seen as particularly significant, and Anglican Evangelicals combined to establish the London College of Divinity in 1863, and halls at Oxford and Cambridge in 1877–81, though these were belittled by other Anglicans as sectional affairs and mere party schemes.[27]

From the 1860s it became fashionable to proclaim Anglican Evangelicalism's decline, decay, and even death. *Macmillan's Magazine* believed that the movement had 'outlived its work' and was 'a falling party'.[28] In his 1868 analysis of Church parties, E. H. Plumptre (professor of exegesis at King's College, London, and later dean of Wells) rejected the prevalent notion that Anglican Evangelicalism was 'effete', but still thought it clear that 'the Evangelical school is, as a whole, losing ground... it does not promise, as it is, to be prominent as an element for good in the future history of the English Church'.[29] Matthew Arnold's *St Paul and Protestantism* (1870) argued that Evangelicalism had long misunderstood the apostle's teaching on predestination, original sin, and justification by faith. He asserted that spokesmen like Ryle and Hugh McNeile (dean of Ripon) held 'as erroneous notions as to what *truth* and *the gospel* really

[21] Charles Beard, *The Reformation of the Sixteenth Century in its Relation to Modern Thought and Knowledge* (London, 1883), p. 414.

[22] 'An Evangelical Manifesto', *Church Times*, 20 July 1877, p. 415.

[23] J. C. Ryle, 'Where Are We?', *The Churchman*, 1 (1879), p. 30.

[24] Edward Garbett, 'The Positive Principle of Protestantism', *Christian Advocate*, n.s. 7 (1873), p. 482.

[25] 'The Evangelical Party and the Age', *Christian Advocate*, 1 (1861), p. 21.

[26] 'Evangelical Scholarship', pp. 679, 681.

[27] Andrew Atherstone, 'The Founding of Wycliffe Hall, Oxford', *Anglican and Episcopal History*, 73 (2004): 78–102.

[28] 'The English Evangelical Clergy', *Macmillan's Magazine*, 3 (1860), pp. 113–14.

[29] E. H. Plumptre, 'Church Parties: Past, Present, and Future', *Contemporary Review*, 7 (1868), p. 329.

is, as Mr Spurgeon or the President of the Wesleyan Conference', but Arnold believed that the Evangelical party in the Church of England had 'done its work' and was a fading power:

> it is losing the future and feels that it is losing it. Its signs of a vigorous life, its gaiety and audacity, are confined to its older members, too powerful to lose their own vigour, but without successors to whom to transmit it.... The best of their own younger generation, the soldiers of their own training, are slipping away from them; and he who looks for the source whence popular Puritan theology now derives power and perpetuation, will not fix his eyes on the Evangelical clergy of the Church of England.[30]

The golden jubilee of the Islington Conference in 1877 provided an opportunity for Evangelicals to celebrate their gains over the previous fifty years, but the *Church Times* prophesied that in the Anglican future, with Evangelicalism eclipsed, 1827 would not be remembered for Islington but for the first edition of Keble's *Christian Year*.[31] When Exeter Hall on London's Strand, long associated with Evangelical societies and their May Meetings, was put up for sale in 1879, the *Saturday Review* saw it as marking the downfall of 'a once powerful party' and Evangelicalism's absorption into broader views of religion.[32] Others mocked Anglican Evangelicalism as 'effete and worn-out', 'as useless as an old almanack or a stranded wreck on a sand-bank'.[33]

The death of prominent Anglican Evangelical spokesmen sparked controversy and soul-searching about the health of the movement. For example, when McNeile died in January 1879, aged 83, *The Times* published an obituary not only of the dean but of his party. He was said to be one of the last specimens of the old Evangelical tradition which was rapidly dwindling away:

> He belonged to a school whose disciples are now few and far between, to a party whose influence has almost ceased to count in current controversies. To men of the present generation, indeed, the old Evangelical party of the Church of England, once so powerful and triumphant, must wear somewhat of the aspect of one of those seaports of ancient fame from which the sea, with all its storms and currents, all its busy burden of life and turmoil and contest, has long since ebbed away.

The newspaper observed that 'the Exeter Hall divine of half a century ago is antiquated and well-nigh obsolete', supplanted by the Tractarians, an ecclesial example of Darwin's doctrine of 'the survival of the fittest'. Evangelicalism had 'decayed' because it 'despised knowledge, discarded taste, and gloried in its

[30] Matthew Arnold, *St Paul and Protestantism; with an Essay on Puritanism and the Church of England* (London, 1870 edn.), pp. viii–ix.

[31] 'An Evangelical Jubilee', *Church Times*, 26 Jan. 1877, p. 49.

[32] 'Exeter Hall for Sale', *Saturday Review*, 9 Aug. 1879, pp. 173–4.

[33] Ryle, 'Where Are We?', p. 33.

want of culture'.[34] These criticisms brought a swift repost from Close and Ryle, who both pointed to the remarkable growth of Anglican Evangelicalism in the half century since McNeile began his ministry. In the 1820s Evangelicals were despised, ridiculed, even persecuted, excluded from positions of influence, with not a dozen Evangelical clergymen in London. By the 1870s there were many more clergy happy to identify themselves as Evangelicals, including bishops and deans. The money raised by Evangelical societies far exceeded that contributed by all other Anglicans put together. There were Evangelical unions in most large towns, and numerous Evangelical conferences. The early Islington Conferences had been accommodated in Daniel Wilson Snr's library, but now three hundred clergy attended. The towns and cities outside London identified as key centres of Anglican Evangelical influence were Manchester, Liverpool, Sheffield, Leeds, Bradford, Hull, Newcastle, Sunderland, Birmingham, Nottingham, Derby, Norwich, Bath, Cheltenham, Bristol, Clifton, and Plymouth.[35] Close insisted: 'we are neither dead nor dying . . . the Evangelical party never was so numerous or so influential as at the present moment. Compared with those days of its veteran founders . . . we are legion.'[36] More provocatively, Ryle affirmed:

> the success of many clergymen of other schools than my own arises mainly from the fact that, wittingly or unwittingly, they often preach the very same doctrines that we do. Sixty years ago they would have been called downright Evangelicals. We have no longer any monopoly of Evangelical truth, and I am not ashamed to say that I thank God for it.[37]

Ryle expounded the question at greater length in *The Churchman*, looking ahead fifty years:

> It may be that sifting, trying times are before us. It may be that numbers may be thinned, and many may desert our cause under the pressure of incessant official frowns, persecution, ridicule and unpopularity. But, come what may, I trust the Evangelical cause will always have a representative body in the Church of England, and a faithful remnant who can stand fire, and stand alone. If gaps are made in our ranks, I hope the cry will always be, as it was in the squares at Waterloo, 'Close up, men, close up; let none give way'.[38]

This debate over Anglican Evangelical vitality was of concern beyond the boundaries of the Church of England. *The Freeman*, a Baptist newspaper, admitted *The Times* was substantially correct and that none could have

[34] *The Times*, 31 Jan. 1879, p. 9.

[35] Letter from J. C. Ryle, *The Times*, 6 Feb. 1879, p. 10; Ryle, 'Where Are We?', p. 33; Bickersteth, *Evangelical Churchmanship*, p. 13.

[36] Letter from Francis Close, *The Times*, 6 Feb. 1879, p. 10.

[37] Letter from J. C. Ryle, *The Times*, 6 Feb. 1879, p. 10.

[38] Ryle, 'Where Are We?', pp. 37–8.

predicted the shift in the balance of power between Evangelicals and Anglo-Catholics since the 1840s; and those even 'who are called Evangelicals are not so Evangelical as were their forerunners'.[39] The *Methodist Recorder* agreed that Anglican Evangelicals were 'undistinguished in the higher walks of scholarship and genius' and had been overtaken by their rivals.[40] From the perspective of Scottish Presbyterianism, John Marshall Lang (father of the future archbishop of Canterbury, Cosmo Gordon Lang) was more sanguine, suggesting like Ryle that many Anglican High Churchmen now preached Evangelical doctrine. Although the 'old war-cries and special watch-words' of the early nineteenth century had passed away, in Lang's view there was no sign of the obsolescence of the 'ever-abiding, ever-authoritative Evangelical theology'.[41]

Amongst Anglican commentators, *The Guardian* declared that Evangelicalism was now 'effete' as an anti-Tractarian protest movement and dwindling in its influence, but Evangelical doctrines concerning salvation by faith in Jesus Christ and the necessity of conversion had pervaded the whole Church of England so in that sense 'the decay of the Evangelical party is the triumph of Evangelicalism as a cause'.[42] *The Rock*, an Evangelical newspaper, was typically pessimistic, with one correspondent arguing by anecdote that Evangelicals were now outnumbered by ritualists and Broad Churchmen, who were entrenched in all the influential positions. In the face of these 'facts', Ryle's claim that Evangelicalism was not in retreat, was dismissed as a 'fond notion' and a delusion.[43] Yet from a ritualist perspective, the *Church Times* admitted that there was life in Anglican Evangelicalism yet: 'on their own showing, these neglecters of churches, preachers of prayers, breakers of rubrics, teachers of false doctrine, are not a moribund sect', but were still flourishing and as ready to fight as ever.[44]

Other prominent deaths led to similar angst. On the decease of Robert Bickersteth (bishop of Ripon) in 1884, *The Spectator* commented that Anglican Evangelicalism 'grows weaker and weaker with every year'. It was fast dying out not only within the Church of England but 'amongst educated men all the world over', because the Evangelical emphasis on conversion and biblical literalism, and their suspicion of sacramentalism, put them out of step with Victorian thought. Their view of religion was 'growing daily less and less tenable, and we do not wonder, therefore, that the worthies of the Evangelical type of Christianity are daily dying off and leaving no successors behind them'.[45] The deaths in 1885 and 1886 of two prominent Evangelical lay

[39] 'The Anglican Evangelicals', *The Freeman*, 14 Feb. 1879, p. 74.

[40] 'Evangelicalism Alleged to be Defunct', *Methodist Recorder*, 14 Feb. 1879, p. 105.

[41] J. Marshall Lang, 'Evangelicalism in the Church of England', *Catholic Presbyterian*, 2 (1879), p. 105.

[42] 'The Decay of Evangelicalism', *The Guardian*, 12 Feb. 1879, p. 200.

[43] *The Rock*, 14 Feb. 1879, p. 127.

[44] 'The Decay of Evangelicalism', *Church Times*, 14 Feb. 1879, p. 107.

[45] 'The Decay of Evangelicalism in the Church', *The Spectator*, 19 Apr. 1884, pp. 513–14.

leaders, the earl of Shaftesbury and the earl of Chichester, both octogenarians, reminded the *Saturday Review* of 'the advanced and growing decay of what was once the dominant religious influence in the Church of England'.[46]

Some Anglican Evangelicals freely acknowledged the decline of their movement, but justified it as, paradoxically, a sign of their success. For example, Anthony Thorold (bishop of Rochester in the 1880s) thought it inevitable that Anglican Evangelicalism had ceased to be 'on the crest of the wave' after finishing its task of 'vitalising the conscience of the Church with zeal for the souls of men, and of disinterring from a deep grave the doctrines of grace'. He admitted that Evangelicals had sometimes unjustly claimed 'a monopoly of the Gospel', but their adversaries in the Church of England had nevertheless 'lit their lamps at its candle, and revived their zeal from its fire'.[47] Others were more despondent. *The Record* lamented Anglican Evangelicalism's 'isolation, supineness, and inactivity'.[48] The *Church Times* in 1893 blamed what it called 'the Evangelical *débacle*' upon 'the absence of any really intellectual school of thought among them, and their lack of touch with the broad life and movement of the English nation'.[49] The newspaper spoke triumphantly of 'the rout of the Evangelicals', declaring that the party was 'now no longer vigorous and fruitful, but reduced to senile repetition of dead formulae, or exhausting its small reserve of strength in hysterical shoutings'.[50] The truth of this historical narrative was seldom tested, but the rhetoric of Evangelical decline had taken firm root in public discourse, even amongst Evangelicals themselves. By the turn of the twentieth century, the expansive confidence typical of Anglican Evangelicalism in the mid-Victorian decades had disappeared, amidst frequent reports of lost ground and the failure to attract new recruits. One clergyman wryly observed: 'Jeremiah must be the patron saint of the Evangelicals; to judge at least by the frequent threnodies with which they wail the chances of their message.'[51]

EVANGELICAL CHURCHMANSHIP

Although this chapter is entitled 'Anglican Evangelicalism', that phrase as applied to the nineteenth century is, of course, anachronistic. 'Anglicanism' was generally used in the Victorian era as a synonym for High Churchmanship,

[46] 'The Decay of Evangelicalism', *Saturday Review*, 27 Mar. 1886, p. 439.

[47] Anthony W. Thorold, *A Charge Delivered to the Clergy of the Diocese of Rochester, at his Second Visitation in 1885* (London, 1885), p. 89.

[48] 'Evangelical Influence in the Church', *The Record*, 15 Dec. 1882, p. 999.

[49] 'The Present Position of the Evangelical Party', *Church Times*, 13 Jan. 1893, p. 33.

[50] 'An Evangelical Undertaker', *Church Times*, 10 June 1892, p. 581.

[51] Herbert Marston, *'The Message of Evangelical Churchmanship to the Present Age', and 'Loosening the Foundations': Addresses* (London, 1906), p. 24.

only one subsection of the Church of England. Thorold, for instance, could write in 1868 that 'The Anglicans are the most numerous, the Liberals the most powerful, and the Evangelicals the most useful.'[52] Victorian Evangelicals in the Church of England described themselves not as 'Anglicans' but as 'Churchmen'. John Miller (rector of St Martin's, Birmingham) was indignant that Tractarians should set themselves up as the 'true Churchmen' when that title properly belonged to Evangelicals.[53]

Evangelicals formed part of a broad coalition in defence of the Protestant heritage of the Church of England, against what they saw as the innovations and intrusions of Tractarianism and ritualism within the establishment.[54] Henry Christmas, editor of the *Church of England Quarterly Review*, coined in 1840 the hybrid term 'Evangelical High Churchmen', for those who were concerned for both 'evangelical truth and apostolic discipline', naming bishops Charles Blomfield and J. B. Sumner as examples of the type.[55] G. S. Faber explained that 'Evangelical High Churchmanship' was a 'just medium' between Tractarianism and Ultra-Protestantism.[56] The Parker Society texts from the Anglican reformers, published between 1841 and 1855, numbered Christmas amongst its team of editors and won wide support from this constituency,[57] though a generation later the *Church Quarterly Review* mocked the volumes as 'unsaleable and unreadable'.[58] Some Evangelicals distanced themselves from these cross-party collaborations. *The Record*, for instance, announced: 'We may as well say that there are Evangelical Papists, as that there are Evangelical-High-Churchmen. Possibly there may be some rare exceptions; but they must be very rare indeed—they must be almost a new race in the world.'[59] The rise of Tractarianism complicated the issue because protestations of loyalty to Church of England tradition could raise suspicions about lack of Evangelical clarity. The promoters of the *Christian Observer* in 1802, the Claphamite journal, promised that its doctrine would be that of the Church of England, as expressed in Edward VI's catechism, Jewell's apologia,

[52] Anthony W. Thorold, 'The Evangelical Clergy of 1868', *Contemporary Review*, 8 (1868), p. 571.

[53] J. C. Miller, *'Subjection; No, Not For An Hour': A Warning to Protestant Christians, in Behalf of the 'Truth of the Gospel' as Now Imperilled by the Romish Doctrines and Practices of the Tractarian Heresy* (London, 1850), p. 13.

[54] John Wolffe, *The Protestant Crusade in Great Britain, 1829–1860* (Oxford, 1991); D. G. Paz, *Popular Anti-Catholicism in Mid-Victorian England* (Stanford, CA, 1992).

[55] 'The Office of a Bishop', *Church of England Quarterly Review*, 8 (1840): 23–4; *The Churchman*, 5 (1841), p. iv.

[56] Quoted in Andrew Atherstone, *Oxford's Protestant Spy: The Controversial Career of Charles Golightly* (Milton Keynes, 2007), p. 317.

[57] Peter Toon, 'The Parker Society', *Historical Magazine of the Protestant Episcopal Church*, 46 (1977): 323–32.

[58] 'Bishop Ryle on the Church of England', *Church Quarterly Review*, 19 (1885), p. 278.

[59] *The Record*, 24 Aug. 1840, p. 4.

and Nowell's catechism.[60] Yet if a journal was launched on the same basis in the 1860s, Thorold observed, some Anglican Evangelicals would greet it as 'mere High Churchism in disguise'.[61]

Some Evangelicals reacted against Tractarianism by emphasizing their Protestantism; others, however, began to emphasize their churchmanship. Thorold urged Evangelical clergy to school their congregations in the nature of Church authority and the distinctive principles of Anglicanism:

> It is really no exaggeration to say, that hardly from one year's end to another is one Evangelical congregation in twenty ever instructed on the essential differences, that distinguish the Church of England from the Nonconformist bodies; the result being that multitudes in our congregations are Churchmen, not by conviction, but by accident; attracted to church, not through any intelligent preference for the Church system, but by the uncertain and personal liking for an individual clergyman, with no answer to give to those who are on the watch to entice them to other communions—and so the easy prey of the Papist, on one hand, or the Plymouth sectaries on the other.[62]

A decade later Edward Garbett (vicar of Christ Church, Surbiton) was more strident in his apologetic: 'It has been thought by many that Evangelical Churchmen have no Church principles, and are little better than Nonconformists within the Church. It is needless to say that this is a total and absolute mistake.' On the contrary, he insisted, Evangelicals were 'as firm and as faithful Churchmen as any within her pale', devoted to apostolic order and apostolic doctrine. Indeed the title deeds of Anglicanism belonged to them: 'We, who are Evangelical Churchmen, believe ourselves to be the true children of the Church of England, and we wish for no other platform of faith and practice than has been afforded us, through the good hand of our God upon us, in her Scriptural formularies.'[63] Elsewhere, Garbett wrote that Evangelicals were not merely a party within the Church of England: 'Now, of this Church, we are not only members, but we claim to be, as Evangelical Churchmen, the truest representatives. Her articles and formularies constitute our platform, and we refuse to accept any other.'[64] The *Christian Observer* likewise declared that Evangelicals were not cuckoos in the Church of England's nest, but held a place there 'as natural as that of a child by the fire-side of his parent'.[65]

[60] *Christian Observer* (1802), p. 9.

[61] Thorold, 'The Evangelical Clergy of 1868', p. 577.

[62] Thorold, 'The Evangelical Clergy of 1868', p. 582.

[63] Edward Garbett, 'Introduction', in Edward Garbett (ed.), *Evangelical Principles: A Series of Doctrinal Papers Explanatory of the Positive Principles of Evangelical Churchmanship* (London, 1875), pp. ix, xvi.

[64] Edward Garbett, 'The Positive Principle of Protestantism', *Christian Advocate*, n.s. 7 (1873), p. 487.

[65] 'On the Present Position of the Evangelical Party in the Church of England', *Christian Observer* (1873), p. 84.

William Sinclair (archdeacon of London) agreed that the 'true and genuine Churchmen' were those who accepted the Reformation settlement of the Church of England, not those who borrowed Roman customs 'under some strange medieval hallucination'.[66] Evangelical clergy published volumes like *Thoughts for Churchmen* (1868), Garbett's *Positive Principles of Evangelical Churchmanship* (1875), and Ryle's *Principles for Churchmen* (1884), spirited defences of the place of Evangelicalism within the established Church as consistent with the truest interpretation of the Thirty-Nine Articles and the Book of Common Prayer. Ryle's volume was savaged by the *Church Quarterly Review* which wondered how he could with integrity remain a bishop in the Church of England and likened him to the comedic figure Mrs Partington, 'twirling her solitary mop against the advancing tide of the Atlantic Ocean'.[67]

The *Christian Observer* combined forces with the *Christian Advocate* in 1875, professing itself to be 'an organ of thoroughly distinctive Church-of-England views', though it soon folded.[68] Its place was filled in 1879 by a new monthly journal entitled, simply and pointedly, *The Churchman*. The first issue's opening essay by Garbett set the journal's tone, seeking to show that historic Evangelicalism since the days of the Clapham Sect was firmly attached to the Church of England, loyal to bishops, respecting the sacraments, and reverent in public worship.[69] The contrasting titles of these two key Anglican Evangelical journals illustrate the ecclesiological shift. At the start of the nineteenth century they chose to emphasize their Christianity, but their descendants at the end of the century felt obliged to emphasize their churchmanship. R. E. Bartlett noticed the trend, warning that these protestations of strict churchmanship were a foolish attempt to conciliate High Church Anglicanism at the expense of relationship with Evangelical Nonconformity. For an earlier Evangelical generation, like Thomas Scott in the 1770s, it was often impossible to discern their denominational allegiance by their doctrinal writings, but the new breed of Evangelicals in the 1870s were quick to profess their loyalty to liturgy and formularies. They so dreaded being stigmatized as Low Churchmen, Bartlett observed, that they now vied with the Tractarians 'in professing devoted and exclusive allegiance to the Church'.[70] As a result they were cut adrift from their natural allies outside the Church of England:

> They are so afraid of being taunted with being bad Churchmen, that they are often even less disposed to a friendly policy towards Nonconformists than their

[66] William Sinclair, 'Current Fallacies in the Church', *The Churchman*, n.s. 7 (1893), p. 603; Seton Churchill, 'In What Does Good Churchmanship Consist?', *The Churchman*, n.s. 8 (1894): 303–12.

[67] 'Bishop Ryle on the Church of England', p. 260.

[68] 'The Church Congress of 1877', *Christian Observer and Advocate* (1877), p. 92.

[69] Edward Garbett, 'The Evangelical School', *The Churchman*, 1 (1879): 1–19.

[70] R. E. Bartlett, 'On the Position of the Evangelical Party in the Church of England', *Fraser's Magazine*, 17 (1878), p. 27.

> High Church rivals, who feel that they, at least, can afford to be civil without any fear of compromising themselves. They are like a man who meets a shabby relation in St James's Street, and who does not like to cut him, but yet is mortally afraid of his friends in the club windows seeing him in unfashionable company.[71]

By the turn of the twentieth century, younger Evangelicals were proud to be known not only as 'Churchmen' but as 'Anglicans'. Herbert Marston (incumbent of Belgrave Chapel, Pimlico) announced:

> We have to declare the Gospel, the whole Gospel, and nothing but the Gospel. But we have to declare it in terms of the Church to which we belong, and in the manner which befits Churchmen.... The Clergy, who speak in her name, are by special honour bound not to shirk the prescribed method. They are not free Evangelistic lances. They are not Methodist preachers. They are Anglicans.... To depreciate the Sacraments; to apologise for the Liturgy; to make light of the order of the Church, are equally signs of bad taste, bad faith, and bad Churchmanship.[72]

One proof of loyal churchmanship was obedience to the rules of the Church and the direction of the bishops. In his 1870 essay on Anglican principles, W. F. Hook (dean of Chichester) criticized both the ritualists ('Romanizers') and the Evangelicals ('Puritans') for the non-natural sense in which they interpreted the Reformation formularies. Evangelicals, he wrote, 'clothe in the garment of Calvinism what the Church has laid before them as plain and simple Catholic truth', and so were inconsistent in their rebuke of ritualism. In Hook's judgement, both should be equally censured: 'if the thumb-screw be allowable to one party, it cannot be withheld from the other'.[73] The rubrics of the Prayer Book were a particular bone of contention, though the *Christian Observer* firmly rejected the suggestion that Evangelicals were guilty of neglecting them.[74] James Bardsley (rector of St Ann's, Manchester) aimed to show in *Mind Your Rubrics* (1866) that the ritualists were the guilty party, not the Evangelicals. He agreed that clergymen ought to be allowed 'reasonable freedom', but 'liberty ought not to degenerate into licentiousness': 'If men may subscribe Protestant Articles and teach Romish opinions—if they may enact Romish ceremonies while they administer a Scriptural service, this would convert the Church into a public scandal, and therefore her doom is inevitable.'[75] Garbett urged: 'We should show ourselves to be Churchmen as well as Evangelicals. We should therefore accept the Church to the utmost as

[71] Bartlett, 'On the Position of the Evangelical Party in the Church of England', p. 29.

[72] Marston, *Message of Evangelical Churchmanship*, pp. 12–13.

[73] W. F. Hook, 'Anglican Principles', in Archibald Weir and William D. Maclagan (eds.), *The Church and the Age: Essays on the Principles and Present Position of the Anglican Church* (London, 1870), p. 36.

[74] 'Alleged Evangelical Ritualistic Irregularities', *Christian Observer* (1869), pp. 161–70.

[75] James Bardsley, *Mind Your Rubrics: Seasonable Thoughts Upon the Rubrics and Other Important Points, for the Consideration of Churchmen* (London, 1866), p. 140.

she is, and show that we are content with her.' This meant accepting even those elements which seemed disagreeable or pointless, without complaint, because they were:

> part of the system to which we are honestly pledged in *foro conscientiae*.... An opportunity now exists of making the platform of the Evangelical body co-extensive with the platform of the Church of England, such as never existed before. But we cannot successfully plead against violations in excess, while we consciously maintain violations in defect.[76]

The Churchman likewise asserted that when a bishop gave instructions concerning the rubrics, they would be followed by all 'loyal, law-abiding Churchmen'. 'Obedience has happily been, and is, a note of the Evangelical School', it insisted.[77]

Another proof of loyalty to the Church of England was a refusal to secede. In 1846, with public attention fixed on the flurry of Tractarian departures for Rome, William Gresley declared that the real danger to the Church of England was the 'evangelical or puritan party' in her midst. He believed Evangelicals were 'Dissenters at heart', teaching 'a mass of heresy', and highlighted the 'utter incompatibility' between their doctrine and their obligations as ordained clergymen.[78] The issue was brought into sharp focus during the bicentenary commemorations in 1862 of the restoration of the Book of Common Prayer and the 'great ejection' of puritans from the establishment. R. W. Dale (Congregational minister in Birmingham) accused Anglican Evangelicals of playing 'fast and loose' with the language of the Prayer Book by interpreting it in a non-natural, non-grammatical sense, just as *Tract Ninety* and *Essays and Reviews* did with the Thirty-Nine Articles. He contrasted the dishonest subscription of Anglican Evangelicals in the Victorian Church of England with the 'incorruptible fidelity' of the two thousand ejected ministers who 'never dreamt of sophistries like these'.[79] Anglo-Catholics likewise did not miss the opportunity to strike at their Evangelical rivals. Evangelicals were 'manifestly inconsistent', declared one Tractarian clergyman, when they tried to juggle Anglican ordination promises with Nonconformist doctrines.[80] By implication, the path of integrity was for Evangelicals to leave the Church of England. C. H. Spurgeon likewise chastised Ryle and his Anglican Evangelical colleagues for their compromise with error, and urged them 'to quit their

[76] Edward Garbett, 'Convocation, Diocesan Synods, and Church Congresses', in Herbert James and others, *Thoughts for Churchmen* (London, 1868), pp. 131–2.

[77] 'Mr Bickersteth's "Thoughts for Today No. 1"', *The Churchman*, 7 (1883), p. 465.

[78] William Gresley, *The Real Danger of the Church of England* (London, 1847 edn.), pp. 17, 26–7, 52.

[79] R. W. Dale, *Churchmen and Dissenters* (Birmingham, 1862), p. 15.

[80] *A Second Letter to the Rev. R. W. Dale, with Reference to the Vindication of the Evangelical Clergy. By a Priest of the Church of England* (Birmingham, 1862), p. 3.

indefensible and dishonourable position, and come out decidedly from all communion with the monster evils of the Establishment'.[81]

There were periodic secessions of Evangelical clergy, such as at Oxford in the early 1830s, or James Shore in the 1840s to found the Free Church of England after his clash with Bishop Phillpotts of Exeter. The secession in 1848 of Baptist Noel (minister of St John's, Bedford Row) also caused a sensation. Further Evangelical departures were threatened during the Gorham crisis, but came to nothing when the Judicial Committee of the Privy Council judged in their favour.[82] The success of ritualism and liberalism only served to heighten Evangelical concerns. One speaker advised the Church Association in 1870 that they should secede together *en masse*, but Garbett rebuked the suggestion because 'the shout of triumph would ring from every Ritualistic platform'. Close was convinced that if Evangelicals seceded they would be signing the 'spiritual death-warrant' of the Church of England. Only persecution would drive them from the establishment, he said.[83] Ryle likewise rejected talk of secession as foolish and premature, insisting that Evangelicals should 'stand fast' and reform the Church from within.[84] He proclaimed that the true principles of the Church of England were 'Protestant and Evangelical', those of 'the glorious Reformation'. Therefore they should not run away even if many clergy were unfaithful to the formularies:

> Away with this talk about secession! Away with this flirting with Plymouth Brethrenism! Let us not play the enemy's game, by deserting the good old fortress, so long as the Articles are unchanged and the pulpit is unfettered.... Rather, like Venn, and Romaine, and Grimshaw, and Berridge, let us man the walls, stand to our guns, nail our colours to the mast, and fight as long as we have a foot to stand on.... Rabbit-hearted Churchmen who are always bolting into holes at the slightest shadow of danger, are the best allies of Ritualism.[85]

Capel Molyneux (incumbent of St Paul's, Onslow Square) came to the opposite conclusion in 1872, seceding from the Church of England as a matter of Evangelical 'duty' because the Judicial Committee of the Privy Council refused to reprimand W. J. E. Bennett's eucharistic doctrines.[86] Yet few followed Molyneux's example. Richard Blakeney (incumbent of Christ Church, Claughton) argued that secession could only be justified by the Church of England's apostasy, and his fellow anti-Catholic polemicist, Michael Hobart Seymour,

[81] 'Churchianity versus Christianity', *The Sword and the Trowel* (1868), p. 85.

[82] Grayson Carter, *Anglican Evangelicals: Protestant Secessions from the Via Media, c.1800–1850* (Oxford, 2001).

[83] 'The Church Association Conference in Liverpool'.

[84] 'The Liverpool Conference', letter from J. C. Ryle, *The Record*, 2 Nov. 1870, p. 2.

[85] J. C. Ryle, *Lessons from English Church History* (London, 1871), p. 45.

[86] Capel Molyneux, *The Bennett Judgment: Our Duty, What Is It?* (London, 1872).

likewise emphasized that there was no perfect Church this side of heaven.[87] Although the nineteenth-century Evangelical secessions were significant, they were eclipsed by the volume of Tractarian secessions to Roman Catholicism, a useful debating point for Anglican Evangelical apologists.

EVANGELICAL COOPERATION

In the wake of the Gorham controversy, Daniel Wilson Jnr (vicar of Islington) proclaimed that the spread of Tractarianism was a greater crisis for the Church of England than any since the Reformation, and called on Evangelicals to take action and get organized.[88] His own Islington Conference played an important unifying role by bringing Evangelical clergy together each January for exhortation by the Evangelical magisterium.[89] Yet more was needed. Alongside the agencies for foreign and home mission, like the Church Missionary Society and the Church Pastoral Aid Society, new organizations sprang into life to defend the Evangelical basis of Anglicanism. The Church of England Clerical and Lay Association for the Maintenance of Evangelical Principles was launched in 1858, followed seven years later by the Church Association which prosecuted ritualism in the courts. Still Ryle called for more to be done, instructing the Islington Conference that Anglican Evangelicals were 'as helpless as a mob'. 'We have numbers, strength, good will, and desires to do what is right; but from lack of organization and generalship, we are weak as water.' He complained that it was difficult to persuade Evangelical clergy to look beyond their own parishes to the needs of the wider Church, likening them to 'hermits' unwilling to leave their caves: 'Episcopalians in theory, they are almost Independents in practice.'[90] Garbett agreed with the diagnosis that Evangelical clergy were 'separated, scattered, isolated, without common communion, common counsels, or the first rudiments of common action', and called urgently for a central union.[91] Not all welcomed the suggestion. Thorold thought there were already plenty of organizations, and more party machinery

[87] Richard Blakeney, *Secession Not Our Duty: or, The Bennett Judgment Examined, in Reply to the Rev. Capel Molyneux* (London, 1872); Michael Hobart Seymour, 'Secession from the Church of England', *Christian Advocate*, n.s. 6 (1872): 800–14.

[88] Daniel Wilson, *Our Protestant Faith in Danger: An Appeal to the Evangelical Members of the Church of England in Reference to the Present Crisis* (London, 1850).

[89] David Bebbington, 'The Islington Conference', in Andrew Atherstone and John Maiden (eds.), *Evangelicalism and the Church of England in the Twentieth Century: Reform, Resistance and Renewal* (Woodbridge, 2014), pp. 48–67.

[90] J. C. Ryle, *We Must Unite! Being Thoughts on the Necessity of Forming a Well Organized Union of Evangelical Churchmen* (London, 1868), pp. 6, 21–2.

[91] Edward Garbett, *The Future of the Church of England* (London, 1872), p. 8; Edward Garbett, *Union Among Evangelical Churchmen* (London, 1871).

'would soon do the work of wild horses, and tear poor Mother Church into a hundred sects'.[92]

A major source of tension within the Evangelical constituency was the extent to which cooperation with Anglicans from other traditions was to be tolerated, or even encouraged. The Church Congress, a voluntary gathering of clergy and laity, without legislative authority, met annually from 1861 in different cities across England and Wales, drawing together Anglicans from a wide spectrum of opinion, though Evangelicals were unsure how to respond. At first the *Christian Observer* stood aloof, criticizing Evangelical attenders for doctrinal compromise. It warned that the Congress movement was trying 'to bridge over the broad abyss which ever must subsist between truth and error', and would lead to 'a fusion of all religious differences in one general mass of lax churchmanship and loose profession'.[93] Wilson also dismissed the congresses as a waste of time, and called Evangelicals to focus instead on preaching 'the plain, simple, old-fashioned truths of the Gospel'.[94] Ryle, however, believed that the congresses were an excellent opportunity for dialogue with Anglicans from other perspectives and thus to lessen prejudice against Evangelicalism.[95] He joked that High Churchmen often understood less about Evangelicalism 'than a native of Timbuctoo knows about skating and ice-creams, or an Esquimaux knows about grapes, peaches, and nectarines'. The common stereotype, he suggested, was of the Anglican Evangelical as a wild person who despises the sacraments, admires dirty churches, cares only about preaching, hates bishops, disapproves of good works, and prefers the company of Nonconformists. Ryle exhorted his fellow Evangelical clergy to attend the congresses so that other Anglicans might see that they too loved the Church of England and that 'we are not all unmannerly, rude Johnsonian bears'.[96] For these collaborations, he was denounced by some Anglican Evangelicals as 'an apostate and a traitor!'[97] From the viewpoint of Evangelical Nonconformity, Spurgeon's *The Sword and the Trowel* warned that the Anglican Congress movement was the yoking of Christ and Antichrist. It mourned that Ryle was 'temporizing in a way which grieves thousands even in his own denomination', and urged him to review his position 'in the light of the Scriptures rather than in the darkness of ecclesiasticism'.[98] Yet Ryle dismissed his critics,

[92] Thorold, 'The Evangelical Clergy of 1868', p. 576.

[93] 'Words of Caution in Reference to the Position of the Evangelical Members of the Church of England at the Present Time', *Christian Observer* (1865), pp. 209–10.

[94] Daniel Wilson, 'Remarks on a Paper by the Rev A. W. Thorold, Entitled "The Evangelical Clergy of 1868"', *Christian Observer* (1868), pp. 755–8.

[95] J. C. Ryle, *Shall We Go? Being Thoughts About Church Congresses, and our Duty with Regard to Them, from the Stand-Point of an Evangelical Churchman* (London, 1878).

[96] J. C. Ryle, *Can a Greater Amount of Unity Be Obtained Among Zealous and Pious Churchmen of Different Schools of Thought?* (London, 1872), pp. 14, 18.

[97] Ryle, *We Must Unite!*, p. 8.

[98] *The Sword and the Trowel* (1879), p. 237.

wryly observing that he was 'not conscious of having imbibed any poison, or caught any theological disease.'[99] The Evangelical non-attenders were chided by *The Times* for their isolationism, as 'a Church within a Church'.[100]

Although Evangelicals claimed for themselves the title of true churchmen, many of them were nevertheless willing to include others within the breadth of the Church of England. Garbett believed that if Evangelicals combined forces with High Churchmen they could prevent sacerdotalism and ritualism from exerting power upon Anglicanism.[101] The wisest limits of Anglican comprehensiveness were a frequent source of debate.[102] Ryle resisted the idea that the Church should become 'a kind of Noah's ark, within which every kind of opinion and creed shall dwell safe and undisturbed'; arguing that such a policy of 'universal toleration' would result in the Church being 'broken to pieces'.[103] Nevertheless, he acknowledged that although Evangelicals represented the best standard of Anglican doctrine, there was room in the Church of England for other schools, provided they kept within the limits of the formularies and did not promote Romanism or Deism. 'I am an Evangelical Churchman', Ryle announced to the Church Congress at Sheffield in 1878, 'and I am not a bit ashamed of it. But I have no sympathy with those who advocate a rigid cast-iron uniformity, and want all churchmen to be, like the rails round Hyde Park, of one unvarying mental height, colour, shape and thickness.' He appealed: 'Let us be as broad as the Creeds and Articles, but not one inch broader.'[104] C. F. Childe likewise warned Evangelicals it would be wrong to condemn all High Churchmen for the ritual extravagancies of Alexander Mackonochie or the doctrinal errors of Bennett. Although some might take Communion fasting, or turn east to face the Creed, they should be welcomed as brethren: 'there is in the High Church party a daily increasing body of Godfearing, devout, nay, essentially Evangelical men; men of prayerful spirit, mortified lives, and holy walk.'[105] Henry Wace (dean of Canterbury), a prominent Evangelical spokesman, went further in 1905 by proposing that rituals be tolerated within Anglicanism if they could be found in the first six centuries of the early Church. It was a creative idea, which the archbishops

[99] Ryle, *Can a Greater Amount of Unity Be Obtained*, p. 17.

[100] *The Times*, 1 Oct. 1878, p. 7.

[101] Garbett, 'Introduction', p. viii.

[102] T. D. Bernard, 'The Comprehensiveness of the Church of England: What Are Its Just Limits?', *Christian Advocate*, n.s. 3 (1869): 652–61; Edward Garbett, 'The Limits of Comprehension', *Christian Advocate*, n.s. 7 (1873): 912–25.

[103] J. C. Ryle, *Principles for Churchmen: A Manual of Positive Statements on Doubtful or Disputed Points* (London, 1884), pp. xxiii–xxiv.

[104] J. C. Ryle, 'The Just Limits of Comprehensiveness in the National Church', in *The Official Report of the Eighteenth Annual Meeting of the Church Congress, Held at Sheffield, 1878* (Sheffield, 1879), p. 132.

[105] C. F. Childe, 'Varying Schools of Religious Thought in the Church of England: Can They Work Together, and To What Extent?', *Christian Advocate*, n.s. 3 (1869), p. 591.

of Canterbury and York picked up, but it failed to win wide backing amongst Wace's own Evangelical constituency because it was a departure from the usual appeals to Scripture or the Reformation formularies.[106]

Despite their reputation for fierce anti-ritualism, some Anglican Evangelicals began to argue that their movement must learn from the aesthetic tastes of the late nineteenth century. Ryle was willing to wear a surplice in the pulpit instead of a black gown, and advocated organs instead of music groups.[107] Bishop Thorold, in a pastoral letter to his clergy in Rochester diocese, announced: 'To try to check Ritualism by discouraging a bright and dignified service, is the wisdom of a mother, who to prevent her boy from being a sailor, never lets him go near the sea.'[108] Likewise F. F. Goe, with an eye to conciliating younger Evangelicals, told the Islington Conference: 'If we protest against harmless diversities in ceremonial with as much vehemence as we protest against false doctrine, we shall weaken our own cause, drive away many whose sympathies are on the side of Evangelical truth, and incur the merited reproach of being unable to distinguish between things that differ.'[109] By the 1880s even *The Record* was counselling that not every 'Anglican' (that is, High Church) innovation should be opposed, such as fashions in church furnishings or the conduct of services: 'Surely it is a waste of strength to fight about such matters, especially when we thus needlessly array against ourselves the whole strength of the popular taste.' Sometimes, when no major doctrine was involved, 'concession is the wisest policy'.[110]

E. H. Bickersteth (vicar of Christ Church, Hampstead, and from 1885 bishop of Exeter) joined the chorus of approval. He told the Southport Conference that there was no good reason to resist the beautifying of church buildings, daily prayers, observance of saints' days, Lenten fasts, flower decorations, and musical services.[111] 'We are often charged with narrowness', he noted. 'The best answer will be a hearty adoption of all that is good in other schools, while cleaving steadfastly to the faith once for all delivered to the saints.'[112] Bickersteth warned that the Anglican Evangelical movement was losing many young people because it was hostile to change, but congregations

[106] Henry Wace and Frederick Meyrick, *An Appeal from the New to the True Catholics, or the Faith and Practice of the First Six Centuries* (London, 1904); Henry Wace (ed.), *An Appeal to the First Six Centuries* (London, 1905); *The Case Against the Proposed Appeal to the First Six Centuries: Letters Contributed to the Record and English Churchman* (London, 1905).

[107] J. C. Ryle, 'Church Music and Singing', *Christian Advocate*, n.s. 5 (1871): 276–7; James Whisenant, 'Anti-Ritualism and the Moderation of Evangelical Opinion in England in the Mid-1870s', *Anglican and Episcopal History*, 70 (2001): 451–6.

[108] Anthony W. Thorold, *A Pastoral Letter to the Diocese of Rochester* (London, 1878), p. 52.

[109] F. F. Goe, 'Evangelical Churchmanship: What Must Be Its Protest?', *The Record*, 19 Jan. 1883, p. 57.

[110] 'Anglicanism: Its Final Issue', *The Record*, 1 Dec. 1882, p. 947.

[111] Bickersteth, *Evangelical Churchmanship*, pp. 8–9, 24–32.

[112] Bickersteth, *Evangelical Churchmanship*, p. 35.

should be free to adopt contemporary tastes '*without holding them more or less Evangelical*, because their usage may not in all points coincide with our own'.[113] It was a sign of moving with the times. Marston declared that Anglican Evangelicals must learn to convey the unchanged gospel message in the language of the twentieth century, not the sixteenth:

> We must be contemporary evangelicals. We are not living in the days of Hooker. Our point of view is not that of the 'Ecclesiastical Polity'.... The messenger of the great message is not bound to parrot ancient shibboleths, in order to prove his orthodoxy; nor to insist on superannuated points of view in order to keep up a show of being in the Protestant succession.[114]

Such sentiments cohered with the position paper in *The Churchman* in 1910 by its new editor Guy Warman (principal of St Aidan's College, Birkenhead), who argued for an Evangelical essentialism which focused on fundamental theological principles unaffected by varieties in ritual or attitudes to biblical criticism.[115] This approach to Evangelicalism was accommodating of the widest diversity of Anglican traditions and signalled the end of the internecine warfare which marked the Victorian age. Nevertheless, amongst Evangelicals it remained a contested position, part of the struggle over the ecclesial identity of the Anglican Evangelical movement which rumbled on throughout the twentieth century and beyond.

CONCLUSION

In 1908 G. R. Balleine (vicar of St James, Bermondsey) published *A History of the Evangelical Party in the Church of England*, which quickly established itself as a classic text. It was a lively narrative of Anglican Evangelicalism's past in the eighteenth and nineteenth centuries but also an apologia and mandate for the future direction of the movement as it entered the twentieth century. Balleine showed little interest in doctrinal definitions or ecclesiastical combat. Instead his portrait was dominated by tales of missionary endeavour, innovative evangelism, and engaged political activism, concerns which mirrored his personal priorities.[116] He was at pains to point out the loyalty of the Evangelical movement to the Established Church, and applauded the fact that even when faced by rampant ritualism, the Anglican Evangelicals 'never dreamed of deserting the ship, even when she seemed to be driving straight upon the

113 Bickersteth, *Evangelical Churchmanship*, p. 11.

114 Marston, *Message of Evangelical Churchmanship*, p. 28.

115 F. S. Guy Warman, 'The Essentials of Evangelicalism', *The Churchman*, 24 (1910): 750–8.

116 Andrew Atherstone, 'George Reginald Balleine: Historian of Anglican Evangelicalism', *Journal of Anglican Studies*, 12 (2014): 82–111.

rocks'.[117] This concern for Evangelicals to invest wholeheartedly in the Anglican project was further demonstrated by his address at the jubilee celebrations of the London College of Divinity on 'The Future of the Evangelical Party':

> Some of the Evangelicals of the past, with all their splendid earnestness in making people Christians, made them Christians of such a vague, indefinite, undenominational type, that whole congregations of them were lost to the Church altogether, and the harvest of much of that noble work has been reaped by other denominations. Is that not a danger that we see still? If we want Evangelicalism to be a power in our own Church in the future, we must make not only Evangelical Christians, but Evangelical Churchmen.[118]

This tension between Christianity and churchmanship lay at the heart of Evangelical struggles over the nature of Anglican identity. The perpetual tussle between doctrine and discipline, and whether it was possible to be both a good Evangelical and a good Anglican, was never satisfactorily settled. In each generation some resolved the tension by downplaying, or abandoning, either their Evangelicalism or their Anglicanism. Others were confident, even strident, in the integrity of their Anglican Evangelicalism, usually by interpreting the Church of England's history and formularies through a Reformation lens. Balleine never lived to see Evangelicalism became 'a power in our own Church', but the Victorian prophecies of the demise and ultimate death of the Anglican Evangelical movement proved premature. After recounting the Evangelical contribution to missions, the alleviation of poverty, education, Bible distribution, Sunday schools, and the deepening of spirituality, one early twentieth-century commentator concluded, 'The plain truth is that the Church of England cannot afford to lose us.'[119]

SELECT BIBLIOGRAPHY

Balleine, G. R., *A History of the Evangelical Party in the Church of England* (London, 1908).

Bebbington, David, *The Dominance of Evangelicalism: The Age of Spurgeon and Moody* (Leicester, 2005).

Carter, Grayson, *Anglican Evangelicals: Protestant Secessions from the Via Media, c.1800–1850* (Oxford, 2001).

[117] G. R. Balleine, *A History of the Evangelical Party in the Church of England* (London, 1908), p. 233.

[118] G. R. Balleine, 'The Future of the Evangelical Party', *The Johnian*, 20 (1914), p. 14; copy at St John's College Archives, University of Birmingham Special Collections, SJC 1/1/2/2/2.

[119] Marston, *Message of Evangelical Churchmanship*, p. 10.

Garbett, Edward (ed.), *Evangelical Principles: A Series of Doctrinal Papers Explanatory of the Positive Principles of Evangelical Churchmanship* (London, 1875).

Ryle, J. C., *Principles for Churchmen: A Manual of Positive Statements on Doubtful or Disputed Points* (London, 1884).

Scotland, Nigel, *Evangelical Anglicans in a Revolutionary Age, 1789–1901* (Carlisle, 2004).

Scotland, Nigel, *'Good and Proper Men': Lord Palmerston and the Bench of Bishops* (Cambridge, 2000).

Toon, Peter, *Evangelical Theology, 1833–1856: A Response to Tractarianism* (London, 1979).

Whisenant, James, *A Fragile Unity: Anti-Ritualism and the Division of Anglican Evangelicalism in the Nineteenth Century* (Carlisle, 2003).

Wolffe, John, *The Protestant Crusade in Great Britain, 1829–1860* (Oxford, 1991).

9

The Oxford Movement and Anglo-Catholicism

James Pereiro

A NEW INTELLECTUAL AND SPIRITUAL ATMOSPHERE

John Henry Newman, in his 'The State of Religious Parties' (*British Critic*, 1839), identified the Oxford Movement as part of a general and widespread intellectual and religious revival of the early nineteenth century, a new and pervasive atmosphere infiltrating all areas of life, 'a spirit afloat... everywhere'.[1] The Tractarians, however, resisted identifying the new spiritual sensibility with the 'spirit of the age'. It was not a transient step in the historical evolution of the human spirit but an expression of man's permanent nature and spiritual needs. Newman felt that the Movement was part of an irresistible and generalized reaction against a prevailing and intellectually impoverishing rationalism which had straitjacketed and done violence to man's nature. Human nature, however, cannot not be held down for long. The inevitable reaction had followed: nature had managed to escape that suffocating embrace and was beginning to breathe freely once again. The Tractarians felt that the contemporary Church of England, emerging from the low ebb of the eighteenth century, was not in a condition to provide for the new spiritual and religious feeling. They were not alone in that estimation. The Evangelicals had advanced similar objections to the routine and un-spiritual character of the generality of the Anglican Church. Even men like Archdeacon Daubeny, a paradigmatic High and Dry Churchman, admitted that the Church of England had settled into a mediocre routine and did not provide for the spiritual aspirations of souls.[2]

[1] John Henry Newman, 'Prospects of the Anglican Church', in *Essays Critical and Historical* (London, 1897 edn.), II, p. 272. He changed the title when republishing the article in this volume of essays.

[2] Charles Daubeny, *Guide to the Church* (Bath, 1830 edn.), p. 242.

The Oxford Movement was born of this desire for a more 'vital' religion. Varied intellectual influences came together in preparing and shaping it. Walter Scott and the Lake Poets were identified by the early Tractarians as having played a part in generating the new sensitivity. The Evangelicals' call to conversion, their insistence on man's personal relationship with God, and on the power of God's redeeming grace had also contributed to create a new and deeper religious feeling, influencing not a few of those later involved in the Oxford Movement.[3] High Churchmanship was, however, from a doctrinal point of view, the fundamental constitutive element in the formation of what became the Oxford Movement. The High Church party had its own revival in the early years of the nineteenth century, particularly around what became known as the Hackney Phalanx, but by the late 1820s and early 1830s it had lost much of its original momentum, and High Churchmen were to welcome the dynamism and early success of the Oxford Movement in spreading many a High Church doctrine.

At Oxford University, the long-standing and well-rooted High Church tradition and the intellectual renaissance of the 1820s provided the right conditions for the emergence of the Movement. Samuel Francis Wood, describing the university at the time, said that a 'considerable intellectual activity manifested itself during the years 1820–1830'. Within Oxford University, Oriel College was the true cradle of this new intellectual awakening. Its common room had gathered together, under the leadership of Provost Edward Copleston, some of the most vigorous intellects in the university, fellows like Richard Whatley, Edward Hawkins, and John Keble.

> The Students were excited to a more intelligent study of the Principles of Logic and Rhetoric by the Elementary works of Archbishop Whately on these subjects; and generally, this Author's writings, whose characteristic it is to sharpen and discipline the intellect without giving it matter to feed and rest upon, were a remarkable preparation for what was to follow. The Ethics of Aristotle also, long a text book in the University, became in the hands of more than one College Lecturer the ground work of a very instructive course of Ethical study. Not that this course was either very extensive or scientific, but it led to much useful reflexion on the formation of moral habits, on their influence on opinions and such like practical points. Bishop Butler's great work 'The Analogy of Religion, Natural and Revealed, to the Constitution and Course of Nature'[4] was also studied; much more for the sake of the poignant suggestions it incidentally contains on the points just named, than as an argumentative defence of Religion.[5]

[3] Robert Wilberforce, *The Evangelical and Tractarian Movements* (London, 1851).

[4] Joseph Butler, *The Analogy of Religion, Natural and Revealed, to the Constitution and Correct Course of Nature* (London, 1736).

[5] Samuel F. Wood, 'Revival of Primitive Doctrine', in James Pereiro (ed.), *'Ethos' and the Oxford Movement: At the Heart of Tractarianism* (Oxford, 2008), p. 253.

Intellectual rigour was accompanied, in Keble's case, by a deep religious sensitivity, which found expression in his popular *Christian Year* (1827). It was around him that the first nucleus of what was to become the Oxford Movement was formed. The reading parties he organized at Southrop during some summer vacations combined the intellectual rigour and religious devotion—within an atmosphere of friendly intercourse between tutor and students—which later characterized the Movement. Keble retired early from Oxford to a pastoral ministry in rural parishes but Hurrell Froude, Robert Wilberforce, and Newman, newly elected to an Oriel fellowship, took up Keble's mantle as college tutors. They bestowed on their pupils—especially those who were more able and endowed with better moral qualities—as much time and effort as was usually given by good private tutors, keeping an account not only of their intellectual but also of their spiritual progress. The tutors' concern and their friendly intercourse with their students were rewarded by the latter with their sincere following and devotion,[6] forging between them strong personal bonds that were to survive university years. Tutors in some other colleges also acted on a similar interpretation of the university statutes but it is doubtful whether they went as far or were as systematic in applying them as their Oriel counterparts.

At the basis of their concept of the tutorial system was Keble's firm conviction that the search for truth could not be separated from the pursuit of goodness. Doing otherwise would lead to intellectual pride, an almost insurmountable obstacle to the attainment of moral rectitude. Lack of moral rectitude, in its turn, would disturb the clear perception of truth, inclining the mind towards error. In essence, Keble's idea amounted to a reversal of the Enlightenment view of intellectual education as leading almost necessarily towards moral uprightness. As far as Keble was concerned, moral uprightness was a fundamental condition for clear intellectual perception: intellectual training could not be dissociated from religious and moral formation.

A MOVEMENT IS BORN

The Oriel tutors' aim was to foster in the students under their supervision—whether destined for the Church or for positions in civil society—intellectual rigour and spiritual maturity. It is unlikely that they had originally conceived the idea of forging a group to exert influence on Church and state. Diverse circumstances seem to have contributed to giving tutors and their students (past and present), the consistency of a group ready to act as such. One of

[6] Thomas Mozley, *Reminiscences, chiefly of Oriel College and the Oxford Movement* (London, 1882 edn.), I, pp. 180–1, 210, 229.

them was the passing of the Catholic Emancipation Act (1829). Peel, the MP for Oxford University, had introduced Catholic emancipation against his previous personally expressed opinion and the wishes of the university. The Tractarians and Oxford Evangelicals campaigned successfully to prevent his re-election. One of the results of this campaign was the marking of boundaries around the pre-Tractarian grouping, distancing them from Provost Hawkins and the other Oriel Noetics, who had supported Peel's candidacy. Tensions between provost and tutors were to escalate in the following years. Hawkins felt, not without reason, that the tutors were taking more and more control of the undergraduates entrusted to them, at the expense of his own authority within the college, and he would in the end stop assigning them new students. The main catalyst, however, for the formation of the Oxford Movement was the Irish Temporalities Act (1833) suppressing several Church of Ireland archdioceses and dioceses. The not-yet-Tractarians, and others with them, felt at the time the need to rescue the Church from the suffocating control of the state. At stake were not only the temporalities of the Church but also its spiritual divine dimension. Keble sounded a not uncertain trumpet call in his Assize Sermon of 1833. It found an echo in many hearts, and Newman, with Froude's support, took in hand the direction of the campaign. He led it with extraordinary vigour and resourcefulness, and his friends and former disciples gathered around him, helping in the initiatives set in motion in order to awaken the Church to the dangers threatening it. Froude was to be prevented from direct involvement in the Movement by the incipient consumption which was to cut short his life; still, his regular correspondence—with Newman, Keble, and others—was a constant source of ideas and encouragement, as well as criticism. Enlarging on one of his own phrases, he could be said to have been the poker of the Tractarian fire in the early years of the Movement.

The Oxford men aimed at awakening the Established Church and nation to the divine character and nature of the Christian dispensation, recalling important and neglected truths. Newman, in his postscript to the 1879 edition of the *Lyra*, wrote that their plan of campaign involved initially a three-pronged strategy: the *Tracts for the Times*, the *Lyra Apostolica*, and the *Church of the Fathers*; the last two being published in monthly instalments in the *British Magazine*. The tracts were meant to take up the theological and controversial side of Christianity, the *Lyra* the ethical, and the *Church of the Fathers* the historical.[7] The tracts were the most visible and influential of their efforts, and were to give the Movement its name. More than forty were produced in the first year, Newman being the main contributor. Their distribution involved friends and sympathizers in an almost capillary campaign to reach the English clergy. The early tracts stressed the divine institution of the Church and the

[7] John Henry Newman, *Lyra Apostolica* (Oxford and Cambridge, 1879), pp. vi–vii.

origin of its divine authority, along High Church lines. They were short and impassioned defences of episcopacy and of apostolic succession. The early Church, they claimed, free from state interference, flourished even under state persecution, without compromising the faith in search of inclusiveness. The tracts soon widened their focus to embrace other topics like the sacramental system (particularly baptism and the eucharist), the rule of faith, the liturgy, and the controversy with Rome. Apostolic succession led naturally to the eucharist: only an episcopal ordination, performed by a bishop in apostolic succession, could guarantee a sacrificial priesthood and the eucharist. The sacramental system and the grace conferred by the sacraments led in turn to a reconsideration of the nature of Christian justification. Pusey's tract on the scriptural views on baptism, published over three consecutive numbers in 1835, brought the topic to public attention. His tract also marked a change of approach. The need for clarion calls to wake up the dormant Church was now passed and the tracts became longer and more learned, as well as less frequent. It also revived the series at a time when public interest was beginning to flag. They continued now to attract a large readership. Newman claimed that in the year to June 1839 they had sold about 60,000 copies of the tracts.[8]

The unambiguous High Church doctrine espoused by the tracts could not but attract controversy. The Evangelical reaction against Pusey's tract on baptism was prompt and unequivocal. Earlier controversies about baptismal regeneration and the nature of Christian justification were still fresh in the minds of many; they now resurfaced. The *Record* led the charge against Pusey's tract and Newman responded to the *Record*'s attacks in a series of letters to the paper, the germ of his *Lectures on Justification* (1839). Just before his controversy with the *Record*, Newman had been involved in an exchange of letters on the rule of faith with a French Catholic priest, the Abbé Jager. These letters were originally published in French periodicals, and Newman later developed the substance of his response to the abbé in his *Prophetical Office of the Church* (1837). In it he criticized the Roman Catholic view of the rule of faith and infallibility and, particularly, the Protestant concept of *sola scriptura*, while defending the Anglican *Via Media*—Scripture and Tradition—that traced its course between Evangelical principles and the tenets of the Church of Rome. The *Lectures* and the *Prophetical Office* defined the Movement's position on the two fundamental points at the heart of the Reformation: justification and the rule of faith.

The *Library of the Fathers of the Holy Catholic Church, Anterior to the Division of East and West*, the great publishing venture of the Oxford Movement, had been conceived by Pusey and Newman in 1836, as a means of spreading Catholic theology. The Fathers witnessed to Vincent of Lerins's rule

[8] Newman to J. W. Bowden, 22 June 1839 (John Henry Newman, *The Letters and Diaries of John Henry Newman* [hereafter *LD*] (Oxford, 1995), VII, p. 97.

of faith: what has been believed always, everywhere, and by all defined the faith of the Church. They were the professed guides of Anglicanism in faith and practice. The Tractarians thought that the Church of England had lost much Catholic doctrine in the foregoing three hundred years by its neglect of the Fathers. It was necessary to go back to them in order to bring to mind the teaching of the Primitive Church. It was not possible to claim continuity with antiquity and, at the same time, be ignorant of its representative writers. The knowledge of Christian antiquity was necessary to understand and maintain orthodox doctrine, and resist heretical error. To their surprise, the archbishop of Canterbury agreed to be its patron, the bishops were among its subscribers, and even some Evangelicals, like Edward Bickersteth, supported the venture. The first volume, St Augustine's *Confessions*, was published in 1838 and some twenty volumes were to appear before 1845.

THE SPRING AND HIGH SUMMER OF TRACTARIANISM

The lines separating Tractarians and Evangelicals had been clearly defined from the first and were never blurred. Their differences may have been put aside when joining together in opposing Peel's re-election or Hampden's appointment as regius professor of theology (1836), but these were only temporary truces to face a common enemy. The front along which Evangelicals and Tractarians faced each other was to extend beyond dogmatic issues like *sola scriptura* and justification. In 1836 Newman was encouraging his London Tractarian friends involved in politics and the professions to counteract the Evangelicals' effort to influence—others would say control—societies like the Pastoral Aid Society or the Society for Promoting Christian Knowledge (SPCK).[9] Some of these laymen took up Newman's invitation and, in alliance with High Churchmen, put forward proposals to change the procedures regulating decision-making about publication policies at the SPCK. As a result, High Churchmen gained control of what to publish but, to Tractarian disappointment, adopted an inclusive stand in order not to offend Evangelical sensitivities. On the other hand, the policies of societies like the Simeon Trust and the Pastoral Aid Society, committed to appoint Evangelical clergy, led the High Churchman Joshua Watson to found in 1837 the Additional Curates Society. Some London Tractarians were elected to its committee.

[9] Newman to F. Rogers, 5 July 1836, *LD*, V, p. 319.

The year 1838 offered these London Tractarians the opportunity of having a wide and deep social influence at national level. The need to improve the education of the people and the possible methods to do so had been discussed for years in Parliament, and been the object of an array of pamphlets and press articles. In 1838 this public concern about the extension of education for the poor offered Gilbert F. G. Mathison, Samuel Francis Wood, and Thomas Dyke Acland the opportunity to approach the National Society for the Education of the Poor (NSEP) with plans to promote the creation of a national system of education under control of the Church. In this they were supported by individuals of widely different persuasions, including among them Gladstone and the Evangelical Lord Ashley. The National Society adopted their plans and co-opted the Oxford men onto its governing committees. The extraordinary expansion of Church schools across the country and the creation of a network of training colleges for teachers during the late 1830s and early 1840s was the direct result of the Oxford men's initiative.[10] Their plans went beyond the scope of the NSEP, aiming at setting up eventually a system of national education, from primary school to university, under the auspices of the Church. They soon realized that it was impossible to recreate a fully developed system of Church education as it had existed before the Reformation. Charles Marriott's effort to set up a college for poor students in Oxford seems to have been the only Tractarian initiative at Oxford University until the creation of Keble College. More successful was the setting up of middle schools. These took their first tentative steps under their inspiration, and later achieved a considerable degree of success and maturity with the foundation of Tractarian-inspired public schools for the middle classes, like those of Nathaniel Woodard.

The year 1838 was, in a certain sense, an *annus mirabilis* for the Oxford Movement, representing perhaps the high water mark of its influence. The Tractarians had committed themselves since 1836 to contribute about a third of the content of the High Church periodical *British Critic*. Newman, however, had larger designs for it. He wanted a review 'conducted, i.e. morally conducted, on the Catholic temper—we want all subjects treated in one and the same principle or basis ... our Editor must be the principle, the internal idea of Catholicism itself, pouring itself outwards, not trimming and shaping from without'.[11] In 1838 Newman, through a daring strategic manoeuvre, obtained editorial control of the review. From that moment, until its closure in 1843, the *British Critic* was to serve as the flagship of the Movement, and its voice—clear and very loud at times—gained a nationwide readership for Tractarian ideas.

The year 1838 also saw publication of the first part of Froude's *Remains*. They appeared in two parts, of two volumes each; the second part coming out

[10] James Pereiro, 'Tractarians and National Education', in Sheridan Gilley (ed.), *Victorian Churches and Churchmen* (Woodbridge, 2005), pp. 249–78.

[11] Newman to E. Churton, 21 Nov. 1837, *LD*, VI, 169–70.

in 1839. At the core of Tractarian thought was the tenet that it was not possible to effect an intellectual reformation without a spiritual one and vice versa. Catholic doctrine without the corresponding Catholic ethos of holiness was destined to have a precarious existence and to be sooner or later unable to preserve its purity and integrity. Froude, for Keble and Newman, was the personification of the Catholic ethos, an ethos of sanctity, and the production of that moral temper was the main aim for the publication of the *Remains*. The reaction, however, disappointed the editors' expectations. The public exhibition of Froude's spiritual battles injured the sensibility of some readers; others were taken aback by his open antagonism towards the English Reformers. Besides, the preface to the second part of the *Remains* put forward a principle which, perhaps unnoticed by many readers at the time, defined one of the fundamental traits of Tractarianism and was to mark the parting of the ways for Tractarians and traditional High Churchmen. The authors claimed that any doctrine or practice demonstrated to be of antiquity called for its reintroduction in the present-day Church.[12] High Churchmen, when later confronted with the results of applying this principle, would counter that the Reformers had already given the authoritative interpretation of antiquity for the Church of England to follow and that the Fathers should now be read within that tradition.

The reaction against the *Remains* took different forms, mostly in print. However, one of them—the Martyrs' Memorial at Oxford—was to be set in stone. The memorial was the brainchild of Charles Golightly who, after an early attachment to Newman and Pusey, had become progressively critical of Tractarian theology and had made it his life-mission to fight for the purity of the English Reformation by unmasking the threat posed to it by Tractarianism. The memorial, promoted in 1838 and built by subscription, was intended as a test of Reformation orthodoxy. None of the Tractarian leaders subscribed to it, not even Pusey who did not share Froude's strictures on the Reformation and the Reformers. The *Remains* checked to a certain extent, at least for a time, the spread of the Oxford Movement's ideas and sowed the first seeds of uneasiness among those High Churchmen who had so far supported it. They had originally been heartened by the growing popularity of the High Church principles championed by the Tractarians; now those principles were in danger of being tainted by association with the 'indiscretions' of Froude's *Remains*. The publication of the *Library of Anglo-Catholic Theology*, mooted in 1839, was intended as High Church ballast for the Movement, proving the Anglican credentials of the ideas put forward by the Tractarians. The committee overseeing the *Library* was predominantly made up of traditional High Churchmen, heavily outnumbering the Tractarians included in it. Newman, Keble, and even Pusey were to approach the project in a rather

[12] Richard H. Froude, *The Remains of the Rev. Richard Hurrell Froude* (Derby, 1839), I, part ii, pp. xi–xiii.

lukewarm way. Although they themselves had used, rather selectively, traditional Anglican divines to support such Catholic ideas on apostolic succession and baptismal regeneration, they would rather not see in print whole works of some of the authors they had quoted because of the non-Catholic views in some of their writings.

DECLINE AND FALL

In spite of the backlash caused by the *Remains*, Newman could say that in 1839 the Movement was at the height of its influence; its doctrines and practice exerted by then a wide and growing sway over the country's religious and social life. Events, however, moved fast, and the year 1841 brought about the most serious check on its progress; one from which it would never fully recover. Its ideas had generated in many clergy and laity alike a deep sense of frustration at the contrast between the Catholic beliefs and feeling they had made their own and the reality of the Anglican Church. Newman's *Tract 90* was an attempt to reassure the Tractarians, and others who sympathized with their ideas, that the Thirty-Nine Articles did not exclude those Catholic doctrines and practices that had become dear to them. The articles, he tried to show, were susceptible of a Catholic interpretation. *Tract 90*, however, proved a futile effort. The unanimous show of episcopal condemnation which followed its publication disqualified it unambiguously. The Anglican Church was Protestant. The promotion of the Jerusalem bishopric (1841), in alliance with Prussian Protestants, seemed to some of the Tractarians to compromise the Catholic character of the Anglican Church.

From the early 1840s Newman was on what he later called 'his Anglican death-bed'. He withdrew from Oxford to Littlemore and there engaged in his last projects as an Anglican, among them the *Lives of the English Saints* and his study of doctrinal development in Christian doctrine. The first had an immediate apologetic purpose. Newman, having failed to reassure Tractarians about the catholicity of Anglican doctrine with his *Tract 90*, tried now to confirm those who were wavering in their allegiance to the Church of their birth by stressing the mark of holiness within it. In Newman's eyes, this had by then become the last-ditch apologetic defence of the Church of England against the claims of Rome. According to the Tractarian theory of religious knowledge, sanctity was not only the safeguard of orthodox doctrine but also the fundamental mark identifying the true Church. A number of Tractarians—including James Anthony Froude—were involved in the *Lives of the Saints*. The project, however, was frowned upon by men like Pusey, Gladstone, and James Hope (later Hope-Scott): it was too Roman, it would simply not do.

As a matter of fact, the first defections to Rome came from among those involved in the *Lives of the Saints*.

Outside Littlemore, controversy continued dogging the Movement. In 1841 Newman had handed the immediate direction of the *British Critic* to Thomas Mozley. From that moment on, the general tone of the *Critic*, and in particular the string of articles published in it by Frederick Oakeley and William George Ward, further alienated those High Churchmen who had already started to distance themselves from Tractarianism after *Tract 90*. Ward's and Oakeley's articles, while heaping criticism on the Church of England in general and on the Reformers in particular, were setting off the Roman Church as the ideal of the Christian Church for Anglicanism to imitate. They could not fail to generate a reaction. William Palmer of Worcester would fly the High Church standard and ride in defence of the Church of England in his pamphlet *A Narrative of Events connected with the Publication of the Tracts for the Times: with Reflections on existing Tendencies to Romanism, and on present Duties and Prospects of Members of the Church* (1843). The title clearly described the pamphlet's message. Palmer avoided criticizing directly the main leaders of the Movement and directed instead his fire onto the writers of the *British Critic*. It had become clear, he wrote, that their message was a subversion of the Anglican Reformation; the writers represented a Trojan horse within the citadel of Anglicanism. All sincere High Churchmen should repudiate the tone and spirit of the review, and defend the Church of their baptism. The *British Critic* did not for long withstand the combined pressure of episcopal disfavour and High Church criticism. It was closed down in October 1843. William Ward, however, would reply to Palmer's strictures and to a large extent confirm them in his *Ideal of a Christian Church* (1844), a jumble of condemnations of the Anglican Reformation and of praises of the Roman system, interspersed with disquisitions about the Tractarian theory of religious knowledge and references to the development of doctrine.

The first defections to Rome took place as early as 1843. They led Newman to resign his incumbency of the university church in Oxford, St Mary the Virgin. By that time, he had published his *University Sermons* (1843), containing among them the recently preached one on the development of doctrine. In the following years, he continued building up his theory of development, and, satisfied that Rome was the true Church of Christ, looked for reception into it in October 1845. Ward had preceded him in September of that same year. Many had remained within the Church of England on Newman's warrant that it was safe to do so. Now that security no longer held and the trickle of conversions to Rome became a steady stream, including some forty to fifty clergymen during the years 1845 to 1847.

The leaders of the Movement who remained in the Anglican Church tried to stem the tide of desertions to Rome by reassuring the anxious and the waverers while trying to give direction to what was left of it. Keble, urged by

Pusey, published his *Sermons Academical and Occasional* (1847) with this aim in mind. They were preceded by a long preface in which Keble appealed to Butler's principles in the *Analogy*, a foundation stone of the Oxford Movement. Keble thought that a wayward and unhealthy desire for certainty in matters of faith had led a certain number of Tractarians to Rome, and he tried to unmask this 'generous' but misguided feeling. The analogy of nature, Butler had said, militated against the possibility of certainty in matters of faith. Probability, in God's plan for man's probation, served as a test of moral rectitude: the believer was to find the path of truth among contrasting claims aided by his moral compass.[13] Keble's words may have held back, at least for a time, some of those experiencing 'Roman difficulties' but it is difficult to assess the actual success of his efforts. In Oxford, Charles Marriott, from 1850 the vicar of St Mary's, tried for his part to fill part of the pastoral vacuum left by Newman, while continuing to edit the *Library of the Fathers*, but was soon removed from that ministry by his illness and premature death in 1858.

The conversions to Rome also had an effect on another scenario, that of the new church built by Pusey in Leeds, St Saviour's. The intention of Pusey was to put into practice the sacramental and devotional dimension of the Movement, and to show that the Church of England could provide for the deeper catholic longings of her children. This full 'sacramental system' involved the frequent celebration of the eucharist in a dignified and solemn manner, stressing the real presence, the offering of confession, and so on. But the initiative came into the world at an inauspicious time, the new church being consecrated two weeks after Newman's conversion to Rome, and it would operate from the outset under a cloud of suspicion. St Saviour's clergy, convinced that they were following apostolic tradition, were ready to labour for a time under the 'external' disapproval of episcopal authority. The Church of England, for the time being, might not teach the 'sacramental system', but they had no doubts that sooner or later she would recognize and make her own Catholic doctrine and practice. They felt, rather optimistically, that Tractarianism, when tolerated, would absorb the Protestant tradition. However, they were not in fact to be tolerated. St Saviour's clergy soon encountered opposition from the bishop of Ripon and of Walter Farquard Hook, the High Church vicar of Leeds. The majority of them deserted the Church of England after the Gorham Judgment of 1850.

The Judgment had presented the remnants of the Oxford Movement with a dramatic crisis. The decision of the Privy Council in the case between Bishop Phillpotts of Exeter and George Cornelius Gorham upheld the legitimacy of Gorham, an Evangelical, denying baptismal regeneration within the Church of England. It was the deathblow for waverers who had survived—some of them

[13] John Keble, *Sermons Academical and Occasional* (Oxford, 1847), pp. x, lxvi–lxvii.

precariously—the crisis of Newman's conversion to Rome. The state had now appropriated to itself the right to define—or rather undefine—the doctrine of the Church of England, and the Church had lodged no complaint against this usurpation. For some this was the ultimate proof of its Erastian character: confirmation that the Church of England was a human not a divine creation. It brought about another significant haemorrhage of Tractarian sympathizers: over sixty clergymen left the Church of England for that of Rome in 1850–1; even more than in the immediate aftermath of Newman's conversion.

DID THE OXFORD MOVEMENT DIE IN 1845?

From then on, many of the converts, Newman included, declared that the Oxford Movement had not succeeded, and could not succeed, in its attempt to make the Church of England Catholic. They felt that the Movement of 1838 had been a gallant effort, but it had failed; it was alien to the national Church, and the Church of England, true to its nature, had reacted by trying to expel it as an alien body. Tractarianism had rejected private judgement; it had waged a vigorous campaign to recover lost or neglected Catholic doctrine, and had performed a providential service by slowing the decline of the Church of England towards rationalism. Unfortunately, the process of dissolution was relentless. The course of the Anglican Church was inexorably downwards: error waxed while truth disappeared; Anglicanism conformed itself to the state of public opinion among the English people. The converts considered that the Movement had been an initiative of the Holy Spirit but that the Spirit's aim transcended the confines of the Church of England. It had familiarized many Anglicans with Catholic doctrine and practice, and, in that way, broken down barriers between them and Rome, facilitating the process of conversion. Those Tractarians who, after recent events, remained faithful to the Church of England could only do so, said the Roman converts, by betraying their own principles, finding refuge in private judgement and the inclusiveness of the establishment, and becoming what they had always abhorred: one more party within the Anglican Church.[14] It was also suggested that, in some cases, family considerations, and the desire not to lose material and social advantage had influenced their decision.

The converts' diagnosis was not to go unchallenged. In 1851 John Mason Neale, a Cambridge graduate of Tractarian sympathies, would dispute the converts' facts and conclusions. The Oxford Movement, he said, had been an intervention of the Holy Spirit in order to restore Catholic doctrine and

[14] John Henry Newman, *Lectures on Certain Difficulties felt by Anglicans in submitting to the Catholic Church* (London, 1850 edn.), pp. 127–34.

practice within the Anglican Church, and to revitalize also its missionary zeal. Its providential character was shown, among other things, by the gradual rediscovery and adoption of Catholic doctrine and principles. Their sudden introduction would have generated a rejection in some, while others might have been led to Rome to seek there what they could not find in the Church of England. The converts were blamed for having set back the progress of Catholic ideas, now contaminated in the public mind by the desertion of many of their supporters. Those who remained in the Church of England had been left with an uphill struggle. They worked under suspicion and, at times, suffered open persecution. What required greater heroism, to leave the Church of England for that of Rome or to remain fighting against the odds for the recovery of the Catholic inheritance of Anglicanism?[15]

The secession of a considerable number of Tractarians to Rome during the period 1845 to 1851 did not put an end to the spread of the doctrines and practices promoted by the Oxford Movement. Catholic doctrine appeared to have a dynamism of its own, independent of the personalities who had initially promoted it. Statistical studies suggest that, in spite of the number of clerical conversions to Rome, Tractarian ideas gathered strength in parishes after 1845. According to Herring, the number of incumbents influenced in different degrees by Tractarianism continued growing during the years 1845–52 and thereafter. Herring's calculation gives 141 Tractarian incumbents for 1845; he reckons that these had become 211 by 1852.[16] These figures require careful interpretation, given the fact that, in the same period, there were almost 140 clerical secessions to Rome.[17] By 1870, according to Herring, there were 442 Tractarian clerical sympathizers among some twenty thousand Anglican clergy.

The Oxford Movement was considerably slower and less influential outside England. The Church of Wales and the Scottish Episcopalians were both small minority Churches in their respective countries. The established Church of Wales numbered less than a quarter of the population in an overwhelmingly dissenting country. The Scottish Episcopal Church, much smaller, was a 'dissenting' church, under a Presbyterian establishment and subject to penal laws until the end of the eighteenth century. The introduction of the Oxford Movement in both countries shared some common characteristics: it was promoted mainly by Oxford-educated clergymen, chiefly from Jesus College in the case of Wales, with the support and financial help of a network of mostly Anglicized landowners connected in many cases by bonds of family or friendship. Such were in Scotland the Marchioness of Lothian, until her conversion

[15] John M. Neale, *Lectures on Church Difficulties* (London, 1871 edn.), pp. 55–69, xi–xxxix; W. J. Sparrow Simpson, *The History of the Anglo-Catholic Revival from 1845* (London, 1832), pp. 288–92.

[16] George Herring, *What Was the Oxford Movement?* (London, 2002), p. 71.

[17] Edward G. K. Browne, *History of the Tractarian Movement* (Dublin, 1856 edn.).

to Rome in 1851, and the Duke of Buccleuch; W. E. Gladstone and James Hope also took a lively interest in the future of Episcopalianism. In Wales Lady Windsor, Lord Tredegar, the Glynnes and Gladstones of Harwarden, the Williams, and the trustees of the Marquis of Bute played a similar role. Tractarianism took root in a pre-existing High Church tradition, tinged with Jacobitism in the case of Scotland. In both, Scotland and Wales, Tractarianism counted on little episcopal support, even though Alexander Penrose Forbes, bishop of Brechin, was to become the first Tractarian bishop in Great Britain. The Scottish Episcopal Church experienced a degree of growth in the years 1839 to 1854, and its new confidence expressed itself in the building of churches and the founding of new congregations. Still, during the nineteenth century, it did not represent more than 3 per cent of the population. Not all of that growth was the result of Tractarian influence, though Tractarianism introduced a new dynamism in Episcopalianism. Something similar happened in Wales. The Oxford Movement established itself in the late 1850s and 1860s, and it soon became increasingly associated with ritualism and the social mission. Although the 1833 crisis of the Church of Ireland had been the immediate reason for the Movement breaking cover, Tractarianism had a very limited success in the country. The Church of Ireland was a small minority in a predominantly Catholic country and was itself largely Evangelical. Still, High Church sympathizers among clergy and laity welcomed the revival of Catholic principles brought about by the Oxford Tracts. These did not lack episcopal support: Bishop Jebb of Limerick had advanced some of those principles, influencing the Tractarians; others like Bishop Mant and Archbishop Beresford were initially sympathetic towards the Movement. This, however, was to flounder in Ireland as a result of the crisis that followed *Tract 90* and the Protestant sense of being under siege by a resurgent Irish Catholicism.

Missions to non-Christian countries were new fields of expansion for Tractarian ideas and practice. Many Anglicans, Tractarians among them, discerned in the accelerating expansion of the British Empire a divine providential dimension. God had granted the empire to Britain that it might spread all over the world the purest form of Christianity, as preserved in Anglicanism. The Society for the Propagation of the Gospel in Foreign Parts (SPG, founded in 1701), and the Evangelical Church Missionary Society (CMS, founded in 1799), which had been active in a minor key during the first part of the century, considerably expanded their operations in Africa and the East in the second. Early Tractarians and High Churchmen, after the American experience, conceived the missionary expansion as taking place under the oversight of missionary bishops independent of the state. The Colonial Bishoprics Fund was established in 1841 in order to endow missionary dioceses. The Junior Clergy Missionary Association, with its strong consciousness of the imperial mission, attracted a later generation of young Anglo-Catholic clergy who channelled their efforts through Universities Missions. The Cambridge Mission to Delhi in the 1870s and the Oxford Mission to Calcutta, begun in 1880, were mainly the work of celibate brotherhoods of priests, graduates of the Universities. Anglo-Catholics took over other SPG initiatives, like those in Central Africa. This was a trend that continued in the last decades of the nineteenth century and in the early years of the twentieth, influenced by the growing acceptance of moderate Anglo-Catholicism and the decline of traditional High Churchmanship. The growing number of Anglo-Catholic dioceses, both in Great Britain and in the missionary field, helped to entrench Anglo-Catholicism in many parts of the empire, not only among the native populations but also among those emigrating to the colonies from the United Kingdom. Some of the new religious orders were also to become active in the missionary field. The Society of St John the Evangelist (SSJE) sent two missionaries to India in 1874. It was a minor presence in the missionary movement and unremarkable by the number of conversions it brought about. However, Benson's idea of a more personal rather than institutional mission activity, carried out by a religious community adopting an indigenous style of life and respect for local custom contrasted with the ideas of Westernization which inspired most missionary ventures.[18]

RITUALISM AND RELIGIOUS LIFE

By the 1860s it was becoming clear that a profound change was in the process of transforming the outward appearance of those who claimed descent from the Oxford Movement. Increasing numbers of clergy were wearing chasubles, celebrating the eucharist facing east, burning incense, and so on. To what an extent this was a logical outcome of the Oxford Movement is a matter still under discussion. The early Tractarians had thought that a formal liturgy was essential to the revival of the Church of England. It should combine a solid doctrinal basis and leave room for the expression of religious emotion, without the 'emotionalism' of the Evangelicals. They were wary, on the other hand, of a ceremonial detached from the theological truths of which it was to be the expression. 'Ceremonialism' could be as obnoxious and deforming as Evangelical excitement, and that for similar reasons. As early as 1839, in response to a young clerical correspondent, a Cambridge graduate, Pusey argued that the wearing of eucharistic vestments at that stage of the Movement was equivalent to beginning at the wrong end; years later, in 1860, he would tell Bishop Tait: 'I

[18] Rowan Strong, 'Origins of Anglo-Catholic Missions: Fr Richard Benson and the Initial Missions of the Society of St John the Evangelist 1869–1882', *Journal of Religious History*, 66 (2015): 90–115.

am in this strange position that my name is made a byword for that with which I never had any sympathy [ritualism], that which the writers of the Tracts... always deprecated.'[19] The Tractarians had a distinct fear that the Movement should become superficial. Even advanced Tractarians like Frederick Oakeley and Frederick William Faber, who in the 1840s were to be criticized for their moderate liturgical innovations, also warned against premature developments in ceremonial, outrunning the slower pace of doctrinal rediscovery.[20] That would contradict the 'principle of reserve', a central Tractarian tenet. God had revealed himself with measure and in a progressive way. He had unfolded the doctrines of revelation in due order and within their proper context, so as not expose beginners prematurely to doctrines for which they were unprepared. The recipients of doctrine would have otherwise been perplexed rather than converted by the sudden exhibition of the whole evangelical scheme. According to the principle of reserve, most early Tractarians believed that the clergy should not introduce liturgical practices which their parishioners were not familiar with before preparing them doctrinally and liturgically. The ritualists, however, thought otherwise: they would teach their parishioners the truths of the Catholic faith through liturgical manifestations which reflected them.

The influential architectural lobby, the Cambridge Camden Society, had identified the point of perfection of Christian piety and worship in the Middle Ages, before its corruption by superstition in the late Middle Ages. Medieval Catholic ethos and doctrine had given rise to Catholic Gothic architecture; they hoped that the process might work in reverse, and that medieval Catholic architecture and ritual would give rise to a more Catholic ethos and doctrine. They had not abandoned the principle of reserve; it had never in fact been part of their intellectual makeup. The medieval Church, rather than the Church of antiquity, was their main inspiration and model; in their terminology, 'ancient usage' did not go beyond the medieval. The Cam was now flowing into the Isis.

The measured innovative approach of early Tractarians when reintroducing neglected rubrics countenanced by the Book of Common Prayer had already been the object of protests, denunciation to bishops, and attacks in the press. Henry Wilberforce at Farleigh and Frederick Oakeley at Margaret Street Chapel (London) were to be the objects of early episcopal scrutiny. Oakeley, the incumbent of Margaret Street Chapel since 1837, had provided the London Tractarians, and a growing congregation attracted by their principles, with a place of worship doctrinally and spiritually inspired by the Oxford Movement, while serving also as a liturgical point of reference for many a clergyman who wanted to import the new spirit and forms into their own parishes. It was not an easy task. Other similar liturgical experiments encountered decided

[19] H. P. Liddon, *Life of Edward Bouverie Pusey*, II, p. 142 and IV, p. 211 (London, 1893 and 1897).

[20] Alf Härdelin, *The Tractarian Understanding of the Eucharist* (Uppsala, 1965), pp. 334–9.

opposition. St Saviour's Leeds, as we have seen, experienced the combined disapproval of bishop and vicar. William J. Bennett, after having built in London one of the jewels of the Gothic revival, St Barnabas Pimlico, was to be chased out of it in 1851 by the combined force of public protests and Bishop Blomfield's censure.

These and other similar instances of opposition failed to stem the tide of liturgical innovation. The work of Archdeacon Robert I. Wilberforce, *Doctrine of the Holy Eucharist* (1853), affirming with great display of scholarship the sacrificial nature of the eucharist and the real presence, gave further doctrinal impulse to liturgical developments. High eucharistic doctrine seemed to call for high liturgical practice. This led the Evangelical Alliance and other ultra-Protestants to step up their watchful vigilance in order to preserve the purity of the Protestant faith. Denunciations and canonical and legal prosecutions followed. The archbishop of York was considering prosecuting Archdeacon Wilberforce because of his eucharistic doctrine and stopped proceedings against him only on receiving his resignation. Wilberforce's fellow archdeacon, George Anthony Denison, 'never a close ally of the Tractarian leaders in early years and best identified as an advanced old High Churchman',[21] was taken to court for sermons of 1853 and 1854 maintaining the real presence. He was condemned as to the substance of his sermons but finally acquitted on a point of law. Bishop Forbes of Brechin, prosecuted in 1857 for the views on the eucharist put forward in one of his charges, was also to be acquitted but did not escape censure. The real presence and the sacrificial nature of the mass were doctrines still beyond the Anglican pale. Change, however, was in the air. The prosecution of William Bennett in 1869 showed how far things had moved on in the intervening years. He was acquitted by both the Court of Arches and the Privy Council. The latter decided that the doctrines of the sacrificial nature of the eucharist, the real presence, and the adoration given to it were not inconsistent with the Thirty-Nine Articles of the Church of England. Paradoxically, this doctrinal latitude within the Anglican Church did not extend to ritualism. It had become a cause of general concern in the 1860s and public opinion led Parliament in 1874 to pass the Public Worship Regulation Act. Prosecutions followed and some priests were imprisoned as a result, the most notable legal case being the prosecution and eventual condemnation of Edward King, bishop of Lincoln, in 1888. The Act, however, was soon discredited and showed itself ineffectual in suppressing ritualism or preventing its spread.

Another striking development associated with the Oxford Movement during the critical years from 1845 to 1851 was the formation of the first Anglican sisterhoods. They were often the result of the cooperation of a Tractarian

[21] Peter Nockles, *The Oxford Movement in Context: Anglican High Churchmanship 1760–1857* (Cambridge, 1994), p. 242.

clergyman and a woman with a calling to the religious life. Their creation responded to the renewed Oxford Movement emphasis on holiness of life and ideals of total dedication to God's service, which had also inspired the proliferation of celibate clergy. Besides, the sisterhoods offered the possibility of useful employment for women who did not feel themselves called to marriage; they also responded to a growing concern for the unprivileged and the search for community organizations engaged in this form of work. The first experiment, the Sisterhood of the Holy Cross in Regent's Park, founded in 1845, was not altogether successful. A number of the nuns, together with their chaplain (William Dodsworth), were to convert to Rome, and in 1858—after some of the nuns had been active in the Crimea as nurses—the congregation was absorbed by the Devonport Sisters of Mercy, to create the Congregation of Religious of the Society of the Most Holy Trinity. The Anglican Sisters of Mercy, founded in 1848 by Priscilla Lydia Sellon and encouraged by Bishop Phillpotts, soon developed a comprehensive network of beneficent initiatives including educational ventures, an orphanage, homes for the poor, and so on. In 1849 Marian Hughes founded the Society of the Holy and Undivided Trinity in Wantage, with the active support of William John Butler, vicar of Wantage, Henry Edward Manning, and Pusey. In spite of the conversions of Manning (1851) and of some of the sisters to Rome, it was to become one of the most flourishing of the now growing number of Anglican sisterhoods, counting some fifty nuns by the 1870s. Among the other later foundations, the Community of St John the Baptist (1852) had a particularly rapid growth, from eight sisters in 1855 to 201 in 1884. The sisterhoods had to overcome the suspicion of Anglicans in general and, in particular, the early opposition of bishops. This did not prevent their growth and involvement in education, caring for the poor and sick, rescue work with street women, and so on. It did not take long for the first orders of contemplative nuns to be established. The greatest growth of religious sisterhoods came in the years 1880 to1910; by the end of the nineteenth century there were several thousand religious sisters in convents all around Britain and overseas.

The foundation of the first male religious orders, leaving aside the erratic efforts of Fr Ignatius of Llanthony, was some twenty years behind the foundation of the early sisterhoods. The SSJE, known as the Cowley Fathers, was the first stable Anglican religious community, being established by Richard Meux Benson and two companions in 1866. They committed themselves to a full round of monastic observance and parochial duties, specializing in parochial missions and retreats. By the end of the century, in spite of their slow growth, they had houses in India, America, and South Africa. Another influential religious order was the Community of the Resurrection (CR). It formed around Charles Gore, then principal of Pusey House (Oxford), and its first members made their profession in 1892. The CR was inspired to a certain extent in the Catholic Oratorian Congregation and, like the SSJE, it was committed to parochial work and missionary outreach, the second becoming particularly prominent after the community moved to Mirfield in 1898. The most prominent of the contemplative male religious orders was the Benedictine Community at Caldey Island, where it finally established itself in 1906, after an early peripatetic existence. It had been a 'bright star in the Anglo Catholic firmament' since its foundation but its life was cut short when its founder and twenty-two of its members joined the Church of Rome in 1913. The last quarter of the nineteenth century and the early years of the twentieth saw the foundation of a considerable number of male and female religious orders, particularly in Britain and the United States. Some of them were of very ephemeral character, but others were here to stay. After encountering early opposition, the religious life was to be one of the enduring contributions of the Oxford Movement to Anglicanism.

ECUMENISM

Tractarian and Anglo-Catholic doctrine of the Church had a natural ecumenical dimension. The Church universal, founded by Christ, was constituted by three branches—Anglican, Orthodox, and Roman—which had preserved apostolic succession and the fundamentals of the faith. The breaches of the original unity, resulting from diverse historical circumstances, without destroying the unity of the Church, had, however, brought about a weakening in each of the branches' hold on its divine endowments and impaired their mission. It was imperative, as a result, to work for re-establishment of the original unity. Traditional High Churchmanship considered that the Church of Rome should reform itself on the model of the Church of England before reunion was to be possible. Others, like Ward and Oakeley, thought that it was the Church of England that was in need of conforming to the pattern of the Church of Rome.

There had been early ecumenical approaches like the failed one of William Palmer of Magdalen College, Oxford to the Orthodox Church and the not much more successful one of the Revd George Spencer, a pre-Tractarian convert to Rome, in his association of prayer for unity. The late 1850s saw, however, a renewed impulse to ecumenical initiative. The Association for the Promotion of the Unity of Christendom (APUC), founded in 1857, grew out of the enthusiasm and sanguine hopes of the Revd Frederick George Lee and Ambrose Phillipps De Lisle, a Catholic layman. The confessed aim of the association was prayer for unity and this uncontroversial objective attracted many to it: Anglican, Catholic, and Orthodox. Lee, Phillips, and some others, were, however, looking beyond prayer for unity. They aspired to an early review by Rome of the vexing question of the validity of Anglican Orders, as a preliminary step on the path towards reunion. It is difficult to estimate the numbers of those who joined the association, as there are no reliable records, but membership grew rapidly. An estimate of the association's membership in its early years set it at about 8,000: 7,000 Anglicans and 1,000 Catholics, plus some Orthodox. Ritualists were the dominant influence within it. The remnants of the Tractarian old-guard—Keble, Pusey, and Isaac Williams—kept their distance from the association, considering it too unrepresentative and Rome-prone.

Harmony among APUC members was to prove short-lived. The *Union Newspaper*, the early organ of the association, under Lee's direction, alienated many High Churchmen because of its advocacy of 'Romish' practices. Its successor, the *Union Review*, trying to assuage Anglican sensitivities, managed to offend Roman ones. The *Union Review*'s implicit and at times not-so-implicit advocacy of the three-branch theory raised doctrinal issues which could not be overlooked. The English Catholic hierarchy, without supporting the APUC, had done nothing at first to discourage Catholic membership of the association. They now felt impelled to intervene. In 1864, the bishops obtained a rescript from Rome condemning the association. The condemnation was renewed in December 1865 after a letter of remonstrance against the rescript signed by 198 Anglicans. Most Roman Catholics then deserted the APUC. It continued its operations but the condemnation left behind an atmosphere of bitterness among many of its Anglican members.[22]

Pusey was now seen as taking up the reins of the ecumenical dialogue with his *Eirenicon* (1865). This was not originally intended as a response to the rescript but as an answer to Manning's claims in *The Workings of the Holy Spirit in the Church of England* (1864). Manning had affirmed that the Church of England rather than being a bulwark against infidelity, as Pusey maintained, had caused the progressive slide of the English people into error. Pusey's *Eirenicon*[23] changed the tone of the ecumenical dialogue, turning it into a detailed examination of controverted Catholic doctrines like infallibility and devotion to the Blessed Virgin. Although responses were to issue from different Catholic quarters, Newman became now Pusey's main correspondent. Their exchanges, however, were mired in their different understandings of the rule of faith. Pusey stood immovable on the *quod semper* of Vincent of Lerins, while Newman rested his case on the theory of development. As a result, their dialogue went round in circles, rarely to meet head on. Two more *Eirenicons* were to follow; the last one—*Is Healthful Reunion impossible?*—

[22] Mark Chapman, *The Fantasy of Reunion: Anglicans, Catholics, and Ecumenism, 1833–1882* (Oxford, 2014).

[23] Edward B. Pusey, *An Eirenicon: In a Letter to the Author of 'The Christian Year'* (London, 1864).

being published in 1870 during Vatican Council I. The council went on to define the infallibility of the Pope that Pusey had feared. He saw it as a disastrous blow to the prospects for reunion, and in 1876 republished his third *Eirenicon* under the revised title *Healthful Reunion as conceived possible before the Vatican Council.*

The dismissal of the APUC and the Vatican Council definitions closed the door to dialogue with Rome. Anglican ecumenical attention turned now to the Eastern Churches and those of the continent which had broken away from Rome, in particular the Old Catholic Church. These episcopal Churches, national in character and deeply anti-papalist, were seen by many Anglicans as more promising partners in dialogue than Rome. The Bonn Reunion Conferences of 1874 and 1875, organized by Professor Ignaz von Döllinger, who had left the Church of Rome after the Vatican Council's definition of infallibility, were a moment of hope. The Bonn Conferences brought together some Anglicans, Orthodox, Old Catholics, and representatives of other Churches. The conferences also marked a convergence of ritualism with traditional High Churchmanship, facilitated by the former's growing anti-Romanism as the result of recent events; for example, this convergence later made it possible for the High Church Christopher Wordsworth, bishop of Lincoln, to join R. F. Littledale and other ritualists in their liturgical conferences at All Saints, Margaret Street. Traditional High Churchmen, like bishops Christopher Wordsworth and Edward Harold Browne, took now a central role in the conferences, as also did Henry Parry Liddon, Pusey's disciple and biographer. The original optimism was short-lived. Pusey, who was not taking part in the conferences, reacted strongly against Orthodox intransigence in respect to the *Filioque*, writing a long pamphlet against its removal from the Creed. The various parties to the conferences drifted inevitably away from each other. Ecumenical paths seemingly closed, the Church of England, for the time being, turned its attention towards building up the Anglican Communion around the globe.

LIBERAL ANGLO-CATHOLICISM AND THE SOCIAL QUESTION

There had been a change in liturgical approach from the early Tractarians to those who claimed descent from the Movement; as the years went by, there would also be considerable doctrinal divergences from traditional Tractarian doctrine. Pusey House had been founded at Oxford in 1884 as a shrine to Pusey and a centre to propagate Tractarian ideas, and Charles Gore was appointed its first principal. His early ideas were initially well within the doctrinal parameters of the Oxford Movement. In 1889, however, he edited the collection of essays published under the title *Lux Mundi*. The volume contained a series of studies in the theology of the Incarnation, central to the Oxford Movement and the subject of Robert Wilberforce's influential book of 1848. However, the forty years since the publication of Wilberforce's book had seen a considerable change of theological method among many of those who claimed descent from the Movement. Some of them, James Mozley among the first, had started to move away from patristic study, with its focus on the recovery of Catholic doctrine, towards a more speculative theology influenced by contemporary philosophy. An unforeseen consequence of this new methodological option was the neglect of an important area of theological enquiry: the theology of the Church. The rich patristic theology of the Mystical Body of Christ which was being rediscovered by the Tractarians in the 1840s was no longer pursued with the same interest, and the doctrines of the Incarnation and the sacramental system failed to produce the ecclesiological fruits that were their natural development. *Lux Mundi*'s openness to the scriptural postulates of the Higher Criticism and its quasi-Hegelian philosophical approach to the Incarnation caused a considerable stir. Many Anglo-Catholics were to attack it. Gore's type of synthesis incorporating biblical criticism and contemporary philosophy while preserving liturgical and sacramental Catholic elements, was, however, to leave a permanent mark on some sectors of Anglo-Catholicism, although many Anglo-Catholics would remain wary of theological liberalism.

An Anglo-Catholic image which has remained in the public's imagination is that of the 'slum priests', mostly celibate, working in Pimlico, in the East End of London, and other similar places in the great industrial cities; gaining the respect and loyalty of their parishioners by their selfless service to spiritual and material needs. The Oxford Movement, however, did not have to wait for the 'slum priests' or the Christian Social Union to develop a social conscience. The recovery of the un-churched urban working class had been the motivation behind Pusey's early initiative at St Saviour's, and had even earlier inspired the involvement of the London Tractarians in the National Society for the Education of the Poor. Besides, recent studies have shown how social concerns, usually allied to a perception of the social evils resulting from the Reformation, were present in the Movement from its early years. The *British Critic* referred frequently to what was called at the time the 'condition of England' and so did much of general Tractarian literature and sermons. These championed a transformation in the relations between the classes, reminding the rich about the obligations of property towards the poor and promoting the improvement of the condition of labour. They felt that the theology of the Incarnation, eucharistic worship, the frequent reception of Communion in the parishes, and the removal of pew rentals were bound to bring about an enhanced awareness of spiritual brotherhood and of social solidarity.[24]

A characteristic Anglo-Catholic pastoral tool in the third quarter of the nineteenth century was parish missions. This initiative, already practised in other denominations, aimed at a revival of parish life and at attracting back the lapsed through an intense and concentrated effort of doctrinal instruction, sacramental practice, and devotional acts. The first missions were organized by Richard Benson, the founder of the SSJE, and Charles Lowder, the 'slum priest' of St Mary's, London Docks. The missions were to become a regular feature in Anglo-Catholic parishes and there were several Anglican brotherhoods—like the SSJE and the Community of the Resurrection—which were committed to this pastoral work. The missions attracted large congregations, and were the occasions of many returning to religious practice, although their long-time effects varied greatly. One of the most spectacular was the Twelve Day Mission to London of 1869. It was organized under Benson's direction and involved some 120 parishes, not all of them Anglo-Catholic.

WHEN DID THE OXFORD MOVEMENT BECOME ANGLO-CATHOLICISM?

Studying the Oxford Movement and Anglo-Catholicism implies having to confront an inescapable question: is Anglo-Catholicism a true development of the earlier Oxford Movement? Hylson Smith saw Anglo-Catholic ritualism and Catholic liberalism as links in the chain of High Churchmanship evolution.[25] Mark Chapman, among the most recent authors, has claimed that Anglo-Catholicism developed out of the Oxford Movement.[26] Those who left for Rome, as we have seen, answered this question very differently. It might be claimed that the remnants of the Tractarian first generation—like Keble, Pusey, Marriott, or Isaac Williams—were overtaken by a new generation which, although recognizing to a certain extent Pusey's nominal leadership, was to follow different principles. Many abandoned the vital connection with patristic theology—as opposed to a mere historical one—while preserving the sacramentalism and devotional dimensions of the Movement. The

[24] Simon A. Skinner, *Tractarians and the 'Condition of England': The Social and Political Thought of the Oxford Movement* (Oxford, 2004), pp. 167–87, 259–64; S. Ives, *The Relative Position and Duties of Clergy and Laity* (Fayetterville, 1844), pp. 7, 19ff.

[25] Kenneth Hylson Smith, *High Churchmanship in the Church of England from the Sixteenth Century to the Late Twentieth Century* (Edinburgh, 1995), p. 175.

[26] Mark Chapman, *Anglicanism: A Very Short Introduction* (Oxford, 2006).

Tractarian theory of knowledge, including the principle of reserve, was also a casualty of the process.

We also need to take into consideration that the term Anglo-Catholicism is not a neutral one. It had a High Church pedigree. In 1838 Palmer had spoken of the Anglo-Catholic masters of the sixteenth and seventeenth centuries and, for example, of the 'Anglo-Catholic theology of the Eucharist'.[27] The *Library of Anglo-Catholic Theology* was a traditional High Church initiative forced upon the Tractarians, not a natural growth of the Movement as the *Library of the Fathers* had been. In 1844 the High Churchman William Gresley published his *Anglo-Catholicism*,[28] where he defined Anglo-Catholicism as the religion of the Church of England; the system of belief and practice the Movement was deviating from. Kaye-Smith in 1927 reinforced this point of view when she wrote: 'if the whole Church of England is not Catholic, it is vain for any party within her to call itself Catholic.'[29] It is difficult to set a clear date when the terms Tractarianism or Oxford Movement gave way to Anglo-Catholicism to describe the Catholic Revival. The change of name, therefore, had implications beyond signifying that the Movement had overflowed the confined limits of Oxford. The new name represented in a certain sense a retreat from advanced Tractarian positions towards traditional High Churchmanship. Besides, later refusals of Pusey, Keble, and Williams to be identified with Anglo-Catholic ritualism or to be involved in the APUC seem to suggest that the old Tractarian guard did not quite recognize them as their true *epigoni*. It is true that Pusey took a leading role in some of the controversies of the time involving ritualism, the doctrine of the eucharist, and ecumenism. But he did so from the outside, in order to defend compromised doctrinal points dear to his heart, like the real presence, the three-branch theory, or the *Filioque*.

Late nineteenth-century Anglo-Catholicism seems to have been the combination of a fourfold genetic inheritance, in which Tractarian elements mixed with Cambridge ecclesiology, traditional High Churchmanship, and liberal theology. These elements, combined in diverse measures and degrees, were to give rise to the different groupings sheltering under the Anglo-Catholic umbrella. The 'Catholic Revival' within the Church of England was more a kaleidoscope than a monochrome phenomenon. The golden age of Anglo-Catholicism was still in the future. They had won many doctrinal and liturgical battles in their search for acceptance within the pale of Anglicanism, and, by the end of the century, they had become an influential force within the Church of England. Some Anglo-Catholics, like Moses from Mount Nebo, thought

[27] William Palmer, *A Treatise on the Church of Christ* (London, 1838), I, pp. vi, 263.

[28] William Gresley, *Anglo-Catholicism: A Short Treatise on the Theory of the English Church* (London, 1844).

[29] Sheila Kaye-Smith, *Anglo-Catholicism* (London, 1927), p. vii; Herbert L. Stewart, *A Century of Anglo-Catholicism* (London, 1929).

themselves able to discern the Promised Land; they could hardly have imagined the glorious post-First World War Congress period. That was to be a time of unbounded optimism, when pastoral success was accompanied by intellectual and artistic distinction. They were then to feel entitled to claim that they had finally entered into their inheritance. The euphoria, however, was to be short-lived.

SELECT BIBLIOGRAPHY

Anson, Peter F., *The Call of the Cloister: Religious Communities and Kindred Bodies in the Anglican Communion* (London, 1964).

Blair, Kirstie (ed.), *John Keble in Context* (London, 2004).

Brendon, Piers, *Hurrell Froude and the Oxford Movement* (London, 1974).

Brown, Stewart J., *The National Churches in England, Ireland and Scotland 1801–1846* (Oxford, 2001).

Brown, Stewart J. and Peter Nockles (eds.), *The Oxford Movement: Europe and the Wider World* (Cambridge, 2012).

Chadwick, Owen, *The Victorian Church*, 2 vols. (London, 1980).

Chapman, Mark, *The Fantasy of Reunion: Anglicans, Catholics, and Ecumenism, 1833–1882* (Oxford, 2014).

Church, Richard W., *The Oxford Movement: Twelve Years 1833–1845* (London, 1891).

Gilley, Sheridan, *Newman and his Age* (London, 1990).

Härdelin, Alf, *The Tractarian Understanding of the Eucharist* (Uppsala, 1965).

Ker, Ian, *John Henry Newman* (Oxford, 1988).

Newman, John H., *Apologia pro Vita Sua*, ed. M. J. Svaglic (Oxford, 1967).

Nockles, Peter, '"Lost Causes and Impossible Loyalties": The Oxford Movement and the University', in M. G. Brock and M. C. Curthoys (eds.), *The History of the University of Oxford*, vol. 6, part 1 (Oxford, 1999), pp. 195–267.

Nockles, Peter, *The Oxford Movement in Context: Anglican High-Churchmanship 1760–1857* (Cambridge, 1994).

Pereiro, James, *'Ethos' and the Oxford Movement: At the Heart of Tractarianism* (Oxford, 2008).

Pereiro, James, *Theories of Development in the Oxford Movement* (Leominster, 2015).

Reed, J. S., *Glorious Battle: The Cultural Politics of Victorian Anglo-Catholicism* (Nashville, 1996).

Simpson, W. J. Sparrow, *The History of the Anglo-Catholic Revival* (London, 1932).

Skinner, Simon A., *Tractarians and the 'Condition of England': The Social and Political Thought of the Oxford Movement* (Oxford, 2004).

Strong, Rowan, *Episcopalianism in Nineteenth-Century Scotland* (Oxford, 2002).

Strong, Rowan and Carole Engelhardt Herringer (eds.), *Edward Bouverie Pusey and the Oxford Movement* (London, 2012).

White, J. F., *The Cambridge Movement: The Ecclesiologists and the Gothic Revival* (Cambridge, 1962).

Yates, Nigel, *Anglican Ritualism in Victorian Britain 1830–1910* (Oxford, 2000).

10

Liberal Anglicanism in the Nineteenth Century

Mark D. Chapman

DEFINITIONS

'Liberal Anglicanism' is a term that is not easily pinned down. It is perhaps best understood as a disposition which seeks to locate the Church within the wider framework of philosophical, social, and political ideas, all of which focus on the pursuit of truth of which the Church is not the sole guarantor. Christianity was not *sui generis* but was part of a shared human quest for truth. Underlying this form of thought was a form of Platonism which understood truth as lying beyond all human knowledge. This implied that the critical faculties of the reasoning mind were accepted as God-given whereby human beings could understand what had been divinely revealed through the generations but which was always open to methodological doubt: nothing could contain the whole of truth, which was ultimately to be found only with God.

There was, of course, nothing new in the application of the critical faculties to the truths of the Church, and Platonism also had a long and venerable history in the Church of England. Nineteenth-century liberal Anglicanism has a long pedigree in the relatively broad-minded and enlightened movements within the Church of England such as the Great Tew Circle, the Latitudinarians, and the Cambridge Platonists of the seventeenth century, and the theologians of the eighteenth-century Enlightenment.[1] Nevertheless, although there are many continuities with the past, nineteenth-century liberal Anglicanism developed in a context which saw rapid modernization, industrialization, and pluralization of society along with the consolidation of 'Church parties', whereby the Church of England became a battle ground of competing visions for what constituted authentic 'Anglicanism'.[2] 'High' and 'Low' Church gradually mutated into

[1] Paul Avis, *Anglicanism and the Christian Church* (Edinburgh, 2002), part two.

[2] Mark Chapman, *Anglican Theology* (London, 2012).

Anglo-Catholic, Evangelical, and a third party which could be described as 'liberal' or Broad Church (or derided as 'Latitudinarian' by critics such as William Ward).[3]

The name 'Broad Church' was possibly coined by A. H. Clough, and later used in a sermon by A. P. Stanley in about 1847.[4] It would seem that Stanley's original use was not intended to designate a Church party, but was a claim that the Church of England encompassed people from a different range of views and was therefore a broad Church. This was the gist of his article written in response to the Gorham Judgment and published in the liberal journal, *The Edinburgh Review*.[5] However, in the famous essay 'Church Parties', published by W. J. Conybeare in 1853,[6] the term was used to designate a third party *alongside* the others. This grouping was also referred to as 'Moderate' or 'Catholic' by its friends, and 'Latitudinarian' or 'indifferent' by its detractors. Conybeare summarized the 'Broad Church' as teaching that the Church was a 'society divinely instituted for the purpose of manifesting God's presence, and bearing witness to his attributes' and 'to realise the ideal of the true Christian brotherhood'.[7] Misquoting a sermon by Thomas Arnold, whom he regarded as the leading figure of the movement, Conybeare noted that the Church 'would remind us daily of God, and work upon the habits of our life as insensible as the air we breathe'.[8]

Conybeare recognized the difficulties of the designation, especially as some of the leading figures, including F. D. Maurice, expended much of their time attacking the notion of Church party and disliked the 'new nickname'. Nevertheless the designation stuck: the 'Broad Church' became the third party which was often defined negatively by those who sought to oppose its rationalizing maxims. Nevertheless, 'Broad Church' is probably a better term than 'liberal', since it emphasizes the ecclesiastical and social dimension of theological thought rather than anything more individualistic. The Broad Churchmen were first and foremost churchmen rather than the sort of liberals and utilitarians against which so many conservatives had reacted in the 1830s.

[3] Wilfrid Ward, *William George Ward and the Oxford Movement* (London, 1889), p. 46.

[4] Arthur Burns, 'Church Parties', in Stephen Taylor (ed.), *An Anglican Miscellany* (Church of England Record Society, vol. 7) (Woodbridge, 1999), pp. 213–385 (p. 235); Owen Chadwick, *The Victorian Church*, 2 vols. (London, 1992), I, p. 544; Tod Jones, *The Broad Church: Biography of a Movement* (Lanham, MD, 2003); Ieuan Ellis, *Seven against Christ: A Study of Essays and Reviews* (Leiden, 1980), p. 2.

[5] 'Report of the judgement in the case of Gorham versus the Bishop of Exeter', *Edinburgh Review*, 92 (1850): 263–92 (p. 266).

[6] Burns, 'Church Parties', p. 341.

[7] Burns, 'Church Parties', p. 343.

[8] Burns, 'Church Parties', p. 342.

THE ROLE OF THE UNIVERSITIES

The rise of the Broad Church movement was closely associated with the reforms of the universities of Oxford and Cambridge in the early nineteenth century: there was a rapid improvement in the quality of teaching and learning, especially in some colleges, most prominently Oriel College, Oxford which became a magnet for serious scholars in all disciplines including theology.[9] The period also saw a series of changes to the union of Church and state which had characterized the old Tory synthesis of throne and altar.[10] The *ancien régime* was increasingly challenged from both inside and outside the Church. The two Anglican universities of Oxford and Cambridge were part of this synthesis, functioning as microcosms of the wider society, and many of their conflicts mirrored those in the wider Church and state.[11] At both the ancient universities as well as the new university at Durham established in 1832, Anglicanism was more than simply a formality: at Oxford undergraduates had to subscribe to the Thirty-Nine Articles on matriculation, and most colleges required compulsory Holy Communion once a term.[12] At Cambridge (and Durham) religious tests were imposed only on graduation.[13] This meant that Dissenters could be admitted, even if they were unable to take their degrees. At Oxford, debates over subscription to the Thirty-Nine Articles of Religion were to the university what Catholic Emancipation had been to the wider state: they continued to provoke controversy throughout the mid-nineteenth century until their final abolition in 1871.[14] About two-thirds of Oxford BAs went on to ordination. The universities also retained close connections with the parishes. On marriage, fellows of colleges, most of whom were clergymen, would frequently move into a parish over which an Oxford or Cambridge college retained the advowson.

Unlike Protestant Germany, where all clergy were subject to a rigorous course in theology, the English universities offered a curriculum of grammar, logic, and mathematics with a modest amount of compulsory theology for all students. Undergraduate theology was not offered until 1870 at Oxford and 1873 at Cambridge. After a reform of the university examination statute in 1800 initiated in part by John Eveleigh (1748–1814), provost of Oriel College,

[9] Daniel Inman, *The Making of Modern English Theology: God and the Academy at Oxford, 1833–1945* (Minneapolis, 2014); David M. Thompson, *Cambridge Theology in the Nineteenth Century: Enquiry, Controversy and Truth* (Aldershot, 2008).

[10] Peter B. Nockles, *The Oxford Movement in Context: Anglican High Churchmanship 1760–1857* (Cambridge, 1994), ch. 1.

[11] H. F. G. Matthew, 'Noetics, Tractarians, and the Reform of the University of Oxford in the Nineteenth Century', *History of Universities*, 9 (1990): 195–225 (p. 197).

[12] Matthew, 'Noetics, Tractarians', p. 195.

[13] D. A. Winstanley, *Unreformed Cambridge* (Cambridge, 1935), ch. 5, esp. p. 313.

[14] 34 Vict. 26. Peter Nockles, 'An Academic Counter-Revolution: Newman and Tractarian Oxford's Idea of a University', *History of Universities*, 10 (1991): 137–97 (p. 152).

Oxford required students to take examinations in grammar, rhetoric, logic, moral philosophy, mathematics, physics, and the Christian religion.[15] To complete a BA, students had to show knowledge of the gospels in Greek, the Thirty-Nine Articles of Religion, and Bishop Butler's *Analogy of Religion*. Even though theology was a relatively modest part of the general arts degree, success in the core disciplines could not compensate for failure in divinity.[16]

The curriculum at both Oxford and Cambridge meant that theology was conceived, at least implicitly, as simply one aspect of a wider conception of truth: theology was a part of general learning. As the century wore on, that general learning became more expansive and teaching improved. Professors would then inspire their students in the pursuit of pure research.[17] Although the higher degrees of Bachelor and Doctor of Divinity remained on the statute book, in practice theology was a *part* rather than the summit of learning. This meant that as university learning expanded through the nineteenth century, so theologians and Church leaders faced a choice of either isolating theology as a sacred science based upon a supernatural revelation, or relating it to the remainder of learning and the educational processes which threatened the distinctiveness of the Church. While there were many efforts to improve the status of theology in the 1830s and 1840s, which led to the foundation of several new professorships,[18] this compulsory element of theology in all Oxford degrees seemed increasingly anachronistic, even if it was not finally abolished until 1931.[19] Following the Roman Catholic example as well as the establishment of the General Theological Seminary in New York in 1817, the dioceses of the Church of England gradually began to establish seminaries (from the late 1830s) to nurture their students in a form of Anglican orthodoxy which many bishops increasingly came to see as under threat from the developments in the universities. Others, however, saw the vital importance of ensuring that theology remained connected with the wider learning.

NOETICS

By 1820 Oriel College, Oxford had become perhaps the most important centre of learning in England. Competitive fellowship examinations meant that it overshadowed the other colleges in terms of its intellectual standing, setting an

[15] Cited in W. R. Ward, *Victorian Oxford* (London, 1965), p. 13.

[16] M. C. Curthoys, 'The Examination System', in M. G. Brock and M. C. Curthoys (eds.), *The History of the University of Oxford* (Oxford, 1997), VII, pp. 339–74 (p. 348).

[17] Inman, *Making of Modern English Theology*, p. 44.

[18] Inman, *Making of Modern English Theology*, pp. 44–5.

[19] Curthoys, 'Examination System', p. 357.

example that would soon be emulated. Under the influence of Edward Copleston (1776–1849), who was elected provost in 1814 (and afterwards became dean of St Paul's and bishop of Llandaff), a group of scholars who shared common interests in theology and wider learning gathered in Oriel. They were quickly given the name 'Noetics'[20] after the highest stage of human intelligence in Plato's *Republic*. Thus, the young Samuel Wilberforce, while an undergraduate at Oriel, wrote to R. H. Froude in 1827 of a 'Noetick School'.[21] The School included Richard Whately (1787–1863), fellow from 1811 and archbishop of Dublin from 1831; Edward Hawkins (1789–1882), Copleston's successor as provost from 1828; and John Davison, fellow of Oriel from 1800. Davison's belief in a progressive revelation proved influential on the scientific thinker Baden Powell, who later contributed to *Essays and Reviews*.[22] Davison was also tutor to Renn Dickson Hampden, fellow of Oriel from 1814 and afterwards bishop of Hereford. On his nomination to the Regius Professorship of Divinity in 1836, a number of conservative opponents campaigned unsuccessfully to prevent his appointment, which became one of the first set pieces of the increasingly partisan divisions in Oxford and the wider Church of England. The charge was that his Bampton lectures of 1832 had tried to strip away some of the doctrinal baggage which, he held, formed no part of the core Christian truth. Indeed in the opening lecture, he claimed that 'Christianity had its beginnings amidst the obstructions of a twofold character: the obstructions of the human heart, and presumption of the human personality.'[23] Similarly, in his *Observations on Religious Dissent* (Oxford, 1834) he supported the abolition of subscription to the Thirty-Nine Articles. While his opponents could not prevent his appointment they nonetheless managed to prevent his preaching to the university and he produced very little academic work afterwards. The Hampden affair provoked bitter polemics, especially from Thomas Arnold, whose article 'Oxford Malignants' was produced directly in response to Tractarian and Protestant opposition.[24]

The Noetics also made an impact on Anglican thinking about political economy, and became trusted advisers to successive governments: Copleston became what Boyd Hilton called a 'clerical counsellor' to Lord Liverpool's

[20] Jones, *Broad Church*, ch. 2; Simon Skinner, 'Noetics', *ODNB*; Richard Brent, *Liberal Anglican Politics: Whiggery, Religion, and Reform 1830–1841* (Oxford, 1987).

[21] Skinner, 'Noetics'; W. Tuckwell, *Pre-Tractarian Oxford: A Reminiscence of the Oriel 'Noetics'* (London, 1909). S. A. Skinner, 'Oriel to Oliver Twist: Noetics and Tractarians at Large', in J. Catto (ed.), *Oriel College: A History* (Oxford, 2013), pp. 371–407.

[22] Pietro Corsi, *Science and Religion: Baden Powell and the Anglican Debate, 1800–1860* (Cambridge, 1988).

[23] R. D. Hampden, *The Scholastic Philosophy Considered in its Relation to Christian Theology* (Oxford, 1833).

[24] Thomas Arnold, 'The Oxford Malignants and Dr. Hampden', *Edinburgh Review*, 63 (1836): 225–39.

governments in the 1820s.[25] Whately became Professor of Political Economy at Oxford, and later established a chair in the subject at Trinity College, Dublin. He also produced lessons in political economy for elementary schools, which was circulated by the Society for Promoting Christian Knowledge (SPCK) across the world.

THOMAS ARNOLD

The most important figure associated with the Noetics on the national stage was Thomas Arnold (1795–1842), fellow of Oriel from 1815, who was appointed headmaster of Rugby School in 1828. He had supported Catholic Emancipation and in 1836 became one of the early fellows of the new University of London, established by the Whig government as a deliberately non-denominational institution. Arnold, who encouraged the introduction of non-denominational Scripture tests, had hoped that this example might influence the progress of the older universities, although in the end he came to realize that the new university was in fact more secular than non-denominational.[26] The vigour and vitality of youth appealed to him from the very beginning of his career and Arnold promoted the expansion of a liberal Anglican education into the public schools on his appointment to Rugby.[27] He remained convinced that a true national Church would put an end to sectarianism and might even embrace Dissent along with Anglicanism.[28] His unified vision of truth embraced the whole nation, its Church and its educational institutions, which he saw as an extension of the post-Reformation English Church: 'The "idea" of my life to which I think every thought of my mind more or less tends is the perfecting of the "idea" of the Edward the Sixth Reformers—the constructing a truly national and Christian Church, and a truly national and Christian system of education.'[29]

For Arnold, who through his life retained a very strong devotion to the person of Jesus Christ, there was a sense of the progressive nature of revelation

[25] Boyd Hilton, *Corn, Cash, Commerce: The Economic Policies of the Tory Governments, 1815–1830* (Oxford, 1977), pp. 79, 94.

[26] Arnold to T. S. Pasley, 16 Feb. 1838, in A. P. Stanley, *The Life and Correspondence of Thomas Arnold*, 2 vols. (London, 1845 edn.), I, p. 437.

[27] David Newsome, *Godliness and Good Learning* (London, 1961); F. D. How, *Six Great Schoolmasters: Hawtrey, Moberly, Kennedy, Vaughan, Temple, Bradley* (London, 1904); Herbert Schlossberg, *The Silent Revolution and the Making of Victorian England* (Columbus, OH, 2000), ch. 5; Mark Chapman, *Theology and Society in Three Cities: Berlin, Oxford and Chicago, 1800–1914* (Cambridge, 2014), ch. 4.

[28] Thomas Arnold, 'Principles of Church Reform', in *Miscellaneous Works* (London, 1845), pp. 257–338, esp. p. 269.

[29] Stanley, *Arnold*, II, p. 12.

through the whole of human history. This meant that it was always limited by time and place, and always expanding: in his well-known *Essay on the Right Interpretation and Understanding of the Scriptures* he could go as far as saying that even Jesus Christ himself 'must often have spoken as a man who possessed no greater knowledge than the men of that time and country'.[30] Similarly, in a sermon on the Psalms, he commented that 'Inspiration does not raise a man above his own time, nor make him even in respect to that which he utters when inspired, perfect in goodness and wisdom.'[31] Human society progressed through a process of enlightenment where people, both at an individual and a more universal level, gradually ascended in their understanding of moral and spiritual truth: 'That God has not thought proper to raise mankind at once to its highest state of moral perfection, any more than individuals are born at once to their maturity, is a matter of actual experience.'[32] Revelation was consequently intimately connected with the process of education: 'The human species has gone through a state of less fulness of moral knowledge, of less enlightened conscience, as compared with its subsequent attainments, just as every individual has done.' Consequently, there had to be a form of training appropriate to the particular state of knowledge, 'not anticipating the instructions of a more perfect state, but improving it in its imperfection; not changing spring into summer, but making of spring the best that could be made of it'. This amounted to a preparation for a perfection which was nonetheless 'not immediately made attainable'.[33] As headmaster, Arnold was quick to draw conclusions about what is appropriate in the education of children: 'while inculcating on a child's mind the principles of Christianity in all their purity, I should hesitate to press upon him all the deductions which follow from those principles, with regard to the various points of his own daily life'.[34]

On this model, Christianity was associated with the fundamental moral discipline required to approach life with a set of ideals and with a mind cultivated by higher ends: Arnold's overriding educational interest was in the pursuit of a universal higher truth through the process of maturing. In a letter from the beginning of his time in Rugby, Arnold wrote that his task was to 'form Christian men, for Christian boys I can scarcely hope to make;... I suspect that a low standard of morals in many respects must be tolerated amongst them, as it was on a larger scale in what I consider the boyhood of the human race'.[35] Education was principally about the formation of the adult

[30] Thomas Arnold, *Sermons Preached Mostly in the Chapel of Rugby School 1828–1831 with an Essay on the Right Interpretation and Understanding of the Scriptures* (London, 1842), p. 286.

[31] Thomas Arnold, *Sermons chiefly upon the Inspiration of Holy Scripture* (London, 1845), p. 147.

[32] Arnold, *Right Interpretation*, p. 287.

[33] Arnold, *Right Interpretation*, p. 287.

[34] Arnold, *Right Interpretation*, p. 288.

[35] Arnold to Tucker, 2 Mar. 1828, in Stanley, *Arnold*, I, p. 88.

Christian character, where mature Christians would be able to think for themselves and thus grasp more of God's revelation. The school was to function as a microcosm of the great Christian task of the education of the human race. The Church was thus to be understood as 'a society for the purpose of making men like Christ', rather than 'an institution for religious instruction and religious worship'. This narrow understanding would rob it 'of its life and universality, making it an affair of the clergy, not of people... of Sundays and synagogues, instead of all days and all places, houses, streets, towns and country'.[36] Arnold's understanding of Christianity permeated far and wide in the Church of England as clergyman headmasters and teachers who shared his educational ideals were appointed to prominent positions in the Church. Two of his successors at Rugby (A. C. Tait and Frederick Temple) went on to become archbishops of Canterbury. The national Church ideal espoused by Arnold, even though it was at times challenged by the other Church parties, continued to be influential in the leadership of the Church through the nineteenth and much of the twentieth centuries. Arnold's own biographer, A. P. Stanley, became a long-serving dean of Westminster (from 1863 until his death in 1881) continuing to espouse liberal causes from the very heart of the establishment.

ESSAYS AND REVIEWS

Despite his untimely death, Arnold remained a powerful influence on the Church of England through the next decades. Indeed, the collected volume *Essays and Reviews* of 1860,[37] the most important product of Broad Church theology, contained many of Arnold's themes. It was to become the most controversial theological book in Victorian England. A collection of seven contributions by scholars connected with Oxford, it was without any editorial input or much particular direction. It was unified around a shared vision which regarded Christianity as simply one aspect of an all-pervasive and unquestioned universal understanding of humanity. While reflecting the wider Oxford general curriculum of classics and history, the contributions also represented the first major effort to apply critical scholarship to the Bible in England, with reviews of a number of prominent books from Germany,

[36] Stanley, *Arnold*, II, p. 13.

[37] *Essays and Reviews* (London, 1860); references to tenth edition (London, 1862), hereafter *ER*. There is now a critical edition with much of the controversial literature: Victor Shea and William Whitla (eds.), *Essays and Reviews: The 1860 Text and its Reading* (Charlottesville, VA, 2000). Ellis, *Seven against Christ*; Josef L. Altholz, *Anatomy of a Controversy: The Debate over Essays and Reviews* (Aldershot, 1994).

where critical scholarship was developing in the more professionalized theological context.[38]

Benjamin Jowett's contribution on 'The Interpretation of Scripture' was the longest and the most influential essay in the volume.[39] As Regius Professor of Greek at Oxford, and shortly afterwards Master of Balliol, Jowett was one of the leading classical scholars of his day, which meant that his views carried weight.[40] In August 1858, Jowett wrote to A. P. Stanley about the invitation he had had from H. B. Wilson, who acted as editor, asking him to contribute to what became *Essays and Reviews*. Although the essayists were working within the 'limits of the Church of England', he noted, they were also 'determined not to submit to this abominable system of terrorism, which prevents the statement of the plainest facts, and makes true theology or theological education impossible'.[41] While he recognized in his essay that the interpretation of Scripture required what Coleridge had called 'a vision and faculty divine', he nevertheless held that 'in the externals of interpretation, that is to say, the meaning of words, the connexion of sentences, the settlement of the text, the evidence of facts, the same rules apply to the Old and New Testaments as to other books'.[42] In short, the reader was to '*interpret the Scripture like any other book*'.[43] Consequently, there was very little to fear from the application of critical scholarship to the Bible. As translator and interpreter of Plato, Jowett was secure in his faith that God's truth could be discovered both inside and outside the Christian tradition. 'The education of the human mind', he wrote, 'may be traced as clearly from the book of Genesis to the Epistles of St Paul, as from Homer to Plato and Aristotle.'[44] As so many of those who entered into the controversy noted, what was at issue was the nature of truth.

A similar approach to truth can be glimpsed in the essay by Frederick Temple (1821–1902), entitled 'The Education of the World'.[45] Temple had been headmaster of Rugby since 1858 and like Arnold he had devoured much German literature. He had also read Coleridge,[46] and Auguste Comte and

[38] Rowland Williams, 'Bunsen's Biblical Researches', *ER*, pp. 59–111; Baden Powell, 'On the Study of the Evidences of Christianity', *ER*, pp. 112–72; John Rogerson, *Old Testament Criticism in the Nineteenth Century: England and Germany* (London, 1984), esp. pp. 180–220.

[39] In *ER*, pp. 399–527.

[40] E. Abbott and L. Campbell, *The Life and Letters of Benjamin Jowett*, 2 vols. (London, 1897); Peter Hinchliff, *Benjamin Jowett and the Christian Religion* (Oxford, 1987); Peter Hinchliff, *God and History: Aspects of British Theology, 1875–1914* (Oxford, 1992), ch. 4.

[41] Abbott and Campbell, *Benjamin Jowett*, I, p. 275.

[42] *ER*, pp. 407–8.

[43] *ER*, p. 458 (Jowett's italics).

[44] *ER*, p. 487.

[45] E. G. Sandford (ed.), *Memoirs of Archbishop Temple by Seven Friends*, 2 vols. (London, 1906); E. G. Sandford, *Frederick Temple: An Appreciation with a biographical introduction by William Temple* (London, 1907); Peter Hinchliff, *Frederick Temple, Archbishop of Canterbury: A Life* (Oxford, 1998).

[46] Sandford, 'Editor's supplement', *Memoirs*, II, pp. 423, 472, 424. Hinchliff, *Frederick Temple*, p. 45.

French Positive philosophy.[47] Even though Temple's essay was one of the least controversial,[48] it revealed a great deal about how Arnold's ideals found expression in the broader interpretation of history: Temple's essay was based on the supposed analogy between the education of the individual and the increasing maturity of the human race. Temple, whose own upbringing was in the context of the early stages of British imperialism, made many assumptions about the relations between the different cultures of the world—at both the individual and the global level there were three stages of human development: childhood corresponded to the period before Jesus' coming; youth and early manhood to Jesus' period on earth; and full manhood corresponded to the period which followed after Christianity was young. Thus even before Christ, there was an opportunity to learn something of God, even if Temple felt that no other stage could ever match the new stage initiated by Christ. Thus the Hebrews 'may be said to have disciplined the human conscience, Rome the Human Will, Greece the reason and taste, Asia the spiritual imagination'.[49]

On this pattern of history, human beings gradually move from the necessary rules of childhood (analogous to the divinely-given Law of the Old Testament) to a situation where instead of mere obedience they begin to exercise their reason through free choice. Temple waxed lyrical about the next stage, the flowering of youth, where emotions are strong and where passion and love run wild. This too gradually disappeared as human beings mature into adulthood. Here they increase in discipline, not by returning to the unthinking legalism of childhood, but through self-legislation according to moral principles, which would gradually lead to self-government and tolerance. The goal of education was about approaching more nearly towards the truth. It was a dialectical process of disentangling toleration from dogmatism 'and to unite toleration, not with indifference and worldliness, but with spiritual truth and religiousness of life'.[50]

Since the goal of religion was to clear away the 'human blunders' that had concealed the truth, so the study of the Bible could be no different in kind from any other truth-seeking intellectual pursuit, and there was absolutely nothing to fear: 'If we have made mistakes, careful study may teach us better. If we have quarrelled about works, the enlightenment of the understanding is the best means to show us our folly.'[51] Education of the human race was thus about growing up, accepting that 'the mature mind of our race is beginning to modify and soften the hardness and severity of the principles which its early manhood had elevated into immutable statements of truth'.[52]

[47] Sandford, *Memoirs*, I, p. 88; see also pp. 55, 78.

[48] Basil Willey, *More Nineteenth Century Studies: A Group of Honest Doubters* (Cambridge, 1956), p. 141; Sandford, *Frederick Temple*, p. 205; Chadwick, *Victorian Church*, II, p. 76.

[49] *ER*, p. 23.

[50] *ER*, pp. 55–6.

[51] *ER*, pp. 57–8.

[52] *ER*, p. 52.

Essays and Reviews provoked a huge outcry on the basis of its seemingly dangerous scholarship, which reinforced the polarization between the Church parties.[53] Such was the tendency to approach Scripture with reverence and awe that more conservative churchmen found it difficult to ask scholarly questions even about genre and textual transmission, which were Jowett's main concerns. For many, the Bible was simply not amenable to the critical pursuit of truth. The book's many opponents included Samuel Wilberforce, bishop of Oxford, who immediately after publication sought to condemn the book's authors by means of the recently revived Church Convocation.[54] Wilberforce was particularly upset that Frederick Temple should have consented to having his essay included alongside what he called the 'scarcely-veiled Atheism of Mr. Baden Powell' and the 'open scepticism and laxity of Mr. Wilson'.[55]

A number of Church leaders from both the Anglo-Catholic and Evangelical ends of the Church began to gather petitions to have the two beneficed clergy who had contributed (Rowland Williams and H. B. Wilson) deprived of their livings, which was one of the few sanctions available. This led to a lengthy court case before the Judicial Committee of the Privy Council on the grounds that they had taught doctrines contrary to their ordination vows. Wilberforce soon went on to orchestrate a discussion among the bishops early in 1861. A number thought that prosecution was necessary, including the old Noetic R. D. Hampden of Hereford, who regarded it as a question of 'Christianity or no Christianity'.[56] Similarly, Edward Pusey, Oxford Regius Professor of Hebrew, thought that the crisis was 'a struggle for the life and death of the Church of England'.[57]

The *Essays and Reviews* controversy demonstrated that the alliance between scholarship and religion was increasingly under strain. In Oxford a number of more conservative churchmen responded to what they saw as the increasing infection of Christian theology by critical thought by creating in 1869 a new undergraduate degree as a bastion of orthodoxy.[58] It was rooted not in a liberal model of education but in the study of the Scriptures and the early Church as the source of all truth. While education might have been a deeply religious activity for men such as Arnold and Temple, it was also clear that the critical

[53] Samuel Wilberforce, 'Essays and Reviews', *Quarterly Review*, 109 (1861): 248–305.

[54] Cited in Standish Meacham, *Lord Bishop: The Life of Samuel Wilberforce (1805–1873)* (Cambridge, MA, 1970), p. 221.

[55] Wilberforce, 'Essays and Reviews', p. 251.

[56] Cited in Reginald G. Wilberforce, *Life of the Right Reverend Samuel Wilberforce, D.D.*, 3 vols. (London, 1882), III, p. 3.

[57] Pusey to Stanley, 23 Feb. 1864, in H. P. Liddon, *The Life of E. B. Pusey*, 4 vols. (London, 1897), IV, p. 63.

[58] See Hinchliff, *God and History*, pp. 100–4; Inman, *Making*, ch. 2.

liberal ethos gradually began to threaten the revealed truths of Christianity. As Temple noted in his 1884 Bampton Lectures (well after his rehabilitation), the doctrine of evolution appears to cut away 'some of the main arguments for that truth' of revelation.[59]

COLERIDGE AND CAMBRIDGE

Liberal Anglicanism also developed in Cambridge. Particularly influential was Samuel Taylor Coleridge (1772–1834), whose somewhat idiosyncratic philosophy proved highly influential. Like Arnold after him, Coleridge regarded Christianity as a form of life rather than a set of doctrines. Discipleship was about growing to maturity through the discipline of what Coleridge called 'manly energy' (*aretēn*).[60] Coleridge's key text, *Aids to Reflection*, is principally a work of educational theory, written 'for the studious young at the close of their education or on their first entrance into the duties of manhood and the rights of self-government'.[61] To be manly, according to Coleridge, was to be mature and to have cultivated the habit of duty. The intellectual sphere was marked by the elevation to a higher plane so that one's understanding should aspire to the perfection of the Christian faith: 'Unless *above* himself he can / Erect himself, how mean a thing is man!'[62] Manly energy had to be cultivated through education. Christianity was consequently measured in terms of practical effects: it was 'not a theory or a speculation . . . but a life and a living process'.[63] This combination of the practical with the intellectual through education in 'manliness' (*thymos*) was closely related to the Greek aristocratic idea of *aretē*, a notion shared by the Greeks, Romans, as well as Renaissance thinkers.

Coleridge's thought was influential on such figures as Julius Hare (1795–1855),[64] tutor at Trinity College, Cambridge, and translator of the German historian Barthold Niebuhr.[65] Hare showed a great interest in German history and theology, particularly Luther. He also befriended the

59 Frederick Temple, *The Relations between Religion and Science* (London, 1888), p. 108.

60 Samuel Taylor Coleridge, *Aids to Reflection in the Formation of a Manly Character on the several grounds of prudence, morality and Religion illustrated by select passages from our elder Divines, especially from Archbishop Leighton* (London, 1825), comment on Aphorism XII, p. 7.

61 Coleridge, *Aids to Reflection*, Preface, p. vi.

62 Coleridge, *Aids to Reflection*, Aphorism X, pp. 5–6.

63 Coleridge, *Aids to Reflection*, Aphorisms on Spiritual Religion, p. 195.

64 N. Merrill Distad, *Guessing at Truth: The Life of Julius Charles Hare* (Shepherdstown, WV, 1979), ch. 8.

65 C. R. Sanders, *Coleridge and the Broad Church Movement: Studies in S. T. Coleridge, Dr Arnold of Rugby, J. C. Hare, Thomas Carlyle and F. D. Maurice* (Durham, NC, 1942), p. 133.

Prussian diplomat-scholar, C. C. J. Bunsen (1791–1860), who published a popularization of Heinrich Ewald's *History of Israel.*

F. D. MAURICE

The most prominent liberal figure emerging from Cambridge at this period was F. D. Maurice (1805–72),[66] who was perhaps the greatest nineteenth-century Anglican theologian. Taking advantage of the possibilities of studying for (but not taking) a degree at Cambridge, Maurice, who came from a Dissenting family, went to Trinity College in 1823. After conversion to the Church of England, he migrated to Oxford, before becoming professor of English literature in 1840 at the new King's College in London, which had been established as a confessional counterpart to University College. He also became professor of divinity in 1846 until 1853, when he published his controversial *Theological Essays*. The principal R. W. Jelf thought them heterodox on account of the 'dangerous tendency'[67] of the purported universalism of his teaching on eternal life. Maurice ended his life as Knightsbridge Professor of Moral Philosophy at Cambridge.

Maurice was the most prolific thinker associated with the Broad Church, even if he resisted the label, and even though his prose can be somewhat contorted which has led to the accusation of muddled thought.[68] His most influential work was *The Kingdom of Christ*, which took the form of a number of letters addressed to Quakers defending the practices of the Church of England.[69] Maurice outlines the various marks or 'signs' of the Church, each of which serves to point the believer away from reliance on self, towards reliance on God. The Church is seen not as a sectarian community of the devout, but as pointing people to their true centre and support.[70] Baptism was aimed at drawing a man 'continually out of himself, to teach him to disclaim all independent virtue, to bring him into the knowledge and image of the

[66] Olive Brose, *F. D. Maurice: Rebellious Conformist* (Athens, OH, 1972); A. R. Vidler, *Witness to the Light: F. D. Maurice's Message for Today* (New York, 1948); A. Michael Ramsey, *F. D. Maurice and the Conflicts of Modern Theology* (Cambridge, 1951); W. Merlin Davies, *F. D. Maurice's Theology* (London, 1964); Jeremy Morris, *F. D. Maurice and the Crisis of Christian Authority* (Oxford, 2008); W. J. Wolf, 'F. D. Maurice', in W. J. Wolf (ed.), *The Spirit of Anglicanism* (Edinburgh, 1982), pp. 49–100.

[67] Morris, *F. D. Maurice*, pp. 117–18.

[68] Stephen Sykes, *The Integrity of Anglicanism* (London, 1978), p. 19.

[69] F. D. Maurice, *The Kingdom of Christ or Hints on the Principles, Ordinances and Constitution of the Catholic Church. In Letters to a Member of the Society of Friends* (first edition, 1837–8) (references are to the edition based on the 1842 edition) (2 vols., Cambridge, 1958). Hereafter *KC*.

[70] See, for example, *KC*, I, p. 284.

Father and the Son'.[71] Similarly, shared liturgies functioned to prevent selfishness in prayer: what was important was that prayer should be *common* since shared forms of worship 'draw us out of the individuality which is our curse and ruin', leading us, 'one and all, to take up our position on the same ground of being justified and redeemed in Christ'.[72]

Drawing on Platonizing thought Maurice held that while all systems, including those of the Church parties, might embrace something of the truth, none could be equated with the whole truth. In a set of lectures published on the different parts of the Prayer Book, Maurice re-emphasized his understanding of the Church and its rites as ways of delivering 'us from Romish dogmatism, and all other dogmatism',[73] towards an absolute need to trust in God. In a letter to his fellow Christian Socialist, Thomas Hughes, Maurice claimed that Evangelicalism was 'a mere religious system constructed by human speculation, made up of crude philosophical notions and popular superstitions, and alien from the revelation of the living and true God which I find set forth in Scripture'.[74] His intention was to deliver the Christian from 'opinions and notions'[75] towards a higher conception of truth which was available to all people. Even though Maurice was deprived of his professorships, he remained an influential theologian, lecturer, and writer. However, as the next section shows, opinions that were acceptable in England were not always acceptable elsewhere.

LIBERALISM IN THE EMPIRE: BISHOP COLENSO

Almost from the time of his consecration as bishop of the new diocese of Natal in 1853 John William Colenso (1814–83)[76] became one of the most notorious figures in the Anglican world. His writings provoked controversies that rivalled those of *Essays and Reviews*. Colenso, who had imbibed the Evangelical atmosphere of Cambridge in the 1830s, studied mathematics there at St John's College. At some point in late 1842 or early 1843 he began to read the writings of Coleridge and Maurice, which led to a change of his religious

[71] *KC*, I, p. 289. [72] *KC* (first edition, 3 vols, 1838), II, p. 231.

[73] F. D. Maurice, *The Prayer Book considered especially in reference to the Romish System: nineteen sermons preached in the chapel of Lincoln's Inn* (1849) (Cambridge, 1966 edn.), pp. 105–6.

[74] Letter of 1861 in Frederick Maurice, *Life of Frederick Denison Maurice*, 2 vols. (London, 1885), II, p. 380.

[75] *KC*, II, pp. 6–7.

[76] George Cox, *The Life of John William Colenso, D.D., Bishop of Natal*, 2 vols. (London, 1888); Peter Hinchliff, *John William Colenso: Bishop of Natal* (London, 1964); Jeff Guy, *The Heretic: A Study of the Life of John William Colenso, 1814–1883* (Pietermaritzburg, 1983); Jonathan A. Draper (ed.), *The Eye of the Storm* (Pietermaritzburg, 2004).

views.[77] Maurice and Colenso quickly became friends, with Colenso imbibing Maurice's universalism.[78] Colenso recognized his indebtedness to Maurice in the preface to his first book of sermons given during his time as incumbent of Forncett St Mary in Norfolk. This amounted to an act of solidarity with Maurice who had been dismissed from his post in 1853.

Colenso, however, never shared Maurice's racial theories. Maurice could not recognize the capacity of those beyond Western civilization to share in an understanding of God. Writing about William Penn, for instance, Maurice criticized the view that 'there is in the savagest Indian a witness for God, that he is to be dealt with as one who knows right and wrong'.[79] In distinction, Colenso was clear that there was an innate witness to the divine in all people regardless of their level of cultural development. Preaching on missionary work among the 'heathen' in a sermon that bore the title, the 'Love of God',[80] he noted all the privileges that had been conferred upon Christians by faith in Jesus Christ, while observing that 'they are not ours in such a sense, as to exclude all others, who have not yet heard of the Gospel of Grace, from any participation in its Blessings'. The universality of God's grace which had been purchased by the blood of Jesus Christ was available to all, whether in England or in the mission field, and was written on the heart of all human beings.[81]

Despite High Church and Anglo-Catholic criticism, there was, however, little inkling of what was soon to come. Indeed, had Colenso remained in his country parish or returned to school teaching (and perhaps ended his days in an English diocese or cathedral) he would have been simply one more representative of the practical Platonism of Arnold and Maurice. But while the controversies provoked by *Essays and Reviews* in the 1860s resembled those that followed the publication of Colenso's *Pentateuch*, this did not prevent Gladstone appointing Temple to the see of Exeter in 1870, and his final move to Canterbury. Whereas Colenso came to be regarded as the heretical chief culprit for the first serious division in the Anglican Communion which led to the calling of the Lambeth Conference in 1867.

What made Colenso's universalism controversial was its translation into the missionary sphere. This was noted by A. P. Stanley, dean of Westminster in a speech in Convocation following Colenso's so-called 'deposition' as bishop of Natal. Stanley commented that since similar views were shared by many others, including some Church Fathers, and himself, they should at 'least deal out the same measure to me that you deal to him'.[82] Colenso's downfall was his missionary context: a concept of a distinct hierarchy of cultures was developing among missionary and evolutionary thinkers, which put an end to

[77] Cox, *Colenso*, I, p. 21. [78] Guy, *The Heretic*, p. 30.
[79] *KC* (3 vols, 1838 edn.), III, p. 313.
[80] F. D. Maurice, *Village Sermons* (London, 1853), p. x.
[81] Maurice, *Village Sermons*, pp. 137–8 [82] Cox, *Colenso*, I, p. 369.

the enlightened perception of the noble savage, even among liberals. Another leading liberal churchman, F. W. Farrar, for instance, schoolmaster at Harrow in the 1850s and 1860s, and later canon of Westminster and dean of Canterbury, adopted a form of universalism, but also maintained an evolutionary view of cultures and languages which meant that it was always tempered by presuppositions about racial superiority. Even though he was one of the few English churchmen to support Colenso through his trials, Farrar could nevertheless write in 1866 that 'the savage is not a stately free, noble creature, presenting the happy spectacle of unsophisticated innocence and primeval liberty, but too generally a wretch, depraved, hideous, and sanguinary'.[83]

This was quite different from Colenso's famous description of the impact of the 'native' on his own thinking. In his lecture to the Marylebone Literary Institute in May 1865, Colenso commented that 'we cannot presume to assert that the human family will never be benefited by light reflected even from the thinkers of Zululand'. Similarly, the question was not 'whether the Zulu nation could benefit from European civilization and the Christian religion, but whether Europe and Christianity might benefit from what the Zulus had to give them'.[84] Although the tone remained patronizing in the famous passage in the first volume of Colenso's study of the Pentateuch, it was nevertheless clear and far-reaching: 'While translating the story of the Flood, I have had a simple-minded, but intelligent, native—one with the docility of a child, but the reasoning powers of mature age—look up, and ask, "Is all that true?"'[85] Similarly, Colenso held, God's forgiveness extended to everyone, Christian and non-Christian alike, even those whose marital customs were different from those of the West.[86] This universalist theme was clearly expressed in his commentary on the Epistle to the Romans written 'from a Missionary Point of View', which, he reported, drew on 'the results of seven years of missionary experience'.[87]

Colenso was attacked initially for his eucharistic theology, which led to the complete estrangement between Colenso and his archdeacon and dean at Pietermaritzburg. This later developed into a series of charges related to the universalism of his Pentateuch commentary. His views provoked the High

[83] F. W. Farrar, 'Aptitudes of Races', *Transactions of the Ethnological Society of London*, 5 (1867), p. 11, cited in Ephraim Mosothoane, 'John William Colenso: Pioneer in the Quest for an Authentic African Christianity', *Scottish Journal of Theology*, 44 (1991): 215–36 (p. 223).

[84] Cited in Peter Hinchliff, 'Ethics, Evolution and Biblical Criticism in the Thought of Benjamin Jowett and John William Colenso', *Journal of Ecclesiastical History*, 37 (1986): 91–110 (pp. 109–10).

[85] J. W. Colenso, *The Pentateuch and the Book of Joshua Critically Examined* (London, 1862), p. vii.

[86] J. W. Colenso, *A Letter to the Archbishop of Canterbury upon the Proper Treatment of Polygamist Converts from Heathenism* (London, 1862).

[87] J. W. Colenso, *The Epistle of St. Paul to the Romans. Newly translated and explained from a Missionary Point of View* (London, 1863), p. v.

Churchman Robert Gray who had been appointed archbishop of Cape Town in December 1853, and who claimed metropolitical powers, into charges of heresy. Colenso was deposed in 1865 by Gray, and formally excommunicated the following year. Colenso's refusal to accept Gray's authority led to a long and technical legal process before the Privy Council, with Colenso managing to hold on to the endowments of his diocese and remaining bishop of Natal. What this revealed was that it was virtually impossible to be a liberal universalist churchman—at least as a bishop—in 'heathen' territory.[88]

FURTHER DEVELOPMENTS

Within the English universities Broad Churchmen began to develop into major scholars as the century wore on. The public school ethos with its non-dogmatic and Platonizing style of Christianity, as represented for instance by James Prince Lee at King Edward School in Birmingham, influenced a number of major authors of the next generations who went on to hold important positions in Church and university. This can be seen in the well-known Cambridge group of J. B. Lightfoot (1828–89), B. F. Westcott (1825–1901), who had been educated at Birmingham (who became successive bishops of Durham), and F. J. A. Hort (1828–92), an Irishman who joined them at Trinity College, Cambridge. At the beginning of 1849 Westcott, who became one of the leading textual critics of his generation, wrote to his future wife that to 'live is not to be gay or idle or restless.... I should say that we live only so far as we cultivate all our faculties, and improve all our advantages for God's glory. The means of living then will be our own endowments, whether of talent or influence; the aim of living, the good of man; the motive of living, the love of God.'[89] For Westcott, as for Arnold, the conception of truth was not restricted to the Church—instead all the human faculties were an aspect of the overall purpose of living which was the glorifying of God.

Inspired by classical scholarship, this Cambridge group devoted themselves to meticulous textual work, producing a revised Greek text of the New Testament, which became the basis of the new English Revised Version. At the same time, the theological implications of such detailed and cautious textual work were regarded by some as overturning some of the more radical scholarship emanating from Germany about the dating of the New Testament, especially that of the great Tübingen patristic scholar, F. C. Baur. Where Baur had seen the differences between the authors of the New Testament as evidence of a conflict in the early Church that had been concealed by what

[88] Hinchliff, *Colenso*, p. 113.

[89] Arthur Westcott, *Life and Letters of Brooke Foss Westcott*, 2 vols. (London, 1903), II, p. 145.

he regarded as the forged letters of Ignatius, Westcott saw diversity as proof of authenticity.[90] Similarly Lightfoot opposed Baur's Hegelianism on the basis of what he regarded as authentic historical study. Unlike some of their German counterparts, the Cambridge school of New Testament scholars was only very modestly liberal, even though they stressed the need to understand the writings of the New Testament in their historical context. Westcott and Lightfoot remained thoroughly orthodox in their theology, regarding history and 'honest criticism' as simply confirming the truths of the Christian faith and the supremacy of Scripture. Compared to more radical movements in Germany, English theology in general remained conservative even where it moved along a cautiously critical path.

At Oxford scholars such as the New Testament scholar William Sanday (1843–1920) and S. R. Driver (1846–1914), his colleague in the Old Testament, concentrated on textual criticism.[91] Nevertheless Sanday mediated a great deal of German scholarship into Oxford, and also introduced the modern research seminar. His *The Life of Christ* was characterized by a sense of fairness, where even the most heterodox views of continental theologians were subjected to critical treatment: 'While I agree more often with my own countrymen, I learn more from the Germans.'[92] Gradually, however, Sanday, who had become Lady Margaret Professor of Divinity in 1895, began to distance himself from traditional historical investigation of the gospels, rooting Christology in psychological theories stemming from Schleiermacher, the American W. P. Du Bose, and William James, which he expounded at length in *Christologies, Ancient and Modern*[93] and *Personality in Christ and Ourselves*.[94] In 1912 Sanday secretly announced his conversion to the 'Modernist cause'.[95] That year also saw the publication of two controversial volumes, the collected volume of a number of Oxford scholars, *Foundations*,[96] and Hensley Henson's *The Creed in the Pulpit*.[97] Particularly contentious in *Foundations* was an essay on 'The Historic Christ' by a member of Sanday's seminar, B. H. Streeter, which appeared to deny the historicity of the

[90] Thompson, *Cambridge Theology*, ch. 5; Stephen Neill, *The Interpretation of the New Testament, 1861–1961* (London, 1964), pp. 33–60; W. G. Kümmel, *The New Testament: The History of the Investigation of its Problems* (London, 1972), ch. 4.

[91] Thomas A. Langford, *In Search of Foundations* (Nashville, TN, 1969), pp. 114–42.

[92] William Sanday, *The Life of Christ in Recent Research* (Oxford, 1907), p. 38.

[93] William Sanday, *Christologies, Ancient and Modern* (Oxford, 1910).

[94] William Sanday, *Personality in Christ and Ourselves* (Oxford, 1911).

[95] See G. L. Prestige, *The Life of Charles Gore* (London, 1935), p. 347.

[96] B. H. Streeter (ed.), *Foundations: A Statement of Christian Belief in Terms of Modern Thought. By Seven Oxford Men* (London, 1912). Keith Clements, *Lovers of Discord: Twentieth Century Theological Controversies in England* (London, 1988), pp. 49–74; Hinchliff, *God and History*, ch.10.

[97] H. Hensley Henson, *The Creed in the Pulpit* (London, 1912).

resurrection.[98] This added to the uproar which had followed the publication of J. M. Thompson's *Miracles in the New Testament* the previous year.[99]

In some ways this controversy marked the end of the dominance of Broad Church critical theology which was increasingly under scrutiny from more conservative and orthodox churchmen from both Anglo-Catholic and Evangelical quarters. Liberal theology was increasingly associated with Germany, which quickly made it very suspicious on account of its association with Germany.

Whether a critical liberal conception of truth was any longer possible within the confines of orthodoxy, however, was a problem that became increasingly pressing as the twentieth century wore on. In the wider society in the nineteenth century there was an increasing sense of the 'secularization of the mind'[100] which meant that some had observed this much earlier, including Thomas Arnold's own son, Matthew, as depicted in his 1867 poem, 'Dover Beach'. By the turn of the twentieth century theology had been sufficiently marginalized in the university and the wider society that many Church leaders and theologians retreated from the wider pursuit of truth into the security of the religious enclave. This proved ever more tempting after the outbreak of the First World War since those who like Sanday sought a religion for the 'cultivated modern man' could easily be labelled as Germanophiles. Consequently, while the remnants of a politically liberal Anglicanism in English society survived well after the war, its expression in theology quickly retreated from the mainstream: Platonism, it seems, which had been dying a slow death through the nineteenth century, finally gave up the ghost in the twentieth.[101]

SELECT BIBLIOGRAPHY

Brent, Richard, *Liberal Anglican Politics: Whiggery, Religion, and Reform 1830–1841* (Oxford, 1987).

Chadwick, Owen, *The Secularization of the European Mind in the Nineteenth Century* (Cambridge, 2008).

Chadwick, Owen, *The Victorian Church*, 2 vols. (London, 1992).

[98] B. H. Streeter, 'The Historic Christ', in *Foundations*, pp. 73–146.

[99] J. M. Thompson, *Miracles in the New Testament* (London, 1911); Clements, *Lovers of Discord*, pp. 49–106; Langford, *In Search of Foundations*, ch. 5; Alan Stephenson, *The Rise and Decline of English Modernism* (London, 1984).

[100] Owen Chadwick, *The Secularization of the European Mind in the Nineteenth Century* (Cambridge, 2008).

[101] Mark Chapman, 'Anglo-German Theological Relations during the First World War', *Zeitschrift für neuere Theologiegeschichte/Journal for the History of Modern Theology*, 7 (2000): 109–26.

Corsi, Pietro, *Science and Religion: Baden Powell and the Anglican Debate, 1800–1860* (Cambridge, 1988).

Distad, N. Merrill, *Guessing at Truth: The Life of Julius Charles Hare* (Shepherdstown WV, 1979).

Ellis, Ieuan, *Seven against Christ: A Study of Essays and Reviews* (Leiden, 1980).

Guy, Jeff, *The Heretic: A Study of the Life of John William Colenso, 1814–1883* (Pietermaritzburg, 1983).

Hinchliff, Peter, *Benjamin Jowett and the Christian Religion* (Oxford, 1987).

Hinchliff, Peter, *Frederick Temple, Archbishop of Canterbury: A Life* (Oxford, 1998).

Hinchliff, Peter, *God and History: Aspects of British Theology, 1875–1914* (Oxford, 1992).

Hinchliff, Peter, *John William Colenso: Bishop of Natal* (London, 1964).

Inman, Daniel, *The Making of Modern English Theology: God and the Academy at Oxford, 1833–1945* (Minneapolis, 2014).

Jones, Tod, *The Broad Church: Biography of a Movement* (Lanham, MD, 2003).

Morris, Jeremy, *F. D. Maurice and the Crisis of Christian Authority* (Oxford, 2008).

Neill, Stephen, *The Interpretation of the New Testament, 1861–1961* (London, 1964).

Newsome, David, *Godliness and Good Learning* (London, 1961).

Sanders, C. R., *Coleridge and the Broad Church Movement: Studies in S. T. Coleridge, Dr Arnold of Rugby, J. C. Hare, Thomas Carlyle and F. D. Maurice* (Durham, NC, 1942).

Shea, Victor and William Whitla (eds.), *Essays and Reviews: The 1860 Text and its Reading* (Charlottesville, VA, 2000).

Thompson, David M., *Cambridge Theology in the Nineteenth Century: Enquiry, Controversy and Truth* (Aldershot, 2008).

Tuckwell, William, *Pre-Tractarian Oxford: a Reminiscence of the Oriel 'Noetics'* (London, 1909).

11

Anglicanism in North America and the Caribbean in the Nineteenth Century

Peter W. Williams

ANGLICANISM IN THE UNITED STATES

The chain of British colonies and former colonies that ran from Newfoundland down the Atlantic coast of North America into the Caribbean provided a veritable laboratory for the development of Anglican Churches outside the mother country during the long nineteenth century. This vast sweep of colonies comprehended a wide variety of climatic and geographical situations, from tundra to tropics. These conditions in turn shaped economic possibilities, from fishing and trapping in what would become Canada to the cotton and sugar crops cultivated by enslaved Africans in the American South and the British West Indies.

The various economic, social, and political complexions of what would become two vast continental nations and a collection of small island colonies and republics provided contexts for national Anglican communities which took shape as colonies morphed into independent countries in which the Church of England no longer enjoyed the established status it had in the English homeland. The variables that shaped these new branches of Anglicanism included the degree of cultural identification still maintained with Britain; ethnic and religious diversity; the role accorded religion by the civil polity; economic and demographic expansion; the presence or absence of chattel slavery; and the degree to which Anglicans were willing and able to accommodate to local cultures and indigenous populations. Throughout the nineteenth century, Anglicans in all of these regions also continued to be affected by developments within the Church of England. How they responded varied considerably over time and across colonial and national boundaries.

The first national Anglican Church outside Britain was the Protestant Episcopal Church in the United States of America (PECUSA). The Episcopal Church—the word 'Protestant' was gradually abandoned—took shape in the wake of the American Revolution, which rendered clerical oaths of allegiance to the British monarch unworkable. After Samuel Seabury, an intransigent Loyalist, managed to obtain episcopal consecration in Scotland in 1784, the way was clear for a new Anglican Church on the American denominational model. Delegates from the newly independent and united thirteen colonies assembled in Philadelphia in 1789 to create a structure for the PECUSA, which would resemble in some important ways the new republic's constitution that was crafted in the same year in the same city. The polity of the PECUSA included a bicameral assembly in which bishops, clergy, and laymen were all enfranchised, and a diocesan and parochial system that reflected this same Whiggish division and balance of powers.[1]

After a fallow post-war period during which the new denomination suffered considerable neglect, new leadership provided invigoration predicated on geographical sectionalism and ecclesiastical partisanship. Bishop John Henry Hobart of New York was the most prominent spokesman for the High Church party during the earlier nineteenth century. Hobart's churchmanship was probably closer to the old 'high and dry' Tory faction of the Church of England than to that of the Oxford Movement, although some of his ideas anticipated and may have influenced those of the latter. His Virginia counterparts, William Meade and Richard Channing Moore, represented the 'low Church' faction, which made common cause with Baptists, Methodists, and Presbyterians in their espousal of the authority of the Bible, the doctrine of the vicarious atonement, and the need for personal conversion—the 'new birth' preached by Anglican itinerant George Whitefield during the Great Awakening of the 1740s. The founding of the General Theological Seminary in New York City in 1817 and the Virginia Theological Seminary on the outskirts of the new nation's capital six years later, provided institutional grounding for the training of a native-born and educated clergy with respectively 'high' and 'low' orientations—as would the founding of a variety of other seminaries later in the century.[2]

One of these seminaries emerged as part of an educational enterprise that demonstrated the PECUSA's entanglement in the sectional strife that would by 1861 immerse the entire nation in a catastrophic civil war. In 1857 Leonidas Polk, the bishop of Louisiana, helped found the University of the South—better known as 'Sewanee'—on a mountaintop in Tennessee as an alternative to the elite colleges of the Northeast for the sons of Southern gentlemen. (Its seminary was established in 1878.) Polk would later die in battle as a major general in the army of the Confederate States of America. Unlike most other Protestant denominations with a presence in both North and South, the PECUSA, which never took an official position on the 'peculiar institution' of slavery,

[1] David L. Holmes, *A Brief History of the Episcopal Church* (Valley Forge, PA, 1993), pp. 50ff.

[2] Holmes, *Brief History*, ch. 3.

remained officially undivided for the duration of the conflict. The bishops of the southern dioceses met separately under the name of the Protestant Episcopal Church in the Confederate States of America, but returned after the war to the national governing body, the General Convention, with little ado.[3]

During the middle decades of the nineteenth century the American West was also in play, as the wide variety of American denominations vied with one another for the allegiance of those who sought economic opportunity in the rich agricultural lands that were opening for settlement as the nation acquired vast tracts first from France, and then from Mexico. The Anglican response to the challenge of the frontier was encapsulated in the quip that 'the Baptists came on foot, the Methodists came on horseback, and the Episcopalians came in parlor cars'. Although some bishops and clergy did make strenuous efforts to establish an Anglican presence in the prairies and mountains, the witticism does point up the affinities of the Episcopal Church with the higher reaches of the American social class system, as well the denomination's predominantly urban character.

Although the Episcopal Church in the nineteenth century found its core constituency among Americans of British birth or descent, it also embraced, at times ambivalently, the numerous other ethnic groups that made up the nation's populace. Although some African slaves owned by Episcopalians attended Anglican worship under white supervision, free blacks tended to reject such formal and usually segregated worship in favour of the more expressive Evangelicalism practised in the Baptist, Methodist, and, later, the 'sanctified' (holiness and Pentecostal) Churches that maintained an institutional presence outside of and parallel to their white counterparts. Some free blacks in the North, however, began to be ordained to the Anglican priesthood, beginning in Philadelphia with Absalom Jones in 1795. Black parishes, which generally attracted the wealthier members of their communities, were also established, such as St Philip's in the Harlem neighbourhood of New York City in 1809. Segregation, formal or *de facto*, remained the rule throughout the nineteenth century, and no person of colour was consecrated for a US diocesan jurisdiction until the era of the First World War.[4]

Anglican outreach to indigenous peoples—never extensive in earlier eras—gained momentum during the decades following the Civil War, as Native Americans were pushed westward onto reservation lands and responsibility for their welfare was entrusted by the federal government to various Christian denominations. Particularly notable among Episcopalians was the work of John Hobart Hare, missionary bishop in what is now the state of South Dakota, whose labours gained numerous converts and, for him, the appellation of 'Apostle to the Sioux'.

[3] Holmes, *Brief History*, pp. 80ff.
[4] Holmes, *Brief History*, pp. 78–87.

Although Episcopal churches and cathedrals began to spring up in Denver, San Francisco, and other western locales during the later nineteenth century, the centres of dramatic growth during this era were the burgeoning cities of the north-east—Boston, Philadelphia, New York—and those growing rapidly in the new industrial zone of the Great Lakes, such as Chicago and Detroit. It was in their wealthier neighbourhoods and suburbs that the Episcopal Church was enhancing its cachet as the denomination of preference not only among established elites but of an urban-industrial upper middle class as well. The concentration of wealth in these parishes and dioceses provided the financial basis for a flurry of church and cathedral building that set the style for other denominations, which vied with Episcopalians to erect splendid urban temples in the Gothic and Romanesque revival modes. Such wealth also promoted the development of a network of private boarding schools on the English model of Thomas Arnold's Rugby, such as Endicott Peabody's Groton (1884) in Massachusetts, which had as their mission the moulding of 'Christian gentlemen' who would provide a cadre of leaders for the industrial elite. Their graduates would in later decades prove remarkably successful in powerful social nodes such as the Wall Street financial district and the US Department of State.

Ecclesiastical factionalism characterized North American Anglicanism during the nineteenth century, especially during its middle and later decades. One dramatic confrontation between 'high'—in the 1830s and after shaped by the Tractarian movement—and 'low'—allied with other Evangelical denominations—occurred in the trials of Benjamin and Henry Onderdonk, the bishops respectively of New York and Pennsylvania. Benjamin was tried in 1844 on charges of 'immoralities and impurities' and suspended from office. His brother Henry was similarly suspended the same year for 'intemperance'. In each case the voting by the House of Bishops followed party lines, with most Evangelicals favouring the conviction of the Tractarian brothers. Subsequent frustrations among the Evangelical faction at what they saw as Anglo-Catholic liturgical and doctrinal abuses resulted in the founding of the schismatic Reformed Episcopal Church in 1873. The western Great Lakes region, especially Chicago and Wisconsin, became a major locus of Anglo-Catholic practice. Nashotah House seminary, founded in 1847 in Wisconsin, became a major institutional centre for what has facetiously been called the 'Biretta Belt' of the Episcopal Church.[5]

The Anglo-Catholic movement was also a spur to the emergence of the Gothic revival as the normative style of the Episcopal Church. Although vestiges of Gothic could be found in early colonial Virginia, the medieval style had been largely displaced by neo-classicism until the advocacy of Gothic by the Ecclesiological movement at Cambridge University as a sort of corollary to Oxford

[5] Holmes, *Brief History*, pp. 107ff.

Tractarianism. During the 1840s Episcopalians, especially in New York and New Jersey, began to build in what they intended to be an authentically medieval style, as exemplified most elaborately in Richard Upjohn's Trinity Church (1845) on Manhattan's Wall Street. Upjohn, who went on to design dozens of churches across the country, also devised an innovative new style—'Carpenter Gothic'—in which traditional Gothic elements such as the pointed-arch window were simplified into a 'board and batten' construction that could be inexpensively reproduced by small rural parishes across the expanding nation.

A reaction to what was often perceived as the dogmatism of Evangelicals and Anglo-Catholics alike was the Broad Church movement, which was, like its counterparts, rooted in British theological currents. Broad Churchmen, however, saw themselves not so much as yet another faction but rather as partakers of a climate of opinion that was open to contemporary intellectual currents such as biblical criticism and evolutionary biology. Prominent among them was Phillips Brooks, a 'prince of the pulpit' who presided over the creation of H. H. Richardson's monumental Trinity Church (1872–7) in Boston's new Copley Square. Brooks chose the Romanesque over the Gothic style for Trinity in the belief that it was historically more appropriate for a Protestant focus on the preached word. Brooks's preaching earned him celebrity status and prompted an influx of Boston's elite Unitarians into the Episcopal Church in response to what they perceived as their own tradition's contrasting lack of vitality.

Another prominent Broad Churchman was New York's William Reed Huntington, whose ecumenical interests represented another of the movement's themes. In an attempt to promote dialogue with other Protestant Churches, Huntington drafted what would become known as the 'Chicago-Lambeth Quadrilateral' (1886, 1888) as a potential set of commonly agreed upon foundations for authority in Christian teaching. His hopes for closer relations with Presbyterians and other denominations were not realized because, in part, of an Anglican insistence on episcopacy; but the Quadrilateral did emerge as a major vehicle for unity within the emergent Anglican Communion in its provision of a common baseline in matters of religious authority.[6]

Both the Broad and Anglo-Catholic camps in the PECUSA became active in the post-Civil War years in responding to the profound dislocations in American society brought about by the concurrent forces of immigration, industrialization, and urbanization. The Episcopal Church provided strong leadership in the interdenominational movement that came to be called the 'Social Gospel', which called for the application of the teachings of Jesus not simply to individual salvation but to the redemption of the social order in all of its dimensions. Much of the inspiration for the Episcopal response to social

[6] Holmes, *Brief History*, pp. 125–6.

issues came from English sources such as the Christian socialism of F. D. Maurice and Charles Kingsley. The 'settlement house', which provided immigrants with social and educational programming as well as political advocacy, was modelled on London's Toynbee Hall. Among others this initiative was promoted by Episcopalians such as Boston's Vida Dutton Scudder, a professor of English at nearby Wellesley College, who founded the Episcopal Church Socialist League in 1911.[7]

Another response to social change in which Episcopalians played a leading role was the 'institutional church', a complex of buildings which provided not only space for public worship but also for a wide variety of social services. Prominent in this movement was St George's at Stuyvesant Square in Manhattan. The rector from 1883 was the Irish-born William Rainsford, who worked together with his senior warden, the financier J. P. Morgan, to address both the spiritual and material needs of the parish's booming immigrant population. By the early twentieth century, most larger cities had institutional churches, both Episcopal and of various other denominations, which filled a major gap in the social safety net later addressed by governmental agencies at various levels in the Depression era.

Other Church leaders promoted systemic reform in the era that took its name from the Progressive drive for the reform of corrupt and unresponsive political systems. Henry Codman Potter, the bishop of New York from 1887–1908, who presided over the weddings of high society, also garnered respect as an effective arbitrator of labour disputes and as an advocate of legal protections for working people. George Hodges, who would later become dean of the Episcopal Theological School in Cambridge, Massachusetts, helped as rector to turn Pittsburgh's Calvary Church into a hotbed of municipal reform activity.

The advent of religious orders in Anglicanism that had its origins in England, rapidly spread to the United States, with an impact on the social and educational spheres as well. Some orders such as the Society of St John the Evangelist (Cowley Fathers) were British transplants, while others, such as the Order of the Holy Cross, originated in the United States—in this case, in the context of a New York City slum ministry in 1884. Its founder, James Otis Sargent Huntington, was attracted to a monastic vocation in the context of a ministry to the urban poor, and worked as an advocate for reformer Henry George's 'Single Tax' movement. Huntington, also a founder of the Church Association for the Advancement of the Interests of Labor (CAIL) in 1887, enlisted Potter and most of the PECUSA's bishops as members, and laid the groundwork for the pursuit of social issues at the institutional level in the national denomination. Huntington's order later turned its efforts towards conducting retreats and establishing boarding schools.

[7] Holmes, *Brief History*, pp. 126–39.

Religious orders for women, beginning with the Sisterhood of the Holy Communion in New York in 1852, provided opportunities for women to pursue careers in education, nursing, and social work in the context of a devotional community. Women, though barred from ordination to the priesthood and diaconate, were also able to pursue careers in the Church as deaconesses, a vocational path pioneered by German Lutherans and adopted by other Protestant denominations as well. The office was deliberately defined so that it would not be construed as a religious order on the Roman Catholic model, which was offensive to Episcopalians with Protestant sensibilities. Deaconesses received training in schools established for the purpose, sometimes attached to cathedrals, and served as social workers in institutional churches as well as nurses, teachers, and missionaries at home and abroad. Their vows were for specific periods, but they were forbidden to marry while serving in the vocation.

Women also provided extensive service as supporters of foreign missions, which the Episcopal Church conducted in China, Haiti, Japan, Liberia, Mexico, and Turkey. As the United States acquired imperial status after defeating Spain in 1898 and relieving it of most of its remaining overseas possessions, the PECUSA began to cultivate missions in this new American empire. Charles Henry Brent served as missionary bishop to the Philippines, and, under the aegis of Bishop Benjamin Henry Whipple of Minnesota, the Church sponsored activity in Cuba and Puerto Rico as well.

Although the Episcopal Church had a legal status no different from that of any other American religious group under the First Amendment to the US Constitution, it did from early on enjoy an informal established status expressed, for example, in its virtual monopoly on the chaplaincy to Congress during the early nineteenth century, and the frequent attendance of US presidents at St John's Church near their official residence, the White House. A major attempt to enhance this status as a *de facto* national church was the drive by Henry Yates Satterlee, the first bishop of Washington, DC, to erect a cathedral that would function as an informal site for national rituals such as presidential addresses and funerals. Other cathedrals such as St John the Divine in New York City and Grace in San Francisco also became civic monuments in the grandeur of their scale and the scope of their decoration. They also represented the centralization of power within the denomination as a whole that was taking place during the early twentieth century.

ANGLICANISM IN CANADA

The fortunes of Anglicanism in North America's other continental nation were shaped by Canada's distinctive history. Although even more vast than the

United States in territory, harsh climate and barren land placed serious limits on the expansion of the Canadian population into its northern reaches. Where religious motives had played a central role in the establishment of several of the colonies that coalesced into the United States, the settlement of the more northward reaches of British North America (BNA) were much more unambiguously commercial in character, especially among Protestants, with Church following empire as one of its ancillaries. The incorporation of a substantial piece of Francophone territory with a largely Roman Catholic population—Quebec—into a part of the British Empire also presented the later task of nation-building with a unique complication. Canada did share with the United States the presence of a substantial and diverse indigenous population, with corresponding challenges of assimilation and evangelization. Where the US political economy was based, directly or otherwise, on the institution of chattel slavery, Canada provided a refuge for some of those who managed to escape from its oppression.

What would in 1867 coalesce into the Dominion of Canada was originally part of British North America. Its religious welfare had in the early period been largely entrusted to the Society for the Propagation of the Gospel (SPG), which continued to be a force in Canadian Anglicanism long after it had withdrawn from the US field. The role of the Church of England did not develop with any uniformity as Canada expanded. It had been established in the Maritime Provinces of Nova Scotia (1758), New Brunswick (1786), and Prince Edward Island (1803), but never in any other part of the incipient nation. The first diocese was formed in Nova Scotia in 1787 with jurisdiction over the whole of BNA. Quebec became the seat of a diocese in 1793. The 1791 Constitution Act that divided the province of Quebec into Upper and Lower Canada—later Ontario and Quebec, respectively—did not accord the Church of England any special privileges, so that no uniform pattern of the relationship between Church and state existed when the time came for an independent national Church. One unique feature of the Canadian system, however, was the creation of the 'clergy reserves', a vast amount of land—much of it unproductive—set aside for the support of Anglican and, for a time, Church of Scotland clergy, in Upper and Lower Canada. Through the efforts of John Strachan, later bishop of Toronto and active member of the 'Family Compact' ruling clique that dominated provincial politics during this period, control of these lands was conveyed to a Clergy Corporation in 1819 and managed by Strachan's allies. After considerable controversy, fuelled by Methodist advocate Egerton Ryerson, income from the lands was distributed more broadly among various Protestant denominations in the 1840s. The system was finally secularized in 1854, although clergy already deriving incomes from them were guaranteed lifetime support.

Loss of support from the SPG, the clergy reserves, and Parliament during the middle decades of the nineteenth century all pointed towards the necessity of inventing a national Anglican Church out of what Alan Hayes has characterized as 'a leisurely and ambiguous system of Church administration' in which power lay scattered among

> primates, metropolitans, bishops, colonial secretaries, the law officers of the Crown, governors, colonial councils of various descriptions, various Canadian courts of law, the Privy Council in England, secretaries of mission societies, vestries, parish clergy and staff, church wardens, General Synod, provincial synods, diocesan synods, the staffs of synodical boards and committees, the imperial parliament in England, the various provincial legislatures, after 1867 the dominion parliament, and other persons and groups.[8]

A number of strains present within Canadian Anglicanism competed to help shape what would emerge in 1893 as what is now known as the Anglican Church in Canada.

One formative influence on the emergence of a distinctively Canadian form of Anglicanism was the influx of Loyalist refugees after the victory of the forces for national independence in the American Revolution. Their in-pouring provided a core of active support for Canada remaining an outpost of English society, culture, and religion, and gave its Anglicanism a distinctively Tory tinge. (It included Charles Inglis, rector of New York's Trinity church, who would become Canada's first bishop, in Nova Scotia.) During its early decades, what would until the twentieth century be known as the Church of England in Canada, was very much in partnership with the enterprise of imperial governance. John Strachan, who in later life became the first bishop of Toronto (1839–67), was born a Scots Presbyterian, but became a member of the 'Family Compact' that held much of the power in Upper Canada during the 1810s to the 1830s and one of the most influential spokesmen for the distinctively Tory version of the role of the Anglican Church in society held by the Loyalists. 'He believed in an ordered society, an established church, the prerogative of the crown, and prescriptive rights; he did not believe that the voice of the people was the voice of God.'[9]

Another part of the distinctively Canadian mixture was the presence of substantial numbers of Irish, a majority of whom were Protestant. (Toronto was the only North American city with more Protestant than Catholic Irish, a sharp contrast with US cities such as Boston and New York.) In 1841, some one-third of the Anglican clergy in Upper Canada (present-day Ontario) were Irish-born, two-thirds of them educated at Trinity College, Dublin.[10] The situation of Anglicanism in Ireland shaped their experience. A large majority

[8] Alan L. Hayes, *Anglicans in Canada: Controversies and Identity in Historical Perspective* (Urbana, IL, 2004), pp. 87, 82.

[9] G. M. Craig, 'John Strachan', *Dictionary of Canadian Biography*, vol. 9 (Toronto, 2003–), online edition <http://www.biographi.ca/en/bio.php?id_nbr=4729> (accessed 8 Aug. 2014).

[10] Hayes, *Anglicans in Canada*, p. 6.

of that nation's population were Roman Catholic peasants who bore an ancestral animosity to what they viewed as alien oppressors, and the oppressors returned the favour. The Church of Ireland was that of the powerful but uncomfortable ruling minority, who felt themselves besieged by papists. The result was an institutional and doctrinal defensiveness, anti-Catholicism, Evangelicalism in churchmanship, and a commitment to establishment. This vocal faction in the Canadian mixture was not ultimately triumphant, but did contribute significantly to the decades of debate over what form Canadian Anglicanism would take once it achieved institutional independence.

By the 1830s it was becoming clear that Canadian Anglicanism was progressively becoming 'disestablished, disendowed, and displaced from the corridors of power and privilege', and was going to have to reinvent itself as a coherent self-governing entity if it was to survive. An 1836 booklet by Thomas Brock Fuller, then missionary in Ontario and later first bishop of the diocese of Niagara, laid out for the first time for public discussion a coherent plan for organizing Church life on a voluntary basis.[11] Although 'high' and 'low' Church—in the older sense of Tory- and Whig-leaning—leaders disagreed strenuously on issues such as the relative power of bishops, a consensus was beginning to develop that the most relevant model for Canadians lay not in England or Ireland but rather with their southern neighbour, which several decades earlier had to settle the issue of how to maintain an Anglican Church in a pluralistic society in which neither aid nor impediment could be expected from the government. Movements towards synodical government by voluntary compact in Australia and New Zealand in the same direction by 1850 also provided important examples of how such restructuring might take place.[12]

The High Churchman Strachan took the lead, convening the first diocesan synod in Toronto in 1853. Approval of such bodies from the Canadian and British governments followed in 1856 and 1857 respectively. The dioceses of Huron, Montreal, and Quebec rapidly followed the synodical path. In 1860 the dioceses of Montreal, Quebec, and Toronto formed the ecclesiastical Province of Canada, with the bishop of Montreal as metropolitan. The next step was an extension of this polity to the entirety of what was emerging during the same years as a transcontinental dominion. Canadian Confederation was achieved in 1867. The 1890 'Winnipeg Scheme' by Charles Jenkins that outlined a plan for a national Church was realized in 1893, when the General Synod came into being. This Church of England in Canada was based on three foundational documents: a 'solemn declaration', a set of 'Fundamental Principles', and a 'Basis of Constitution'. The result closely resembled that of the PECUSA in many aspects, save for some of the nomenclature: bicameral, with episcopal, clerical, and lay representation, and a primate elected by the House of Bishops.

[11] Hayes, *Anglicans in Canada*, p. 84.

[12] Hayes, *Anglicans in Canada*, p. 88.

Canadian Anglicanism was demographically and geographically rooted, not surprisingly, in the original centre of Anglophone settlement, so that the earliest dioceses were located in the Maritimes, Quebec, and Ontario. Its spread beyond this core was a response, on the one hand, to the impulse to evangelize indigenous peoples and, on the other, to the opening up of the Canadian west to settlement by native Canadians and newer immigrants—in the nineteenth century still mostly from Britain. The task of evangelization was divided between the SPG, which served those in territory under British rule, and the Church Missionary Society (CMS). A major undertaking of the CMS was missionary work in the north-west, or 'Rupert's Land', which since 1670 had been under the control of the Hudson's Bay Company. No European settlement took place there until the early nineteenth century, but in 1820 John West, a CMS missionary, was appointed by the Company to serve a territory that for some time included virtually all of Canada outside the eastern provinces. West and the CMS missions and schools that followed were quite successful in working with the Cree from their base in Red River, and the Henry Budd College for the Ministry at The Pas, Manitoba, is named for one native convert who was ordained to the Anglican priesthood in 1853. Beginning in the 1880s, the government began to employ Canada's Churches to maintain residential schools for Indians, an enterprise that generated considerable controversy in subsequent years in both Canada and the United States over coercive methods employed to 'civilize' and 'Christianize' indigenous peoples.

The first of Canada's ecclesiastical provinces was that of Canada, founded in 1860, and later subdivided in 1912 to form the Province of Ontario, while retaining the Maritimes and most of Quebec. As the Canadian west became more settled, the Province of Rupert's Land was created in 1875. The settlement of British Columbia, which had no churches or clergy prior to 1849, was stimulated by the discovery of gold in 1858 and the completion of the Canadian Pacific Railway in 1885. Missionaries were provided by the SPG, the CMS, and the Colonial and Continental Church Society. A gift from a wealthy Englishwoman, Angela Burdett-Coutts, established the new diocese of British Columbia, for which she named the first incumbent, George Hills, in 1859, illustrating continuing reliance on British patronage. It was here that one of the most divisive public events in the Canadian Church's history took place, illustrating that the deep lines of partisanship that had divided Anglicans in Britain and the United States were now having their impact on Canada as well. At the consecration of the Christ Church Cathedral in Victoria in 1872, the archdeacon of Vancouver preached in a manner that indicated sympathies with the Oxford Movement, which provoked a public cry of outrage from Edward Cridge, the cathedral's dean. This outburst led to a formal censure from Bishop Hills followed by Cridge's removal from office. The latter responded by leading most of his congregation, including the governor of the

Hudson's Bay Company, into the schismatic American body, the Reformed Episcopal Church.[13]

Although Anglican cathedrals certainly predated the partisan controversies of the nineteenth century and were not confined to High Churchmen, cathedrals in this period could be an 'outward and visible sign' of ecclesiastical partisanship, since their presence itself testified to the importance of the episcopate, a major theme of the Tractarian movement. Nineteenth-century cathedrals were almost always designed in the Gothic revival mode, which for Ecclesiological Society enthusiasts, who often shared Tractarian views, was rich in sacramental significance. One of the first acts of John Medley as bishop of Fredericton, New Brunswick, in 1845 was to commence work on Christ Church Cathedral. Medley, while serving as a rector in Exeter (UK), had published in 1841 a short book entitled *Elementary Remarks on Church Architecture*, which was endorsed by the Ecclesiologists. He engaged the Exeter-born Frank Wills, who was to design Gothic revival churches throughout the United States, as his architect. The cathedral was modelled on St Mary's, Snettisham, in Norfolk, a move also approved by the English arbiters of church style. Edward Feild, who became bishop of Newfoundland (including the Bermudas), was another champion of Tractarian principles, and set about, among other things, making his diocese free of English financial support. In 1846 he enlisted the prominent English Gothic architect George Gilbert Scott to design and, at a distance, supervise construction of St John the Baptist Cathedral in St John's.[14]

The rift between 'Church party' (the old High Churchmen and the Tractarians) and the 'Evangelical party' (old Low Churchmen and newer Evangelicals) manifested itself in a variety of other ways among decentralized Canadian Anglicans, including parallel and competing hymnals, mission boards, Sunday school curricula, newspapers, and seminaries. A major example of the latter occurred in Toronto, where the High Church Trinity College (1852) provoked a reaction in the founding by Evangelicals first of Huron College (1863) in London, Ontario, followed by Wycliffe College in 1877. The latter institution had begun as the Anglican institution of King's College in 1827, with John Strachan as its first president; but in 1849 had received a new name together with a secularized status.[15]

During the nineteenth century Canadian Anglicanism had recapitulated the United States Anglican experience, moving from a Church that had been established to some degree and in some places during the colonial

[13] Hayes, *Anglicans in Canada*, pp. 123–4.

[14] Phoebe B. Stanton, *The Gothic Revival and American Church Architecture: An Episode in Taste* (Baltimore, MD, 1968), ch. 4; Hayes, *Anglicans in Canada*, p. 125, and Document 29, pp. 261–4.

[15] Hayes, *Anglicans in Canada*, p. 66 and ch. 4.

period—which ended several decades later in Canada—to one denomination among many that possessed equal standing under the law. The Church of England in Canada, had, in response to both internal and external pressures, adopted many of the features of the polity that had earlier been forged by the PECUSA. In both nations Anglicans were associated with the wealthier and better-educated social strata, and enjoyed some of the aura of informal establishment. There were, however, some nuanced differences between the United States and Canadian experiences. The United States from its beginnings had enacted and enforced a much stricter and clearer delineation between the realms of Church and state than had been the case in Canada; even though the latter nation has, ironically, become in the long run a more 'secular' nation. Anglicans in particular had never experienced the severity of the rupture between Britain and its colonies that had been the case with US Episcopalians, as the continued use of the official name of 'Church of England in Canada' indicated. Canadian Anglican identity was more evolutionary than revolutionary, in keeping with a national reputation for social harmony.[16]

ANGLICANISM IN THE CARIBBEAN

Christianity had been introduced into the Caribbean by Christopher Columbus, who had interpreted his mission within the apocalyptic framework of the radical Franciscan tradition. The native peoples of the larger islands (Great Antilles) were rapidly exterminated through disease and warfare, and the region became a staging area for the Spanish conquest of its New World empire. Repopulation occurred in the wake of the 'Sugar Revolution', which transformed the economy of the islands and was made feasible through the labours of imported enslaved Africans. The sugar plantation emerged during the seventeenth and eighteenth centuries as the dominant institution of island life, especially in the British colonies.

The island of Hispaniola in the Greater Antilles had long been divided into French and Spanish colonies which emerged in the nineteenth century as the independent nations of Haiti (1804) and the Dominican Republic (1821). Historically under Roman Catholic hegemony, the religious loyalties of these nations have been divided between traditional Catholicism and hybrid Euro-African religions such as Vodun (Voodoo). In these areas Anglicanism entered the scene only at a relatively late date, and from other Caribbean islands and the United States rather than directly from Britain.

[16] Hayes, *Anglicans in Canada*, pp. 68–9; Marguerite Van Die, 'Canada: Church and State', in Charles H. Lippy and Peter W. Williams (eds.), *Encyclopedia of Religion in America* (Washington, DC, 2010), I, pp. 377–85.

The moving spirit behind Haitian Anglicanism was the African American priest James Theodore Holly, who came from a northern free black family and worked as an abolitionist. Holly was ordained in Michigan, worked with escaped slaves in Canada, and served a black parish in New Haven, Connecticut, as well as a period as American consul in Liberia. In 1861 Holly led an emigrant group from New Haven to Haiti, with considerable loss of life from disease. There he established a mission without the backing of the Episcopal Board of Missions consisting primarily of American blacks, which became the core of *L'Eglise Orthodoxe Apostolique Haitienne*. This was recognized as a diocese by the Anglican Communion in 1870. In 1874 Holly was named Missionary Bishop of Haiti by the PECUSA, thus becoming the first Episcopal bishop of African descent. After Holly's death in 1911, at which time Haitian Anglicans numbered some two thousand, Haiti became a missionary diocese of the PECUSA, presided over by Euro-American bishops.

Anglicanism entered the Dominican Republic through the influx of sugar workers from smaller Caribbean islands during the later nineteenth century. Some of these immigrants were educated, and brought with them the Book of Common Prayer. Benjamin Isaac Wilson arrived from St Croix in the British Virgin Islands in 1891 as a self-appointed missionary. With Holly's support, Wilson organized Holy Trinity Church at San Pedro de Macrís, and was ordained to the priesthood in 1898. After Holly's death, jurisdiction passed to Bishop Charles Colmore in Puerto Rico.

In the latter colony, the forerunner of Holy Trinity parish was organized around a nucleus of non-Roman Catholics in 1869 in Ponce, primarily for immigrants from other islands in the British West Indies. Four years later an iron and wood church was imported from Liverpool, and operated only under strict governmental regulations which prohibited, for example, the ringing of its bell. Another mission on the island of Vieques was founded in the 1880s by Joseph Bean, a black Bermudan government worker. Originally under the supervision of the bishop of Antigua, these congregations came under the jurisdiction of the Episcopal Church after the American annexation of the island in 1892. In 1901 Puerto Rico became a missionary district, with its first bishop, James Haart Van Buren, sent the following year.

Cuban Anglicanism had two sources, both in the United States. On the one hand, Bishop Henry Benjamin Whipple of Minnesota, who was also a strong advocate for Native Americans, visited Cuba in 1871 and began to advocate an American presence there. The result was the appointment of the priest Edward Keeney to a ministry to English-speakers, which was not warmly received by the Spanish government. During the same years a number of congregations among Cuban immigrants to the United States in cities such as New York and New Orleans began to develop, with native Cubans gaining American ordination and returning to their homeland to establish ministries there, while also advocating Cuban independence. After the American occupation the PECUSA in 1904 sent Albion W. Knight as the first missionary bishop.[17]

The Anglican presence was, not surprisingly, much more pronounced in those parts of the Caribbean that were British colonies. The general pattern followed on most of the islands was the imposition of British control during the seventeenth or, occasionally, the eighteenth century, with the establishment of the Church of England following in its wake. As in Virginia and other North American colonies, no resident bishop existed during this period; instead, the bishop of London was nominally in charge of Anglican religious life. The governors of the individual colonies exercised *de facto* episcopal power, and island legislatures played important roles in the administration and financing of Church life, including those civil functions which had historically been entrusted to Church of England parishes. The SPG provided many of the clergy, but was unable to supervise them closely because of the realities of local lay control. The clergy tended to identify closely with the English 'plantocracy' that owned the plantations and their forced labourers, and who exercised *de facto* control over all aspects of island political and economic life, including the Church. Although the planters were vastly outnumbered on most of the islands by slaves of African origin, the latter had no say in island affairs, and clergy for the most part did not concern themselves too zealously with the slaves' spiritual or material well-being.

By the later eighteenth century the religious composition of the islands began to become more complex, paralleling in some ways the situation in the American southern colonies. Although the SPG was concerned with religious training for the slaves, it ran into resistance from the planters—tobacco in Virginia, sugar in the British West Indies—who feared that slaves might equate Christian baptism with manumission and political enfranchisement. The Great Awakening in the American colonies introduced a new kind of Evangelical energy into colonial Protestantism, challenging Anglican complacency and bringing the message of the gospel to black and white alike. The spread of the Baptist version of Christianity from the mainland to the islands and the work of Methodist and Moravian missionaries among island blacks began to challenge the religious hegemony previously enjoyed by the Church of England, which had been overwhelmingly the domain of the white settlers. The interaction of Christianity with African traditions—arguably stronger in the islands, where the percentage of black population was much higher than in the American South—produced various hybrid religions, fluid in their oral character and socially marginal existence. In addition to the small populations of Jews and Roman Catholics in the British West Indies, these Evangelical and

[17] A. Hugo Blankinship, Jr, 'The Episcopal Church of Cuba', ch. 48 in Ian Markham, J. Barney Hawkins, Justyn Terry, and Lesley N. Steffensen (eds.), *The Wiley-Blackwell Companion to the Anglican Communion* (Hoboken, NJ, 2013).

creolized versions of Christianity raised a formidable challenge to Anglican religious hegemony, with social and political implications as well.

Two other forces emanating from the British imperial government had profound implications for the development of Anglicanism in these islands during the nineteenth century. The first was ecclesiastical reorganization. As on the mainland, many members of the planter elite feared the appointment of a bishop because it might put some unwanted limits on *de facto* lay control of the Church, the addition of extra expenses, and the potential evangelization of the lower, primarily black, orders of society. In 1824 bishops for the islands were finally named, with Christopher Lipscomb appointed to Jamaica (including the Bahamas and Honduras), and William Hart Coleridge to Barbados and the Leeward Islands (including Guiana, Trinidad, Tobago, and the Windward Islands). New dioceses for Antigua, Guiana, and Nassau, all part of the British Caribbean system, would come at mid-century. The planters' anxieties were allayed in part by a compromise through which bishops would select clergy, who would then be inducted into parishes by the colony's governor.

The other major development with profound implications for island society, including the Church, was the movement in Britain that began to develop in late eighteenth-century Britain against the institution of slavery. The involvement of the Church of England in this movement with respect to the British West Indies began in a significant way in 1783 with Bishop Porteus of London calling upon the SPG to address the conditions of the residents on the Codrington Estates which they held in Barbados. Various religious and ideological strains converged in England that resulted in Parliament's passage of the Slave Trade Act, which in 1808 attempted to outlaw—with considerable but imperfect success—the importation of African slaves into the British Empire. The formation of the Anti-Slavery Society by Evangelical William Wilberforce and others, together with the so-called Baptist War in Jamaica in 1832, prompted Parliament to abolish slavery itself the following year, with compensation for slaveholders and an 'apprenticeship' system which was ostensibly intended to prepare liberated slaves for new lives as freed people. Full emancipation was achieved in 1838. Anglican clergy were not generally supportive of these developments, since they were socially and economically allied with the slave-holding plantocracy and the majority had been involved in slave management themselves. Even missionary work was suspect as having the potential for planting thoughts of equality.[18]

The further development of Anglicanism in the British West Indies during the nineteenth century might best be charted by attention to the two colonies that were first to have resident bishops, namely, Jamaica and Barbados. During the eighteenth century such Church of England presence as there was—the

[18] Catherine Hall, *Civilising Subjects: Colony and Metropole in the English Imagination, 1830–1867* (London, 2002), p. 77.

SPG never became an effective force—was intended for the benefit of the colonial officials and garrisons in the principal settlements of Spanish Town and Kingston; the planters and their estate staffs were too scattered to be able to attend parish services regularly. In Kingston, only about 8 per cent of worshippers attended Church of England services, with Roman Catholics and various Protestant Dissenters accounting for the large majority of the population.[19] It was only with the advent of Bishop Lipscombe in 1824 that the Church of England presence was significantly enhanced. Lipscombe ordained sixty-six priests and seventy-three deacons—all of British provenance—and consecrated thirty-one new churches during his episcopate, which lasted until his death in 1843.[20] Lipscombe also extended the Church of England's presence far into the countryside, providing religious instruction to slaves and ministry to whites scattered in rural parishes.

A defining event for the island was the 'Christmas Rebellion' or 'Baptist War' of 1831–2, although Baptist missionaries actually had nothing to do with it. Its leader, Samuel Sharpe, was a 'native Baptist', that is, an Afro-Jamaican who, with many of his followers, had developed an interpretation of Baptist Christianity shaped by their own experience and heritage. The rebellion, which originated as a peaceful act of resistance against unjust working conditions, escalated into a widespread armed revolt that was suppressed quickly and brutally by British forces. A counter-revolutionary movement emerged in the form of the Colonial Church Union (CCU), led by the Anglican clergyman George Bridges—described by a contemporary as 'intolerant, intransigent, and totally without charity'—which waged war against Dissenters, destroying Baptist chapels and harassing their clergy.[21]

The CCU was an extremist group, and was soon outlawed, and revulsion against its tactics helped steer Anglo-Jamaican sentiment towards emancipation. Lipscombe not Bridges represented the mainstream of the Anglican presence. Even though the Clergy Act of 1825, re-enacted several times subsequently, compelled Lipscombe to share authority over clergy with the royal governor, he moved quickly to consolidate episcopal authority over the Jamaican Church. He took seriously, within the limits of the paternalistic mindset of the day, the imperial mandate to bring slaves within a 'community of feeling' through the agency of the Church of England—a vague and implausible task given the indifference or resistance of the non-British population—and tried to rein in the work of the CMS, whose itinerant

19 Shirley O. Gordon, *God Almighty Made Me Free: Christianity in Preemancipation Jamaica* (Bloomington, IN, 1996), p. 10.

20 'The History of the Diocese of Jamaica and the Cayman Islands', website of the Anglican Diocese of Jamaica and the Cayman Islands. <http://www.anglicandioceseja.org/?page_id=50> (accessed 8 Aug. 2014).

21 Robert J. Stewart, *Religion and Society in Post-Emancipation Jamaica* (Knoxville, TN, 1992), p. 33.

strategies struck Lipscombe as subversive of institutional authority. The tensions between them were not resolved until the withdrawal of the CMS presence in the 1840s. The SPG followed suit in 1866 in protest over the Church's failure to promote a native clergy.[22]

The vision of Lipscombe and his immediate successors did not extend as far as a native, or even a creole, clergy; they preferred recruits who had been educated at Oxford, Cambridge, and Dublin. The experience of Robert Gordon, the first black Jamaican to be ordained to the priesthood, was a case in point. Born in 1830 to probably free Methodist parents, he presented himself in 1853 for ordination, but was deflected by an unacceptable offer to prepare him for missionary work in West Africa at Codrington College in the Bahamas. He eventually obtained ordination in Canada, and was appointed to a parish in England. He later publicly attacked the Jamaican Church for its refusal to accept native clergy, espousing the role of Afro-Creole nationalist. Like his US counterpart James Holly, Gordon found the colour line in New World Anglicanism a barrier that was impossible to cross.[23]

The era of the US Civil War encompassed two further defining moments in Jamaica's attempt to contain two societies whose demarcation was drawn on a mixture of racial, social, religious, and economic lines. The Great Revival that began in 1860 again combined elements of Evangelical—especially Baptist—Christianity with the African tradition of Obeah and its creole offshoot, Myal, resulting in extreme physical manifestations that alarmed white Christian missionaries as a potentially benign force that had escaped their control. This manifestation of cultural restlessness was followed in 1865 by the Morant Bay Rebellion, a protest against the selling-off of abandoned estate lands and evicting the small farmers living there as squatters. Again, Native Baptists were involved in the leadership, including Paul Bogle, who was executed after the revolt's rapid suppression. An alarming aspect of the episode was the death of a Church of England clergyman who also held the office of custos, a local official with a variety of civic duties. The revival and the rebellion in close succession together united both Church of England and Dissenting clergy in a common revulsion against religious and political enfranchisement for blacks. The Church of England's existence as an enclave of English society and culture in the islands would continue well into the following century.

In 1869, the oft-renewed Clergy Act, which had established the Church of England in Jamaica with a nod towards local autonomy, was not renewed, and the Jamaican Church was on its own. An 1870 act of the Jamaican legislature created an 'Incorporated Lay Body of the Church', with 'gradual disendowment'. The first synod of this new ecclesiastical entity was held the same year, with financial support from the laity and friends in England. The size of the

[22] Stewart, *Religion and Society*, pp. 1–5.

[23] Stewart, *Religion and Society*, pp. 97ff.

diocese had been diminished with the creation of the diocese of Nassau, which included the Bahamas and the Turks and Caicos Islands in 1861. In 1883 the Province of the West Indies was established, including the dioceses of Jamaica, Barbados, Guyana (1842), Antigua (1842), Nassau and the Bahamas (1861), the Windward Islands (1869), Trinidad and Tobago (1872), and British Honduras (1891). Enos Nuttall, who had become Jamaica's bishop in 1862, assumed the title of the province's primate in 1893, and later archbishop in 1897.[24]

If the Church of England had been an outpost of Englishness in Jamaica, it was if anything more so in Barbados. Fondly known by some as 'Little England', Barbados maintained an Established Church until 1969, three years after its emergence as an independent nation within the British Commonwealth. A small English-born elite had controlled Barbadian society and its sugar-dominated economy since the colony's seventeenth-century origins. (In 1871 the census revealed that the colony's population was 10 per cent white, 24 per cent 'coloured', and 65 per cent black.) Prior to William Coleridge's arrival as bishop in 1824, the colonial governor had controlled clerical appointments, and vestries dominated by local elites had extensive civil responsibilities, including education and poor relief as well as church maintenance. Pew rentals, which had also been a feature in the US South, continued in use until the twentieth century as a material expression of the racial and class stratification that characterized Barbadian Church life as well as the broader social order.[25]

The appointment of a bishop for Barbados in 1824 led to the predictable tensions between that office and an entrenched clergy who had become comfortable as part of the established 'plantocracy'. In 1868 Britain ended payments for clergy salaries, and the 1872 Bishop's Reappointment Act ensured that Church support would now come from tax monies and that the legislature would be firmly in control of the institution. The clergy continued to be predominantly British and white, although an occasional English-trained black such as E. S. Thorne, appointed as a rector in 1884, might slip by if demonstrating the proper social attitudes. They demonstrated little interest in theological pursuits or social change, being content with ministering to the needs of the planter class, who made up a minority of the population but a majority of church-goers.

Under Bishop John Mitchison (1873–91), the Barbadian Church became more active in the realm of education, a function which had traditionally been part of the Church's work in the British West Indies. In 1875 Mitchison headed the colony's Commission on Education, which led to a more coordinated educational system for the island. Perhaps the most distinctive feature of Anglican life in Barbados was Codrington College, which had been established

[24] 'The History of the Diocese of Jamaica and the Cayman Islands', website.

[25] Kortright Davis, *Cross and Crown in Barbados: Caribbean Political Religion in the Late 19th Century* (Frankfurt, 1983), pp. 54ff., 69.

through the legacy of two slave plantations to the SPG by Christopher Codrington in 1710. Opened in 1745 and initially providing both a general education and preparatory studies for the sons of the plantocracy planning to continue their studies in England, it shifted gears in the nineteenth century to become exclusively a theological college, one of the first in the Anglican world. In 1875, at Mitchison's initiative, it became affiliated with the University of Durham, from which its degrees were granted until 1958. Mitchison, whose attempts at imposing moral discipline did not sit well with the Barbadian clergy, returned to England in 1891.

Anglicanism in the British West Indies during the nineteenth century underwent a number of important structural changes that resulted in more regional control of Church government but which never succeeded in moving adherence to the Church of England beyond the plantocracy, who generally resisted episcopal efforts directed towards freedom, evangelization, and education of their non-British labourers. They and the local clergy, almost uniformly of British descent, maintained an alliance directed at sustaining the system of production of labour which benefited them all in its distinction between privileged English and exploitable Africans. Although the Church survived, the loyalties of most of the population lay with the Evangelical groups who had originally reached out to them and who provided them with empowering roles in religious life, or with the Afro-Caribbean hybrid movements that combined features of the Evangelical and African heritages.

The nineteenth century was thus characterized by a movement towards an independent Anglicanism throughout what had originally been British North America. The degree to which a genuinely autonomous version of Anglicanism was achieved varied according to the particular circumstances of each region, including the relationship of Church to state; the extent of *de facto* and *de jure* religious pluralism; the relationship of residents of English stock to other, especially enslaved African, populations; and the cultural and political hold which Britain maintained upon the nation at large and the Anglican community in particular. Although significant examples of Anglican sympathies with social reform and ministry to minorities did in fact exist, Anglican Churches tended more generally to draw from and identify with the interests of local elites, while maintaining a strong bond of sympathy with the Church of England and its traditions.

SELECT BIBLIOGRAPHY

Bourgeois, Michael, *All Things Human: Henry Codman Potter and the Social Gospel in the Episcopal Church* (Urbana, IL, 2004).

Butler, Diana Hochstedt, *Standing against the Whirlwind: Evangelical Episcopalians in Nineteenth-century America* (New York, 1995).

Carrington, Philip, *The Anglican Church in Canada* (Toronto, 1963).

Davis, Kortright, *Cross and Crown in Barbados: Caribbean Political Religion in the Late 19th Century* (Frankfurt, 1983).

Dayfood, Arthur Charles, *The Shaping of the West Indian Church 1492–1962* (Gainesville, FL, 1999).

Dean, David M., *Defender of the Race: James Theodore Holly, Black Nationalist Bishop* (Boston, MA, 1979).

Donovan, Mary Sudman, *A Different Call: Women's Ministries in the Episcopal Church, 1850–1920* (Wilton, CT, 1986).

Frey, Sheila R. and Betty Wood, *Come Shouting to Zion: African American Protestantism in the American South and British Caribbean to 1830* (Chapel Hill, NC, 1998).

Gordon, Shirley O., *God Almighty Make Me Free: Christianity in Preemancipation Jamaica* (Bloomington, IN, 1996).

Guelzo, Allen C., *For the Union of Evangelical Christendom: The Irony of Reformed Episcopalians* (University Park, PA, 1994).

Hayes, Alan L., *Anglicans in Canada: Controversies and Identity in Historical Perspective* (Urbana and Chicago, IL, 2004).

Higman, R. W., *A Concise History of the Caribbean* (Cambridge and New York, 2011).

Holmes, David L., *A Brief History of the Episcopal Church* (Valley Forge, PA, 1993).

Katerberg, William H., *Modernity and the Dilemma of North American Anglican Identities, 1880–1950* (Montreal, 2001).

Paz, Juan Ramón de la, 'La Historia de la Iglesia Episcopal de Cuba'. <http://anglicanhistory.org/wi/cuba/> (Project Canterbury, 2001).

Porter, Andrew, *Religion versus Empire? British Protestant Missionaries and Overseas Expansion, 1700–1914* (Manchester and New York, 2004).

Stewart, Robert J., *Religion and Society in Post-Emancipation Jamaica* (Knoxville, TN, 1992).

Westfall, William, *Two Worlds: The Protestant Culture of Nineteenth-Century Ontario* (Kingston and Montreal, 1989).

12

Anglicanism in Sub-Saharan Africa, *c.*1829–1910

Emma Wild-Wood

In 1828 St George's Cathedral was erected in Free Town, Sierra Leone. It stood as a symbol of confident, prayerful expectation of Anglican expansion in a tiny enclave of migrant Christianity that was barely a generation old. Elsewhere in sub-Saharan Africa Anglicanism was present only in chaplaincies to British companies and their garrisons, a spiritual service to British mercantile interests. During much of the nineteenth century Anglican activity emanated from discrete locales in coastal regions and thus this chapter is organized geographically. By the early twentieth century, however, it reached towards the centre of the continent. In 1906 the Malek mission in Sudan was inaugurated; in 1909 St Peter's Cathedral, Likoma Island, Lake Nyasa, was completed; in 1910 the diocese of Northern Rhodesia was begun; and the settlement of a colonial boundary ensured an Anglican presence in the Belgian Congo. This spread of Anglicanism involved complex encounters of peoples, of ideas, expectations, and spirituality. If the building and name of St George's Cathedral indicates an expectation of continuity with traditional Anglican institutions and governance, the mission-focused Christianity developing on the Sierra Leone peninsular suggests that situational contingency and local shaping of Anglicanism made its expansion possible.

This chapter portrays the first shoots of an African form of Anglicanism as rooted in cross-cultural relationships which encouraged an adoption and adaptation of European structures, beliefs, and practices in response to local, social, and spiritual needs. Even at its most local, Anglicanism in sub-Saharan Africa connected across regions and continents. African adherents of Anglicanism were attracted to the universal claims of the Christian faith; their membership of the Anglican Church served to tighten the fictive kin relationships 'in Christ' across the globe. A study of Anglicanism in nineteenth-century Africa therefore entails a balancing of the local with the transnational as Africans and Europeans moved into, across, and out of the continent, exchanging new beliefs and practices.

Earlier studies of Anglicanism in Africa focused on the work of European and North American missionaries and their mission agencies. Active in sub-Saharan Africa were the Church Missionary Society (CMS), the Society for the Propagation of the Gospel (SPG), the Universities' Mission to Central Africa (UMCA) and, by 1910, numerous smaller Anglican societies and non-denominational agencies for whom Anglicans worked. Where bishops were present, they exerted great personal influence in developing ecclesial policy but they were too few in number to affect significantly the ways in which religious change took place. Mission agencies expected that African Christians' knowledge of their own context made them particularly effective missionaries. Whilst European prejudice and unrealistic expectations often prevented Africans from taking leadership positions, recent historiography has recognized the impetus of African Christians in evangelism, education, and inculturation. African laity, catechists, and priests, often employed by mission agencies, bridged cultural divides to facilitate the implantation of the Anglican Church.

The encounters which shaped African Anglicanism can be seen in the following overlapping influences. The enslaved, the recently freed, and the dislocated encountered abolitionist missionaries who propounded a theology which read *imago Dei* through an Enlightenment lens and declared a common humanity and universal salvation in Christ. This humanitarian message was compelling for many Africans. It was also used to encourage British intervention in the continent. Secondly, Africans with a cosmopolitan outlook encountered literacy, new technologies, and social ideas offered in a package with Christianity. Many understood these to be useful in their changing societies and adapted such novelties to their own needs. Thirdly, Africans encountered pervasive European power. Whilst this transcended Anglicanism, one cannot overlook the particular relationship of Anglican missionaries to the nation at the forefront of anti-slavery enforcement because of its global mercantile dominance. Anglican missions frequently preceded British imperial rule, yet missions called upon British political and economic interests when they considered them beneficial for evangelism, abolitionism, and civilization. Some pleaded for British 'protection' against slavery, paganism, insecurity, or Muslim incursion only to discover that their goals were often at odds with those of colonial administrators. Where Anglican missionaries were critical of British rule, they were usually loyal critics, adopting the role of negotiators and using metropolitan contacts to militate against its excesses. Missionaries were useful allies for some Africans; others considered them arrogant and intrusive. Finally, Africans encountered new forms of religious belief and practice and engaged in a process of sifting their own familiar categories and novel Anglican categories to develop their own response. This process was often easier for those who were already engaged in the first and second sets of encounters; the dislocated and cosmopolitan frequently became messengers to more settled or internally cohesive communities who were less curious, or indeed hostile, towards novelty. As they joined the Anglican Church, Africans explored ways in which it provided divine sustenance for living in altered circumstances, and how far cultural norms which remained precious could be reconciled within it.

WEST AFRICA

Anglicanism was first present in the eighteenth-century cosmopolitan coastal ports. The first African Anglican clergyman, Philip Quaque, was an SPG chaplain to the Royal Africa Company's castle on the Gold Coast (1766–1816).[1] He aspired to be a missionary and teacher to the African population, but often his engagement was hampered by the company's trading interests in slaves, gold, and mahogany. His attempts to mediate between cultures frequently left him isolated and misunderstood by his extended family, the SPG, and the Company employees. After his death, Quaque was replaced by British chaplains. In the nineteenth century the SPG worked in coastal towns on the Gold Coast, in colonial posts, and along railway routes bringing valuable freight to the coast. The development of a native Anglican Church was not officially initiated until 1904 when Nathaniel Hamlyn became the first bishop of Western Equatorial Guinea, by which time the Methodist Church was thriving and the Anglican Church was regarded as '*abanmu asor*', 'the Church of the Castle, the government's Church'.[2]

The most significant expansion of the Anglican Church began north-west of the Gold Coast and was intimately connected to the anti-slavery campaigns of the late eighteenth and early nineteenth centuries. The peninsula of Sierra Leone had been declared a British colony in 1787 for the purpose of resettling freed-slaves. A group of 'Black poor' from London was followed, in January 1792, by freed-slaves who had settled in Nova Scotia after the American War of Independence. They brought from the slave plantations the Methodist and Baptist traditions of the American Great Awakening. In 1800 Maroons from Jamaica joined them in Freetown. The settlers perceived themselves to be returning home to Africa, but their Atlantic-Christian culture was little appreciated by the peoples among whom they settled. Their cause was

[1] Edward E. Andrews, 'Christian Missions and Colonial Empires Reconsidered: A Black Evangelist in West Africa, 1766–1816', *Journal of Church and State*, 51 (2010): 663–91.

[2] John S. Pobee, 'The Anglican Church in Ghana and the SPG', in Dan O'Connor and others, *Three Centuries of Mission: The United Society for the Propagation of the Gospel 1701–2000* (London, 2000), p. 411.

facilitated by prominent Church of England philanthropists, particularly members of the Clapham Sect, who developed the Sierra Leone Company in 1792 to encourage legitimate trade and provide protection for the settlers. They also ensured that in 1804 Sierra Leone became the first mission field of the CMS. More freed-slaves arrived from 1808 after the British Parliament abolished the slave trade in 1807. The Royal Navy patrolled the West African coast intercepting slaving vessels and bringing the human cargo to Sierra Leone. Some whom the navy liberated came from as far away as Kongo; many had been casualties of the Yoruba wars, taken as slaves by Fulani and Yoruba raiders and bought by Portuguese traders for the transatlantic market. The peninsula became a Crown Colony in 1808, after the Sierra Leone Company foundered, in order to promote legitimate trade and protect against regional hostility and slaving. British rule was not immediately perceived as a threat to self-determination.

By 1825, 18,000 re-captives had been settled in villages along the Sierra Leone peninsula. In 1840 the figure was 67,000. A small number went to Bathurst, Gambia, a British colony since 1816. Over the nineteenth century they became known as Krio and formed a literate and influential elite whose corporate identity was largely Christian. Many Krio became Anglicans, partly because the CMS educated about four-fifths of the population by supplying the colony with more missionaries than other societies and collaborating closely with the colonial administration. Governor Charles McCathy, a keen supporter of mission agencies, resourced the CMS's involvement in his scheme of 'parishes', each with a church and school, through which re-captives could obtain immediate aid, housing, new skills, work, marriage partners, and so on. They also heard preaching on freedom in Christ, a persuasive message for the previously enslaved. By the 1850s two-thirds of the population of the colony professed Christianity.[3] Those who settled in Gambia joined the Anglican chaplaincy established for European traders and the military. When it closed in 1880 the small Anglican community was served by a priest from the Sierra Leone diocese until they developed their own leadership from the 1930s.[4] Abolitionism and the repatriation of free blacks in the United States also precipitated the foundation of an Episcopal Church in Liberia from 1838, along with larger Methodist and Baptist Churches. Between 1806 and 1816 the CMS prioritized work among the Susu people of Rio Pongas, present-day Guinea. But the influx of freed-slaves to Freetown, high missionary mortality rates, the hostility of slave traders, and the strength of Islam caused the abandonment of the project until 1855, when it was

[3] Jehu J. Hanciles, *Euthanasia of Mission: African Church Autonomy in a Colonial Context* (London, 2002), p. 7.

[4] Martha T. Frederiks, *We Have Toiled All Night: Christianity in the Gambia, 1456–2000* (Zoetermeer, 2003), pp. 213–15.

re-established by West Indian missionaries as a thank offering for the 150th anniversary of the Anglican Church in the Caribbean.

The early CMS mission in Sierra Leone was an international organization, largely staffed by German Lutheran men, many of whom had married British or African American women. The first two missionaries, Melchior Renner (active 1804–21) and Peter Hartwig, were instructed to establish a Christian community, 'exhibiting to the Natives the practical influence of Christianity in regulating the tempers and the life'.[5] The Evangelical Christianity they espoused expected individual commitment to faith, Bible study, prayer, and corporate worship within a monogamous family and companionate marriage. A call to transformation of all aspects of life initially had more success among those who had undergone dislocation. The Krio became enthusiastic learners of new skills by which to improve their situation. The development of educational institutions was a significant part of the work of the CMS, integral to its evangelistic aims. Literacy enabled Bible reading, but also job opportunities as clerks, lawyers, and staff for colonial government.

Primary and secondary schools developed gender-specific curricula common in the Western world at the time. Elizabeth Renner, née Richards (d. 1826), a freed-slave from Nova Scotia, was involved in the mission education of girls from 1808. She aimed to make them 'chaste, decent, and honest' wives for the new class of educated men emerging in the colony, and to show them 'such necessary works as are needful for females brought up in this country'.[6] Some scholars understand mission education, often accompanied by a disciplinary regime, as the imposition of social control; girls' education receives particular opprobrium as instruction into unequal Western gender expectations.[7] Others suggest that missionary women shifted the norms of the metropole, reinventing expectations rather than replicating them.[8] Either way, Africans adopted and adapted received Western forms of domesticity, childcare, and marriage along with literacy, numeracy, and Christian education.

Prominent among the educational establishments was Fourah Bay College (est. 1816). By 1825 it provided an academic syllabus for boys only, one which would allow them to work in the Church, commerce, and colonial administration. By 1876, the college was affiliated to Durham University which awarded its degrees. Most clergy were educated at Fourah Bay and from their number the development of Anglicanism in Sierra Leone and Nigeria

[5] Eugene Stock, *History of the Church Missionary Society*, 4 vols. (London, 1899), I, p. 84.

[6] Letter from Elizabeth Renner, 12 Feb. 1802, quoted in Samuel Abraham Walker, *Missions in Western Africa among the Soosoos, Bulloms &c being the first undertaken by the Church Missionary Society for Africa and the East* (Dublin, 1845), p. 363.

[7] Fiona Leach, 'African Girls, Nineteenth-Century Mission Education and the Patriarchal Imperative', *Gender and Education*, 20 (2008): 335–47.

[8] Fiona Bowie, Deborah Kirkwood, and Shirley Ardener (eds.), *Women and Missions: Past and Present—Anthropological and Historical Perceptions* (Oxford, 1993).

was assured. Whilst many families ensured that between their children a variety of professions were represented, the close connection between education and the Church encouraged ministerial vocations. Three brothers of one family went into the priesthood, working in Sierra Leone, Lagos, and the Niger. The careers of Henry, Nathaniel, and Samuel Johnson span the second half of the nineteenth century; they taught in schools, and carried out translation, pastoral, and mission work. Henry (1840–1901) became archdeacon of Upper Niger in 1878. Samuel (1846–1901) wrote *A History of the Yorubas* (1921), which was instrumental in the formation of the corporate and Christian identity of a hitherto disparate group of peoples.[9]

Many freed Africans around Freetown developed commercial links with their areas of origin. Some found their families and shared with them their Christian faith. The development of trade and family links between Sierra Leone and the Yoruba and Igbo areas paved the way for missionary activity and establishment of the Church in Nigeria. As early as 1839 Krio traders petitioned the British government to establish a colony in Badagri for these purposes, and they assisted the much-vaunted Niger Expedition of 1841 through prayer and financial giving. British mission supporters, led by Thomas Fowell Buxton, a prominent abolitionist, urged the government to support the expedition in order to encourage non-slaving commerce and the importation of 'civilization' and Christianity to the Niger River basin. Buxton appealed for a sharing of Britain's 'blessings' because 'we owe Africa a debt which our utmost efforts can never wholly cancel'.[10] Swayed by humanitarian fervour and economic advantages the British government agreed to the project. The expedition did not yield the expected results and almost two-thirds of the European participants died, although most of the Africans remained healthy. In Britain it was considered a fiasco. Yet it shaped the way in which the Anglican Church developed in what is now Nigeria. Sierra Leone became a missionary base, the 'native pastorate' providing missionary personnel who were supported by Krio traders.

In 1825 one of Fourah Bay College's most famous alumni entered, a recaptive called Ajayi who took the name of his British sponsor, Samuel Crowther. Samuel Ajayi Crowther (*c.*1809–91) was a CMS representative on the Niger Expedition and made a significant contribution to its research. He had already contributed to the language work of the CMS in Freetown, developing the mission's concern to communicate and evangelize in the vernaculars by collecting Yoruba and Temne vocabularies. He went to Britain for training, was ordained priest in 1843, and was among the first of many

[9] Kehinde Olabimtan, *Samuel Johnson of Yorubaland, 1846–1901: Identity, Change and the Making of a Mission Agent* (Oxford, 2013), pp. 15–19.

[10] [Thomas Fowell Buxton], *Abridgement of Sir T. Fowell Buxton's Work on the African Slave Trade and its Remedy* (London, 1840), p. 8.

African clergy who visited Britain and developed direct relations with Church leaders and personnel at the CMS headquarters. His close association with Henry Venn (1796–1873), secretary of the CMS, was to influence Venn's visionary thinking about mission policy. Whilst Venn's expectation of a moratorium on mission, and of an indigenous self-governing, self-supporting, self-perpetuating Church often ran aground on local contingencies and missionaries' growing mistrust of African leadership, it remained a CMS ideal. On returning to West Africa, Crowther, with Henry Townsend (1815–86), and C. A. Gollmer (1812–86), opened a new mission at Abeokuta among the Egun Yoruba, followed by missions at Onitsha, Igbebe, and Badagri. The first baptism took place at Abeokuta in 1848. Igbo were also numerous in Sierra Leone and traded in their region of origin. They petitioned the CMS committee to establish a mission in the area and supported a further expedition in 1853. The first missionaries settled in the area in 1857 and included Igbo-Krio like the Revd John Christopher Taylor (*c.*1815–80). Their work took place alongside, and sometimes in competition with, Catholic and Presbyterian missions already in the area.

The spread of new missions over large areas of West Africa necessitated a regional episcopal see. In 1852 the first bishop of Sierra Leone, O. E. Vidal, was consecrated and, before he died in 1855, he presided over the first ordination of clergy in Freetown. But the high mortality of European bishops hampered the development of the Church; Vidal and several of his successors were unable to complete clergy training or visit all parts of their vast diocese. It further demonstrated the need for local leadership. In 1863 the Native Pastorate Church was formed, which was self-supporting and distinct from the CMS organization. By 1881 only the bishop among the clergy in Sierra Leone was European. In 1898 the native pastorate assumed responsibility for mission work in the Sierra Leone hinterland, which had been declared a British protectorate in 1886. While in 1864 Crowther was consecrated Missionary Bishop of the Niger Territory, it came at a time when those Europeans who considered Africans unprepared for leadership roles were becoming more numerous and forceful. Crowther's episcopacy was, therefore, impeded by racial prejudice and the contingencies of approaching colonial rule.

The Niger mission became embroiled in the European scramble for West Africa and the increasing mistrust it generated between Europeans and Africans over leadership and finance. The last of the Yoruba wars finished in 1877 and British companies competed for access to trade routes. Across Africa missionaries desired dissociation from arms and alcohol trading and greater autonomy of movement from commercial ships on which they had hitherto relied for transportation. To this end calls for missionary vessels were common. Crowther's petition for a vessel resulted in his obtaining the *Henry Venn*. It came, however, with a European manager who prioritized trade and exploration and had scant respect for Crowther. Futhermore, Crowther's pastoral approach to his clergy was criticized by Europeans as insufficiently robust. In 1879 the management of the Niger mission was handed to the European-dominated finance committee in Lagos. In the 1880s a number of new, younger CMS missionaries accused Crowther of inability to discipline his clergy, and his power was further eroded. In 1890 Crowther declared the Niger Delta Pastorate to be self-governing within the Anglican Communion and under direct control of Canterbury, but the suspicion and accusations had broken him and he died at the end of the following year. Taylor and Henry Johnson were also casualties of the scandal. The arrogance of certain British missionaries demonstrated their captivity to the racial assumptions of the age and their conviction of the superiority of holiness-influenced Evangelicalism.

Crowther's episcopate, however, also saw the growth of the Anglican Church. Before the advent of colonial rule the establishment of good relations with local rulers was important for the success of the missions, and Crowther won the trust of a number of these leaders through whom he hoped to influence wider society. Some leaders were intrigued by the claims of Christianity, its novel technologies, its way of approaching divinity through one divine mediator rather than a pantheon of spirits and divinities, and its contribution to community well-being and flourishing. One example of differences surrounding the local encounter with Christianity comes from the island of Bonny. A significant palm oil trading port, it was ruled by a merchant-king whose political power depended on economic success. Claimants for the kingdom and their supporters invested in different religious traditions in order to structure society and to empower their political and economic ambitions. William Dappa Pepple (d. 1866) believed that Christianity offered necessary spiritual power for the modern challenges that his kingdom faced and originally approached the United Presbyterian Mission of Calabar. His rival, Jaja of Opado (*c.*1821–91), exiled Pepple and rejected Christianity as impractical and damaging for trade, considering that it exaggerated the value of universal literacy. Jaja insisted that binding trade agreements should take the form of oaths to local deities, thus protecting local traders by excluding Christian Igbo businessmen. They in turn supported the Pepple faction which mounted another attack and defeated Jaja. In 1865 Pepple invited the CMS to start a mission, and he and his heir worked closely with Dandleson Crowther (1844–1938), son of Samuel Ajayi, and archdeacon of Lower Delta from 1874. Jaja remained suspicious of missionary and foreign commercial intrusion in Opado state and was eventually arrested and exiled by British colonial forces. The appropriation of Anglicanism in Bonny and the Niger area was contested within the complex political and commercial dynamics of small states.

The encounter with Anglicanism in Yorubaland and the Niger flourished for a number of reasons: Krio returnees influenced their kin; war and migration developed new social organizations; inhabitants of new towns were attracted to the novel ideas and technologies demonstrated by the Krio and the mission stations; and projects of literacy and translation which had begun in Sierra Leone found audiences often desirous of disseminating their own cultural traditions. From the mid-nineteenth century the skills of writing and translation no longer remained the preserve of coastal ports but were available upriver. Church presses not only produced Christian literature in English and vernaculars but also collections of proverbs, histories, newspapers, and journals on current affairs. The development of a literate social class was part of a cultural conversion to Christianity in which the Anglican Church played a significant role. The acceptance of Western bio-medicine was another element of this process; men like Samuel Crowther junior and the fourth Johnson brother, Obadiah (1849–1920), trained as doctors in the United Kingdom. They introduced new comprehensions of healing and the human body with the medicine they administered. Some converts, keen to embrace the changes of their new life adopted a suspicion of local art, music, and stories, perceived to maintain connections with their pre-Christian life. Yet the shifts in culture were not all one way. Others sifted the demands made upon them, choosing which ones they would respect. As converts reordered their social and spiritual lives they also reconfigured Christianity. Translation necessitates rendering ideas and stories into new thought forms and is part of the process of rooting Christianity and inculturating it in a new society. Translations of the Prayer Book accompanied those of the gospels and became the mainstay of Anglican worship. Taylor translated much of the New Testament into Igbo by 1860 and also worked on the Union Igbo Bible (1906), whilst Crowther rendered significant sections of the Bible and Prayer Book into Yoruba. He also gathered and published local proverbs. Thus traditional forms of wisdom, biblical ideas of nationhood, and literate forms of communication all contributed to new, cohesive forms of Yoruba and Igbo identity.

The process of sifting the Krio and the CMS form of Christianity was propounded by an emerging urban Christian elite who consciously wished to shape their faith as an African religion. James 'Holy' Johnson (*c.*1836–1917) was ardent in his articulation of African Christianity and autonomy whilst remaining within the Anglican Church. He was a priest in the native pastorate of Sierra Leone from 1866 until 1874 when he became minister of St Paul's, Breadfruit, in Lagos, a British colony since 1861. Johnson became superintendent of the Interior Yoruba Mission in 1876 before returning to Breadfruit in 1880. From 1886 he joined the Legislative Council in Nigeria, where he was an open critic of imperialism. In 1900 Johnson became assistant bishop of the Niger mission and Benin territories, serving until his death in 1917. His sobriquet 'Holy' was bestowed in recognition of his strict, ascetic spirituality which he combined with a fervent commitment to African culture and pan-Africanism. Johnson promoted an autonomous, self-supporting Church unencumbered by European control, and the evangelization of Africa by

Africans. To facilitate African leadership he raised funds to endow the Niger mission and end dependency on England. Johnson was a close associate of the prominent pan-Africanist, Presbyterian minister, and, briefly, employee of the CMS, Edward W. Blyden (1832–1912). In 1873 in Sierra Leone Blyden supported Methodists and Baptists who had formed their own African Churches in the 1840s and urged Anglicans to separate from the Church of England. He came to Lagos to repeat the call in 1891 as Crowther's episcopate faced opposition. Some Anglicans formed the United Native Anglican Church. Whilst Johnson hosted Blyden, he opposed every attempt at division within Anglicanism, preferring to attempt change from within. He wished to develop a nation and a Church with African philosophies and African theology, entering into dialogue with traditional diviners and incorporating Yoruba religious names into Christian baptismal rituals.

The opinions of West African Anglicans diverged on the relation of Christianity with African cultures, traditional religions, and politics, but Krio Christians and the CMS missionaries were uniformly exercised about Islam. Long present in West Africa, Islam experienced a resurgence in the nineteenth century. At a church conference held in Freetown in 1871, the subject was presented as 'Our Mohammedan and Heathen Population—The Duty of the Church in Relation to Them'. One response was to send Henry Johnson to learn Arabic in Jerusalem (1873–6) in order to translate the Bible. Crowther, in his book *Experiences with Heathens and Mohomedans in West Africa* (1892), advocated engaged and respectful apologetics.[11] But as British rule spread, the administration feared that proselytism would jeopardize collaborative relations with Muslim rulers in the north and accordingly limited missionary activity; the single CMS station among the Hausa at Zaira was viewed as an irritant. This policy discouraged the exploratory and cordial African interreligious engagement of previous decades.

The collaboration of the CMS with Krio church leaders and traders had, by the twentieth century, established a growing Anglican Church in West Africa. Yet the hardening racial attitudes of Europeans almost destroyed it. Most missionaries no longer held to the early ideals of international Christian equality and, adopting systems of racial hierarchies, began to compare Africans to children under their tutelage. A few maintained relations with Africans that allowed a critique of such notions. The African response was various; some rejected the Church, some accepted European tutelage, others attempted to disentangle it from missionary control or Western civilization believing that British imperial influence distorted the gospel.

[11] Andrew F. Walls, 'Africa as the Theatre of Christian Engagement with Islam in the Nineteenth Century', in David Maxwell with Ingrid Lawrie (eds.), *Christianity and the African Imagination* (Leiden, 2002), pp. 49–54.

SOUTHERN AFRICA

Concepts of racial hierarchy also influenced the culture of the Anglican Church in Southern Africa. The SPG's commitment to improving the godliness and orderliness of colonial societies ensured attention to the pastoral care of British settlers early in the nineteenth century. But its mission to Africans was fully implemented only later in the century. Early African actors in and around the Church were required to fathom the religious entanglements between Europeans associated with the appropriation of their land and those who sought to ameliorate their lives or support claims for self-determination.

During the Napoleonic Wars the Cape Colony passed from the Dutch to the British, who, in their second occupation from 1806, established an Anglican garrison chaplaincy. Likewise, the islands of Mauritius and the Seychelles developed a small Anglican presence from 1810 and 1814 respectively in the wake of the British conquest of the French-held islands. The SPG sent nine chaplains to the Cape Colony in the 1820s under the jurisdiction of the bishop of Calcutta. The ecclesiastical institution expanded after the arrival in 1848 of Robert Gray (1809–72), previously secretary to the SPG, as bishop of Cape Town. In 1853 the dioceses of Natal and Grahamstown were instituted, followed by Bloemfontein in 1863. Controversially, a bishop of Pretoria was consecrated in 1878 during a short-lived interlude of British control of the Republic of Transvaal; an appointment influenced by colonial ambition which flouted Afrikaner opposition to an Anglican presence. The original clandestine land purchase by Bishop Wilkinson of Zululand was augmented through the deployment of clergy in the gold-rush towns and cemented after the South African War of 1899. Land and mineral resources attracted a large number of British settlers who wished to maintain their lifestyle and rule. Many found in the Anglican Church a social and spiritual vehicle for achieving that aim. It became for many migrants a home-from-home and they imported forms of worship, architecture, and arguments to which they were greatly attached. Prominent settlers supported missionary evangelism and education, although they were wary of missionary work that challenged the racial ordering of society in the colonies. Notable among missionaries were the religious orders of women, like the Community of St Michael and All Angels (1874) in Bloemfontein; and of men, such as the Community of the Resurrection (1902) in Johannesburg. They pioneered education, medicine, and care for migrant workers in the burgeoning towns, and in the case of the latter, developed a crucial role in the training of black clergy.

Tensions arose through the SPG's eclectic recruitment process. The society engaged clergy from throughout the United Kingdom and from different types of churchmanship who, at a time when Anglicanism was becoming more partisan, travelled with their party convictions.[12] The consequent arguments demonstrate the peculiar ecclesiastical issues facing Anglicanism as it spread across the globe which, whilst not absent in other areas of Africa, were rarely as acute as in South Africa. In 1870 the Church of the Province of South Africa (CPSA) was incorporated under Gray as the archbishop of Cape Town, gaining a hard-won autonomy from the Church of England in matters of doctrine, practice, and Church discipline. There was an irony in this independence; Gray used the British systems in South Africa to develop a Church that declared its autonomy from them. In obtaining its autonomy, the Church became the site for fissures which contributed to the perceived need for addressing episcopal governance in the colonies. The complexity of the constitutional issues and the variety of opinions expressed by clergy of Catholic, Liberal, and Evangelical persuasions have often eclipsed the local development of the Anglican Church in the historiography.

Gray, influenced by the Oxford Movement, was concerned with the perceived liberal and Erastian tendencies in the Church of England. He promoted governance by synods and considered it proper to have a metropolitan in Africa rather than defer to the bishop of London. When the bishop of Natal, John Colenso (1814–93), wrote controversial commentaries on Romans (1861) and the Pentateuch and Joshua (1862), Gray assumed the authority to summon Colenso to a tribunal, convict him of heresy, and excommunicate him. Colenso rejected the process, appealing to the Privy Council in England to try his case, a course of action abhorrent to Gray's Tractarian sensibilities. The Privy Council's decision was unsatisfactory; it denied Colenso a particular see but affirmed his episcopate. For some time there were two bishops in Natal. Supporters of Colenso maintained an institution distinct from the CPSA—the Church of England in South Africa. A much smaller body, it attracted not only those of a liberal persuasion but also Evangelicals, with whom Gray had an earlier disagreement about baptismal regeneration. The public nature of this debacle and its demonstration of the inadequacies of dealing with ecclesiastical controversies arising in the colonies precipitated a meeting in 1867 of all the bishops in the emerging Anglican world, from which the decennial Lambeth Conferences developed.

Whilst Gray worked towards an independent Church, John Colenso attempted to engage with African thought and custom. The irony of Colenso's position was that he insisted on the legal jurisdiction of the Church of England while accepting African social norms as contextually Christian. His writings were influenced by F. D. Maurice's social concern and biblical criticism and by the Zulu people among whom he worked. Colenso was not alone among

[12] Joseph Hardwick, 'Anglican Church Expansion and the Recruitment of Colonial Clergy for New South Wales and the Cape Colony, c.1790–1850', *The Journal of Imperial and Commonwealth History*, 37 (2009): 361–81.

missionaries in studying African culture: a scholarly tradition of cultural and linguistic research ran through the modern missionary movement. He was, however, unusual in the extent to which he allowed a study of Zulu belief and customs to influence his theological thinking and preaching. He was concerned about the social demands placed upon converts and rejected the normal insistence on monogamy as a condition for baptism, believing it made forsaken wives vulnerable. More controversially, he believed that the Zulu had already received salvation and needed to accept Christ simply in order receive assurance. The ecclesiastical scandal meant that his style of thoughtful engagement with theology and culture was side-lined, although he and his daughter, Harriette (1847–1932), continued their defence of African rights. To gain a profound comprehension of the language, they worked closely with a number of Zulu, including converts William Ngidi and Mgema Fuze who both married two wives. Ngidi, one of Colenso's few converts, was initially an enthusiastic itinerant preacher who explained the harmony between Zulu and Christian beliefs. Eventually, however, he returned to Zulu beliefs, shunning the religious accommodation he once espoused. The Anglican Church had little impact on the cohesive society of the Zulu until sometime after the destruction inflicted by the Anglo-Zulu war (1879). Whilst community conversion to Christianity often occurred among the dispossessed and distressed, those who provided Christian succour in South Africa often had, at best, an ambiguous relationship with the forces that meted out destruction. Colenso was again unusual in the strength of his criticism of British treatment of the Zulu.

The Xhosa had suffered the threat of European incursion since the eighteenth century and, even though the London Missionary Society (LMS) and the Moravians had taken their part, Xhosa society was undermined by its impact. Xhosa attempts to alter their fortunes caused further disaster which ironically strengthened the influence of the Anglican Church among them. In 1857 the Xhosa completed a year-long slaughter of their cattle and crops, following prophecies that this would lead to the resurrection of their ancestors who would overthrow white domination and bring renewed purity and unity to their nation. This catastrophe cannot simply be interpreted in religious terms as old belief giving way to new: the prophecies were a synthesis of Xhosa belief and Christian symbols that promised the imminent arrival of a messiah, resurrection of the dead, and political salvation for the Xhosa. Whilst the action demonstrated the determination to reject European intrusion, the prophecies melded Christian and Xhosa tropes to inspire collective response to rapid socio-political change.

Tragically, the cattle killings caused famine and disease in which over 20,000 Xhosa died and survivors understood the prophecies to have failed. As they faced societal devastation and explored new possibilities of communal belonging many responded to the aid organized by Bishop Henry Cotterill

(1812–86) at the four Anglican mission stations and thus became Anglican members. The mission stations nurtured social change, gradually developing an African middle class through clergy and teacher training and schools, like the prestigious St Matthew's at Keiskama Hoek in the Eastern Cape. However, as a schoolgirl rebellion at Bloemfontein demonstrates, Xhosa wished to maintain certain priorities in education: in 1877 the girl-boarders, backed by their parents, refused to clean laundry for whites and demanded more food, more academic lessons, and more church services. Education, in their view, should not prepare them for domestic servitude; many aspired to be teachers and nurses.[13]

The Anglican leadership was concerned about racial tensions among its members. The Provincial Missionary Conference in 1892 brought to the attention of the CPSA the ill treatment of Africans, the seeming indifference of European settlers to mission, and the challenges to Church unity of ministering in segregated society. In reality a two-tier, segregated Church emerged in which the 'tension between principled inclusiveness and missional effectiveness' was apparent.[14] The impulse to form separate congregations also came from Africans who wished to develop their own styles of worship, in their own languages, and to articulate their social and political concerns without interference. Ethiopianism gained prominence at the end of the nineteenth century. A form of independency inspired by biblical references to Africa (e.g. Ps. 68:31), the ancient Christian kingdom of Ethiopia, and political pan-Africanism, it preceded the explosion of Zionist Churches in the twentieth century that developed distinct liturgical and ritual structures which resonated with African practices. One initiative within the Anglican Church was the Ethiopian Order. James Mata Dwane (1848–1916) of the Ethiopian Church sought communion with the Anglican Church because of its claims to apostolic succession. He sought an autonomous black Church which responded to African spirituality within a broad Anglican tradition, understood as part of the Church universal. The CPSA would only countenance a subordinate relationship. Nevertheless, in 1899 members of the Ethiopian Church agreed to the formation of an Order of Ethiopia within the Anglican Church, with Dwane as the provincial. Although the CPSA wished to see itself as a symbol of unity in a divided land, racial mistrust and inequality ran through it. The constitution of the independent Union of South Africa in 1910 further institutionalized segregation within the state. It also marked the end of a mutually supportive relationship of British imperialism and Anglicanism in South Africa.

[13] Modupe Labode, 'From Heathen Kraal to Christian Home', in Bowie et al., (eds.), *Women and Missions*, pp. 126–44.

[14] Peter Lee, *Compromise and Courage: Anglicans in Johannesburg, 1864–1999* (Pietermaritzburg, 2005), p. 13.

In another response to colonialism and segregation some missionaries aspired to work in areas untainted by colonial intrusion, imagining a pristine Africa would respond more positively to the gospel if it avoided the moral and political contamination of settlers and British companies. Bishop George Knight-Bruce (1852–96), who led the beginning of the mission in Matabeleland, was one such individual. His paternalistic vision involved obtaining vast tracts of land so Anglicanism could predominate over the forces of Western modernity and other missionary societies entering the area. He believed that mission-farms could protect local people and financially support the Church in a system akin to the British glebeland. Knight-Bruce resented Cecil Rhodes's British South Africa Company's interest in Matabeleland. He attempted to maintain an impartial position in the Anglo-Ndebele war of 1893 and was dismayed by the capture and exile of King Lobengula Khumalo (1845–94). As European settlers and Catholic and Methodist missions entered the region Knight-Bruce's aspirations could not be fulfilled and he resigned. Subsequently the SPG clergy, in the shifting power dynamics of emerging colonialism, negotiated their work alongside other missions and with the colonial authorities in Southern Rhodesia and accepted the Company's money for their work.

Accompanying Knight-Bruce were a number of African catechists, including a missionary whose work has been immortalized in the life of the Anglican Church in Zimbabwe, Bernard Mizeki (*c.*1860–96). Originally from Portuguese East Africa, he migrated to Cape Town, where there was a sizeable community of fellow 'Mozbiekers' often sought by explorers and missionaries as guides and interpreters in their areas of origin.[15] Like others, Mizeki converted to Christianity and was noticed by the Cowley Fathers (Society of St John the Evangelist) who sent him to Zonnebloem College for five years where his gift for languages was honed. In 1891 Mizeki volunteered to travel with Knight-Bruce. Mizeki and Frank Ziqubu, a Zulu, began work near Umtali with only a few goods with which to barter for food. For five years Mizeki learned Shona and formed good relations with the people, kept the Anglican daily office, and farmed a plot of land for his subsistence. He married the granddaughter of chief Mangwende but was murdered three months later in a Shona uprising against colonial incursion. Although local villagers warned him of the danger, he refused to flee, and the accounts of the supernatural disappearance of his body added to the honour given to him. His martyrdom is commemorated on 18 June at the site of his death. Lily Mutwa, Mizeki's widow, became a catechist in her own right, attending St Monica's school in Penhalonga for women and girls from 1904 before organizing women's work in Rusapi from 1907. As a migrant to the Cape Colony, Mizeki had already

[15] Patrick Harris, 'Making Mozbiekers: History, Memory and the African Diaspora at the Cape', in Benigna Zimba, Edward Alpers, and Allen Isaacman (eds.), *Slave Routes and Oral Tradition in Southeastern Africa* (Maputo, 2005), p. 113.

made a number of cultural and religious transitions and he expected that through his brokership the Shona would do the same. He made judgements about the rectitude of local practices; cutting down some trees in a sacred grove and carving crosses on others, whilst also incorporating local stories of the supreme deity into his preaching on Christ and instructing European missionaries on Shona customs. Mizeki's approach represents an African appropriation of Christianity which demanded significant rupture from traditional practices, but understood Shona theistic belief as a *praeparatio evangelica* in which the seeds of the gospel would grow.

The Anglican situation in southern Africa can be contrasted with Madagascar where the SPG began a small mission in 1864. The LMS had been active on the island since 1818 and by the end of the 1860s the Merina rulers had adopted Protestant Christianity, making mission education compulsory for their subjects. A significant part of the SPG's work was the network of girls' schools established by Emily Lawrance (Mauritius 1867–74, Madagascar 1874–99) and Gertrude M. King (1900–19). The schools were intended to rescue girls from the prostitution rife in the rum trading ports of the east coast, and to produce young women able to become teachers, evangelists, or to marry Malagasy catechists. The French–Malagasy wars led to French rule in 1895 and Protestants assumed a dissenting role vis-à-vis the colonial state. The SPG missionaries had greater reservations about the French colonial regime than did many of their counterparts about British interests in southern Africa. They, like other mission agencies who were neither nationally nor ecclesiastically close to imperial authority, developed a sharper critique of colonialism as immoral and anti-Christian.

In 1857 a new Anglican society was formed, the Universities' Mission to Central Africa. David Livingstone, in a gesture of practical ecumenism not untypical of the missionary movement, appealed to the English universities and Trinity College, Dublin, to support a mission which would address the Arab and Portuguese slave trade and the conflicts between different ethnic groups that slavery invoked. Livingstone famously revived earlier calls for 'legitimate commerce' and the 'civilizing' work of literacy and bio-medicine to accompany Christian mission. The near universal admiration for Livingstone aided the positive perception of the missionary enterprise in Britain. The UMCA was episcopally led from the start. C. F. Mackenzie, who had been archdeacon in Natal (1855–9), was consecrated in Cape Town by Gray, an act which demonstrated Gray's position as metropolitan with authority for regions beyond imperial control. A number of Mozbiekers were part of the expedition team as was Livingstone who introduced them to local chiefs. The team discovered that the quest for land, gold, ivory, and slaves had destabilized the area beyond their expectations. The Nyanga had fled the northwards advance of the Ngoni in about 1825, crossing the Zambezi into Nyasaland. Now they were slave-raided for the Portuguese and Arabs by the Yao, who themselves had been previously raided. Their displacement caused famine and disease. The missionaries were reluctantly drawn into the conflict and they too fell victim to sickness. By 1863 Mackenzie and others were dead and the situation was deemed too volatile to perpetuate missionary work. The UMCA relocated to the island of Zanzibar. It was to be some years, and via the exertion of British influence on the Sultan and traders of Zanzibar, before Nyasaland was considered sufficiently stable to resume the original work.

EAST AFRICA

Anglican missions arrived in East Africa in the mid-nineteenth century before the advent of British imperial rule. As in West Africa, trafficked Africans, who had encountered Christianity through liberation from slavery, provided committed staff for the first Anglican missions on the east coast of Africa. Two initiatives began in the year 1864.

The CMS bolstered its fragile presence around the seaport of Mombasa with Africans freed by the Royal Navy and settled and educated at the CMS mission at Nasik, near Bombay, India. In all, forty Africans agreed to return to the continent as missionaries, recruited as church leaders, builders, and artisans. First among them were William Jones, Ishmael Semper, George David, and sisters Pricilla and Polly Christian. They joined German missionary Johannes Rebmann (active 1846–75), who had been the companion of Johann Ludwig Krapf (1810–81). These two men had dedicated themselves to Swahili Bible translation and begun the slow task of establishing relations with local leaders, seeking permission to work in their areas of jurisdiction. Krapf came to Mombasa (1844–53) after working in Ethiopia. He developed a vision of a chain of missions across the continent and convinced the CMS of its feasibility. It was to remain an inspiration for sixty years until colonial borders solidified. However, much of the long-term evangelization and church planting on or near the coast was carried out by the confident and mobile 'Bombay Africans'. William Jones (*c.*1840–1904), for example, having started working for the CMS, spent three years with the UMCA, before returning to the CMS and then going to India for a further three years. By 1874 he was based at Rabai, Mombasa, and by the 1880s he led a congregation of five hundred baptized members with thousands of adherents.

The second initiative arose from the UMCA's relocation to Zanzibar. The eventual erection of Zanzibar Cathedral (completed 1880) on the site of the old slave market, its altar replacing the whipping post, was considered symbolic of victory over the slave trade. The UMCA began, however, with the education of freed-slaves, establishing in 1864 a boys' school for the training of evangelists, and in 1865 a girls' school for the education of suitable Christian wives. By 1870 the first pupils of St Andrew's, Kiungani, were made sub-deacons, reviving an early Church position. Sub-deacon Francis Mabruki, five other freed-slaves, and two English missionaries established Magila mission on the mainland. In 1879 the cutting of the Dar es Salaam–Nyasa road was begun, making the original mission area of the Shire more accessible. In 1880, W. P. Johnson and four Kiungani graduates began Ruvuma mission on the north-eastern shores of Lake Nyasa. Six years later Cecil Majaliwa, the first African priest of the UMCA, went to Chitangali in Ruvuma. Missionary expectation that freed-slaves could act as cultural brokers, developing rapport in every society, were sometimes disappointed. Many had lost their mother-tongue and the kinship ties so important to the social fabric of village life. Others had grown accustomed to the climate and urban lifestyle of Zanzibar and felt ill at ease in the villages. However, individuals like Majaliwa picked up the language quickly, visited local people, and learnt their customs. Majaliwa further showed his commitment by remaining in Chitangali when it was attacked. He gained the respect of village heads and established schools and churches among the Yao and the Makonde. The chief of Chitangali, Barnaba Matuka, was converted and two of his sons, Johanna Abdallah and Cypriani Chitenge, were later ordained, becoming a second generation of African priests. Majaliwa's semi-retirement to Zanzibar in 1897 earned him criticism from Europeans who expected him to continue missionary work on the mainland and has overshadowed his significant engagement in Ruvuma.

Another African priest of the UMCA whose work has been recorded was Leonard Kamungu (*c.*1870–1913). An early product of the Likoma mission, he graduated from Kiungani in 1897 and worked in a number of places in Tanganyika and Nyasaland. To celebrate the UMCA's jubilee, the diocese of Northern Rhodesia was proposed and funds raised. Leonard Kamungu was among the early staff of the diocese and, before his untimely death, baptized ninety-six people in Msoro. Events of his life were recorded in his letters to a supporter in Britain and form the basis of a short biography. His explanations of his ministry and appeals for prayers from British Christians indicate the extent to which Kamungu saw himself participating in an international movement which bound its members together in a common cause.[16]

In 1873 Sir Bartle Frere (1815–84), a senior colonial administrator, negotiated a treaty outlawing the slave trade with Sultan Barghash of Zanzibar (r. 1870–88). Frere regarded as inefficient the slow work of translation and building relations with local communities and suggested the CMS provide a home and artisanal skills for re-captives. Thus the settlement of Freretown was created. In 1875 the first 271 people arrived, over half of whom were children, and came under the tutelage of the Revd and Mrs W. S. Price. Freed-slave

[16] D. Y. Mills, *An African Priest and Missionary* (London, 1914).

villages frequently imposed a disciplined paternalism, and have subsequently been criticized for permitting only limited freedom for their residents.

Other slaves managed to escape their captors independently and established autonomous fugitive villages. Their dislocation from their previous societies encouraged interest in the liberative message and new technologies of Christianity. The leader of one group, Abe Sidi, was converted through Rebmann's first convert, Abe Gunja, and influenced three villages in the 1860s and 1870s. Godama, Fulladoyo, and Mwaiba are considered the first African Christian communities in East Africa and were prosperous and well-ordered with a vigorous church life. Sidi (Gunja's son) and Isaac Nyondo (Polly Christian's husband) conducted services and administered law and order with occasional oversight from other Bombay Africans, until Sidi was decapitated by Swahili forces in a raid in 1885. The relative autonomy of the village churches came to an end in 1895 when the CMS imposed white missionary control.

The CMS and the UMCA made slow but steady progress in Kenya and Tanganika. Work started among the Kikuyu in 1900 and in Western Kenya in 1906. As the missions developed and the health and habitat of European missionaries improved, the relative status and standard of living of African church workers declined and relations between the Africans and Europeans deteriorated. Paternalism and 'trusteeship' became key concepts in British rule in Africa. Missionaries, whilst frequently mitigating the worst of colonial intrusion, assumed supervisory roles and superior attitudes.

This shift in attitudes was slower in one area of East Africa, partly because of its particular history of conversion and partly because of its Church leadership. The rapid growth of the Anglican Church among the Baganda and neighbouring kingdoms from the 1870s was intertwined with the factional politics of a centralized state wishing to change its internal order. King Muteesa I (r. 1856–84) ruled over a confident and expanding kingdom which, from the 1860s, had developed trade with the Arabs and an interest in Islam. Muteesa welcomed contact with other foreigners and the visit to him by H. M. Stanley (1841–1904) precipitated missionary involvement. The CMS sent missionaries in 1877, and the Roman Catholic White Fathers arrived in 1878. Young men at court were intrigued by literacy and technological innovations brought by the missionaries and a number converted. When Muteesa died there was a struggle for the control and direction of the kingdom among Traditionalists, Muslims, and Christians. The Christians split into 'English' and 'French' factions and, by 1893, the Anglicans had gained political dominance. During the upheaval three significant events occurred. One was the killing of young Christian pages at court who demonstrated commitment to their faith and encouraged others to follow. Another was the establishment of a local council to lead the nascent Church which confidently took charge when missionaries left. The third was the exile and flight of Christians to neighbouring areas where they shared their faith with others. This exile anticipated organized evangelization by 'native teachers' from the mid-1890s onwards. It was facilitated in many regions by the alliance between the Baganda and the British, except in areas like Bunyoro where their suppression of dissent was so rapacious that the population did not convert, or became Catholics. By 1910 a confident, local Church was developing into a quasi-established Church in many areas of present-day Uganda. Apolo Kaggwa (1865–1926), the Protestant first minister, encouraged close relations between Church and state. Many of his chiefs were Anglicans; Hamu Mukasa (1871–1956), for example, supported evangelistic work and wrote Bible commentaries. Many CMS missionaries took a close interest in Ugandan cultures; *The Baganda* (1911) by Revd J. Roscoe (1861–1932) remains a classic anthropological work. Roscoe and Kaggwa collaborated closely in research and Kaggwa published a number of historical and anthropological works in Luganda.

Bishop Alfred Tucker (1849–1914) of the CMS arrived in Kampala in 1890 determined to ensure that the initial African-led growth of the Church was maintained. When the diocese of Eastern Equatorial Africa was divided in 1897, Tucker chose to be bishop of Uganda. He followed Venn's vision of a self-propagating, self-governing, and self-funded Church. Against some missionary opposition he ensured the Church operated independently of the CMS and developed a policy of ordaining committed evangelists, regardless of their prior training. One Ganda who benefited from this approach was Apolo Kivebulaya (*c.*1865–1933) who was ordained a priest in 1903 after eight years as evangelist and deacon. Stories of his missionary endeavours in Toro and the Ituri forest recounted in magazine articles and biographies were told to inspire British Christians to follow in his footsteps.

CONCLUSION

The twentieth century would see exponential growth in the Anglican Church in sub-Saharan Africa that was hardly anticipated in 1910 when it was still numerically small and structurally fragile. Yet the history of the nineteenth century indicates the influence and attraction of the Church, permitting an enquiry into reasons for African adherence to, and rejection of, Anglicanism. With few exceptions this question is rarely asked, partly because it is subsumed by a broader examination of Christian conversion.[17] Many Africans became Anglicans for reasons that transcended denominational interest; because it was the first mission in the area or the best resourced. Western

[17] John Karanja, *Founding an African Faith: Kikuyu Anglican Christianity 1900–1945* (Nairobi, 1999).

education and bio-medicine were attractive to many. Those intrigued by such resources did not always convert but they often recognized spiritual power in the material benefit of new technologies. Some leaders, like King Muteesa, sought alliances with missionaries who were nationally connected to economic and political influence, either because they desired access to that power, or because they required a sympathetic negotiator with it. So Anglican missionaries, like Bishops Tucker and Knight-Bruce, found themselves brokering colonial relations or protesting against colonial intrusion. In different contexts, Anglicanism could be seen to offer either an innovation to the present religio-political imagination with only a modest deviation from the status quo, or a radical intrusion upon the familiar with resources to transform life for better or worse: on the Island of Bonny it was understood both ways by different actors. Certainly the involvement in the spread of Anglicanism by African migrants, freed-slaves, and young people suggests that some forms of dislocation or search for alternatives were significant: a Krio culture developed in Sierra Leone; and in Buganda political modernizers identified in Christianity the possibility of rupture from the old system and were willing to fight for it. Among the Kikuyu of Kenya generational fissures were highlighted by the arrival of Christianity; young people gained assertiveness through their conversion.

Those Africans most committed to evangelism invariably preached change. They introduced literacy, bio-medicine, and new forms of construction and sanitation. They adopted a translated version of the Book of Common Prayer (often published by the SPCK), ecclesiastical vestments, and church ornament of metropolitan Anglican churches. But they did so in ways which resonated with local interest and cultural norms. European missionaries were familiar with the thirty-fourth article of the Church of England that permitted local practices in prayer and worship, but few shared Colenso's confidence about which local customs were edifying; assumptions about the degradation caused by 'heathenism' ensured a cautious approach. African catechists and priests, however, brokered the introduction of new ideas and technologies by identifying connections with the familiar. Kivebulaya, for example, described himself as a diviner and the Bible as a divining tool, he described books as 'the spears which protect us',[18] and he used the chief's sacred drum to call to Christian worship, thus appropriating local societal power and symbolism whilst simultaneously challenging it. His use of the Prayer Book developed its potential as an oral rite even whilst he emphasized literacy. A new religious narrative provided mechanisms for the perennial concern about access to spiritual power for well-being and dealing with daily life. Even for those exhorting transformation there was resonance with prior religious beliefs and practices.

[18] Apolo Kivebulaya, Diary, 3 June 1925, Africana Collection, Makerere University.

Distinctions have been noted between the Evangelical and Anglo-Catholic missionary societies, promoting individual conversion and biblical reading on the one hand and Christian community and liturgy on the other. But these emphases may not have been so apparent to nineteenth-century Africans: CMS missionaries aimed to form Christian communities and they used the Prayer Book in worship; likewise the SPG and the UMCA expected to see in their converts' evidence of transformed lives and also developed projects of Bible translation. African critique by the end of the nineteenth century was usually aimed at the unwillingness of missionaries to relinquish control. As colonialism took hold and missionaries' longevity and living standards improved, their relationships with Africans became less equitable. Some Africans severed missionary links but retained Anglican aspects of worship. Anglicanism left a legacy in those Churches that borrowed its forms but, from the 1890s, established themselves as independent of its jurisdiction.

Since Anglican Christianity could rarely dissociate itself from British economic and political influences, even when it wished to, it attracted those whose cosmology expected spiritual and political forces to be interdependent. The hierarchical structure of the Church could be readily understood by those societies which possessed similar strata. Anglicanism was also attractive to those who sought to develop an internationalist perspective. It provided one way of being modern. From Crowther to Kamungu, African clergy visited and corresponded with counterparts in Britain. They had opportunities to travel and to develop the fictive kinships propounded in the message of universal salvation in Christ. James Johnson, for example, perhaps remained in the Anglican Church because his pan-Africanist commitments sought a confident African identity for international engagement rather than a rejection of international connections. The history of sub-Saharan Anglicanism until 1910 is one of the entanglement of nations and peoples at a time of rapid social change. Many Africans sought spiritual communities that responded to contemporary life and its novelties—for some the Anglican Church fulfilled that role.

SELECT BIBLIOGRAPHY

Abimbola, Adedoyin Olabisi, 'Missionary Encounters and the Development of Yoruba Women's Spirituality, 1842–1930', PhD thesis, University of Liverpool, 2008.

Adiele, Shed N. (ed.), *The Niger Mission: Origin, Growth and Impact 1857–1995* (Aba, Nigeria, 1996).

Ajayi, J. F. Ade, *Christian Missions in Nigeria, 1841–1891: The Making of a New Elite* (Evanston, IL, 1969).

Barnes, Andrew E., *Making Headway: The Introduction of Western Civilisation in Colonial Northern Nigeria* (Rochester, NY, 2009).

Chidester, David, *Religions of South Africa* (London, 1992).

Elpick, Richard and Rodney Davenport (eds.), *Christianity in South Africa: A Political, Social and Cultural History* (Claremont, South Africa, 1997).

Farrant, Jean, *Masonaland Martyr* (Cape Town, 1966).

Glasson, Travis, *Mastering Christianity: Missionary Anglicanism and Slavery in the Atlantic World* (New York, 2012).

Hanciles, Jehu J., *Euthanasia of Mission: African Church Autonomy in a Colonial Context* (London, 2002).

Hinchliff, Peter, *The Church in South Africa* (London, 1968).

Johnson, T. S., *The Story of a Mission, The Sierra Leone Church: First Daughter of CMS* (London, 1953).

Karanja, John, *Founding an African Faith: Kikuyu Anglican Christianity 1900–1945* (Nairobi, 1999).

Lee, Peter, *Compromise and Courage: Anglicans in Johannesburg, 1864–1999* (Pietermaritzburg, 2005).

O'Connor, Dan and others, *Three Centuries of Mission: The United Society for the Propagation of the Gospel 1701–2000* (London, 2000).

Peel, J. D. Y., *Religious Encounter and the Making of the Yoruba* (Bloomington, IN, 2000).

Pobee, John S., *The Anglican Story in Ghana: From Mission Beginnings to Province of Ghana* (Kaneshie-Accra, Ghana, 2009).

Porter, Andrew (ed.), *The Imperial Horizons of British Protestant Missions, 1880–1914* (Grand Rapids, MI, 2003).

Porter, Andrew, *Religion versus Empire? British Protestant Missionaries and Overseas Expansion, 1700–1914* (Manchester, 2004).

Prevost, Elizabeth E., *The Communion of Women: Missions and Gender in Colonial Africa and the British Metropole* (Oxford, 2010).

Sannah, Lamin, *West African Christianity* (Maryknoll, NY, 1983).

Suberg, O. M., *The Anglican Tradition in South Africa: A Historical Overview* (Pretoria, 1999).

Tengatenga, James, *The UMCA in Malawi: A History of the Anglican Church 1861–2010* (Zomba, Malawi, 2010).

Welch, Pamela, *Church and Settler in Colonial Zimbabwe: A Study in the History of the Anglican Diocese of Mashonaland/Southern Rhodesia, 1890–1925* (Leiden, 2008).

Wilson, George H., II, *The History of the Universities' Mission to Central Africa* (London, 1936).

Zvobgo, Chengetal J. M., *A History of Christian Missions in Zimbabwe, 1890–1939* (Gweru, Zimbabwe, 1996).

13

Anglican Mission in the Middle East up to 1910

Duane Alexander Miller

This chapter will explore the issue of Anglican identity in the Middle East up until the Edinburgh Conference of 1910. From Henry Maundrell's eighteenth-century journey from Aleppo to Jerusalem to Henry Martyn's well-known efforts at translation and evangelism in Persia from 1811, some Anglicans had been to the Middle East, and many more read about their journeys. But the nineteenth century was a period of intentional missionary work by the Church of England and its allies in mission. Because of this, the topic of Anglican identity is best investigated by studying the wide variety of missions that were active. Missions in Egypt and Iran will be briefly noted, but the main focus is on the American Episcopal mission to Constantinople and the Protestant-Anglican mission centred in Palestine. The chapter argues that there were a wide variety of different conceptualizations of what it meant to be Anglican, that sometimes these conflicted, and that the Middle East provided a testing ground for different and contesting visions of what it means to be an Anglican.

ASIA MINOR AND PERSIA

Horatio Southgate: Missionary Bishop of the Episcopal Church (USA) in Istanbul

The Protestant Episcopal Church of the United States was late to enter into the world-wide Protestant missionary movement. The Church of England already had the Society for the Propagation of the Gospel (SPG), founded in 1701, the Church Mission Society (CMS), founded in 1799, and the London Jews Society (LJS), formed in 1809; and the most influential of all missionary boards in the

United States, the American Board of Commissioners for Foreign Missions (ABCFM), was chartered in 1812 as a mostly Presbyterian and Congregationalist body. Not until 1821 was the Domestic and Foreign Missionary Society (DFMS) organized. After 1835, technically speaking, every Episcopalian was a member of said society, and in 1846 it was legally incorporated under New York law. It was the DFMS that would supervise the missionary work of Horatio Southgate.

Horatio Southgate was born in Portland, Maine, on 5 July 1812 to a Congregationalist family. While studying at Andover Theological Seminary he changed his affiliation from Congregationalism to the Protestant Episcopal Church of the United States. On conclusion of his seminary studies he was ordained as a deacon in 1835 and went on his first mission.

The first period of Southgate's missionary career, like many other contemporary missionary endeavours, was one devoted to exploration. It lasted from 1836 through 1839, and resulted in the publication of his *Narrative of a Tour through Armenia, Kurdistan, Persia, and Mesopotamia* (1844). Prior to this, communication with the geographically isolated ancient Churches of Asia was often difficult. 'When travel became more possible in the nineteenth century, with the peace following the Revolutionary and Napoleonic wars, and the building of railways, coupled with Britain's economic and imperial expansion, Anglican contact with the Orthodox world inevitably increased.'[1] At the time large swathes of Asia, and the Ottoman Empire in particular, were largely a mystery to Europeans and Americans. So before establishing permanent missions it was necessary to send teams to explore.

Before departing for his first, exploratory, mission in 1836, Southgate gave a homily at the Church of the Ascension in New York on 3 April, the evening of Easter Sunday that year. The title of the sermon was 'Encouragement to Missionary Efforts among Mohammedans'.[2] This homily presented Southgate's early concepts of mission and the role of an Episcopalian in the mission field. In it he openly called for evangelism directed at Muslims, and in doing so rejected the common approach to mission in the Muslim world, including that of the American Board. That strategy, prevalent in the nineteenth century, has been given the title of the Great Experiment by Robert Blincoe, which is analogous to the missionary strategy that Vander Werff calls the 'via the Eastern Churches strategy' for evangelizing Muslims. The Great Experiment

[1] Geoffrey Rowell, 'Eastern Horizons: Anglicans and the Oriental Orthodox Churches', in Nigel Aston (ed.), *Religious Change in Europe, 1650–1914: Essays for John McManners* (Oxford, 1997), p. 382.

[2] Horatio Southgate, *Encouragement to missionary effort among Mohamedans: a sermon by the Rev. Horatio Southgate, Jun., missionary of the Protestant Episcopal Church in the United States of America, to Persia, etc.; to which are annexed an account of the meeting held at the Church of the Ascension on the evening of Easter Sunday, April 3, 1836; with the address delivered thereat by the Rev. Mr Southgate, and his letter of instructions* (New York, 1836).

aimed at the eventual evangelization of the large Muslim population of the Ottoman Empire and Persia, but in an indirect manner. Evangelizing Muslims was, in the Ottoman Empire, illegal. Converting from Islam to Christianity (or any other religion) was generally considered a capital crime. As Bernard Lewis explains, 'The excommunicated unbeliever is not only damned in the world beyond; he is outlawed in this world. He is deprived of all legal rights and barred from all religious offices; his very life and property are forfeit. If he is born a Muslim, his position is that of an apostate, a dead limb that must be ruthlessly excised.'[3] Furthermore, all the schools of Shari'a agree that the male apostate must be slain, and the basis of this law comes directly from a verified saying of the Prophet himself: 'Whosoever changes his religion, slay him.'[4] Given these dangers and difficulties, the Western missionaries soon became convinced that engaging in direct evangelism of Muslims was not viable. But they often found pockets of Christians—Church of the East, Orthodox, Armenians, Copts—throughout the lands they were exploring. These ancient Churches, often described as 'decayed' and 'superstitious', must be reformed, and then, it was believed, these indigenous Christians, with their knowledge of the local languages and customs, would evangelize their Muslim neighbours and masters. There was a general consensus that the Great Experiment was the best missionary strategy for the Ottoman Empire and Persia. Scores of schools, hospitals, and dispensaries were founded throughout the East with the vision of accomplishing this goal.

Southgate, in his sermon, took issue with the Great Experiment strategy. He outlined his reasons for advocating *direct* evangelism of Muslims, arguing that Persians, rather than Arabs or Turks, should be targeted. Some of his key points were as follows: that if the Muslims convert then it would be a small thing to complete the evangelization of the rest of the world;[5] Persian Muslims had a long tradition of enquiry and religious curiosity;[6] Persians did not have the same bloodlust of the Arab founder of the religion, and thus Christianity suited them better;[7] Islam was in a state of superstitious decline ('not unlike that of the Romish Church'), and should be replaced by Christianity;[8] and the Ottomans were willing to interact with Europeans and Americans more than was the case in the past.[9] His final reason was that 'they have always been, and still are, almost entirely neglected by the Christian Church'.[10]

But this vision of direct Episcopal mission to Muslims was abandoned by Southgate after his first exploratory mission, which ended in 1839. As he wrote in his *Narrative*: 'While the author was pursuing his inquiries among the

[3] Bernard Lewis, 'Some Observations on the Significance of Heresy in the History of Islam', *Studia Islamica*, 1 (1953), p. 59.

[4] *Sahiih Al Bukhari* 4:52:260.

[5] Southgate, *Encouragement*, p. 5.

[6] Southgate, *Encouragement*, p. 9.

[7] Southgate, *Encouragement*, p. 15.

[8] Southgate, *Encouragement*, p. 16.

[9] Southgate, *Encouragement*, p. 19.

[10] Southgate, *Encouragement*, p. 24.

Mohammedans, he soon found his mind drawn, almost unconsciously, to the state of the Eastern Churches, and his interest became, at length, so deeply excited in their behalf, that he devoted to them all the attention which the more immediate duties of his work permitted.'[11]

After the conclusion of his first exploratory mission (1836–9) the topic of evangelizing Muslims appears to have been forgotten. Rather, upon his return to the United States he proposed that the mission should be centred in Constantinople, not Persia, and that the focus of his ministry should be on the existing Eastern Christians there rather than on Muslim evangelism. He was ordained to the priesthood in 1839 and returned to Constantinople—this was the commencement of his second and longer mission (1840–9).

Southgate's correspondence indicates that he was preoccupied with the protection, improvement, and revivification of the ancient Churches for their own sake, and not with the view that they would then evangelize Muslims. 'The Romanist has no scruple in invading the Eastern Churches, drawing off their members, preaching schism, inculcating error. The Latitudinarian[s are . . .] breaking up the foundations of these ancient communions, violating their integrity, preaching schism also in another direction, and teaching a neglect of everything that we hold most sacred in the Church's institutions.'[12] He appears to have been using the term 'Latitudinarian' to refer to Evangelical missionaries in general. Moreover, 'The position which we [the Episcopal mission], as a Church, have assumed here, is the only one which can save the Eastern Churches from rationalism and infidelity on the one hand, or a degrading superstition on the other.'[13]

Southgate believed that the ancient Churches—Armenian, Greek Orthodox, Syriac Orthodox—were threatened by enemies on all sides: the Roman Church; a non-episcopal, non-sacramental Evangelicalism; and finally the irreligious rationalism of modernity. His strategy revolved around the education of clergy and that staple of missionary work, translation. He opened a small seminary and his goal, never completely brought to fruition for various reasons, was to train clergy for the ancient Churches. He was adamant that he did not want to establish a separate Protestant millet, nor had those been his instructions from the DFMS. When he did accept converts, they were only from the Uniate churches, like Peter Hazzar, formerly a Chaldean Catholic. In 1844, during a visit back to the United States, he was consecrated to the missionary episcopate—a newly created office—of the Dependencies and

[11] Horatio Southgate, *Narrative of a Tour through Armenia, Kurdistan, Persia and Mesopotamia* (New York, 1840), I, p. vi.

[12] Horatio Southgate, 'Letter from Horatio Southgate to the Rev Dr Coxe, dated Aug 1, 1847, from San Stefano', *The Spirit of Missions*, 12 (1847), p. 437.

[13] Horatio Southgate, 'Bishop Southgate's Report', *The Spirit of Missions*, 12 (1847), p. 415.

Dominions of the Sultan of Turkey. Southgate was the first person to hold the office and would be the last.

It was during this second mission that he ran into trouble with some missionaries from the American Board. The immediate occasion was Southgate's translating for an Armenian a passage from the *Missionary Herald*. It was part of a communication from one of the missionaries in which were 'some free remarks as to whether a division in the Armenian church were or were not practical and desirable'.[14] Those American missionaries wrote to the American Board complaining about what they considered to be Southgate's change of behaviour after his first mission—for instance during his first mission as a deacon he had taken Communion from one of their non-Episcopal ministers, but upon his return he would no longer do so. They also complained about his 'personal unfriendliness, and . . . his interference with their work'.[15] At a time of particular tension among the Armenians he sided with the Armenian Apostolic Church over the Armenians who had left or were thinking of leaving to form a new Congregationalist-style community.

> Taking upon himself the role of defender of the Armenian church, he seized every opportunity to warn Armenians against Western Evangelical influences, and to make them realize that the Evangelicals were without the traditional fasts and historic Christian observances, and that they lacked what he felt the Eastern churches considered essentials of a church, namely, episcopacy, confirmation, and liturgies; all of which were both held and valued by the Episcopal church.[16]

Southgate attempted to justify himself in two short publications, *The Vindication of the Rev H. Southgate* (1844) and *A Letter to a Friend* (1845). While Southgate's mission was supervised by the DFMS, he was responsible for raising most of his income, and these controversies led to a decline in the funds available for his ministry.

Perhaps this sort of tension was inevitable—it was a fundamental question of identity. Southgate had been given directions by his board and by the presiding bishop not to proselytize and to 'keep steadily in view the unity of the Church'.[17] But he was faced with a conundrum: as an Episcopalian, with whom did he belong? On the one hand the Americans were, like the Anglicans, born of the Protestant Reformation and inherently suspicious of all things 'Romish'. Moreover, they upheld the Christological doctrines promulgated at Ephesus and Chalcedon. On the other hand, Southgate had the ancient non-Chalcedonian Churches which were sacramental, episcopal, held tradition in high regard, and very importantly, they were not Papists.

[14] *The New Englander Review*, 3 (1845), p. 249.

[15] Plato Shaw, *American Contacts with the Eastern Churches* (Chicago, 1937), p. 54.

[16] Shaw, *American Contacts*, p. 60.

[17] Charles Bridgeman, 'Mediterranean Missions of the Episcopal Church from 1828–1896', *Historical Magazine of the Protestant Episcopal Church*, 31 (1962), p. 107.

Southgate was, as a Christian who had repudiated a congregational ecclesiology, perhaps more sensitive to some of these issues than other Protestants, and he had clear instructions to liaise with and edify the ancient Churches. In the end he aligned himself with the Eastern Churches, only accepting converts from the Papists, and, in the case of Michael Jamala, using that priest as a missionary to Mosul to strengthen the non-Uniate Eastern Christians. Both Southgate's ecclesiology and his mandate from the board in the United States precluded making Anglicans of these indigenous Christians.

During his episcopate Southgate engaged in several activities to strengthen the indigenous Churches: in addition to his embryonic seminary, he had multiple works translated into local languages,[18] especially Armenian, and supported the distribution of missionary literature and the Book of Common Prayer in various local languages. While other missions finally decided that the culture and hierarchical nature of the indigenous Churches could not be reformed (according to their model of reformation), Southgate never gave up. He had left one unconventional theory of mission behind—direct evangelism of Muslims—for another wherein he understood himself to be the defender of the ancient Churches against the onslaught of Rome, congregationalism, and secularism. The ancient Churches were, in his view, more authentic expressions of Catholic Christianity than the sectarianism espoused by the ABCFM missionaries.

After the tension in the United States occasioned by the complaints of the ABCFM missionaries and the dysfunctional and impractical funding system of the foreign missions board of the DFMS, Southgate decided to discontinue his work there. He resigned from his position as missionary bishop on 12 October 1850.[19] That same year the DFMS officially closed Constantinople as a mission field. Southgate went on to be elected as bishop of California and bishop of Haiti, but he turned down the positions, and died in 1894.

It is difficult to see how Southgate's missionary episcopate can be construed as a success. Neither his seminary nor his episcopal see continued after his departure. He left a body of translated works, a record of his travels, and a good deal of animosity between missionaries and even among his fellow Episcopalians.

Missions in Persia

Anglicans were also active in Persia. Fourteen years after the publication of William Carey's *Inquiry*, Henry Martyn arrived in India, but his journeys

[18] For a complete list see Kenneth Cameron, 'The Oriental Manuscripts of Horatio Southgate', *Anglican and Episcopal History*, 10 (1941): 57–61.

[19] Donald Armentrout and Robert Boak Slocum, *An Episcopal Dictionary of the Church* (New York, 1999), p. 497.

would eventually take him to Persia where he would translate the Bible into Persian. Other explorations took place, like that of George Percy Badger in 1842, sponsored by the SPG and SPCK, but did not result in a permanent mission.[20] Badger's recollections were published as *The Nestorians and their Rituals with the Narrative of a Mission to Mesopotamia and Coordistan in 1842–1844* (London, 1852).

The indigenous and ancient Church present in Persia at the time was known in the nineteenth century as the Assyrian Church of the East. In the literature of the day these Christians were often called Nestorians, because they supposedly followed the lead of Nestorius (d. 431), the Patriarch of Constantinople who argued against the title *theotokos* or 'God bearer' for Mary, preferring to call her 'Christ bearer'. The ecumenical Council of Ephesus in 431 found that Nestorius was in error, and the Church of the East did not accept the ruling of Ephesus.

The major sustained Anglican initiative in this region was the Anglo-Catholic Archbishop's Mission to the Assyrians which lasted from 1884 through 1915. The mission consisted mainly of education, translation, and supporting the Church of the East, which had been losing membership to the American Presbyterian missionaries in the region. The presence of the Anglo-Catholics who had arrived to 'defend the Nestorians against the Americans' became a source of tension. Scholarship and translation were what the Anglicans had to offer, but what the Church of the East wanted was a powerful political sponsor to provide schools, a printing press, funding, and security from Muslim Kurdish raids.[21] The Anglican missionaries were concerned with demonstrating the Christological orthodoxy of the Church of the East, and in so doing provide 'an early example of the now commonly accepted ecumenical principle of endeavoring to reach behind the rigidities of opposed doctrinal formulae to a common understanding of faith'.[22] Athelstan Riley (1858–1945), native of London and member of Anglo-Catholic wing of the Church, was one of the backers of the mission. He was clear that 'The mission has no intention of making Anglicans of the Assyrians, of forcing upon them our Prayer-book, or of teaching purely Anglican theology. It takes its stand upon the teaching of the universal and undivided Church of Christ, and with this limitation desires to interfere with nothing in this ancient national Church.'[23]

In 1897 about 20,000 of the 25,000 members of the Church of the East confessed the doctrine of Ephesus and Chalcedon and received the

[20] Rowell, 'Eastern Horizons', p. 388.

[21] Robert Blincoe, *Ethnic Realities and the Church: Lessons from Kurdistan, a History of Mission Work, 1668–1990* (Pasadena, CA, 1998), p. 95.

[22] Rowell, 'Eastern Horizons', p. 383.

[23] Athelstan Riley, 'The Assyrian Church, a paper read at the Wolverhampton Church Congress, October 1887' (1887), p. 4. <http://anglicanhistory.org/england/riley/wolverhampton1887.html>, accessed 25 Dec. 2012.

political-religious sponsor they had desired from Orthodox Russia. The Patriarch requested that the Anglicans depart, which they did, leaving some fifty schools to the Church of the East and Russians.[24] The Church of the East supposed they had found a foreign patron and protector in the Russians, leaving no room for their competitors, the English. The chief lasting product of the Assyrian Mission was competent scholarship on the language and liturgy of the Church of the East.

The CMS was also active in Persia, recognizing it as a mission field around 1876. The CMS mission would eventually unfold into one of the most interesting and diverse Anglican dioceses in the region, including numerous converts from Islam, Judaism, Baha'ism, as well as Armenian converts to Protestantism. Robert Bruce of Dublin had proposed a work in Persia in 1869, and by the time that missionaries had arrived the vision of mission as 'reviving' the ancient, indigenous Church had faded, and they were more willing to simply found their own Church. In 1883 the celebrated Bishop French of Lahore, passing through Persia, confirmed some sixty-seven people and ordained the Armenian Minas George to the diaconate. By 1900 the CMS had missionaries in Shiraz, Yazd, and Kerman and hospitals and schools were built.[25]

As with other places the CMS focused on educational and medical missions. It was here in Persia that Southgate's bolder initial strategy actually proved somewhat feasible. 'Between 1900 and 1907, over 100 adult Muslims had the courage to face opposition and receive baptism... The number of inquirers increased and in 1911 alone, CMS baptized over 100 converts from Islam.'[26]

While much of the growth took place after 1910, the foundation was in place for an Evangelical Anglican presence that would eventually become the diocese of Iran. The conjunction of converts from Islam and the production of a lasting (if persecuted) Anglican diocese point to one of the more successful missions in the Muslim world—one that drew on education, medicine, translation, and evangelism across religious borders.

PALESTINE AND THE TRANS-JORDAN

The Protestant bishop in Jerusalem had three bishops before it became the exclusively Anglican bishop in Jerusalem. After a hiatus a fourth bishop, this

[24] Blincoe, *Lessons from Kurdistan*, p. 104.

[25] Yahya Aramjani, 'Christianity: viii: Christian Missions in Persia', in *Encyclopaedia Iranica* (2011). <http://www.iranicaonline.org/articles/christianity-viii>, accessed 20 Dec. 2012.

[26] Lyle Vander Werff, *Christian Mission to Muslims: The Record—Anglican and Reformed Approaches in India and the Near East, 1800–1938* (Pasadena, CA, 1977), p. 167.

one Anglican alone, was consecrated. Of these four bishops, three had a lasting effect on the diocese. They were Michael Solomon Alexander, Samuel Gobat, and George Francis Popham Blythe. The third bishop did not live long enough to make a lasting impact. The other three bishops represented the ethos of their respective missionary societies, with sometimes conflicting goals. In seeking to better understand Anglican identity in the formative days of missionary work in the Trans-Jordan, it is possible to see in these three bishops archetypes or representatives of three different visions for what it meant to be Anglican.

Michael Solomon Alexander (1841–5)

Alexander had been a rabbi before his conversion to Christianity. He was only bishop for four years (1841–5) but nonetheless his mission, the LJS, was instrumental in making Jerusalem into a modern city and building the first Protestant church in Palestine.[27] His goal was to create and shepherd a Hebrew congregation on Mount Zion, and he was well-qualified for this work, speaking Hebrew, English, and German. This congregation was to embody 'pure, Christian worship in the Holy City. Heretofore, the only Christian forms of worship regularly supported in Jerusalem have been the corrupt Latin, Greek, and Armenian services.'[28] This vocation to make Jews into Christians in Jerusalem was millenarian in character; 'converted Jews, collected in the Holy Land, would pave the way for the second coming of the Messiah'.[29] Alexander was an Evangelical churchman, and his great vision was for the evangelism of Jews. This sets him and his companions apart from later Anglicans, and results in an understanding of the role of the bishop as a missionary and evangelist. While he seems to have taken little or no interest in preaching to Muslims (a dangerous activity under Ottoman rule), he was zealous to make Rabbinic Jews into Christian Jews. During his four-year episcopate he was able to operate fully on a sacramental level, including ordaining Hebrew Christians to the diaconate and priesthood, confirming, burying, and marrying.[30] The LJS opened a press, a school, and a hospital.[31] They commenced the construction of Christ Church in the Jaffa Gate, the first Anglican building in Jerusalem.

[27] Kelvin Crombie, *For the Love of Zion: Christian Witness and the Restoration of Israel* (Bristol, 2008).

[28] *Foreign Missionary Chronicle*, 8 (1840), p. 101.

[29] Heleen Murre-van den Berg (ed.), *New Faith in Ancient Lands: Western Missions in the Middle East in the Nineteenth and Early Twentieth Centuries* (Leiden, 2006), p. 154.

[30] Crombie, *Love of Zion*, pp. 119, 120.

[31] Yaron Perry, *British Mission to the Jews in Nineteenth-Century Palestine* (London, 2003), p. 142.

Alexander and his episcopal successors were active in welcoming foreign dignitaries and important visitors. This was expected by a person who represented the Church of England and hence the British crown, as well as the Lutheran Church of Prussia, and hence the Prussian crown as well. Through his work and that of his fellow LJS missionaries resident in or around Jerusalem, like the industrious Dane Hans Nicolayson and Dr Edward MacGowan (1795–1860), a small Jewish convert congregation was established on Mount Zion. In Alexander's thought the bishop was, like the apostles themselves, charged with preaching the Christian message to those who had never heard it.

These activities roused other forces. Moses Montefiore funded a Jewish Hospital so the impoverished Jews would not be forced to seek medical care with the missionaries. Catholic France and Orthodox Russia were likewise concerned when they saw that the English had positioned both a bishop and consulate in Jerusalem. The Catholics had maintained the Latin Patriarch of Jerusalem as a titular and honorary office since the fall of the Latin Kingdom of Jerusalem, but in 1847, five years after Alexander's arrival in the city, Pope Pius IX issued the bull *Nulla Celbrior* and so re-established a residential Patriarch in the person Joseph Valerga (d. 1872).

These Protestant missionaries and the new consulate attracted the attention and jealousy of the other major players in Europe who saw in Jerusalem a ripe field for contest, investment, and development. Consulates were opened in the city: Prussia in 1842, France and Sardinia in 1843, the United States in 1844, and Russia in 1858.[32] The Orthodox Patriarch of Jerusalem who 'generally lived in the greater comfort of Constantinople', visiting his flock from there, was compelled to take up a more permanent residence in the city.[33]

Samuel Gobat (1846–79)

Samuel Gobat to this day remains an immensely influential figure in the history of the Diocese of Jerusalem. Gobat was a French Swiss CMS missionary who had served in Abyssinia and then Malta, and was an 'excellent Arabic student... and a devout but somewhat narrow evangelical of the Continental type'.[34] He was nominated by the Prussian crown in accordance with the agreement to establish the Jerusalem bishopric between the Prussian Lutherans and the English Church. While he continued to work with the LJS

[32] Charlotte van der Leest, 'Conversion and Conflict in Palestine: The Missions of the Church Missionary Society and the Protestant Bishop Samuel Gobat', PhD thesis, Leiden University, 2008, p. 36.

[33] Charles Bridgeman, 'Michael Solomon Alexander: First Bishop of the Church of England in Jerusalem (1841–1845)', *Historical Magazine of the Protestant Episcopal Church*, 12 (1943), p. 37.

[34] Bridgeman, 'Alexander', p. 39.

he was sometimes suspicious of Jewish converts.[35] It was Gobat who made the pivotal decision to officially request that the CMS send missionaries to his vast diocese. While Gobat continued the diplomatic role of the Protestant bishop, his invitation to the CMS led to the viable Arabophone churches and schools of his diocese, such as the Bishop's School in Jerusalem opened in 1847.[36]

The Protestant bishopric had not been established with the intention of proselytizing Christians from the ancient Churches of the area, but Gobat and the CMS missionaries did not appear to find much of value in the ritual and iconophilia of those ancient Churches.

> Gobat held himself obliged to set up a church-structure for the Arab folk—almost wholly from the (Greek) Orthodox population—when on his view the situation required it by virtue of their adoption of his form of faith. From the 1860s, beginning in Nazareth, came the creation of Anglican 'parishes' and the ordaining of Arab clergy. The Anglicans, one might say, had church congregations in spite of themselves and yet also because of themselves.[37]

With the arrival of the CMS the prestige of the LJS as the representative of British Christianity was eroded.

The CMS missionaries came armed with the asset of educated missionaries able to meet this need, and would go on to found churches and schools all across the Trans-Jordan region of Greater Syria. That the Protestants could start schools was probably as attractive to the local Christians as their 'pure' and 'reformed' evangelical faith. In Gobat's memoirs and collected letters and in the CMS archives we find multiple instances of requests from Arabophone Christians for the Protestants to send a priest and teacher, and to start a school for them. As early as 1848 Gobat was corresponding with Christians in Nablus/Shechem about establishing a school for them there. In 1850 he received letters from Nazareth (then a majority-Christian city) requesting that he found a church and a school. In 1851 the CMS started its missionary work in the diocese according to the request of Gobat, and in that same year he received a request from the Christians in the ancient agricultural and administrative centre of Al Salt, located in modern-day Jordan, to 'take them under my care'.[38] By 1860 a new mission station had been founded in Bethlehem. By 1860 Gobat reported in his yearly circular letter that small congregations existed in Ramleh and Nablus, and reported eight Jews being baptized. He also mentioned that he had a missionary in Aintab (present-day Gaziantep in modern Turkey), 'formerly an Archbishop of the Armenian Church' named Megerdich, whom he refers to in the same passage as

[35] Perry, *Mission to the Jews*, p. 100. [36] Perry, *Mission to the Jews*, p. 102.

[37] Kenneth Cragg, *The Arab Christian: A History in the Middle East* (Louisville, KY, 1991), p. 133.

[38] Samuel Gobat, *Samuel Gobat, Bishop of Jerusalem: His Life and Work* (London, 1884), p. 281.

'Archbishop Megerdich'.[39] Likewise he calls him 'Archbishop' with no qualifications. This would appear to mean that Gobat had accepted the validity of his holy orders from the Armenian Apostolic Church.

By 1862 the CMS had abandoned their work in Egypt. In 1871 Christ Church in Nazareth became the first consecrated church building of what is today the diocese of Jerusalem. While the bishops of the diocese often worked from and ministered in the Christ Church Jerusalem compound, that property never did belong to the diocese.[40] At the consecration of the Christ Church in Nazareth Gobat also ordained to the diaconate the first indigenous Arabophone Christians in his diocese: Michael Ka'war and Seraphim Boutaji, both of them converts from the Greek Catholic Church.[41] Three years later St Paul's in Jerusalem was completed for Arabophone Christians there. In 1879 Samuel Gobat died, and, like Alexander, was buried near Jerusalem. While the LJS remained active during his bishopric their accomplishments among Jews did not have the enduring consequences of Gobat's entrepreneurial ministry. But Gobat's willingness to actively proselytize among ancient Christian Churches would not become a lasting facet of the identity of the Anglican and Lutheran Christians in the region.

The third bishop of the diocese was Joseph Barclay. Born in Ireland and of Scottish ancestry, he only served a brief two years as bishop (1879–81). His tenure was brief, but it was during his episcopate that the English–Prussian agreement was formally dissolved in 1886, and as of that year there were, according to Richter, 217 Protestants in Jerusalem who were born Jews.[42]

George F. P. Blyth (1887–1914)

In 1887 George Blyth was consecrated as Anglican bishop in Jerusalem, the first Englishman to hold the position. He was also the first person to be only an Anglican bishop, as the Lutherans now desired a bishop of their own. Additional funding from the CMS and LJS would make this possible, as the Prussian funds were no longer available.[43] Blyth was viewed as too High Church and ritualistic by the CMS and LJS missionaries, and he was not zealous to continue the legacy of proselytizing Orthodox converts to

[39] Gobat, *Samuel Gobat*, pp. 360, 361, 380.

[40] Duane Alexander Miller, 'Christ Church (Anglican) in Nazareth: A Brief History with Photographs', *St Francis Magazine*, 8 (2012): 696–703.

[41] Malcolm White, 'Anglican Pioneers of the Ottoman Period: Sketches from the CMS Archives of Some Arab Lives Connected with the Early Days of the Diocese of Jerusalem', *St Francis Magazine*, 8 (2012), pp. 295, 296.

[42] Julius Richter, *A History of Protestant Missions in the Near East* (New York, 1970 [1910]), p. 255.

[43] Perry, *Mission to the Jews*, pp. 139, 140.

Anglicanism. At the time of his consecration there were two churches in Jerusalem—Christ Church owned and operated by the LJS, and St Paul's, which was under the CMS missionaries. '[W]hen Blyth was unsuccessful at controlling them, he attempted to work around them.'[44] And so he established the Jerusalem and the East Mission (JEM), and built his own church.

Blyth took control of the diocese after a period of six years of vacancy which, according to a veteran missionary priest of the diocese, had 'left every one [CMS and LJS] liberty to do what was right in his own eyes'.[45] Estelle Blyth, his daughter, relates that upon arriving in Jerusalem her father faced two main difficulties: 'Proselytism and the position of the native clergy'.[46] It was the proselytism of Gobat and his CMS missionaries that had helped to create the indigenous Arab-speaking Church. On at least two occasions Blyth was asked by groups of Arab Christians to be received as Anglicans, both of which requests he turned down. One group was from Bethlehem and another, some 5,000 Christians, from Beirut.[47] In both cases he tried to reconcile the Arab Orthodox Christians to the Orthodox prelates. It is difficult to picture Gobat taking this course of action. Blyth jealously guarded the prerogatives of the Orthodox Patriarch of Jerusalem. This goal of mending relations with the Orthodox had been a priority since before he arrived in Jerusalem, and was clearly enunciated in the sermon preached at his consecration to the episcopate.[48]

In 1899 he built and then expanded what is today called the Cathedral Church of St George the Martyr, but he never called it that. Rather, it was called the Collegiate Church of St George the Martyr, as he held the conviction that the Church of the Holy Sepulchre was the cathedral church. He also was scrupulous in always referring to himself as the Anglican bishop *in* Jerusalem. Desiring to respect the Orthodox tradition of baptism by immersion he had a baptismal pool installed in the church. An indication of the warm relations between the Anglican and Orthodox bishops is that when some of the Orthodox girls attending the school near St George's requested to be able to take Communion during chapel, he first required that they get permission from the Patriarch, and permission was granted. A Catholic scholar in 1910 observed that, all in all, 'Bishop Blyth and his archdeacons are conciliatory to all the Eastern Churches and on excellent terms with the Orthodox patriarch.'[49]

[44] Duane Alexander Miller, 'The Installation of a Bishop in Jerusalem: The Cathedral Church of St George the Martyr', *Anglican and Episcopal History*, 76 (2007), p. 549.

[45] Bridgeman, 'Alexander', p. 41.

[46] Estelle Blyth, *When we Lived in Jerusalem* (London, 1927), p. 14.

[47] Beresford Potter, 'In Memoriam—Bishop Blyth', *Bible Lands*, 4 (Jan. 1915).

[48] Edward Bickersteth, *Thy Kingdom Come: A Sermon Preached in Lambeth Palace Chapel on March 25, 1887 on the Consecration of the Ven. G. F. P. Blyth Archdeacon of Rangoon to the Bishop of the English Church in Jerusalem and the East* (London, 1887).

[49] Adrian Fortescue, 'Jerusalem (After 1291)', in *The Catholic Encyclopedia* (New York, 1910). <http://www.newadvent.org/cathen/08364a.htm>, accessed 19 May 2012.

Blyth and the CMS missionaries did not get on very well as the missionaries had become accustomed to the lack of a bishop, and they did not welcome his oversight. Blyth (and others) were scandalized about what they perceived as the poor CMS treatment of the native clergy. Estelle Blyth describes them as being in a state of practical servitude and relates that they were not permitted to interact directly with the CMS office in London, but that all their communications had to go through their local CMS superiors. In one mission, native clergy had to wait for the CMS woman missionary to arrive at church before they could begin the liturgy. The sermons of the native clergy had to be checked by CMS representatives before they could be preached. The churchmanship of the CMS missionaries was lacking, in Blyth's view, one of their missionaries telling him that saints' days were obsolete. In their turn, CMS missionaries were offended by the ritualism of the new bishop and his friendliness towards the Orthodox Patriarch. '[Blyth] insisted that the priest should turn to the east during the saying of the creed, that lighted candles should be on the altar, that wine should be mixed with water at the eucharist, that the celebration of the eucharist should be only in the morning, and the like.'[50] On his part, Blyth complained that the CMS presented for Confirmation individuals who had received the Orthodox chrism at the time of their baptism. Richter concludes, 'There was therefore the unedifying spectacle in Jerusalem of two parties in the Anglican Church, working on different principles.'[51]

Blyth was a great builder and fundraiser. Upon noting that the congregation in Haifa was renting he raided funds and bought them land and a church building, a school, and mission house. St Mary's in Cairo was also built during his episcopate.[52] Estelle Blyth relates that her father would rise early each morning to write letters to Anglican prelates around the world, seeking gifts and contributions for the construction of his diocese. The institution of the Good Friday Offering, which continues to this day in the Episcopal Church of the United States, was part of this effort.[53] Blyth would lay each letter on the church altar before sending it off by post.

In 1901 the CMS opened a new hospital in Nablus.[54] In Nazareth a girls' school and an orphanage were started, and those eventually came under the CMS as well. In 1905 the Palestine Native Church Council was formed. This represented an important step towards indigenous leadership for the Arabophone Christians, as it was not under the direct authority of the CMS. 'The foundations were laid in the last years of the Ottoman period for increasing Arab-Anglican control of their own affairs, something that would have

[50] Richter, *Protestant Missions*, p. 246. [51] Richter, *Protestant Missions*, p. 246.
[52] Potter, 'Bishop Blythe'. [53] Bridgeman, 'Alexander', p. 42.
[54] Murre-van den Berg, *New Faith*, pp. 133–50.

important reverberations for the entire twentieth century.'[55] In 1907 Canon Sterling of the CMS in Gaza opened a new hospital there. Medical missionaries of the CMS were also active in Acre, Salt, and Karak. As of 1910 there were in all fifty-four schools with some 3,000 students. The CMS had fourteen (male) missionaries, five of whom were medical missionaries, and thirty-one missionary women. The CMS church membership was 2,323, which would not have been the entire diocesan membership since the LJS had their own work, and much of the expatriate membership would not be counted, including the congregation worshipping at St George's in Jerusalem or St Mark's in Alexandria.[56]

These three bishops, in spite of their very different understandings of their missions and ministries, managed to establish a viable, if fragile, Anglican presence. By 1910 it must have seemed that things were going well in spite of internal controversies—churches had been built, Jews and Arabs had become Anglicans, and relations with the historical Churches had been mended.

MISSION IN EGYPT

After an aborted start in Egypt (1818–62), the CMS reopened the work, most significantly sending Dr Frank Harpur who founded a hospital there. St Mark's in Alexandria had been founded as a congregation in 1830s, and had a building by the 1850s.[57] Major developments in Egypt, however, would have to await the arrival of talented and creative missionaries Douglas Thornton and Temple Gairdner in Cairo, who experimented with evangelizing Muslims. By 1890 all three of these CMS missionaries were in Egypt, though Thornton died prematurely. Also, until 1921 the aim of the CMS mission was to revitalize the Coptic Orthodox Church rather than create an indigenous Anglican community, in contrast to their proselytism in Palestine. Nor does it appear that the bishops from Jerusalem devoted a great deal of time to ministry in Egypt: 'There was not much episcopal oversight until 1905, when the Bishop in Jerusalem built St Mary's Church in Cairo and also schools in the same compound.'[58]

However, the Anglican presence in Egypt was, on the whole, an imperial one, aimed at providing English churches for English expatriates who arrived

[55] Seth J. Frantzman, Benjamin Gleuckstadt, and Ruth Kark, 'The Anglican Church in Palestine and Israel: Colonialism, Arabization and Land Ownership', *Middle Eastern Studies*, 47 (2011), p. 105.

[56] Richter, *Protestant Missions*, p. 253.

[57] Bridgeman, 'Alexander', p. 35.

[58] Gordon Hewitt, *The Problems of Success: A History of the Church Missionary Society 1910–1942, Volume One in Tropical Africa, the Middle East, at Home* (London, 1971), p. 304.

there particularly following the British occupation of Egypt in 1882. Consequently, with Anglican churches being primarily English-speaking churches, in a mission that did not aim at creating indigenous churches, notwithstanding the CMS missionaries, and a minimum of episcopal oversight—there is little ground for speaking of 'Egyptian Anglicanism' until well after 1910. Gairdner, an intriguing and brilliant character who 'faced intractable things with a joy that was never quenched',[59] would go on to make a substantial contribution to the theory and practice of Christian witness to Muslims. His multifaceted witness to Muslims extended to writing such plays as 'Joseph and his Brothers', and 'Passover Night'.[60] But his influence would not be felt until after the Edinburgh Conference, which he attended, and based on which he wrote *Echoes from Edinburgh 1910: An Account and Interpretation of the World Missionary Conference*. Therefore a detailed discussion of his ministry does not belong in this chapter. Suffice to say that his influence on the practice of evangelistic mission to Muslims would be substantial among (mostly non-Anglican) Evangelical missionaries who would witness by the second half of the twentieth century the largest ever movement from Islam to Christianity.[61]

WHAT DID IT MEAN TO BE ANGLICAN IN THE NINETEENTH-CENTURY MIDDLE EAST?

From the beginning this issue was confusing and contested. The three bishops in Jerusalem outlined here were types for three larger models of mission, and thus, identity. Alexander and the LJS saw their mission as an eschatological sign that the parousia was near because Jews were being restored to the Holy Land, and because (they hoped) the influx of Jews to the Church would fulfil Paul's claim in Romans 11.[62] Their greatest accomplishment—that of playing a key role in making Jerusalem into a modern city—was not one they had purposed at all. Their greatest goal—of establishing a Jewish congregation on Zion—was barely accomplished, and at great cost. Other missions (Hebron, Jaffa, Safed) were all unsuccessful in the long term.

Gobat embodied the energetic and unapologetically Evangelical wing of Anglican Christianity. He had few qualms about converting or welcoming indigenous non-Jewish Christians, and by inviting the CMS to be active in

[59] Kenneth Cragg, 'Temple Gairdner's Legacy', *International Bulletin of Missionary Research*, 5 (Oct. 1981):164–7.

[60] Vivienne Stacey, 'Anglicans in the Household of Islam', *St Francis Magazine*, 3 (2008), p. 1.

[61] Duane Alexander Miller, 'Living among the Breakage: Contextual Theology-Making and Ex-Muslim Christians', PhD thesis, University of Edinburgh, 2014, pp. 90–3.

[62] Rowell, 'Eastern Horizons', p. 382.

Palestine he made one of the most formative decisions for the diocese. The LJS was allowed to continue with its ministry, even if the cause of evangelizing Jews was not championed by Gobat, who expressed suspicion regarding the motives of Jewish converts and enquirers.

If Gobat was instrumental in opening the doors of an Anglican Protestantism to the indigenous Arabophone Christians, Blyth shut them. He saw his mission as repairing the relations with the other ancient Churches and offering them, in his own words, 'a clear conception of what Anglican worship and doctrine profess' according to 'what is legal and usual in the Church at home'.[63] This sense of mission—bishop as ambassador and statesman, we might call it—did not fit with the mission or identity of the LJS or CMS. So he formed his own mission, built his own church, expanded it, and built his own seminary. He made of Jerusalem an international centre for global Anglicanism before the term was in common use, in part by giving bishops from wealthy dioceses in the Anglophone world honorary titles and inviting them to various solemnities.

Anglican mission in the Middle East was a laboratory, a place for experimentation. Individuals and agencies in the mission field were not often as closely supervised as English or American clergy at home. So the mission field of the Middle East became an arena wherein the disputations going on in the West among the Churches and within Anglicanism could be written large and tested. The fact that Alexander, Gobat, and Blyth could all have been bishops of the same diocese yet have such very different concepts of what Anglican mission signified is evidence for this. The archbishops' mission to the Assyrians and Southgate's mission in Constantinople both led to the odd scenario wherein Anglican clergy were opposing the missionary work of Protestants and siding with the ancient, indigenous Churches. Southgate's experiment led to the bizarre scenario of a bishop with no clergy to oversee, and Blyth arrived in Jerusalem only to find that he controlled none of the churches there. Some of the missionary goals were, to put it lightly, unconventional—the LJS mission to evangelize Jews, an ecumenical *Protestant* diocese, or having an Anglican bishop *in* Jerusalem, but not *of* Jerusalem.

And what of the indigenous Christians who decided to become Anglicans? While many of the documents and texts we have are from missionaries (or edited by missionaries), we do know enough to make a few general points that seemed to characterize many of the Arabophone or Jewish converts. The first is that we find in Gobat's letters and documents that when requests arrived from Arab towns, it was for a cleric *and* a teacher. Protestants (and then Anglicans) were clearly associated with education, so when Gobat established

[63] 'Consecration Sermon (1898)', in Judith Lidberg, *One Hundred Years: A Cathedral Presence in Jerusalem* (Jerusalem, 1998 [?]), p. 77.

a school in Nablus it actually attracted Christians from other villages to *move* to the city in order to 'send their children to a Christian school'.[64]

A second point is that it appears there was sometimes confusion about precisely what rights came with being a member of the Church of England. Did it also mean that such a person had special rights as a subject of the British monarch and head of the Church of England? Such issues led to tension in Jerusalem in relation to some Hebrew converts during Alexander's episcopate.[65] One particularly interesting hint comes from a note from a CMS evangelist (and later priest) who was instrumental in the founding of Anglican congregations on the east bank of the Jordan in places like Fuheis and Salt. In the second half of the nineteenth century the Ottoman government was just beginning to establish real control over what had been a lawless region, and before this political assertion mission work on the east bank was difficult if not impossible.[66] In 1879 Chalil Jamal, reporting on his work in Fuheis, a Christian village, wrote, 'Some three months ago, I received more than two invitations from the heads of families there, to go and make them *Ingleez* [English] as they say.'[67] What did this mean? How did these Orthodox Christians understand what it meant to be Anglican? It is hard to say with certainly, but in common parlance the Orthodox Patriarchate of Jerusalem was run mostly by Greek bishops, and thus the Church and its Christians were simply called the Church of the Greeks (*kaniisat al rum*). Because of this usage it is probable that the Fuheis Christians understood themselves to be moving from a Greek Church to an English Church, and just as the Greek Church had Greek bishops and privileged the Greek language, so the English Church would do something similar. But unlike the Greek Church, the English Church would open a school for them too. Not until later would the concept of having a church led by and for the indigenous Christians become a powerful influence, though an indication of this development is found in the formation of the Palestine Native Church Council in 1905.

If indigenous Anglican converts benefited from the schools and the missionaries who preached 'the reformed Gospel', they must have been disappointed by how they were treated by their previous Churches. CMS records contain numerous allegations of corruption and violence on the part of the Orthodox and Latin Churches and charges that Protestants were taxed more heavily than other Christians. Moreover they were often deprived of their role in governing their own towns and were not allowed to place representatives in the town councils.[68] CMS missionaries like John Zeller decried that the

64 Gobat, *Samuel Gobat*, p. 255.

65 Sybil Jack, 'No Heavenly Jerusalem: The Anglican Bishopric, 1841–83', *Journal of Religious History*, 19 (1995): 191–203.

66 White, 'Anglican Pioneers', pp. 298ff.

67 Quoted in White, 'Anglican Pioneers', p. 308.

68 van der Leest, *Conversion and Conflict*, pp. 221–4.

firmans from the Ottoman authorities in Istanbul 'guaranteeing' the rights of Protestants were ignored.

In sum, the different groups and individuals represented here all had specific ideas of what it meant to be an Anglican Christian, and many of them tested out those theories in the mission field. The mission field of the Middle East allowed them to experiment with concepts related to eschatology, evangelism, ecclesiology, and ecumenism (among others) in a scope and manner that would not have likely been permitted or possible back at home.

SELECT BIBLIOGRAPHY

Ainsworth, William Francis, *Travels and Researches in Asia Minor, Mesopotamia, Chaldea, and Armenia* (London, 1862).

Blincoe, Robert, *Ethnic Realities and the Church: Lessons from Kurdistan, a History of Mission Work, 1668–1990* (Pasadena, CA, 1998).

Bridgeman, Charles, 'Mediterranean Missions of the Episcopal Church from 1828–1896', *Historical Magazine of the Protestant Episcopal Church*, 31 (1962): 95–126.

Bridgeman, Charles, 'Michael Solomon Alexander: First Bishop of the Church of England in Jerusalem (1841–1845)', *Historical Magazine of the Protestant Episcopal Church*, 12 (1943): 31–43.

Coakley, J. F., *The Church of the East and the Church of England* (Oxford, 1992).

Cragg, Kenneth, *The Arab Christian: A History in the Middle East* (Louisville, KY, 1991).

Crombie, Kelvin, *For the Love of Zion: Christian Witness and the Restoration of Israel* (Bristol, 2008).

Gairdner, W. H. T., 'The Christian Church as a Home for Christ's Converts from Islam', *Muslim World*, 14 (1924): 235–46.

Gobat, Samuel, *Samuel Gobat, Bishop of Jerusalem: His Life and Work* (London, 1884).

Jack, Sybil M., 'No Heavenly Jerusalem: The Anglican Bishopric, 1841–83', *The Journal of Religious History*, 19 (1995): 191–203.

Miller, Duane Alexander, 'Christ Church (Anglican) in Nazareth: A Brief History with Photographs', *St Francis Magazine*, 8 (2012): 696–703.

Miller, Duane Alexander, 'The Installation of a Bishop in Jerusalem: The Cathedral Church of St. George the Martyr, 15 April 2007', *Anglican and Episcopal History*, 76 (2007): 549–54.

Murre-van den Berg, Heleen (ed.), *New Faith in Ancient Lands: Western Missions in the Middle East in the Nineteenth and Early Twentieth Centuries* (Leiden, 2006).

Perry, Yaron, *British Mission to the Jews in Nineteenth-Century Palestine* (London and Portland, OR, 2003).

Pikkert, Pieter, *Protestant Missionaries to the Middle East: Ambassadors of Christ or Culture?* (Hamilton, ON, 2008).

Richter, Julius, *A History of Protestant Missions in the Near East* (New York, 1970 [1910]).

Rowell, Geoffrey, 'Eastern Horizons: Anglicans and the Oriental Orthodox Churches', in Nigel Aston (ed.), *Religious Change in Europe, 1650–1914: Essays for John McManners* (Oxford, 1997), pp. 381–97.

Southgate, Horatio, *Encouragement to missionary effort among Mohamedans: a sermon by the Rev. Horatio Southgate, Jun., missionary of the Protestant Episcopal Church in the United States of America, to Persia, etc.; to which are annexed an account of the meeting held at the Church of the Ascension on the evening of Easter Sunday, April 3, 1836; with the address delivered thereat by the Rev. Mr Southgate, and his letter of instructions* (New York, 1836).

van der Leest, Charlotte, 'Conversion and Conflict in Palestine: The Missions of the Church Missionary Society and the Protestant Bishop Samuel Gobat', PhD thesis, Leiden University, 2008.

Vander Werff, Lyle L., *Christian Mission to Muslims: The Record—Anglican and Reformed Approaches in India and the Near East, 1800–1938* (Pasadena, CA, 1977).

White, Malcolm, 'Anglican Pioneers of the Ottoman Period: Sketches from the CMS Archives of Some Arab Lives Connected with the Early Days of the Diocese of Jerusalem', *St Francis Magazine*, 8 (2012): 283–314.

14

Episcopal Establishment in India to 1914

Robert Eric Frykenberg

RELIGIOUS INSTITUTIONS AND THE INDIAN EMPIRE

How the East India Company dealt with ambiguities of ruling over expanding domains within a highly complex multi-faith empire, as recently shown with meticulous care by Penelope Carson,[1] was never fully comprehended by Anglicans. The Company, from its humble beginnings in 1600 as a tiny private venture struggling for survival down to its blood-soaked demise in the wake of the Great Rebellion of 1857, always depended heavily upon Indian manpower, money, and methods. Out of necessity, the Company's Raj made itself the guardian of all pukka religious and social institutions under its sway. Religion in India was a matter too crucial for meddling by Lords Spiritual of England.

The Company's first foothold was codified in a 1639 golden *sāsanam*. Inscribed in the Sri Venkateswara Temple at Tirupati, this granted dominion over a tiny strip of shoreline. A small gold coin (*hūn*, aka 'pagoda'), bearing the image of the same deity, legitimized the Company's authority over a tiny domain. This fledgling settlement soon grew into the city-state of Madras.[2] Similar grants soon brought Bombay and Calcutta into being. Thereafter, with the spread of more and more 'small hard pieces' of local influence and territorial acquisition, the sway of the Company's empire rested on an ever more elaborate patchwork of contracts and treaties combined with military conquest. From three city-states founded in seventeenth century—Madras, Bombay, and Calcutta—a vast imperial system emerged. By the second decade of the nineteenth century, the Company ruled one of the largest empires in the world. A military machine consisting of hundreds of thousands of soldiers and

[1] Penelope Carson, *The East India Company and Religion, 1698–1858* (Worlds of the East India Company, Vol. 7) (Rochester, NY, 2012), pp. xii, 279.

[2] C. S. Srinivasachri, *History of the City of Madras* (Madras, 1939), pp. 26–36; R. Sathianathaier, *Tamilaham in the 17th Century* (Madras, 1956), pp. 40–8; William Foster, *The Founding of Ft. St. George* (London, 1920), pp. 1–24.

a civil administration run by as many native civil servants held it together. Regiments of sepoy infantry, sawari cavalry, and native artillery from elite warrior communities provided security for a regime manned by a vast bureaucracy of native Indian gentry. The 'steel frame' of roughly a thousand 'heaven born' Europeans that ruled, did so not so much by force as by collaboration and acquiescence.

By as early as the 1780s, great wealth had accrued to the *mahajans* (gentry) of each presidency. In Madras, such affluence was celebrated by the *Sarva Deva Vilāsa* or 'Celebration of the Gods'.[3] This remarkable document attributed the power of Madras to local deities, in whose names magnificent new temples were being built, and to which famous poets and dancers were being drawn. Under Madras Regulation VII of 1817, and similar regulations for Bombay and Bengal, the Company took formal responsibility for all pukka religious and sacred institutions. Company servants managed endowments (*ināms*) for thousands of hallowed shrines, temples, pilgrim sites, for daily and annual ceremonials, festivals, and processions (*melas*, *tirnāls*, *tirthas*, and *yātras*), as well as monastic schools (*mathas*), dancing girls (*devadasis*), and musical institutions. The Company also cared for the management of Islamic institutional endowments (under *inām* and *waaqf* land tenures), as well as for Christian and other religious institutions. Institutions of each and every religious community, in varying degrees, remained under the 'protection' of the Company.[4] The very stability and viability of the entire imperial system depended upon support from intricately and, at times, precariously balanced networks of religious support and toleration. Within highly complex multi-faith contexts the Indian Empire was, in fact, a 'Hindu Raj'.[5] 'Hindu', in this sense, related both things native to India, as well as things religious and to an increasingly specific set of institutions that came to be known as 'Hinduism'. This system of official support for vast religious endowments is what Anglican episcopacy encountered upon its arrival in 1814.

The Company opposed any form of established Christendom within its domains. While some 665 chaplains had served its stations and ships from 1601 to 1858, clergy had hitherto been loath to leave comfortable benefices in England for the hazards of India. Few had taken home fortunes. Many had died overseas. Prior to the Restoration, Anglican chaplains had mingled with

[3] V. Raghavan, 'The *Sarve-Deva-Vilasa*: A Critical Historical Study', *Adiyar Library Bulletin*, 21 (1957) and 22 (1958), is an incomplete palm-leaf manuscript of 86 leaves.

[4] Chandra Y. Mudaliar, *The Secular State and Religious Institutions in India: A Study of the Administration of Hindu Public Religious Trusts in Madras* (Wiesbaden, 1972); *State and Religious Endowments in Madras* (Madras, 1974); Franklin A. Presler, *Religion and Bureaucracy Policy and the Administration for Hindu Temples in South India* (Cambridge, 1987).

[5] Robert Eric Frykenberg, 'The Emergence of Modern "Hinduism" as a Concept and as an Institution: A Reappraisal With Special Reference to South India', in Gunther-Dietz Sontheimer and Hermann Kuke (eds.), *Hinduism Reconsidered* (New Delhi, 1989 edn.), pp. 82–107.

Puritans, Congregationalists, and Dissenters; but contacts with Christians of India, whether St Thomas Christians, Armenians, or Catholics (whether under the *Padroado* in Goa or of the *Propaganda Fide* in Rome), had remained minimal. Anglican chaplains, merely Company employees, had enjoyed few temporal powers.[6] An occasional chaplain had tried to spread the gospel among 'benighted heathen', but Company policy opposed missionary activity or interference with local institutions. This attitude never changed, and persisted as long as the British Raj lasted.

HANOVERIAN-PIETIST ANGLICANISM

The eighteenth century brought a significant change—a bifurcation between anti-missionary policy and actual practice in India. After the Peace of Westphalia in 1648, blended Pietist and Enlightenment impulses spread to England from the Pietist centre of Halle, augmented by Moravian and Huguenot refugees, the Glorious Revolution, and the Hanoverian Succession. The leading Pietist, August Hermann Francke, blended Enlightenment and devotion by calling for personal faith acquired by reading both the Word of God and the Word of Nature. Essential for this was universal literacy in one's mother tongue. Consequently, out of Halle came schools for orphans and the poor. Model schools, *Kindergarten* and *Kunst under Wunder Kammer*, multiplied and brought mass literacy. Impulses that later engendered the Great Awakening in America and Evangelical awakening in Britain arrived in India as early as 1706.

The Danish-English-Halle Mission (DEHM) of Tranquebar was a radical innovation—an international collaboration between three royal cousins: Frederick IV of Denmark, Anne of England, and Sophia of Hanover. Anglicans, alarmed by 'Papist' claimants to the throne and by the expansionist policies of Louis XIV, reached out to other Protestant 'national' Churches of Europe, especially to affluent Huguenots and Pietists who had settled in London. The Society for Promoting Christian Knowledge (SPCK), a voluntary agency for support of charity schools formed by the Revd Thomas Bray in 1698, reflected this new ethos. Francke himself was a founding member. So too was his influential disciple, Anton Wilhem Böhme, chaplain to Prince George of Denmark and Princess Anne, who published an English translation of Francke's *Pietas Hallensis* in 1701—the very year that the Act of Settlement assured a Protestant succession to the throne and Bray also formed the Society for the Propagation of the Gospel in Foreign Parts (SPG).

[6] Daniel O'Connor, *The Chaplains of the East India Company, 1601–1858* (London, 2012).

In 1706, two disciples of Francke, Bartholomaeus Ziegenbalg and Heinrich Plütschau, arrived in Tranquebar (*Tarangambadi*). After mastering Tamil, they established model 'charity schools' (*dharmappallikkūm*), trained 'teacher-pastors', and set up presses to publish biblical, literary, scientific, and technological texts. The two-way flow of cultural interactions between India and Europe they engendered increased the Enlightenment both to the East and the West. Ziegenbalg, with his command of classical and colloquial Tamil, exhaustively studied local lore and assiduously gathered palm-leaf manuscripts.

Böhme's *Propagation of the Gospel in the East* (1709) prompted the SPCK to set up a 'Malabar Committee', with Ziegenbalg and Plütschau as corresponding members. So a three-way collaboration began, with missionaries trained in Halle, appointed in Copenhagen, and sent out from London. Tamil fonts cast in Halle went to Tranquebar aboard English vessels, along with books, paper, and ink. Contact with Eastern Churches also prompted the making of fonts for 'Arabick... used in the East Indies'.

The result was an amalgam of anomalies: an Anglican mission in India staffed by German Lutheran missionaries. Delicate diplomacy was continuously required to iron out difficulties of blending Anglican with Pietist doctrine. Mutual respect for different forms of Protestantism was not easy, especially over the ordination of Tamil pastors. Yet, SPCK control remained remarkably light. This anomaly lasted for as long as a Hanoverian monarch sat on the English throne. Chaplains of George I, George II, and George III came from Halle and sustained royal faith, piety, and support. Between 1706 and 1845, sixty-six Halle missionaries, ordained in Copenhagen, preached in the palace of St James en route to Tranquebar. Some thirty of these were supported by the SPCK.[7]

ANGLICAN EPISCOPACY AND CONFORMITY

Establishment of Anglican Christendom within the Indian Empire began in 1814. Within the Company's Charter Renewal Act of 1813 was a clause providing for limited admission of missionaries into British India. Anglican indifference and neglect towards India had already begun to give way before rising tides of Evangelicalism, both Anglican and Nonconformist.[8] Prior

[7] Robert Eric Frykenberg, 'The Halle Legacy in Modern India: Information and the Spread of Education, Enlightenment, and Evangelization', in *Missionsberichte aus Indien im 18 Jahrhundert. Ihre Bedeutung für die europäische Geistesgeschichte under ihr wissenschaftlicher Quellenwert für die Indienkunde* (Halle, 1999), pp. 6–29.

[8] Rowan Strong, *Anglicanism and the British Empire, c.1700–1859* (Oxford, 2007), pp. 123–7.

efforts of Charles Grant, William Wilberforce, and the 'Clapham Sect' for insertion of a 'pious clause' in the Charter Renewal Act of 1793 had failed. Evangelical disciples of Charles Simeon of Cambridge had then been sent to India as 'missionary chaplains'—by means of patronage exercised by 'Saints' among Company directors. New voluntary missionary societies—the Baptist Missionary Society (BMS, 1792), the London Missionary Society (LMS, 1795), and the Church Missionary Society (CMS, 1799)—had strenuously lobbied Parliament for the same cause. Claudius Buchanan, made vice-provost of the new College of Fort William in 1800 by Lord Wellesley, the governor-general, had been dismayed to find so few places for Anglican worship in India. His *Memoir on the Expediency of an Ecclesiastical Establishment for India, both as a Means of Perpetuating the Christian Religion among our own Countrymen and as a Foundation for the Ultimate Civilization of the Natives* (1805) had sounded the alarm. Anglicans in India were being bypassed by foreigners and Dissent. Anomalies of Hanoverian-Pietist Anglicanism, epitomized by SPCK collaboration with Copenhagen, Halle, and Tranquebar, then cut off by a Napoleonic Europe, began to wane in the face of a less flexible Anglicanism.

Initial episcopal efforts 'to set to order things that are wanting' did not go well.[9] Without a pre-existing diocese, a royal letter patent had to be issued. Expenses for the episcopal establishment in India could be charged to the Government of India's Ecclesiastical Department without undue concern about public opposition in India. After all, Company revenues had already long supported Hindu and Muslim establishments. But for Indian revenues to pay for evangelizing activities was an entirely different matter. Every governor-general, from Warren Hastings onwards, had adamantly, and repeatedly, rejected attempts to impose Anglicanism upon the Company's subjects in India, and would continue to do so.[10]

Thomas Fanshawe Middleton, the first bishop of Calcutta, having arrived almost surreptitiously, found himself frustrated. He could not appoint, discipline, dismiss, or ordain chaplains, missionaries, and native clergy. All chaplains who came to India did so under licences issued by the archbishop of Canterbury and the bishop of London; and in India, they were assigned positions by local governments of the Company. Nor was the Government of India about to submit to dictates from bishops in England. When a Danish royal charter enabling William Carey, the Baptist missionary, to establish Serampore College in 1818 embarrassed Middleton, he responded by establishing Bishop's College in 1820. For staffing this college, he turned to the SPG. For the first time, the SPG was to replace DHEM/SPCK missionaries

[9] Fred D. Schneider, 'Parliament, the East India Company, and the Calcutta Bishopric', *Church and State*, 16 (1974): 51–71.

[10] Bernard Palmer, *Imperial Vineyard: The Anglican Church in India under the Raj* (Lewes, 1999).

with Anglican clerics. After Middleton died in 1822, remaining SPCK positions in South India were also taken over by the SPG in 1826.[11] Yet Anglican recruitment lagged. Years would pass before Anglican missionaries arrived in strength.

In 1832, five years after the tragic drowning of Bishop Reginald Heber and the deaths of his two successors, Daniel Wilson became the fifth bishop of Calcutta. In 1836, he also became the first metropolitan bishop of India and the East in a diocese that stretched as far as Cape Town and Sydney. Ceaseless efforts to impose Anglican conformity and increase Anglican dominion would mark the thirty-six years of his entire career.

CAMPAIGNS AGAINST 'HEATHENISM' AND IDOLATRY

Outrage marked the earliest years of formal Anglican engagement with religion in India. Charles Grant and Claudius Buchanan railed against entrenched customs such as female infanticide, widow burning, hook-hanging, and human sacrifice.[12] But little was done to wade into such dangerous waters until Lord William Bentinck became governor-general in 1827. With support from social reformers such as Raja Ram Mohan Roy, 'inhuman and superstitious practices' such as female infanticide and widow-burning (*sati* aka *suttee*) were abolished. But Hindu reformers supported this measure at the risk of their lives. A storm of opposition erupted, coming from the very elites upon whom the Raj depended for support. Over thirty thousand Calcutta gentry (*bhadralok*) signed a 'Sacred Petition' protesting against the violation of their ancient 'religious freedoms' and interference in their 'eternally hallowed and time-honoured tradition' of burning widows.[13]

The dust of this disturbance had hardly settled when a broad Anglican attack was mounted against official support for 'Satanic' heresy and idolatry. A memorial initiated by Daniel Corrie, formerly archdeacon of Calcutta who had become bishop of Madras, and signed by hundreds of the Company's European civilian and military officers, protested against official involvement in 'heathen' and 'idolatrous' practices. Management of tens of thousands of

[11] Victor Koilpillai, *The SPCK in India, 1710–1985* (Delhi, 1985), p. 43.

[12] Charles Grant, *Observations on the State of Society among the Asiatic Subjects of Great Britain, with particular respect to Morals and the means of improving it* (1792); Claudius Buchanan, *Christian Researches in Asia* (1811) and *An Apology for Promoting Christianity in India* (1814).

[13] At the Council Chamber, Whitehall, the 7th Day of July 1832. Submitted by a Committee of the Lords of His Majesty's Most Honourable Privy Council: National Archives UK, London: Register (P. C.), vol. 312, fos. 404–19.

temples, pilgrim shrines, and ceremonies depended directly upon Company revenues. Hundreds of thousands of corvée labourers were being forced into pulling temple cars (*rath yātras*); and thousands of temple dancing-girls (*devadasis*) were being forced into 'immoral' thraldom. Christian officers, obliged to participate at festivals, had to stand guard and salute deities in violation of their consciences.

The Government of India's reaction to this petition was swift and severe. Officers were summarily disciplined or dismissed outright. Bishop Corrie was censured. Sir Peregrine Maitland, Commander-in-Chief of the Madras Army, was forced to retire. In London, his Anti-Idolatry Connexion League launched a pamphlet campaign.

COLLABORATION WITH THOMAS CHRISTIANS

Bishop Daniel Wilson's attempt to impose Anglicanism upon Thomas Christians of Cochin and Travancore (now Kerala) also went wrong. Thomas Christians are the broad category of Christians in India who canonically trace their origins to the apostle in 52 CE. Since their sacred scriptures are in Syriac, and many have, at various times, received their training and ordination from the Catholicos heading the Church of the East in Mesopotamia, many such Christians are also known as 'Syrian' Christians. A smaller subcategory of such Christians are known as *Malankara Nazranis* (from Nazarenes). This exclusive elite community trace their origins to 345 CE when their leader, Thomas of Kinayi, received lands for 400 Christian families from the Perumal (Emperor) of Kerala.

Formal ties with *Malankara Nazranis* had begun in 1806. Claudius Buchanan, engaged in a diplomatic mission on behalf of the governor-general, Lord Richard Wellesley, had been given an audience in the palace of Mar Dionysius I (aka Divannasios I). His promise to the High Metran (or metropolitan bishop), of a CMS seminary at Kottayam providing basic training for priests (*kattanars*), and a Malayalam translation of Holy Writ for every pulpit, was welcomed. In response, he received a thousand-year-old copy of the Syriac Scriptures.

All went well for a dozen years. Literacy among *kattanars* increased, as also did positions for Christian civil servants within the two kingdoms of Cochin and Travancore. But by 1818, Thomas Christian elites increasingly resented the highhanded and paternalistic actions of the CMS missionaries and their excessive influence upon prelates within the Syrian Church. When Hindu elites reacted against excessive patronage of Christians within the governments of Cochin and Travancore, blame for the consequent persecution of Christians fell upon the CMS missionaries. Bishop Reginald Heber tried to smooth relations and resolve the disputes. But Bishop Wilson's insistence upon conformity to Anglican norms of apostolic order and doctrine, and Anglican encroachments upon Malankara customs, went too far. At a synod convened at Mavelikkara in 1836, three decades of Anglican–Syrian collaboration were abruptly terminated. Struggles over the Kottayam seminary property followed.

Two groups of reform-minded Thomas Christians broke away from the High Metran, Dionysius IV (Divannasios IV, aka Mar Thoma XII: 1829–52). The smaller group became Anglican. The larger, while committed to ancient traditions, preserved reforms initiated at Kottayam College. These Malankara reformers were led by Abraham Malpan of Maramon. Abraham sent his nephew Mathew to obtain a formal *statikon* (or commission of appointment) from the patriarch of Antioch (in Mardin). This action of bypassing election by Indian congregations, a procedure that had been in existence since the Oath of Koonan Cross in 1653, led to litigation. Mathew Athanasios's elevation as the Mar Thoma High Metran was ultimately ratified by the Maharaja in Cochin in 1852.[14] Thereafter, the CMS missionaries turned their attention to the lowest of the low caste peoples, the abolition of slavery, mass conversion, and basic education. Cordial relations between Anglican Thomas Christians and these reformed Mar Thoma were maintained.[15]

TIRUNELVĒLI AND 'THE RHENIUS AFFAIR'

Mass conversions to Christianity began in Tirunelvēli Country in 1799. Three disciples of Christian Friedrich Schwartz of Thanjāvur—Rasa Clarinda (aka Kohila), Sathiyanathan Pillai, and Chinnamutthu Sundaranandam David—aided by Christian Wilhelm Gericke and Joseph Daniel Jänicke who were both DHEM/SPCK missionaries—had led thousands of Nadars (aka Shanars) into the faith. Whole villages had turned Christian, converting temples into chapel-schools. Persecutions by Hindu landlords (*zamindars*) inspired these new Christian communities to form 'Villages of Refuge'. But by 1806 leadership had faltered, and fledgling communities struggled for survival. Help came in 1816, when James Hough arrived in Palaiyankottai. This chaplain-missionary, and disciple of Charles Simeon, tried to resuscitate village chapel-schools out of his own pocket. When he pleaded for the CMS Committee of Correspondence in Madras for help, the committee sent Karl Theophilus Ewald Rhenius. Rhenius, a Prussian ex-military officer, had become imbued with the spirit of

[14] Leslie Brown, *The Indian Christians of St. Thomas: An Account of the Ancient Syrian Church of Malabar* (Cambridge, 1982 edn.), pp. 125–6, 140–3.

[15] C. P. Mathew and M. M. Thomas, *The Indian Churches of Saint Thomas* (Delhi, 1967).

Halle and trained at Johann Jänicke's Missionary Seminary in Berlin. Later described by Bishop Robert Caldwell as 'one of the ablest, most clear-sighted, practical, and zealous missionaries that India had ever seen', Rhenius is renowned as the 'Apostle of Tirunelvēli'.[16]

The strategy of this brilliant, charismatic, and dynamic figure was to organize a highly disciplined force of local Tamil leaders so as to systematically spread the gospel into every corner and segment of society. His inspired and rigorously drilled 'pilgrims' (*desanthari*) went out in pairs to each and every village. Scores of those who worked with him were led by such lieutenants as David Pillai Asirvatham, John Devasagayam, and Savarirayan Pillai who would meet monthly in Palaiyankottai for renewal. Some 371 village chapel-schools were established, each with its own pastor/teacher bringing literacy for both boys and girls.[17] Two high schools and a seminary trained leaders, pastors, and teachers. Voluntary self-help societies—for health and welfare, for orphans, widows, and the poor, and for running a printing press—cultivated inter-faith amity with other communities. In each of hundreds of local Christian communities a prayer bell sounded every dawn and dusk. When persecution erupted, new 'villages of refuge' were established. Like-minded missionaries from the continent flocked to join Rhenius. While doing all this, Rhenius not only strove to produce a more perfect Tamil translation of the New Testament, but erected a towering place of worship (now known as Holy Trinity Cathedral) in Palaiyamkottai.

Rhenius did not easily fit into the Anglican mould. Welcoming Bishop Wilson to India, he reported on rapid increases in the number of Tirunelvēli Christians. Urgently in need of more Tamil pastors, he also reported recently ordaining seven young men whom he had carefully trained. This action, taken under local authority that DHEM/SPCK missionaries had practised for a century, received a sharp rebuke from the bishop. Rhenius had violated the Anglican policy of exclusive episcopal ordination by bishops in the apostolic succession, which had been confirmed as Anglican doctrine since 1662. Henceforth all local pastors were to be strictly bound to receive Anglican orders from an Anglican bishop. A hurt and stung Rhenius responded to his rebuke by publishing a review entitled *The Church: Her Daughters and Handmaidens, her Pastors and her People, etc.* (1834) and another pamphlet calling for a more tolerant 'Union of Christians . . . in spreading the Gospel'. Rhenius wrote: 'When my fellow-labourer [J. Schnarre] and I were sent out to India, twenty-one years ago, no question was ever put to us on the subject of

[16] J. L. Wyatt (ed.), *Reminiscences of Bishop Caldwell* (London, 1894), p. 99.

[17] Stephen Neill, *A History of Christianity in India 1707–1858* (Cambridge, 1985), p. 509; Julius Richter, *A History of Missions in India* (Edinburgh and London, 1908), pp. 422–3, 160.

conformity to the Church of England.'[18] Two CMS missionary officials were sent to Tirunelvēli. They hand-delivered a severe letter informing Rhenius that his connection with the CMS was at an end; and that since the territory where he had worked now 'belonged to the CMS', he should forthwith depart from Tirunelvēli.

Rhenius, heartbroken, never fully recovered. Neither did the Tamil congregations of Tirunelvēli, nor the world-wide following that had been supporting his work. On 15 December 1836, at a new 'village of refuge' endowed by David Pillai Asirvatham and christened 'City of Salvation' (*Suvrisesha-puram*), a special house was set aside and dedicated for the use of Rhenius. It was there that he died two years later, exhausted by over-exertion in the completion of his new Tamil translation of the New Testament—his final legacy to Tamil Christians.

'The Rhenius Affair' provoked consternation far and wide. Heated pamphlets were exchanged. Some local congregations, 'Westside People' or *Melpakkatha*, including people of Dohnavur, seceded. Blaming Rhenius's death on Anglicans, a splinter movement of 'Hindu-Christians' turned against missionary colonialism. 'Eastside People' or *Kilppakkathār* remained with the CMS and the SPG. Some alienated German missionaries were persuaded to return to the mission. The Rhenius system itself continued to grow and flourish beyond all expectations. Despite such paternalistic CMS overlords such as Edward Sargent and John Thomas, gifted Tamil Christian leaders multiplied and a diaspora of Tirunelvēli Pietist influence spread ever more widely.[19] In North Tirunelvēli new and separate SPG campaigns were launched in 1845 by Thomas Ragland;[20] and in Nagarcoil to the south, LMS and Leipzig missions soon thrived, recruiting some disaffected congregations. Jesuit missions, having recently returned, also greatly benefited from what had happened.

Thus it was that Anglican conformity and dominion replaced the old Hanoverian collaboration.[21] Robert Caldwell, the SPG scholar who, along with Edward Sargent of the CMS, would later become one of two suffragan bishops of Tirunelvēli,[22] lamented: 'Americans and Germans are doing far more for India, proportionately... than English churchmen'.[23] But even as late as 1852 ninety-nine German missionaries were still supported by Anglican

[18] *Farewell Letter of Mr Rhenius to the Church Missionary Society, after Receiving his Dismissal* (London, 1836); and *Memoir of the Rev. C. T. E. Rhenius*, ed. Julius Rhenius (London, 1841), pp. 501–3.

[19] William Kemm, *John Thomas: Missionary to South India* (Delhi, 2010).

[20] *A Memoir of the Rev. Thomas Gajetan Ragland: Fellow of the Corpus Christi College, Cambridge, and Itinerating Missionary of the Church Missionary Society in North Tinnevelly, South India* (London, 1861).

[21] Richter, *History*, pp. 159–60.

[22] Y. Vincent Kumaradoss, *Robert Caldwell: A Scholar-Missionary in Colonial South India* (Delhi, 2007).

[23] Robert Caldwell, *Lectures on the Tinnevelly Missions* (London, 1857), pp. 21–2.

societies, as against 138 English missionaries. Germans put Anglicans to shame. They knew more about India. This, Caldwell felt, was a national disgrace. Yet, even as Hanoverian Anglican Pietism of the old DHEM–SPCK shrank, a newly rising Anglican colonialism prevailed—at least for a while.

CASTE ABOLITION AND CONFORMITY

For as long as Serfoji Maharaj reigned and the SPCK German missionaries remained active, high-born Tamil Pietists in South India flourished. Yet, their status was assailed by egalitarian pressures. In 1826, after SPG missionaries had taken over the SPCK positions, they remounted the attacks against 'heathen' and 'Satanic' customs that had been perpetuated by their predecessors, and the single institution they singled out as the very heart of evil was caste. Yet, when faced with attacks against caste, Bishop Heber defended the prevailing traditions. Tamil Christians who worshipped 'together separately' were no different than Christian gentry in America or Europe whose slaves or servants sat and worshipped separately—where masters attended morning worship while servants prepared dinner and attended evening worship, or sat separately during morning worship.[24]

Two years after Heber's death, Vedanayagam Sastriar (1774–1864), the most remarkable Pietist and Evangelical poet of the nineteenth century, published his 'Dialogue on the Difference of Caste'.[25] In St Peter's Church, the imposing building funded by the Maharaja, different castes had always been seated in different quadrants of nave and transept: Europeans on benches, Vellalars on grass mats, and Paraiyars on stone floors—with women or children sitting separately, by birth and status. Sastri saw nothing wrong with Communion being taken 'together separately'. A Christian, he declared, was no mere abstraction; nor were birth (*jāt*) and lineage (*vamsha*). Each person belonged to an earthly family—each with distinct birth and blood, face and name, style and tongue.[26] Humanity, created and redeemed by God, was no mere intellectual category. Each life embodied an earthly culture—and 'birth'

[24] Reginald Heber, 21 March 1826: Madras Public Consultation/P (Tamil Nadu Archives: vol. 620: 1155–67), paras 2–5; Thomas Robinson, *The Last Days of Bishop Heber* (London, 1830), pp. 321–5.

[25] Vedanayagam Sastriar, *Jātiyacaracampavinai* (Tanjore, 1829); *'Sadipedaga Sambaveney': Dialogue on the Mode of Junior or Modern Missionaries of Communing with Tamil Christians and the Reproaches Contained in Their Various Books which They Publish* (Tanjore, 1834).

[26] D. Dennis Hudson, *Protestant Origins in India: Tamil Evangelical Christians 1707–1835* (Grand Rapids, MI, 2000), pp. 140–72; Indira Viswanathan Peterson, 'The "Bethlehem *Kuruvanci*"', in Judith M. Brown and Robert E. Frykenberg (eds.), *Christians, Cultural Interactions, and India's Religious Traditions* (Grand Rapids, MI, 2002), pp. 9–36.

(caste). No single life could remain immutable. But change, ever possible, mainly came slowly, even painfully.

In 1833, Bishop Daniel Wilson decreed the banning of caste. But when Paraiyar Christians were ordered to sit on mats used by Vellalars, Vellalar worshippers abandoned churches and withdrew their children from schools. Seven hundred Vellalars in Vepery who refused to share the common cup and bread with people of low birth were excommunicated. When a dying Vellalar youth in Thanjāvur was denied the eucharist, three thousand promptly left congregations in which their forbearers had long worshipped. Another objector was flogged so badly that a physician was required. Petitions before the governor, Sir Frederick Adam, and the governor-general, Lord William Bentinck, described humiliations, fines, imprisonments, and beatings administered by local magistrates upon requests by missionaries. When Bishop Wilson scolded the government for interfering 'in purely spiritual matters', he was roundly rebuked.[27]

George Uglow Pope, the Anglican (SPG) missionary sent to Thanjāvur in 1851, determined to eradicate caste. Blaming this 'handy-work of Satan' on the Tranquebar missionaries, he saw Vedanayagam Sastriar—disciple of Schwartz, classmate of Serfoji Maharaja, renowned writer of classic epics who had composed hundreds of hymns and who as principal had run the Thanjāvur schools for sixty years—as epitomizing the lax non-conformity of the old DHEM/SPCK (Hanoverian Anglican) system.[28] Vedanayagam was summarily dismissed. Vedanayagam, for his part, accused SPG missionaries of committing four great atrocities: tampering with Tamil scripture, replacing older versions; forcing all Christians into one caste, and then denying the eucharist and excommunicating all who refused; banning hallowed customs, such as flowers for weddings and funerals; and removing Tamil lyrics and music from Tamil worship services.[29]

The damage resulting from the bishop's decree would long outlast him, amidst increasing religious tensions in which the Company's Raj was perpetually caught in the middle. Unable to adequately satisfy any community—Christians, Hindu, or Muslim—its final years were fraught with fending off irreconcilable religious forces. In 1857, the Great Rebellion (or Mutiny) brought the East India Company to a blood-spattered end. Among the first to be killed as Delhi erupted in violence was Midgley Jennings. The constant rantings against 'devilish' idolatry by this SPG missionary-chaplain

[27] Susan Billington Harper, *In the Shadow of the Mahatma: Bishop V. A. Azariah and the Travails of Christianity in British India* (Grand Rapids, MI, 2000), pp. 93–115.

[28] Anon., *The Lutheran Aggression, A Letter to the Tranquebar Missionaries, Regarding Their Position, Their Proceedings; and Their Doctrine* (Madras, 1853).

[29] Hudson, *Protestant Origins in India*, pp. 148–72.

and disciple of the Oxford Movement had been notorious in the Mughal capital ever since his arrival in 1851.[30]

In such a world, Anglican Christendom in India could not prevail. Governors-general of India, from Warren Hastings onwards, had repeatedly warned against introducing episcopacy or any officially supported Christian institutions. Anglican actions against caste had exacerbated tensions, and alienated Indian Christians. Years later, commenting on Bishop Wilson's actions, Bishop Eyre Chatterton of Lahore would observe: 'Everywhere the English missionaries were most unpopular; hundreds of catechists [pastor/ teachers] resigned; and the excitement was so great [that] the governor-general [Lord William Bentinck] himself questioned the bishop's wisdom.'[31] Assaults against Christians of South India perpetrated by Bishop Daniel Wilson, and Pope's treatment of Thanjāvur Christians, especially his dismissals of Rhenius and Vedanayagam, had brought more harm than good. Bishop Wilson and Vedanayagam died in the same year—1858—even as the fires of the Great Rebellion were raging. By then, Pietist missionaries of the Leipzig Mission, led by Karl Graul (1814–64), had been replacing the last Halle/SPCK missionaries for over a decade.

DOWNWARD FILTRATION AND UPWARD FULFILMENT

The Great Rebellion, or Mutiny, of 1857–8, was pivotal. The attitudes and aspirations of the Anglicans were altered. Blame fell on missionaries, tracing their aggressiveness and arrogance as far back as the Vellore Mutiny of 1806.[32] Warnings against intrusions into socio-religious customs had been incessant.[33] Attempts to establish an Anglican polity within a multi-faith Raj as complex as India were now seen to require extraordinary caution. 'Enlightenment' and 'secularization', stressing literacy, higher education, and tolerance were now to be fostered. The Queen's Proclamation of 1858, replacing Company rule with that of the Crown-in-Parliament, stressed this outlook. From

[30] O'Connor, *Chaplains of the East India Company*, p. 134.

[31] Eyre Chatterton, *A History of the Church of England in India since the Early Days of the East India Company* (London, 1924), p. 165.

[32] R. E. Frykenberg, 'New Light on the Vellore Mutiny', in Kenneth Ballhatchet and John Harrison (eds.), *East India Company Studies: Papers Presented to Professor Sir Cyril Philips* (London, 1986), pp. 207–31.

[33] John Bruce Norton, *The Rebellion in India: How to Prevent Another* (London, 1857); Sir Syed Ahmad Khan, *The Causes of the Indian Revolt* (English translation, 1873); Michael P. Adas, 'The Meaning of Mutiny: A Critical Bibliographical Study of the Interpretive Literature on the Indian Mutiny of 1857–1858', MA thesis, University of Wisconsin, 1968.

this time onwards Anglican rhetoric became more restrained. The next metropolitan bishop, George Edward Lynch Cotton (1858–66), pledged two 'indispensable' objectives: 'better understanding of the old religions of India', and 'dealing fairly and kindly' with different Christian communities of India.[34] Compulsory Bible lessons imposed on non-Christian students by non-Christian teachers would end. Fewer confrontational disputes with acute Hindu or Muslim minds would occur. Cotton's successor, Robert Milman (1816–76), mastered Bengali, Hindi, and Urdu, but exhausted by incessant travel he died in Lahore. Not until 1898 did this pattern of episcopal demise end so that a bishop might actually retire to his homeland. Dioceses were too vast, so new ones were created—Madras (1835) and Bombay (1837); Colombo (1845), followed by separate sees at Lahore and Rangoon (1877), Travancore/Cochin (1879), Chota-Nagpur (1890), Lucknow (1893), Tinnevelly/Madura (1895), Nagpur (1903), and Dornakal (1912).

Yet, by the first decade of the 1900s, a serious anomaly grew up that foreshadowed the end of any Anglican 'establishment' in India. The irregular status of many new bishoprics, supported by private endowments, revealed deep contradictions of a 'tacit consent' between Church and state. Anglican polity as the state Church of India became a dead letter and was seen as altogether 'specious', and moves towards the dismantling of such pretensions and connections to the state in India began but were not completed until 1930.[35]

ENLIGHTENMENT AND EDUCATION OF ELITES

While the CMS and SPG missionaries continued to spread the gospel, both in North and South India, and built schools so as to increase literacy among low-born peoples, both societies increasingly focused upon reaching high-born elites. Few among such elites were Christians, but many were anxious for their children to acquire modern education and proficiency in English. Elite demands for modern education in English had prompted Christian Friedrich Schwartz to found the earliest English medium schools at Thanjāvur, Shivaganga, and Ramnad in the 1780s. These, subsidized by the Company, and run by Vedanayagam Sastriar for sixty years, were early glimmerings of modern Enlightenment. By the 1790s, the Company was supporting elite colleges in Delhi, Calcutta, and Varanasi, as later in Pune, that blended oriental and modern learning.

[34] Chatterton, *History of the Church of England*, p. 233.
[35] Harper, *The Shadow of the Mahatma*, pp. 111–14, 125–6.

Contrary to much historiography, English was never a colonial imposition upon hapless subjects. Rather, elite, high-born communities, wishing to preserve or enhance their already high positions, would not be denied. Most missionaries strove for basic literacy in vernacular languages for the 'lower orders'; but higher education, in English, enhanced prospects for India's gentry. High tuition fees effectively barred admission of 'lower orders' into such institutions of higher learning. But, by the 1870s, policies of 'downward filtration' were being blended with ideals of 'upward fulfilment'.[36] Thereafter, liberal theologies stressed 'dialogue' whereby religious truths would bring 'mutual understanding' of a 'common humanity'. In the fullness of time it was thought, in this way all would accept the gospel of Christ. Mutual co-option would bring cultural and religious harmony.[37]

The 1854 Education Despatch of Sir Charles Wood, Secretary of State for India, by providing 'grants-in-aid' to private schools, signalled a pivotal change for educational systems of India. Even so, equal emphasis on tax-supported vernacular education for schools in the countryside (*mufassal*) matched English higher education in cities. Since most modern educational institutions were run by missionaries, their schools became the main beneficiaries of the grant-in-aid system. Calcutta and Madras gentry (*bhadralok* and *mahajans*) were assured that traditions of oriental learning and English education would be expanded, and that modern universities would prepare India's youth for entry into various modern professions, sciences, and technologies.[38]

Advanced, exclusively English medium colleges, founded by Alexander Duff in Calcutta, John Anderson in Madras, and John Wilson in Bombay during the 1830s, were followed, after the establishment of universities in 1858, by a number of newer, Anglican-led institutions of advanced learning. These were to be found among some 250 modern colleges, of varying quality and religious affiliation, that came into being throughout India. Anglican colleges stretched unevenly from Kottayam and Machlipatnam to Calcutta, Agra, and Lahore. Among them, no single institution achieved more distinction, nor epitomized a more eclectic scholarly Anglicanism than St Stephen's College, Delhi.[39] It developed from a proposition of Brooke Foss Westcott,

[36] George Norton, *Native Education in India* (Madras, 1848), pp. 44–52.

[37] Eric J. Sharpe, *Not to Destroy but Fulfil: The Contribution of J. N. Farquhar to Protestant Missionary Thought before 1914* (Gleeup, Sweden, [1965]); J. N. Farquhar, *The Crown of Hinduism* (Oxford, 1813); John P. Jones, *India's Problem: An Essay toward the Interpretation of Hinduism and the Re-Statement of Christianity* (London, 1909).

[38] Bruce Tiebout McCully, *English Education and the Origins of Indian Nationalism* (New York, 1940), pp. 131–42.

[39] Nandini Chatterjee, 'Creating a Public Presence: The Missionary College of St. Stephen's, Delhi', in *The Making of Indian Secularism: Empire, Law and Christianity, 1830–1960* (London, 2011), pp. 109–33.

then regius professor of divinity at Cambridge and later bishop of Durham. Westcott was inspired by the work of Thomas Valpy French in Agra and Lahore, and proposed a new SPG college in Delhi. An avid reader of oriental philosophy, he held that no proper understanding of Christianity could ignore other religions. A small band of Oxbridge scholars dedicated to 'fulfilment theology'—the proposition that other religions are vouchsafed a partial revelation of God which finds fulfilment in the completeness of Christ[40]—would try to replicate Origen's Alexandria on the banks of the Jumna. The Cambridge Brotherhood, led by Samuel Scott Alnutt, opened the college in 1881.[41] Little did the founders realize that there would soon be a New Delhi and that this shift of India's capital would put them at the strategic centre of India. Two figures with strong nationalist convictions emerged at St Stephen's College—Charles Freer Andrews and Sushil Kumar Rudra.[42] They became fast friends. Indeed, Andrews would face down the SPG leaders to secure Rudra's appointment as principal of the college. This Bengali Anglican from a non-Brahman family would have a long and successful tenure.

Ironically, the grant-in-aid system of education initiated in 1854 would eventually undermine Christian missions. Most students at elite missionary schools and colleges came from families of affluent upper-caste *mahajans* who were not Christian. Such students were taught, more and more, by Indian teachers who also were not Christian. Younger generations of missionaries coming to India by the end of the nineteenth century, being more theologically broad-minded products of a post-Darwinian intellectual climate that enshrined 'scientific' Enlightenment, increasingly diluted claims of the gospel with 'civilization'. As funding pressures were exacerbated by dwindling voluntary contributions from 'home', missionaries tended to enhance the secularizing content of what was being taught in their schools.[43] A pattern emerged of increasing numbers of non-Christian Indian teachers, while European missionaries found themselves relegated to positions that were administrative or supervisory. In short, the 'grant-in-aid' system profoundly altered the agendas of academic institutions run by missionaries. Both explicitly and implicitly, orthodox Christian theology became marginalized within many schools and colleges.

[40] 'Christ the fulfiller' is extolled in T. E. Slater's *The Higher Hinduism in Relation to Christianity* (1909) and J. N. Farquhar's *The Crown of Hinduism* (1913); Sharpe, *Not to Destroy, but to Fulfil*; Brian Stanley, *The World Missionary Conference, Edinburgh 1910* (Grand Rapids, MI, 2009), pp. 205–47.

[41] C. M. Millington, *'Whether we be Many or Few': A History of the Cambridge/Delhi Brotherhood* (Bangalore, 1999).

[42] Hugh Tinker, *The Ordeal of Love: C. F. Andrews and India* (Delhi, 1979); Daniel O'Connor, *A Clear Star: C. F. Andrews and India, 1904–1914* (New Delhi, 2005), pp. 37–8.

[43] Hayden J. A. Bellenoit, 'Missionary Education, Knowledge and North Indian Society, *c.*1880–1915', DPhil thesis, University of Oxford, 2005.

As a consequence, what emerged out of elite mission colleges such as St Stephen's were classes of increasingly progressive and secularized nationalists. In addition, as the public influence of college-educated Indian Christians increased, so too their relationships with public institutions became more complex, convoluted, and sensitive.[44] Attempts to help peoples who were oppressed, landless, poor, and stigmatized brought new voluntary associations, both Christian and non-Christian, into competition with each other. The resulting dilemmas would never be fully or satisfactorily resolved.[45]

CELEBRATED HIGH-BORN CHRISTIAN LEADERS

Anglican emphasis on elite communities of North India led to the emergence of a number of high-profile Indian Christians. Those who were Anglicans, however, tended to have conflicted relations with the Church, and so some went their own way. One of the earliest, and most remarkable and renowned, was a disciple of the Simeonite chaplain Henry Martyn (1781–1812). Sheikh Salah Abdul Masih (1776–1827) came from a devout and prominent, upper-class (*ashraf*) family in Delhi. Thoroughly trained in Persian and Arabic, his path to faith began with reading Martyn's Urdu translation of the New Testament. After baptism in 1811 he became a co-worker of yet another Simeonite chaplain, Daniel Corrie. Seeking to influence Muslim elite (*ashraf*) communities, especially in Agra and Lucknow, he worked with the CMS. Yet, even as his fame spread, he realized that, despite invitations to royal *durbars*, or into *umara* and *'ulama* homes, his life was in danger. Pietist ordination in 1820 was followed, in 1825, by episcopal ordination from Bishop Heber. Engaged with ongoing disputations (*munazaras*) in Lucknow, he died suddenly and mysteriously after returning home to care for his ailing mother.[46]

Maulvi 'Imad ud-din (1830–1900) was the most noteworthy Anglican missionary to Muslims of India. Descended from traditions of high learning, he began as a Muslim preacher at the central mosque (*jama masjid*) of Agra. His anti-Christian rhetoric fuelled tensions between local *ulema* and missionaries. Later, as a wandering *faqir* in search of meaning, Urdu scriptures led him to the Christian faith. Ordained an Anglican clergyman and serving as a CMS missionary, he strove to convince upper-class Muslims that the *Injil* (gospel) could bring any person to God. In his Urdu publications,

[44] Chandra S. Mallampalli, *Christians and Public Life in Colonial South India, 1863–1937* (London, 2004).

[45] Jeffrey Cox, *Imperial Fault Lines: Christianity and Colonial Power, 1818–1940* (Stanford, CA, 2002); John C. B. Webster, *The Christian Community in Nineteenth Century North India* (Delhi, 1976).

[46] Avril Powell, *Muslims and Missionaries in Pre-Mutiny India* (London, 1993).

he declared that 'mission theology' was inadequate for Muslim–Christian understanding.[47]

Krishna Mohan Banerjea (1813–85), like many Calcutta gentry (*bhadralok*), became fluent in English. He had turned agnostic, if not atheist, before becoming a Christian. Baptized in 1832 by Alexander Duff, he received Anglican ordination in 1836 and pastored a city congregation until 1852. He then took a post at Bishop's College where he taught philosophy and wrote works challenging Brahmanical lore and the Brahmo Samaj. His *Dialogues on Hindu Philosophy* (1861) and service as chaplain to the bishop brought him acclaim.[48]

Brahmabandav Upadhyay (1861–1907),[49] another Bengali Brahman, was baptized an Anglican in 1891 but later became a 'Hindu' Roman Catholic. Abandoning his original name of Bhawani Charan Banerjea, and donning the saffron robes of an itinerant mendicant, he wanted Christian faith to conform to Vedic philosophy, and thus to reclaim India's ancient monotheism. Seeing himself as 'Hindu' by birth and 'Christian' by rebirth and ritual purity, his theology fitted 'fulfilment' fashions of the day. If Christianity in India were to last, it would need to be firmly rooted in the soil of India.

Nilakantha [Nehemiah] Sastri Goreh (1825–95) was a Chitpavan Brahman. While on pilgrimage in Varanasi, he encountered missionaries.[50] His Đ~stratattvavomormaya (1844) aimed to vanquish Christian thought. Instead, John Muir's *Mataparikṣha* radically altered his thinking. Muir was a devout Scottish Presbyterian and government officer and his irenic work was in Sanskriti verses entitled 'The Investigation of Religion' which marked a new, more tolerant attitude to Hinduism. Goreh's baptism in 1848 caused a public furore among elite Hindus. Migrating into High Church Anglicanism, he visited England in the 1850s as tutor to Maharaja Duleep Singh of Punjab. There he met Professor Max Müller and Queen Victoria. In his *Saddarshan Darpan*,[51] he pioneered the use of Sanskriti categories so as to refute non-Christian arguments. After his ordination in 1870, he increasingly worked with the Society of St John the Evangelist.[52] His sage counsel in 1873

[47] Powell, *Muslims and Missionaries*; Ernst Hahn, *The Life of the Rev. Malawi Dr. 'Imad ud-din Lahiz* (Vaniyambadi, 1978).

[48] T. V. Philip, *Krishna Mohan Banerjea, Christian Apologist* (Madras, 1982).

[49] Timothy C. Tennant, *Building Christianity on Indian Foundations: The Legacy of Brahmabandav Upadhyay* (Delhi, 2000); B. [Brahmachari Rewachand] Animananda, *The Blade: Life and Work of Brahmabandhab Upadhyay* (Calcutta, [1945]).

[50] Richard Fox Young, *Resistant Hinduism: Sanskrit Sources on Anti-Christian Apologetics in Early Nineteenth Century India* (Vienna, 1981), pp. 101ff.; C. E. Gardner, *The Life of Father Goreh* (London, 1900).

[51] Translated as *A Christian Response to the Hindu Philosophical Systems*, and re-introduced by K. P. Aleaz (Kolkata, 2003).

[52] Rowan Strong, 'Origins of Anglo-Catholic Missions: Fr Richard Benson and the Initial Missions of the Society of St John the Evangelist, 1869–1882', *Journal of Religious History*, 66 (2015): 103–8.

helped to convince Pandita Ramabai that Christian belief could be rationally grounded.

Pandita Ramabai [Medhavi Dongre] (1858–1922) was perhaps the most accomplished Indian Christian of her day.[53] A veritable 'Mahatma', she acquired an amazing blend of learning and insight. This wisdom rested upon a prodigious memory, instilled by her father who suffered for daring to transmit sacred Sanskriti lore to a female. Drilled for hours each day from infancy, she could recite an enormous corpus of lore, including grammars, dictionaries, and classical texts. In 1878 astounded *pandits* of Calcutta before whom she extemporaneously composed Sanskrit poetry pronounced her a *Pandita*, and added *Saraswati*. Her deep opposition to the Hindu treatment of women turned into a life-long campaign. After breaking caste and marrying a Bengali Kayastha attorney, she went with him to Assam. There she stumbled upon a Bengali Gospel of Luke. Soon widowed and caring for an infant daughter, she was invited to Pune by the social reformer Govind Ranade. There, while championing women's rights, she learned English with the wife of her host. Their teacher, an Anglo-Catholic nun from the Community of St Mary the Virgin (CSMV), Wantage, named Miss Hurford, used the Bible as a textbook. In 1882, invited to the CSMV's centre in Wantage, Ramabai accepted on condition that she might teach Sanskrit to fledgling missionary nuns. It was there that she was baptized. It was there also that, after a stormy relationship with the Mother Superior, she would later write: 'I have just with great efforts freed myself from the yoke of the Indian priestly tribe, I am . . . unwilling to place myself under a similar yoke.'[54] Baptism did not 'oblige a person to obey rules of uninspired men' but bound one 'only to Christ'.[55] As both 'Hindu' and 'Christian', Ramabai avoided all denominations but founded what became the Mukti (liberty) mission. With world-wide support, this rescued high-caste child widows but later reached out to all downtrodden women. Even as a spirit-filled revival broke out at Mukti and attracted wide attention she remained serene and increasingly retreated into scholarship. She had just completed a vernacular and less Sanskriti translation of the Bible into Marathi when she died.

Sadhu Sundar Singh (1889–1928?) was Sikh-Christian convert.[56] His initial abhorrence of Christianity was followed in 1904 by a stunning vision of Christ

[53] Meera Kosambi (ed. and trans.), *Pandita Ramabai Through Her Own Words* (Oxford, 2000); Robert Eric Frykenberg, 'Biographical Introduction', *Pandita Ramabai's America* (Grand Rapids, MI, 2000), pp. 1–54.

[54] Ramabai to Sister Geraldine (Ladies College, Cheltenham, 12 May 1885), in S. B. Shah (ed.), *Letters and Correspondence of Pandita Ramabai* (Bombay, 1977).

[55] Ramabai to Sister Geraldine, 7 Nov. 1885.

[56] A. J. Appasamy, *Sundar Singh* (London, 1958); C. F. Andrews, *Sadhu Sundar Singh* (London, 1934); Mrs Arthur [Rebecca Jane] Parker, *Sadhu Sundar Singh* (London, 1918); B. H. Streeter and A. J. Appasamy, *The Sadhu: A Study of Mysticism and Practical Religion* (London, 1921).

and baptism in Shimla. He soon donned the saffron robe of a mendicant, or *sadhu*. Instead of adapting to Western modes he declared, 'Indians need the Water of Life, but not the European cup.' Devoting himself to working among remote hill peoples, as a *bhakta* (one who follows the path of personal, pietistic devotion known as *bhakti*), he preferred ascetic and ecstatic utterances over the stuffy preaching of 'missionary churches'. Narratives of his daring adventures, dangers, and hardships, and his miraculous acts of healing appeared in Punjabi and Urdu publications; and then gained attention in the wider world. In 1918, speaking invitations came from abroad, and books about him appeared. C. F. Andrews became a close friend, as did B. H. Streeter and A. J. Appasamy. Appasamy, in *The Sadhu* (1921), saw him as a 'living mystic' or 'bhakti saint' whose analogies, anecdotes, and parables carried hidden meanings. Invited to England on a speaking tour, he was made much of by Anglicans whom he visited; but while several Anglicans identified themselves with him, his own identity remained vague. Sceptics, such the Jesuit Henry Hosten, warned against letting any *maharishi* or *swami* ('lord') divert attention from Christ. Sundar Singh's last years were marred by controversy and misunderstanding. In ill-health, he made a final mission to Tibet, in April 1929. This ended in his disappearance and he was never found.

CONCLUSION

Under Anglican (CMS and SPG) authority, Tamil Pietism not only survived, but thrived. This unique form of Tamil Christian *bhakti* (devotionalism), despite aggravations suffered in Thanjāvur and Tirunelvēli, could not be suppressed, confined, or defined by alien mores modelled in Europe. While no single language or culture could ever be inherently sacred, Tamil Pietists learned from experience that their language was capable of more perfectly expressing their faith. Various distinct Christianities emerged in India. The path blazed by Vedanayagam Sastriar, for example, would soon be followed by H. A. Krishna Pillai's epic *Irakshaniya* V~ttirikam. This work, modelled on *Pilgrim's Progress*, would eloquently demonstrate how Tamil appropriations of Christian truth could creatively enhance, rather than diminish, classic Christian verity.

What began in the Tamil south spread to the peoples of Kerala, to Kannadika and Telugu peoples, to Bombay (now Maharashtra and Gujarat), and thence north to the Indo-Gangetic Plain, stretching from Punjab eastwards beyond Assam. Fresh 'mass' movements broke out among lowly (*ãvarna*) communities in the late nineteenth and early twentieth centuries. Wholesale conversions took place among aboriginal tribal (*ãdivasi*) peoples on the forested and mountainous frontiers of the north-east. Virtually all such movements occurred among non-Anglicans. Nevertheless, Anglicans, while heavily engaged with elite communities, also benefited by proximity to mass movements led by non-Anglican missionaries. Such was the case with converts from the lowest castes—e.g. Chuhras of Punjab, Bhangis and Chamars of U.P. (United Provinces of Agra & Oudh), Mahars of Central and Western India, Madigas and Malas of the Telugu of the eastern south, and Paraiyars and Pulaiyars of the deep south. In every case, converts from these communities were absorbed into Anglican churches.[57]

Thus, while the Noble College (CMS) catered to upper caste, mainly Brahman students of Andhra, low caste Madigas and Malas began to turn Christian during the 1870s, along with some middle caste Kammas and Reddis. These movements, initially led by American Baptist and Lutheran missionaries, spilled over into the CMS work of Henry Watson Fox around Bezwada (aka Vijayawada).[58] Yet, nowhere did Madiga/Mala conversions become more significant than in Dornakal. The movement in Dornakal was led by Bishop Vedanayagam Samuel Azariah (of Megnanapuram, Tirunelvēli).[59] Azariah, the protégé of Bishop Henry Whitehead of Madras, became Anglicanism's first Indian bishop in 1912. Whitehead, like Bishop Reginald Copleston (1902–13), was an avid student of religions in South India. Heading the Oxford Mission to Calcutta that began in 1879, two years after the Cambridge Mission to Delhi, he tried to resuscitate the by then moribund Bishop's College. That such ardent Anglo-Catholics could become equally ardent supporters of ecumenism and mass evangelism can be seen as a harbinger of things to come, foreshadowing the disestablishment of 1929/1930. One missionary critic wondered how bishops, as 'State Officials' in India pledged to strict religious neutrality, could directly engage in evangelizing activity.[60] The large accessions in Dornakal posed a crisis that could only be resolved by disestablishment. Azariah, like Rudra, was an ardent nationalist; but unlike Rudra and Andrews, both friends of Gandhi, he evoked the opposition of Gandhi. Gandhi saw events in Dornakal as draining away voters from the 'Hindu majority'; and, hence, as a threat to *swaraj*—'self-rule' or 'self-government'.[61] As Indian Christian leaders joined the national movement, Anglican Christendom in India became impossible. Azariah himself would become the champion of a national Church. Ecumenical union would run through Tranquebar (1919) and end with the founding of the Churches of South India and North India. Strivings for an Anglican Christendom in India would cease; but Anglican episcopacy would remain.

[57] John C. B. Webster, *A History of the Dalit Christians of India* (San Francisco, 1991).

[58] H. V. Elliott, *A Memoir of the Rev. Watson Fox, B.A., of Wadham College, Oxford, Missionary to the Teloogoo People* (London, 1850).

[59] Harper, *In the Shadow of the Mahatma*, pp. 120–33.

[60] Bernard Lucas, *Harvest Field*, XXXII, 9 (1912).

[61] As defined in *Chambers 20th Century Dictionary* (Edinburgh, 1983), p. 1305.

SELECT BIBLIOGRAPHY

Brown, Judith M. and Robert E. Frykenberg (eds.), *Christians, Cultural Interactions and India's Religious Traditions* (Grand Rapids, MI, 2002).

Chatterton, Eyre, *A History of the Church of England in India since the Early Days of the East India Company* (London, 1924).

Cox, Jeffrey, *Imperial Fault Lines: Christianity and Colonial Power in India, 1818–1940* (Stanford, CA, 2002).

Frykenberg, Robert Eric, *Christianity in India: From Beginnings to the Present* (Oxford, 2010).

Frykenberg, Robert Eric (ed.), *Christians and Missionaries in India: Cross-Cultural Communication since 1500, with Special Reference to Caste, Conversion, and Colonialism* (Grand Rapids, MI, 2003).

Harper, Susan Billington, *In the Shadow of the Mahatma: Bishop V. S. Azariah and the Travails of Christianity in British India* (Grand Rapids, MI, 2000).

Kaye, John W., *Christianity in India: A Historical Narrative* (London, 1855).

Kosambi, Meera (ed. and trans.), *Pandita Ramabai: Through Her Own Words* (Delhi and Oxford, 2000).

Kumaradoss, Vincent, *Robert Caldwell: A Scholar-Missionary in Colonial South India* (Delhi, 2007).

Mallampalli, Chandra, *Christians and Public Life in Colonial South India, 1863–1937* (London, 2004).

Millington, C. M., *'Whether we be Many or Few': A History of the Cambridge/Delhi Brotherhood* (Bangalore, 1999).

Muthuraj, Jospeh G., *We Began in Tranquebar*: volume I: *SPCK, the Danish-Halle Mission and Anglican Episcopacy (1706)*; volume II: *The Origin and Development of Anglican-CSI Episcopacy in India (1813–1947)* (Delhi, 2010).

Neill, Stephen, *A History of Christianity in India 1707–1858* (Cambridge, 1985).

Newbigen, Leslie, *Foolishness to Greeks: The Gospel and Western Culture* (Grand Rapids, MI, 1986).

Newbigen, Leslie, *The Gospel in a Pluralist Society* (Grand Rapids, MI, 1989).

Paul, Rajaiah D., *Chosen Vessels: Lives of Ten Indian Christian Pastors of the Eighteenth and Nineteenth Centuries* (Madras, 1961).

Richter, Julius, *A History of Missions in India* (Edinburgh and London, 1908). Translation of *Indische Missionsgeschichte* (1906) by Sydney H. Moore.

Studdert-Kennedy, Gerald, *Providence & the Raj: Imperial Mission and Missionary Imperialism* (New Delhi, 1998).

Sundkler, Bengt, *Church of South India: The Movement Towards Union, 1900–1947* (London, 1954).

15

Anglicanism in China and East Asia, 1819–1912

Philip L. Wickeri

CHINA

The Christian tradition in East Asia began with the arrival of missionaries from the Church of the East (the so-called Nestorians) in the late seventh century in Chang'an (Xi'an), the capital of China's Tang Dynasty. The Church of the East attempted to establish a Church and adapt to Chinese culture, but the extent to which it attracted Chinese adherents remains unclear. The mission was active in China until the end of the ninth century, but it suffered persecution, and all that survived were some of their monuments and writings that inspired subsequent generations of Western missionaries and Chinese Christians. In the thirteenth century, the Church of the East again came to China and established churches, primarily among non-Han Chinese peoples. Sorghaghtani Beki (d. 1252), the mother of Kublai Khan, became a Christian voice for religious toleration at the ruling Mongol court. Franciscan envoys and missionaries came around the same time. Both traditions continued until the fifteenth century, after which they also disappeared from the scene.

Beginning in the late sixteenth century, Matteo Ricci and the Jesuits initiated a sustained dialogue with Chinese culture and built churches all over the country. Franciscans and Dominicans came somewhat later, but they opposed the Jesuits' approach to engagement with Chinese culture. By the late seventeenth century, Roman Catholics were present in many parts of the Qing Empire. However, in 1715, Pope Clement XI condemned the Chinese Rites of the Jesuits, favouring the more European views of the other religious orders. When he heard of the reaction in Rome, the Yongzheng Emperor no longer allowed Catholic missionaries of any kind to continue their religious work. Christianity all but disappeared for a third time. However, Jesuit and Chinese writings from this period on theology, science, geography, and many other subjects are extensive.

It is important to recall the early attempts to establish Christianity in China, both because they have shaped the history of Chinese Anglicanism, and because they are regarded by Anglicans to be part of a catholic tradition that they share.[1] This early history also illustrates an enduring theme in Anglican history: the encounter between Christianity and non-Western cultures. In China, with its long and turbulent history, the foreignness of Christianity and the need for indigenization or contextualization has been a continuing challenge for Anglicanism.

The arrival of Robert Morrison in Macau in 1807 began a new era of Christian mission in China. From then until the mid-twentieth century, missionaries from many countries and Churches, Protestant, Catholic, Orthodox, and Anglican, came to China to spread the gospel. Throughout this period, the development of Chinese Christianity was both facilitated and impeded by the forces of colonialism and empire. All Christian Churches benefited from their association with Western cultural aggression against China. Protestant Churches developed slowly, but they continued to be seen as foreign or colonial.[2] Indeed, it could be said that Anglicanism, more than other Protestant denominations, was closely linked with the Anglo-American project to carve out a sphere of influence in China, making use of their superior military, political, and economic power.

Morrison was a Presbyterian sent to China by the London Missionary Society and employed as a translator by the East India Company. He pioneered Protestant translation work, and prepared the way for those who would follow.[3] One of the earliest terms he (or one of his Chinese assistants) suggested for the translation of 'Christianity' was *shenggonghui*, or 'Holy Catholic Church'.[4] The translation was consistent with what had been written in the early creeds and suggested the universality of the faith for those who had never heard of Christianity. However, the transliterated term *jidujiao*, the religion of Christ, became the preferred term for Protestants to differentiate themselves from the Roman Catholics who had been in China since the sixteenth century and who were known as the religion of the 'Lord of Heaven' (*tianzhujiao*). Protestant Churches and mission societies also wanted to differentiate themselves from one another. By the mid-nineteenth century, denominational names were fixed, and *shenggonghui* became the accepted name for the Church that British Anglican and American Episcopalian missionaries were trying to establish in China.[5]

[1] Shiu Keung Lee, *The Cross and the Lotus* (Hong Kong, 1971).

[2] Norman Etherington (ed.), *Missions and Empire* (Oxford, 2008).

[3] Christopher A. Daily, *Robert Morrison and the Protestant Plan for China* (Hong Kong, 2013); Christopher Hancock, *Robert Morrison and the Birth of Chinese Protestantism* (London, 2008).

[4] Robert Morrison, *Daily Order of Morning Prayer Throughout the Year* (Malacca, 1818).

[5] G. F. S. Gray with Martha Lund Smalley, *Anglicans in China: A History of the Zhonghua Shenggong Hui (Chung Hua Sheng Kung Hui)* (New Haven, CT, 1996).

The first Anglican priests in China were not missionaries, but chaplains attached to the British East India Company in Macau, sent to serve the foreign community. Morrison and the Anglicans did not always see eye to eye. In one letter he writes:

> High church people, priests and laymen, have goaded me by sneers and implied insults. I suppose such is a specimen of their general behaviour and will be so as long as Church and State are joined—and will even survive it—for the same sects there, like the papists look with scorn on all others. Now in the midst of this evil, I would not drive away the liturgical services of older time. They never get angry. They always, by the Press, breathe benevolence and love.[6]

But Anglican and Protestant missionaries from other denominations, especially those from Britain and the United States, generally worked well together in the early decades of the nineteenth century.[7] In 1821 George H. Vachell, an Anglican priest, conducted the funeral for Morrison's first wife, Mary, while Morrison was still away in Canton.[8] Macau was the entry point for missionaries from the Western missionary societies in the early nineteenth century, just as it had been for the Roman Catholics who went to China three hundred years earlier. Only after the First Opium War and the signing of the Treaty of Nanking (1842) were missionaries legally able to establish themselves in other parts of China.

THE AMERICAN EPISCOPAL CHURCH MISSION IN NINETEENTH-CENTURY CHINA

The Domestic and Foreign Missionary Society of the Protestant Episcopal Church in America appointed its first missionaries to China in 1835.[9] Henry Lockwood and Francis R. Hanson arrived in Canton late that year, but they were met with hostility by the local population and were unable to do any work, or even study the Chinese language.[10] They relocated to Singapore, and

[6] Letters from his father, the Revd Robert Morrison (1824–1834), 118/2 Macao, 21 March 1834. Endorsed 'March 23, 1834', Wellcome Library Western Manuscripts and Archives, MS5829. This quotation was called to my attention by Professor John Carroll, Hong Kong University.

[7] Murray A. Rubenstein, *The Origins of the Anglo-American Missionary Enterprise in China, 1807–1840* (Lanham, MD, 1996).

[8] Lindsay and May Ride, *An East India Company Cemetery: Protestant Burials in Macao* (Hong Kong, 1998), p. 234.

[9] Meimei Lin, 'The Episcopalian Missionaries in China, 1835–1900', PhD thesis, University of Texas at Austin, 1994.

[10] 'The Mission to China: From the Missionaries, the Rev. Messsers Hanson and Lockwood', *The Spirit of Missions*, 1 (1836): 79–81.

then to Batavia, to work among overseas Chinese, seeing this as a way to prepare for future work in China. Both left Asia after just a few years, and the work of the mission fell to William James Boone (1811–64), who had been appointed a missionary in 1837. Boone may be regarded as the founder of the American Church Mission (or the Protestant Episcopal China Mission, PECM), as the China branch of the Domestic and Foreign Missionary Society.

Boone and his wife moved the mission back to China in 1840, settling first in Macau, and then, in 1842, in Amoy (Xiamen). In 1844, Boone was consecrated bishop of Amoy and other parts of China by the Protestant Episcopal Church in the United States of America.[11] He thus became the first bishop of China outside the East Syrian or Roman Catholic tradition. He was also the first bishop in the Anglican Communion consecrated for strictly foreign service. Together with several missionary colleagues and their families, Boone moved to Shanghai the following year, and this became the base of the PECM. Shanghai, like Amoy, was one of the treaty ports open to foreign missionaries after the Treaty of Nanjing (1842), where they enjoyed the privileges of 'extraterritoriality' (exemption from Chinese law) extracted by the foreign powers. The city became the base of most Churches engaged in missionary work in China. There was little anti-foreignism in Shanghai in the 1850s and 1860s, and even the Taiping Rebellion (1850–64), the most widespread and destructive movement in nineteenth-century China, had little effect on the Foreign Settlement and mission work there.

Boone was joined by other United States missionaries and clergy, most of whom were from Virginia Theological Seminary. They established churches, contributed to the translation of the Bible and the Book of Common Prayer (American version), and began educational and medical services. Boone ordained the first Chinese priest, Huang Guangcai, in 1863, who had been previously ordained a deacon in 1851. He had accompanied the Boone family on their trip to America in 1843–6, where Bishop Boone was raising funds and support for their work in China, and later became the first Christian convert in the PECM. Huang served as priest in the PECM for more than three decades. Unlike many other missions, it was PECM policy to encourage Chinese leadership in the Church.

The work of the PECM declined during the American Civil War because of the lack of funding, and the number of missionaries was reduced from twenty-eight to six. With the treaties ending the Second Opium War in 1860, missionary work in China expanded, and by 1864 there were more than two hundred missionaries representing twenty-four Churches and societies of all denominations. Bishop Boone died in 1865, and his successor Channing Moore Williams (1829–1910) was named missionary bishop of both China

[11] Gray, *Anglicans in China*, p. 10.

and Japan. Williams was in Tokyo at the time he was made bishop, but he returned to Shanghai to preside over a growing diocese and missionary force. During Williams's tenure, there were more confirmations than in the previous twenty years combined. More Chinese also became enrolled in church schools, and foundations for a church hospital were laid. Bishop Williams established himself in Tokyo in 1869, and thereafter visited China on a yearly basis. This was an interim solution due to the shortage of personal until the full separation of Japan from the diocese of Shanghai in 1873.

Beginning in 1868, the PECM began work in the central Chinese city of Wuchang, in what later became the diocese of Hankow (1901). Bishop Logan H. Roots (1870–1945), the second bishop of Hankow, had a long and distinguished career as both churchman and prominent figure in Chinese social and political circles unlike most Anglican and Episcopal bishops. In 1910, the PECM started a third diocese in Anqing in the province of Anhui, where mission work had been going on for some time. The three dioceses brought together American Episcopalian work up and down the Yang-Tze (Yangzi) River, creating a network of churches, schools, hospitals, and social service centres.

Although small in the number of adherents (never more than two or three thousand members), the PECM became influential in the social and intellectual life of late nineteenth-century China. This may be attributed to its top-down approach to mission work. The PECM was interested in the training of an elite Chinese who would become leaders in Church and society. Already in the nineteenth century, Episcopalians had begun to train renowned priests and church workers, as well as first-class educators, scholars, and professionals.[12] To accomplish the task of preparing a Chinese Christian elite, the Domestic and Foreign Missionary Society sent out missionaries, most of whom were involved in education.

Among these was Lydia Mary Fay (1804–78), who came to China when she was forty-six, far older than most Western missionaries entering the mission field.[13] She was put in charge of a boarding school, and for almost thirty years was a pioneering educator in Shanghai. Fay studied Chinese every day, and became widely recognized as both a linguist and a sinologist. In 1876 she helped to start Duane Hall, a secondary school which later became part of Shanghai's St John's College, the predecessor of St John's University. Fay worked alongside other PECM missionaries, women and men, who contributed to the reputation of the mission as a leading educational institution. It should be added that the PECM pioneered in sending well-educated single

[12] Edward Yihua Xu, 'The Protestant Episcopal China Mission and Chinese Society', in Philip L. Wickeri (ed.), *Christian Encounters with Chinese Culture: Essays on Anglican and Episcopal History in China* (Hong Kong, 2015), pp. 25–46.

[13] Ian Welch, 'Lydia Mary Fay and the Episcopal Church Mission in China', *International Bulletin of Missionary Research*, 36 (2012): 33–7.

women missionaries to China; most other societies did not do so until the late nineteenth century.

Due to the strong interest of the PECM in the development of Chinese leadership it ordained Chinese priests much more quickly than any of the British missionary societies. Among the outstanding priests and Chinese intellectuals from this period was Yen Yun-ching (Yan Yongjing, 1838–98). One of the first Chinese to study in the United States, Yen became a renowned educator, translator, and advocate for social justice.[14] He was regarded as the equal of his missionary colleagues, and enjoyed the same salary and benefits as they, something that was unusual in the nineteenth century. Yan helped to start Boone University in Wuchang, and was also the first principal of St John's College in Shanghai (1879).

The creative force behind that college was Samuel I. J. Schereschewsky (1831–1906), who became one of the most well-known missionaries of nineteenth-century China. He was a Lithuanian Jew who converted to Christianity after emigrating to the United States.[15] Schereschewsky went to China in 1859, and soon moved to Peking, where he was the first American missionary. There he did language study and urged all missionaries to study Chinese 'seven hours a day' as he had done. A gifted linguist, Schereschewsky helped translate the Bible and the first full Chinese edition of the Book of Common Prayer. This he translated with Bishop John Burden from the Church of England; it was based on the 1662 English Prayer Book, but also contained elements from the 1789 American version. Schereschewsky became the third bishop of Shanghai in 1877 (he had declined the appointment twice, before and after the resignation of Bishop Williams), but his gifts were never in administration. Together with his successor, he effectively defended the Church in the 'Ritualism controversy' (1882–3), when some Evangelical missionaries opposed the introduction of more liturgical services in Shanghai parishes. Schereschewsky strongly believed in mission through higher education, and in the necessity of a native ministry. He expanded the work of Chinese catechists and priests in the churches. The college he founded on the outskirts of Shanghai grew to become St John's University (incorporated in 1907), one of the best Christian institutions of higher education in China.[16]

[14] Edward Yihua Xu, 'Westernization and Contextualization: A Study on Three Pioneering Chinese Pastors of the Sheng Kung Hui in China', in Peter Chen-Main Wang (ed.), *Contextualization of Christianity in China: An Evaluation in Modern Perspective* (Sankt Augustin, Germany, 2007), pp. 183–206.

[15] James Arthur Muller, *Apostle of China: Samuel Isaac Joseph Schereschewsky, 1831–1906* (New York, 1937); Irene Eber, *The Jewish Bishop and the Chinese Bible: S. I. J. Schereschewsky, 1831–1906* (Leiden, 1999).

[16] Xu Yihua, 'St. John's University, Shanghai as an Evangelising Agency', *Studies in World Christianity*, 12 (2006): 23–49; Xiong Yuezhi and Zhou Wu (eds.), *Sheng Yuehan Daxue Shi* [History of St. John's University] (Shanghai, 2007).

William James Boone (1846–91), son of the first Bishop Boone, succeeded Schereschewsky and resolved the many internal difficulties facing the PECM. There had been some dissatisfaction with Bishop Schereschewsky among the seasoned missionary leadership, who tended to be more conservative theologically. Bishop Boone was similar to his predecessor theologically, but was a capable administrator, and was more familiar with the history of PECM work in Shanghai. He also expanded work in education, and was succeeded by Frederick Rogers Graves (1858–1940). His episcopate of forty-four years made him the longest serving bishop in China. He was a capable administrator with a rigid frame of mind. Nevertheless, Graves fostered friendly relationships with the British societies, and played a leading role in efforts toward Church unity examined in the following. However, by the 1920s, he had alienated the Chinese clergy who wanted a faster pace of devolution and indigenization.

THE CHURCH MISSIONARY SOCIETY AND OTHER BRITISH SOCIETIES IN CHINA

From Britain there was a separate missionary beginning, one that began with the founding of the British Crown Colony of Hong Kong in 1842. Hong Kong, because of this imperial possession, would continue to have a special place in Chinese Anglican history right up to the present day. In 1843, Vincent Stanton was appointed Colonial Chaplain to Hong Kong. He had been in South China some years before, having gone out on his own because he was too young and impetuous for missionary service. He was even imprisoned by the Chinese during this earlier stay. With his new appointment, he began to organize the Anglican community in Hong Kong, and took tentative steps to reach out to the Chinese community.

In 1807 the CMS set up a fund to reprint the Hans Sloane Chinese Bible at the British Museum. This was a partial translation done by Roman Catholics in the eighteenth century, a copy of which Robert Morrison used to begin his own study of Chinese. The CMS later contributed to the evangelical work of the controversial German missionary Karl Gutzlaff on the China coast. But the CMS wanted to become more directly involved in evangelistic work in China, though it was not until 1836 that the first CMS missionary went to Singapore, 'and thence to make journeys to Chinese ports as he might find possible'.[17] This exploration did not amount to much. Eight years later, CMS missionaries George Smith and Thomas McClatchie went to China on an exploratory visit.

[17] Eugene Stock, *The History of the Church Missionary Society: Its Environment, Its Men and Its Work*, 3 vols. (London, 1899), I, p. 468.

They toured South China and eventually settled in Shanghai.[18] By this time, Stanton had already begun to raise funds for St John's Cathedral and St Paul's College in Hong Kong, both of which were opened in 1849.[19]

That same year the diocese of Victoria was created by letters patent, and George Smith appointed the first bishop. His was the largest diocese in the world at that time for it included all of China plus Japan. But it was a claim that ignored the PECM, already well established in Shanghai. However, the Americans, after some negotiation, agreed that the bishop of Victoria would have jurisdiction over British clergy in the city. The letters patent authorized the diocese to provide oversight and pastoral care to members of the Church of England only, but both Bishop Smith and the CMS missionaries who followed him were very much interested in evangelism in China. CMS work had already begun in the treaty port city of Foochow (Fuzhou), which would become an important centre for Anglican work in China. The early bishops of Victoria spent much of their time in Fukien (Fujian), Kwangtung (Guangdong), and other parts of South China.

In 1872, the diocese of Victoria was reduced to China south of the twenty-eighth parallel, and Smith's successor, Bishop Charles Alford (1816–98), resigned over what he considered a slight to his authority. He was succeeded by John Shaw Burdon (1826–1907), who already had considerable experience in China and was a linguist and China scholar. In South China the CMS had an approach to mission which was much the opposite of that of the PECM. It was grassroots oriented, but the missionaries were always in control. In Fujian and Guangdong, the CMS started many rural churches and service centres, and schools were also important in the cities. Notwithstanding their grassroots approach the CMS did not promote Chinese leadership as quickly as the Americans, and by the end of the century there were only six Chinese priests in Fukien and one in Hong Kong. This may reveal a difference in approaches to indigenization and trust in a 'native clergy' between British Anglicans and the more flexible American Episcopalians.

The PECM and CMS did cooperate on areas of common interest, the most important of which was in translation work. Joseph Schereschewsky and John Burdon became friends in Peking when they were engaged in language study—Burdon was the first Anglican missionary in the capital city, and Schereschewsky sometimes spoke at CMS services. By the late 1860s, they had translated most of the Book of Common Prayer (BCP) into Chinese, and the full translation was published in 1872. Schereschewsky and Burdon used the Roman Catholic term for God (*tianzhu*) in their translation, but the more

[18] George Smith, *A Narrative of an Exploratory Visit to East of the Consular Cities of China and to the Islands of Hong Kong and Chusan in Behalf of the Church Missionary Society in the Years 1844, 1845, 1846* (London, 1847 edn.).

[19] George B. Endacott and Dorothy E. She, *The Diocese of Victoria, Hong Kong: A Hundred Years of Church History, 1849–1949* (Hong Kong, 1949), pp. 1–14; Stuart Wolfendale, *Imperial to International: A History of St. John's Cathedral, Hong Kong* (Hong Kong, 2013).

common mainline Protestant term for God (*shangdi*) was eventually adopted by Anglicans. There were many other versions of the BCP translated or partially translated in the nineteenth century, but the 1872 Chinese BCP became the most widely accepted. It was authoritative because of the elegance of its literary Chinese and its acceptance by both the CMS and the PECM. Burdon and Schereschewsky also worked on Bible translation as part of a committee that included representatives from several other denominations.

Other British missions entered China in the second half of the century, the most important of which was the Society for the Propagation of the Gospel in Foreign Parts (SPG), which began work in Peking in 1863. This beginning ended after only one year, and it was not until 1874 that the SPG would again start work in North China. The SPG mission was supported from 1880 onward by the North China and Shantung Mission Association, a society based in England and primarily involved in fundraising activity. Charles Perry Scott (1847–1927) was consecrated as bishop of Peking in 1880, after an anonymous gift had been made in England for the bishopric of North China, and he served for thirty-three years. His diocese included five Chinese provinces. By this time the CMS had been working in North China for seventeen years, but without much success, and it handed over its twenty-six church members to the care of the SPG. The SPG established schools and engaged in welfare work, but the church itself never became very large compared with other parts of China or other Protestant bodies in Peking, perhaps because too little attention was devoted to personal or direct evangelism, and missionary energy was directed to building up the church, schools, and welfare agencies as institutions. In 1903, Shantung (Shandong) became a separate diocese under the authority of the SPG. The first bishop of Shantung, G. D. Iliff, emphasized the need for mission and evangelism to be done by the Chinese themselves, drawing on the ideas of Henry Venn. He set up the first training schools in North China for this purpose.

Roland Allen (1868–1947), the best-known SPG missionary, took Venn's idea of establishing a Church run by and for Chinese even further. He went to China in 1895, and stayed until a few weeks after the end of the Boxer Uprising in 1901. He went back to China for a few years later, but was invalided home. The Boxers (or Righteous and Harmonious Fists) were a nativist collection of rebels who set out to drive foreigners and Christianity out of China, but in the end were defeated and humiliated by foreign armies. In part, as a result of his first-hand experience of the Boxers, Allen later wrote about 'the imperialism of missions in China' and the missionary movement as embracing a dominating ideology for the subjugation of non-Western peoples and their emerging Churches.[20] Allen developed a trenchant critique of the missionary movement

[20] Roland Allen, 'The Imperialism of Missions in China', *The Living Church* (26 Jan. 1929), pp. 435–6.

that was far ahead of its time. His radical approach was for missionaries to go to a place and then leave once they had set up a local church. However, there were few Anglicans who paid attention to Allen at the time.

Other Anglican mission societies also entered the China field.[21] The Church of England Zenana Mission (CEZMS), founded in India, was a women's missionary society that worked closely with the CMS. It began work in Fukien (Fujian) and South China in 1884, sending single women missionaries to do 'women's work for women'. The Dublin University Mission began to send male missionaries to Fukien in 1887, also in cooperation with the CMS. They were university graduates who initially worked mainly in the area of education.

British and Commonwealth Anglicans also participated in interdenominational societies that sent missionaries to China. These included the Society for Promoting Female Education in the East (FES), which began work in China very early (1837). The women sent out by FES tended to be fiercely independent and involved in education and welfare work.[22] Their goal was to raise the status of women, and so they often came into conflict with the male-only ecclesiastical hierarchies. The YMCA and the YWCA went to China in the late nineteenth century, and had both Anglican and Episcopal staff who were unrelated to the PECM or the British societies.

The most important of the interdenominational societies was the China Inland Mission (CIM), founded by James Hudson Taylor (1832–1905) in London in 1865. The CIM was an international Evangelical faith mission based in China but supported by 'home centres' in many countries. It was not a denomination, but it became the largest Protestant mission in China, working at the grassroots, in remote regions inland, and far away from the growing urban centres. The CIM cooperated with the CMS and other societies, and Evangelical Anglicans were attracted to the CIM with its emphasis on revivalism, direct evangelism, and conversion of the heart. The Australian CIM was founded in 1890 and would send Anglican missionaries to China and Hong Kong for the next half-century. Anglicans in the CIM took responsibility for the diocese of Western China, started in 1895.

The CMS became the largest Anglican missionary society in China, although it had nowhere near the number of missionaries as the CIM. The number of CMS dioceses grew in the late nineteenth century. The Mid-China diocese was created in 1880, and it later divided into West China (Sichuan, in 1895) and Chekiang (Zhejiang, in1909); Fukien (Fujian, in 1906); and

[21] R. G. Tiedemann, *Reference Guide to Christian Missionary Societies in China: From the Sixteenth to the Twentieth Century* (Armonk, NY, 2009).

[22] Patricia P. K. Chiu, 'Female Education and the Early Development of St. Stephen's Church, Hong Kong (1865–1900s)', in Wickeri (ed.), *Christian Encounters with Chinese Culture*, pp. 47–64.

Kwangsi-Hunan (in 1909). A special area of interest was work with leprosy, and the CMS established important leprosaria in Kwangtung and Chekiang (Zhejiang).[23] Bishop George E. Moule (1828–1912) was the first bishop of Mid-China, and he developed Chekiang into a strong diocese second only to Fukien. Bishop Moule was joined in CMS work by his brother, and the Moule family became well known in Britain for both their mission work and sinological interests. The CMS was also active in opposing the continuing opium trade. In part because of the society's efforts, Archbishop Frederick Temple issued a statement against the opium trade at a special meeting held at Lambeth in 1902.

By the end of the nineteenth century, the coastal province of Fukien, which was under CMS jurisdiction, had the largest number of Anglicans in China—almost 13,000 adherents. There were 169 CMS schools and 224 Chinese workers in the diocese,[24] including fifteen native clergy. Most of the male missionaries were related to the Dublin University mission, and many of the women were related to the CEZMS. Fukien, by the middle of the twentieth century, had almost half the total number of Anglicans in China. Anglicans, however, were never more than 10 per cent of the Protestant population in Fukien at any time. Anglican liturgy was not accessible to rural people and those with limited education were attracted by the simplicity and fervour of other denominations, including Methodists, Presbyterians, and indigenous Protestant Churches who were also active in the province.

The expansion of the missionary presence in Fukien and elsewhere sometimes generated hostile responses from many sectors of the local Chinese populace. The Boxer Rebellion in the north was but one example of this. More broadly, 'missionary cases' involving Christians from many denominations were taken to the courts or resolved in international negotiations from the 1860s onward. These cases were seen by Chinese as examples of foreign meddling in Chinese affairs.[25] Chinese political and religious interests, the landed gentry, and traditional intellectuals opposed Christianity and its association with the foreign powers and privileges granted by the unequal treaties that ended the Opium Wars. Missionaries were often the only foreigners that Chinese came into contact with, and their presence and activity sometimes provoked violent attacks against them and their Chinese converts. The largest case involving Anglican (CMS) missionaries was the Huashan-Kutien Massacre in Fukien in 1895, in some sense comparable to the Boxer Rebellion.

[23] Zhou Donghua, 'The Anglican Church and the Treatment of Leprosy in Modern Fuzhou', conference paper, Learning from the Past, Looking to the Future: Anglican-Episcopal History in China and Its Impact on the Church Today (Hong Kong, 7–9 June 2012).

[24] Ryan Dunch, *Fuzhou Protestants and the Making of a Modern China, 1857–1927* (New Haven, CT, 2001), p. 20.

[25] Paul A. Cohen, *The Missionary Movement and the Growth of Chinese Anti-Foreignism, 1860–1870* (Cambridge, MA, 1967 edn.).

Sparked by the anti-foreignism of a local religious group, several missionary families were killed.

As a British possession, Hong Kong was by and large spared from violent anti-foreignism. The diocese of Victoria was seen as the colonial bishopric for the British possession of the island of Hong Kong, Kowloon, and the New Territories (leased in 1898). The first six bishops of Victoria were all CMS men, and the society's presence in Hong Kong continued well into the twentieth century. Although the diocese was initially under the Colonial Office, it was, in effect, disestablished and disendowed by government decree in 1892. Henceforth, the Church in Hong Kong would increasingly develop its own means of support, although education and social service work would continue to receive government funding and patronage. By the end of the century, the CMS had established only three Chinese churches in Hong Kong, but a new consciousness of the need for a Chinese Anglicanism was slowly beginning to develop.

Anglicans also played an important role in establishing a mission to seafarers, in Hong Kong and other cities on the China coast.[26] Closely related to this work were the chaplaincies established in the treaty ports along the China coast for the English residents. In the late nineteenth century, Bishop Hoare (1851–1906) of the diocese of Victoria regularized and expanded the work of these consular chaplaincies.[27] This work developed out of the close relationship between the Church of England and its missionaries and British government agencies and officials in China.

JAPAN

It is possible that missionaries and merchants from the Church of the East visited Korea and Japan in the Tang Dynasty, but no incontrovertible evidence of their presence has ever been found. Francis Xavier is seen as the founder of Roman Catholic missionary work in Japan in the sixteenth century. That Church flourished there for more than a century, but with a change in government it suffered severe persecution and was driven underground. Japanese Catholics were then cut off from the rest of the Church until the mid-nineteenth century.

Commodore Matthew Perry of the United States Navy opened Japan for foreign residence and commerce in 1854. Five years later, John Liggins and

[26] Stephen Davies, *Strong to Save: The Story of the Mariners' Club, Hong Kong: 1863–2013* (Hong Kong, forthcoming).

[27] G. A. Bunbury, 'Episcopate of Bishop Joseph Charles Hoare, 1898–1906', Hong Kong Public Records Office [henceforth HKPRO], HKMS 94-1-5, fos. 3–4.

Channing Moore Williams went to Nagasaki from China to become the first United States Episcopalian missionaries in the country. They at first worked mainly among English and American businessmen and their families, because the government forbade religious work among the Japanese people, and in any case they did not speak Japanese. Liggins had to leave Japan because of ill health. Williams lived in a Buddhist temple, and spent much of his time studying the Japanese language and translating the Book of Common Prayer from the draft Chinese version into Japanese. He opened the first Episcopal church in Nagasaki in 1864.

Japan had already been claimed in 1849 as part of the Diocese of Victoria and Bishop George Smith made a visitation in 1860 to survey the territory, but cautioned against beginning missionary work there because of Japan's isolation.[28] It would also spread the resources of an already hard-pressed mission too thinly. His successor Bishop Alford also visited Japan in 1868 and met with Williams, but also made no effort to begin mission work in Japan. The Meiji Restoration of 1867 opened up the country to trade and commerce, and missionary work among the Japanese could begin.

British interest in Japan had been stirred by the Loochoo Naval Mission on the Ryukyu Islands (then under Chinese suzerainty). This mission supported the work of B. J. Bettelheim from 1845 to 1854, but it was discontinued after that. The CMS began its Japan mission in 1868 with the arrival of George Ensor, the first British missionary in the country. The first SPG missionaries, William Ball Wright and Alexander Croft Shaw, arrived in Yokohama in September 1873. By this time, Japan was no longer part of the diocese of Victoria, if it ever really had been. But, as in China, the Episcopal Church, the CMS, and the SPG worked independently, with little direct cooperation with one another.

Channing Moore Williams became Episcopal missionary bishop of China and Japan in 1866, and resided in China for three years. He moved from Shanghai back to Japan in 1869, although he still had oversight over the work of the PECM in China. He was made bishop of Edo (now Tokyo) in 1873, and there he lived for the next twenty years. No longer involved in China (after 1874) Bishop Williams devoted his energy to work among the Japanese people and the study of Japanese language and culture. With missionary colleagues recently arrived from the United States, he started parishes and mission stations in different parts of the country, recruited lay missionaries, established schools, and laid the foundation for St Luke's Hospital. In 1874 he personally began St Paul's University in Tokyo (later Rikkyo University and the only Anglican-related university in the country).

[28] George Smith, *Ten Weeks in Japan* (London, 1861).

CMS work was initially centred in Osaka, but it quickly established mission stations in Tokyo and Kyoto. The society also initiated work among the Ainu, the indigenous people of Japan. John Batchelor began this pioneering work in the northern island of Hokkaido in 1880. Many Ainu became Anglicans, but Batchelor also worked to safeguard and preserve Ainu culture. The work of the SPG in Japan was not as extensive as that of the CMS, but SPG missionaries also established churches and schools in different parts of the country. Priests from both the CMS and SPG served British congregations in Tokyo, Yokohama, and Kobe. Overall, neither the Episcopal Mission, the CMS, nor the SPG made much progress in the 1870s.

The 1880s were a time of consolidation and development. The goal of Anglican work was to build a strong Church as a foundation for later expansion.[29] The Japanese Book of Common Prayer was published in 1882, and, because the Episcopal Church, the CMS, and the SPG all had a share in its translation, it was accepted all over the country. The first two Japanese deacons, Nobori Kanai and Masakazu Tai, both graduates of Tokyo Theological School, were ordained the following year. In 1886, Edward Bickerstaff was consecrated bishop of Japan and had authority over both CMS and SPG areas. He got along well with Bishop Williams, and the two worked to bring all Anglican work together and form a national Church. The first General Synod of the *Nippon Sei Ko Kai* (the Holy Catholic Church of Japan) was held in 1887.[30]

Although mission work in Japan had begun much later than China, the Anglican Church was established there much earlier. This was because Japan was a smaller and more homogeneous country, which in turn facilitated communication among the different mission societies. It was estimated that at this time the Church had about 1,300 Japanese members, a very small percentage of the total number of Japanese Christians. By 1894, the Church had six dioceses, each of which was related to one of the four constituent missionary bodies—which from 1888 included the Anglican Church of Canada which began work in Japan under the *Nippon Sei Ko Kai*.

Bishop Williams retired in 1893, but because of his love of Japan and the Church he helped to found he continued to live in Kyoto until 1908, two years before his death in the United States. While Williams was identified with the Japanese Church more than anyone else among the foreign leadership, the *Nippon Sei Ko Kai* remained dependent on foreign resources and clergy well into the twentieth century. This was one reason for the slow development of Japanese Anglicanism. At the same time, by the end of the nineteenth century the Church had found a niche in Japanese religious and cultural life as a

[29] A. Hamish Ion, *The Cross and the Rising Sun*. Volume 2: *The British Protestant Missionary Movement in Japan, Korea, and Taiwan, 1865–1945* (Waterloo, ON, 1993).

[30] Henry St. George Tucker, *History of the Episcopal Church in Japan* (New York and London, 1938).

community that became known for its contributions to education, modernization, and the spiritual life of the people.

KOREA

Korean Confucian scholars had brought Christianity to Korea during the Joseon (Chosun) Dynasty in the early seventeenth century after their study of the new teachings and their baptism in Peking. The Catholic Church grew through persecution, and, by the end of the nineteenth century it was firmly established in the country. Korea began to open up to foreign trade and missionary work later than either China or Japan, and, as a small country caught between three great powers, it remained isolated, a 'hermit kingdom'. The first resident Protestant missionary and his family arrived in 1884, and over the next decades the number of Presbyterian and Methodist missionaries grew rapidly. In 1880 Anglican missionaries from Japan visited Korea, and in 1885 the CMS sent two Chinese catechists from Fukien to work in Busan. But they were able to do very little in the short time they were there.

In 1887, English bishops from North China and Japan visited Korea and wrote a report to the archbishop of Canterbury urging him to start a Korean mission. His response was positive. Less than two years later, on All Saints' Day, 1889, the Church of England mission in Korea began when Archbishop Edward White Benson (1829–96) consecrated Charles John Corfe (1843–1921) as missionary bishop of Chosun (Korea) in Westminster Abbey. Bishop Corfe arrived the next year accompanied by two doctors and established his residence in Seoul. He was also missionary bishop of Manchuria until 1891, when it reverted to the Chinese diocese of North China. By the end of 1891 the Korean mission had two priests, two deacons, and two ordinands. The mission was supported largely by the SPG, both financially and in terms of personnel. Unlike China and Japan, there were no competing Anglican societies (the CMS withdrew its catechists upon the arrival of Bishop Corfe). While most Protestant missionaries in Korea were American, the Anglican missionaries were English and were among the very few Englishmen in the country.

Bishop Corfe was a strong Anglo-Catholic and organized the mission in Korea as if it were a missionary order.[31] His early work was in many ways similar to that of Anglican beginnings in China and Japan. He established the Church of St Michael and All the Angels in Seoul in 1890; built two

[31] John Charles Corfe, *The Anglican Church in Korea* (Seoul, 1905); Mark Napier Trollope, *The Church in Korea* (London, 1915).

hospitals in Seoul, one for men and one for women, and one in Chemulpo (Incheon); and started schools, social work centres, and orphanages in Seoul and neighbouring cities. Corfe devoted himself to language work, and required a high standard of fluency for new missionaries. He also placed a high value on respect for Korean culture. The Bible had already been translated into Korean, and so Bishop Corfe devoted his attention to work on liturgy and Anglo-Catholic literature. The missionaries he recruited were all celibate, Anglo-Catholic, and well-educated. The Society for the Sacred Mission (SSM) sent missionaries beginning in 1896, but they stayed only for a few years. Almost all other early missionaries were from the clergy sent by the SPG, except for the doctors and women teachers who were laypeople.

The Sino-Japanese War of 1894–5 was a time of hardship for the Korean people as it marked the beginning of the fifty-year Japanese occupation, but missionaries were allowed to continue their work as before. Korean nationalism was on the rise, but anti-colonialist sentiments were directed against Japan not the Western powers. One result of the war was the influx of Japanese into Chemulpo. In response, the mission in Korea began work with Japanese immigrants there, even though it lacked resources to do this effectively. In addition, work among the Japanese went against the tide of a growing anti-Japanese Korean nationalism.

Work among Koreans grew slowly, and Bishop Corfe baptized the first Anglicans only in 1897 when, for the first time, the liturgy was celebrated in Korean. Incense was introduced at the first service, which had not been common practice in either China or Japan. As an Anglo-Catholic, Corfe insisted on the use of incense in the liturgy, and felt it would be culturally appropriate in a Korean setting where incense was used in Buddhist and folk religious rituals. By the time of Bishop Corfe's retirement in 1904, there had been two hundred baptisms. Many of these were from the mission station at Kangwha Island, off the coast of Chemulpo.

In Korea and Japan, as well as in China, the Anglican community was small in comparison with the missions and Churches of other denominations. The Anglican liturgy and inherited tradition demanded more of local Christians than what was expected in other Churches. Unlike the Catholics and other Protestants, Anglicans and Episcopalians expected a high level of literacy among communicants. This limited their growth in rural areas especially. Still, the Churches in each country had distinctive emphases—in education, churchmanship, medical work, and literary ventures. Anglican missionaries in China, Japan, and Korea expended great effort in studying the local culture and language. And with Christians from other Protestant traditions, they contributed to modernization by their very presence in the country, something that was valued by the people whom they had come to serve, whether Christian or not.

TOWARDS THE 'HOLY CATHOLIC CHURCH OF CHINA' (CHUNG HUA SHENG KUNG HUI)

There was both cooperation and competitiveness among Protestant missionaries in nineteenth-century China. Continuing appeals for Christian unity accompanied the consolidation of Church institutions and denominational interests. Moreover, as Chinese nationalist aspirations came into increasing conflict with Western interests, all Christian organizations faced new challenges.

American Episcopalians and the various Anglican mission societies had come to China and begun their work without any central direction or even consultation. They generally worked alongside each other, although there were differences in mission policies, as well as jurisdictional disputes, primarily over questions of diocesan boundaries, episcopal jurisdiction, and transfers from one diocese to another. As the different dioceses and missionary areas became more familiar with one another's work, there were also disagreements about Church terminology and liturgy, and which version of the Chinese Prayer Book to use.

Already in 1853, Bishop Boone conceded authority over English clergy and laity in Shanghai, a PECM area, to Bishop Smith of the CMS. Bishops Boone and Smith became good friends, but this was not always the case in the nineteenth century, when questions of nationality, churchmanship, and even personal style inhibited closer cooperation. Even the creation of diocesan boundaries and the areas of mission activity were done on an *ad hoc* basis, and bishops from other parts of the country were informed after the fact.

The first meeting of British and American bishops in China (and Korea) was not held until April 1897, in Shanghai.[32] This was at the initiative of Bishops Graves and Scott. All of the bishops in China were present, except for Victoria where the see was about to fall vacant. Because Korea had been under Chinese suzerainty, Bishop Corfe was also at this first Shanghai meeting. Different resolutions were passed on Church terminology. Curiously, it was resolved that 'Anglican' should be rendered *conggu jiaohui* (the 'Church that follows antiquity'). But the term never caught on and the resolution was overturned in favour of the commonly accepted *shenggonghui* ('Holy Catholic Church') at the next bishops' meeting. The desirability of a common Prayer Book was discussed, but no decision was made. The bishops met again in 1899, and the major decision made at this conference was that the bishops would not become involved in local politics, even though this possibility was allowed

[32] *Letter and Resolutions of the Conference of the Anglican Communion in China* (Shanghai, 1897–9); *Letter and Resolutions of the Conference of the Bishops of the Anglican Communion in China and Hong Kong* (Shanghai, 19–23 Oct. 1903); *Report and Resolutions of the Conference of the Anglican Communion in China and Hong Kong* (Shanghai, 1907, 1909).

under the unequal treaties and the extraterritorial laws, and had been practised by the Roman Catholic hierarchy. This was a wise decision made on the eve of the Boxer Rebellion and in response to the growing anti-foreignism and interference of Churches (particularly the Roman Catholic hierarchy) in Chinese political affairs. The next conference of bishops did not meet until 1903, when two new dioceses were represented, and it was agreed that future conferences should include representatives of Chinese and foreign clergy. The 1907 conference decided that lay representatives from each diocese should be invited, and that a draft constitution should be prepared for a General Synod. Lay representation would increase the number of Chinese at the proposed General Synod. In ten years, the PECM and the British mission societies had finally decided to proceed with the founding of a Church.

Also in 1907, the Church of England in Canada was asked to begin work in Henan. Henan was the last of the historic eighteen provinces in China proper to have an episcopal see. The first bishop was William C. White (1873–1960), a Canadian priest who had been working with the CMS in Fukien. He brought with him several co-workers from that province, and the first Communion service in Henan was celebrated in Fukien dialect. The ancient city of Kaifeng became the centre of the new diocese. Kaifeng was also the centre of a declining Chinese Jewish community, and Bishop White developed a close and supportive relationship with Jewish families in the city.[33] He was to be the only non-Chinese bishop the diocese ever had.

The long-standing jurisdictional dispute between the Americans and the English in Shanghai was finally settled. We have seen that the bishop of Victoria was given authority over English clergy in Shanghai in 1853. In 1872, Shanghai came under the bishop of Mid-China (later the diocese of Chekiang). This was an irregular situation. Finally, in 1908, an agreement drafted by the archbishop of Canterbury was signed at Lambeth Palace by the relevant English and American bishops, putting the English congregations under the bishop of Chekiang, and all Chinese parishes up and down the Yang-Tze River under the PECM bishops of Shanghai and Hankow. This was a matter of foreign missionary jurisdiction, but it did have implications for Chinese Christians for they were also required to negotiate between the different missions when they moved between dioceses.

The Centenary Mission Conference held in Shanghai in 1907 to celebrate the arrival of Robert Morrison as the first missionary to China in 1807 saw almost 1,200 representatives gather from most of the Protestant groups active in China. Anglican missionaries were well represented and Bishop Graves chaired the Executive Committee. The conference was dominated by American and British missionaries, and, in terms of indigenization, not much

[33] William Charles White, *Chinese Jews: A Compilation of Matters Relating to the Jews of K'aifeng Fu* (Toronto, 1942).

had changed over the past century. No Chinese were invited, and the call for Christian unity was limited to programmes for cooperation and comity among Western missionary organizations. This clearly went against what the PECM had been trying to do since its arrival in China.

The movement for the creation of a Chinese Church had become more urgent for Chinese Anglicans, even though this had not been on the agenda at the interdenominational Centenary Mission conference. Two years later, the 1909 Conference of the Anglican Communion in China and Hong Kong included eight bishops (all foreign), fifteen foreign and thirteen Chinese clergy, and fifteen Chinese laity. Given the standards of the time, Chinese Christians were well represented. The draft Constitution and Canons for the General Synod were approved, written largely by Bishop Scott (SPG) of the diocese of North China. These drafts were sent to diocesan synods or synods for comment and ratification. The Committee on 'Local Adaptation' submitted a report emphasizing the need for the indigenization of church architecture, marriage and burial rites, and liturgical dress, as well as the consideration of special services for Chinese festivals.[34] Anglicans in China would continue to struggle with these issues, but indigenization questions were now on the table.

On 26 April 1912, the Chung Hua Sheng Kung Hui (the Holy Catholic Church of China) was formally constituted at St John's pro-cathedral in Shanghai. The pro-cathedral was located on the campus of St John's University, which by this time had already become an outstanding institution of higher learning. This was the first non-Roman Catholic national Church body formed in China. Representatives of all the Anglican and Episcopal churches and mission societies in China were present, including ten of its eleven bishops. There were an estimated 30,000 baptized Church members at the time, and many more adherents.[35] The new Church included three dioceses from the PECM (Shanghai, Hankou, and Wuhu (later Anking)), five dioceses that were associated with the CMS (Victoria-South China, Fukien, West China (Sichuan), Chekiang, and Kwangsi (Guangxi)-Hunan), two dioceses established by the SPG (North China and Shandong), and one diocese under the Church of England in Canada (Henan). Bishop Scott was elected first chairman of the House of Bishops, and Bishop Logan Roots from the PECM was elected vice-chairman. Chinese was to be the one and only official language, although synod documents were in both Chinese and English. There was a resolution on the need for local adaptation,[36] further developing the issues that

[34] 'Report of the Committee on Local Adaptation, Presented to the Conference of the Anglican Communion held in China, March 27th to April 6th, 1909', HKPRO, HKMS 94-1-6.

[35] Stock, *History of the Church Missionary Society*, IV, pp. 294–5; Kenneth Scott Latourette, *A History of Christian Missions in China* (New York, 1929), p. 664.

[36] *Constitutions and Canons of the Chung Hua Sheng Kung Hui Together with the Report of the General Synod, and the Report and Resolutions of the Conference of the Anglican Communion in China and Hong Kong Held at Shanghai, April 18th–26th, 1912* (Shanghai, 1912).

had been raised from the 1909 conference report. Although leadership and funding were still in the hands of the PECM, the CMS, the SPG, and other societies, with important decisions made by their boards in New York and London, in 1912 the page had been turned and a Chinese Church had been founded.[37]

SELECT BIBLIOGRAPHY

Corfe, John Charles, *The Anglican Church in Korea* (Seoul, 1905).

Eber, Irene, *The Jewish Bishop and the Chinese Bible: S. I. J. Schereschewsky, 1831–1906* (Leiden, 1999).

Endacott, George B. and Dorothy E. She, *The Diocese of Victoria, Hong Kong: A Hundred Years of Church History, 1849–1949* (Hong Kong, 1949).

Gray, G. F. S. with Martha Lund Smalley, *Anglicans in China: A History of the Zhonghua Shenggong Hui (Chung Hua Sheng Kung Hui)* (New Haven, CT, 1996).

Ion, A. Hamish, *The Cross and the Rising Sun*. Volume 2: *The British Protestant Missionary Movement in Japan, Korea, and Taiwan, 1865–1945* (Waterloo, ON, 1993).

Lin, Meimei, 'The Episcopalian Missionaries in China, 1835–1900', PhD thesis, University of Texas at Austin, 1994.

Manross, William Wilson, *A History of the American Episcopal Church* (New York, 1950).

Rubenstein, Murray A., *The Origins of the Anglo-American Missionary Enterprise in China, 1807–1840* (Lanham, MD, 1996).

Stock, Eugene, *The History of the Church Missionary Society: Its Environment, Its Men and Its Work*, 3 vols. (London, 1899).

Tiedemann, R. G., *Reference Guide to Christian Missionary Societies in China: From the Sixteenth to the Twentieth Century* (Armonk, NY, 2009).

Tucker, Henry St. George, *History of the Episcopal Church in Japan* (New York and London, 1938).

Wickeri, Philip L., *Christian Encounters with Chinese Culture: Essays on Anglican and Episcopal History in China* (Hong Kong, 2015).

Xu, Edward Yihua, 'Westernization and Contextualization: A Study on Three Pioneering Chinese Pastors of the Sheng Kung Hui in China', in Peter Chen-Main Wang (ed.), *Contextualization of Christianity in China: An Evaluation in Modern Perspective* (Sankt Augustin, Germany, 2007), pp. 183–208.

[37] I wish to express my thanks to Dr Rowena Ruiwen Chen and Ms Katie Webb for their research assistance in the preparation of this chapter.

16

Anglicanism in Australia, *c.*1829–1910

Hilary M. Carey

Anglicanism in Australia developed rapidly from 1829 with the arrival of William Grant Broughton (1788–1853) as archdeacon of New South Wales replacing the fractious Thomas Hobbes Scott (1783–1860). In the course of the next eighty years the Church of England would grow from a chaplaincy to convicts and settlers to the strongest denomination in an independent, federated Australia with some significant missionary outreach to Aborigines and rural people throughout the continent. Aspirations for an Anglican ascendancy would rise and fall as other Churches jostled for primacy, but the Church of England asserted itself as the largest and most diverse of the emerging nation's Christian denominations.

The creation of a liberal, free community from a society made up largely of convicts and former convicts was a substantial achievement. It required not just the will of government in both London and the colonies, but also the development of a cultural and social infrastructure robust enough to cope with the tides of emigrants and economic change that they brought in their wake. The pressure for change accelerated after the presentation of the three Bigge Reports (1822–3), the government enquiry into the condition of the colony of New South Wales, which recommended that free settlers be admitted in larger numbers but also that the convict transportation system remain in place, though with modifications to make it more regimented and punitive.[1] The number of convicts transported began to increase in the 1830s and so did the problems they created for integration with the free settler economy and society. The society being created also came at a considerable cost to the Aboriginal peoples of Australia who were displaced by the new arrivals who chose, overwhelmingly, to replant their home Churches as part of the settler colonies of a new British world.

[1] J. J. Eddy, *Britain and the Australian Colonies 1818–1831: The Technique of Government* (Oxford, 1969), p. 256.

These were times of rapid change in the British metropole, as the effects of Catholic emancipation, mass emigration, and an effective constitutional revolution overturning the old regime were felt at home and the colonies. The direct impact of this in the Australian colonies was the creation of a climate strongly resistant to any attempt to transplant the old system of conservative and aristocratic party privilege in Church and state. For this reason the appointment of Archdeacon Scott was more or less an unmitigated disaster. Scott resigned and was replaced by William Broughton, first as archdeacon and then as the first and only bishop of Australia. Broughton was also a traditionalist and advocate of establishment but he gave paternal support to the spiritual aspirations of those colonists on the lower rungs of society.

In London, the Colonial Secretary Lord Bathurst was receptive to the idea that the colonies should have a more formal ecclesiastical governance with Anglican bishops and state-subsidized Anglican schools for the many. The senior government chaplain, Samuel Marsden, who had important supporters, most notably William Wilberforce, was also actively trying to improve the ecclesiastical and educational provision for the colony, though with less sympathy for the imposition of a Tory High Churchman as bishop. In correspondence with Governor George Arthur of Van Diemen's Land, Marsden decried the low state of religion and morals but praised the potential of the rising generation: 'by educating the children of all ranks we may hope that the Population will improve in morals'.[2] Despite such ambitious plans, the idea that a free society should necessarily be Anglican did not have the support of the large Dissenting population, whether Catholic, Presbyterian, or Methodist, to name just the major groups.

Broughton was aware from the beginning of the challenges he faced. In the charge he delivered shortly after his arrival to the clergy of his archdeaconry he laid out the character of his Church: 'The great purpose of the gospel, stated in a few words, is to bring man to God.'[3] Yet in the colony, clergy and churches were few and distances between them were great, while few gave priority to religious matters. Broughton called for the sanctification of the Sabbath, the observation of public prayer making use of the resources and precedent of the missionary societies, and for literature and religious education using the Society for Promoting Christian Knowledge (SPCK). With these tools he hoped to address the needs of convicts whom he urged clergy to seek out 'since they will hardly make the first advance'; and the Aboriginal inhabitants. He concluded with the aspiration that the Church of England should become

[2] Marsden to Arthur, 15 June 1827. Photostat copy, Oxford, Bodleian Library USPG Papers [henceforth USPG], C/AUS/TAS 4.

[3] W. G. Broughton, *A Charge Delivered to the Clergy of the Archdeaconry of New South Wales at the Primary Visitation, Holden at Sydney, in the Church of St James, on Thursday, the 3d of December, 1829* (Sydney, 1830), p. 7.

the 'mother of Missionaries who should attempt the recovery of this unhappy generation'.[4] More practically Broughton launched himself into a lifelong campaign to entrench Anglican institutions into the fabric of colonial life by building churches, recruiting clergy, and co-opting the active support of the colonial government. In a letter to Governor Franklin in Van Diemen's Land he urged the construction of a church large enough to include both the free and convict people together.

> The convict population is unworthy and vile enough I admit, but are *we* so pure under an all-seeing eye as to venture to pretend that in a moral and religious estimate we form a separate class from them as we do in our political capacity? 'I trow not!' Well then, I say that as they, outwardly at least, have not ceased to be members of the Christian Church, they have a right to participate in its outward privileges and visible ordinances; and we have no right to banish them from the general assembly of the congregation.[5]

Broughton saw this participation in communal religious service as a key part of the reformative training by the Established Church in the colony.

The colonial Church had been patronized by sympathetic governors but lacked the resources to expand to meet the needs of the whole society, particularly in relation to education. Under Governor Ralph Darling in the 1820s, there was a short-lived experiment to remedy these inadequate ecclesiastical resources through the Clergy and School Lands Corporation (usually known at the Church and School Corporation) which bestowed one-seventh of the land in the colony for the exclusive benefit of the Church of England; clergy reserves were established at the same time for Van Diemen's Land where they created similar controversy.[6] Similar attempts to endow an established Anglican Church in Canada through the mechanism of the clergy reserves were overthrown at much the same time. In the aftermath of the overthrow of these arrangements, the Church of England was effectively disestablished, a reality not all Anglican clergy in the colonies accepted readily.[7] However, this led in most cases to a strengthening of autonomy from the colonial state, and greater financial security as colonial governments provided generous support for education and clerical provision based on a denomination's share of the population.

[4] Broughton, *A Charge Delivered*, p. 32.

[5] Broughton to Sir George Arthur, 6 Aug. 1830. USPG, C/AUS/TAS 4.

[6] Kelvin Grose, 'What Happened to the Clergy Reserves of NSW?', *Journal of the Royal Australian Historical Society*, 72 (1986): 92–103; Kelvin Grose, 'Scott Arthur and the Clergy Reserves in Van Diemen's Land', *Journal of the Royal Australian Historical Society*, 75 (1989): 179–89; Alan Wilson, 'The Clergy Reserves: "Economic Mischiefs" or Sectarian Issue?', *Canadian Historical Review*, 42 (1961): 281–99.

[7] Rowan Strong, 'The Colonial Religion of the Anglican Clergy: Western Australia 1830–c.1870', *Journal of Religious History*, 38 (2014): 91–114.

The means favoured by Broughton to solve perennial problems of under-supply of clergy and religious literature was through appeal to the older missionary societies: the Society for the Propagation of the Gospel (SPG) and the SPCK. In 1838, the SPG offered to provide generous salaries and annuities to candidates offering to go out to New South Wales and Van Diemen's Land as chaplains. The society had no shortage of candidates who immediately came forward to offer themselves for the twenty positions on offer. The SPG was the first to recognize that the future of the colony would be the free colonists, who now included respectable ticket-of-leave men and their descendants who needed and valued education for their children.

The decline of exclusive support for the Church of England did not mean the end of state funding for religion. In fact Anglicans benefited markedly from the new regime of multiple establishments which was brokered by the liberal Irish-born governor of New South Wales, Richard Bourke (1777–1855).[8] The Church Acts for New South Wales (1836) and Van Diemen's Land (1837) provided for the various Churches on the basis of their population. This ensured that Anglicans received the most though Catholics, Methodists, Presbyterians, and Jews all benefited from state funding. The end of convict transportation to New South Wales in 1840 put a further break on government support for religion. In that year Lord John Russell wrote to the archbishop of Canterbury rejecting his request for additional religious instruction for the convicts in New South Wales and the Church of England.[9] But before the flow had ceased, the colony was provided with dozens of handsome churches. Many of the new Anglican churches were constructed in the Gothic Revival style following the aspirational designs of leading British architects, including Augustus Pugin. English architects with substantial Australian careers included Edmund Blacket, who designed many churches in Gothic style for the Sydney diocese, and William Butterfield who designed St Paul's Cathedral in Melbourne.[10] The period of multiple establishments came to an end in the 1860s when sectarian objections to state funding for education led to the withdrawal of support for religious schools.

[8] David Stoneman, 'For the Honour of God and the Good of Man', *Journal of Religious History*, 38 (2013): 341–55.

[9] Russell to Archbishop of Canterbury, 8 Aug. 1840. USPG C/AUS/GEN 1.

[10] Joan Kerr, 'The Development of the Gothic Taste in New South Wales: As Exemplified in the Churches of the Colony from the Beginning of Settlement up to the Establishment of the Victorian Gothic Revival Style at the End of the 1840s', MA thesis, University of Sydney, 1976; G. A. Bremner, *Imperial Gothic: Religious Architecture and High Anglican Culture in the British Empire, c.1840–1870* (New Haven, CT, 2013).

ABORIGINES

Besides the convicts, the other object of Broughton's special hopes for Anglican ministry were the Aborigines. As it was on other frontiers in the Atlantic and British worlds, it proved more difficult to provide for indigenous people from the traditional resources of the SPG and the SPCK. The first missionary efforts to Aboriginal people had been spearheaded either by concerned individuals or by the major non-Anglican Protestant missionary societies including the London Missionary Society and the Wesleyan Methodist Missionary Society. The Secretary of the Church Missionary Society (CMS), Dandeson Coates, was an ardent advocate for an Anglican CMS mission to be advanced in both New Zealand, where it was soon highly successful, and Australia, where it was a good deal less so. In Van Diemen's Land there were no formal missions, only the ambiguous salvage work of G. A. Robinson, a former Methodist schoolteacher.[11] It was not until 1832 that the CMS succeeded in initiating the first Anglican mission to the Aborigines which was located at Wellington Valley, then the innermost point of the Australian frontier. Broughton refused to support the licensing of missionaries accredited by the bishop of London and the CMS to the Wellington station and was rankled about the arrival of clergy who refused to accept his standing as diocesan.[12] His intransigence lost him the support of Samuel Marsden, who nevertheless never opposed him on any other matter, and the governors, who saw him as an expensive encumbrance on the colonial establishment who could not adapt to the colonial reality.

The Wellington Mission was not blessed with success and struggled with the lack of episcopal sanction as well as hostility from the colonists who resented the mission's access to land. It was also starved for funding and personnel. The colonial reputation of the missionaries plummeted when they reported on the catastrophic impact of European settlement and the sexual predation of Europeans—including convict shepherds—on Aboriginal women. The missionaries reported on the disastrous impact of so-called European civilization in the colony and declared that there was 'nothing but Missionary effort to save the wretchedly corrupted Natives from becoming extinct'.[13]

Following the closure of missions to the Aborigines by all the major British missionary societies there were limited efforts to try again with local diocesan funding supplemented by private philanthropy. Important Anglican initiatives usually with the intent of 'saving the remnant' were located in South Australia

[11] N. J. B. Plomley (ed.), *Friendly Mission: The Tasmanian Journals and Papers of George Augustus Robinson, 1829–1834* (Hobart, 1966).

[12] Hans Cnattingius, *Bishops and Societies: A Study of Anglican Colonial and Missionary Expansion, 1698–1850* (London, 1952).

[13] D. Coates to Lord Glenelg, 31 Oct. 1838. National Archives UK, CO 201/280, fo. 131.

at Poonindie (1850), Lake Tyers in Victoria (1861), and Yarrabah in Queensland (1892). Many of these efforts were associated with individuals of striking temperament and unconventionality.[14] Anne Camfield conducted the Albany Native Institution in her own home with some assistance from Archdeacon John Wollaston, the SPG, and the Western Australian government. The Yarrabah mission was notable for the efforts of the controversial missionary John Gribble. With his wife Mary, John Gribble operated the Warangesda mission on the Murrumbidgee largely supported by private donations. He was invited to open a mission at Carnarvon in Western Australia by Bishop Henry Parry, where he wasted little time in publishing accounts of atrocities, physical abuse, kidnapping, and sexual exploitation of Aborigines by pastoralists.[15] While not without foundation, Gribble was a polemicist and his writing was open to challenges from local settlers on the grounds of veracity and sensationalism. Vigorously attacked by the establishment newspaper *The West Australian*, Gribble was dismissed by Parry for abandoning his station and ignoring the instructions of both his bishop and the missions committee. In 1894, the South Australian government closed Poonindie and sold its land to local farmers. It was the height of the depression and competition for land was intense. However, it represented the last remaining Anglican mission of this era. New initiatives would not emerge until well into the new century. At the same time, Australian men and women were active as missionaries with the CMS and the (Anglican) Australian Board of Missions in locations throughout the Pacific.

NEW BISHOPRICS: COLONIAL BISHOPRICS FUND

Beginning in the 1840s Broughton's original vast diocese of Australia was divided and new bishops appeared. Some, like Broughton, came armed with letters patent and claims for oversight of all clergy, including missionaries and convict chaplains. This asserted authority soon brought them into conflict with both the government and the members of the missionary societies, many of whom were reluctant to place themselves entirely at the disposal of the colonial bishop, particularly if they were receiving a government salary. In 1841 George Selwyn became bishop of New Zealand and Australian bishoprics followed: Francis Nixon for Tasmania in 1842, Augustus Short to Adelaide, Charles Perry to Melbourne, and William Tyrell to Newcastle in 1847.

[14] John W. Harris, *One Blood: 200 Years of Aboriginal Encounter with Christianity, a Story of Hope* (Sutherland, New South Wales, 1994 edn.).

[15] J. B. Gribble, *Dark Deeds in a Sunny Land, or, Blacks and Whites in North-West Australia* (Nedlands, Western Australia, 1987).

Matthew Blagden Hale (1811–95) arrived as bishop of Perth ten years later in 1857 and Edward Tufnell (1814–96) in Brisbane in 1859, reflecting the expanding lines of colonial settlement. The Australian colonies were major beneficiaries of the Colonial Bishoprics Fund (1840–1) and without this source of funding it seems likely that Australia, like the American colonies, would have been dominated by Methodists or other Dissenters. The fund made it possible to create leaders for the colonial Church without the expense and political entanglements of letters patent. Rowan Strong sees this as creating 'a new imperial paradigm of engagement with the British Empire'.[16] That the Church of England remained the largest Church in Australia (though with no more than 40.4 per cent of the population in 1901) until the 1980s was due in no small degree to the revival of the missionary spirit which saw possibilities and aspirations for a new Anglican missionary age in the settler colonies.[17] Well-organized denominational societies and a commitment to support the colonial Churches underpinned the central place which the Church of England retained in Australian social, cultural, and public life throughout the long nineteenth century.

CONFERENCE OF BISHOPS, 1850

Australian dependence on the Church of England was one factor in the slow emergence of an independent Australian Anglican Church, something achieved by the Wesleyan Methodists as early as 1851. There were nevertheless important innovations which were trialled early in Australia and later impacted elsewhere in the Anglican world. One of the most significant was the meeting of the six bishops of Australia and New Zealand, who met under the hospitality of Bishop Broughton in Sydney in October 1850. This meeting was prescient in suggesting the need for a more formal organization of colonial bishops but it would take many years to achieve synodical governance in Australia.[18] One significant achievement of the 1850 meeting was the creation of the Australian Board of Mission (ABM) which was restructured many times.[19]

[16] Rowan Strong, *Anglicanism and the British Empire, c.1700–1850* (Oxford, 2007), pp. 218–21.

[17] W. W. Phillips, 'Religion', in Wray Vamplew (ed.), *Australians: Historical Statistics* (Sydney, 1987), pp. 436–46, 465–6.

[18] Bruce Kaye, Tom Frame, Colin Holden, and Geoffrey R. Treloar (eds.), *Anglicanism in Australia: A History* (Melbourne, 2002), pp. 43–6.

[19] David Hilliard, *God's Gentlemen: A History of the Melanesian Mission, 1849–1942* (Brisbane, 1978); David Hilliard, 'Colonialism and Christianity: The Melanesian Mission in the Solomon Islands', *Journal of Pacific History*, 9 (1974): 93–116; David Hilliard, 'Bishop G. A. Selwyn and the Melanesian Mission', *New Zealand Journal of History*, 4 (1970): 120–37.

A constitution for a national Church in Australia of the Anglican Communion was still some decades away. There was agreement to form a general synod in 1872 and this met every five years, but was only able to make recommendations to the separate dioceses. Throughout the nineteenth century tensions between Evangelical and non-Evangelical parties frustrated moves to create a national communion with its own metropolitan bishop.

The tenacity with which the constitutional connection binding the colonial Churches to Canterbury was asserted was not inconsistent with striving for colonial autonomy, and there were connections between moves for colonial self-rule and that for independent Church management. In 1866 one of the first acts of the new Parliament of New South Wales was to enable the Church to manage its property. Despite the absence of an overarching organization, dioceses and bishops found different ways to create denominational infrastructure. Personnel continued to be recruited from England and Ireland and the SPG endowed bishoprics along the rural frontier. These included Goulburn (1863), Grafton and Armidale (1867), Bathurst (1869), Ballarat (1875), North Queensland (1878), Riverina (1884), and Rockhampton (1892).[20]

Anglican aspirations to be the Church for the rising nation seemed increasingly unrealistic, but the dioceses devised flexible modes of governance that engaged the laity and clergy. Denominational infrastructure including metropolitan cathedrals, elite secondary schools, and university colleges ensured that Anglicans remained visible and dominant in the professions and the elite of colonial society. Royal visits, state funerals, and other ceremonies ensured that the Anglican Communion and its elegant metropolitan cathedrals were given quasi-establishment status.

THE RURAL FRONTIER

Attempts to remain in contact with settlers as they pushed ever further inland were a deep concern for the colonial Church. Challenges included communication and distance but also rivalry with other Churches, notably the Methodists and Catholics who had more nimble forms of frontier development. George Alfred St Clair Donaldson (1863–1935), bishop of Brisbane, saw the outback bush itself, with its endless isolation, as a pastoral challenge and without romance. 'There are isolated families; the boundary-riders; the rabbit-fence

[20] H. W. Tucker, *The Spiritual Expansion of the Empire: A Sketch of Two Centuries of Work Done for the Church and Nation by the Society for the Propagation of the Gospel in Foreign Parts* (London, 1900 edn.), p. 124.

men; the swagmen. How can we reach them? What can we do to relieve the soul-destroying monotony and loneliness of their lives?'[21] By this stage the bishop and his clergy were already making the transition from emigrants and pioneers to identification with the colonial Church. Evangelical clergy with an appetite for rural ministry in the colonies were recruited with the support of the Colonial and Continental Church Society, formed in 1851 from the union of the Newfoundland School Society and the Colonial Church Society which had begun as a mission to Aborigines in Western Australia.[22] This would later (1919) be reforged by a group of Sydney Anglicans as the Bush Church Aid Society which would, in time, become the largest Australian organization ministering to 'the bush', providing missionaries, deaconesses, and hostel workers in remote parts of Australia.

'The bush' was also invoked by the mainstream of the Church of England through the ministry of the Bush Brothers.[23] Nathaniel Dawes (1843–1910), the first Anglican bishop of Rockhampton, provided the initiative for the Bush Brothers in the aftermath of the 1897 Lambeth Conference. There were eventually seven brotherhoods located in different dioceses in Queensland and New South Wales where there were bishops sympathetic to the celibate ideals of the brotherhood. For their recruits the brotherhoods drew heavily on England and on an ideal of imperial self-sacrifice combined with manly, outdoor energy. The brothers attracted some outstanding men and some went on to become bishops. George Halford, later to succeed Dawes as bishop of Rockhampton, founded the Brotherhood of St Lawrence in Longreach, Queensland, in 1897. The Brotherhoods of St Paul (1902) in Gayndah (later Charleville), St Barnabas in Charters Towers for Northern Queensland (1902), and the Brotherhood of the Good Shepherd for New South Wales soon followed. Memoirs by former Bush Brothers, such as D. H. S. Matthews or J. W. Eisdell, were an important means to bring new recruits to the movement.[24]

[21] St Clair Donaldson in *Brisbane Church Chronicle*, cited in Charles T. Dimont and Francis de Witt Batty, *St. Clair Donaldson, Archbishop of Brisbane, 1904–1921; Bishop of Salisbury, 1921–1935* (London, 1939), p. 48.

[22] Hilary M. Carey, *God's Empire: Religion and Colonialism in the British World* (Cambridge, 2011), pp. 148–76; Joseph Hardwick, *An Anglican British World: The Church of England and the Expansion of the British Settler Empire, c.1790–1860* (Manchester, 2015), p. 34.

[23] R. A. F. Webb, *Brothers in the Sun: A History of the Bush Brotherhood Movement in the Outback of Australia* (Sydney, 1978); Ruth Frappell, 'The Australian Bush Brotherhoods and Their English Origins', *Journal of Ecclesiastical History*, 47 (1996): 82–97.

[24] J. W. Eisdell, *Back Country: Or the Cheerful Adventures of a Bush Parson in the Eighties* (London, 1936); D. H. S. Matthews, *A Parson in the Australian Bush* (London, 1909).

WOMEN AND CHARITABLE WORK

The work of women also expanded in the later decades of the nineteenth century. There had always been a role for women of higher rank, exemplified in the work of governors' wives such as Mrs Eliza Darling (Sir Ralph was governor in New South Wales from 1836 to 1844 although not viewed with much sympathy by current generations).[25] Eliza followed traditional philanthropic opportunities to improve conditions for convict women at the female factory and education for convict children. She founded the Female School of Industry to provide economic alternatives to prostitution. More substantial contributions were made by missionary wives, deaconesses, and women's religious orders which were active in Australian dioceses where there were sympathetic bishops. The voluntary labour of Anglican women was given organizational expression in parish auxiliaries, participation in the choir, and decorating churches. As parishes became more feminized—something which was noticeable to observers by the later decades of the nineteenth century—there were more opportunities. The Mothers' Union (MU) had been established in England by Mary Sumner in the 1870s. In Australia, it was established first in the diocese of Tasmania in 1892 where it enjoyed the patronage of Maud Montgomery, the wife of Bishop Montgomery, and it soon expanded to the other colonies. At this stage it was one of a tiny number of national women's organizations and by 1912–13 had over 2,000 members.

Women were also active in rural ministry, education, and in outreach to the poor. Queensland and Victoria provided a sympathetic field for Anglican sisterhoods who ran schools and provided a ministry for single women in the Anglo-Catholic tradition. The largest of the Anglican sisterhoods was the Community of the Holy Name, founded in Melbourne in 1888 for work in poor districts. The Society of the Sacred Advent in Brisbane mostly conducted schools. The English Sisters of the Church came to Sydney in 1892 and branched out to Melbourne and Perth (1901) where they worked in schools and among the poor. A smaller group of women were trained in the Evangelical tradition at the Church of England Deaconess Institution in Sydney which first opened in 1891.

[25] Elizabeth Windschuttle, '"Feeding the Poor and Sapping Their Strength": The Public Role of Ruling-Class Women in Eastern Australia, 1788–1850', in Elizabeth Windschuttle (ed.), *Women, Class and History: Feminist Perspectives on Australia 1788–1978* (Melbourne, 1980), pp. 53–79; Anne P. O'Brien, *God's Willing Workers: Women and Religion in Australia* (Sydney, 2005).

SOCIAL LEADERS

By the 1880s, Church authorities were expressing increasing concern about the decline of religious engagement, particularly in the rapidly expanding cities of south-eastern Australia.[26] While the colonies continued to promote themselves as a rural destination in advertising aimed at potential British emigrants, the typical Australian by the turn of the century was a city dweller. The census of 1900 shows that cities held over half the population, almost double that in 1860. Sustained economic growth had attracted emigrants and new urban industries as well as slums and poverty. But nostalgia for the bush fuelled the sales of nationalist literary magazines such as *The Bulletin* which extolled the rugged masculinism of the 'lone hand' and the anti-clerical stereotype of the bush parson. Urban missions sought to reach those who had fallen out of traditional parish-based networks. The Anglicans came to this work rather later than more socially-minded denominations such as Methodists, but by the time of the 1890s depression there were mechanisms in place which began to make inroads into dominant older forms of charitable patronage and philanthropy.[27] In Melbourne the Revd Horace Tucker attempted to create settlements for the urban poor. In Sydney, the social strand in Anglicanism was exemplified in the central city ministries of clergy such as F. B. Boyce (1844–1931) and R. B. S. Hammond (1870–1946) who advocated social housing and teetotalism.[28] Social activism also revived the flagging fortunes of inner city parishes which were losing population as young families moved away to new suburbs.

EMPIRE AND NATION

As the nineteenth century drew to a close, the Church of England was closely entwined with moves to create a national federation of the Australian colonies.[29] In 1898, as Australians were gathering themselves for the first popular vote on federation, Henry Hutchison Montgomery, bishop of Tasmania from 1889 to 1901, promoted the potential of the proposed union to his congregations in Hobart. Montgomery urged his flock to accept the federal union because it would encourage the union of the British race which he saw as

[26] Anne O'Brien, *Philanthropy and Settler Colonialism* (Basingstoke, 2015), p. 90.

[27] Rowan Strong, 'An Antipodean Establishment: Anglicanism in Australian society 1788–c.1934', *Journal of Anglican Studies*, 1 (2003): 61–90.

[28] B. G. Judd, *He That Doeth: The Life Story of Archdeacon R. B. S. Hammond* (London, 1951).

[29] Luke Trainor, *British Imperialism and Australian Nationalism: Manipulation, Conflict and Compromise in the Late Nineteenth Century* (Cambridge, 1994).

the precursor to the spiritual expansion of British Anglicanism. In this way, Australian federation was one step towards the great international union of British Anglicans for which Montgomery yearned.[30]

The 1908 Pan-Anglican Congress was the high point of Anglican imperialism and swept up Australian churchmen. The meetings culminated in a great thanksgiving service in St Paul's during which a massive 'thank offering' of £333,208 was given up for the worldwide needs of the Anglican Church. While generally opposed to the secular manifestations of imperial sentiment, the Australian Church benefited from the public exposure and publicity of the Pan-Anglican Congress.

The last decade of the nineteenth century was also a time for anniversaries and memorials in the colonies. In Australia, the sense of colonies and Churches coming of age was also marked by a series of jubilees. The Melbourne diocese chose to recognize 1897 as a fiftieth jubilee of the consecration of Bishop Perry, the first bishop of Victoria (1847), with the happy coincidence that this year was also the Queen's Diamond Jubilee.[31] The motivation for this was partly financial, hence the invitation to consider the jubilee as a time of 'thankfulness and liberality',[32] but it was also a sign of the general awakening to institutional maturity in the Australian Anglican Church. There was pride that the Australian bishops, together with Bishop Gray of Capetown, and Bishop Selwyn of New Zealand, were among the first Anglican bishops to be established in the British world. In his analysis, Robert Bosher is no doubt correct to point out that the Pan-Anglican Congress was effectively able to build on existing empire-mindedness and the glamour of the imperial capital at the height of the imperial age.[33] The Congress hymn was unashamedly jingoistic:

God of our England's glory
And Empire near and far...
O Lord! We thank Thee on this day
For the deep joy when many meet
Brethren from Britains far away
Who find the old Church sweet.[34]

[30] Steven Maughan, 'Imperial Christianity? Bishop Montgomery and the Foreign Missions of the Church of England, 1895–1915', in Andrew Porter (ed.), *The Imperial Horizons of British Protestant Missions, 1880–1914* (Grand Rapids, MI, 2003), pp. 32–57.

[31] *The Age*, 28 June 1897.

[32] *The Age*, 10 Mar. 1897.

[33] Robert S. Bosher, 'The Pan-Anglican Congress of 1908', *Historical Magazine of the Protestant Episcopal Church*, 23 (1954): 126–42.

[34] Bosher, 'The Pan-Anglican Congress of 1908', p. 130.

CONCLUSION

In Australia the Church of England was, by century's end, the pre-eminent Christian denomination in the new Australian federation and many did find this connection 'sweet'. Yet the Church was insecure about its place in the new order. It had confidently addressed social tensions created by urbanization and the challenge to older forms of mission created by mass emigration. However, it was less sure about the Australian reality in which there was a mixed economy of rival British Churches without a tradition of establishment or significant government aid to religion. Certainly, the Church had successfully expanded to fill the new national borders—but it lacked a distinctive Australian voice. At century's end, the Anglican message of imperial unity and British loyalism continued to resonate with most Australians. Through their elite schools and the Anglican colleges attached to the older universities, the Church of England exerted disproportionate influence on elites within the Church, government, and judiciary. However the pattern set by explosive settler colonialism in the second half of the nineteenth century would soon be blown away by the Australian response to war.

SELECT BIBLIOGRAPHY

Barrett, John, *That Better Country: The Religious Aspect of Life in Eastern Australia 1835–1850* (Melbourne, 1966).

Border, Joseph Thomas Ross, *Church and State in Australia, 1788–1872: A Constitutional Study of the Church of England in Australia* (London, 1962).

Bremner, G. A., *Imperial Gothic: Religious Architecture and High Anglican Culture in the British Empire, c.1840–1870* (New Haven, CT, 2013).

Breward, Ian, *A History of the Australian Churches* (Sydney, 1993).

Breward, Ian, *A History of the Churches in Australasia* (Oxford, 2001).

Carey, Hilary M., 'Gladstone, the Colonial Church and Imperial State', in Hilary M. Carey and John Gascoigne (eds.), *Church and State in Old and New Worlds* (Leiden, 2011), pp. 155–82.

Carey, Hilary M., *God's Empire: Religion and Colonialism in the British World* (Cambridge, 2011).

Dimont, C. T. and F. de Witt Batty, *St. Clair Donaldson, Archbishop of Brisbane, 1904–1921; Bishop of Salisbury, 1921–1935* (London, 1939).

Eddy, J. J., *Britain and the Australian Colonies 1818–1831: The Technique of Government* (Oxford, 1969).

Frappell, Ruth, 'The Australian Bush Brotherhoods and Their English Origins', *Journal of Ecclesiastical History*, 47 (1996): 82–97.

Gladwin, Michael, *Anglican Clergy in Australia, 1788–1850: Building a British World* (Woodbridge, 2015).

Hardwick, Joseph, *An Anglican British World: The Church of England and the Expansion of the Settler Empire, c.1790–1860* (Manchester, 2015).

Harris, John W., *One Blood: 200 Years of Aboriginal Encounter with Christianity, a Story of Hope* (Sutherland, New South Wales, 1994 edn.).

Hilliard, David, *Godliness and Good Order: A History of the Anglican Church in South Australia* (Netley, South Australia, 1986).

Judd, Stephen and Kenneth Cable, *Sydney Anglicans: A History of the Diocese* (Sydney, 2000).

Kaye, Bruce, Tom Frame, Colin Holden, and Geoffrey R. Treloar (eds.), *Anglicanism in Australia: A History* (Melbourne, 2002).

O'Brien, Anne P., *God's Willing Workers: Women and Religion in Australia* (Sydney, 2005).

Roe, Michael, *Quest for Authority in Eastern Australia, 1835–1851* (Melbourne, 1965).

Strong, Rowan, *Anglicanism and the British Empire, c.1700–1850* (Oxford, 2007).

17

Anglicanism in New Zealand and the South Pacific

Allan K. Davidson

New Zealand and the South Pacific islands are further away from England than almost any other part of the world, and yet they were profoundly shaped by English Anglican missionary and colonial forces. The beginnings of permanent European settlement in New Zealand were inextricably linked with Samuel Marsden, chaplain in New South Wales, and his inauguration of missionary work among Māori, the country's indigenous inhabitants. In Australia Marsden was caught up in political controversies and criticized for his role as a magistrate and his extensive agricultural endeavours, but in New Zealand he gained a reputation as an almost patriarchal figure among Māori. Marsden's Evangelical commitment and connections encouraged the Church Missionary Society (CMS) to appoint its first English agents, sent anywhere in the world, to New Zealand. Founded in 1799 as a voluntary society 'upon the *Church-principle*, not the *High* Church principle',[1] the CMS initially lacked episcopal support and clerical recruits. In appointing lay artisans, Marsden argued that their civilizing activities would raise Māori moral and industrial habits, making them more receptive to the gospel. Civilizing and Christianizing were not an either/or, but Marsden's emphasis initially downplayed the latter dimension.

William Hall, a carpenter, and John King, a shoemaker, were chosen by Marsden on his visit to England in 1808 when he secured CMS support. He had already established a close relationship with Te Pahi, a leading Māori chief from the Bay of Islands who visited New South Wales in 1805. Te Pahi's young relative, Ruatara, who Marsden had previously met, was on the ship returning with Marsden to Australia. A strong mutual friendship developed, reinforced

[1] Charles Hole, *The Early History of the Church Missionary Society for Africa and the East to the end of A.D. 1814* (London, 1896), p. 31.

by Marsden's hospitality to Ruatara at Parramatta and the help he gave in introducing Ruatara to new agricultural techniques.

The mission's beginning was delayed by the sacking of the *Boyd* in 1809 in a reprisal action by Māori against ill-treatment by Europeans. King and Hall were joined by Thomas Kendall, a school teacher, in 1813. A preliminary voyage to New Zealand by Hall and Kendall in mid-1814 and an invitation by Ruatara encouraged Marsden to commence the mission. Anglican beginnings in New Zealand were based on an engagement between missionaries and *tangata whenua*, people of the land, which over subsequent decades evolved in multiple ways.

For Marsden there was a strong relationship between the gospel and national identity. On Christmas Day 1814, at Ruatara's village where the mission party arrived a few days earlier, he described the English flag flying above Rangihoua as 'the signal for the dawn of civilization, liberty, and religion . . . and flattered myself they would never be removed till the natives of that island enjoyed all the happiness of British subjects'.[2] He led worship and preached from the text, 'Behold! I bring you glad tidings of great joy' (Luke 2:10). Ruatara had made the arrangements for the service and attempted to explain Marsden's sermon to Māori. Sadly for the mission, Ruatara died in March 1815 shortly after Marsden departed for Australia. Ruatara has become known as *Te Ara mō te Rongopai*—'The Gateway of the Gospel'.[3]

The mission struggled in its early years with internal conflict and external pressures. The leading Bay of Islands chief, Hongi Hika, as the mission's protector, was involved in tribal fighting using newly acquired muskets in devastating raids against traditional enemies. Kendall, accompanied by Hongi, and another chief, during a visit to England, helped by Professor Samuel Lee, was able to construct a Māori grammar, crucial in both understanding and translating the language. While in England Kendall was ordained. After his return, his adultery and musket-trading provoked his dismissal. The arrival of the Revd Henry Williams in 1823 brought on-the-spot leadership giving impetus to evangelization, itineration, teaching, translation, and peace-making. Henry's brother William joined the mission in 1826 bringing considerable linguistic skills.[4]

Following Hongi's death in 1828 Māori showed an increasing interest in Christianity. The release of slaves, captured during the 'musket wars' and brought to the north where they learnt about Christianity, resulted in a

[2] J. R. Elder (ed.), *The Letters and Journals of Samuel Marsden 1765–1838* (Dunedin, 1932), p. 93; J. R. Elder (ed.), *Marsden's Lieutenants* (Dunedin, 1934).

[3] Ken Booth, *For All the Saints: A Resource for the Commemorations of the Calendar* (Hastings, New Zealand, 1996), pp. 152–6.

[4] Judith Binney, *The Legacy of Guilt: A Life of Thomas Kendall* (Auckland, 2005 edn.); Caroline Fitzgerald (ed.), *Te Wiremu: Henry Williams—Early Years in the North* (Wellington, 2011).

remarkable spontaneous indigenous-led spread of Christianity throughout the country. Piripi Taumata-a-Kura, for example, returned to the east coast of the North Island where, on his own initiative, he became a teacher and preacher. One expression of the increasing interest in Christianity was learning to read and write. Newly translated portions of the Bible and Prayer Book, and the printing undertaken by William Colenso from 1834, with the whole New Testament available from 1837, fed this interest. Leaders, such as Nopera Pana-karaeo in Kataia, Tamihana Te Rauparaha, and Matene Te Whiwhi from the Kapiti Coast on the south-western coast of the North Island, and Wiremu Tamihana Tarapipipi Te Waharoa in the Waikato, acted as evangelists among their own people and missionaries to others.

Historians have disagreed over the reasons why Māori after their initial disinterest in and rejection of Christianity, from the 1830s became Christians in large numbers. 'Conversion' was on a continuum from those who fitted the missionaries' expectation of an individual experience of saving grace, to those who blended Christian ideas and practices into tribal life. Literacy was one attraction, along with access to new knowledge and material goods. The missionaries' advocacy of peace, after intense inter-tribal conflict, found a response within Māori society.[5]

From the latter part of the 1830s the leadership of capable ordained missionaries in the North Island such as William Williams on the east coast, Alfred Brown in the Waikato and Bay of Plenty, Robert Maunsell in the Waikato, Octavius Hadfield on the Kapiti Coast, and Richard Taylor in Whanganui, together with the establishment of mission stations consolidated this missionary expansion. Missionary wives, for example, Marianne Williams and Jane Williams were influential, particularly among women and children. CMS missionaries maintained collegial relationships with Wesleyans who commenced work with CMS support in 1822. But the arrival of French Catholic Marist missionaries in 1838 under the leadership of Bishop J. B. F. Pompallier resulted in local rivalries between people being caught up in European denominational allegiances.[6]

During his last visit in 1837, the year before his death, Marsden noted that 'The prospect of success to the Mission is very great.'[7] By 1840 thirty-eight male CMS missionaries had come to New Zealand, including nine ordained priests and five single women.[8] Anglican missionaries were, however, in a

[5] Timothy Yates, *The Conversion of the Māori: Years of Religious and Social Change, 1814–1842* (Grand Rapids, MI, 2013).

[6] Caroline Fitzgerald (ed.), *Letters from the Bay of Islands: The Story of Marianne Williams* (Auckland, 2004); Cathy Ross, *Women with a Mission: Rediscovering Missionary Wives in Early New Zealand* (Auckland, 2006).

[7] Elder (ed.), *Letters and Journals*, p. 522.

[8] Church Missionary Society, *Register of Missionaries (Clerical, Lay, & Female), and Native Clergy from 1804 to 1904* (London, 1904); Robert Glen (ed.), *Mission and Moko: Aspects of the*

somewhat anomalous situation respecting ecclesiastical jurisdiction. Prior to the proclamation of British sovereignty, ordained clergy were nominally under the bishop of London, but geographical distance made nonsense of this. When W. G. Broughton, the first Anglican bishop in Australia, visited New Zealand in 1838–9, he ordained Octavius Hadfield as a priest, confirmed Māori converts, and consecrated church and burial grounds. As a High Churchman he justified his actions on the basis of his inherent rights deriving from episcopal ordination.

Concerns were increasingly raised by missionaries about the detrimental impact of Europeans, or Pākehā as Māori called them, who were settling in the country. Missionaries were instrumental in 1831 in a petition signed by thirteen northern chiefs to King William IV requesting protection against possible French annexation. Through their personal links in London, the missionaries contributed to the parliamentary reports and debates on aboriginal rights in the late 1830s, and opposition to the colonization schemes devised by William Wakefield.

Although the CMS was a voluntary organization within the Church of England, its leaders were committed to the establishment relationship between Church and state. That was seen in the role Anglican missionaries played in the creation of the New Zealand colony. In 1839 the Colonial Office dispatched Captain William Hobson to secure cession of sovereignty from Māori, assume control of land transactions, and make provision for Māori welfare; he was instructed to look to the missionaries for support. The former British Resident, James Busby, worked with Hobson in drawing up a Treaty which was translated into Māori by Henry Williams and his son Edward. The Treaty of Waitangi was presented by Hobson to Māori on 5 February 1840 with Williams acting as the interpreter for the day's debate. Missionary support ensured Māori acceptance on 6 February. Bishop Pompallier's intervention secured the recognition of religious toleration as an unwritten article. In the following months, Williams and other missionaries assisted in obtaining signatures from over 500 chiefs throughout the country, leading to Hobson's proclamation of British sovereignty. Since 1840 there has been much debate over the Treaty, the differences between the Māori and English versions, its impact on Māori and their loss of land, and their exercise of *rangatiratanga* or chiefly autonomy. The vital involvement of Anglican missionaries in this foundational national event continues to attract critical attention.[9]

In 1840 a promising Anglican Māori Church, worshipping in the Māori language was emerging. The Pākehā population was estimated at 2,000, while

Work of the Church Missionary Society in New Zealand 1814–1882 (Christchurch, 1992), pp. 193–212.

[9] Keith Newman, *Bible & Treaty: Missionaries Among the Māori—A New Perspective* (North Shore, New Zealand, 2010); Claudia Orange, *The Treaty of Waitangi* (Wellington, 1987).

Māori numbered over 70,000. Within twenty years Māori were overtaken by Pākehā. By 1910 New Zealand's population reached over one million, but Māori declined to a low point of some 42,000 in 1896. Missionary dominance in New Zealand affairs in 1840 was rapidly sidelined as Māori were swamped by Pākehā settlers. There was considerable incompatibility between missionary Christianity, with its commitment to Māori, and colonial Christianity, which was linked to the aspirations of migrants who desired land to advance themselves.[10]

George Augustus Selwyn's ordination as 'Bishop of New Zealand' in 1841 brought missionary and colonial episcopal oversight together. He was the first appointee of the Colonial Bishoprics Fund, which was inaugurated by Charles Blomfield, the bishop of London, to promote and endow colonial bishoprics. Selwyn's stipend was funded equally by the CMS and the Colonial Office. Educated at Eton and St John's College, Cambridge, Selwyn was shaped by traditional High Church theology, emphasizing apostolicity, catholicity, and episcopal authority. He was sympathetic to, although not a supporter of, the Oxford Movement, and was a member of the Cambridge Camden (Ecclesiological) Society. He worked closely with CMS Evangelicals although they regarded his churchmanship with suspicion. Henry Venn, the CMS secretary, and Selwyn tussled over issues of Church authority and the control of the missionaries. Venn, with his ideas about the autonomy and independence of the missionary Church was disappointed with Selwyn's slowness in ordaining Māori and promoting indigenous leadership. The first Māori ordained was Rota Waitoa, as deacon in 1853 and priest in 1860.[11]

Selwyn arrived in 1842, impressing CMS missionaries by his youthfulness (he was thirty-three) and energy; he became something of an archetype for Victorian muscular Christianity. The College of St John the Evangelist, first at the CMS mission at Waimate in 1843, and then in Auckland from 1844, was to be the 'key and pivot' of his diocese—a multi-level institution with a seminary, Māori teachers' and boys' schools, grammar school, and infant department. Alongside this were a hospital, building and printing departments, and a farm with students and staff engaging in 'useful industry' to gain practical skills to help them live in a colonial environment. Disagreements with the CMS and their missionaries, settler prejudices against mixed-race schooling, concerns about leadership, and finally a homosexual scandal contributed to the College's closure in 1853. St John's, some of its constituent parts and its endowment, found new life through a variety of institutions over subsequent decades.[12]

[10] Allan K. Davidson, 'The Interaction of Missionary and Colonial Christianity in Nineteenth Century New Zealand', *Studies in World Christianity*, 2 (1996): 145–66.

[11] Allan K. Davidson (ed.), *A Controversial Churchman: Essays on George Selwyn, Bishop of New Zealand and Lichfield, and Sarah Selwyn* (Wellington, 2011).

[12] Allan K. Davidson, 'Useful Industry and Muscular Christianity: George Augustus Selwyn and His Early Years as Bishop of New Zealand', in R. N. Swanson (ed.), *The Use and Abuse of Time in Christian History* (Woodbridge, 2002), pp. 289–304; G. A. Selwyn, *Are Cathedral*

Freed from the constraints of establishment, Selwyn rejoiced in the 'power to mould the institutions of the church from the beginning according to true principles'.[13] On the basis of his episcopal ordination, and in what some thought was a breach of royal prerogative, he appointed archdeacons to provide regional oversight, and called clerical synods in 1844 and 1847. Australasian bishops met in conference in Sydney in 1850, where Selwyn advocated provincial and diocesan autonomy, and clerical and lay participation in governance. Influenced by democratizing pressures from leading laymen and aware of the constitutional structure of the American Protestant Episcopal Church, Selwyn negotiated with CMS leaders, and consulted with crown officials in England and Church people in New Zealand about Church governance. The constitutional convention held over a month in Auckland in 1857 included Henry Harper, the recently appointed bishop of Christchurch, clergy, and leading laity. Voluntary compact was accepted as the basis for Church membership, with synodical government endorsed at both national and diocesan levels. Bishops, clergy, and laity sat together, although they voted in separate houses. Fundamental provisions entrenched the 'formularies': the Book of Common Prayer, the Ordinal, the Thirty-Nine Articles, and the Authorized Version of the Bible. For its time, the constitution was innovative in governance and conservative in liturgy and theology. The exclusion of Māori from the constitutional deliberations reflected how Selwyn was dealing with a peculiarly Anglican issue of separation of Church and state and the CMS concern to protect Māori interests. The participation of leading missionaries was seen as providing a CMS voice. The end result, however, was that Māori from the 1860s were assimilated within the Pākehā church structures.

The arrival of emigrants and increasing alienation of Māori land provoked tension and eventually conflict. Māori *rangatiratanga* or sovereignty resulted in polarization between *kaupapa* or loyal Māori and those asserting their autonomy. In the Bay of Islands in 1844–5 Anglican Māori were divided by a conflict which erupted in which Hone Heke, a baptized member of the Church, and his men, cut down a flagpole flying the Union Jack four times, symbolically rejecting British sovereignty. Henry Williams was criticized by Māori for the government's failure to observe the Treaty, and by Pākehā for being too friendly to Māori. Governor George Grey, who arrived in 1845, and Selwyn, unjustly discredited Williams and other missionaries, who were accused of excessive and questionable land purchases from Māori. Although Williams justified his purchases as fair and made on his children's behalf, he

Institutions Useless? A Practical Answer to this Question, Addressed to W. E. Gladstone, Esq. M.P. (London, 1838); Allan K. Davidson, *Selwyn's Legacy: The College of St John the Evangelist, Te Waimate and Auckland—A History, 1843–1992* (Auckland, 1993).

[13] H. W. Tucker (ed.), *Memoir of the Life and Episcopate of George Augustus Selwyn*, 2 vols. (London, 1879), II, p. 83.

was dismissed from the CMS. Williams was reinstated in 1854 but by then the damage to the northern missionaries' influence had been done.

Selwyn and leading Anglicans were caught between advocating for Māori and supporting the settler community. These tensions multiplied in the 1850s. New Zealand gained responsible government in 1852 but Māori were excluded from participation. The inspirational Anglican chief, Wiremu Tamihana in the Waikato, who built his own Christian village and acted as a peace-maker, drew on the example of Samuel and Solomon to encourage the recognition of a Māori king in 1858 as a means of maintaining law and order among Māori and protecting their land. Selwyn and many missionaries were initially supportive. Settler pressure to acquire land, however, resulted in fighting in Taranaki in 1860 over an unjust purchase. An Anglican pro-Māori group led by Archdeacon Octavius Hadfield, the former chief justice Sir William Martin, and Selwyn vehemently criticized government actions.

The increasingly aggressive government policy, first in Taranaki, and then from 1863 in the Waikato resulted in a war that went on for ten years. The King Movement, or *kīngitanga*, was now questioned by Anglican leaders as challenging the Queen's sovereignty. Selwyn's role as a chaplain to the colonial troops undermined his credibility among their Māori opponents. Many rejected missionary Christianity and were caught up in indigenous religious movements combining Christian teaching and traditional cultural values. Missionary loyalties were tested and often compromised. C. S. Völkner, the CMS missionary at Opotiki, gave information to the governor on Māori leading to his 'trial' as a spy and murder by disaffected Māori in March 1865. The war seriously damaged confidence in the Anglican Church among Māori in the middle portion of the North Island.[14]

Nominally the Anglican Church for a brief period included about 50 per cent of the Pākehā population, but from the 1870s until after the First World War averaged between 40 and 42 per cent. The largest number of emigrants came from England. Providing clergy and buildings was a huge challenge for a colonial society. The Church never had establishment status in New Zealand although its leaders often assumed a *de facto* establishment role.[15]

Selwyn's large diocese was progressively subdivided from 1856. The first bishops, Henry Harper in Christchurch, Edmund Hobhouse in Nelson, and C. J. Abraham in Wellington, were linked to Selwyn by Eton and Oxbridge

[14] Bronwyn Elsmore, *Mana from Heaven: A Century of Maori Prophets in New Zealand* (Auckland, 1999).

[15] Allan K. Davidson and Peter J. Lineham, *Transplanted Christianity: Documents Illustrating Aspects of New Zealand Church History* (Palmerston North, 1989), pp. 181–2; Allan K. Davidson, 'Colonial Christianity: The Contribution of the Society for the Propagation of the Gospel to the Anglican Church in New Zealand 1840–80', *Journal of Religious History*, 16 (1990): 173–84; G. A. Wood, 'Church and State in New Zealand in the 1850s', *Journal of Religious History*, 8 (1975): 255–70.

connections. William Williams's ordination as bishop of Waiapu at the first General Synod in 1859 reflected the accord Selwyn negotiated with the CMS. The separation of the diocese of Dunedin from Christchurch proved to be troublesome. Henry Jenner's selection as bishop, his premature consecration by the archbishop of Canterbury in 1866, and endorsement by Selwyn backfired when Dunedin opposition was mounted against Jenner's ritualistic sympathies. Harper became primate after Selwyn's departure in 1869 and he presided over both the diocesan and general synods rejecting Jenner. This vote was an expression of New Zealand's ecclesiastical autonomy from the Church of England with Jenner the unfortunate victim. S. T. Nevill was consecrated as bishop of Dunedin in 1871, a position he held for nearly fifty years.

Initially, there was a contest over the respective powers of the general (national) and diocesan synods. Christchurch, with its large endowments gained from its beginnings as a Church of England settlement, ensured that dioceses with their annual synods became the Church's powerbase. Antipodean Anglican identity brought together British and Irish strains, with Broad to Low Church predominating. Diocesan bishops imprinted their own character on their dioceses. Nelson diocese under A. B. Suter, its second bishop, developed a distinctive Evangelical character. Christchurch was regarded as a very English city with the site for its cathedral at its centre and institutions such as Christ's College reflecting the English model of public schools. The contribution of Anglicans to primary and secondary education, however, was divided between their own schools and the larger state system, which from 1877 in the face of sectarianism was committed to primary education that was 'free, secular and compulsory'. Intense loyalty to the crown and empire was expressed in uncritical support for British imperial causes, notably in the South African War. But sabbatarianism and an active prohibition movement were led by Protestant Churches without extensive overt Anglican involvement.

Following Selwyn's activist episcopacy, the Church at a national level was largely apolitical. Triennial general synods, the lack of a permanent primatial see, and a succession of ageing primates limited the Church's impact on national life. Anglicans fell silent in the face of Māori protest over the continuing alienation of their land, notably with the peaceful prophetic movement at Parihaka in Taranaki in the 1870s and 1880s. Initially, the Waiapu diocesan synods conducted their proceedings in Māori. Following the wars of the 1860s and the relocation of the bishop to Napier, English was used in the synod meetings. Attempts to gain episcopal leadership for or by Māori made no progress. When Williams resigned as bishop of Waiapu in 1876 a plea for a Māori to be elected as bishop fell on deaf ears. The attempt in 1880 to have a suffragan bishop of Auckland appointed for Māori work was rejected on the grounds of the unity of the races, and the hope that they would work together.

Diocesan Māori Church Boards provided Māori with an opportunity to discuss matters concerning themselves, but their voices were largely absent at the synodical decision-making level. Eventually in 1898, after several attempts, provision was made to ensure Māori representation at diocesan synods. Attempts to achieve this at the General Synod in 1901 and 1913 failed. The conclusion of CMS grants in 1902 led to the appointment of a Māori Mission Board in 1904 to finance Māori work, but it had no Māori members. By 1910, 100 Māori had been ordained deacons and of these sixty-four had become priests. Te Rau College was established in Gisborne in 1883 for training Māori ministers from all the North Island dioceses using the vernacular. From the early twentieth century, however, the use of English in teaching increased. Te Aute College, founded in 1854 by Samuel Williams, and reopened in 1870 under the leadership of its headmaster, John Thornton, was successful in stimulating Māori leadership in social and political areas through the Te Aute College Students' Association. A new generation of prominent Anglican Māori political and church leaders were influenced by this.[16]

ANGLICAN NEW ZEALAND

Migrant communities often conserve the religious traditions they bring to a new land. That was true of New Zealand Anglicans in their worship, church architecture, and theology. Although their seasonal world was turned upside down, Christmas, observed in summer, reflected northern hemisphere symbolism. Few attempts were made to re-envision Christianity from within their new context. Adaptations were made in using wood for church buildings, resulting in the timber-framed 'Selwyn Churches' inspired by the Gothic Revival with their steep shingled roofs, while several unique Māori churches blended European architecture and Māori carving and weaving.[17]

Anglicans described themselves in 1857 as 'The United Church of England and Ireland in New Zealand'. Following disestablishment in Ireland the title was changed in 1874 to 'The Church of the Province of New Zealand' with the appendage, 'commonly known as the Church of England'. This identity was reinforced by recruiting English clergy and bishops. Of the fifteen bishops in New Zealand up until 1910, twelve were born in England, one in Ireland, one in Scotland, and one, Leonard Williams, the third bishop of Waiapu, in

[16] G. H. D. Connor, 'Whāia te Atuatanga: Theological Education, Textbooks, Te Rau College, Cultures and Contexts', MA thesis, Massey University, 2012.

[17] Colin Brown, *Vision and Reality: Christchurch's Cathedral in the Square* (Christchurch, 2000); C. R. Knight, *The Selwyn Churches of Auckland* (Wellington, 1972); Richard A. Sundt, *Whare Karakia: Māori Church Building, Decoration & Ritual in Aotearoa New Zealand 1834–1863* (Auckland, 2010).

New Zealand. A Provincial Board of Theological Studies, established in 1874, provided curricula and examinations for clerical training which ensured uniformity with an almost exclusive dependence on English theological texts. The debates over ritualism and the trial of Henry Carlyon, the incumbent in Kaiapoi, who was found guilty in 1877 of practices and doctrine contrary to Church teaching, mirrored English disputes without the intensity and extent of division found in England. The demands of the Church in a pioneering context, the moderating influence of bishops and the relative freedom for parishes and their clergy to develop their own ethos helped mitigate, if not prevent, ritualistic and theological divisions.

Church leadership was in male hands, with, in contrast to England, an expanded role given to laymen in parish and diocesan oversight and in acting as lay readers to overcome the shortage of clergy. Women were active in supporting roles through pastoral and children's work, charitable and community service. Exceptionally, Sarah Selwyn, Mary Ann Martin, and Caroline Abraham joined their husbands in protesting vigorously against land injustice in 1860. Although New Zealand in 1893 was the first country in the world to give women the vote, it was another thirty years before Anglican ecclesiastical franchise was extended to women. In Auckland from 1883, the Women's Home, with Eliza Cowie, the bishop's wife its first superintendent, provided a refuge for prostitutes and unmarried mothers. The Community of the Sacred Name under the leadership of Sister Edith was brought to Christchurch by Bishop Churchill Julius in 1893. The following year, the Mission to the Streets and Lanes of Auckland was formed with a commitment to minister to children and the poor. This became the Mission of the Good Shepherd in 1900 and the Order of the Good Shepherd in 1905. Only a small number of women committed themselves to religious vocations, but orphanages and other benevolent institutions, both within and without the Church, drew on considerable support from church women.[18]

THE PACIFIC

The Anglican presence in the Pacific beyond New Zealand was constrained by Selwyn's recognition of comity. The London Missionary Society was active in the Pacific from 1797 and Methodists from 1822. Despite the heavy demands of New Zealand, Selwyn claimed a mandate deriving from Archbishop William Howley's valedictory description of New Zealand 'as the central point of a system extending its influence in all directions . . . over the islands

[18] Margaret McClure, *Saving the City: The History of the Order of the Good Shepherd and the Community of the Holy Name in Auckland, 1894–2000* (Auckland, 2002).

and coasts of the Pacific'.[19] Recalling the debt of the Church in England to Augustine, Selwyn in 1847 held out the vision of New Zealand forming a 'Missionary centre' where Polynesian youths could be gathered and carry to their people 'the strictest knowledge, and the most confirmed faith'.[20] Lacking financial resources and manpower, Selwyn inaugurated the Melanesian mission in 1849 with an innovative missionary strategy. Sailing his little schooner to the New Hebrides (Vanuatu) and New Caledonia, he brought five young men back to St John's College. Voyages to the New Hebrides and Solomon Islands, recruiting and returning scholars became an annual pattern. This approach lessened problems posed by malaria and other endemic diseases, the plurality of languages in Melanesia, and the hostility facing Europeans. The strategy's weakness lay in the ineffectiveness of young men and women, who had lacked status in their own societies, becoming evangelists among their own people.[21]

John Coleridge Patteson was recruited by Selwyn to take over the leadership of the mission. He was consecrated without letters patent in 1861 as 'Missionary Bishop of the Western Isles of the South Pacific Ocean'. Melanesia became a missionary diocese of the New Zealand Church. Patteson's extraordinary linguistic skills were advantageous given the many languages in Melanesia. He also built on Selwyn's positive attitude towards Melanesians emphasizing their shared common humanity. A distinguishing characteristic of the mission from its more Evangelical counterparts was the way it valued indigenous cultures. An attempt to set up a supporting Australasian Board of Missions failed and in its initial decades the mission depended heavily on English and family support.

In 1861 the headquarters moved from St John's College to Mission Bay in Auckland, and in 1867 to Norfolk Island which was closer to the islands with a more favourable climate. Mota, an island language, was adopted as the mission's lingua franca. While committed to developing an indigenous Church, the public school model of education, the Prayer Book approach to worship, and the Christian pattern of marriage meant that the mission reflected an Anglicized Church blueprint. European labour traffickers in the northern New Hebrides and Solomon Islands disturbed local communities, contributing to the murder of Bishop Patteson at Nukapu in 1871. Patteson was rapidly recognized as a martyr, giving the mission prominence in Anglican circles.[22]

[19] Tucker, *The Life of Bishop Selwyn*, I, p. 85.

[20] [G. A. Selwyn], *A Charge Delivered to the Clergy of the Diocese of New Zealand at the Diocesan Synod in the Chapel of St. John's College, on Thursday, September 23, 1847* (London, 1849), p. 20.

[21] Allan Davidson (ed.), *The Church of Melanesia 1849–1999: Marking the 150th Anniversary of the Founding of the Melanesian Mission* (Auckland, 2000); David Hilliard, *God's Gentlemen: A History of the Melanesian Mission, 1849–1942* (St Lucia, Australia, 1978).

[22] David Hilliard, 'The Making of an Anglican Martyr: Bishop John Coleridge Patteson of Melanesia', in D. Wood (ed.), *Martyrs and Martyrologies* (Oxford 1993), pp. 333–45.

After an interval of six years under the leadership of the mission's scholarly headmaster Robert Codrington, John Selwyn, son of the founder, was consecrated bishop of Melanesia. Throughout the remaining century the mission continued annual voyages with the exchange of students. Summer schools during which missionaries lived with local people deepened contacts. Employment of women missionaries on Norfolk Island to work with Melanesian girls and young women was motivated in part to provide 'Christian wives for Christian lads'.[23] The ordination of George Sarawia as the mission's first deacon in 1868 and priest in 1873 did not lead as quickly to the indigenous Church Patteson had envisaged. Following Patteson's death, a growing paternalism resulted in greater dependency on European missionaries. Underneath the external Church influences traditional Melanesian forces remained strong, as Sarawia's involvement on his home island of Mota in the *sukwe* cult, a men's secret society, indicated. During Cecil Wilson's episcopate, 1894 to 1911, the mission began work in Queensland among Melanesian labourers and settled European missionaries permanently in the islands. The mission's dominance in the islands was challenged by missionaries from other Churches and its growing European staff displaced earlier emphases on the locally led Church.

In Fiji, where Methodists were active from 1835, an Anglican colonial chaplaincy was begun by William Floyd at Levuka in 1870. Nevill, bishop of Dunedin, independently advocated Anglican intervention, looking forward in 1886 to an 'Oceanic Province' with more bishops and missionary activity. Suter investigated Polynesia for the New Zealand Church resulting in no immediate action. Harper as primate, while sensitive to Methodist claims, hoped the issue would be addressed at the Lambeth Conference in 1888; nothing came of this.

The annexation of Hawai'i by the United States in 1898 precipitated its bishop, Alfred Willis, to look towards Tonga to continue his episcopal ministry. At the age of sixty-six, after thirty years in Hawai'i, Willis arrived in Tonga in June 1902. The Anglican congregations gathered around Willis were small. While Nevill as acting-primate in 1902 recognized Willis as 'Missionary Bishop of Tonga', the Society for the Propagation of the Gospel (SPG) were reluctant to endorse him.[24]

The growing Melanesian community working in the Fijian sugar plantations along with the arrival of indentured Indian labourers gave Anglicans a

[23] Janet Crawford, '"Christian Wives for Christian Lads"', in Allan Davidson and Godfrey Nicholson (eds.), *'With all Humility and Gentleness': Essays on Mission in Honour of Francis Foulkes* (Auckland, 1991), pp. 51–66.

[24] Allan K. Davidson (ed.), *Tongan Anglicans 1902–2002: From the Church of England Mission in Tonga to the Tongan Anglican Church* (Auckland, 2002); Stephen L. Donald, *In Some Sense the Work of an Individual: Alfred Willis and the Tongan Anglican Mission 1902–1920* (Hibiscus Coast, Auckland, 1994).

missionary thrust alongside their colonial chaplaincy. T. C. Twitchell's appointment in 1908 as missionary bishop in Polynesia under the jurisdiction of the bishop of London recognized the need for episcopal oversight. The SPG then began supporting Willis whose title was eventually regularized in 1913 as 'Assistant Bishop for Tonga'.

CONCLUSION

Anglicans in New Zealand in 1910 still mirrored their English origins in their worship, ministry, and ethos. Contrasting features with England were their assertion of ecclesiastical autonomy, synodical government, and lay leadership. While the emerging Māori Church of 1840 was assimilated under the dominant Pākehā structures, it continued in its ministry and local life to retain distinctive Māori characteristics. Similarly, Anglican identity in the Melanesian mission and Polynesia reflected some local features, but its leadership, governance, and worship mirrored its Church of England origins. Anglicanism had been transplanted to the South Pacific but was still taking root.

SELECT BIBLIOGRAPHY

Bester, R. (ed.), *Harvest of Grace: Essays in Celebration of 150 Years of Mission in the Nelson Diocese* (Nelson, 2010).

Binney, Judith, *The Legacy of Guilt: A Life of Thomas Kendall* (Auckland, 2005 edn.).

Bluck, John (ed.), *The Gift Endures: A New History of the Waiapu Diocese* (Christchurch, 2009).

Brown, Colin, Marie Peters, and Jane Teal (eds.), *Shaping a Colonial Church: Bishop Harper and the Anglican Diocese of Christchurch* (Christchurch, 2006).

Davidson, Allan K. (ed.), *A Controversial Churchman: Essays on George Selwyn, Bishop of New Zealand and Lichfield, and Sarah Selwyn* (Wellington, 2011).

Davidson, Allan K. (ed.), *Living Legacy: A History of the Anglican Diocese of Auckland* (Auckland, 2011).

Davidson, Allan K., *Selwyn's Legacy: The College of St John the Evangelist, Te Waimate and Auckland—A History, 1843–1992* (Auckland, 1993).

Davidson, Allan K. (ed.), *Tongan Anglicans 1902–2002: From the Church of England Mission in Tonga to the Tongan Anglican Church* (Auckland, 2002).

Davidson, Allan K., Stuart Lange, Peter Lineham, and Adrienne Puckey (eds.), *Te Rongopai 1814: 'Takoto te pai!' Bicentenary Reflections on Christian Beginnings and Developments in Aotearoa New Zealand* (Auckland, General Synod Office, 2014).

Davidson, Allan K. and Peter J. Lineham, *Transplanted Christianity: Documents Illustrating Aspects of New Zealand Church History* (Palmerston North, 1989).

Elder, J. R. (ed.), *The Letters and Journals of Samuel Marsden 1765–1838* (Dunedin, 1932).

Elder, J. R. (ed.), *Marsden's Lieutenants* (Dunedin, New Zealand, 1934).

Evans, John H., *Churchman Militant: George Augustus Selwyn, Bishop of New Zealand and Lichfield* (London and Wellington, 1964).

Evans, John H., *Southern See: The Anglican Diocese of Dunedin New Zealand* (Dunedin, New Zealand, 1868).

Fitzgerald, Caroline (ed.), *Letters from the Bay of Islands: The Story of Marianne Williams* (Auckland, 2004).

Fitzgerald, Caroline (ed.), *Te Wiremu: Henry Williams—Early Years in the North* (Wellington, 2011).

Glen, Robert (ed.), *Mission and Moko: Aspects of the Work of the Church Missionary Society in New Zealand 1814–1882* (Christchurch, 1992).

Hilliard, David, *God's Gentlemen: A History of the Melanesian Mission, 1849–1942* (St Lucia, Australia, 1978).

Limbrick, Warren E. (ed.), *Bishop Selwyn in New Zealand 1841–68* (Palmerston North, 1983).

Morrell, W. P., *The Anglican Church in New Zealand: A History* (Dunedin, 1973).

Newman, Keith, *Bible & Treaty: Missionaries Among the Māori—A New Perspective* (North Shore, 2010).

Ross, Cathy, *Women with a Mission: Rediscovering Missionary Wives in Early New Zealand* (Auckland, 2006).

Tucker, H. W. (ed.), *Memoir of the Life and Episcopate of George Augustus Selwyn*, 2 vols. (London, 1879).

Williams, R. W. K., *George Augustus Selwyn (1809–1878): Theological Formation, Life and Work* (Farnham, 2014).

Williams, William, *Christianity Among the New Zealanders* (London, 1867).

Yarwood, A. T., *Samuel Marsden: The Great Survivor* (Carlton, Victoria, 1977).

Yates, Timothy, *The Conversion of the Māori: Years of Religious and Social Change, 1814–1842* (Grand Rapids, MI, 2013).

18

Anglicanism in Latin America, 1810–1918

David Rock

In post-independence Latin America, the British Episcopal Church, as it was first known, required the presence of English merchants and settlers and of a supportive political environment but only the Rio de la Plata region met these conditions to a sufficient degree. In liberal Buenos Aires, freedom of worship preceded the Catholic Emancipation Act of 1829 in Britain itself but elsewhere British mercantile connections were weaker, liberalism was less developed, and all forms of Protestant worship lagged.[1] Anglicanism extended its range after 1860 as British investment flowed into the continent. The British built railways on the Argentine pampas; they opened mining camps on the Chilean coast, the Peruvian highlands, and Minas Gerais in Brazil; they developed nitrate fields in northern Chile and rubber plantations in the Amazon region.[2] In such areas a few score English-born technicians and managers sometimes attended Anglican chapels. In the later nineteenth century too, Anglican mission stations appeared in Patagonia and Tierra del Fuego in the far south, and in the Chaco, the desert covering western Paraguay and a large slice of northern Argentina. Protestant Episcopal missions from the United States and the South American Missionary Society (SAMS) based in Britain created new Anglican clusters in Brazil, Argentina, and Chile.[3] A map reproduced from the SAMS *Magazine* of the 1890s showed mission stations in Ushuaia (then called Ooshooia), Keppel Island on the Falkland Islands, Rosario, Córdoba, Concordia, Frayle Muerto, Bahía Blanca, Chupat Colony,

[1] Juan B. Alberdi, 'Bases y puntos de partida para la organización de la República Argentina', in Alberdi, *El pensamiento política latinoamerican* (Buenos Aires, 1964), pp. 14–26.

[2] Edward Every, *The Anglican Church in South America* (London, 1915); Rory Miller, *Britain and Latin America in the Nineteenth and Twentieth Centuries* (London, 1993); David Rock, 'The British in Argentina', in Robert Bickers (ed.), *Settlers and Expatriates: Britons over the Seas* (Oxford, 2010), pp. 18–44.

[3] Thomas Bridges, *Los Indios del Ultimo Confín: Sus Escritos para la South American Missionary Society* (Ushuaia, Tierra del Fuego, 2001), p. 27.

and Patagones—all in Argentina; four stations existed in Uruguay in Montevideo, Fray Bentos, Salto, and Paysandú; another five in Brazil at São Paulo, Santos, Pernambuco, Rio de Janeiro, and Rio Grande; and four in Chile at Santiago, Chañaral, Lota, and Puchoco. Until after the First World War, the Church remained almost exclusively Anglophone with little contact with Latin American people. 'Our object is internal, to help ourselves, not external, to attack others', declared Bishop Edward Every, the Church's principal figure at the time, as he emphasized its exclusively ethnocentric focus.[4]

The confined spaces of Anglicanism partly reflected the hostility of the vernacular Catholic Church. Everywhere, the Catholic clerics and their allies fought to keep all forms of British influence at bay. They opposed British commerce and lobbied to prolong the religious intolerance of the colonial period. When they failed to eliminate the Anglicans, the Catholics forced them to disguise their places of worship as private houses. They prohibited Catholic children from attending Anglican schools and opposed non-Catholic burial grounds. They objected whenever British residents married Latin American women in non-Catholic services and insisted that children of mixed marriages were raised as Catholics. On occasion, as in Cuba before independence in 1898, they urged the authorities to refuse the right of residence to non-Catholics. As a result, Anglicanism commonly functioned in segregated and even semi-clandestine forms. Even in relatively supportive Buenos Aires, the early British settlers before 1820 were sometimes forced to dispose of the dead in the Rio de la Plata because Catholic priests prevented their burial onshore in local cemeteries.

The Anglican Church became an ethnic institution both by choice and by metropolitan imposition. English residents wanted to import the Church but to keep it to themselves. British governments regarded the early chapels as instruments of control and stabilization over the expatriate communities, as 'patriotic institutions rather than religious . . . corporations', and as a means to promote trade.[5] The Erastian model diminished after 1860 when a larger British population and a flow of private resources from Britain enabled stronger and independently financed Anglican chapels. In the later nineteenth century, the SAMS created a diocesan structure but geographical barriers and limited resources impeded its development. In their early years, the chapels evolved separately from one another. In their later years, their continuing sense of autonomy and independence reflected the cellular, disconnected structure of the British communities throughout the region.

[4] Bishop Edward Every, quoted in Paula Seiguer, 'Identidad y Protestantismo: Los Immigrantes de Origen Inglés Vistos a Través de sus Revistas, Buenos Aires, 1900–1910', *Sextas Jornadas sobre Colectividades* (Buenos Aires, 1998).

[5] Every, *Anglican Church*, p. 13.

A CONTINENTAL SURVEY

Anglican services were first held among English merchants who migrated to Latin American ports during the Napoleonic Wars and their aftermath. Broadly speaking, they were modelled on Portuguese practice since the seventeenth century. In Oporto, English merchants were permitted their own religious observances by treaty but forbidden to flaunt them in public or to proselytize among the general population. In Latin America in the absence of chapels and clergy, in early years the congregations met informally in private residences, once more following Portuguese precedent. Laymen, consuls, ship captains, or naval chaplains conducted services. Anglicanism first achieved recognized standing in Rio de Janeiro. Its admission to that city became a condition of Article 12 of the trade treaty of 1810 between Britain and Portugal following the French occupation of Portugal and the escape of the Portuguese monarchs to Brazil under British protection.[6] In 1810–30, Rio became a major market for British goods and an emporium of British re-exports, although Catholic clerics resisted the construction of the small Anglican chapel until the early 1820s. Conditions in Rio resembled Oporto where from the late seventeenth century the British were allowed to worship privately but prohibited from constructing a chapel.[7] After 1830 conflicts between Britain and Brazil over the slave trade, and over slavery itself, deterred British settlers and impeded the Church's development. By 1839, only one service a week was held in the Anglican chapel. In 1876, American Methodists purchased the modest, attractive neo-Gothic structure and in 1881 sold it on to Baptists.[8]

Anglicanism developed a tenuous existence among British merchants in north-eastern Brazil, where slavery also remained deeply entrenched. In Pernambuco, a chaplaincy formed in 1811 but the arrival of the first chaplain was delayed until 1822; the laying of the chapel's foundation stone was further postponed until 1838. In Bahia, the Church developed to a very modest level in the nineteenth century and shrank around 1900 as the area stagnated and the remnants of the British community assimilated.[9] Following the abolition of Brazilian slavery in 1888 and the growth of British investment, members of the British community constructed a second Anglican chapel in Nichtheroy, a city adjacent to Rio de Janeiro. At the turn of the century other chapels appeared in

[6] Douglas Milmine, *The History of Anglicanism in Latin America* (Tunbridge Wells, 1994), p. 38.

[7] John Delaforce, *The Factory House at Oporto* (Bromley, 1990), p. 9.

[8] George Kritschke, *História da Igreja Episcopal Brasileira* (Rio de Janeiro, 1949), p. 21.

[9] Every, *Anglican Church*, p. 69; Louise H. Guenther, *British Merchants in Nineteenth Century Brazil: Business, Culture, and Identity in Bahia, 1808–1850* (Oxford, 2004), pp. 65–83, 146.

São Paulo and the port of Santos based on a mix of British and American worshippers, and in the rubber region of the far north in Belem where imported workmen mainly from Barbados comprised the bulk of the congregation. Overall, Anglicanism achieved minimal standing in Brazil. In one thousand pages of facts, figures, and photographs on Brazil published by Lloyd's Bank of London in 1913, mention of the Anglican Church was limited to half a sentence.[10]

In 1807, British forces briefly held Montevideo on the east bank of the Rio de la Plata. At that time the British and Foreign Bible Society distributed Bibles but as the British left the city the Catholic bishop ordered them to be handed in for destruction.[11] In the mid-1840s, Montevideo became the site of a chapel founded by Samuel Fisher Lafone, a Liverpool-born Anglican of Huguenot descent who became a wealthy and powerful South American merchant-rancher. Lafone lived in Buenos Aires until 1833 when he secretly married an upper-class Creole woman in a non-Catholic ceremony. A *cause célèbre* of the era, the marriage caused a furore among Catholics that helped force Lafone to move to Montevideo.[12] A dozen years later he constructed Holy Trinity Chapel on his estate on the Montevideo shoreline as part of his effort to promote a sense of community among local British residents. Sixteen years after Lafone's death in 1871, the Uruguayan government expropriated the site forcing the Anglicans to abandon the church building and vacate the cemetery. The removal of the remains took place during a smallpox epidemic that caused the death of the chaplain.[13] In Paraguay, the remotest republic in the wider Rio de la Plata region, the formation of the Anglican Church (as opposed to the Anglican missions in the Paraguayan Chaco) was delayed until 1913. In this venue, the Church assimilated the vestiges of the New Australia Colony founded twenty years previously as an experiment in Utopian Socialism by Australian and British migrants.[14]

The Pacific coast proved an even less propitious environment for Anglicans than the Atlantic. After independence in the 1820s, Chile developed a liberal movement as commerce and mines attracted European merchants, seamen, and prospectors. Several Anglican chaplains attempted to minister in the port of Valparaíso but none found a firm footing. In 1829 pro-clerical conservatives seized power from the liberals, terminating any potential opportunity to

[10] Reginald Lloyd and others, *Twentieth Century Impressions of Brazil: Its History, People, Commerce, Industries and Resources* (London, 1913), p. 645; Every, *Anglican Church*, p. 75; Alan K. Manchester, *British Preeminence in Brazil: A Study of European Expansion* (Chapel Hill, NC, 1933), p. 86.

[11] John Owen, *The History of the Origin and First Ten Years of the British and Foreign Bible Society*, 3 vols. (London, 1816), I, p. 368.

[12] David George, *Historia de la Iglesia Anglicana en la Argentina* (Buenos Aires, 2010), pp. 11–12.

[13] Every, *Anglican Church*, p. 42.

[14] Every, *Anglican Church*, p. 48.

establish an Anglican church. For several decades, governments of Chile applied the Anglophobe principle attributed to Juan Egaña, a local conservative leader: 'without religious uniformity, the country will become a republic of merchants rather than citizens'. Legally sanctioned religious toleration in Chile was delayed until 1854 and the opening of an Anglican chapel until 1858. Meanwhile, the chaplain of the British Pacific fleet based at Valparaíso conducted intermittent services onshore.[15] Although Valparaíso remained a principal centre of Anglo-Latin American commerce for many decades, its modest Anglican chapel functioned without an organ until 1903. In Santiago de Chile, the national capital, an Anglican chaplaincy appeared belatedly in 1904. Other small chapels to the south near Concepción founded by British settlers received support from the SAMS. A temporarily thriving Anglican church appeared in Punta Arenas on the western mainland side of the Straits of Magellan. A British community several hundred strong serviced passing ships until the opening of the Panama Canal in 1914 or worked on the great sheep ranches of southern Patagonia.[16] Lastly, the Anglican Church of St Michael and All Angels appeared in 1903 in the northern nitrate port of Iquique.[17]

British commerce flourished in Lima, but again Anglicanism faced hostile officialdom.[18] Article 2 of the Peruvian constitution of 1834 declared: 'The religion of the Republic is Roman Catholic, which the State will protect by every Christian means and will allow none other.' By 1914 the city of Lima contained seventy churches in a population of 300,000, but none was Anglican. In Colombia, Ecuador, Venezuela, and Central America, countries and regions the British never penetrated on any important scale, mere traces of Anglicanism appeared. They included a mission station in Costa Rica during a brief gold mining boom in the 1830s and another station founded by the SAMS in the late 1860s in Panama. In Venezuela, the British consul set up a chapel and a cemetery in 1834, but an Anglican church was delayed until 1909. A work published in 1877 mentions Anglican missions in Panama, Callao, the Chincha Islands (off the coast of Peru), Coquimbo (Chile), and Paysandú (Uruguay) but offers no further description of their origins or progress.[19]

Hostility to the Anglican Church prevailed in Cuba and Puerto Rico, the two surviving remnants of Spain's American empire. Anglophone communities of

[15] John Mayo, 'The British Communities in Nineteenth Century Chile: Engagement and Isolation', in Oliver Marshall (ed.), *English-Speaking Communities in Latin America* (Basingstoke, 2000), p. 196.

[16] Every, *Anglican Church*, pp. 86–95; Laurie Nock, 'The British and their Descendants in Chilean Patagonia', in Marshall (ed.), *English-Speaking Communities*, p. 206.

[17] Every, *Anglican Church*, p. 98.

[18] Every, *Anglican Church*, p. 113.

[19] Milmine, *Anglicanism*, pp. 58–95; John Marsh and Waite H. Stirling, *The Story of Commander Allen Gardiner, R.N., with Sketches of Missionary in South America* (London, 1877 edn.).

shopkeepers, artisans, and small farmers lived in Cuba but all non-Catholic worship was banned under traditional Spanish law shaped by the Counter-Reformation. In this venue too, services had to be conducted in private, commonly by visiting naval chaplains. Multiple religious disputes occurred in nineteenth-century Cuba affecting baptism, marriage, and burials, and the rights of residence of non-Catholics.[20]

The few Britons in Mexico belonged to merchant houses in Mexico City and the Caribbean port of Veracruz. In 1815–55, conservatives dominated the powerful Mexican Church stifling potential competitors. American missionaries founded the first Episcopal Church congregations during *La Reforma*, a liberal campaign of the mid-1850s to destroy the economic and financial power of the Catholic Church and expropriate its enormous land assets. Some British mining prospectors, commonly Cornishmen, entered Mexico during the mid-century period but left few marks. In the 1860s, clerical influence revived temporarily under the French-backed regime led by Emperor Maximilian leaving the small American missions in peril. Liberals dominated the eras of Benito Juárez ending in 1872 and of Porfirio Díaz in 1876–1910 leading slowly to more favourable conditions. The Episcopal Church Mission founded in 1865, renamed the Mexican Episcopal Church in 1892, became closely identified with Henry Chauncey Riley, an Anglo-Chilean. In 1893–5, his influence, derived from his past residence in the United States, led to the construction of Christ Church chapel in Mexico City.[21] For long periods of the late nineteenth century, diplomatic relations between Britain and Mexico were suspended. From 1900 British investment flowed into Mexico but never on a sufficient or sustained scale to promote many institutions of British origin. In Mexico, Anglicanism in its original English form remained limited to a closeted and infinitesimally small minority.[22]

THE EPISCOPAL CHURCH IN BUENOS AIRES

The Church put down strongest roots in Buenos Aires, a city that became the nodal point of British enterprise, commerce, and investment in Latin America. From an early date many Britons considered this city and the surrounding Rio

[20] Luis Martínez-Fernández, 'Crypto-Protestants and Pseudo-Catholics in the Nineteenth Century Hispanic Caribbean', *Journal of Ecclesiastical History*, 51 (2000): 347–65.

[21] Alpha Bechtel, 'The Mexican Episcopal Church: A Century of Reform and Revolution', MA thesis, San Diego State College, 1966; Sarem Navarrete and Constanza Patán Tobío, *Inventario del Archivo Parroquial Antigua Christ Church* (Mexico City, 2009); Milmine, *Anglicanism*, pp. 50–4.

[22] Barbara A. Tenenbaum and James M. McElwen, 'From Speculative to Substantive Boom: The British in Mexico, 1821–1911', in Marshall (ed.), *English-Speaking Communities*, pp. 51–79.

de la Plata the most attractive part of Latin America, which formed 'a striking contrast with the slavery and squalid misery of [Rio of Janeiro]'.[23] Attracted by plentiful food, a pleasant climate, and a free labour market with high wages, hundreds of Irish and Scots soldiers deserted from the British forces during the attempts to seize Buenos Aires in 1806 and 1807. British visitors who arrived after the revolution of 1810 against Spanish rule noted the weak standing of the Catholic Church compared with other parts of Spanish America. James Thomson, a Scottish Baptist missionary and educator working on behalf of the British and Foreign Bible Society, wandered the entire country handing out Bibles in Spanish translation. Less successfully, he went to Chile and Gran Colombia where the Catholic clergy resisted more strongly.[24] In the 1820s, the liberals of Buenos Aires headed by Bernardino Rivadavia provided the British with civil liberties in an effort to develop trade.[25] Rivadavia instituted freedom of worship and offered land grants to northern European Protestant settlers (although he failed to deliver the land). Of the early British settlers, around half were English-born potential Anglicans mostly from Liverpool and London and their respective environs; Lowland Scots and Midland Irish, respectively Presbyterians and Catholics for the most part, comprised the other half in roughly equal measure. The influx of migrants produced a British and Irish community of around 3,000, which included hundreds of artisans, mechanics, shopkeepers, and seamen. Numerous female migrants enabled the formation of an ethnic community. The British community of Buenos Aires contrasted with the smaller, less well-rooted, more exclusively male, and easily assimilated British population in other principal South American ports.

British Foreign Secretary George Canning played a leading part in promoting the Anglican Church in Buenos Aires. At his instigation, in 1823–4 Parliament granted diplomatic recognition to several newly independent Spanish American states including the United Provinces of South America, the forerunner of modern Argentina. Canning appointed Woodbine Parish as consul in Buenos Aires ordering him to request the government to protect 'not only the enjoyment of civil rights but the unmolested exercise of religious Worship' for British settlers. He urged the consul to warn the settlers not to stir opposition by attempting to convert Catholics. Parish should advise

[23] Sir Woodbine Parish, *Buenos Ayres, and the Provinces of the Rio de la Plata; Their Present State, Trade, and Debt; with Some Account from the Original Documents of the Progress of Geographical Discovery in Those Parts of South America during the Last Sixty Years* (London, 1839), p. 104.

[24] James Thomson, *Letters on the Moral and Religious State of South America; Written during a Residence of Nearly Seven Years in Buenos Ayres, Chile, Peru, and Colombia* (London, 1827).

[25] David Rock, 'Porteño Liberals and Imperialist Emissaries in the Rio de la Plata: Rivadavia and the British', in Matthew Brown and Gabriel Paquette (eds.), *Connections after Colonialism: Europe and Latin America in the 1820s* (Tuscaloosa, 2013), pp. 207–22.

British residents to 'avoid offensive or ostentatious displays of Religious worship . . . show deference and submission to Government, under whose protection they live, with strict obedience to the Laws, and the most scrupulous Respect for the Customs, Usages and Institutions Civil and Religious of the Inhabitants'.[26]

These principles were incorporated into the Treaty of Amity, Commerce and Navigation of 1825 between Britain and the United Provinces, which granted the British freedom of worship and exempted them from military service and forced loans. They were permitted to build churches on an understanding that non-Catholic worship would be kept behind closed doors. The 1825 treaty shaped the development of the British community and its churches throughout Argentina for more than a century.[27] Its religious component enshrined the view that 'faith, conscience, trust, reputation' stood at the heart of all mercantile transactions and that the Church would help to promote them.[28] The treaty acknowledged that the Anglican Church and any other non-Catholic denominations would be confined to the European settler communities.

In 1825 too, Parliament passed the Consular Chaplaincy Act (6 Geo. IV c 87) promising subsidies to the Anglican Church and to British cemeteries and hospitals in foreign ports. The Act was intended to benefit sojourning merchants and sailors, although Canning wanted to promote permanent British communities in Latin America in the interests of British trade.[29]

The Canning era spurred the construction of a large Anglican church in the United Provinces half-funded by the British government and located in the commercial heart of Buenos Aires. After several years of planning and fundraising, the provincial government assisted the Anglicans to purchase a plot of land on the site of a former convent. In 1831 they inaugurated the Episcopal British Church of St John the Baptist, an impressive and expensive building with Doric columns designed by Richard Adams, a young British-born architect.[30] Intended to display the wealth and status of the British mercantile interest, the building embodied Canning's expectation that the United Provinces would play a major role in future British commerce. Parish viewed the church correctly as 'a Monument of British Influence in Buenos Ayres—the only place in Spanish America where for many years to come it is likely that the Exercise of our Protestant Worship will be publickly tolerated'.[31]

[26] Foreign Office to Parish, 23 Apr. 1824. National Archives UK [henceforth NAUK], FO 6/4.

[27] Parish, *Buenos Ayres*, 396.

[28] Peter Mathias, 'Risk, Credit and Kinship in Early Modern Enterprise', in John J. McCusker and Kenneth Morgan (eds.), *The Early Modern Atlantic Economy* (Cambridge, 2000), pp. 15–37.

[29] C. K. Webster, *Britain and the Independence of Latin America, 1812–1830: Select Documents from the Foreign Office* (Oxford, 1938), p. 157.

[30] Parish, *Buenos Ayres, and the Provinces of the Rio de la Plata.*

[31] Parish to Foreign Office, 20 Apr. 1831. NAUK, FO 6/32.

St John's church and other so-called consular chapels stood outside the jurisdiction of the archbishop of Canterbury. Consul Parish and his successors managed affairs locally, while Charles Blomfield, the bishop of London, licensed the churches on behalf of the British government and exercised a distant supervisory control. In the late 1820s, Blomfield lobbied for more resources for the consular chapel in Buenos Aires by stressing its role in arresting the acculturation of British settlers. He warned that unless Anglicanism strengthened its influence, Britons would baptize their children in the Catholic Church, and 'the natural consequence [will be] their own accession to its Communion, and this is still more commonly the case with those who marry the women of the country'.[32] According to Blomfield, the functions of the Church in Latin America included promoting endogamy, defending the use of the English language, and setting up barriers against cultural absorption; in his view, Anglican clergymen abroad ought to function as ethnic leaders. Writing at the end of the nineteenth century about the Scots, James Dodds held that throughout Latin America their history 'has been largely a religious one, for it is unquestionably the Christian faith that has united Scotsmen into a community in these Republics'.[33] The Anglicans performed the same role of expatriate community-building as the Scots Presbyterians.

In 1824 Parish reported 'the very great want felt here of the presence of an English clergyman... [Many British residents] had families which they are naturally anxious to see brought up and instructed in the Religion of their own country'.[34] John Armstrong, a former missionary trained by the Society for Promoting Christian Knowledge, became the first resident Anglican cleric to minister in Buenos Aires (and very likely in Spanish America). He arrived in 1826 at the behest of English merchants after a short career in British Honduras (Belize). His experiences exemplified the travails of the Anglican Church during its early days even in the relatively supportive environment of Buenos Aires. His hopes of strong local support and easy success were unrealized. The Church depended on resources from English merchants whose position grew perilous during the recession and civil war of the late 1820s. Armstrong accepted a salary in paper currency whose depreciation at the time he was installed sharply reduced his real income. He founded the Buenos Ayrean School Society but commercial recession stifled its development. He was soon reduced to running a Sunday school free of charge and working as a private tutor.[35]

[32] Blomfield to Foreign Office, 16 Feb. 1829. NAUK, FO 6/28.

[33] James Dodds, *Records of the Scottish Settlers in the River Plate and their Churches* (Buenos Aires, 1897), p. vii.

[34] Parish to Foreign Office, 17 May 1824. NAUK, FO 6/4.

[35] *British Packet*, 26 Apr. 1828.

In correspondence with Blomfield, he detailed his struggles to enhance the Anglican congregation against competition from Scottish Presbyterians.[36] Initially Armstrong ran his school with William Brown, a Presbyterian minister, but friction impaired long-term collaboration. While Brown sought to introduce the Calvinistic practices of the Scottish parochial schools, Armstrong manoeuvred although with little success to entice several hundred Presbyterians into the Anglican fold. In this sectarian contest, Armstrong's relative weakness against Brown derived partly from the relative instability of English residents compared with the Scots. The former arrived as aspirant merchants who ultimately intended to leave Buenos Aires and return home, while many of the latter, like Brown himself, had migrated to South America indefinitely. As early as the 1820s, a few wealthy English merchants preferred to educate their children in England while the more modestly placed Scots relied on local schooling. In 1839 Brown established St Andrew's Scotch School, which outlived a string of weak Anglican rivals.

Both the Anglican and the Presbyterian Churches enjoyed establishment legal status in Britain. In the late 1820s, Woodbine Parish accentuated sectarian conflict by denying requests by Brown for a British government subsidy for the Presbyterians on the same terms as the Anglicans. They contended that the Act of 1825 applied only to sojourning merchants and sailors, and not to 'Emigrants [like many of the Scots] who by forming permanent Settlements in Foreign Countries, must sooner or later be looked on as Aliens'.[37] After lobbying in London, in 1831 the Presbyterians did obtain the desired subsidy on the same terms as Anglicans.[38] Over the following twenty years, the Presbyterian congregations grew larger than the Anglicans to judge by the size of the matching funds each received from the British government. For a time both Churches faced struggles as Canning's vision of expanding Latin American trade failed to materialize. In most of the period 1829–52, Juan Manuel de Rosas ruled Buenos Aires as an autocrat amidst intermittent civil war and foreign naval blockades, including that of 1845–7 in which the British Navy participated. In 1841, so-called Episcopal Commissioners, who were merchants holding offices in the Protestant Church, pleaded for a larger British subsidy to revive its flagging fortunes. As they noted, 'many of the heads of Commercial Houses have withdrawn themselves from the City and the fortunes of all foreign residents have been much diminished by the depreciation of our money and the frequent occurrence of political convulsions'.[39] Despite the unfavourable climate, the Churches clung on to their

[36] Blomfield to Foreign Office, 16 Feb. 1829. NAUK, FO 6/28.
[37] Parish to Foreign Office, 24 Dec. 1827. NAUK, FO 6/20.
[38] Dodds, *Scottish Settlers*, p. 182.
[39] Episcopal Church leaders to Foreign Office, 14 Dec. 1841. NAUK, FO 6/80.

modest congregations recruited in the port and commercial districts of the city.

In 1842, Armstrong abandoned St John's church and re-emigrated to Canada. His successor Barton Lodge left an important mark in 1844 when he helped create the British Hospital, later considered one of the most prestigious institutions founded by the British throughout Latin America. In its early days, the hospital became another bone of contention between Anglicans and Presbyterians as Brown opposed the proposal. He was concerned the Scots would have to pay for an institution few would be allowed to use. Under the rules of the British subsidy, access to the hospital was limited to the sojourners, who were mainly English, and would exclude the settlers, who were commonly Scots. Brown argued for the sick being supported by private charity to avoid having to make contributions to an institution from which Scots would obtain small benefit. For some years, the hospital functioned as a hospice for cirrhosis-scarred seamen. An annual report for 1848 noted that 70 per cent of deaths that year resulted from alcoholism.[40] During its first twenty years, the hospital excluded women patients. As Brown had indicated, it would only treat the all-male sojourning merchants and seamen and would refuse to treat the settlers who included all the women.

In 1815–45, the English predominated in the Anglophone population. During the agrarian crisis in Ireland that peaked during the Potato Famine of the late 1840s, the number of Irish Catholics in the province of Buenos Aires surpassed both the English and the Scots, remaining the largest of the three ethnicities into the 1880s. Irish and Scottish settlers became closely attached to sheep farming. Their respective ministers, Father Antony Fahy and James 'Padre' Smith, Brown's successor as the Presbyterian minister, won renown for their journeys across the pampas by horseback to visit their rural parishioners. At this point, the Anglican clerics were less well known as rural travellers because 'Englishmen are rarely here other than in [urban] mercantile pursuits.'[41] Celtic rural dwellers in Argentina included the predominantly Congregationalist and Baptist Welsh community founded in 1865 one thousand miles south of Buenos Aires on the Chupat (or Chubut) River in Patagonia.

In 1850–70, expanding British commerce with Buenos Aires fuelled an increase in the English-born urban population. As one indicator, the British government subsidy paid to the Anglicans grew from £291 in 1846 to £444 in 1854.[42] By the 1860s, scores of young Englishmen were being contracted to work in Buenos Aires as clerks or trainee merchants. Walter Heald, who went to Buenos Aires in mid-decade to work in a merchant house, typified the

[40] *British Packet*, 8 July 1848.

[41] Michael G. Mulhall, *Handbook of the River Plate; comprising Buenos Ayres, the Upper Provinces, the Banda Oriental, Paraguay* (Buenos Aires, 1869), p. 14.

[42] Minister to Foreign Office, 5 Feb. and 22 Mar. 1859. NAUK, FO 6/220.

young middle-class English migrants of the period. On arrival, he joined a British club providing a reading room, library, and restaurant. He became a Freemason, a keen sportsman, and an assiduous member of the Anglican Church. He further exemplified the English migrants of the period by marrying an Anglo-Argentine woman from a prominent mercantile family.[43] Smaller in number than the Irish Catholics and Scots Presbyterians, groups with stronger rural offshoots, the Anglicans nevertheless occupied an entrenched position.

ANGLICAN CONSOLIDATION

In 1860–1913, every British institution in Latin America betrayed the impact of private foreign investment. Around 60 per cent of total British investment in Latin America flowed into Argentina to build railways and tramways, water and sewage works, harbour installations, land companies, and meat-packing plants. By the First World War, British investment in Argentina stood at around half that in the United States and double that in Brazil. Buenos Aires had now become the 'capital of the most progressive republic [of Latin America], the greatest city and trade centre of the whole continent, the objective of steamship lines of the great European nations, and similarly the starting point of an ever increasing network of railways'.[44] By Bishop Edward Every's estimate, the British population of Argentina in 1914 stood at 50,000.[45] It was considered by all as the largest such community at the time outside the British Empire and the United States.

The Buenos Aires Great Southern Railway and the Bank of London and the River Plate, both founded in 1862, pioneered the myriad British firms that appeared in the Rio de la Plata. The firms were followed by their employees. Church and consular marriage registers listed growing numbers of clerks, bookkeepers, accountants, and occupations linked to the railways like surveyors and engineers. The newcomers were mainly young Englishmen like Heald 'from our public schools, or from Oxford and Cambridge'.[46] Conservative in their political views and imperialist in sentiment, they also became great enthusiasts for sports, clubs, and British churches and schools. Many returned to Britain to marry and brought their wives back to Argentina. Alternatively, numerous marriages like Heald's took place between British migrants and Anglo-Argentine women. As the offspring of these

[43] Walter Heald, *Private Diary of Walter Heald*, Rylands Library, University of Manchester, GB 133 Eng MSS 1217.

[44] Every, *Anglican Church*, p. 17.

[45] Every, *Anglican Church*, p. 10.

[46] Edward Every in *The Diocesan Magazine* (Buenos Aires, 1907), p. 66.

unions, Anglo-Argentine children grew increasingly visible from the 1890s, while English-language schools, some with Anglican connections, proliferated.

Clusters of British settlement appeared in secondary cities headed by Rosario, Montevideo, and Bahía Blanca, and in more distant cities like Mendoza, Tucumán, Asunción del Paraguay, and Concepión in the southern part of the Central Valley of Chile.[47] By the late nineteenth century, Britons were migrating into rural Argentina in much larger numbers. They took positions as managers and bailiffs on modernizing cattle *estancias*, where they undertook the improvement of livestock, the development of irrigation, or the introduction of new crop rotations. The Anglican Church followed the men in the guise of the so-called camp chaplaincies, a system similar to earlier practices among the Irish and Scots in which the clergy moved from one locale to another. Travelling between destinations by train and riverboat, as well as by horse and carriage or mule-back, the chaplains penetrated far into northern and western Argentina and the contiguous republics.

In Argentina in particular, government at every level upheld freedom of religion unflaggingly. Hundreds of thousands of European immigrants were flowing into Buenos Aires, mainly Italians and Spaniards, although non-Catholic northern Europeans formed a substantial minority. The latter founded numerous Protestant churches that local Roman Catholics no longer possessed the will or the power to resist. In 1873 the British government terminated most of the subsidies to the Church in Argentina under the Act of 1825 arguing that their congregations were large and wealthy enough to stand alone. By the early 1880s, church revenues were rising. St John's church in Buenos Aires rented out larger numbers of pews and received more income from offertories; the installation of stained glass windows and the advent of a sung eucharist followed.[48]

New chapels appeared in the suburbs of Buenos Aires and in several inland cities. Following a disastrous yellow fever epidemic in 1871, wealthier Britons resettled in the village of Flores about eight miles west of the city centre, which became the site of flourishing sports clubs and of St Peter's church. As Flores grew congested in the 1890s, the British moved to Belgrano, a northern neighbourhood with similar easy rail access to the city centre. By 1914, the Flores community had been almost abandoned and St Peter's required external subsidies to stay alive, while Belgrano acquired distinction for its clubs, mansions, schools, and St Saviour's Anglican church.[49] West of Buenos Aires stands Hurlingham, a village founded in 1888 as the site of the leading

[47] Reginald Lloyd (ed.), *Twentieth Century Impressions of Argentina* (London, 1911).
[48] *Standard*, 15 Apr. 1882; 8 Aug. 1883; 14 Apr. 1885.
[49] *Standard*, 1 Apr. 1896.

sporting club of British origin throughout Latin America.[50] By 1900, Hurlingham village contained houses of gabled windows, trim hedges, and verdant lawns. Weekday bridge parties complemented the weekend sports. A prestigious girls' school and lastly St Mark's church appeared. Thanks partly to the church (in this case shared with the Presbyterians) Hurlingham became 'as English a colony as you would wish to find'.[51]

As suburbanization increased, many British employees moved south across the Riachuelo, a narrow river marking the boundary between the federal capital established in 1880 and the province of Buenos Aires. Clusters of British settlement sprang up linear fashion around the suburban stations of the Great Southern Railway. They included Lomas de Zamora, the site of Holy Trinity church, the largest Anglican chapel in this area founded in 1889 following a donation of land by Henry A. Green, a leading figure in the Bank of London and the River Plate.[52] Among the southern suburbs, Quilmes, the site of All Saints Anglican church, retained the popularity among British residents it had first acquired in the 1840s among Scots and Irish settlers.

The greater significance of Quilmes to Anglicans stemmed from St George's College, a school for boarders and day pupils founded in 1897 by Canon J. T. Stevenson, a South African-born Anglican. The school started with slender resources, but quickly developed into an emblematic institution in the British community. It taught British values with a pronounced imperialist slant and promoted English sports led by cricket and rugby. Focusing on 'the training of the moral sense', it sought to inculcate 'the sense of honour, the spirit of obedience and sacrifice, the capacity for cooperation and all the qualities... which have invested Great Britain with a pre-eminence in the government of native races the world over'.[53]

The college replicated English public schools except that it could not legally apply corporal punishment. Its Anglican connections became visible in its neo-Gothic chapel completed shortly before the outbreak of the First World War. Following their exit from St George's at the age of fourteen, a few boys progressed to schools in England, commonly to Haileybury near the city of Hertford, and from there to a leading British university. But most ex-Georgians remained in Buenos Aires to become apprentices and trainees in British firms. Anglicanism overtly influenced several other suburban schools including St Hilda's College, a girls' school founded in Hurlingham in 1912 under Stevenson's auspices.

Outside the capital city the new chapels and chaplaincies depended on subsidies from the SAMS enhanced by contributions from British companies.

[50] Jeremy Simpson in <http://www.hurlinghamclub.org.ar/historia.php>.

[51] *Standard*, 6 Oct. 1914.

[52] B. J. Townsend, *The History of Holy Trinity Church, Lomas* (Buenos Aires, 1936).

[53] J. T. Stevenson, *The History of St. George's College, Quilmes* (London, 1936), p. 127.

St Bartholomew's, the principal parish outside Buenos Aires, was established in Rosario de Santa Fe in 1868. This city developed rapidly as steam shipping facilitated commerce along the Rio Paraná and grain production expanded throughout the surrounding rural areas. The chapel building was inaugurated in 1876 (and consecrated in 1879), although the subsidies continued until 1897.[54] In the 1870s, Anglican clergymen established St Bartholomew's School, which differed from St George's College (founded about twenty years later) by admitting pupils of mixed ethnic background. The relatively small numbers of British families in Rosario, and the greater instability of the British population compared with Buenos Aires, encouraged the school to adopt a more flexible admissions policy. The practice also reflected the willingness of the SAMS to engage more fully with the general population without actively proselytizing among people baptized as Catholics. In Rosario, the British pooled resources to form the Anglo-German Hospital and to maintain a cemetery. Inevitably, the First World War destroyed these ties.[55]

Rising to a total of twenty-nine clergy by 1912, Anglicanism grew for a time into the largest non-Catholic denomination in Argentina.[56] Two SAMS-supported chapels appeared near Rosario alongside workshops maintained by the Central Argentine Railway, and another in Córdoba, two hundred miles north-west of Rosario, where a camp chaplaincy was established.[57] Chaplaincies appeared north of Rosario on the Paraná and Uruguay rivers; two chapels were established in the far south among English railway workers in the Welsh community of Chubut and at Rio Gallegos, an area of vast sheep ranches originally populated by former residents of Scottish origin from the Falkland Islands. The far north-western province of Jujuy, two thousand miles distant from Rio Gallegos, became the site of Leach's Argentine Estates Ltd, a British company founded in the 1870s to develop sugar cane plantations. At San Pedro, Jujuy, St George's chapel provided a place of worship for up to two hundred imported British managers, botanists, and irrigation engineers.[58] Anglicanism affected the development of other institutions. Irish nuns long administered an orphanage in Buenos Aires that admitted all English-speaking children. As the Irish diaspora of the 1840s assimilated, the Anglicans took over the care of orphans. In 1897, a former SAMS missionary founded The Allen Gardiner Homes in Rosario. In 1906, he moved the institution to a less expensive and more attractive site in the province of Córdoba.[59]

[54] *Standard*, 19 Aug. 1876, 19 Aug. 1879.

[55] George, *Iglesia Anglicana*, p. 39; P. L. Falconer, *Centenary of St. Bartholomew's Church: A Brief History* (Rosario, 1968).

[56] *Diocesan Magazine*, vol. 2, 1911.

[57] George, *Iglesia Anglicana*, pp. 36–9.

[58] *Diocesan Magazine*, 1912, p. 331.

[59] *Standard*, 28 Sept. 1904, 9 June 1911.

MISSIONARIES AND BISHOPS

The SAMS played a major role in the late nineteenth-century expansion of Anglicanism. The society was founded by Allen F. Gardiner, widely considered the Church's most notable figure in nineteenth-century South America. Gardiner's published work is *A Visit to the Indians* (1841). Extensive citations from his unpublished journals appear in Anon., *The Martyrs of the South: A Brief Sketch of the Late Captain Allen F. Gardiner, RN: His Missions, His Companions, and the Death of the Party in Tierra del Fuego* (1852) and John Marsh and Waite H. Stirling, *Gardiner* (1867). An informative narrative is Arnoldo Canclini, *Allen Gardiner, Marinero, misionero, mártir* (1979). Gardiner's career began during the Napoleonic Wars as a naval officer. He first visited Rio de Janeiro in 1814 where the most degraded forms of slavery he witnessed left a lasting impression. In subsequent years, he landed in many ports in the Indian and Pacific oceans while growing steadily aware of his missionary vocation. In the mid-1830s, he spent an extensive period in Natal where his efforts to establish an African mission failed. Henceforward he devoted his attention to South America, which he referred to as the 'forgotten continent'. He began searching for remote indigenous peoples untouched by contact with Christianity or Western civilization. In several voyages between 1838 and 1850, he visited numerous South American ports on the Atlantic and Pacific, the Chaco and Tierra del Fuego. His travels, recorded in journals, included a journey across the Andes by mule-back accompanied by his wife and two children and an arduous crossing of the Atacama Desert through Bolivia. Gardiner remained curiously reluctant to settle, citing hostile indigenous peoples, opposition from Catholics, his limited linguistic abilities, his married state, and eventually his advancing age. He wanted to scout out the opportunities for missionary work but leave to others the task of establishing and maintaining the missions.

However, by 1850 (at the age of fifty-six), he fixed on Tierra del Fuego. Previous visitors to this region, notably Charles Darwin in the voyage of the *Beagle* fifteen years previously, had dismissed the Fuegians as 'probably the lowest of the human race' but they attracted Gardiner on these same grounds as a formidable challenge to missionaries. The Fuegians lived in isolation but were less nomadic than the mainland Patagonian Indians to the north, whose way of life defeated all missionary efforts. In the 1840s, Gardiner laid out a strategy for missionary work on Tierra del Fuego. As a first step, he would establish a base on the Falkland Islands where a British colony formed in 1833, and transport several Fuegians there for conversion and acculturation.

> Happily for us and, I trust, eventually for the poor Indians, the Falkland Islands are now under the British flag... Making this our headquarters, I purpose... bringing back with me two or three Patagonian lads in order to teach them English, and then prepare them to become interpreters to the

> missionaries who, we trust, may eventually serve amongst them. Who can tell but the Falkland Islands, so admirably suited for the purpose, may become the key to the aborigines of both Tierra de Fuego and Patagonia?

He intended to promote an exchange of languages between the missionaries and the Indians and train the Indians to work on the secondary stations on Tierra del Fuego. Acculturated Indians would also assist the task of evangelization.[60] Gardiner founded the Patagonia Mission Society but failed to raise sufficient funds in Britain to carry out his two-stage plan. In late 1850, he took a small party and two small barges directly to Tierra del Fuego. Step by step, morbid journals narrated the ensuing disaster. Unaccountably, the party left many of its powder supplies and provisions on the ship that deposited them on the island. They fled hostile Indians but moved to a point along the coast where ships rarely passed. Rough seas almost destroyed their barges. Fish and game proved scarce. One by one the men starved, with Gardiner himself the last man to die.

Opinions were divided on Allen Gardiner. Some dismissed him as incompetent or suicidal while others lauded him as a martyr. His death sparked efforts to fulfil his aspirations led by George Pakenham Despard, a Bristol clergyman. Contributions swelled to the Patagonia Missionary Society, which in 1868 became the South American Missionary Society. Following Gardiner's death, progress proved slow. In 1854, the society obtained a land grant on Keppel Island, a north-western islet on the Falklands. From here, expeditions to Tierra del Fuego led to Indians living with the missionaries, where the two eventually learned each others' languages. In 1859, a second exploratory landing on Tierra del Fuego provoked another disaster when Indians killed nine members of the British expedition. In 1862, an attempt to establish a mission in Patagonia on the Rio Santa Cruz failed. After almost twenty years of persistent effort, in 1869 Waite H. Stirling, a clergyman associated with Despard, led the first successful expedition from Keppel Island to Tierra del Fuego, where he survived for almost nine months with Indian assistants.[61] In 1871, Thomas Bridges, who had assumed leadership of the Keppel Island mission, succeeded Stirling as the head of the mission station at Tierra del Fuego. Living with his wife and children on the site of the city of Ushuaia, Bridges remained in Tierra del Fuego for almost fifteen years mastering the language of the Yamana, the island's principal indigenous ethnic group. The early life of the missionary's son, E. Lucas Bridges, among the coastal Yamana and the inland Ona peoples, inspired the book *Uttermost Part of the World*, a

[60] Marsh and Stirling, *Commander Allen Gardiner*, p. 23.

[61] Frederick Macdonald, *Bishop Stirling of the Falklands: The Adventurous Life of a Soldier of the Cross* (London, 1929).

remarkable work of wilderness and ethnographic exploration.[62] Contact with the Anglican missionaries, however, became a prelude to the destruction of the indigenous peoples of Tierra del Fuego. In the 1880s, Argentine and Chilean sheep farmers settled on the island. Their arrival sparked demographic collapse among the Indians and the ultimate termination of the mission.

From the late 1880s, the attention of the SAMS shifted to the Chaco region at the far northern extremity of Argentina overlapping into Paraguay, an area to which Gardiner first drew attention in the 1840s. The penetration of missionaries began in 1889 among the Lengua-Mascoy tribes west of the Rio Paraguay from a river base known as Riacho Fernández. The Chaco missions became closely identified with Wilfrid Barbrooke Grubb, a Scottish Anglican, whose thirty-five-year missionary career began on the Falkland Islands before he proceeded north. In the Chaco, his willingness to trek hundreds of miles into unknown territory and live among the Indians in isolation led to his reputation as the 'Livingstone of South America'. He survived hostile insects, unpredictable climates, festering disease, alligator attacks, and a damaging attack by a disaffected Indian. Like Thomas Bridges on Tierra del Fuego, Grubb mastered various indigenous languages by laboriously compiling dictionaries. Eight years elapsed before he made his first convert to Christianity and many more before he met his ambition to establish a self-supporting and self-expanding Church. In his later career, he worked from the opposite western side of the Chaco among the Toba and Matacos, who two centuries earlier had been the targets of Jesuit missionaries. Grubb claimed to have wrought a social revolution as measured by the decline of infanticide, drunkenness, and 'indecency'—'changing the savages into civilised members of the community'. He was opening up the Chaco to development but sounded the alarm about the destruction of the habitat and of the ill-effects of using the Chaco Indians for seasonal labour by Leach Brothers of Jujuy and other companies.[63]

Following the proclamation of a republic and the disestablishment of Roman Catholicism in Brazil in 1889, the Protestant Episcopal Church of the United States created several missionary churches in Rio Grande do Sul at Porto Alegre. Their steady growth underscored the difference between British and American branches of the Church. The original British model established by the consular chaplaincies sought to protect the ethnicity of its congregations of British origin and descent, while the American offshoots of the Church became immersed in native Latin American society. In Brazil, the Church evangelized, ordained locally born priests, and adopted a vernacular liturgy, practices in sharp contrast with its British Anglican forerunners. In

[62] E. Lucas Bridges, *Uttermost Part of the Earth: A History of Tierra del Fuego and the Fuegians* (New York, 2007 edn.).

[63] W. Barbrooke Grubb, *A Church in the Wilds* (London, 1914).

1898, the American Episcopal Church appointed Lucien Lee Kinsolving, one of the original missionaries, as bishop to signal its existence outside the British-dominated diocesan structure. By the mid-1920s, the Porto Alegre Church maintained thirty-two mostly Brazilian ministers, ninety churches, and 3,000 communicants, numbers far greater than any cluster of British origin outside Buenos Aires.[64]

The formation of an Anglican diocese in South America began on the initiative of the SAMS. In late 1869 Waite Stirling, the pioneer of the mission in Tierra del Fuego, became bishop of the Falkland Islands, a title extended to include 'South America' when the consular subsidies terminated. Nominally, his diocese covered the entire subcontinent except British Guiana. As bishop, Stirling continued missionary work from the Falkland Islands. He visited Church outposts in Brazil at Morro Velho in the state of Minas Gerais and the American missions at Porto Alegre, and maintained contact with his appointee Grubb in the Chaco.[65] In 1881 the republics of Argentina and Chile settled the frontier line in Tierra del Fuego by treaty and set up their respective authorities. Soon after, Stirling denounced the treatment of the Indians on the island although to no effect.[66] The bishop commanded limited influence in Buenos Aires where local Anglicans representing previous generations of British settlers viewed him unfavourably as a Low Church evangelist who threatened their autonomy. Towards the end of his tenure, the resources he received from the SAMS gradually strengthened his position.[67]

Edward Every, the patrician-born second bishop of the Falkland Islands and South America, owed his appointment in 1902 to the SAMS although he identified with the resident British alone. Beyond supporting the Missions to Seamen founded in Buenos Aires in 1905, he performed no missionary or evangelical work. Every enjoyed no more success than Stirling in welding his vast diocese together or creating a stable financial base. In 1907 he subdivided the jurisdiction into separate eastern and western spheres with an anomalous dispensation that the South Atlantic Falkland Islands became the capital of the western Pacific jurisdiction stretching from Tierra del Fuego along the entire Pacific coast. The reform failed and Every ultimately reassumed responsibility for the entire continent. His diocese received £5,000 a year, about half its revenue, in subsidies from the SAMS, which performed on a tenfold scale the same role as the British government under the consular chaplaincies.[68] St John's church in Buenos Aires became Every's diocesan capital. He gave the residence the unusual title of a pro-cathedral—a form of cathedral in the

[64] Kritschke, *Igreja Episcopal*; Every, *Anglican Church*, p. 129; Milmine, *Anglicanism*, pp. 37–44.

[65] Macdonald, *Stirling*, pp. 148–52, 217.

[66] *Standard*, 4 Mar. 1883.

[67] Macdonald, *Stirling*, p. 221; George, *Historia Anglicana*, pp. 26–35.

[68] Every, *Anglican Church*, pp. 148–50.

making—lest the Catholics accuse him of transgressing the terms of the 1825 treaty. By 1912, he had introduced skeletal diocesan institutions. The pro-cathedral became his base for unending excursions to far-flung Anglican communities, commonly no more than individual families, widely scattered in the continent. In *Twenty-Five Years in South America* published in 1929, he reflected on his 'life of constant travel, such as are granted to few others, over an area which formed the greatest Anglican diocese in the world'.[69]

Every became a rich source of information about the British living in South America. He shared a common criticism of his compatriots before the First World War (which wartime experience belied), that the British lacked community spirit and operated as 'unrelated groups of individuals and families with little natural cohesion'.[70] Although he sometimes complained about his compatriots, a sense of class and ethnic superiority permeated his opinions. In the Chilean nitrate fields, 'it gave me a thrill of pride to know that when there were two or three young Englishmen of the public school type in charge, there was seldom trouble'. In Buenos Aires, he criticized the British for 'going about as a superior race, associating only with each other, having their sports grounds clubs, schools, churches, just as if they were in their own land'.[71] Yet he exhorted his countrymen to stay aloof from the rest of the population. Intermarriage became the greatest potential error, which would lead to Englishmen being 'lost to the community'. In the event of marriages between British men and Latin American women, it became crucial to bring up the children in England since 'language is a most potent factor either in separating or uniting people'. He warned that British women who married Latin American men stood to lose all their property as well as their British nationality; moreover, under Latin American law they had no entitlement to the nationality of their husbands.[72] Education became key to preserving ethnic loyalty, and Every stood solidly behind Stevenson's efforts to promote St George's College. At the end of his career in the mid-1930s, when British influence was declining throughout Latin America, his ethnocentricity strayed far to excess. He lamented that South Americans would never match British standards for 'moral reasons: our sturdiness of character and racial superiority—the superiority of our civilisation'. Visiting Barbrooke Grubb's mission villages in Paraguay, he reported that 'never before had I faced so large a purely heathen congregation and spellbound I watched the inscrutable dark faces, wondering reverently what the Holy Spirit was effecting with them, as the missionary delivered his message. What point of contact did he find with them? How far were these dull minds capable of understanding?'[73]

[69] Edward Every, *Twenty-Five Years in South America* (London, 1929), p. 1.

[70] Every, *Twenty-Five Years*, p. 69.

[71] Every, *Twenty-Five Years*, pp. 8, 19, 79.

[72] *Diocesan Magazine*, Apr. 1912.

[73] Edward Every, *South American Memories of Thirty Years* (London, 1933), pp. 42, 119.

William Case Morris, a near contemporary and colleague of Edward Every, became his opposite by transcending the taboos rooted in the 1825 treaty to prohibit contact between the Anglican Church and the Latin American population. Born in England, Morris lived briefly as a child in the early 1870s in a utopian religious community in Paraguay. When the community collapsed, his family settled in Buenos Aires. As a young missionary tied initially to Methodism, he worked for a time in the rough, hybrid seafaring community of the Boca district of the city. Morris converted to Anglicanism during a visit to England when the SAMS offered to assist his missionary work. In Buenos Aires in 1898, he founded the Escuelas Evangélicas Argentinas and created a small church in the Palermo district, one of the few Anglican foundations as yet to conduct services in Spanish. He plucked orphans from the streets, up to seven thousand at any given time, providing them with food, shelter, and education.[74] He enlisted the support of Argentine governments and several eminent political leaders including Bartolomé Mitre, a former president of the republic. His forthright appeal for funds at Christmastime 1917 continued until his death in 1932: '100,000 [Argentine pesos] are needed at once' he declaimed. 'Six thousand, two hundred children require our immediate help.'[75] Morris stood out as an extraordinary figure, too unusual within the British community and distanced from it to command much affection. His background and career proved unique. The support of the secular liberals he commanded such as Mitre and of later presidents had no parallel in Argentina and very few throughout Latin America.

CONCLUSION

The development of the Anglican Church in nineteenth-century Latin America illustrated the principal zones of British penetration and its degree of intensity in different parts of the region. North of the equator, Anglicanism developed scarcely any presence at all while south of the equator it became heavily concentrated in the Rio de la Plata. Throughout the period 1806–1920, Buenos Aires remained the core site of Anglicanism; smaller Anglican outposts in provincial Argentina, Chile, Brazil, and Uruguay followed in descending order. The third quarter of the nineteenth century marked a division in the Church's development. In the earlier period of the consular chaplaincies, Anglicanism existed as a subsidized outpost of a foreign state. In this form, its functions emphasized a secular mission of linking its members together in the interests of British commerce.

[74] *Standard*, annual reports from 4 July 1901.

[75] *Standard*, 5 Dec. 1917.

The Church changed substantially after 1860 with the flow of foreign investment, the abolition of the consular subsidies, and the rise of the SAMS. In this period the salience of Buenos Aires grew even more pronounced as it became, at least nominally, the capital of a continental diocese. The consolidation of Anglicanism illustrated new areas of urban and rural settlement, the evolution of the railways, and the diffusion of British investment. Anglican schools headed by St George's College instanced the pervasive imperialist mentality of the period after 1900. The era too marked the growth of the Anglican missions in Tierra del Fuego and the Chaco through the inflow of British resources from the SAMS. As the SAMS achieved pre-eminence, the Church drew closer to potential Latin American constituencies if only as yet to a limited degree. At heart the Anglican Church remained, as Bishop Every portrayed it, an ethnically exclusive institution serving the interests of the British commercial and investment economies.

SELECT BIBLIOGRAPHY

Bridges, E. Lucas, *Uttermost Part of the Earth: A History of Tierra del Fuego and the Fuegians* (New York, 2007).

Dodds, James, *Records of the Scottish Settlers in the River Plate and their Churches* (Buenos Aires, 1897).

Every, Edward, *The Anglican Church in South America* (London, 1915).

Every, Edward, *South American Memories of Thirty Years* (London, 1933).

Gardiner, Captain Allen F., *A Visit to the Indians on the Frontiers of Chile* (London, 1841).

George, David, *Historia de la Iglesia Anglicana en la Argentina* (Buenos Aires, 2010).

Grubb, W. Barbrooke, *A Church in the Wilds*, edited by H. T. Morrey Jones (London, 1914).

Marsh, John and Waite H. Stirling, *The Story of Commander Allen Gardiner, R.N., with Sketches of Missionary in South America* (London, 1877 edn.).

Miller, Rory, *Britain and Latin America in the Nineteenth and Twentieth Centuries* (London, 1993).

Milmine, Douglas, *The History of Anglicanism in Latin America* (Tunbridge Wells, 1994).

Parish, Sir Woodbine, *Buenos Ayres, and the Provinces of the Rio de la Plata; Their Present State, Trade, and Debt; with Some Account from the Original Documents of the Progress of Geographical Discovery in Those Parts of South America during the Last Sixty Years* (London, 1839).

Rock, David, 'The British in Argentina', in Robert Bickers (ed.), *Settlers and Expatriates: Britons over the Seas* (Oxford, 2010), pp. 18–44.

Stevenson, J. T., *The History of St. George's College, Quilmes* (London, 1936).

Thomson, James, *Letters on the Moral and Religious State of South America; Written during a Residence of Nearly Seven Years in Buenos Ayres, Chile, Peru, and Colombia* (London, 1827).

19

Music and Anglicanism in the Nineteenth Century

Jeremy Dibble

Anglicanism, not only in Britain but in various corners of the world, is justly admired for its musical tradition, discipline, deportment, training, and professionalism, in addition to its distinctive hymnody, psalmody and carols, anthems, and service music. The consolidation of such attributes ultimately finds its roots in the nineteenth century when so many of the practices, values, and customs we take for granted today were devised and established. Yet it took the best part of a century for these factors to take shape and they did so under the influence of a complex matrix of factors—a tension between the two theological polarities of High and Low Church practice, the role of clergy, choir, organist, organ, and congregation, the role of musical instruction, the cross-fertilization of the two seminal *loci* of parish church and cathedral, under the panoply of the two larger issues of ecclesiastical reform and Romanticism.

THE EARLY NINETEENTH CENTURY AND THE INFLUENCE OF THE OXFORD MOVEMENT

As Nicholas Temperley has explained, music in the English parish church emerged from the eighteenth century with a renewed, indeed reformed commitment to the singing of hymnody and psalmody.[1] For the majority of congregations, the repertoire was largely predicated on Sternhold & Hopkins's *Old Version* of the metrical psalms (established since the Reformation) and

[1] Nicholas Temperley, *The Music of the English Parish Church* (Cambridge, 1979), pp. 204ff.

Tate & Brady's *New Version*, first published in 1696, and, while it proved financially challenging to country parishes, the aspiration of most churches was to install and own an organ to accompany the singing. On the Evangelical wing, however, the influence of the Methodists' new-found spontaneity of worship, in which the maxim of 'singing for all' reawakened an old hostility to the central role of the choir,[2] gave rise to a new breed of simple tunes, ones which were at once more comprehensible and more singable than those of the former West Gallery tradition of fuging tunes, and many of which found their origins in secular music. The place of the congregation in parish churches as a musical agency was therefore paramount; there was even room in some churches for the *chanting* of psalms and canticles, a revolutionary (pre-Tractarian) practice to which the most extreme Protestants objected as a relic of Popery. Above all, however, this style of musical worship placed emphasis on the individual Christian experience with its sense of emotion and immediacy, an approach from which the traditional High Churchman, loyal to the dignity of the Book of Common Prayer, recoiled owing to a distrust of emotions as 'enthusiasm' or zealotry.

In contradistinction to congregationalism, the aspiration for the High Churchman was for the imitation, indeed the emulation, of cathedral practice, with a view to the improvement of music as an *aesthetic* experience. Perhaps the most potent example of this was at Leeds parish church where Walter Hook sought to establish daily choral services in a style later advocated by John Jebb's *The Choral Service of the United Church of England and Ireland being an Inquiry into the Liturgical System of the Cathedral and Collegiate Foundations of the Anglican Communion* published in 1843. Jebb, in many ways a forerunner of the Oxford Movement, abjured what he perceived as the cacophony of congregational singing. He was fervent believer in the notion of the professional, paid choir, in surplices, singing, not from the gallery but from the chancel (an innovation often associated with the Oxford Movement, but actually established by Hook's predecessor, William Fawcett, in 1818.[3] For Jebb, such a choir was *intercessor par excellence*, and he advised Hook (whose achievements were all the more remarkable in that they took place in a dissenting city) to establish a choral model in 1841 which was later imitated by similarly aspiring churches in London and in a number of other sizeable industrial towns.

While Jebb's *Choral Service* sought to promote the principle of exclusively choir-led worship, it also lamented that the standard of cathedral choral worship had fallen into what seemed like irreparable decay. There are many accounts of how parlous cathedral chapters had become in their control of aberrant choral vicars who, in many instances, enjoyed a freehold status (i.e. a

[2] Temperley, *English Parish Church*, p. 209.

[3] Bernarr Rainbow, *The Choral Revival in the Anglican Church* (Oxford, 1970), p. 27.

job for life) and were either absent or often represented by unapproved deputies. This was certainly the case in many cathedrals, including St Paul's in the 1840s and 1850s as experienced first-hand by the young John Stainer, a chorister at the cathedral.[4] The organist and bibliophile Edward Francis Rimbault wrote to the editor of the *Musical World* in November 1842, lamented the neglect into which the choirs of St Paul's and the Chapel Royal had fallen, and wondered why cathedral deans cared so little about musical standards.[5] As a passionate disciple of Jebb's ideal, the irascible S. S. Wesley, embittered by a catalogue of bad experiences at the hands of cathedral chapters, used his tract of 1844, *A Few Words on Cathedral Music* (1849), as a means of channelling his pent-up frustration.[6] Much of this corrosion of attitudes had been caused by poor pay, and a *laissez-faire* (and often non-resident) cathedral clergy, who, unconcerned about singing, benefited from an unreformed system of remuneration where funds were siphoned away to clerical salaries instead of into music and the welfare of choristers.

Much of this degeneration was addressed by the Dean and Chapter Act of 1840, though reforms and their effects on cathedral choirs took several decades to bring about change; in the meantime, the lives of numerous deans throughout the country were harried by the persistent champion of the chorister, Maria Hackett, who brought shame to many cathedrals for neglecting their duty of responsibility to chorister education and well-being. Hackett began her activities in 1811 with a letter to the bishop of London about the appalling treatment of the choristers at St Paul's where she was a parishioner. Later she sent copies of her *Brief Account of Cathedral and Collegiate Schools, with an Abstract of their Statutes and Endowments* to every cathedral in 1827. Although legal action proved too costly, her visits to almost every cathedral foundation meant that deans and chapters could not ignore her or her cause. Jebb's ideal continued to be put into practice at Leeds (where Wesley resided as organist between 1842 and 1849) and remained a landmark at a time when the Cathedral Commissioners had embarked on a major investigation of cathedral foundations. They reported in 1854, two years before Frederick Ouseley founded (and financed) St Michael's College, Tenbury, in Worcestershire, the first collegiate foundation since the Reformation, devoted to a high ideal of the performance of Anglican choral service.

The establishment of St Michael's took place in the wake of reforms instigated by the Tractarians in the 1830s, though, as Temperley has stated, it was not to the Oxford Movement that the imperatives of the choral service

[4] Jeremy Dibble, *John Stainer: A Life in Music* (Woodbridge, 2007), pp. 7ff.; Philip Barrett, *Barchester: English Cathedral Life in the Nineteenth Century* (London, 1993), pp. 166ff.; Nicholas Temperley, 'Cathedral Music', in Nicholas Temperley (ed.), *The Blackwell History of Music in Britain: The Romantic Age 1800–1914* (Oxford, 1988), pp. 172–4.

[5] *The Musical World*, 17 (1842), p. 375.

[6] Peter Horton, *Samuel Sebastian Wesley: A Life* (Oxford, 2004), pp. 163–9.

owed their revival, for many of the strictures were already in place. Nevertheless, the Oxford Movement's influence could be conspicuously felt in a number of significant areas. As part of a renewed zeal to restore order to the liturgy, there had also been a new desire to re-establish the larger schemata of the lectionary and the Church year, factors which had a profound effect on the specific choice of anthems, service music, and, as will be mentioned later, hymnody. Directors of music, influenced by the enthusiasm and guidance of their Tractarian masters, would no longer aspire to predicate their choice of music on what was practically possible (which often meant performing with the available resources from week to week); instead, the Church calendar and feast days would direct what was to be sung. Similarly the Oxford Movement's later increased ardour for ritualism, the importance of the entire Communion service (rather than its more curtailed current form), and a newly-discovered respect for the eucharist inevitably encouraged a greater role for music within the liturgy and the composition of service music and specific themes of anthems and hymns. Furthermore, the Romantic fervour out of which the Oxford Movement was born also witnessed a rediscovery of the Church's older musical traditions, in particular plainsong and the advocacy of music of the sixteenth and early seventeenth centuries, notably of the music of Tallis, Byrd, and Gibbons. The championing of music composed before 1650 for worship had formed part of William Crotch's influential essays at Oxford some years before the Tractarian 'revolution',[7] and his values were defended by Frederick Ouseley, Thomas Helmore, precentor and vice-principal at St Mark's College, Chelsea and a well-known advocate and publisher of plainchant, and the Motett Society, founded in 1841, to propagate the virtues of old Church music. It was, however, the physician and amateur musician Robert Druitt who set out many of the fundamental principles of Tractarian musical worship in his *A popular tract on church music, with remarks on its moral and political importance*, published in 1845. Druitt, who was appalled by the standard of parish music, founded the Society for Promoting Church Music (SPCM) along with the *Parish Choir*, the Society's official journal.

MERBECKE AND THE ZEAL FOR PLAINSONG

The Tractarian passion for plainsong was also accompanied by the rehabilitation of the sixteenth-century John Merbecke's *Booke of Common Praier*

[7] William Crotch, *Lectures on the History of Music written between 1798 and 1832* excerpts as *Substance of Several Courses of Lectures* (London, 1831); Peter Huray and James Day (eds.), *Music and Aesthetics in the Eighteenth and Early-Nineteenth Centuries* (Cambridge, 1981), pp. 427–42.

Noted, which set the Anglican liturgy to a semi-rhythmical monophony derived largely from old chant. In fact it was Jebb who initially drew attention to the importance of Merbecke in 1841, but it was William Dyce who issued a modified version, adapted for his edition of *The Order of Daily Service* published in 1843; others by William Pickering and Edward Rimbault rapidly followed. The enthusiasm for Gregorian chant was also taken up with special alacrity by members of the Cambridge Camden Society, later known as the Ecclesiologists. Many of them, powerfully motivated by a rejuvenated interest in Gothic architecture and 'primitive' art, espoused a medieval vision of robed men and boys chanting the service, ideally without organ (an instrument which, for the most extreme apologists, was a nuisance). Yet, although congregations (who, unlike Jebb's model) were *not* to be excluded from choral participation in the liturgy (a central principle of the Tractarians), they were only familiar with harmonized chant, organ accompaniment, and some form of rhythmic framework, all of which militated against the medieval dream towards which so many Ecclesiologists aspired. In addition, there was the problem of language, for Gregorian chant had only ever been sung to Latin, whereas, within the Anglican liturgy, English was *sine qua non*.

Nevertheless, the advocates of chant were not to be discouraged. Walter Kerr Hamilton, curate and later incumbent of St Peter-in-the-East at Oxford, got his congregation to chant the canticles (as prepared by his organist, Alexander Reinagle), but he was soon encouraging them to sing Gregorian chants. After becoming bishop of Salisbury, Hamilton continued to promote his preference for Gregorian music along with the view that congregational participation was the 'great end to be aimed at' and that 'a choir should be used as to help bring about this blessed result'. Moreover, harmony, he claimed, was a bad and meretricious association which needed to be expelled from worship.[8] Another advocate of Gregorian music was Frederick Oakeley, former chaplain of Balliol College, Oxford, a dyed-in-the-wool Tractarian and admirer of Newman's and John Rouse Bloxam's ritual practices at Littlemore. At Margaret Chapel in London, where he became minister in 1839, he sought the help of the former Magdalen College chorister, Richard Redhead, in order to form a small choir of boys and men.[9] At first the chanting was to Anglican chant, but, in 1843, with the joint publication of *Laudes diurnae* by Oakeley and Redhead, the congregation were able to sing Gregorian music from a fully pointed psalter. Ideas about the practice and notation of Gregorian music were scant in the early days of the Tractarian revival, so figures such as Oakeley had to rely on *Cantica Vespera* (London, 1841), a publication by Vincent Novello, organist of the Sardinian Embassy Chapel in London. Such was the level of

[8] Walter Kerr Hamilton, *Church Music: A Sermon, Preached at the Church of St Mary, Sturminster… on Thursday, April 12, 1860* (Salisbury, 1860), pp. 9–10.

[9] Rainbow, *Choral Revival*, pp. 18–25.

liturgical and musical observation at Margaret Chapel that it attracted many Tractarian followers, including the future prime minister William Gladstone.[10] Other attempts to adapt plainsong were made by Edward John Hopkins at the Temple Church in London where plainchant melodies were adapted to a form of Anglican chant, much appreciated by the congregation.[11]

It was, however, at St Mark's College, Chelsea, that plainsong gained its most significant fillip. Under the aegis of John Hullah, who fostered important new methods of sight-singing, and the college's Tractarian vice-principal, Thomas Helmore, a graduate of Magdalen Hall, Oxford (1837–40), who had been deeply impressed by the *Tracts for the Times*, a small choir of boys (from the model school) and men sang unaccompanied daily choral services. These services included plainsong, Anglican chants (from Boyce's *Cathedral Music*), and Tallis's litany and responses combined with English (and Italian) sixteenth- and seventeenth-century anthems and service music.[12] Students at the college, originally founded to train teachers for the National Schools, were also expected to take part in the services together with the congregation, which formed part of a broader musical education designed to be used in parochial schools. This was significant enough in terms of the college's dissemination of musical excellence; but perhaps the most important consequence of Helmore's work was his adaptation of plainsong into English, which required several years of trial and experiment. This resulted in a landmark publication, the *Psalter Noted* (1849) which was duly expanded the following year in *A Manual of Plainsong*. Though it remained an authoritative text, which was revised by Brigg and Frere in 1902, the *Manual*'s archaic notation of four lines, old clefs, black longs, breves and semibreves preserved a medieval ideal (derived essentially from Dyce's antiquarian *Order of Daily Service*) which was strangely impractical for its users.[13]

FROM PARISH TO CATHEDRAL: A COMPROMISE

Gregorian chant, early music, and their place within the richer matrix of ritualism undoubtedly had its followers among the more extreme Anglo-Catholics. Among them were W. J. E. Bennett of St Paul's, Knightsbridge, and St Barnabas, Pimlico, a founding member of the SPCM, who instituted sung Matins, Litany, and Communion, and took as his guide the musical teachings of Helmore, and even after the 1850 Pimlico 'anti-popery' riots and Bennett's resignation, services continued in much the same form. Helmore

[10] Rainbow, *Choral Revival*, p. 16.

[11] Rainbow, *Choral Revival*, pp. 39–41.

[12] Rainbow, *Choral Revival*, p. 50.

[13] Temperley, *English Parish Church*, p. 261; Rainbow, *Choral Revival*, pp. 79–86.

continue to proselytize his belief in the 'true church music' until his death in 1890. In London, a number of important churches—All Saints Margaret Street, St Alban's Holborn, and St Mary Magdalene Paddington—adhered to Helmore's standpoint.

Yet, in spite of its neo-medieval enthusiasm, this vision of choral worship failed to attract the majority, and by the 1880s the passion for Gregorian music had begun to wane, in spite of the efforts of the London Gregorian Association (founded in 1870) to consolidate its position. In fact, in spite of the more publicized conflict between High and Low Churchmanship, a middle ground had evolved between the two which was also perceived as a uniting force for the national Church, in which the cathedral model of choral worship, led by a professional, surpliced choir and organist (now invariably qualified through the College of Organists, founded in 1864) was adopted by all parties. The High Churchmen already had their model from Leeds, Tenbury, and St Andrew's Wells Street, while Evangelicals clearly saw the leading of singing psalmody as an improvement; as for the Broad Churchman, a service with music guided essentially by the choir, yet with a degree of congregational participation in the hymns, retained an attractive message.

The splendour of the choral service was, for many, the outward sign of a more prosperous, educated, industrial society. Indeed, its apogee is perhaps best epitomized by the growth of Diocesan Choral Festivals (or in the case of the capital, the London Church Choir Association) where thousands of singers from local choirs would coalesce once a year to sing services on a truly grand scale. These major collective, religious, and artistic events would often involve the commissioning of new works such as Hubert Parry's anthem 'Hear my words, ye people' (1894).

The irony, however, was that the 'cathedral model' itself derived its lead, not from the cathedrals, but from the upward trajectory of musical performance in the parish churches. Indeed, Ouseley, addressing the Church Congress in 1872, remarked that little difference in standards existed between them.[14] In truth, little improved in the cathedrals during the first half of the nineteenth century, and many of the developments and expectations enjoyed in the parish churches had not reached them. In the college chapels of the ancient universities, things were somewhat mixed. In Cambridge, St John's College and Trinity College benefited from the services of Thomas Attwood Walmisley (who also served Great St Mary's), who trained his choristers with some efficiency. The music at King's, however, was in a pitiful state of atrophy. Similarly at Oxford, there were three collegiate institutions with music—New College, Christ Church, and Magdalen—which were thought well of locally, though in reality the standard of singing and discipline was poor. Walmisley, a

[14] Frederick A. G. Ouseley, *Proceedings of the Church Congress* (Leeds, 1872), p. 326.

thoroughly capable musician, was succeeded by John Larkin Hopkins, an able if unimaginative individual. At Oxford, chapel music languished under an aged Walter Vicary as *informator choristarum* at Magdalen, the lacklustre William Marshall at Christ Church, and the one-legged Stephen Elvey who, carried around in a bath chair, also played at St John's and the university church of St Mary the Virgin. Only with the arrival of the nineteen-year-old John Stainer in 1860 did reforms at Magdalen come about.[15] Stainer had come from Tenbury where he had been organist since 1857 and he entered Oxford at a time when the university was undergoing major structural changes.[16] A man of rare talent, Stainer brought energy to the changing regime at Magdalen. Though he had known a Broad Church atmosphere at Tenbury, he warmed to the more ritual Tractarianism influenced by Bloxam in Magdalen chapel as well as to the Tractarian atmosphere of St Mary the Virgin where he succeeded Elvey.[17] Bloxam's influence at Magdalen was considerable, not only in observing a High Church approach to the liturgy but also in promoting the welfare of the choristers whose role he believed was crucial to the chapel's success and prestige. In this regard he oversaw the erection of a new choir school in 1851 and was responsible for the appointment of sympathetically High Church schoolmasters. Through his love of tradition, he helped to revive the old Magdalen tradition of singing from the Magdalen Tower on May Morning, and Christmas entertainments of carols for the choristers.[18] Thanks also to Bloxam's guiding hand, a choir of sixteen choristers and eight professional lay clerks sang daily Matins and Evensong and there was choral Communion on a significant number of important Sundays and feast days throughout the Church year. In a matter of years, Stainer had further raised the standards at Magdalen with regular practices for both boys and men, a systematic rota of chants for psalms and musical services, and anthems (some of them specially composed by Stainer himself) that complied with the Church calendar.

In 1872, with the vacancy of the organist's post at St Paul's Cathedral, Stainer was head-hunted by a triumvirate of Tractarians, Canon Henry Parry Liddon, Canon Robert Gregory, and the Dean, Richard William Church, three men who had major designs on reform of the choir and saw Stainer as the means of realizing this goal. Within three years massive changes had been effected, thanks in part to the commutation of funds from ecclesiastical reforms and the skilful handling of the cathedral's finances by Robert Gregory. From twelve boys, the number had been increased to thirty-six, and a new choir school was opened in early 1875 whose new regime gave renewed fillip

[15] Dibble, *John Stainer*, pp. 63ff.

[16] W. R. Ward, *Victorian Oxford* (London, 1965), p. xiii.

[17] Dibble, *John Stainer*, p. 71.

[18] Robin Darwall-Smith, 'Magdalen and the Rediscovery of Christmas', *Magdalen College Record* (2001): 92–102; Dibble, *John Stainer*, pp. 75–8.

to the much-valued musical education that a choristership could provide. School holidays were introduced as well as free afternoons which were filled by services for lay clerks only. The six unruly vicars-choral had been brought to heel by the threat of their abolition by an Act of Parliament, and by the addition of a further twelve men, no longer with rights of freehold but with proper pension provision. Formal processions, the adoption of cassocks and surplices, vestry prayers, chorister inductions, weekly practices, and fines for non-attendance were copiously instituted. In addition there were printed weekly music lists, regular Sunday choral Communion, a notable expansion of musical repertoire, biennial music reports, the introduction of *Hymns Ancient & Modern*, carols, and orchestral services which included Mendelssohn's *St Paul* for the Patronal Festival, Bach's *St Matthew Passion* during Holy Week, and commissioned anthems and services for the Festival of the Sons of the Clergy. Soon the choir of St Paul's had replaced Leeds as the High Church model and one towards which not only cathedrals aspired but parish churches as well.

MUSICAL REPERTOIRE FOR THE CHORAL SERVICE: THE MAKINGS OF A NATIONAL HERITAGE

Concomitant with the growth of choral worship in Anglicanism was the mass production of music on a scale never witnessed before. In particular, the efforts of Vincent Novello, an English Catholic with a background in Church music (he was organist to the Sardinian, Spanish, and Portuguese embassy chapels between 1796 and 1822), vocal music in score (both in notation and Tonic Sol-Fa) became widely available across the spectrum of abilities, rendering the old system of cathedral partbooks redundant. This in turn spawned an industry of practical Church music, a wealth of psalm chant books, hymnals, service music, and anthems, many of them easy for parish use and designed for competent organists and choirs singing in harmony.

The romantic aptitude of composers such as S. S. Wesley and Thomas Attwood Walmisley, along with John Goss's later anthems were most popular. The Mozartian sonata forms of many of Goss's creations link his style with the more Georgian eloquence of Thomas Attwood, though much of Attwood's Church music has disappeared from the repertoire with the exception of 'Come, Holy Ghost', 'Turn thy face from my sins', and the delicious minuet style of 'Turn thee again, O Lord, at the last', all of which have a strong classical bent. Works by Goss such as 'If we believe that Jesus died' and 'O Saviour of the World' derive their pathos from Romanticism. Greatest of his generation was, however, S. S. Wesley. With a background in theatre music, he brought a new, vivid, harmonic vocabulary to his Church music, placing emphasis not only on the new chromatic resources available, but also on the enhancement of diatonic dissonance. His practical short anthems, 'Wash me throughly' (distinctly redolent of Spohr) and the rondo 'Thou wilt keep him in perfect peace' are deeply expressive, as is the *a cappella* 'Cast me not away from thy presence'. Numbering among his medium-size anthems is 'Blessed be the God and Father', best known perhaps for its verse 'Love one another' and its dramatic fugato conclusion 'The word of the Lord endureth forever'; though equally fine is the eight-part 'To my request and earnest cry' now little heard. But Wesley's finest music is contained in his large-scale verse anthems such as 'The wilderness', 'Let us lift up our heart', and 'Ascribe unto the Lord' which are of such dimensions that they cannot practically be sung liturgically, save for shorter excerpts. In concept they are more cantata-like with their substantial solo verses, often (like 'Thou, O Lord God' from 'Let us lift up our heart') couched in elaborate instrumental forms symptomatic of the concert hall. The same can be said of Walmisley's full-length anthems of the 1830s and 1840s and Stainer's larger anthems such as 'Awake, awake put on thy strength' and 'They were lovely and pleasant in their lives' composed for use at Magdalen College between 1860 and 1872. Service music also required careful handling, and among the most significant compositions was Walmisley's Evening Service in D minor (*c.*1855) for its structural tightness of verse construction, its independent organ accompaniment, its archaic, yet romantic harnessing of synthetic plainsong, and its use of modal harmony. By the end of the 1870s, the 'supremacy of instrumental music', central to the trend of German Romanticism, motivated Charles Villiers Stanford's radical Morning, Communion, and Evening Services in B flat (1879), and A (1880), and anthems such as 'The Lord is my shepherd' (1886). The highly original nature of Stanford's sacred works lies in the emphasis on symphonic design, organic development of the musical material, and, in the case of the service music, a broader matrix of thematic musical references across the entire scheme of the day. Added to this, a further mark of true genius is its retention of a practicality of length and ease of use. Stanford's services, among some of the most original Church music of its era, became the model for others such as Hubert Parry, Charles Wood, John Ireland, T. T. Noble, and Edward Bairstow.

While the growth of anthems and service music for the choral service may have been one major symptom of Anglican ingenuity and creativity, another was without doubt the extraordinary eruption of psalmody and hymnody. Originally the preserve of the Methodists at the end of the eighteenth century, enthusiastic hymn-singing was taken up by the Anglican Evangelicals in the early nineteenth century, led by figures such as Thomas Cotterill of Sheffield, whose *Selection of Psalms and Hymns for Public and Private Use, adapted to the Services of the Church of England*, first published in 1810, ran to many editions. The Anglican chant had, by the 1850s, reached its apogee with a flood of new chants, the publication of chant books, and, perhaps most importantly, the more universal systematization of pointing (as represented by Stainer's *Cathedral Psalter* in 1875 with an authority conferred by its editorial committee of John Stainer, James Turle, and Joseph Barnby).[19] But whereas psalms were more generally the more complex preserve of the choir, the hymn, one of the oldest established forms of musical worship, was an entity in which choir and congregation, across the theological spectrum, could unite. As the Church also began to loosen its long-held control over what hymn texts could be sung, the *Old* and *New Versions* began to be abandoned in favour of new tunes and new poetry. During the 1850s publications such as Bickersteth's *Christian Psalmody*, Kemble's *Selection of Psalms and Hymns*, and Mercer's *Church Psalter and Hymn Book* had wide circulations; while John Mason Neale's *The Hymnal Noted* enjoyed popularity among the High Church and Anglo-Catholics. Mercer's book also established a new trend, that of placing the four-part harmony on two staves: a practice which only served to encourage the practice of singing in harmony.

It was with the issue in 1861 of *Hymns Ancient & Modern* edited by Baker and Monk, that hymnody representing the various wings of Anglicanism came together within the covers of one book and where hymn text and hymn tune became an inseparable unity. Monk's musical influence came down in favour of the 'ancient' rather than the modern—plainsong melodies, German chorales, old English tunes—but he did himself contribute seventeen contemporary tunes such as EVENTIDE ('Abide with me'), twelve of which had texts by prominent Tractarian poets—Lyte, Baker, Caswall, Faber, Heber, Chandler, Neale, Williams, and Moultrie. More auspiciously, seven tunes were contributed by John Bacchus Dykes of which ST CUTHBERT, MELITA, HOLLINGSIDE, HORBURY, and NICAEA have became internationally well known. Dykes, justly described by Temperley as 'the most important Tractarian composer of hymn tunes',[20] authored a style of hymn that was truly romantic in the use of its resources; indeed, so popular did it become that, in the 1875 revised edition of *Hymns Ancient & Modern*, more than fifty of Dykes's tunes were included. Emotional in its inventive deployment of chromatic harmony, it sought to move the hymn into a new orbit in which attributes of other genres such as partsong, cantata, and oratorio were detectable, where the organ played a key role, and where the ethos of singing hymns not only galvanized the love of *harmony* but also advanced a sense of *performance*. A further consequence of the hymn's importance to choir and congregation alike was its new position of prestige for composers. Indeed, so seriously was the hymn taken that it spawned *Julian's Dictionary of Hymnology* in 1899, and the

[19] Rainbow, *Choral Revival*, p. 297.

[20] Temperley, *English Parish Church*, p. 250.

notion of 'collected hymns' became the mark of composers such as Barnby (1897), E. J. Hopkins (1901), Stainer (1899), and Dykes (1902).

In tandem with the huge popularity of the high Victorian hymn tune came the recognition of the carol. Valued by the antiquarian, and thoroughly disseminated by Stainer's *Christmas Carols New and Old* (published between 1867 and 1878), the carol had nevertheless been excluded from formal worship on the grounds of its secular associations, that is until clerical pressure came from figures such as Richard Chope and Sabine Baring-Gould in *Carols for Use in Church: During Christmas and Epiphany* (1875) who believed in its pedagogical power to teach the doctrine of the Incarnation.[21] In 1878 Stainer oversaw the introduction of a carol at the end of Evensong during the octave of Christmas at St Paul's. Other cathedrals began to introduce carols at Evensong on Christmas Eve, but it was at Truro Cathedral in 1880 that the Nine Lessons and Carols, drawn up by Bishop Edward Benson as another ideal fusion of choir and congregational participation, was born. The Festival of Nine Lessons and Carols at King's College, Cambridge was not introduced until 1918 when, after its first broadcast in 1928, it swiftly became a national institution. Many may also have realized that they were tapping into a tradition, which, along with Anglicanism's unique repository of hymnody, anthems, and service music, possessed, not to say fashioned, enormously potent national characteristics of beauty, order, mystery, and quiet contemplation, on which the twentieth-century Anglican *via media* of choral worship would capitalize.

SELECT BIBLIOGRAPHY

Adelmann, Dale, *The Contribution of Cambridge Ecclesiologists to the Revival of Anglican Choral Worship 1839–62* (Aldershot, 1997).

Barrett, Philip, *Barchester: English Cathedral Life in the Nineteenth Century* (London, 1993).

Chope, R. R. and H. S. Irons (eds.), *Carols for Use in Church: During Christmas and Epiphany* (London, 1875).

Cole, Suzanne, *Thomas Tallis and His Music in Victorian England* (Woodbridge, 2008).

Darwall-Smith, Robin, 'Magdalen and the Rediscovery of Christmas', *Magdalen College Record* (2001): 92–102.

Dibble, Jeremy, *John Stainer: A Life in Music* (Woodbridge, 2007).

Hamilton, Walter Kerr, *Church Music: A Sermon, Preached at the Church of St Mary, Sturminster... on Thursday, April 12, 1860* (Salisbury, 1860).

Horton, Peter, *Samuel Sebastian Wesley: A Life* (Oxford, 2004).

[21] S. Baring-Gould, 'Christmas Carols', in R. R. Chope and H. S. Irons (eds.), *Carols for Use in Church* (London, 1875), p. xxiii.

Huray, Peter and James Day (eds.), *Music and Aesthetics in the Eighteenth and Early-Nineteenth Centuries* (Cambridge, 1981).

Hymns Ancient & Modern and Henry William Baker: A Herefordshire Vicar and His Hymn Book (Leominster History Study Group, 2013).

Rainbow, Bernarr, *The Choral Revival in the Anglican Church* (Oxford, 1970).

Temperley, Nicholas, 'Cathedral Music', in Nicholas Temperley (ed.), *The Blackwell History of Music in Britain: The Romantic Age 1800–1914* (Oxford, 1988), pp. 171–213.

Temperley, Nicholas, *The Music of the English Parish Church* (Cambridge, 1979).

Ward, W. R., *Victorian Oxford* (London, 1965).

Zon, Bennett, *The English Plainchant Revival* (Oxford, 1999).

20

Anglican Art and Architecture, *c*.1837–1914

Ayla Lepine

Church art and architecture and the interaction between religion and the arts in Victorian Britain and its empire have been important and fruitful avenues for recent scholarship, though much remains to discover and interpret. Debates are fresh and topics remain under-researched regarding the presence of Anglican sensibility in relation to art institutions such as the Royal Academy, art movements such as the Pre-Raphaelites and their wider circle, and architectural projects beyond the tight network of patrons and architects creating buildings within the Church of England's diverse expressions in Britain and the empire. The Victoria and Albert Museum's 1971 exhibition of Victorian Church art contained an unprecedentedly wide variety of Anglican material, and its catalogue remains an important resource for identifying makers and designers.[1] In 1984, the Pre-Raphaelites exhibition at Tate Britain touched on religious themes within their work, but only lightly. In the 1990s, publications by Mark Crinson and Christopher Webster highlighted the early impacts and global scope of Ecclesiology, a powerful movement collaboratively founded by clerics and architects that reshaped the style and meaning of Church architecture in relation to the Church of England's institutional development.[2] More recent art historical scholarship, such as Tim Barringer's 2005 monograph *Men at Work: Art and Labour in Victorian Britain* and Michaela Giebelhausen's *Painting the Bible*, published in 2006, productively complicate the relationship between religion, empire, style, and the production of art and architecture that explored Anglican themes in a global context. The major Pre-Raphaelite

[1] John Pope-Hennessy and others, *Victorian Church Art*, exhibition catalogue (London, 1971).

[2] Mark Crinson, *Empire Building: Orientalism and Victorian Architecture* (London, 1996); Christopher Webster and John Elliott (eds.), *A Church as it Should Be: The Cambridge Camden Society and its Influence* (Donington, 2001).

exhibition of 2012–14, which took hundreds of objects from London to Washington DC, Moscow, and Tokyo, included a major thematic section dedicated to 'Salvation' in which visual culture of Christianity, modern life, and industrial labour were closely connected.[3] Michael J. Lewis's survey of the Gothic Revival and Geoffrey Cantor's explication of the importance of religion within the Great Exhibition of 1851 also offer valuable perspectives on style, theology, and the Church of England at the height of the Victorian period.[4] An introduction to the firms, religious workshops, and key techniques and designers for ecclesiastical embroidery, written by the textile historian Mary Schoeser in 1998, is a key publication foregrounding the diversity of textiles used in Anglican spaces in the nineteenth century. Though published over half a century ago, Peter Anson's *The Call of the Cloister* continues to be the authoritative survey on men's and women's Anglican religious communities in Victorian Britain and its imperial territories. Anson's *Fashions in Church Furnishings* also continues to offer an insight into changing tastes attendant on Anglican liturgical, theological, and architectural change between the mid-nineteenth and mid-twentieth centuries. In nearly all cases, scholastic focus has been on social and religious history, and thus there is limited engagement with art and architecture in relation to the rise of monastic life within Anglicanism in the nineteenth century.

Texts like these also foreground the need for further research in the intersections of Anglican institutions and liturgy and the decorative arts. In Alex Bremner and Michael Hall's extensive studies of the Gothic Revival, style and Anglicanism are tightly interwoven.[5] Broader publications on the significance of religion and the arts, by Douglas Adams, Graham Howes, and Sally Promey to name but a few of the leading scholars in this growing field, assist in the formation of new art and architectural historical interpretations of Anglican objects and spaces.

The history of Anglican art and architecture in the nineteenth century is therefore a multi-dimensional history that must be viewed in relation to numerous interlacing phenomena. This chapter focuses on two art and architectural movements that were very significant in shaping and expressing Victorian Anglicanism. These are the rise of Pre-Raphaelitism from its establishment in 1848 and its transformation of religious painting; and the Gothic Revival and its impact on architecture within and outside Church of England networks. Both the Pre-Raphaelites and the Gothic Revival were controversial,

[3] Tim Barringer and others (eds.), *The Pre-Raphaelites: Victorian Avant-Garde*, exhibition catalogue (London, 2012).

[4] Michael J. Lewis, *The Gothic Revival* (London, 2000).

[5] G. Alex Bremner, *Imperial Gothic* (New Haven, CT, 2013); Michael Hall, *George Frederick Bodley and the Later Gothic Revival in Britain and America* (New Haven, CT, 2014).

popular, and transformative within the Victorian period, straddling geographies, denominational diversity between Evangelical and Anglo-Catholic beliefs, and international activities and movements within and beyond Anglicanism. Both movements intersected in their application and effects within art, architecture, and design. As Tim Barringer observes, the Pre-Raphaelites were not allied with a single Anglican group: 'the views of each of the major religious factions—the Oxford Movement, Broad Church, and Evangelical groups—can in turn be associated with particular Pre-Raphaelite works.'[6] Moreover, the imperial project and empire's interaction with art and architectural development must be considered alongside the significance of theological education, mission, and monasticism as religious activities with direct outcomes for patronage, production, and debate within the arts. Offering key case studies in Anglican art and architecture within Britain and its imperial territories, I aim to demonstrate that a distinctively Anglican aesthetic emerged and flourished across the Victorian period and beyond the threshold of the twentieth century.

As the Church historian Frances Knight declares, throughout the nineteenth century both Christian iconography and Christian theology were in states of major transformation.[7] Knight has also compellingly argued that while the nature and threat of hell was at the forefront of Victorian thinking until *c.*1860, after this mid-century turn—which coincided with the arrival of the Aesthetic Movement and an emphasis on beauty's uncoupling from a firm and rigid morality—heaven was the prime concern for the Victorian religious mind from *c.*1860 until the turn of the twentieth century.[8] Anxieties regarding identity, salvation, resurrection, and judgement in the midst of the Church of England's controversial bifurcations and ever-present ambitions within regional, national, and imperial culture, were diversely and stimulatingly expressed in art and architectural terms. Questions regarding salvation, resurrection, and suffering pervaded Victorian theology and Anglican art. Architects such as George Gilbert Scott, William Butterfield, George Edmund Street, George Frederick Bodley, and John Loughborough Pearson transformed Britain and its empire, punctuating it with Gothic spires at a swift pace. Artists including John Everett Millais, William Holman Hunt, Ford Madox Brown, and Elizabeth Siddall explored religious themes in their work with a renewed energy to combine historicism, realism, and religious symbolism for an eager market of buyers and viewers.[9]

6 Tim Barringer, *Reading the Pre-Raphaelites* (New Haven, CT, 1998), p. 110.

7 Frances Knight, *The Nineteenth-Century Church* (Cambridge, 1996), p. 47.

8 Knight, *Nineteenth-Century Church.*

9 Elizabeth Prettejohn (ed.), *The Cambridge Companion to the Pre-Raphaelites* (Cambridge, 2012).

MATTER OF FAITH: MAPPING ART AND ARCHITECTURAL TRENDS

There are several key turning points that were formative for the gestation of Anglican art and architecture in the nineteenth century. Catholic emancipation in 1829 and the Oxford Movement in 1833 inaugurated a vibrant and risky new wave of theological possibility. The arts were engaged with these developments from the outset: Augustus Welby Northmore Pugin published his polemical *Contrasts* in 1836 with a new edition in 1841, and a fast-paced output of other Gothic Revival projects and writings followed until his death in 1852. The Cambridge Camden Society was founded in 1839 to promote a new science of church building and historical understanding of pre-Reformation European traditions in architecture, music, theology, and the arts more broadly. It swiftly gained an impressive host of members ranging from bishops to architects. Their journal, *The Ecclesiologist*, was one of the most influential publications of its time, and when the group re-formed as the Ecclesiological Society in the 1840s it swiftly became a mouthpiece for art and architectural religious transformation in Britain and throughout the empire. The Great Exhibition of 1851 brought many sacred traditions into contact as never before, and art and architecture moved to the epicentre of the monarchy and government's articulation of productivity, industry, taste, and art institutions.

In 1849, John Ruskin published *The Seven Lamps of Architecture*, and this was followed by his revolutionary perspectives on history, tradition, and revivalism laid out in *The Stones of Venice*, which appeared in three volumes between 1851 and 1853. An essay within it on 'The Nature of Gothic' was the single greatest influence upon architectural adherence to interpretations—however diverse—of the Gothic style in the nineteenth century.[10] With the rise of ritualism through the 1860s and the steady importance of Evangelical organizations in the midst of major cultural change within and outside England's religious landscape, art and architectural contributions increasingly took on a political and at times controversial heft.

Meanwhile, Evangelical dialogue on art and identity took new forms with the growth of middle-class wealth throughout the Victorian period. As the historian Deborah Cohen explains, 'Things had moral qualities. Urged on by clergymen who preached that beauty was holy, Victorians evaluated the merits of sideboards and chintzes according to a new standard of godliness. A correct purchase could elevate a household's moral tone; the wrong choice could exert a malevolent influence.'[11] The material world of the arts and the heavenly

[10] William Morris, 'Preface', *The Nature of Gothic* (London, 1892).

[11] Deborah Cohen, *Household Gods: The British and Their Possessions* (New Haven, CT, 2006), p. x; R. W. Dale, *The Old Evangelicalism and the New* (London, 1889), p. 36; Chandra Mukerji, *From Graven Images: Patterns of Modern Materialism* (New York, 1983).

world of the soul was as crucial a relationship for Evangelical Anglicans as for Anglo-Catholics. In his popular *Recreations of a Country Parson* (1861), the Evangelical clergyman Andrew Boyd made a case for the spiritual qualities of design and the arts in every Evangelical home: 'We are all moral chameleons; and we take the colour of the objects among which we are placed.'[12] Moral chameleons took many hues, and often fought one another's interpretations of the holiness of beauty in the Victorian public arena of both Church and state.

In 1874, religion was debated hotly in Parliament, and the Public Worship Regulation Act came down heavily on Anglo-Catholic liturgical practices. In the same year, three prominent Gothic Revival architects formed Watts and Company, which provided the vessels, textiles, and fashionable interiors that were associated with the ritualist practices that many within and outside the government were seeking to quash and condemn.[13] By the time of Queen Victoria's Diamond Jubilee in 1897, the pageantry's marriage of religion and empire on the steps of St Paul's Cathedral foregrounded the increasingly firm and established aesthetic of Anglicanism's rediscovery of medievalism in the midst of the British Empire's climax, prior to the onset of deep anxiety regarding both ideological and military conflict zones worldwide at the turn of the twentieth century and towards the Great War.[14] Against the pressures of the Crimean War in the 1850s and the Second South African War of 1899–1902, artists and architects explored the dimensions of Anglican religious experience in a rapidly changing world. As William Holman Hunt's third version of *The Light of the World*, his groundbreaking painting of Christ knocking at the door of vulnerable humanity, circled the globe on its tour from Britain to New Zealand, Canada, South Africa, and Australia between 1905 and 1907, its appearance's wild popularity marked the establishment of an Anglican aesthetic—diverse, certainly, but discernible—which had emerged in the 1830s and revolutionized British Church art and architecture across a century.

EXHIBITING ANGLICANISM

Among the most significant events in Victorian art was the Great Exhibition. In May 1851, the Great Exhibition of the Works of Industry of All Nations

[12] Andrew Boyd, 'Concerning the Moral Influences of the Dwelling', in *Recreations of a Country Parson* (London, 1861), p. 241.

[13] Ayla Lepine, 'On the Founding of Watts & Co', in Dino Franco Felluga (ed.), *BRANCH: Britain, Representation and Nineteenth-Century History*. Extension of *Romanticism and Victorianism on the Net*. <http://www.branchcollective.org/?ps_articles=ayla-lepine-on-the-founding-of-watts-co-1874>, accessed 1 Aug. 2014.

[14] Angus Trumble and Andrea Wolk-Rager, *Edwardian Opulence*, exhibition catalogue (New Haven, CT, 2013).

opened to the public in London's Hyde Park. It also drew art, design, and architecture into contact with discourses of commodification, religion, and politics in a thoroughly modern Victorian arena. Housed within a giant greenhouse structure dubbed the Crystal Palace by the popular *Punch* magazine, the exhibition showcased a material world glittering with modern promise.[15] Over six million people flooded in to see the exhibition and take part in this unprecedented event.

For art and architectural historians, the Great Exhibition tends to be explored in relation to the engineering feat of the Crystal Palace's vast glass and metal construction, the articulation of the British Empire through commodities and rituals of display, and the values of nationhood in transnational contexts becoming clarified and debated as never before. This monumental event in the history of international exhibitions and global politics is usually discussed in secular terms. As the stained glass historian Jim Cheshire writes, 'the fact that this famous event was beyond the control of the church makes it particularly significant . . . the Great Exhibition was a profoundly secular affair with a strong commercial flavour'.[16] While not ecclesiastically controlled *per se*, the exhibition was, however, a highly significant phenomenon in relation to Anglican art and architecture. Religious objects, including sculpture, stained glass, metalwork, books, and textiles, were on show in several arenas; chief among these was the Medieval Court designed by the Roman Catholic architect and designer Augustus Pugin. Bibles and objects associated with Christianity from sculpture to metalwork and stained glass were displayed as objects of devotion and craftsmanship.[17] As reports attested and as the painter Henry Selous depicted in his vast group portrait of the inaugural proceedings, the archbishop of Canterbury blessed the exhibition at the culmination of an ornate ceremonial procession during its May 1851 opening day.[18] Many religious groups saw the exhibition as an opportunity for mission and evangelism. In the writer and clergyman Charles Kingsley's sermon in St Margaret's Westminster on 4 May 1851, he asked if the exhibition could be 'anything but a matter of personal gain or curiosity, for national aggrandisement, insular self-glorification, and selfish—had almost said, treacherous—rivalry with the very foreigners whom we invited as our guests?'[19] Preachers throughout

[15] Isobel Armstrong, *Victorian Glassworlds* (Oxford, 2008).

[16] Jim Cheshire, *Stained Glass and the Victorian Gothic Revival* (Manchester, 2004), p. 155.

[17] Geoffrey Cantor, 'On Display: The Building, Its Contents, and English Protestantism', in *Religion and the Great Exhibition* (Oxford, 2011), pp. 102–27.

[18] *Athenaeum* (5 June 1852), p. 633, *Art Journal* (1852), p. 262; Sir Henry Cole, *Fifty Years of Public Work* (1884), I, p. 179; C. Wood, *Victorian Panorama* (repr. 1976), pp. 1, 11, quoted in <http://collections.vam.ac.uk/item/O8820/the-opening-of-the-great-oil-painting-selous-henry-courtney/>, accessed 10 May 2014.

[19] Charles Kingsley, 'Fount of Science', in *Sermons on National Subjects* (London, 1852), p. 112.

Britain took on the exhibition as a topic for sermons with a very wide range of interpretations of the event's spiritual and theological dimensions.

The frontispiece for the *Official Descriptive and Illustrated Catalogue* of the Great Exhibition displays a range of figures of all ages and many attributes—including a musician, a knight, labourers, and poets—arranged in an ascending arc around the *contrapposto* Britannia, who lightly embraces a youth carrying a bough of peace. In the topmost corners of the image, an inscription reads 'The Earth is the Lord's and all that therein is. The compass of the world and they that dwell therein.' These provocative words from Psalm 24 are situated at the heart of the grand production of the Great Exhibition, consecrating it and declaring that everything within it and all who contribute to it are enmeshed in a Christian world-view sustained and supported by the British monarchy and the exhibition's commissioners. As the historian Geoffrey Cantor has demonstrated, the significance of religion in and around the Great Exhibition must not be underestimated. Along with many denominations and sacred traditions, Anglicans used the exhibition and the Crystal Palace's array of spectacles as an opportunity to preach, publish, evangelize, and engage with visual and material cultures of empire to further their particular world-view.

The Great Exhibition opened up new debate regarding monarchy, empire, and Anglican faith via its sheer range of religious material on offer, including Bibles and sacred objects. An Evangelical perspective on the Victorian mission field is evident in Thomas Jones Barker's 1863 painting, *The Secret of England's Greatness*. The artwork depicts Queen Victoria presenting a Bible to an anonymous African, potentially based on Ali bin Nasr, Governor of Mombasa.[20] His presence does not refer to Mombasa in particular, however, and while the Queen and her prime minister are instantly recognizable, the African figure stands instead as an allegory of Anglican mission within the British Empire. The Bible Victoria offers is, of course, the sacred Scripture that constitutes the 'secret of England's greatness'. This is an especially Anglican gesture, connecting the central importance of Scripture with the unique character of the Church of England's Defender of the Faith. A Bible's portability, as the historian John Plotz asserts, was part of its power as a conveyor of religious meaning and experience across varied terrains, cultures, and social factors as empire evolved as an enmeshed and unstable system of encounter.[21]

This series of encounters in relation to Anglican identities were materialized within the complex sculptural programme of the Albert Memorial. This monument, festooned with gold, marble, metalwork, and semi-precious stones

[20] 'The Secret of England's Greatness', National Portrait Gallery. <http://www.npg.org.uk/collections/search/portrait/mw00071/The-Secret-of-Englands-Greatness-Queen-Victoria-presenting-a-Bible-in-the-Audience-Chamber-at-Windsor>, accessed 10 Aug. 2014.

[21] John Plotz, *Portable Property: Victorian Culture on the Move* (Princeton, NJ, 2009).

combining Gothic Revival and Classical stylistic details, featured a reliquary-like Gothic canopy within which a representation of the Prince Consort holding the *Catalogue* of the Great Exhibition was relatively informally positioned. Four sculptural groups representing four imperial continents that sent materials for displays at the Crystal Palace surround the central memorial canopy, placing monarchy in the centre of imperial reach. The Gothic canopy is surrounded by a flurry of triumphant angels, and its highest point terminates in a large cross pointing heavenward. The connection between the Exhibition of 1851, the sacred character of monarchy, the Christian context of mourning, and the links between London and empire are all enshrined at the Albert Memorial on the edge of Hyde Park.

The Great Exhibition's proceeds fed directly into the foundation and collections for the South Kensington Museum, a complex that eventually became the Natural History Museum, the Victoria and Albert Museum, and an array of interconnected sites for learning and culture in and around the South Kensington area of London. As Carol Duncan points out in *Civilising Rituals*, the rise of the museum is a distinctly nineteenth-century phenomenon, and museums were designed and curated with a quality of holy ritual in mind. Duncan explains, 'The museum's sequenced spaces and arrangements of objects, its lighting and architectural details provide both the stage set and the script... The situation resembles in some respects certain medieval cathedrals where pilgrims followed a structured narrative route through the interior, stopping at prescribed points for prayer or contemplation.'[22] Duncan connects what she calls the 'art museum as a performance field' to religious experience, explaining that religious ritual and cultural ritual were conflated in these modern spaces so crucial to nineteenth-century architectural, visual, and material culture.[23] Amongst the public collections becoming established within Britain, connections between religion, the arts, and the Church of England in particular were consistently produced, refined, and communicated.

ANGLO-CATHOLICISM AND THE ARTS

In addition to global spectacle and imperial sculpture, activity within religious life itself was instrumental in shaping the aesthetics, materials, and meanings of Anglican art and architecture. Among these major Victorian shifts few were more significant for the arts and architecture than the rise of Ecclesiology and the impact of the Oxford Movement. The emergence of Anglo-Catholicism began with the Oxford Movement and its leading figures, John Keble, John

[22] Carol Duncan, *Civilizing Rituals: Inside Public Art Museums* (London, 1995), p. 12.
[23] Duncan, *Civilizing Rituals*, p. 12.

Henry Newman, and Edward Bouverie Pusey. But with the exception of Keble's poetic and artistic sensibilities, these theologians were not especially concerned with forging connections between a renewed understanding of Anglicanism and a new path for art and architecture. Rather, the emergence of Ecclesiology in the late 1830s and 1840s was to provide the aesthetic response—and a surprisingly coherent and stringent one—to Oxford Movement radical shifts in belief, practice, and corporate worship. One of the key features of Anglo-Catholic artwork is the revival of *Opus Anglicanum*, technically sophisticated and ornate embroidered ecclesiastical textiles that had reached their high point of production in the fourteenth century in England. These textiles were revived to accompany and embellish Anglo-Catholic liturgy, in which the altar, the clergy, and the eucharist took a central ritualized role. Books such as Charles Walker's *The Ritual Reason Why* (1868) and Ernest Geldart's *A Manual of Church Decoration and Symbolism* (1899) encouraged and explained the revived use of ecclesiastical textiles from banners to maniples in Anglo-Catholic liturgy.[24] Most of these textiles were made by women in the nineteenth century, often in the context of Anglo-Catholic religious communities. As Julie Melnyk explains, 'The revival of religious communities and mysticism, together with an emphasis on women's biological role, offered opportunities for theological participation and for the formation of a separate women's theological culture.'[25] Historians including Susan Mumm and Carmen Mangion have written extensively on the unique contribution of nuns, women deacons, and lay women to the visual culture and institutional transformation of Anglicanism in the nineteenth century.[26]

Religious communities were both art and architectural patrons and producers, and they contributed to a distinctive Anglican aesthetic. From the early Oxford Movement sisterhood near Regent's Park founded by E. B. Pusey to the highly successful sisterhoods of the Society of St Margaret founded in East Grinstead by John Mason Neale in 1855, and the Community of St John the Baptist in Clewer founded by Harriet Monsell and Thomas Carter in 1852, these groups fused a renewed interest in pre-Reformation modes of religious life with countless opportunities for new architecture and works of art on an impressive scale. Architects including G. E. Street, G. F. Bodley, and J. D. Sedding worked alongside sisterhoods to design convent architecture and to produce textiles and furnishings. Though male monastic groups were far rarer than women religious, another community that contributed to the

[24] Mary Schoeser, *English Church Embroidery, 1833–1953* (London, 1998).

[25] Julie Melnyk, 'Women, Writing and Theological Cultures', in Sue Morgan and Jacqueline de Vries (eds.), *Women, Gender and Religious Cultures in Britain, 1800–1940* (London, 2010), p. 37.

[26] Susan Mumm, *Stolen Daughters, Virgin Mothers: Anglican Sisterhoods in Victorian Britain* (London, 2001); Carmen Mangion, 'Women, Religious Ministry and Female Institution Building', in Morgan and de Vries (eds.), *Women, Gender and Religious Cultures*, pp. 72–93.

distinctive Anglican aesthetic in art and architecture was the Society of St John the Evangelist (SSJE). Founded in Oxford in 1866, the SSJE was the first Anglican monastic community in history. From a small cohort of three Anglo-Catholic priests, the brotherhood swiftly expanded to create new religious missions in the United States and India. The SSJE had a close working relationship with George Frederick Bodley, who most likely designed the 1880s SSJE vestments and who provided designs for the Society's church and cloisters in Oxford, conceived and constructed between 1896 and 1904. The distinctive art and architecture of Anglican monasticism participated and continues to survive in a constant productive tension between the local and the global, and the expression of private devotion and public mission.[27]

In addition to the Ecclesiologists who established their Society in Cambridge, the Oxford Society for Promoting the Study of Gothic Architecture (founded in 1839), and the annual Church Congress papers on architecture and the arts were key voices for the Gothic Revival and for focusing upon key issues within Anglican art and architecture more broadly. Within Ecclesiological circles, the Anglo-Catholic politician and critic A. J. B. Beresford Hope perhaps did more than anyone to attempt to articulate the anxious question of style in relation to Anglican identity. Religion and architecture particularly intersected over the concept of 'development', which has been expertly discussed by architectural historians including Michael Hall and Carla Yanni.[28] A keen interest in theories of evolution, geology, and theological exploration into truly new systematic territory combined to produce Gothic Revival churches in which features such as structural polychromy expressed a simultaneity of meanings regarding the tensile strength of Christianity, the unfolding of the relationship between God and humanity across history, and the revealing of divine presence and Providence in the natural world.[29] These circulating themes crystallized in buildings such as George Edmund Street's St James the Less in Pimlico, John Loughborough Pearson's bold new cathedral for Truro in Cornwall, and chief among them William Butterfield's assertive High Victorian masterpiece All Saints, Margaret Street in London. These architects, along with G. F. Bodley, William White, Sophy Gray, and others, were also regularly and deeply involved in the creation of a distinctly Anglican Gothic Revival architectural series of styles in which British architectural forms and

[27] Martin Smith, *Benson of Cowley* (Oxford, 1980); A. Lepine, 'Sacred Beauty: G. F. Bodley's Designs for Oxford and Cambridge', PhD thesis, The Courtauld Institute of Art, 2011.

[28] Michael Hall, '"Our Own": Thomas Hope, A. J. B. Beresford Hope and the Creation of the High Victorian Style', in Rosemary Hill and Michael Hall (eds.), *The 1840s* (London, 2008), pp. 60–75; Carla Yanni, *Nature's Museums: Victorian Science and the Nature of Display* (Princeton, NJ, 2005).

[29] Michael Hall, 'What Do Victorian Churches Mean?', *Journal of the Society of Architectural Historians*, 59 (2000): 78–95; Neil Jackson, 'Clarity or Camouflage? The Development of Structural Polychromy in the 1850s and early 1860s', *Architectural History*, 47 (2004): 201–26.

ecclesiological ideology took shape within the distinctive circumstances of colonial territories from Canada and India to New Zealand and South Africa.[30] In London, the foundation stone for All Saints was laid in 1850, and its primary patron was Beresford Hope himself, though he and Butterfield were not consistently in agreement regarding the church's architectural features.[31] With prolific use of multi-coloured stone, tiles, brick, stained glass, textiles, and a sumptuous east wall painted with images of saints and the life of Christ by William Dyce, All Saints was designed to be a multi-sensorial, fully immersive space in which the materiality of Anglo-Catholic identity, revolutionary and controversial as it was, could be keenly felt. It was to religious architecture what the Pre-Raphaelites were to religious art in Victorian Britain.

THE PRE-RAPHAELITE REVOLUTION

In 1848, with Europe torn by political upheaval and multiple pressures of modernity contributing to rapid progress and deep conflict, the Pre-Raphaelite Brotherhood banded together in London. Recent scholarship by Alison Smith, Jason Rosenfeld, Tim Barringer, Caroline Arscott, and Diane Waggoner has offered revelatory insights regarding Pre-Raphaelitism in relation to belief, morality, and the arts in nineteenth-century Britain. The Pre-Raphaelites' primary priority was to paint differently from their Royal Academy contemporaries, marshalling new chemical pigments, the emergent technology of photography, innovative approaches to literature, nature, and history, and a strong sense of historicism and medievalism which valued the art and sensibilities they found in artwork produced before Raphael and the Italian Renaissance. Among their first actions was to draw up a list of 'immortals'. This roll call of figures from across diverse histories and backgrounds also had an internal ranking system. Shakespeare received three stars and Chaucer was awarded two, but chief among these powerful lives was Jesus Christ, who alone was granted four stars. As Michaela Giebelhausen has noted, the Pre-Raphaelites and William Holman Hunt in particular succeeded in cultivating a fresh and compelling way of depicting Jesus as 'at once immediate, human and divine'.[32]

Among Holman Hunt's numerous images concentrating on the life of Jesus, none was more famous than *The Light of the World*. Hunt's painting was completed in 1853 and was described by John Ruskin as 'one of the noblest

[30] Bremner, *Imperial Gothic*, pp. 185–226.

[31] Paul Thompson, *William Butterfield* (London, 1971), p. 349; Roger Dixon and Stefan Muthesius, *Victorian Architecture* (London, 1978), pp. 204–9.

[32] Michaela Giebelhausen, 'The Religious and Intellectual Background', in Prettejohn (ed.), *Cambridge Companion to the Pre-Raphaelites*, p. 70.

works of sacred art produced in this or any other age'. In the painting, Christ wears an alb, jewelled and embroidered cope, and crown of thorns. Though these elements are typically associated with an Anglo-Catholic symbolic vocabulary, the Evangelical John Ruskin suggested that by placing Christ within an English orchard the real meaning of the painting was that Christ is 'a living presence among us now'.[33] In Hunt's painting, Christ carries a lantern, which is the only significant light source, illuminating the tangled vegetation of the isolated orchard with an eerie gleam. The resurrected Christ's right hand is poised to knock upon a door with no keyhole and no handle—the door of the human soul can only be opened from within. Hunt was a devout and Evangelical Anglican, and his painting constitutes a visual exegesis of the scriptural passage (which was printed in the catalogue when the painting was shown at the Royal Academy in 1854): 'Behold, I stand at the door, and knock; if any man hear my voice, and open the door, I will come in to him, and will sup with him and he with me.'[34] Hunt would paint a further two versions of *The Light of the World*. The earliest is in a specially designed side chapel at Keble College, Oxford, produced by J. T. Micklethwaite and integrated with the assertive and vivid brickwork of William Butterfield's Gothic college. The final version, begun in 1899, toured Britain's colonies between 1905 and 1907 and was seen by tens of thousands. It was installed in St Paul's Cathedral. Throughout the last half of the nineteenth century it steadily gained what Tim Barringer argues is 'a place as an official icon of English Protestantism'.[35]

Ford Madox Brown's *Work* (1852–65) connected hearty male labour with the sacred in a distinctively Evangelical and Christian Socialist manner. The social strata of London are all present, from the work-shy aristocracy in the background to the muscular foregrounded labourers digging a road in Hampstead. They are overseen by F. D. Maurice and Thomas Carlyle, and it is Carlyle's famous phrase in his 1843 book *Past and Present* that is clearly evoked in Madox Brown's painting: 'For there is a perennial nobleness, and even sacredness, in work'.[36] Moreover, Madox Brown's work of art—his own painterly labour—was exhibited accompanied by a quotation from Genesis 3:19, 'In the sweat of thy face shalt thou eat bread'. Madox Brown, together with his Pre-Raphaelite artistic circle who were also invested in the close ties between labour and salvation, also explored this theme in relation to more discernibly Anglo-Catholic iconography. His *Our Lady of Good Children* (1847–61) combined Romanesque interior details, a cloth of honour, and a Renaissance-inspired pair of Madonna and child figures only to turn this holy

[33] John Ruskin, *Modern Painters*, quoted in Michael Wheeler, *Ruskin's God* (Cambridge, 1999), p. 124.

[34] Revelation 3:20.

[35] Barringer, *Reading the Pre-Raphaelites*, p. 118.

[36] Thomas Carlyle, *Past and Present* (London, 1843); Tim Barringer, *Men at Work: Art and Labour in Victorian Britain* (New Haven, CT, 2005).

and admittedly all too ordinary image into a meditation on a mother's role as caretaker in a far more practical sense. Attended by an angel, the Virgin is giving the Christ child a meticulous bath. In Madox Brown's 1865 one-man show, the title of the work was listed in the catalogue as *Oure Ladye of Saturday Night*.

The combination of reverent symbolism with a shocking attention to the quotidian characterized much Pre-Raphaelite art which focused on biblical themes, from John Everett Millais's *Christ in the House of His Parents* to Madox Brown's *Jesus Washing Peter's Feet*, and the fearful look of uncertainty in the red-haired teenage virgin confronted by a muscular Annunciation angel in Dante Gabriel Rossetti's *Ecce Ancilla Domini!* Though the Pre-Raphaelites were by no means exclusively religious painters or painters of religion, their profound and lasting impact upon Anglicanism and the arts is undeniable. Although Madox Brown's *Our Lady of Good Children* evidently interacts with histories of religious representation, the artist cautioned, 'To look at it too seriously would be a mistake. It was neither Romish nor Tractarian, nor Christian Art (a term then much in vogue) in intention; about all these I knew and cared little, it was merely *fanciful*, just as a poet might write some Spencerian [*sic*] or Chaucerian stanzas.'[37] As Giebelhausen explains in *Painting the Bible*, the Pre-Raphaelite preoccupation with religious subject matter was a way of producing radical and arresting works of art for a public too used to an unchallenging visual framework for religious iconography. Religious art was, in part, a deliberate shock tactic from the avant-garde of Pre-Raphaelite Victorian Britain.

AN EXPANSIVE ANGLICAN VISUAL CULTURE

The emergence, maintenance, and diverse developments of a distinctively Victorian Anglican identity across Britain and its empire was a complex and ever-shifting terrain within which a cluster of art and architectural phenomena helped to define a dominant yet often vulnerable and contradictory factional religious culture. By studying Pre-Raphaelite and Gothic Revival approaches to religious spaces and imagery in particular, a nuanced transnational understanding of the significance and the intricacy of Anglican visual culture and built environments begins to come to light.

The relationship between the British Empire and religious art and architecture has been fruitfully explored by scholars including Mark Crinson and Alex

[37] Ford Madox Brown, *The Exhibition of Work and Other Paintings* (1865), catalogue reprinted in Kenneth Paul Bendiner, *The Art of Ford Madox Brown* (University Park, PA, 1998), pp. 131–56 (p. 143).

Bremner, whose attention to collaboration, conflict, style, and patronage has shed significant light on how transculturation took place in the midst of architectural change and development.[38] Increasingly, the roles of architectural sculpture and the decorative arts as modes of imperial visual communication are also receiving substantial academic attention.[39] Moreover, different modes of living and expressions of Anglican identity are also receiving long-awaited academic attention, drawing new aspects of art and architectural history into view.

Henry Alexander Bowler's *Can These Dry Bones Live?*, completed in 1855, depicts a Victorian young woman in a black shawl leaning on a tombstone in a churchyard, contemplating skeletal fragments. She is alone, surrounded by the lush greenery and grassy grave markers of the seemingly rural parish. The story from Ezekiel seen in traditional Christian exegesis as addressing the question of resurrection with a resounding 'yes', is turned into a rhetorical uncertainty in this mid-Victorian painting. By 1901, the tone of British art could be more theologically ambiguous still. John Byam Liston Shaw's *The Boer War 1900–1901, Last Summer Things Were Greener* depicts a lone woman in a rural scene, though unlike Bowler's figural composition Byam Shaw does not present us with a churchyard. The title refers to the Anglo-Catholic Christina Rossetti's poem, *A Bird Song*. In Byam Shaw's painting, a figure stands by a stream with an unravelled ball of wool held loosely in her hand, recalling a loved one who has died in the imperial war in South Africa. An affirmative answer to the question 'Can these dry bones live?' is more elusive still within this frame, but it remains thick in the atmosphere as a complicated uncertainty. What may be gleaned from these two works of art fifty years apart, which depict single female figures pondering absence, death, and the afterlife? As the searching questions of life, love, and death were articulated afresh on the brink of the twentieth century, the layered connections between painting and the Church became more expansive, encompassing, and even flexible rather than becoming increasingly fixed within a conventional framework of iconography and symbolism. Like Anglicanism itself, the works of art touching upon core issues within the Church and Victorian life were diverse yet distinctive in style and subject matter as markers of identity, declaring the substance of Anglican faith and understanding for a shifting and factional yet united and unprecedentedly powerful and global Church of England.

[38] Bremner, *Imperial Gothic*; Mark Crinson, *Empire Building: Victorian Architecture and Orientalism* (London, 1996).

[39] Barringer, *Men at Work*, pp. 243–312; Michael Hatt and Jason Edwards (eds.), *Sculpture Victorious*, exhibition catalogue (New Haven, CT, 2014).

SELECT BIBLIOGRAPHY

Anson, P. F., *Fashions in Church Furnishing, 1840–1940* (London, 2006).

Barringer, Tim, *Men at Work: Art and Labour in Victorian Britain* (New Haven, CT, 2005).

Barringer, Tim, *Reading the Pre-Raphaelites* (New Haven, CT, 2012).

Bremner, G. A., *Imperial Gothic: Religion, Architecture and High Anglican Culture in the British Empire* (New Haven, CT, 2013).

Brooks, Chris, *The Gothic Revival* (London, 2000).

Cantor, Geoffrey, *Religion and the Great Exhibition of 1851* (Oxford, 2011).

Crinson, Mark, *Empire Building: Orientalism and Victorian Architecture* (London, 1996).

Dixon, Roger and Stefan Muthesius, *Victorian Architecture* (London, 1978).

Giebelhausen, Michaela, *Painting the Bible: Representation and Belief in Mid-Victorian Britain* (Aldershot, 2006).

Hall, Michael, *George Frederick Bodley and the Later Gothic Revival in Britain and America* (New Haven, CT, 2014).

Hill, Rosemary, *God's Architect: Pugin and the Building of Romantic Britain* (London, 2008).

Lepine, Ayla, 'On the Founding of Watts & Co., 1874', in Dino Franco Felluga (ed.), *BRANCH: Britain, Representation and Nineteenth-Century History*. Extension of *Romanticism and Victorianism on the Net*. <http://www.branchcollective.org>.

Lewis, Michael J., *The Gothic Revival* (London, 2002).

Morgan, Sue and Jacqueline de Vries (eds.), *Women, Gender and Religious Cultures in Britain, 1800–1940* (London, 2010).

Pope-Hennessy, John et al., *Victorian Church Art*, exhibition catalogue (London, 1971).

Prettejohn, Elizabeth (ed.), *The Cambridge Companion to the Pre-Raphaelites* (Cambridge, 2012).

Schoeser, Mary, *English Church Embroidery, 1833–1953* (London, 1998).

Sladen, Theresa and Andrew Saint, *Churches, 1870–1914* (London, 2011).

Wheeler, Michael, *Ruskin's God* (Cambridge, 1999).

White, James, *The Cambridge Movement* (Cambridge, 1962).

21

Anglicans, Science, and the Bible in the Nineteenth Century

Diarmid A. Finnegan

It is not easy to precisely determine the significance of science to nineteenth-century Anglicanism or the significance of Anglicanism to nineteenth-century science. Both science and Anglicanism were subject to radically transformative social, political, technological, and ideological forces. The consequent dramatic changes to Anglican and scientific culture were pervasive and profound. Moreover, both Anglicanism and science were, in many ways, intimately related. On one account, science increasingly occupied cultural territory previously dominated by an Anglican establishment. From the early nineteenth century, powerful advocates for the authority of science pushed against the public reach and range of Anglican interests in order to carve out greater influence for a scientific and secular *mentalité*. Such an account, however, risks obscuring as much as it reveals. The growing cultural influence of science in nineteenth-century England, and in other parts of the world where Anglicanism flourished, cannot be understood without a careful account of initiatives that owed much to Anglicans and Anglican modes of thought and operation.

What was true at the level of cultural contests and compacts was also true at the level of ideas and attitudes. Various 'flashpoints' between science and Anglican beliefs can be easily identified throughout the long nineteenth century. Much energy was given to attempts to demonstrate the incompatibility of scientific and Anglican thought worlds and to efforts to defend their commensurability. This more combative account of the intellectual relationship between Anglicanism and science also hardly tells the whole story. At the level of ideas, the relationship between science and Anglicanism in the nineteenth century turns out to be an influential case of religious thought providing terms, concepts, and modes of thinking that were conducive to, as well in tension with, scientific enquiry.

To illustrate the complexity of the unfolding relationship between Anglicanism and science throughout the nineteenth century, this chapter concentrates on two broad areas of intellectual enquiry, namely natural theology and evolution. In both cases, Anglican involvement in their development was profound. This involvement took a variety of forms—some more constructive and others more critical or censorious. While natural theology in all of its diverse guises enjoyed the sustained support of leading Anglican thinkers and authors throughout the nineteenth century, some of the most caustic critiques came not from a growing cadre of scientific critics but from various camps within the Church of England. Evolutionary theory generated significant theological concerns and was strongly resisted, particularly when applied to human origins and human society. Yet it was also given a distinctly Anglican 'hue' through efforts to use it as a theological and cultural resource to maintain and express the relevance and reliability of Christian belief to modern thought and modern society.

As the final section of this chapter makes clear, debates about the religious significance of science became increasingly 'global' as the century progressed. Certainly, science and Anglicanism were both caught up in a rapidly globalizing world. Missionary anthropologists were among those who experienced the increasing global reach of science and Anglicanism within a single frame and, partly as a consequence, made their own distinctive contributions to linked debates about evolution, anthropology, and Anglican mission. It was unavoidable that the terms of those debates were set as much by colonial as by metropolitan experiences and priorities. Here, again, it is impossible to disentangle the changing shape of Anglicanism and the rapidly evolving nature of science or to abstract either from wider and increasingly global influences. The global scale, however, is not where this chapter begins. Instead, we start with a watch on a heath in the work of a noted English divine.

ANGLICAN NATURAL THEOLOGIES

There is little doubt that the Revd William Paley's 1802 work, *Natural Theology*, helped to shape in fundamental ways scientific and religious discussions throughout the nineteenth century. His inference from perceived design in nature to a divine designer—famously compared with someone coming upon a watch on a heath and inferring from it the existence of a watchmaker—not only consolidated certain conceptions of science and theology but also, later in the century, acted as a foil for promoting alternative accounts of 'purpose' in nature. Paley's work was, however, neither original nor unique. It represented one example of a venerable, if unstable and contested, tradition of arguing from the appearance of coordinated mechanisms or contrivances in nature to operation of a supernatural intelligence.

Nevertheless, Paley's *Natural Theology* was undoubtedly among the more prominent natural theological texts to appear at the beginning of the nineteenth century. While it was not novel in any radical sense, it was a product of Paley's own characteristic blend of Anglican theology. If Paley's declared aim was to demonstrate the existence and natural attributes of the Creator, his text lent support to the latitudinarian and utilitarian theology promoted in his other celebrated works. For Paley, the rational pursuit of the greatest general happiness could unveil God's will for human society and morality. In the same way, natural theology uncovered God's beneficent design in nature through the use of human reason. As such, it was not only a bulwark against revolutionary atheism and deistic rationalism but was also an antidote to pietistic enthusiasm and ritualistic excess. It provided a stable foundation for Christian belief and brought an awareness or vivid impression of the divine into everyday life. Paley presented natural theology as a vital propaedeutic for doctrinal instruction and as an exercise that sensitized the observer to the divine presence in nature. Discerning the work of the Creator in nature was not, in Paley's presentation, a purely intellectual enterprise but one that led, through the creation of vivid 'impressions', to moral improvement.[1]

The influence of Paley's *Natural Theology* measured in terms of sales figures—in Britain over 90,000 copies were in circulation by 1859—was clearly extensive.[2] If it was not, in fact, used in Cambridge's curriculum and more cited than read as the century moved on, it nevertheless functioned as a powerful cultural marker.[3] Moreover, Paley's work prompted others to demonstrate the power, wisdom, and goodness of God displayed in his works even as scientific understandings shifted and accumulated.

In 1830, the bequest of £8,000 made by the Eighth Earl of Bridgewater, Frank Henry Egerton (1756–1829), gave a significant financial boost to the natural theology enterprise in Britain through the 1830s. Bridgewater's sizeable bequest was given to support work that unfolded, 'by all reasonable arguments', the 'Power, Wisdom and Goodness of God as manifested in the Creation'.[4] The publication between 1833 and 1836 of the eight volumes that

[1] Niall O'Flaherty, 'The Rhetorical Strategy of William Paley's *Natural Theology* (1802): Part 1, William Paley's *Natural Theology* in Context', *Studies in History and Philosophy of Science Part A*, 41 (2010): 19–25.

[2] Jonathan R. Topham, 'Biology in the Service of Natural Theology: Paley, Darwin, and the Bridgewater Treatises', in Denis R. Alexander and Ronald L. Numbers (eds.), *Biology and Ideology from Descartes to Dawkins* (Chicago, 2010), p. 92.

[3] Aileen Fyfe, 'The Reception of William Paley's *Natural Theology* in the University of Cambridge', *British Journal for the History of Science*, 30 (1997): 321–35.

[4] Cited in Jonathan R. Topham, 'Science and Popular Education in the 1830s: The Role of the Bridgewater Treatises', *British Journal for the History of Science*, 25 (1992): 397–430; 'Beyond the

made up the Bridgewater Treatises evidenced not only the widespread appetite for natural theology but also the unstable mix of metaphysical and theological assumptions that informed a significant British intellectual tradition. The eight authors, chosen by the President of the Royal Society with the assistance of the archbishop of Canterbury and the bishop of London, were all Anglicans apart from Thomas Chalmers, a Church of Scotland clergyman. All to one degree or another paid homage to Paley but all, again to varying degrees, offered versions of natural theological argumentation that departed from some of Paley's core assumptions or emphases.

The most significant divergence from Paley's account was found in Peter Mark Roget's treatise on physiology. Roget's stress on laws of form in nature shifted attention away from the functionalism that marked Paley's work. God's design was evident through the discovery of homologous forms that occurred across a range of otherwise widely different species and indicated to the natural theological eye the structuring effects of a divine blueprint. The Cambridge philosopher and Anglican cleric William Whewell also underlined the importance of the laws of nature and the 'divine legislator' behind them. This was not, however, a radical departure from Paley. In the closing section of his Bridgewater Treatise Whewell directly paraphrases Paley's argument that law 'supposes an agent... without [which] the law can have no efficacy, no existence'.[5] Even so, an emphasis on laws or regularities more than teleology or adaptations helped to open up space for a different form of natural theology and aided those wanting to distance themselves from a design argument reliant on functionalism. This lead was followed by the Anglican anatomist Richard Owen, for instance, who impressed on his readers the importance of morphological laws and archetypal plans to promote an Anglicized version of transcendental morphology more usually associated with pantheistic evolutionism.[6]

The departure of other Bridgewater authors from Paley took a rather different course. William Kirby, author of volume seven—*The History, Habits and Instincts of Animals* (1835)—espoused a form of natural theology encouraged by his association with the Hackney Phalanx, an influential group of High Churchmen. Kirby was also influenced by the Hutchinsonian philosophy that at least some members of the Phalanx were in sympathy with. In his introduction, Kirby, after a lengthy refutation of Lamarckian evolution echoed the Anglican naturalist and theologian John Hutchinson by arguing that natural philosophical as well as religious truths could be found in Scripture

"Common Context": The Production and Reading of the Bridgewater Treatises', *Isis*, 89 (1998): 233–62.

5 William Whewell, *Astronomy and General Physics Consider with Reference to Natural Theology* (London, 1839), pp. 361–2; cf. William Paley, *Natural Theology* (London, 1802), p. 447.

6 Nicolaas Rupke, *Richard Owen: Biology without Darwin* (Chicago, 2009).

and nature, God's two books. In Scripture, physical truths were veiled from the common mind in the form of figures and allegory. But the discerning reader, by hunting out physical truths hidden behind the letter of Scripture, could add significantly to understanding of the world of nature. Kirby's approach avoided Paley's more utilitarian bent and allowed him to detect in nature much more of God's character and in Scripture much more of nature's hidden orderings than figures like Paley would allow. Kirby's variant of natural theology (if it can correctly be described as part of that tradition) has been interpreted as a defence of High Church Toryism.[7] Whether or not that adequately captures Kirby's motivations and meaning, it underlines the fact that the political and cultural correlates of natural theology were by no means fixed or singular.

Kirby's efforts to discover scientific truths in Scripture shared something in common with another line of thought that flourished in the same period as the Bridgewater Treatises, namely scriptural geology. A product of a view of the opening chapters of Genesis as a source of scientific as well as theological truths, scriptural geology was championed in the 1820s and 1830s by a number of Anglicans including the clergymen George Bugg, William Cockburn, and Thomas Gisbourne. Such scriptural geologists were convinced that Genesis straightforwardly communicated physical truths about the origin and age of the earth and of life. In this respect, advocates of the science directly discoverable in Scripture differed from those like Kirby who did not think that scientific truths could be identified by simply reading the 'letter' of the biblical text. As Ralph O'Connor shows, while their views were widely ridiculed at the time (and have been frequently dismissed by historians since), scriptural geologists were highly effective popularizers of geological knowledge. Further, as O'Connor argues, keeping in view the publications of those who believed that the nascent science of the earth directly confirmed, and was confirmed by, the Bible's account of creation helps make sense of better-known efforts of clerical geologists such as Adam Sedgwick and William Buckland to promote geological enquiry.[8] Simply put, Buckland and Sedgwick endeavoured to beat the scriptural geologists at their own popularizing game.

Beyond defending the scientific authority of Scripture in the context of early nineteenth-century intellectual culture, the idea that the Bible had direct and significant things to say about living nature and that living nature could illustrate scriptural or spiritual truths had relevance within more devotional or liturgical settings. Scriptural botany was more often concerned with identifying, describing, and interpreting the plants of the Bible than it was with

[7] John F. M. Clark, 'History from the Ground Up: Bugs, Political Economy and God in Kirby and Spence's *Introduction to Entomology*', *Isis*, 20 (2006): 28–55.

[8] Ralph O'Connor, 'Young Earth Creationists in Early-Nineteenth-Century Britain? Towards a Reassessment of Scriptural Geology', *History of Science*, 45 (2007): 357–403.

combating efforts to wrest botany from religious influence. Books like John Kitto's *Thoughts among Flowers* (1847) used descriptions of individual plants to convey moral and religious lessons. Here botanical science was pressed into religious service by increasing the biblical literacy of readers but also promoted the scientific study of plants far beyond the confines of university-based researchers or expert practitioners.

Whatever the popular reach of scriptural science, it was natural theology in its more standard or classical guise that proved to be a critical rhetorical resource for an elite group of 'gentlemen of science' anxious to demonstrate the conformity between science and Anglican theology. This was particularly apparent in the discourse surrounding the founding of the British Association for the Advancement of Science in 1831.[9] Here, natural theology served at least two functions. First, it anchored the association in an intellectual tradition long nurtured by the Church of England and Ireland and thus helped to sustain the cultural authority of Anglican thought. This was unsurprising given the large proportion of founding members who were Anglican clerics. Second, however, it was used to broaden the association's appeal and to supply a 'non-sectarian' basis for the pursuit of science over and above denominational rivalry. Thus constituted, the association was reformist and latitudinarian in tone and in practical effect.

A variety of Anglican commentators, noting this, excoriated the association for being a kind of alternative or anti-Church and a vehicle for inculcating infidelity. William Cockburn, for example, used the meeting of the British Association at Newcastle in 1838 as an occasion to attack the dangers of the 'peripatetic philosophy' that it peddled. The association, in promulgating novel ideas that contradicted the plain sense of Scripture, aided the 'widespreading plague of infidelity' and put the faith of the 'mixed assemblies' it attracted at grave risk.[10] Five years later, he issued another invective against the association when it met (for the second time) in York. As dean of York Minster, Cockburn took the opportunity to 'defend the Bible' against the association's leading geologists (and prominent Anglican clergymen) William Buckland and Adam Sedgwick.[11]

If Cockburn's aim was to defend Scripture, the Tractarian supporter John William Bowden sought to preserve the attractions and influence of the Church. In a lengthy critique published in 1839, Bowden argued that the association dangerously mimicked the Church in uniting people around a shared goal. His concern was less with the clash between scientific discovery

[9] Jack Morrell and Arnold Thackray, *Gentlemen of Science: Early Years of the British Association for the Advancement of Science* (Oxford, 1981).

[10] William Cockburn, *A Remonstrance... upon the Dangers of Peripatetic Philosophy* (London, 1838), p. 24.

[11] Morrell and Thackray, *Gentlemen of Science*, pp. 243–5; Nicolaas Rupke, *The Great Chain of History: William Buckland and the English School of Geology (1814–1849)* (Oxford, 1983).

and revealed religion than with the potential of the association, in an age of intense religious disagreement, to 'put scientific fellowship in place of the communion of the Church'.[12] Bowden's invective against the association also reflected a suspicion of natural theology expressed in other works such as William Irons's *On the Whole Doctrine of Final Causes* (1836). Science, in the estimation of figures like Bowden and Irons, could not help cultivate moral or religious virtues and was liable, if given too great an importance, to lead to infidelity. John Henry Newman's letters to *The Times* in 1841 attacking the secularizing tendencies behind Peel's support for the Tamworth Reading Room continued this line of critique.

Despite criticism from various quarters within the Anglican fold, the British Association rapidly became the leading forum for the public discussion of scientific ideas in early Victorian Britain. Attracting thousands to its week-long meetings each year, it helped to forge a new relationship between scientific and public culture and, in its early years, maintained the 'Baconian compromise' between God's two books—Scripture and nature—that had so strongly informed its founding constitution.[13] It signalled the success and social significance of a distinctly Anglican account of the relations between science, public culture, and the Christian religion. In setting the terms for what counted as scientific orthodoxy, the association also prescribed limits on what claims science could make with respect to core religious convictions. This dual function endured until at least 1860. Up to that point, Anglican clergymen were prominent in the running of every scientific section and made significant contributions to the overall governance of the organization.

The growing popularity of science, indicated not only by the success of the British Association but also by the burgeoning number of local scientific societies and rapidly expanding market for books on the subject, presented additional opportunities to address new audiences with a natural theology amenable to, and born of, moderate Anglicanism. Despite severe criticisms, Anglican natural theologies continued to appeal to a mass audience. As Bernard Lightman has shown, Anglican clerics such as Ebenezer Cobham, Francis Orpen Morris, Charles Kingsley, and T. W. Webb were writing scientific books with a distinctly natural theological colouring from the 1840s. The sales figures register their significance at least in terms of indicating and encouraging a widespread appetite for popular science in a natural theological mode. Astonishingly, Cobham's *A Guide to the Scientific Knowledge of Things Familiar*, first published in 1847, had sold an estimated 113,000

[12] John William Bowden, 'The British Association', *British Critic*, 25 (1839), p. 19.

[13] James R. Moore, 'Geologists and Interpreters of Genesis in the Nineteenth Century', in *God and Nature: Historical Essays on the Encounters between Christianity and Science* (Berkeley, CA, 1986), pp. 322–50.

copies by 1874.[14] The popularity of these writers contributed to making science an acceptable and alluring subject among the Victorian reading public and helped to imbue scientific pursuits with religious meaning.[15]

Anglican clergymen who made a publishing success of the presentation of science framed by natural theology were part a much larger constituency composed of 'parson naturalists,' who were themselves part of an older tradition most famously embodied in Gilbert White (1720–93). Often leading members of local natural history societies, such figures more occasionally rose to national prominence through their expert contributions to a variety of scientific specialisms and learned societies.[16] Operating outside the confines of a scientific elite, these figures helped to solidify a general sense of conformity and communion between science and Anglican Christianity.

The general sense of harmony between science and revealed religion promoted by Anglicans at all levels of intellectual culture was, of course, frequently disturbed by others who deployed science as a weapon to attack the religious or social status quo. These disturbances were by no means restricted to the second half of the nineteenth century. It would be a mistake, then, to impose a straightforward chronological narrative of decline on what was a vibrant, diverse, and enduring tradition of promoting science as an ennobling study of God's handiwork and an integral component of a dominant form of Anglican identity. If that traditional Anglican formula combining science and religion faced resistance throughout the century, it also, in new contexts and guises, persisted and thrived. That was true, as the next section shows, even in the face of the emergence of evolution as a credible and increasingly influential scientific theory.

ANGLICANS AND EVOLUTION

Transformism before Darwin

Of all the scientific developments that stirred discussions among Anglican thinkers, it was evolution that provoked the most sustained and varied reaction. The subject of evolutionary development, whether cosmic or organic, had already been a lively topic of discussion in the closing decades of the eighteenth century. William Paley's allusions to evolution in his *Natural*

[14] Bernard Lightman, *Victorian Popularizers of Science: Designing Nature for New Audiences* (Chicago, 2007), p. 64.

[15] Aileen Fyfe, *Science and Salvation: Evangelical Popular Science Publishing in Victorian Britain* (Chicago, 2004).

[16] Patrick Armstrong, *The English Parson Naturalist: A Companionship between Science and Religion* (Leominster, 2000).

Theology are worth mentioning, not because they were necessarily representative of early Anglican responses, but because they help to indicate that the better-known debates that occurred later in the century had a long and often unacknowledged history. Paley's remarks are also telling because they registered what was a relatively common response to evolutionary explanations among Anglicans throughout the nineteenth century, namely that it was not necessarily 'atheistic' but nevertheless had to be treated with circumspection. Paley did not think the formation of species through the operation of natural laws, mechanisms, second causes, or the activation of pre-programmed 'appetencies' threatened the conviction that an explanation of nature's operations had to include reference to divine intelligence.[17] Nevertheless, his worry was that such schemes would undermine the detailed search for final causes in nature discernible in particular cases rather than in more general or abstract terms. This, Paley felt, would undermine the effectiveness of the science of nature to cultivate an appetite for revealed religion.

A more general anxiety about the threat evolutionary theory posed for natural theology had a strongly political bearing. Natural theology, at least as perceived by some of its more virulent critics and more politically conservative proponents, not only provided a propaedeutic for Christian belief but also helped to maintain a sense of a naturally ordered and hierarchical human society. This, at any rate, was a key motivating force behind the savage critiques of natural theology issued by artisanal workers in late Georgian London. These 'Red Lamarckians', to borrow Adrian Desmond's provocative descriptor, mobilized the latest evolutionary thinking to pour scorn on a Tory-tinged natural theology that kept the lower classes in their fixed or preordained places.[18] Evolution thus provided a weapon to attack patrician dominance and ecclesiastical privilege. Already in 1820s London, then, evolution was becoming a placeholder for debates about social change that encouraged the emergence of a proto-socialist science set against a divinely ordered nature or a religiously sanctioned class-based society.

The subject of the compatibility of Christian views of creation and theories of evolutionary change became a highly charged topic of national debate after the publication in 1844 of the anonymous *Vestiges of the History of Creation*. The book, which argued that life, like the cosmos itself, had gradually evolved from primitive beginnings, became a sensational bestseller. James Secord, in detailing the reception of *Vestiges* among the clerical professoriate in Oxford and Cambridge, reveals how the book threatened the compromise worked out between science and Anglican natural theology that had provided the social as

[17] Paley, *Natural Theology*, pp. 439–73; Alister E. McGrath, *Darwinism and the Divine: Evolutionary Thought and Natural Theology* (Chichester, 2011).

[18] Adrian Desmond, *The Politics of Evolution: Morphology, Medicine and Reform in Radical London* (Chicago, 1989).

well as intellectual rationale for the British Association.[19] The savage review of *Vestiges* by the Woodwardian Professor of Geology, Adam Sedgwick, put on full display a theological conservatism that had been called into question by those critical of his attack on William Cockburn years previously. If Sedgwick's response was more extreme than most, his fear that *Vestiges* would provide evidence of the infidel tendencies of scientific pursuits and tell against efforts to raise the profile of science within universities was shared by his academic colleagues in Cambridge. William Whewell, for example, while regarding Sedgwick's intervention as overheated, offered his own sustained and highly critical assessment of *Vestiges* to the reading public.

In contrast, it is perhaps not surprising that more liberal Anglican commentators found cause to welcome *Vestiges* and the strongly progressivist philosophy that it helped to promote. Although the Revd Baden Powell, Savilian Professor of Geometry at Oxford, did not comment publicly on *Vestiges* when it first appeared he was predisposed to view it favourably. Powell had already hinted in his *Connexions between Science and Religion* (1838) that species need not be thought of as created directly by divine fiat and had emphasized the operation of natural laws as the best explanation of natural phenomena.[20]

Perhaps more unexpected was the fact that a number of leading figures within the Tractarian movement, of which Powell was an arch-critic, were also able to use *Vestiges* to buttress a particular account of the relationship between Anglican theology and science.[21] Richard William Church, for example, declared himself more troubled by criticisms levelled at *Vestiges* than the arguments presented in its favour. In comments published in the *Guardian* in 1846, Church argued that the scientific critics of *Vestiges* shared a metaphysics that unnecessarily opposed 'natural order' to a 'scriptural and popular' account of divine action and thus, following Paley's 'starveling argument', looked for 'a heap of exceptions' likely to be shown to be unexceptional as science progressed.[22] Church called for a return to a scholastic metaphysics of creation that did not place restrictions on inductive science but provided a philosophy of nature compatible with a Christian doctrine of creation. If this was done, Church saw little threat from an evolutionary account of life to orthodox Christian belief.

The varied reactions to *Vestiges* reflected not just the differential play of theological ideas but were also shaped by efforts to promote certain understandings of Anglican identity. Increasingly, evolution and Anglicanism

[19] James Secord, *Victorian Sensation: The Extraordinary Publication, Reception and Secret Authorship of Vestiges of the Natural History of Creation* (Chicago, 2000).

[20] Pietro Corsi, *Baden Powell and the Anglican Debate* (Cambridge, 1988), p. 274.

[21] Secord, *Victorian Sensation*, pp. 256–8.

[22] Reprinted in Mary C. Church (ed.), *Occasional Papers* (London, 1897), pp. 59, 65.

became entangled, making it harder to use the former as a weapon to attack the latter. Alliances as well as antagonisms between advocates of evolution and defenders of Anglicanism multiplied. It is well to keep this in mind in turning to the Anglican agnostic and evolutionist, Charles Darwin.

Darwin and Anglicanism

In writing *On the Origin of Species*, Charles Darwin was deeply concerned to avoid the kind of controversies that erupted following the publication of *Vestiges* and went to some lengths to appease religious critics. If his famous text sought to undo what he termed 'the ordinary doctrine of creation', it also was designed to leave room for a theistic evolutionism of the kind already in circulation through the efforts of figures like Baden Powell. The epigram from William Whewell's Bridgewater Treatise that appears on every edition of *On the Origin of Species* declared that 'events [in the material world] are brought about not by insulated interpositions of Divine power, exerted in each particular case, but by the establishment of general laws'. While Whewell was not willing to extend this argument to the origin of life and its myriad forms, he nevertheless acknowledged that Darwin's book deserved respect and careful consideration. Darwin's pleasure in this response and in the more active support for his evolutionary proposals from other Anglican clergymen discloses something of the importance of his own attitude towards Anglicanism in shaping how he presented his science to a wider public.

Darwin's personal relationship with the Anglican Church is both revealing in its own right and, immediately after Darwin's death in 1882, provided material for positive Anglican responses to science and evolution. From birth, Darwin's life was intimately connected with the Anglican Church. While Unitarianism and religious scepticism exercised a formative influence during childhood, Darwin was baptized in an Anglican church and later, after medical training in Edinburgh, began studies in Cambridge that formed the preliminaries for ordination as a clergyman. If Darwin did not pursue that course beyond completing his BA degree in January 1831, Anglican structures of belief and praxis and Anglican clergymen remained an important influence. As Darwin's correspondence reveals, he participated fully in Anglican structures at a local and global level. His involvement in the parish of Down included close friendship with the curate, John Brodie Innes, and for many years Darwin gave an annual donation to the South American Missionary Society. These connections expressed Darwin's appreciation of the social values embedded in Anglicanism rather than a commitment to orthodox Anglican belief.[23] In 1871, for example,

[23] Paul White, 'Darwin's Church', in Peter Clarke and Tony Claydon (eds.), *God's Bounty: The Churches and the Natural World* (Woodbridge, 2010), pp. 333–52.

Darwin withdrew his support for the local school when the curate—no longer his friend John Innes—insisted that pupils recite the Thirty-Nine Articles.[24]

This resistance to an enforced orthodoxy but sympathy towards the Church as a cultural institution was enough to allow Darwin to be buried in Westminster Abbey without creating any major controversy within the Church of England.[25] George Prothero, chaplain to the Queen and preacher at Darwin's funeral, was able to present 'the greatest man of science of his day' as a man in whom 'lived that charity which is the very essence of the true spirit of Christ'. Darwin, the evolutionist and agnostic, was offered to the nation as an exemplar of Christian moral culture.

If the Church of England was able to describe Darwin as a Christian gentleman of science after his death, it proved harder to stage-manage an official response to Darwin's theory of evolution. The difficulties began early, not least with the fall-out from the exchange between Samuel Wilberforce and Thomas Henry Huxley during the Oxford meeting of the British Association for the Advancement of Science in 1860. It should be said, however, that the exact nature of the exchange remains disputed and only patchily recorded by contemporary sources. What is clear is what the exchange was not. It was not in any straightforward sense a 'victory' for science over obscurantist Anglican religion.[26] Bishop Samuel Wilberforce was too accomplished a rhetorician to set himself against science as such. Drawing on the work of Richard Owen, Britain's leading comparative anatomist, Wilberforce countered Darwin's claims with those of another scientific authority. Many, of course, did think Wilberforce was being duplicitous and saw his motives as ultimately about protecting the Church's, and his own, interests. But among those more cynical observers were a number of Anglican clergymen who had their own reasons to dislike the bishop. It is telling, too, that during the same meeting of the British Association, Frederick Temple—then headmaster of Rugby School and later to become archbishop of Canterbury—preached a sermon in which he made a plea for allowing science latitude to pursue truth without risk of theological censorship. Another revealing reaction to Wilberforce's panegyrics was ascribed to the prominent Anglican botanist Charles Babington. A committed and devout Evangelical Anglican, Babington was deeply suspicious of Darwinism, a stance he retained throughout his long life. In this sense, he was aligned with Wilberforce. Yet in 1860 Babington decried Wilberforce's

[24] Janet Browne, *Charles Darwin: The Power of Place* (New York, 2002), p. 455.

[25] James R. Moore, 'Charles Darwin Lies in Westminster Abbey', *Biological Journal of the Linnean Society*, 17 (1982): 97–113.

[26] On this, see, for example, John Hedley Brooke, 'The Wilberforce–Huxley Debate: Why Did it Happen?', *Science and Christian Belief*, 13 (2001): 127–41; David N. Livingstone, 'Myth 17: That Huxley Defeated Wilberforce in their Debate over Evolution and Religion', in Ronald L. Numbers (ed.), *Galileo Goes to Jail and Other Myths About Science and Religion* (Cambridge, MA, 2009), pp. 152–60.

departure from 'fact and argument', and welcomed with 'glee' Huxley's attack.[27] Babington saw in Huxley's response a commitment to scientific rigour that he felt was lacking in Wilberforce's arguments. Taken together, these Anglican reactions to the Wilberforce–Huxley exchange underline the complex nature of the event and of the relations between Anglicanism and science.

In many respects, what exactly happened in Oxford is of less importance than how it was later represented and remembered. It was a turning point not because Darwin's bulldog, Huxley, trounced the bishop, but because it was narrated like that in later accounts. Quite quickly it came to symbolize a growing campaign to wrest science from ecclesiastical control using evolution as the weapon of choice. The later nineteenth century witnessed the emergence within the British Association and in other elite intellectual circles of a 'scientific priesthood' that, if not rejecting religion as such, certainly combated ecclesiastical privilege, censure, and barriers to educational attainment, as well as presenting science as an 'extra-Christian' or secular activity.[28] This campaign crystallized around the X-Club, a London-based coterie of men of science committed to expanding the cultural authority of scientific learning.

It would be mistaken, however, to exaggerate the success of the X-Club and their supporters or to study them in isolation from other trends within the Church of England and Ireland and within wider society. To regard the efforts of agitators such as Huxley, John Tyndall, Herbert Spencer, and John Lubbock as marking a radical rupture from the efforts of Anglican figures to create new forms of consilience between scientific and moral culture is too imprecise. As Paul White has argued, Huxley and a wider circle of scientific naturalists cooperated with prominent liberal Anglicans to promote, particularly through educational reform, a new cultural arrangement that gave science and progressive thought a much more prominent place and role in national culture. There was sufficient shared ground and personal friendship between liberal churchmen such as Frederic Farrar, Arthur Penrhyn Stanley, and Benjamin Jowett and the 'scientific naturalists' to work towards the reform of a wide range of institutional structures and to attempt to create a 'single community of diverse, but complementary, elites'.[29]

The alliances forged between Anglican figures and a scientific elite were reflected in the positive support given to Darwin's theory of evolution in the decades after *On the Origin of Species* appeared. Among the most vocal supporters was the novelist, naturalist, and historian, the Revd Charles Kingsley. On reading *On the Origin of Species* Kingsley happily extended Whewell's

[27] Anna Maria Babington (ed.), *Memorials, Journal and Botanical Correspondence of Charles Cardale Babington* (Cambridge, 1897), p. xx.

[28] Thomas Henry Huxley, 'On Descartes' "Discourse Touching the Method of Using One's Reason Rightly and of Seeking Scientific Truth"', *Macmillan's Magazine*, 22 (1870): 69–80.

[29] Paul White, 'Ministers of Culture: Arnold, Huxley and Liberal Anglican Reform of Learning', *History of Science*, 43 (2005), p. 126.

'general laws' to the 'self-development' of life finding that conception of creation a 'loftier one' than constant interventions in nature by the deity. In articulating this, Kingsley provided Darwin with a 'capital paragraph' to demonstrate that his book need not 'shock the religious feelings of anyone'.[30] Kingsley continued to promote the compatibility between Darwinian evolution and Christian belief until his untimely death in 1874. Through novels, lectures, and sermons, Kingsley presented a post-Darwinian version of natural theology to a wide audience, and acted as a kind of scientific chaplain to agnostics such as Huxley.

Yet for all Kingsley's enthusiasm for Darwinism, he did find his 'religious feelings' disturbed in later encounters with Darwin's evolutionary ideas. As Piers Hale has recently argued, while Kingsley was quite prepared to admit that humans had evolved from ape-like ancestors, he could not subscribe to Darwin's account of human evolution, as expressed in the *Descent of Man* (1871).[31] What troubled Kingsley was the idea that Christian civilization had gradually emerged from more 'savage-like' human cultures. To recount an evolutionary history of the human body was one thing. To also provide an evolutionary explanation of human morality was another. For Kingsley, savage cultures were explicable in terms of an innate human tendency towards moral degradation. He could not see how moral culture emerged, without supernatural assistance, from a primal savage state. It is also worth noting that this broadly Christian understanding of the origins of morality and moral degeneracy was accompanied in Kingsley's thinking by an ugly racialist twist.[32] Unlike some other Anglican defenders of a providentialist understanding of human evolution, Kingsley argued that science had confirmed what he took as the pre-eminently biblical view that competition between races and the destruction of the 'less favoured' was a 'universal law of living things'.[33]

The same general anxiety about the impact of Darwin's account of human evolution can be detected in figures who represented a different theological constituency than the one most often associated with Kingsley. But how it was expressed and to what ends differed markedly. A sermon preached by Edward Pusey in 1878 entitled 'Un-science, not science, adverse to faith' provides one example. Pusey's sermon was an important statement on science and evolution by a senior Anglican figure known for his vigorous and controversial defence of theological orthodoxy in an Anglo-Catholic mode. While Pusey

[30] Cited in Piers J. Hale, 'Darwin's Other Bulldog: Charles Kingsley and the Popularization of Evolution in Victorian England', *Science and Education*, 21 (2012): 977–1013.

[31] Piers J. Hale, 'Chance and Contingency in the Evolution of Man: Mind and Morals in Charles Kingsley's *Water Babies*', *Journal of the History of Biology*, 46 (2013): 551–97.

[32] Jonathan Conlin, 'An Illiberal Descent: Natural and National History in the Work of Charles Kingsley', *History*, 96 (2011): 167–87; William Kelley, 'Nature and Religion: Recovering Charles Kingsley', *Journal of Ecclesiastical History*, 65 (2014): 620–9.

[33] Charles Kingsley, *Scientific Lectures and Essays* (London, 1880), p. 324.

made it clear that he did not consider an evolutionary account of life to be scientifically established, he pointed out that its truth or falsity was of little theological consequence. The creation by evolution of plants and animals would, he averred, simply confirm 'no other than the teaching of our Western theology since S. Augustine'. In this he echoed others who had called upon Augustine to demonstrate the general compatibility of organic evolution and a Christian doctrine of creation.[34] It was when evolution was applied to the 'soul of man' that the trouble began. Darwin's theory of descent seemed to Pusey to demand an understanding of human origins and history that contradicted core theological convictions. In particular, it undermined the idea that humans had been made in the image of God and that the fallen state of humankind was not according to nature but had been caused by sin. To embrace Darwin's theory of descent would mean locating the origin of the 'moral law' in a 'struggle for existence in which the stronger ever extirpated the weaker'. This, to Pusey, would destroy Christian morality and the Christian understanding of humanity. Like Kingsley, Pusey denied that humans could, unaided, cultivate Christian morality. Pusey, however, stressed 'civilized degradation', a far worse form of moral degeneracy than any 'savage' society. He dismissed human empires ('that grow, swell and vanish') and gloried in the empire of Christ. That empire, rather than extirpating the weak, took as the 'sceptre of its power' the 'gibbet of slaves, the execration of the world'.[35] For Pusey, such morality could have no naturalistic cause or explanation.

Evangelical Anglicans, albeit in a different theological idiom, expressed similar concerns about evolution, particularly when applied to humans. A long-standing antagonism towards evolution in general and human evolution in particular can be detected in the contributions made by Anglicans and others in the publications associated with the Victoria Institute and the Christian Evidence Society, two Evangelical organizations founded in the 1860s to combat threats to Christian belief from the rather nebulous advance of 'modern thought'. A representative example of this Evangelical antagonism to evolution can be found in the work of the Revd Thomas R. Birks. A leading Evangelical theologian and Professor of Moral Philosophy at Cambridge from 1872, Birks steadfastly opposed evolution in a number of books, articles, and lectures that aimed to defend the Bible against 'modern thought'. Birks was particularly critical of the 'nomotheists' who sought to reconcile evolution and Christian belief through an appeal to creation by natural law. Such a view, Birks suggested, might be regarded as 'a wise scheme of Providence, if the purpose of God were only to develop a race of self-satisfied atheists'. However, Birks was convinced that it did not do justice to the biblical testimony that creation plainly declared the glory of God. For Birks, it was vital to insist that

[34] Ernan McMullin, 'Darwin and the Other Christian Tradition', *Zygon*, 46 (2011): 291–316.
[35] Edward Bouverie Pusey, *Un-science, not Science, Adverse to Faith* (London, 1878).

all species of plants and animals were created directly and, in particular, that 'the creation of man was distinct from that of animals, and latest in time'.[36]

For all the widespread scepticism among Evangelical Anglicans about evolution, particularly as applied to humans, some did tentatively hold to the view that, should human evolution be verified scientifically, it would remain possible to hold to the truth of the early chapters of Genesis. The leading physicist and Evangelical Anglican, George Gabriel Stokes, remained unconvinced by evolutionary theories of human origins but conceded that the 'supernatural modification of a previously existing animal' did offer a way of reconciling biblical and scientific accounts.[37] In this Stokes, like other fellow Anglicans, aligned himself with the Catholic zoologist St George Mivart and the naturalist Alfred Russel Wallace, who, against Darwin, argued that natural selection did not provide a sufficient explanation of human nature. To explain the intellectual and moral capacities of humans required some appeal to supernatural intervention.

There were others, however, who argued that the Christian theist had no theological reason to prefer Wallace and Mivart's account to Darwin's. The Anglican theologian Aubrey Moore, for example, argued that Wallace's proposal rested on the questionable premise that unaided natural processes had formed plants and (non-human) animals.[38] To Moore's mind, this contradicted a Christian metaphysics of creation that emphasized God's constant cooperation with secondary causes. If this Christian understanding of causality was allowed, then there was nothing at stake theologically in the debate between Darwin and Wallace over whether or not humans had emerged without the direct intervention of a higher intelligence. If the 'soul' had emerged gradually and without direct divine intervention, that did not make it any less God's intended creation. Moore also reminded his readers of the centuries-long dispute between 'traducianists' and 'creationists' over the origin of individual human souls.[39] There was no more cause for concern over the equally intractable question of the origination of the soul of the first humans.

Despite such efforts to demonstrate the potential compatibility of Darwinian and Christian understandings of human origins, problems remained. One especially stubborn difficulty was raised early on by another of Darwin's clerical correspondents, Leonard Jenyns. Just a few weeks after the publication of *On the Origin of Species*, Jenyns wrote to Darwin and admitted that while he could 'embrace [the] theory in part' he could 'hardly see what sense of meaning is to be attached to Gen: 2:7 & yet more to vv. 21. 22, of the same

[36] Thomas R. Birks, *The Scripture Doctrine of Creation* (London, 1873), pp. 136, 183.

[37] Cited in David B. Wilson, 'A Physicist's Alternative to Materialism: The Religious Thought of George Gabriel Stokes', *Victorian Studies*, 28 (1984), p. 91.

[38] Richard England, 'Natural Selection, Teleology, and the Logos: From Darwin to the Oxford Neo-Darwinists, 1859–1909', *Osiris*, 16 (2001): 270–87.

[39] Aubrey Moore, *Science and the Faith: Essays on Apologetic Subjects* (London, 1893), p. 210.

chapter, giving an account of the creation of *woman*'.[40] The creation of Adam from the dust of the earth suggested to Jenyns an immediate creation of the first man. The more detailed description of the creation of the first woman from Adam's side was even more difficult to reconcile with the view that humans, male and female, had evolved from pre-human progenitors. This exegetical conundrum was picked up decades later by Thomas Huxley precisely in order to criticize what he regarded as the disingenuous liberalism exhibited by the authors of *Lux Mundi*, a collection of essays by Anglo-Catholic thinkers (Aubrey Moore among them) to reconcile orthodoxy with modern thought.[41] To Huxley, the fact of Eve's formation from Adam was a fundamental tenet of Christian belief not least because, according to Matthew's gospel, Christ reaffirmed it. Yet, according to modern science, it was 'monstrously improbable'.[42] The *Lux Mundi* essayists, Huxley judged, were too quick to suggest that the early chapters of Genesis made no claims plainly to report historical or scientific facts.

Perplexity over how to read the Genesis account of the creation of the first woman in the light of Darwin's theory of evolution was widely shared. Moreover, the perplexity was sharpened and given a political bearing due to its relevance to long-running parliamentary debates about marriage to a deceased wife's sister. The prohibition of this union had been enshrined in canon law in 1604 and had passed into common law in 1835. For the rest of the nineteenth century, constant calls in and out of Parliament were made for its repeal. It was the idea that man and wife formed 'one flesh' that provided for many the theological basis for the prohibition. A man's sister-in-law became, in effect, his blood relative due to the indissoluble physical union with his wife. Behind these convictions, which found detailed expression in the table of kindred and affinity in the Book of Common Prayer, was an interpretation of the Genesis 2 account of the formation of the first woman, 'taken out of the man' and thus 'flesh of his flesh and bone of his bones'. For a number of the bishops and other Anglican commentators, there was something about the precise way in which the woman was formed that secured the mystical and physical reality of the marriage bond. As Jenyns had hinted, it was easier to reconcile evolution with the account given of the creation of Adam from the dust of the earth than it was to find room for the evolution of Eve.

What is apparent, then, is that where there were concerns about the implications of evolutionary theory for Anglican belief, these tended to revolve

[40] Cited in Diarmid A. Finnegan, 'Eve and Evolution: Christian Responses to the First Woman Question, 1860–1900', *Journal of the History of Ideas*, 75 (2014): 283–305.

[41] On *Lux Mundi*, see Peter Hinchliff, 'Separate Spiritual Truths: The Essays in *Lux Mundi*', in *God and History: Aspects of British Theology, 1875–1914* (Oxford, 1992), pp. 99–121.

[42] Cited in Finnegan, 'Eve and Evolution'.

around the figure of the human. The perceived consequences for theological anthropology of emerging theories of human evolution stirred up significant anxieties—not least because of the challenges such theories were thought to pose to the teaching and authority of the Bible on questions of human origins and gender relations. At the same time, discussions about human evolution also supplied opportunities for rethinking or reconstructing Christian doctrine or promoting a political theology of race and empire. It remains to be shown that Anglican debates about evolution, anthropology, and theology were not restricted to the intellectual 'centre' but were evident across an increasingly 'global' Anglican sphere of influence. It is certainly worth briefly exploring what a more global history of the relations between Anglicanism and science in the long nineteenth century might involve.

Evolution, Anthropology, and 'Global Anglicanism'

Until relatively recently, the historiography on science and religion in the nineteenth century has, with some notable exceptions, concentrated on debates that occurred within the metropole rather than colonial settings. Calls for a 'global history' of science and religion have begun to challenge this dominant scholarly view.[43] There are certainly good reasons to apply a 'global' optic to Anglican contributions to debates about science and the Bible in the long nineteenth century—an archetypal 'age of empire' and globalization. Anglicans were not only deeply involved in the project of empire but were also working to forge a 'global communion' in ways that overlapped with other sorts of globalizing projects, religious and secular. The emergence of the Lambeth Conferences and the vibrancy and global reach of Anglican missions were among the many expressions of this and both helped to cultivate conversations about science and religion shaped by inter-cultural exchange. And of all the scientific topics, it was evolution, particularly as applied to anthropology and philology, that again dominated these more dispersed or relocated discussions about science and Anglican belief.

The controversial career of John William Colenso was one of the most prominent manifestations of the confluence of mission, evolution, biblical criticism, and an emerging and contested 'global' Anglican identity. Colenso represented a liberal voice in a colonial setting but he also made a significant contribution to debates about science, evolution, and the Bible in Britain. Underlying Colenso's controversial account of the first six books of the Bible was a commitment to accommodating religious beliefs to recent scientific

[43] Sujit Sivasundaram, 'A Global History of Science and Religion', in Thomas Dixon, Geoffrey Cantor, and Stephen Pumfrey (eds.), *Science and Religion: New Historical Perspectives* (Cambridge, 2010), pp. 177–98.

developments. This commitment was also couched in a declared dedication to making Christian faith relevant to non-European cultures in ways that were true to the findings of science. In the preface to his *Pentateuch and the Book of Joshua Critically Examined* (1862), Colenso recalled 'an intelligent native' (the Zulu catechist and translator William Ngidi) asking him whether the account of Noah's flood was true.[44] It was, Colenso reported, his difficulties in answering that question based on the findings of geological science that prompted his more systematic and extensive enquiry into the historical veracity of the opening books of the Bible.

As is well known, Colenso's interest in the latest scientific developments and his concern not to shirk questions about the Bible's historical veracity even in the mission field made him a controversial figure in Britain and in South Africa. His heresy trial in South Africa may have collapsed under the weight of disputes over the legitimacy of newly emerging structures of ecclesiastical jurisdiction in the colonies, but it confirmed his status as a leading representative of liberal and progressive Anglicanism. It is not unexpected, then, to find that Colenso, along with promoting the latest results of biblical criticism, was sympathetic to an evolutionary account of human origins and dismissed efforts to query it on merely biblical grounds. At the same time, he persistently defended the necessity of missionary work by arguing that an evolutionary view of human origins and cultural development supported a view of non-European populations as capable of moral and intellectual improvement.[45] Colenso argued that if human civilizations had emerged from a primitive and 'savage' state, then there was every reason to believe that, with the assistance of Christian missions, an African civilization would emerge. In countering a more fatalist view that appealed to Darwinian evolution to point to the inevitability, or even desirability, of the extinction of 'weaker races'—one, as noted, that Charles Kingsley tended towards—Colenso contributed to efforts to make Darwinism palatable to a liberal Anglican constituency in the metropole and to converts to Anglicanism in Natal.[46]

Colenso's views on evolution, fashioned as they were between England and Natal, indicate one way in which evolution became a topic of debate in venues well beyond Britain. Another somewhat later indication that such debates were exercising those responsible for managing the Anglican Church beyond Britain and Ireland came in the form of an extended discussion during the

[44] John W. Colenso, *The Pentateuch and the Book of Joshua Critically Examined* (London, 1862), p. vii.

[45] Peter Hinchliff, 'Ethics, Evolution and Biblical Criticism in the Thought of Benjamin Jowett and John William Colenso', *Journal of Ecclesiastical History*, 37 (1986): 91–110.

[46] John W. Rogerson, 'Colenso in the World of Nineteenth-Century Intellectual Ferment', and Gwilym Colenso, 'The Pentateuch in Perspective: Biblical Criticism in its Colonial Context', both in Jonathan A. Draper (ed.), *The Eye of the Storm: Bishop John William Colenso and the Crisis of Biblical Inspiration* (Pietermaritzburg, 2003), pp. 127–35 and pp. 136–67 respectively.

1888 Lambeth Conference. Included among its business was the discussion of a report 'On definite teaching of the faith to various classes' formulated and tabled by Frederick Temple, then bishop of London. Temple's report included among its recommendations that holding the opening chapters of Genesis to be 'a vision of allegory' should be considered a legitimate opinion for the believer, and that countenancing 'mistakes of fact' in the Bible should not be thought a threat to religious veracity. Emerging as they did from Temple's Bampton lectures, these suggestions were designed to help those burdened by the apparent discrepancy between the Bible and modern science, particularly evolutionary accounts of human origins. The report was debated at length with strong opposition being voiced alongside tentative agreement. The discussion reveals a diversity of opinion across an emerging global Anglican Communion. William Webber, bishop of Brisbane, backed the report in full. Henry Whipple, bishop of Minnesota, rehearsed some standard theological concerns about reading the opening chapters of Genesis as mere allegories. Edward Ralph Johnson, bishop of Calcutta, questioned the wisdom of formally and publicly addressing the issue at all. These deliberations terminated in a vote over whether the report should be printed or not. With forty-five supporting this and fifty-nine opposing it, the report remained unpublished and demonstrated a spectrum of opinion of the subject across Anglicanism's wider spheres of influence.[47]

In many respects, the Lambeth discussions remained detached from colonial realities and did not register the difference colonial situations made to Anglican attitudes towards science in general and evolution in particular. More telling, perhaps, were the efforts of a number of missionaries to contribute to the development of anthropological science through their prolonged residence among indigenous peoples. Among the most notable were the Revd Henry Callaway (1817–90) and the Revd Robert Henry Codrington (1830–1922). Both missionaries were in dialogue with leading British anthropologists, including Max Muller and Edward Tylor, but both resisted an evolutionary paradigm for understanding the peoples they studied.

Henry Callaway's ethnographical descriptions of the groups he lived with and observed at the Society for the Propagation of the Gospel's settlement at Springvale in the Province of Natal were offered as contributions to the emerging science of comparative religion. Writing shortly after Callaway's death, Marian Benham, his biographer, presented his comparative ethnography as a pure form of inductivism unfettered by theoretical preconceptions. Callaway himself pointed out the benefits and the dangers of being a missionary anthropologist, noting that a missionary's immersion in the lives of a particular cultural group gave him/her an advantage over anthropological

[47] Gregory P. Elder, *Chronic Vigour: Darwin, Anglicans, Catholics and Development of a Doctrine of Providential Evolution* (Lanham, MD, 1996).

theorists, but he also worried that the missionary impulse was likely to work against a more objective view of alien cultural practices. Yet for all his emphasis on avoiding the blind spots of a missionary point of view, Callaway's account of African religious sensibilities and beliefs correlated with his own theological convictions. As a moderate High Church Anglican, Callaway was opposed to a Calvinist understanding of the fallen human condition and was averse to the excessive ritualism of Tractarianism without repudiating the importance of liturgical worship.[48] Against bleaker versions of Calvinism, Callaway stressed anthropological evidence for the innate spiritual receptivity of indigenous African groups to theological truths even while pointing out the distortive effects of ritualism and superstitious custom, whether Christian or not.

Given his relatively conservative theological leanings, it is not surprising that Callaway found evolutionary progressivism promoted by his bishop, John William Colenso, unpalatable. More specifically, Callaway used anthropological science to counter Colenso's arguments for the toleration of polygamy, by arguing that his own sustained observation of polygamy in practice overturned Colenso's more benign assessment of its social effects. Further, Callaway opposed Colenso's programme of reworking Christian belief in African terms. In this dispute, it was philological science that proved to be an important aid. Callaway cautioned against using indigenous terms to convey fundamental theological categories until their precise meaning had been determined. Callaway argued, for example, that the Zulu term Colenso adopted for God did not, in fact, refer to any kind of deity or divine spirit but rather identified a primitive ancestor.[49] By stressing the capacity of Africans to embrace the Christian message and Christian morality, in resisting speculation in the interests of inductive observation, and in holding that Christianity contained permanent truths rather than shifting meanings subject to a process of adaptation and evolution, Callaway comprehensively resisted principles and forms of thought that were frequently supported by the general evolutionism which suffused late Victorian anthropological discourse.

Similar sentiments and arguments can be found in the writings of the Revd Robert Henry Codrington, a leading player in the Anglican Melanesian mission between 1871 and 1888.[50] As well as sharing with Callaway a sense

[48] Rowan Strong, 'Continuity and Change in Anglican Missionary Theology: Dr Thomas Bray and the 1910 World Missionary Conference', *Journal of Postcolonial Theory and Theology*, 2 (2011): 1–32.

[49] David Chidester, '"Classify and Conquer": Friedrich Max Müller, Indigenous Religious Traditions and Imperial Comparative Religion', in *Beyond Primitivism: Indigenous Religious Traditions and Modernity* (New York, 1997), pp. 71–88.

[50] Sara Sohmer, 'The Melanesian Mission and Victorian Anthropology: A Study in Symbiosis', in Roy MacLeod and Philip F. Rehbock (eds.), *Darwin's Laboratory: Evolution and Natural History in the Pacific* (Honolulu, 1994), pp. 317–38.

of the potential and pitfalls of missionary anthropology, Codrington also emphasized the importance of resisting the imposition of theoretical preconceptions on the subjects of ethnographic description. He was particularly critical of John Lubbock's seminal text, *The Origin of Civilisation*, noting on reading it that 'the savages of scientific men recede further and further from my experience'.[51] This inductivism allowed Codrington to stress the benefits of anthropology for missionary work (in understanding the lives of those who came under the care and attention of the mission) and to avoid more speculative concerns with the origins and nature of religious beliefs and language. In many respects, Codrington was working within an older tradition of ethnological enquiry associated with the Evangelical Anglican James Cowles Prichard, which stressed not just the single origin and unity of the human race but also the parity between different racial groups in terms of intellectual and linguistic aptitude. As with Callaway, Codrington resisted the dominant evolutionism that characterized late nineteenth-century anthropology.

Of course, not all Anglican figures in the colonies were sceptical of evolutionary science. Colenso was one example of a leading clergyman who, in a qualified way, promoted evolution as an established intellectual theory that demanded serious consideration. But lay Anglicans also forged a relationship between evolution and colonial Anglicanism in ways that wedded scientific authority to modified forms of Christian belief. In New Zealand, for example, the geologist and biologist Frederick Wollaston Hutton (1836–1905) proved instrumental in promoting Darwinism as the most plausible scientific explanation of the diversity and biogeography of living forms, but in a way that emphasized the compatibility between evolutionary science and 'revealed religion'. Hutton had championed Darwinism as a young man, writing an early positive review of *On the Origin of Species* and had vehemently opposed fellow Anglican critics of Darwinism such as Adam Sedgwick. From his arrival in New Zealand in 1866, Hutton continued to promote Darwinism in the face of religious objections. He did this, however, not in order to distance himself from his own Anglican upbringing but to demonstrate the validity of an accommodationist approach to evolution and Christian belief, one that adjusted how doctrinal commitments were expressed or formulated in order to make room for the new science of evolution. As John Stenhouse has argued, Hutton successfully persuaded a number of leading religious thinkers in New Zealand to adopt a version of theistic evolution that emphasized divine immanence within an ordered creation.[52] In this Hutton was replicating a

[51] Cited in Helen Gardner, 'Defending Friends: Robert Codrington, George Sarawia and Edward Wogale', in Kate Fullagar (ed.), *The Atlantic World in the Antipodes* (Newcastle upon Tyne, 2012), p. 154.

[52] John Stenhouse, 'Darwin's Captain: F. W. Hutton and the Nineteenth-Century Darwinian Debates', *Journal of the History of Biology*, 23 (1990): 411–42.

fairly common stance among Anglicans in Britain. That did not make the New Zealand context irrelevant. The political overtones of Hutton's Christianized Darwinism were in sharp contrast to the use made of evolutionary terminology by other British settlers. These actors appealed to the 'struggle for existence' and 'extirpation of weaker races', to argue that Māori extinction was inevitable, thus undermining a more humanitarian view of settler–indigenous relations.[53] Like Colenso, Hutton presented a more benign form of Darwinism that not only propped up his own Anglican convictions but also lent support to the upholding of Māori rights in the face of aggression by Pākehā settlers.

CONCLUSION

It is possible to argue that there was a 'colonial difference' in how Anglicanism and science were brought into combination.[54] In those contexts where Anglican identity was less clearly tied to the apparatus of the state, the Anglican Church was not the target of a sustained campaign to wrest cultural authority from it. Frank Turner's thesis that the primary goal of a group of elite men of science was to dismantle the state-sanctioned authority of the Church of England certainly suggests that where the state's power to enshrine the Church's cultural authority was weaker, there was less cause for a concerted attempt to undermine the public credibility of theological claims. That may have facilitated both the persistence of a pre-evolutionary understanding of life and the promotion of a theistic evolutionism that supported Anglican interests.

This thesis is suggestive, but it does not fully register the complex causes behind the relations that developed between science and Anglicanism through the nineteenth century. Those relations were situated within, and shaped by, overlapping conglomerations of personal, institutional, and intellectual interests and cannot be fully understood using 'colonial' or 'metropolitan' terms of reference. This also means, more generally, that the historian looks in vain for the Evangelical, High Church, Tractarian, or Broad Church attitude towards scientific developments or scientific culture whether in the Anglican 'centre' or elsewhere. Theological positions and scientific claims did not stay still and, as with the reactions found among Christian thinkers in other denominations, were also strongly shaped by local circumstances.[55] This is true not only when

[53] John Stenhouse, 'Darwinism in New Zealand, 1859–1900', in Ronald L. Numbers and John Stenhouse (eds.), *Disseminating Darwinism: The Role of Race, Place, Religion and Gender* (New York, 1999), pp. 61–89.

[54] I owe this suggestion to Dr John Stenhouse.

[55] David N. Livingstone, *Dealing with Darwin: Place, Politics and Rhetoric in Religious Engagements with Evolution* (Baltimore, MD, 2014).

science and Anglicanism are viewed separately but, perhaps yet more so, when brought into relation. What can be stated with confidence, however, is the importance of science in shaping Anglican belief and identity and the importance of Anglican identity and belief in shaping science. This chapter has pointed to some of the ways in which that mutual influence was made manifest but much more remains to be done to fully explicate how wide and deep it really was.

SELECT BIBLIOGRAPHY

Brooke, John Hedley, *Science and Religion: Some Historical Perspectives* (Cambridge, 1991).

Corsi, Pietro, *Baden Powell and the Anglican Debate* (Cambridge, 1988).

Desmond, Adrian, *The Politics of Evolution: Morphology, Medicine and Reform in Radical London* (Chicago, 1989).

England, Richard, 'Natural Selection, Teleology, and the Logos: From Darwin to the Oxford Neo-Darwinists, 1859–1909', *Osiris*, 16 (2001): 270–87.

Lightman, Bernard, *Victorian Popularizers of Science: Designing Nature for New Audiences* (Chicago, 2007).

McGrath, Alister E., *Darwinism and the Divine: Evolutionary Thought and Natural Theology* (Chichester, 2011).

Moore, James R., 'Charles Darwin Lies in Westminster Abbey', *Biological Journal of the Linnean Society*, 17 (1982): 97–113.

Morrell, Jack and Arnold Thackray, *Gentlemen of Science: Early Years of the British Association for the Advancement of Science* (Oxford, 1981).

Rupke, Nicolaas, *The Great Chain of History: William Buckland and the English School of Geology (1814–1849)* (Oxford, 1983).

Rupke, Nicolaas, *Richard Owen: Biology without Darwin* (Chicago, 2009).

Secord, James, *Victorian Sensation: The Extraordinary Publication, Reception and Secret Authorship of Vestiges of the Natural History of Creation* (Chicago, 2000).

Topham, Jonathan R., 'Beyond the "Common Context": The Production and Reading of the Bridgewater Treatises', *Isis*, 89 (1998): 233–62.

White, Paul, 'Ministers of Culture: Arnold, Huxley and Liberal Anglican Reform of Learning', *History of Science*, 43 (2005): 115–48.

22

The Feminization of Nineteenth-Century Anglicanism

Susan Mumm

CONTINUITY AND CHANGE

The feminization of the Anglican Church in the nineteenth century must be placed in the broader context of the gradual feminization of Christianity in the English-speaking world overall. As Callum Brown reminds us, a demonstrable gender imbalance in Sunday worship in Britain was some four hundred years old by the start of the twentieth century, although the volume of commentary on the point swells markedly after 1800. In addition to forming the majority of congregations, by the start of the nineteenth century earlier ideas about the earth-bound nature of women had given way to a general belief that they were the more spiritual sex.[1] Brown claims that 'femininity and piety become conjoined discourse after 1800',[2] and although his own research focuses on Evangelical and Dissenting thought, the observation is true of all branches of Anglicanism in the period. The Anglican Church's strongest response to the gender imbalance in the Victorian pew was the development of the concept of muscular Christianity, whose best-known (and perhaps also most extreme) proponent was the clergyman and writer Charles Kingsley. Although much was written and said about muscular Christianity emphasizing the 'masculine' virtues of Christ, of Christian men, and of the Church Militant as a counterbalance to the femininity of Anglican adherents, it appears to have had little impact on the diurnal parish life of the Anglican Church in England and the

[1] Callum G. Brown, 'Masculinity and Secularization in Twentieth-Century Britain', in Yvonne Maria Werner (ed.), *Christian Masculinity: Gender and Religion in Northern Europe in the Nineteenth and Twentieth Centuries* (Leuven, 2011), p. 49.

[2] Callum G. Brown, *The Death of Christian Britain: Understanding Secularization 1800–2000* (London, 2009 edn.), p. 88.

colonies, being played out primarily in boys' schools and in the world of amateur sport.[3]

Feminization, when applied to nineteenth-century Anglicanism, is a complex and multi-faceted concept. A narrow focus on one aspect of the historical record isolated from other elements will produce an argument about the nature and extent of feminization that becomes demonstrably false when placed in a broader and more representative context. A great deal depends on two key definitions, which Victorian cultural commentators defined in such varying and self-serving ways that the concepts underlying them could be, and were, used both as attack and as defence: *feminization* (an anachronistic term that was not used at the time: 'effeminacy' was a common near-equivalent, and was applied to both female and male behaviour) and *Anglicanism*. Despite the contradictory and complex evidence, some key themes emerge.

The strongest theme that can be identified is that of feminization as a development and as a developer. In other words, the feminization of the Anglican Church in this period occurred as a series of incremental changes rather than as a series of innovations, although a handful of new initiatives are evident. If the focus of the historian is the development of the work of laywomen, especially in the part of the voluntary sector devoted to Church associations, then considerable feminization is evident over the course of the nineteenth century. One striking aspect in the growth of laywomen's work for the Church is how frequently proponents of this development laid claim to the Anglican nature of their organizations, while opponents employed definitions that kept women's work outside of the limits of the sanctioned circle. Conversely, if attention is paid primarily to the ordained ministry, there is virtually no evidence of feminization in this period at all. Victorian gender hermeneutics were biased towards denying women any official or leadership role in the work of the Church, and this did not change in this period. Even the undoubtedly influential Ladies' Association of the Society for the Propagation of the Gospel in Foreign Parts (formed *c.*1866), was in 1900 'not yet formally a part of the Society, but a recognized and indispensable auxiliary to it'.[4]

Women's work for the Anglican Church in the nineteenth century presented a complex blend of traditionalist continuity and innovative boundary-pushing, within an overall context of religious and social conservatism. However, the sheer volume of activity undoubtedly spurred a qualitative change, and actual innovations caused the status quo to be questioned more widely and more persistently after the 1870s. Despite the varying attitudes towards women in the

[3] Brown, *Death*, pp. 96–8.

[4] H. P. Thompson, *Into All Lands: The History of the SPGFP 1701–1950* (London, 1951), p. 236.

Anglican and Episcopalian Churches of Britain, the United States, and the colonies, there is little evidence that the sister Anglican Churches developed on distinct lines during the years before the end of the long nineteenth century. In all the Anglican Churches, continuity was expressed through the relatively stable relationship between the worker and the decision-makers. This meant that while there was a growing range of activities for women, power in Church matters did not appreciably shift. There were more opportunities for female activity but not much scope for female authority. Authority remained firmly in the hands of father, husband, or clergyman. The single exception to this, although a striking one, was the development of Anglican sisterhoods with their alternative authority structure, culminating in the mother superior and her council of sisters.

As indicated before, if it were a simple question of charting the growth of activity, or even of church attendance, then Anglicanism shows a decided feminizing trend from the 1840s onward. In addition to more work for the Church being performed by women, the range of their contributions broadened, and cooperation between cognate women's societies became increasingly evident. Cooperation is evident in the growth of organizations as opposed to individual parish visiting under the direction of local parochial authority. Examples of the growth of cooperative Anglican women's work include, in order of decreasing intensity of commitment, the sisterhoods (the first were founded in the 1840s, with over one hundred in operation by 1900), the deaconess orders (several were established after mid-century), the Anglican wing of the Young Women's Christian Association (1855, later to merge with the other organization of the same name), the Girls' Friendly Society (1875), the Ladies' Association for the Care of Friendless Girls (1878), and the Mothers' Union (1876). There were many more as well, but these are probably the largest and best known of the groups actually founded by Anglican women for religio-social purposes during the century.

ROLES AND WORK FOR WOMEN

Another simple measure of Anglicanism's increasing feminization in this period is the increasing preponderance of women in parish congregations. While it is unfortunate that the 1851 Census of Religious Worship did not request the gender breakdown of congregations, it is clear from other published sources that it was perceived as a weakness in the Victorian Church that most congregations were increasingly made up of women. These female laypeople could not be realistically excluded from all organized Church activity. An accompanying set of debates, aside from the propriety or scriptural basis for the work of women, gave rise to arguments about whether such work could be truly Anglican.[5] The compatibility of women's work and Anglican identity was challenged on several grounds. Could work initiated by anyone outside the Church's ordained leadership ever be considered authorized? What was official work for the Church: how far did it extend beyond the ordained ministry and who could lead it? If the socio-religious work of laymen could be defined as Anglican, could the similar work of laywomen be denied that status? Did work have to be official, or authorized, to be truly Anglican? These questions were still being earnestly debated during the meetings of the Pan-Anglican Congress in 1908 and were still in the course of resolution during the inter-war period.[6]

The work of Anglican women in establishing and staffing Anglican agencies for women, girls, and children is a major part of the great expansion of voluntary work across society in the period. A publication of the 1890s lists the roles for women within Anglicanism as: district visiting, Sunday school teaching, church music, parochial clubs, missionary societies, study circles, rescue and preventative agencies, sisterhoods, deaconess institutions, the Girls' Friendly Society (GFS), and the Mothers' Union. This list is reasonably close to being comprehensive, although it does omit a few specialist activities, such as Anglican Bible women (an initiative copied from Nonconformity), and the local societies that collected money for Bibles as a way of encouraging both devotion and thrift among the poor. We could also include the Ladies' Penitentiary Association and the Ladies' Association for the Care of Friendless Girls. Some agencies depicted themselves as resolutely Anglican despite mixed memberships. As well as the GFS, the White Cross Army (later the White Cross League) made claims to be considered as an Anglican society. Both the GFS and the White Cross certainly saw the label of Anglicanism as important not only to their identity, but also to their growth and to the respect accorded them.

It is possible to argue that the women who founded or managed or staffed these activities were consciously or unthinkingly broadening the range of what women could do under the authority and with the approval of the Anglican Church, while expanding the roles available to laywomen in response to social and religious need. However, it is equally reasonable to argue that with their focus on the need and the work, they would not have recognized this picture of their significance and would have rejected it. Overall, the picture is dominated by role expansion and activity expansion rather than activity that could be seen as explicitly feminist. In other words, pragmatism permitted women into

[5] Susan Mumm, '"A Peril to the Bench of Bishops": Anglican Sisterhoods and the Church of England, 1845–1908', *Journal of Ecclesiastical History*, 59 (2008): 62–78.

[6] Central Committee of Women's Church Work, *Younger Women and the Church of England* (London, 1916); Cyril C. B. Bardley (ed.), *Women and Church Work* (London, 1917); H. S. Marshall (ed.), *Pastoralia for Women: A Book for Women by Women* (London, 1934).

spheres of religious activity through expediency much more than it did through belief that their work was desirable. However, as the century drew to a close, there is increasingly evident a real, but considerably muted, sense that women's work entitled them to a say in its organization and management. However, increased opportunities for women to work did not coincide with opportunities to lead. In the few instances where this was seen as the century came to an end, the gift of limited and contingent authority was bestowed based on uncontestable expertise in the work, despite the drawback of the expert being a woman. The small number of women who were promoted to positions of leadership in mixed-gender societies (usually in front-line service in mission or social work) had to demonstrate a level of expertise high enough to overcome the obstacle of gender bias.

A major element of the expediency of women's work for their faith was that it was freely offered. Unpaid work carried with it positive connotations in the eyes of Victorian commentators: sacrifice, offering, higher social class, affluence, and amateurism. Paid work for the Church was literally non-existent for women, with the exception of female missionaries, who notoriously received a pittance, if single, and nothing at all, if married. All of this was in striking contrast to the clerical career.

Any consideration of whether, and how, Anglicanism feminized in the nineteenth century has to be understood in the context of Victorian beliefs about natural behaviour, scriptural teaching, the historic practice of the Church, and what was considered to be socially desirable. Victorian Christians, including and perhaps especially Anglicans, happily assumed that their social practice was as close to Christian perfection as any society had ever achieved. Countless sermons, pamphlets, newspaper articles, and books (while identifying areas for national improvement), stressed that English home life, relationships with servants, public service, and professional ethics, were all infinitely superior to those of less favoured nations, and this demi-perfection was normally associated with the peculiar genius of the Anglican *via media*.[7] This permitted social and religious conservatives to argue that family ties were as sacred, and as binding, as religious vocation in any form. This argument then made it possible to insist that all familial duties must be satisfied before a woman could be considered independent enough to dedicate herself to work for the Church. Some historians make much of the equality of souls arguments in explaining the growth of women's work in the Victorian Church. This was the position, firmly based in mainstream Christian theology, that since Christ died to save all, both men and women, their souls were equally precious.[8] However, these historians often overlook the fact that the equality of souls idea

[7] H. O. Wakeman, *What Has Christianity Done for England?* (London, 1886), pp. 11, 17–18.

[8] Leonore Davidoff and Catherine Hall, *Family Fortunes: Men and Women of the English Middle Class, 1780–1850* (Chicago, 1987).

meant that women could be adequately represented by men, as the soul itself was without sex or gender. William Temple (later to become archbishop of Canterbury) made an interesting argument that male/female difference actually made recognizing women's work more important, instead of relying on the standard position that Christianity set equal value on the souls of both sexes. Believing that there were fundamental differences between the sexes, Temple argued that society suffers if both perspectives are not fully represented in Anglican social service.[9] Many Anglican laywomen followed Temple's line by choosing to justify their work by emphasizing their difference, rather than their similarity, to men.

As has been suggested earlier, in all areas of Anglican women's work, an important distinction was made between single and married women. Even if still living at home, parental authority (with some exceptions) sat more lightly on single adult women, who could commit themselves to parish work as part of their normal routine, and could plan their time accordingly. Married women, even those with servants, found themselves pulled away from church work by the demands of pregnancy, motherhood, and family nurture. Additionally, even the childless and affluent married woman could not consider her time her own to the extent that would permit her to take up work for the Church without her husband's permission and approval. This difference between married and single women played itself over time by the establishment of a pattern where every innovation in women's church work was pioneered first by single women. Some, such as religious orders, remained by their very nature the province of the unmarried. Celibacy was defended on both practical and symbolic grounds. The acceptance of laywomen as full-time workers for the Church was contingent on women being able, and willing, to demonstrate that no family tie or domestic duty was being neglected by their self-dedication. This was justified by arguing that Scripture taught that family ties were in themselves religious obligations. Women without home ties were believed to be the only women who were free to pursue full-time devotion to a cause. Symbolically, the lack of husband and children was seen as enabling women to replace these loved objects with devotion to a whole category of people, usually children or the poor. This was construed as a kind of spiritual motherhood. Married child-free women of high social standing were important as workers (and in the case of the GFS and Mothers' Union, as founders), but their ability to devote their time to their work always remained somewhat contingent. The founder of the Mothers' Union, Mary Sumner, for example, did not begin her work until her children were grown; most other key figures in the early history of these movements were childless.

[9] W. Temple, 'Cooperation Between Men and Women in Social Work', in *Pan Anglican Papers: The Church and Its Ministry* (London, 1908).

As has been mentioned earlier, the unthinking acceptance of the supremacy of family obligation meant that the expansion of women's work within Anglicanism during this period made a strong connection between full-time work and vowed or unvowed celibacy. Thus professional women's work became informally linked to celibacy as well, while marriage and amateurism went hand in hand. Even in the state sector (relatively small at this time: more women professionals worked under the auspices of the Church of England than for secular agencies until the 1890s), women teachers, doctors, and social workers were expected to remain single, as were nurses. Although celibacy was not required of the clergy in the post-Reformation period, the Anglican women's communities that sprang up in the 1840s and beyond required celibacy of their members. As their Roman Catholic counterparts did, Anglican sisterhoods demanded a vow of life-long celibacy at the time of profession. Deaconess orders varied in respect of this vow, from a promise that continued as long as they remained in the role of deaconess, to vows indistinguishable from those of monastic orders.

Like sisterhoods, deaconesses worked without official sanction and without any official definition of the role. While more acceptable as a concept than sisterhoods, because the term could be traced back to the New Testament, the deaconess movement was assessed as only partially successful due to the Church not understanding it as a vocation, seeing it instead as a free supply of trained servants for parish work. The arguments for the celibacy of deaconesses were entirely practical and protective of the supremacy of home duties. At the end of the Victorian era it was estimated that there were between three and four hundred Anglican deaconesses in the Anglican Communion overseas, and about three hundred in the United Kingdom.[10] Some branches of the Anglican Church, particularly the Church in the colonies and the dioceses led by Anglo-Catholic bishops, became noticeably more accepting of women's full-time work in the final decades of the century but remained resistant to any form of female leadership. Colonial dioceses were chronically short of leisured women, as well as being disproportionately led by bishops who had been influenced by the Tractarians. They looked to sisterhoods and deaconess orders as standing in the place of regular parish workers, as well as being more willing, due to their Anglo-Catholic leanings, to accept the legitimacy of the communal life chosen by these women. The Church overseas also benefited from the colonial success of the GFS, with its emigration society and its hostels for young female emigrants in many of the major ports of arrival in the colonies. The GFS was an Anglican society founded by Mary Townsend in 1875. Townsend was the childless wife of a wealthy layman, who established a society for girls which mirrored the parish and diocesan organization of the

[10] Georgina A. Gollick, 'The Training of Women Missionaries', read at the Lambeth Conference in July 1897, published in Jan. 1898, p. 28.

Church of England, easing its acceptance and ensuring its popularity. It had enrolled 100,000 members by 1900.

At the other end of the spectrum from celibate sisters and emigrating GFS members was the parochial ideal of women, geographically and domestically anchored, serving as voluntary assistants to assist the parish clergyman, whether in town or country. In terms of volume of activity, district visiting, as it was often called, dwarfed even the activities of the GFS. Women of the middle and upper classes were assigned small territories within the parish, and charged with regularly visiting all the families within that area. They distributed tracts and advice, read to the family, and reported back to the clergyman cases of want, illness, and other problems that might necessitate a visit from the priest or some form of assistance. District visiting was the most conservative form of religious feminization, involving as it did a vast army of church workers, unpaid, untrained, and extremely visible at parish level. The feminine roles enacted by the visitor changed remarkably little over the century, although the responsibilities of the clergyman's wife also demonstrated little change with the passage of time.

Clergymen's wives occupied an interesting religious and social niche. Clergy wives and daughters were the only women workers whose directors combined both natural and spiritual authority in a single personality, where both religious and familial duty dictated obedience. Advice manuals dispensing idealized role models for the wives of Anglican clergymen make it clear that a wife's work in the parish was an expected part of her role, with some reduction in involvement during peak childbearing years. One such work, in a section headed 'hints to the clergyman's wife relative to her active exertions among the poor', devotes individual chapters to a wide range of expected activities: cottage visits, sick visiting, the running of schools, religious education of children outside of the school setting, cottage and farmhouse reading, operating the parochial library, and concludes with a chapter of advice on delegated authority: in short, how clergy wives should mentor the poor to engage in charitable pursuits among those even lower down the social scale.[11] Even in parishes where minimal voluntary support was given, the Sunday school was invariably part of the outreach. Sunday school education was largely a female domain from very early on, although classes for adolescent boys were run by men whenever a suitable volunteer was willing, or could be pressed into service. Most other Sunday schools were female-staffed, although overseen by the parish priest. In rural parishes and in urban ghetto districts, the parson's wife and daughters were assumed to be responsible for overseeing these classes, and often, in the remoter parts of the countryside, for providing the tuition themselves. Clergy wives appear to have accepted these duties as

[11] [Francis Edward Paget], *The Owlet of Owlstone Edge: His Travels, His Experience, and His Lucubrations* (London, 1856), p. viii.

part of the commitment involved in marrying a parson, and assumed the functions demanded of them to the extent that their families and health would permit.

The only point of complete agreement among the manuals devoted to preparing women for work in parishes was in their uniform insistence on complete subordination of women workers to the clergyman, whether that clergyman was their own husband or a raw curate. Pages are often written about the dangers of female leadership, criticizing everyone from queens down to heads of sisterhoods with unhesitating misogyny. 'Wherever women are left to the uncontrolled exercise of their own will, there from very wantonness, from very dread of control, they seem to go wrong and to exercise a despotism at once too foolish, and too capricious to be endured.'[12] The ideal was a life given up entirely to the demands of others: 'she will toil on unnoticed till the heat and burden of the day are over: and then she will flee away, and be at rest. There will be no paragraph about her in the "Times": perhaps her only earthly memorial will be in the parish register of burials.'[13]

Cultural and religious commentators on women's ministry tended to emphasize an ideal where the parish reigned supreme as an organizing principle. The parish was seen as the organizing unit for women's work when it was under proper control, precisely because it provided for close control by the local clergy. The parish was also a key constraint, because not all women's work could be contained by its boundaries (a good deal of it grew to be organized at the national level), and attitudes and ability at parish level varied markedly. Parish work became broader, but not deeper, as rural parishes depopulated in some regions and urban parishes became more demanding places to work. In some urban areas, the flight of the middle classes left entire parishes without lady volunteers to assist the clergyman and to staff the activities of the church. In other areas, affluent middle-class parishes found themselves embarrassingly oversupplied with women workers, who were however available only sporadically and as their other duties permitted. Some East End London parishes were entirely staffed by women volunteers who commuted there from their homes in the West End.

Parochial oversight was seen by the Church's leadership and conservative laypeople as the defining factor of the Anglican way, regardless of the relative quality of the overseer and overseen. Advice manuals for women workers routinely alleged that chosen oversight could hide an unruly or rebellious spirit in the district visitors or other lady philanthropists. Lengthy and repeated warnings in these publications against working too independently suggest that subservience did not come naturally to all Anglican district visitors. Advice manuals emphasized common themes. All the factors which might

[12] [Paget], *Owlet*, p. 216. [13] [Paget], *Owlet*, p. 232.

give women church workers authority—social class, wealth, intelligence, age, experience—were as nothing when compared to the spiritual and gendered authority of the curate, even if his talents were meagre. Ability was not seen as bestowing the right to decide one's own work. The ideal parochial worker 'willingly appears to work as if she were *under* him [the curate], even in those parts of the work in which she may be better accomplished than he is'.[14] While all women working at parish level were expected to limit themselves to approved activities, even greater restrictions were imposed on parish volunteers who were young. A number of the district visiting manuals suggest appropriate tasks for young women, such as teaching in schools or running clubs, carefully steering clear of the household visiting that could have exposed them to immorality, crime, or simply to extreme poverty.[15]

The right of the parish priest to rule the workers seems to have lain more lightly on laymen, where they attempted such work. There appear to have been no Victorian manuals offering advice to young male visitors. The manuals in existence consistently refer to their readership as female, and to district visitors as women. If men worked as parish visitors, advice on how they should do it was not given, or at least not published. One very liberal source, generated by the Maurician Christian socialists, comments in passing that there is nothing in district visiting that makes it unsuitable for men, but implies that men do not undertake it. The only publication from the period that I can find that deals systematically with the organization of men's voluntary work for the Church at parish level (and it is proposing it rather than describing work already in existence), comments as an afterthought in its final pages, 'the laity of this neighbourhood, after they have duly organized their Association, should obtain, if possible, the sanction of their own Minister, and that of the Chief Pastor of the Diocese'.[16] This attitude is very different from that displayed towards laywomen.

One of the important shifts in the role of women was linked to their increasing dominance in the religious education of children. As the century progressed, the Church shifted from a 'catechism and release' approach, which essentially took children through confirmation and then treated them as adults, free to decide their own religious affiliation, to one where post-catechumens were nurtured into an ongoing relationship with their religion. This involved elements of both mentorship and education, and women dominated the organizations that were intended to keep girls and young women from lapsing. While a number of these organizations were, or became, non-denominational, the GFS remained resolutely all-Anglican throughout the

[14] W. R. Collett, *Woman's Work in the Church* (London, 1863), p. 14 (emphasis in original).

[15] J. L. L. Davies, 'District Visiting', in *Lectures to Ladies on Practical Subjects* (Cambridge, 1855), p. 118.

[16] 'Suburban Churchwarden', in *What Are the Laity Doing? Or, Lay Organization the Want of the Church* (London, [1867]), p. 11.

century and beyond. One of the two organizations that formed the fledgling Young Women's Christian Association was Anglican, although after merger with the other YWCA it became non-denominational early in its history. Many other such groups, such as the Metropolitan Association for Befriending Young Servants were dominated by Anglican women, but never established a clearly Anglican brand identity. This may also have been the case with the societies for women's emigration, founded by Anglican women but not seen as Anglican associations.

As discussed earlier, when looking beyond the parish, almost all Anglican women's work was directed towards the assistance of girls and women, and the largest single agency established during the century was undoubtedly the GFS. The GFS has been described as the first Anglican organization designed for and run by laywomen. It was intended, in part, to bridge the gap between the schoolroom and marriage, as it was open only to single girls and women. Membership peaked in 1913, with about 40,000 Associates (upper-class Anglican women who provided local leadership and who could be married, although most were not) and 200,000 girl members who, although GFS was open to all Christian girls, were predominantly Anglican. Whole-of-life care for Anglican women became available when Mary Sumner founded the Mothers' Union in 1885, which was intended to recruit Anglican married women (GFS members had to resign on marriage). Sometimes it 'degenerated' into a society for women whose Anglicanism was not demonstrated in Sunday attendance: one clergyman wrote to his bishop in 1901 'I've been compelled to "kill" the local branch of the Mothers' Union' for that reason.[17] (And apparently, kill it he could.) The Girls' Diocesan Association was another group established as much to occupy devout women as to support Anglican girls; and a more liberal group, the Young Women's Help Society, was founded in 1880 as an offshoot of the GFS. These organizations offered, in varying degrees, a broad range of Anglican assistance to women and girls: employment registries, clubs and recreation rooms, hostels, vacation homes, literacy training, and opportunities for protected immigration. Their only forays into political activity were the purity campaigns of the 1880s, when a wide array of Anglican societies, in company with associations from other faiths, lobbied the British government in an ultimately successful campaign to raise the age of sexual consent from thirteen to sixteen.

The GFS is of interest because it was generally conceded to be Anglican despite allowing Christian girls of any denomination to become members.[18]

[17] Margaret Houlbrooke, *Rite Out of Time: A Study of the Ancient Rite of Churching and its Survival in the Twentieth Century* (Donington, 2011), p. 42.

[18] Vivienne Richmond, '"It is Not a Society for Human Beings but for Virgins": The Girls' Friendly Society Membership Eligibility Dispute 1875–1936', *Journal of Historical Sociology*, 20 (2007): 304–27.

This policy was shared by the White Cross Army, and thus throws into high relief the question of who decides Anglican identity. The White Cross was a fascinating all-male purity movement led by an Anglican woman, Jane Ellice Hopkins, which recruited hundreds of thousands of men (of any faith) between the 1880s and the First World War. Hopkins, the co-founder (with Bishop Lightfoot of Durham) remained throughout its existence the only woman associated with it, as it was thought that campaigning on such an explicitly sexual subject tainted her reputation. The tenuous nature of its Anglican identity is highlighted by the fact that Hopkins, on Lightfoot's advice, always attempted to organize diocesan meetings for the bishop and clergy before holding a mass meeting. It was clear that official Anglican support and sanction remained important to her, as well as being tactically and politically astute. When the White Cross Army amalgamated with the Church of England Purity Society in 1891 (in itself a tacit acknowledgement of its legitimacy as an Anglican organization), the public role accorded to Hopkins was swiftly withdrawn. Sue Morgan argues that despite such set-backs, the 'revolutionary' leadership of churchwomen set the Anglican agenda for the agencies associated with sexual reform movements.[19] However, the clergy remained uneasy and suspicious of women-run organizations, even where those organizations were charities. Women were instructed that they should not aspire to roles in management (even if the charity were all-female) but could 'carry out practical work under proper direction'.[20]

The Church Missionary Society was the primary forum in which Anglican women in this period could function as overseas missionaries. By 1897, 253 women missionaries (not including wives of missionaries) were associated with the CMS.[21] By 1900, the second largest Anglican missionary society, the Society for the Propagation of the Gospel in Foreign Parts (SPG), had 186 women in the field. Membership in the SPG was formally opened to women in 1921. All women volunteers for the mission field were by this date undergoing a form of training, and the earlier expectation that only upper-class women were useful abroad was breaking down. Working-class women with 'such knowledge of the English language as would make the acquisition of another probable'[22] were being accepted and were arriving in the mission field after two years of language and mission training. Regardless of class, single women missionaries fought a battle for acceptance long after married men's wives were performing all the functions of a missionary, but without the stipend or official recognition of their contribution. Many early women missionaries

[19] Sue Morgan, '"Wild Oats or Acorns?" Social Purity, Sexual Politics and the Response of the Late-Victorian Church', *Journal of Religious History*, 31 (2007), p. 160.

[20] Collett, *Woman's Work*, p. 19.

[21] Gollick, *Women Missionaries*, p. 39. See Thompson, *Into All Lands*, p. 235.

[22] Gollick, *Women Missionaries*, p. 40.

were unpaid and all worked in a situation where their status was unclear. They were authorized by a missionary society, but it was alleged that they laboured 'without status in the Church and without authorization from the archbishops or bishops'.[23] Overseas, female missionaries replicated the work of women in parishes at home. They did not preach or serve in sacramental roles. Even those qualified as doctors were depicted as handmaidens and assistants of the clergy in the exercise of spiritual authority.[24]

Victories in the area of governance, either at home or abroad, were very few. By the end of the nineteenth century women were able to hold the office of churchwarden, and the Representative Church Council had agreed that the franchise of parochial church councils should be extended to women. It was still being discussed by the Convocation of Canterbury (Lower House) whether 'women should receive all rights or privileges granted to laymen' while the First World War was raging.[25]

EFFETE ANGLICANISM

Moving from the growing work of women in Anglicanism to the second major theme of this chapter, we turn to the feminization of the culture of the Church itself. Allegations that Anglicanism was becoming infiltrated by feminine modes of thought, practices, and preferences became widespread after the emergence of the Anglo-Catholic party as an effective minority within the Church (approximately 1850). Some forms of women's work that developed during the period were strongly associated with Anglo-Catholicism, and that in the minds of many laymen was associated with John Henry Newman, who dominated the formative period of the movement before his conversion to Catholicism. Almost equally notorious was Newman's reputation of being the most feminine of men, a trait which caused him to be both loved and despised by his contemporaries.[26]

Cultural criticism of Anglicanism, especially in Britain, focused on a perception of its increasing 'effeminacy'. Antagonists portrayed an effeminate Anglicanism strongly associated with the Anglo-Catholics, and clumped together beliefs that Church of England worship was becoming too attractive to women, was increasingly welcoming to effete men, and was thus off-putting to masculine men. One need only think, for example, of the well-known *Punch*

[23] Gollick, *Women Missionaries*, p. 23.

[24] Gulnar Eleanor Francis-Dehqani, *Religious Feminism in an Age of Empire: CMS Women Missionaries in Iran, 1869–1934* (Bristol, 2000), pp. 39–43, 109–13.

[25] A. Maude Royden, *Women and the Church of England* (London, [1916]), p. 23.

[26] Geoffery Faber, *Oxford Apostles: A Character Study of the Oxford Movement* (London, 1942), pp. 30–5.

cartoon where one curate, surveying his comrade in his new vestments, clasps his hands and exclaims with ecstasy at the becoming nature of the garment. The cartoon was published in an 1866 issue of *Punch*. It is headed 'Height of Fashion' and the caption reads: 'Ardent Ritualist: "Oh, Athanasius, it's charmingly becoming!"'[27] Even at the end of the nineteenth century Protestant/Anglo-Catholic conflicts were still routinely depicted as a 'struggle between masculine and feminine styles of religion'.[28] Opponents of Anglo-Catholicism used the high percentage of women in the congregations as evidence that the religion offered within the walls was sentimental, rather than intellectual, emotional rather than rational, and generally suspect simply because it did appear to be disproportionately attractive to women. The increasing elaboration of church decoration, ornate ritual, and the growth of church music were all blamed for driving away 'manly men' as well.

Even the new discipline of psychology had an explanation for what it depicted as near-universal abandonment of the Church by young men, noting that only 7 per cent were regular attenders, while women were the mainstays of both church work and congregations: 'the qualities demanded are the feminine ones of love, rest, prayer, trust, desire for fortitude to endure—traits not involving ideals that must stir young men . . . The Church has not learned to appeal to the more virile qualities.'[29]

CONCLUSION: THE OUTLIERS AND THE MAINSTREAM

Reflecting on both worship and women's work for the Church, it is possible to see a pattern where the more extreme practices have the effect of making moderate practices acceptable over the course of time. Sisterhoods are a good example of this: they served as lightning rods, attracting enormous criticism, while the cooperative work of women who remained in their family homes while working for the Church became increasingly acceptable, almost by force of contrast. They seemed moderate and amenable to authority in comparison with the sometimes autocratic, and invariably controversial, mothers superior. One of the ironic results of the anti-sisterhood cultural commentary was that it forced spokesmen into being more approving of women's other work in the

[27] *Punch* (22 Dec. 1866), p. 258.

[28] David Hilliard, 'UnEnglish and Unmanly: Anglo-Catholicism and Homosexuality', *Victorian Studies* (Winter 1982), p. 190.

[29] T. R. W. Lunt, 'Preparation of the Young for Personal Service in the Work of the Church', in *Pan Anglican Papers* (London, 1908), SG Group 3, 2, citing the work of G. Stanley Hall, the father of the psychological study of adolescence.

Church. It seemed necessary to admit that women were the natural source of staff for refuges, orphanages, Sunday schools, women's missions, and so on, thus legitimizing roles that had only been tacitly accorded approval before. So while sisterhoods were buffeted by accusations of being disobedient and unnatural, laywomen found themselves able to expand their roles within Anglicanism with less opposition and less scrutiny. This can be seen as an example of how the advanced guard allows the centre of gravity to gradually shift, in this case in a more woman-oriented direction, although with great difficulty and considerable slowness.

Late Victorian discourse within Anglicanism began to acknowledge the immense expansion of activity and of efficiency of women's work for their Church:

> an extraordinary amount of good work has been quietly and unostentatiously, voluntarily and gratuitously, achieved by women. Among the unrecorded Saints of the Church of Christ, there are hundreds of names of wives, widows, and daughters of clergymen, and of single women, who in obscurity have dedicated their lives and their substance to the promotion of the kingdom of God in our own country and in heathen lands.[30]

Pay and official recognition were still not offered, but increasingly the value and the scale of the more conservative work began to be acknowledged.

Overall, it is reasonable to assert that the Anglican Church did undergo significant feminization during the nineteenth century, although this was not desired, or planned, by the Church itself. Much of the grudging acceptance of women's contribution can be seen as an unintended consequence of earlier developments that the Church had viewed with great concern: for example, the exemplars of responsible female leadership in the sisterhoods and the politicization of some Anglican churchwomen through their experience of the social purity movements. It is also true that congregations and communicant lists became steadily more female in composition as the century drew to a close, although this was because of male withdrawal from the pews rather than a positive increase in female participation. But even as it reached its numerical peak and was poised for limited acceptance, Anglican women's work for the Church was about to decline. As many historians have noted, social changes, accelerated by, but not originating in, the First World War, contributed to the decline of Anglican charities, especially those run by women. In 1916, Maude Royden was able to explain why: 'There was a time when religious work was almost the only avenue for a woman's energies, but now the world is all before her where to choose.'[31] Most Anglican women with a sense of vocation chose to be welcomed by agencies outside the Church rather than to be marginalized inside it.

[30] Gollick, *Women Missionaries*, p. 22.
[31] Roydon, *Women and the Church*, p. 13.

SELECT BIBLIOGRAPHY

Brown, Callum, *The Death of Christian Britain: Secularization 1800–2000* (London, 2009 edn.).

Gill, Sean, *Women and the Church of England from the 18th Century to the Present* (London, 1994).

Harrison, Brian, 'For Church, Queen and Family: The Girls' Friendly Society 1874–1920', *Past and Present*, 61 (1973): 107–38.

Hilliard, David, 'UnEnglish and Unmanly: Anglo-Catholicism and Homosexuality', *Victorian Studies* (Winter, 1982): 181–210.

Jones, Timothy Willem, *Sexual Politics in the Church of England, 1857–1957* (Oxford, 2013).

Koven, Seth, *Slumming: Sexual and Social Politics in Victorian London* (Princeton, NJ, 2004).

McEwan, Muriel Lynn, 'Ministering in Affliction: The "Brown Deaconesses" of the Church of Scotland 1888–c.1948', PhD thesis, Open University, 2004.

Mitchell, Patricia Mary Clyne, 'The Girls' Friendly Society, 1875–1900', PhD thesis, Open University, 2003.

Morgan, Sue, '"Wild Oats or Acorns?" Social Purity, Sexual Politics and the Response of the Late-Victorian Church', *Journal of Religious History*, 31 (2007): 151–68.

Mumm, Susan, '"A Peril to the Bench of Bishops": Anglican Sisterhoods and the Church of England, 1845–1908', *Journal of Ecclesiastical History*, 59 (2008): 62–78.

Mumm, Susan, *Stolen Daughters, Virgin Mothers: Anglican Sisterhoods in Victorian Britain* (London and New York, 1999).

Reed, John Shelton, *Glorious Battle: The Cultural Politics of Victorian Anglo-Catholicism* (Nashville, TN, 1999).

23

Anglican Economic and Social Engagement

Jane Garnett

> Twenty-one years ago Karl Marx wrote: 'The English Established Church will more readily pardon an attack on thirty-eight of its thirty-nine articles than on one thirty-ninth of its income'. Today there are probably more followers of Karl Marx in the Church of England than in any other church organisation in the world.

The American Christian Socialist Revd W. D. P. Bliss of Boston was opening an article published in 1888 on 'Socialism in the Church of England'.[1] Deliberately provocative, he was also signalling what he saw as a welcome shift of emphasis within the Church. Intellectual and political debate across the world about the meaning of socialism and its relationship to individualism was intense at this point and into the early twentieth century; and Christian socialism, variously conceived, was presented by many as a dynamic means of transcending that dualism. In 1891 Bliss was to found the American branch of the Anglican Christian Social Union (CSU, started in Britain in 1889). The first volume of Marx's *Capital*, in the preface to which the comment cited by Bliss comes, was published in 1867, the year of the first Lambeth Conference, which was preoccupied with questions of liturgy and Church order, rather than the Church's responsibility in the face of social problems (which were to be the focus in the Conference of 1888). But it would be misleading to see this as emblematic of too sharp a contrast, either in terms of chronology or of the development of Anglican preoccupations. Whilst few Anglicans in fact ever became exactly 'followers' of Marx, many, throughout the nineteenth century, in different idioms, languages, and contexts, identified comparable questions of value and utility to those which Marx addressed, and engaged in their own critiques of the principles underlying classical political economy. These issues

[1] W. D. P. Bliss, 'Socialism in the Church of England', *Andover Review*, 10 (1888), p. 491.

were an integral part of repositioning Anglicanism in its new and rapidly changing national and transnational contexts. For many, they raised comparably significant, maybe even more profound, questions of authority than did debates about the constitution and governance of the Anglican Communion. How could Anglicans build theologically and pastorally on their distinctive religious identity to confront the challenges of expanding capitalism?

The reference to Marx is a reminder of the cosmopolitanism of the Anglican intellectual world. Much has been made of the impact of new technologies of communication on the development of transnational cultures from the last quarter of the nineteenth century, and it is true that there was a significant proliferation of discursive media. The university world expanded considerably at this point, and there was frequent movement of people and ideas to and fro, within the empire and beyond.[2] The Anglican Communion became much larger over the period—growing from forty-eight dioceses (none outside Britain) in 1784 to 251 in 1908. But earlier nineteenth-century Anglican social and economic thought was itself cross-cultural. Missionary and trading networks fostered the multi-directional transmission of people and ideas; Evangelicalism developed in self-consciously global ways, and developed publishing ventures—the Bible Society, the Religious Tract Society—to support the extension and reinforcement of Christianity; High Church and more liberal or Broad Church Anglicans, as well as Evangelicals, read widely and had personal links with North American and continental European social theologians and activists. Popular books, pamphlets, and lectures (such as those given under the auspices of the YMCA at Exeter Hall in London, 1848–68) were published simultaneously or almost simultaneously in different parts of the world. Works on commercial ethics by American Evangelicals—Henry Boardman, Henry Ward Beecher, William Sprague, and Edwin Freedley—were widely read and reviewed by the British Evangelical press, and the American *Merchants' Magazine* published extracts from popular British works.[3] Periodicals associated with different Church parties—the *British Critic*, *Christian Remembrancer*, *Christian Observer*, *Church of England Monthly Review*—whilst they could be theologically pugnacious, were not narrowly sectional. The *Contemporary Review*, founded in 1866 as the Church counterpart to the secular *Fortnightly*, attracted a range of influential writers on social, economic, and theological themes, reviewed widely and acquired a strong international reputation. Later in the century the *Economic Review*, the organ of the Anglican Christian Social Union (CSA), provided a forum for

[2] Tamson Pietsch, *Empire of Scholars: Universities, Networks and the British Academic World, 1850–1939* (Manchester, 2013); Simon J. Potter, 'Webs, Networks and Systems: Globalization and the Mass Media in the Nineteenth- and Twentieth-Century British Empire', *Journal of British Studies*, 46 (2007): 621–36.

[3] Richard Carwardine, *Transatlantic Revivalism: Popular Evangelicalism in Britain and America, 1790–1865* (Westport, CT and London, 1978, 2006).

international debate alongside, and in interaction with, explicitly transatlantic journals like the *International Journal of Ethics*, published in Chicago, or the *Quarterly Journal of Economics*, out of Harvard. All these (and others in France and Italy, building on Catholic social theory[4]) were specifically set up in the 1890s with the purpose of developing systematic thought on the ethical basis of economic life and of making ethics intrinsic rather than extrinsic to economic thinking. The *International Journal of Ethics* and the *Quarterly Journal of Economics* had no particular religious association, but engaged seriously with religious motivation as part of the framework of economic understanding.

The influential British historical economist Herbert Foxwell[5] was invited to contribute an article on 'The Economic Movement in England' for the second volume of the *Quarterly Journal of Economics* in 1887. Fiercely critical of the legacy of Ricardo and of the materialist emphasis of the previous generation of economists, he outlined what he took to have been healthy reactions against it. In the same critical category he put economic theorists like his colleague Alfred Marshall and mentor William Stanley Jevons; historical, biological, and German metaphysical conceptions of social evolution (including Marx's); and moral and humanistic critiques, within which he cited the abolition of slavery, opposition to the 1834 Poor Law, the Christian socialism of the Anglican and Methodist Churches, and the writings of John Ruskin and William Morris. Keen to regain a methodological holism, he argued that:

> Tending as it does, to stimulate the economic imagination and to incite to patient research, the apparent reaction against economic teaching will prove, in the long run, to have greatly aided its reconstruction and widely extended its influence.[6]

In the longer run, and certainly in the heyday of positivistic social scientific confidence in the mid-twentieth century such a hope was to be dashed; but into the early twentieth century his perspective was credible, respected, and widely shared amongst those who thought seriously about the development of the economy.

Foxwell was pointing to a tradition of moral criticism which was well established in Anglicanism, as well as in other Christian denominations. As in other aspects of its identity, Anglican social and economic thought fell on a wide spectrum from conservative to radical. It constituted a field of debate rather than a homogeneous or hegemonic position. It was marked by a high degree of methodological rigour, and conviction that thinking about the

[4] e.g., *La Réforme Sociale*, *Revue Sociale Catholique*, *Rivista Internazionale di Studi Sociali*.

[5] A. L. Bowley, 'Foxwell, Herbert Somerton (1849–1936)', Revd Richard D. Freeman, *Oxford Dictionary of National Biography* (Oxford, 2004). <http://ezproxy.ouls.ox.ac.uk:2204/view/article/33239>, accessed 25 Aug. 2014.

[6] Herbert Foxwell, 'The Economic Movement in England', *Quarterly Journal of Economics*, 2 (1887): 84–103.

economy could not be separated from fundamental questions about the functioning of society and the values by which that society wished to live: questions of the quality of life. It followed that for those who took theology seriously, there was serious concern for theological coherence in approaches to thinking about the economy. This point requires emphasis, because strikingly persistent anachronism has dogged modern scholarship on nineteenth- and twentieth-century economic thought, and there has been too little conversation between historians of political economy whose background is in economics and historians of religious and theological ideas. It has thus been possible to continue to suggest that Christian ethical engagement with the economy was either unscientific and sentimental or simply derivative, denying it independent methodological traction; and to project a twentieth-century definition of economics onto the nineteenth century. A. M. C Waterman's book of essays of 2004, presented as a contribution to closer interaction between historians of economics and religion, tends ironically to end up reinforcing the divide: the author's own teleology of nineteenth-century secularization (the corollary of a mid-to-late twentieth-century social scientific world-view) occluding what was in fact a much richer understanding of the nature and scope of economics in the late nineteenth and early twentieth centuries.[7] A collection of essays of 2008 on political economy (in its turn reflective of a widening early twenty-first-century economic lens)[8] marks a welcome desire to take seriously religiously-motivated economic criticism, but it too draws on a limited knowledge of nineteenth-century religious historiography. In developing a discussion of some of the wealth of Anglican economic and social thought over the long nineteenth century, this chapter furthers the conversation now opening up again between economists and moral philosophers, which in many respects reprises much earlier confrontations of utilitarianism and a relational 'ethics of care'.[9]

Concerns about social ethics and political economy were integral to debates about Anglican identity as a whole which developed in the early decades of the nineteenth century—in response to American independence, the intellectual and socio-political aftermath of the French Revolution, union with Ireland, the expanding British Empire, the repeal of the Test and Corporation Acts and Catholic Emancipation in 1828–9, and consequent constitutional challenges. It is in part because of the intensity of Church party tensions in the 1830s–1850s, and their long historiographical legacy, that both the nature and the

[7] A. M. C. Waterman, *Political Economy and Christian Theology since the Enlightenment* (Basingstoke, 2004), ch. 13, 'Establishment Social Thinking'; cf. his earlier *Revolution, Economics and Religion: Christian Political Economy, 1798–1833* (Cambridge and New York, 1991).

[8] Bradley Bateman and H. Spencer Bauzhaf, 'Keeping Faith, Losing Faith: An Introduction', *History of Political Economy*, 40 (2008): 1–20.

[9] Martha Nussbaum and Amartya Sen, *The Quality of Life* (Oxford, 1998); Virginia Held, *The Ethics of Care: Personal, Political and Global* (Oxford, 2005).

chronology of Anglican social and economic thought in the nineteenth century have been distorted. The Anglican Christian socialism of the 1840s and 1850s associated with Frederick Denison Maurice and Charles Kingsley was not on the whole controversial in Anglican circles for its confrontation of difficult issues of individual and social responsibility, nor even for its direct engagement with the language of socialism—Maurice's commitment to 'the conflict we must engage with sooner or later with the unsocialist Christians and the unchristian Socialists'[10]—but for the theology which underpinned it.[11] Evangelicals and High Churchmen were contemporaneously constructing social and economic ethics rooted in their respective theologies, which they often perceived and presented as more rigorous, provoking in turn Broad Church criticisms of Evangelical and Tractarian/Anglo-Catholic narrowness and dogmatism.[12] All have tended to be taken too much at face value.[13] What they were all contributing to was a complex debate about the place of Anglican influence in the world, in the face of what seemed increasingly urgent challenges, both moral and ecclesiological. Whilst individual manifestations of it waxed and waned, and there were distinct moments of self-conscious revival,[14] the debate continued to develop throughout the century and into the next.

A fundamental issue was the epistemological and moral status of political economy, whose laws by the 1830s threatened to claim a universal hegemony. Assimilated to a Christian natural theology, an interrelationship between the providential order and economic progress could seem to validate a synergy between the pursuit of individual self-interest and social good, and a happy affinity between Christian and utilitarian impulses. The concerns of critical Anglican clergy and laypeople were not just with the intellectual plausibility of political economy, but with the moral and psychological effects of such a belief in self-acting economic laws. In a rapidly expanding economy which was yet subject to sudden and intense fluctuations, this could lead alternately to complacency, to a damaging sense of human impotence, or to a compartmentalization of values between the marketplace and other spheres of activity. People might begin to turn away from a religious frame of reference because it could not help them to address the challenges of ordinary moral experience. Given that Britain's national reputation was bound up with the beneficence of

[10] Frederick D. Maurice (ed.), *Life of Frederick Denison Maurice*, 2 vols. (London, 1884), II, p. 35.

[11] *Christian Observer*, 50 (1850), p. 871.

[12] John R. Seeley, 'The Church as a Teacher of Morality', in W. L. Clay (ed.), *Essays on Church Policy* (London, 1868), pp. 267–75; [W. J. Conybeare], 'Church Parties', *Edinburgh Review*, 200 (1853): 273–42.

[13] Torben Christensen, *Origin and History of Christian Socialism 1848–54* (Aarhus, 1962).

[14] David M. Thompson, 'The Christian Socialist Revival in Britain: A Reappraisal', in Jane Garnett and Colin Matthew (eds.), *Revival and Religion since 1700* (London, 1993), pp. 273–95.

her economic progress, and that this was conceived as inherently related to the values of a Christian, and in fact broadly Protestant religious system, it was increasingly realized that there was considerable scope for ethical slippage between these interlinked categories. Apart from affecting the moral and social health of the nation (and thereby in turn undermining economic progress), such slippage would also affect Britain's reputation abroad (and her expanding global ambitions). Such a challenge was felt by all Christians: Protestant Nonconformists defending the moral dynamic of the Protestant conscience; Catholics critical of aspects of capitalist culture which seemed corrupted by Protestant individualism; Anglicans from across the theological spectrum who related their discussion of political economy to their respective conceptions of Anglican authority. As Britain's economic model spearheaded capitalist expansion world-wide, the ramifications of these debates were widely felt.

At a formal academic level in England, debate had begun in the late 1820s and 1830s in Oxford and Cambridge, self-conscious epicentres of Anglican intellectual authority, and educators of the British and imperial political elite. In Oxford, Richard Whately, concerned especially after 1829 with the project of constructing a stronger intellectual rationale for the Christian identity of the university (under a broad liberal Anglican umbrella), demarcated the scientific realm of political economy (whose conclusions were susceptible to deductive logic) from that of policy and practice (where religious moral authority could and should apply)—a standpoint which was essentially to support that of J. S. Mill. The conceptual implications of such a division were challenged by William Whewell and Richard Jones in Cambridge, who drew on new understandings of the simultaneous interactions of elements provided by chemistry to affirm a more holistic approach to political economy.[15] At an academic level, however, this sort of insight remained undeveloped, and the writings of Ricardo and Mill, provided with a Christian framework by Whately and others, continued to dominate political economy in English universities until the late 1860s and 1870s. Yet it is important to see this academic culture within a wider context, and to recognize the richness and complexity of critical debate which took off outside the curricula of the ancient universities, and which had a lasting theoretical and practical influence both within and beyond them. The two worlds were not in fact so separate. Whately recognized the importance of popular education for general reform: his book *Easy Lessons on Money Matters for the Use of Young People* (1833), derived from his lectures on political economy, was distributed through the SPCK and translated into many languages (including Māori and Japanese). In his role as archbishop of Dublin from 1831, he instituted a systematic promotion of political economy

[15] William Whewell, *On the Universality of Definitions* (London, 1832), p. 266; William Whewell (ed.), *Literary Remains, Consisting of Lectures and Tracts on Political Economy, of the late Rev. Richard Jones* (London, 1859), pp. 598–600.

(from university to elementary schools) as an agent of social progress, associated with an inclusive ideology of beneficent Anglican cultural hegemony—a modernizing strategy with analogies in British India and Australasia.[16] The encounter of a universalizing economic ideology conceived in an Anglo-Scottish environment with the radically different economy and culture of southern and western Ireland was to provoke the development of a critical counter-cultural Irish political economy at a popular and academic level, in Anglican as well as Catholic circles.[17] This stressed the significance of cultural and religious particularities, and specifically underlined communal as opposed to individualistic imperatives in the Irish context. It was not coincidental that two of the earliest historically grounded academic challenges to classical political economy in English circles were to come from Anglican Dublin: from Thomas Cliffe Leslie and James Kell Ingram in the 1860s and 1870s. As well as being grounded in awareness of historical differences in Ireland, they were to draw on a wide range of social thought and experience from within England and beyond, in France, Belgium, and the German states over the previous decades. Ireland was also to be a point of comparative reference in heated policy debates over poverty, in which Whately was engaged, as were many other Anglican clergy and laity from diverse theoretical vantage points. J. B. Sumner, from 1828 to 1848 bishop of Chester (from 1848 archbishop of Canterbury), who was a member of the Poor Law Commission behind the 1834 Poor Law Amendment Act, had published in 1814 *A Treatise on the Records of Creation, and on the Moral Attributes of the Creator*, an influential work of natural theology on which Whately drew in the development of his ideas on political economy. In his own diocesan educational projects and ecclesiastical charges, which were also more widely disseminated, Sumner's religious message was a conservative Evangelical Malthusianism, increasingly challenged and debated by fellow Evangelicals as well as members of other Church parties.

Religious opposition to the principles of the 1834 Poor Law (one of Foxwell's examples of important challenges to political economy), building on the perception that it embodied the most corrupting assumptions of political economy and utilitarianism, was intense and variegated. It illustrates very clearly both the widespread Anglican resistance to what was seen as the spread of market values and the theological specificity of the critiques developed.

[16] Norman Vance, 'Improving Ireland: Richard Whately, Theology, and Political Economy', in Stefan Collini, Richard Whatmore, and Brian Young (eds.), *Economy, Polity, and Society: British Intellectual History, 1750–1950* (Cambridge, 2000), pp. 181–202; Richard Brent, 'God's Providence: Liberal Political Economy as Natural Theology at Oxford 1825–62', in Michael Bentley (ed.), *Public and Private Doctrine* (Cambridge, 1993), pp. 85–107.

[17] Thomas A. Boylan and Timothy P. Foley, *Political Economy and Colonial Ireland: The Propagation and Ideological Function of Economic Discourse in the Nineteenth Century* (London, 1992).

Tractarian hostility to the 'never-wearied, never-satisfied, pursuit of Mammon... to the exclusion of all deep, all holy, all calm, all reverent thoughts'[18] found voice in sermons, tracts, and fiction, as well as in the pages of the *British Critic*, published in Oxford under Tractarian control from 1838 to 1843. The vibrant social theology thus formed built on Tractarian founding principles of spiritual renewal, incarnationalism, and the reassertion of apostolic authority in opposition to liberalism and Erastianism.[19] It involved criticism of what were perceived as both High Church and Evangelical compromises with the world. It shared features with romantic, paternalist High Tory medievalism, but its distinctiveness lay in its affirmation of the Church and of the parish as the only agents of amelioration. The New Poor Law's institution of an administrative system of unions which cut across established parish boundaries and undermined the principle of parochial responsibility was anathema. Socially conservative, the Tractarians were religiously and morally radical. When Frederick Oakeley called the Bible 'a *levelling* Book', this was not a plea for social but for spiritual equality—for the Church to reclaim its proper role as the defender of the poor.[20] The Tractarian appeal for a transformation of public attitudes was in this respect very comparable to that called for by Kingsley and Maurice, or by many Evangelicals, but the nexus of this transformation was a different ecclesiology of Church and state in each case. Maurice's theology envisioned a national Church which in its very breadth—conceptually and historically defined—embodied the principle of divine immanence. The commitment to social and moral activism on behalf of the poor, and to the promotion of working-class associations and education, was rooted in a sacramental inclusivity. When Kingsley preached a sermon in London on *The Message of the Church to Labouring Men* in 1851, very shortly after the 1848–9 European revolutions, and used the language of liberty, equality, and fraternity (in their 'fullest, deepest, widest, simplest meaning'), his was not a call for social upheaval but for the grasping of social and environmental responsibility. But his framing of the sacraments could be seen as a challenge to orthodox teaching: 'Baptism works no miracle; it proclaims a miracle which has been from all eternity... In that font is a witness for education and for sanitary reform.'[21] Both Tractarian and Mauricean sacramentalism, in their several but analogous ways, were to underpin an ongoing Anglican

[18] John Henry Newman, *Parochial and Plain Sermons*, 8 vols., ed. W. J. Copeland (London, 1868), VIII, p. 160.

[19] S. A. Skinner, *Tractarians and the 'Condition of England': The Social and Political Thought of the Oxford Movement* (Oxford, 2004).

[20] Frederick Oakeley, *The Dignity and Claims of the Christian Poor: Two Sermons* (London, 1840), pp. 15–16.

[21] Charles Kingsley, *The Message of the Church to Labouring Men* (London, 1851), pp. 21, 23; cf. Frederick D. Maurice, 'On Preaching to the Poor', in *Sermons Preached in Lincoln's Inn Chapel*, 2 vols. (London, 1860 edn.), II, pp. 314–15.

impetus to critical engagement with political economy. Meanwhile, a burgeoning Evangelical social activism took root in a variety of distinctive theological forms at the same period; grounded both in re-articulation of the atonement and the Incarnation, and in a strengthened sense of the sanctification of the nation and the temporal world as a whole.[22]

One of the most characteristic Evangelical responses to concerns about poverty was also to focus on the duties of those with wealth. Encouraged by the formation in 1856 of the American Systematic Beneficence Society, in 1860 its British counterpart was founded on an interdenominational basis; the inaugural meeting was presided over by Sir Culling Eardley, president of the Evangelical Alliance. In its emphasis on the necessarily interrelated systematization of individuals' commitments to hard work (and business success), fair treatment of employees, family responsibilities, church and charitable giving of not just money but time, it encouraged a higher degree of moral rigour in the construction of a coherent religious life. Instead of focusing on the moral degradation of the poor (as the New Poor Law did), or on concerns about their de-motivation through indiscriminate giving (as the Charity Organization Society, founded in 1869, was to do), the Society shifted the spotlight to problematize the moral and religious state of those with resources to give and responsibility for others. Although the cultural hegemony of *laissez faire* economics, and the assimilation of its laws to Christian natural theology, meant that these members of the middle classes were the less likely to realize it, they were in fact the social group most vulnerable to its demoralizing and corrupting effects: they urgently needed to examine their consciences.[23]

Evangelicals (Anglican and Nonconformist), disproportionately represented in the business community, and aware that this profile could lead to an unfortunate association in the public mind between commercial expediency and Evangelical hypocrisy, were particularly concerned to develop detailed ethical guidance for their own communities. But they also wanted to contribute to a wider debate about the utilities and values which should properly be involved in the development of more sophisticated economic models and in interrelated reflection on the relationship between legal regulation and the role of trust. In the form of sermons, pamphlets, exemplary biography, and periodical literature, as well as more lengthy philosophical and theological

[22] Ralph Brown, 'Victorian Anglican Evangelicalism: The Radical Legacy of Edward Irving', *Journal of Ecclesiastical History*, 58 (2007): 675–704; Boyd Hilton, 'Evangelical Social Attitudes: A Reply to Ralph Brown', *Journal of Ecclesiastical History*, 60 (2009): 119–25; Ralph Brown, 'Evangelical Social Thought', *Journal of Ecclesiastical History*, 60 (2009): 126–36; Martin Spence, 'The Renewal of Time and Space: The Missing Element of Discussion about Nineteenth-Century Premillennialism', *Journal of Ecclesiastical History*, 63 (2012): 81–101.

[23] Jane Garnett, '"Gold and the Gospel": Systematic Beneficence in Mid-Nineteenth-Century England', in W. J. Shiels and Diana Wood (eds.), *The Church and Wealth: Studies in Church History 24* (Oxford, 1987), pp. 347–58.

treatises, they provided a sustained and serious contribution to economic debate from the 1840s onwards, providing a fertile ground for the reception of Ruskin and other critics who sought to widen economic discourse in the later part of the century.[24] They underlined how fundamentally commercial confidence depended on assumptions about ethical behaviour, itself at least partly religious in origin. Legal reformers indeed argued that inadequate or impossibly cumbersome legal structures could themselves have the paradoxical effect of encouraging commercial immorality.[25] Evangelicals contributed to parliamentary debate in the 1850s and 1860s on the reform of bankruptcy legislation and the establishment of limited liability, in both of which contexts there was a complex interplay between the encouragement of large-scale enterprise and the critical role of individual responsibility. Distinctions between legitimate and illegitimate trading needed to be made with reference to how scrupulously accounts had been kept, credit-worthiness monitored, moral principles maintained over the longer term, not just at the moments of crisis when resort to the law would be triggered.[26] This required a more refined set of legal principles than currently operating, as well as a higher degree of ethical accountability. In other areas of commercial legislation, the bar was deliberately set very low: the law regarding adulteration of goods was very limited on the ground that competition was the best regulator. Moralists pointed out, though, that, even apart from the risks to public health, at stake here was the reputation of the entire trading community, and by extension of the nation as a whole.[27] The pioneer and promoter of joint stock banking, J. W. Gilbart, whose works on banking in England, Ireland, and America were extremely influential, set out the collective moral and religious responsibilities of public companies with reference to detailed scriptural exegesis: he urged that public companies should endeavour to promote each other's interest, and that banking and insurance companies should be 'pitiful', being as accommodating as possible when honest clients were in trouble.[28] Keen to disseminate principles of corporate responsibility, he endowed the Gilbart Lectures at King's College, London, which took place annually from 1872 until 1998.

In 1868 F. D. Maurice gave a series of lectures at Cambridge, published in 1869 as *Social Morality*. Drawing on the methodology of his *Kingdom of Christ*

[24] See Jane Garnett, 'Evangelicalism and Business in Mid-Victorian Britain', in John Wolffe (ed.), *Evangelical Faith and Public Zeal: Evangelicals and Society in Britain 1780–1980* (London, 1995), pp. 59–80.

[25] Jane Garnett, 'Commercial Ethics: A Victorian Perspective on the Practice of Theory', in Christopher Cowton and Roger Crisp (eds.), *Business Ethics: The Practice of Theory* (Oxford, 1998), pp. 117–38.

[26] *Christian Observer*, 1858, p. 82; *Record*, no. 3499, 10 Jan. 1859, p. 2.

[27] *Record*, no. 3049, 25 Feb. 1856, p. 2.

[28] J. W. Gilbart, *A Practical Treatise on Banking*, 2 vols. (London, 1849 edn.), II, pp. 687–8; cf. pp. 674–9. Also his *The Moral and Religious Duties of Public Companies* (London, 1846).

of 1838, he invoked a series of historical examples to develop his argument both for the mutual interdependence of the individual and the collective, and for the overarching and sustaining reality of the universal Kingdom of Christ. Individual, family, nation, and Church were providentially intertwined, each realizing its moral integrity in the interrelationship of part and whole. In the development of his analysis, Maurice deployed a deconstructed notion of gender to underline the complex mutuality of the domestic and the civil, and to resist conventionally binary understandings of the feminine and the masculine; such a focus on gender was to inflect the most imaginative critiques of classical political economy in the second half of the nineteenth century.[29] Distinctively rooted in his own theological background, Maurice's language and points of reference were characteristic of the 1860s, and his concerns were to resonate widely at this point. He drew on Henry Maine's *Ancient Law* (1861) on the individual and the family, and engaged critically with then-fashionable Comtean positivism. In his own first lecture series, Maurice's successor as Knightbridge Professor of Moral Philosophy, the Evangelical T. R. Birks, took on J. S. Mill as his critical target in developing his arguments for a more morally integrated political economy.[30] A utilitarianism which represented society as simply an aggregate of individuals was being challenged philosophically to an increasing extent at this period both by historical work and by evolutionary thinking predicated on organic conceptions of society, in which it was more possible to develop ideas of altruism and of common good.[31] For both the religiously committed and the agnostic, methodological individualism and deterministic evolutionism posed equivalent difficulties for a dynamic sense of moral agency and purpose. The revival of philosophical idealism, associated especially with T. H. Green in Oxford in the 1870s and 1880s, was to provide an impetus behind renewed religious confidence, and (in opposition both to absolute idealism and to crude materialism) the development of new forms of Christian moral philosophy. The study of history was inherently bound up with questions of religious and national identity, and of the cultivation of critical self-understanding. All of these debates related to the Church's critical confrontation of the liberal individualism on which capitalism was built, at a time when social investigation and increased awareness of economic complexity themselves suggested refinements of conceptual approach.

The relationship between individual religious purpose and social morality was thus fundamental to Anglican as to non-Anglican intellectual reflection. It

[29] Jane Garnett, 'Political and Domestic Economy in Victorian Britain: Ruskin and Xenophon', in Collini et al. (eds.), *Economy, Polity and Society*, pp. 205–23.

[30] T. R. Birks, *First Principles of Moral Science* (London, 1873), pp. 142–63.

[31] Charles D. Cashdollar, *The Transformation of Theology, 1830–1890: Positivism and Protestant Thought in Britain and America* (Princeton, NJ, 1989); Thomas Dixon, *The Invention of Altruism: Making Moral Meanings in Victorian Britain* (Oxford, 2008).

also needs to be emphasized (not least as another aspect of an embodied intellectual history) that this period was a moment also of renewed emphasis on the necessary interrelationship between thought and action, the theoretical and the practical. Vindicating the role of the critic in 1864, Matthew Arnold stressed the particular contemporary dangers of heedless (and headlong) activity.[32] F. D. Maurice's disciple, the housing and environmental reformer Octavia Hill, concurred, and emphasized the role of training and the cultivation of understanding as a process which was itself intrinsically morally transformative. She pleaded further (in Mauricean idiom) for the practical invigoration of ideas as living principles, rather than nostrums frozen in dogma.[33] More widely, members of the Anglican Church debated the need both to respond thoughtfully to new ideas, and to articulate responses in such a way as to fuse the theoretical and the experiential. This in turn implied fresh consideration of the Church's own organizational models and histories and their relationship to the individual and civil society within Britain and in the wider Anglican Communion. Different forms of association and affinity were argued for and practised, but the principle of association was fundamental.

Anglican Evangelicalism built strongly on its own history in this context. Interrelated Evangelical networks of the sort which had flourished in the late eighteenth and early nineteenth centuries, grounded in intense piety and a fervent sense of moral responsibility, continued to proliferate well into the twentieth century, manifesting a strong and deliberative synergy between theological seriousness, practical activism, and wider consciousness-raising whose significance has often been underplayed. As one example among many, the philanthropic and reformist activities of the Noel, Buxton, and Kinnaird families had world-wide ramifications. Self-consciously maintaining the traditions of their respective families, Sir (Thomas) Fowell Buxton and his wife, Lady Victoria (née Noel), worked together in political and social service, supporting, among other organizations, the British and Foreign Anti-Slavery Society (of which he was president from 1899), the Church Missionary Society, and societies concerned with the welfare of Africans. Sir Thomas and his brother were members of the Commons Preservation Society and campaigned from 1866 to save Epping Forest. From 1895 he was Governor of South Australia, where he promoted education and awareness of Aboriginal land rights, and hosted the first convention to discuss the constitution of a united Australia; Lady Kinnaird established girls' clubs, and was founding

[32] Matthew Arnold, 'The Function of Criticism at the Present Time' [*National Review*, 1864], Essays in Criticism, First Series in *Complete Prose Works of Matthew Arnold*, 11 vols., ed. R. H. Super (Ann Arbor, MI, 1962), III.

[33] Octavia Hill, 'Blank Court; or, Landlords and Tenants', *Macmillan's Magazine*, 24 (1 May 1871): 458–9; cf. *Octavia Hill's Letters to Fellow-Workers 1872–1911*, ed. Robert Whelan (London, 2005), pp. 266–7, 115, 247–8, 291–2, 511; *Life of Octavia Hill as Told in her Letters*, ed. C. E. Maurice (London, 1913), pp. 33, 535.

president of the Mothers' Union in South Australia. As a niece of Emily Jane Kinnaird, the founder of the YWCA, Victoria Buxton was also an active supporter of that organization in Adelaide. From the Kinnairds' house in London, Bible reading and a large number of Evangelical societies (such as the British Ladies' Female Emigration Society and the Christian Colportage Association) and campaigns (including one in 1871 against the slave trade on the West African coast) were spearheaded. Lady Kinnaird was a key participant in the Evangelical revivals of 1859–60 and 1873–4, and later much involved in the Mildmay Conferences. She was particularly engaged with women's education in India, a cause which her daughters were to continue to promote. One of her daughters, Emily, as well as helping to enable the YWCA to expand internationally, took a leading role in creating the Council of Women Workers (later the National Council of Women), and was energetically concerned with boosting women's skills and influence. Noel Buxton, one of the sons of Fowell and Victoria, in addition to continuing the campaign for the worldwide abolition of slavery, worked extensively on the international stage from the very early twentieth century, culminating in his role as president of the Save the Children Fund from 1930 to his death in 1948. His cousin, Conrad Noel, inspired by Maurice's sacramental universalism, but also by his father's interests in Romanticism and by his family's Evangelical activism, was to become the radical Christian socialist vicar of Thaxted (from 1910). Evangelical family histories might, as in this last case (and as has more generally been assumed to have been the norm), be transmuted into new religious or secular forms,[34] but many in fact maintained and renewed their specifically Evangelical impetus in new and developing forms of social engagement.

Reflection on Anglican history was deeply practical. Only an understanding of human experience in the past could underpin conviction in the present. The relationship between the Church, the nation, a wider history of the Christian Church, and the universal kingdom of Christ bore both on the authority of Anglicanism and the responsibility of individual Anglicans. How could individual and social energy be mutually harnessed in the service of a higher principle than self-interest and materialism? How could Anglican association best be articulated within a growing world-wide communion? Different theologies and ecclesiologies drove varied interpretations in a rich debate which in turn informed social and economic theory and practice, in part through a more complex engagement with the history of the Reformation and the Catholic pre-Reformation world. A range of examples is indicative of some of the further contours of this debate from different theological perspectives. The High Church William Stubbs, hostile to excessive faith in the rise of Parliament, as also to over-Protestant interpretations of the Reformation, saw

[34] Cf. Christopher Tolley, *Domestic Biography: The Legacy of Evangelicalism in Four Nineteenth-Century Families* (Oxford, 1997).

the historic apostolic Church in England as the cradle of civil liberties, defining nation and individual through the parochial and diocesan structure.[35] As specific reinforcement of the dynamic potential of a national Church, his High Church narrative of Anglican continuity from the Anglo-Saxon period could find surprising affinities with, as well as occasions for debate over, the radically Arnoldian conception of the parish as a little nation developed in theory and in lived experience in London by his slightly younger Oxford contemporary W. H. Fremantle.[36] The explicit cosmopolitanism of Fremantle's notion of Anglicanism building up from the local to the global through concentric circles of Christian energy, as well as his celebration of the founding ideals of New England religious culture, made his work resonate particularly in an American context.[37] Stewart Headlam, founder of the Anglo-Catholic lay and clerical Guild of St Matthew in 1877, had been inspired by Maurice's lectures as an undergraduate, and alongside a ritualist sacramentalism wanted to align the Anglican Church incarnationally with the labour movement in the promotion of social justice.[38] J. M. Ludlow, Kingsley's and Maurice's Christian socialist colleague—by religious affiliation a French Protestant, Anglican by association—wrote in the *Contemporary Review* in 1872–3 two influential articles drawing a line of continuity between medieval parish guilds and modern friendly societies. In their embodiment of vibrant religious mutuality and voluntarism, the maintenance of such bodies was, he argued, the secret of a healthy state.[39] This was the age of both the parochial and extra-parochial club, and the role of such associational culture as a social and educational microcosm of the wider Church was seen to be equally vital by those who held pluralist and consensual views of Church and state.

Meanwhile the British, imperial, and non-British potentialities of Anglicanism were bound up with wider concerns about social and economic ethics. James Anthony Froude, often wrongly categorized as a Protestant apologist and disregarded in his ongoing Anglican affinity, criticized the way in which the history of the Reformation had been abused by Protestants as well as Catholics, and especially castigated Protestant complacency which supported an unthinking liberalism in nineteenth-century Britain. As editor of *Fraser's Magazine* he published a series of articles on political economy by Ruskin

35 William Stubbs, *Clericalism: A Sermon* (1881), p. 11.

36 W. H. Fremantle, *The World as the Subject of Redemption* (London, 1883), p. 335; Paul T. Phillips, 'The Concept of a National Church in Late Nineteenth-Century England and America', *Journal of Religious History*, 14 (1986): 26–37.

37 Fremantle, *The World as the Subject of Redemption*, pp. 227–30, 322–5.

38 Stewart Headlam, *The Service of Humanity* (London, 1882); Sidney Webb, 'Socialism in England', *American Economic Association*, 4 (1889): 34–9.

39 J. M. Ludlow, 'Gilds and Friendly Societies', *Contemporary Review*, 21 (1872–3): 553–72, 737–62; Cf. Daniel Weinbren, 'The Good Samaritan Friendly Societies and the Gift Economy', *Social History*, 31 (2006): 319–36; Dan Weinbren and Bob James, 'Getting a Grip: The Roles of Friendly Societies in Australia and Britain Reappraised', *Labour History*, 88 (2005): 87–103.

(after the controversial articles which became *Unto This Last* had been discontinued in the *Cornhill Magazine*), and also gave space to the Irish political economist Cliffe Leslie who criticized from an Irish perspective the principles of free-market economics dominant in England. Froude's idea of commonwealth, developed in *Oceana* (1886), was especially significant for an integrated understanding of the reciprocities of Church, nation, and empire. He argued that the empire was a moral and spiritual test: the Church had the potential (not yet realized, in his view), through the exercise of a better understanding of the dynamics of its own history as well as that of the colonies, to help build creative energies at the periphery, not just direct them from the metropolis. The progressive constitutional, social, and moral narrative of British imperialism had reached its Liberal Anglican imperial apogee in J. R. Seeley's *The Expansion of England* (1883). With just as strong a view of the Christian nation—to him the nation was a Christian nation or it was nothing—Froude was much more refined in probing the dangers of a complacent reliance on such a belief. He compared unfavourably the role of the Church of England in the West Indies with that of the Catholics in Dominica, and cited critically a High Anglican sermon in Melbourne which had extolled England's providential role of representing the spirit of Christ: 'It was good to tell us to exhibit Christ's spirit; but was flattering our vanity the best way to bring us to it?'[40]

Anglican contributions specifically to the study of economic history in this period were significant for complicating linear progressive narratives and challenging the validity of universal economic laws; in doing so, they provided an impetus both to social and political action and to theoretical redefinition. They drew on and fostered cross-cultural conversations within Anglican or Episcopalian circles, and tended, in an imperial context, as Froude's perspective did, to support federal cooperation and interaction. In 1888 the committed lay Anglican W. J. Ashley was to move from Oxford to the University of Toronto to be the first Professor of Political Economy (combined with constitutional history). His inaugural lecture proclaimed that *laissez faire* was no longer 'acceptable as a general principle... each case... must be decided on its merits', and with reference to a wide range of considerations. Into the early twentieth century the teaching of economics, commerce, and politics in Toronto were intertwined with economic history and geography, modern languages, and accountancy. The universities of Toronto and Birmingham, where Ashley was to move in 1901 to be Professor of Commerce (having gone to Harvard as the first Professor of Economic History in the world in 1892),

[40] James A. Froude, *Oceana; or, England and her colonies* (London, 1886), p. 98; cf. Jane Garnett, 'Protestant Histories: James Anthony Froude, Partisanship and National Identity', in Peter Ghosh and Lawrence Goldman (eds.), *Politics and Culture in Victorian Britain* (Oxford, 2006), pp. 171–91.

were pioneers within the British Empire of undergraduate commerce degrees, grounded in theory, organizational practice, and general cultivation (in deliberate contradistinction to American courses in 'scientific management').[41] Such an approach to commerce was intended to provide humane training for leaders and citizens. Whilst in America, Ashley became a friend of Richard Ely, who, like William Bliss, had converted to Episcopalianism through being inspired by the ideal of a national Church. Particularly influential seems to have been the liberal ecclesiology of Thomas Arnold and A. P. Stanley, in part mediated through William Fremantle's *The World as the Subject of Redemption* and awareness of Fremantle's parochial work in London to invigorate lay social activism. Bliss and the Wellesley academic and settlement worker Vida Scudder (both passionate Mauriceans) were to found the Christian Socialist Church of the Carpenter in Boston. Ely followed through the international potential of a world-wide Christian society into support for transnational organizations (like labour unions) and ideas of world federation. A historicist and idealist, like Ashley also informed by German economic thought, his *Introduction to Political Economy*, which sold half a million copies, opened with the affirmation that Christianity provided 'our highest conception of a society which embraces all men'.[42] The English economic historian and clergyman William Cunningham, also strongly influenced by Maurice, taught alongside Ashley at Harvard in 1899. Both took their strong inductivist and historicist principles with them to North America, where they were affirmed in the context of a stronger historical tradition of institutional economics. Both became supporters of tariff reform, as part of a convinced social imperialism grounded in a rationale which was simultaneously economic and Anglican.

All these individuals, on both sides of the Atlantic, were involved in the Anglican CSU. Founded in Britain in 1889, it was dedicated to the cultivation of an associational culture which could foster serious and informed debate and perform a religiously and morally educative role—the outworking of Anglican renewal. It operated through branches in towns and cities (sixty-eight in Britain by 1911), which were themselves broken down into sub-branches. The same theme was discussed each year, and the perspectives of different places were compared and debated: the historical method in action. Affiliates in the United States, Canada, Australia, and New Zealand proliferated in the

[41] Ian M. Drummond, *Political Economy at the University of Toronto: A History of the Department 1888–1982* (Toronto, 1983); A. B. McKillop, *Matters of Mind: The University in Ontario, 1791–1951* (Toronto, 1994); W. J. Ashley, *Commercial Education* (London, 1925).

[42] Richard T. Ely, *Introduction to Political Economy* (1889); cf. *The Past and the Present of Political Economy* (Baltimore, MD, 1884); Luigi Bradizza, *Richard T. Ely's Critique of Capitalism* (New York, 2013); Donald E. Frey, 'The Impact of Liberal Religion on Richard Ely's Economic Methodology', in Bradley W. Bateman and H. Spencer Bauzhaf (eds.), *Keeping Faith, Losing Faith: An Introduction, History of Political Economy*, 40, supplement (2008): 299–313.

1890s. Local social investigations (for example into housing conditions) were sponsored, settlement houses set up, and—most innovatively—'white lists' of honest tradespeople in each area were published to assist responsible consumer behaviour and thus encourage honourable trading practices and the improvement of quality. The Executive Annual Report of 1898 noted the publication of white lists in Oxford, Birkenhead, Leeds, Leicester, Manchester, and London (Leicester's included 235 firms, Manchester's 700, London's 500).[43] As well as organizing public debates, and publishing pamphlets on specific issues, from 1891 to 1914 the British CSU published the *Economic Review*, designed to 'infuse economic thinking with history and Christian faith'. Its editors were W. J. H. Campion,[44] one of the contributors to the incarnationalist essays of 1889, *Lux Mundi* (also secretary to the Oxford House Settlement in Bethnal Green, London); the Canadian John Carter, who had come over to Oxford in the mid-1880s, served his curacy in the East End of London, and returned to Oxford as librarian of Pusey House (and honorary secretary of the CSU); and L. R. Phelps, Oxford tutor and city councillor who lectured on economics to generations of those studying for entry to the Indian and Sudanese civil services. In 1892 they were joined by Hastings Rashdall, a liberal churchman and historically minded moral philosopher who stressed the importance of developing a specific and differentiated ethical casuistry.[45] All were committed to the Church's role in active citizenship and the wide extension of education. In 1896 the *Commonwealth* was established as a more popular periodical, funded by a businessman who, in 1894 and 1895, had attended the Lent sermons—published as *Lombard Street in Lent*—organized by the CSU in the City of London.

The first editorial of the *Economic Review* declared its intention to address 'Economic Morals from the Point of View of Christian Teaching'. Acknowledging the combined legacy of Evangelicalism and Tractarianism as models of the force of personal religion and corporate church life, they also commended Aquinas (on whom Ashley had written for Palgrave's *Dictionary of Political Economy*) for his precision, subtlety, and—most importantly, as they articulated it—demonstration of the impossibility of drawing a sharp line between the spheres of the economic moralist and of the scientific economist. Aquinas here stood for an understanding of economics as an integral part of the religious and moral order. Serious engagement with historical and contemporary Catholic thought was to be a consistent thread. Asserting that for the Anglican Church as a whole to be socially effective the prerequisite was

[43] Oxford, Pusey House: CSU, Central Annual Report, 1898, cit. A. A. Eckbert, 'The Social Thought of the Christian Social Union, 1889–1914', MLitt thesis, Oxford University, 1990, p. 29.

[44] Jane Garnett, 'Lux Mundi Essayists', *ODNB*.

[45] Jane Garnett, 'Hastings Rashdall and the Renewal of Christian Social Ethics, c.1880–1920', in Garnett and Matthew (eds.), *Revival and Religion since 1700*, pp. 297–316.

knowledge, they outlined their intention to include reports on British and foreign legislation, and summaries of periodical and other socio-economic literature from around the world, as well as giving space to a range of intellectual, ideological, and theological positions.

The CSU attempted to find a mean between individualism and socialism, interpreted very much in the terms of a Christian Aristotelianism—the relation between the part and the whole in pursuit of an agreed end. In an article in the *Economic Review* in 1895, Henry Scott Holland proclaimed that 'individuality, itself, is social to the core. It springs out of society... we are all Aristotelians here.'[46] This emphasis informed a broader resistance to all normatively dualistic ways of thinking—to the separation between the religious and the secular, the theoretical and the practical. J. M. Ludlow celebrated Maurice's significance in this respect, adducing as emblematic of his holistic vision the ways in which he embodied a union between feminine and masculine principles.[47] From innumerable angles, attempts over-sharply to distinguish the theoretical and deductive from the inductive and ethical in economic thinking were deplored. Whilst the Cambridge economist Alfred Marshall's influential neo-classical *Principles of Economics* (1890) had extended the range of economic utilities, the economic historian William Cunningham pointed out that this did not alter the fundamental problems raised by the methodology of classical political economy: if ethical considerations were to be simply included as one element in an economic law which stated how we assume people will act, this would be a disastrous accommodation.[48] Christian moral philosophy demanded the judgement of motive, whereas Marshall believed that the economist could only study mental states through their manifestations, and if they provided evenly balanced incentives to action, he treated them *prima facie* as for his purpose equal. Cunningham was to reiterate in 1910: 'The new Political Economy does not really leave room for the operation of Public Spirit or the Sense of Duty, because it professes to take account of them as utilities, and merges them all in the calculation of expediencies.' This led to theoretical imprecision, but also to a regrettable practical impact on the public mind.[49] Rejecting systems built on rights or contract, CSU members emphasized the reciprocal effect of the part upon the whole, and the sacrificial duties owed between constituent members of a community. Sacrifice, purpose, and personality were rooted in Christ's work within all aspects of social, economic, and political life. In the emphasis on bringing such points down from the level of abstraction and making them morally engaging for

[46] Henry S. Holland, 'The Church of God and Social Work', *Economic Review*, 5 (1895), p. 7.

[47] J. M. Ludlow, 'Some of the Christian Socialists of 1848 and the Following Years', *Economic Review*, 3 (1893): 490–4.

[48] William Cunningham, 'A Plea for Pure Theory', *Economic Review*, 2 (1892): 25–40.

[49] William Cunningham, *Socialism and Christianity* (London, 1910), p. 14.

individuals, these Anglican commentators saw a reinforcement and working through of a broader defence of their faith. The re-articulation of fundamental doctrines such as those of the Incarnation and the atonement in new terms was inherently interrelated to their engagement with the moral challenges of the socio-economic world. Here, too, there was a need to combat not just materialism and naturalism, but also the newer philosophical and psychological tendencies towards both absolute idealism and subjectivism. In every aspect of these debates, there was an emphasis on the rejection of extremes and absolutes, as being incompatible with the complexities of human experience.

The Pan-Anglican Congress of 1908 in London was the culmination of much Anglican work over the previous decades, and was in particular emblematic of the CSU's dedication to the wide diffusion of knowledge which should underpin informed debate and action, among clergy and laity.[50] It shared the CSU's commitment to the explicit intertwining of social responsibility, prayer and devotion, and to engaging the radical force of penitence. It was an extraordinary event, in preparation from 1902, involving 1,000 delegates, 5,000 members (and 1,500 supplementary members), in addition to which thousands of free tickets were issued for each of the daily and evening sessions; it was estimated that 46,000 people were involved in one way or another. There was extensive daily international press coverage, which was subsequently reprinted in book form.[51] Discussion in individual dioceses was encouraged years ahead of the Congress, sermons were given,[52] and papers written for consideration at it, which were published in cheap editions in 1908, each paper with an appended reading list.

> The success of a Congress depends not only on the expert knowledge and eloquence of the speakers, but also on the general level of intelligence among the audience. Every member of the Congress, by means of some previous study, should be in a position to appreciate the fundamental principles at the root of every Christian discussion.[53]

The rhetoric of the Congress invoked the desire to deepen 'a sense of corporate life throughout the world', and proclaimed its distinctiveness from purely clerical or bishops' conferences.[54] This was global Anglicanism writ large—a collective 'effort at self-realization'[55]—and the input of the lay constituency

[50] Cf. V. H. Stanton, 'Christianity and Social Duty', *Economic Review*, 3 (1893): 87–101.

[51] *Pan-Anglican Congress, 1908. Special Report of Proceedings, &c reprinted from The Times* (1908), 6d.

[52] A. B Mynors, E. G. Ingham, and J. H. Ellison, *Sermons on the Pan-Anglican Congress*, ed. W. H. Hunt (London, 1908).

[53] *Pan-Anglican Papers: Being Papers for consideration at the Pan-Anglican Congress, 1908* (London, 1908), back cover.

[54] *Pan-Anglican Congress*, 5 vols. (London, 1908), I, p. 1; H. J. Wilmot-Buxton, *Dreams and Realities: A Sermon on the Pan-Anglican Congress* (London, 1908), pp. 7–9.

[55] W. E. Gibraltar, 'The Pan-Anglican Congress', *Irish Church Quarterly*, 1 (1908): 274–90.

was strongly felt. At many points in the preliminary papers and in the published proceedings, stress was laid on the ways in which the Congress in itself embodied the principles of cosmopolitan energy and debate which it was concerned to promote. Ideas and moral purpose were reinforced through the very process of mutual engagement. In her paper on 'Sweating', the trade unionist and social reformer Gertrude Tuckwell welcomed the Congress as a solvent of dogmatism about the laws of political economy—a means of effecting the cross-cultural research which could refine economic understanding through an awareness of difference of circumstance and historical context. She cited specific examples of minimum wage policies from Australia and New Zealand. Her further point was that only through such serious work of comprehension of economic wrongs and needs would the Church fulfil its role as the Church of the people. This was more than just a plea for self-preservation: it was an articulation of what she asserted as the fundamental rationale of the Church as an institution.[56]

It was symbolically significant that Section A of the Congress was designated 'The Church and Human Society', and attracted particularly large numbers. The moment to confront this theme seemed opportune, in terms of manifested collective will, but more so by virtue of the scale of the challenge: Henry Scott Holland pointed to the acute delocalization, dehumanization, and abstraction of contemporary capitalism, and the need to get a grip on power dynamics in their practical specificity. The Congress offered a valuable context in which to share experience and information, and to practise some applied theology. The global reach of capitalism diffused responsibility, whilst also making it more difficult to grasp:[57] a bicycle-manufacturer could run a model factory, 'but has the rubber for his tyres been wrung by fire and sword from the natives of the Congo?'[58] In specific imperial contexts clear evidence could be presented of economic and social injustice, on which the Church was challenged to take a stand. The Revd Charles Freer Andrews, vice-principal of St Stephen's College, Delhi discussed the moral dimensions of Britain's economic relations with India in crisp fiscal particularities, and found them wanting. More broadly, he criticized the degree to which native Indian enterprise and leadership were being deterred. Civilization was being imposed from without rather than developed from within (as was successfully happening in Japan). He urged that the Church should raise 'no uncertain voice' against what he saw as the general Anglo-Indian intolerance of racial equality, and pointed out that a Church in India which aspired to be national would need to focus on understanding a whole new series of economic and moral issues

[56] G. Tuckwell, 'Sweating', *Pan-Anglican Congress*, II, Part II (Papers), SA 3(e), pp. 25–31.

[57] *Pan-Anglican Congress*, II, pp. 78–82.

[58] C. R. Buxton, 'Companies and Conscience: Justice and Dividends', *Pan-Anglican Congress*, II, Part II (Papers), SA 4(a), pp. 1–4.

raised by the *Swaraj* movement (the philosophy of self-rule through community developed by Gandhi).[59] Andrews combined something of the prophetic urgency of his Irvingite background with the theology of B. F. Westcott to ground his radical conception of fellowship and the sacrificial imperative of friendship.[60] In 1914 he was to renounce his priesthood and work alongside Gandhi and Tagore for the future of India.[61]

Other speakers suggested that just as Britain had much to learn from other countries in the 'new' world, those countries could potentially avoid some of the errors of the first industrial revolution, or build on already tested responses to socio-economic challenges. This could be expressed in different rhetorical styles, and with differential degrees of critical edge. In relation to housing policy, Alderman Thompson commented that:

> Here in England we have much to undo, as well as much to do. In Canada, Africa, and Australia, there are still greater opportunities that are given by new countries. Will the Church see to it that the new countries do not reproduce the evils of the old, but that as their towns grow up and their fields are tilled, the people shall be free at least from the grosser evils of industrial civilization?[62]

The language of uncorrupted territory drew on a long-standing religious debate about the impact of agricultural and industrial development on the natural environment, in which there had been significant cross-fertilization across the empire (partly through missionary channels) as well as between America and Australasia.[63] In her summing up of one of the women's meetings (preceding the main Congress) on 'The Child in relation to Home and State', the chair, the religious writer Mary Carus-Wilson, was sharper and more combative in tone. She observed that child labour was spreading with industrialization into India, Egypt, and East Africa, and that:

> As we are a Pan-Anglican Congress, we have got to tell our American sisters that the evils of child-labour in their crudest form are rampant in the Southern States of America, and that they have got to be dealt with as they have been dealt with in other countries long ago.

[59] C. F. Andrews, 'India and England: Some Moral Aspects of the Economic Relation', *Pan-Anglican Congress*, II, Part II (Papers), SA 5(c), pp. 51–8.

[60] B. F. Westcott, *Social Aspects of Christianity* (London, 1887); C. F. Andrews, *What I Owe to Christ* (London, 1932).

[61] Hugh Tinker, *The Ordeal of Love: C. F. Andrews and India* (London, 1979, 1998); Leela Gandhi, *Affective Communities: Anti-Colonial Thought, Fin-de-Siècle Radicalism, and the Politics of Friendship* (Durham, NC and London, 2004), pp. 13–18.

[62] W. Thompson, 'The Housing Problem', *Pan-Anglican Congress*, II, SA 3(i).

[63] James Beattie and John Stenhouse, 'Empire, Environment and Religion: God and the Natural World in Nineteenth-Century New Zealand', *Environment and History*, 13 (2007): 413–46; Leigh E. Schmidt, 'From Arbor Day to the Environmental Sabbath: Nature, Liturgy and American Protestantism', *Harvard Theological Review*, 84 (1991): 299–323.

Quick to guard against complacency at home, she concluded by emphasizing that reform was still required in many aspects of English life.[64] Examples of Anglican failings and hypocrisies were indeed outlined in a variety of contexts, from neglect of Aboriginal customs in Australia to the iniquities of Britain's continued pursuit of the opium trade with China.[65] In this, as in other areas of comparative analysis, uncomfortable issues were opened up, but the premise of the Congress was to provide such discursive potential, in the hope that more effective Anglican positions could be arrived at.

Both the specific role of women and the gender assumptions of the Church were exposed as controversial in the very decision to hold a series of separate women's meetings. It was emphasized that in doing so the intention was not to contravene the agreed principle that the main proceedings were open and relevant to all, but to open up a forum for discussion in which more women could join. Louise Creighton, the chair, was at various points trenchant in her affirmation that men's and women's questions were indivisible, whilst criticizing the Church for its privileging of men's roles in mission work, at home and abroad: recognition of the role of highly educated women in the Church should provide a model for a state more built on gender equality. She made a subtle and culturally sensitive point in underlining how serious were the consequences of such failure, given the challenge of enabling Eastern women to 'keep the best gifts of her social system, and yet attain to the full liberty of a Christian woman'. This was not just about missionary effectiveness, but about wider social responsibility. Analogously, the predominant emphasis of the women's meetings was on the ways in which attention to domestic values as well as domestic responsibilities should underpin a broader social and mental shift of perspective, and on the role of the Church in influencing public opinion in this direction. Creighton tactfully but firmly reproached the bishop of Missouri for a conservative commendation of women's role in the family. Seconded by William Temple, she underscored that the family was neither an end in itself nor an uncomplicated good, but both a microcosm of, and metaphor for, the working out of wider human interrelationships.[66] In countless such ways, debates were opened up which had significant potential for generating moral energy.

In some respects, the 1908 Congress represented a high point of intellectual and organizational sophistication in the Anglican Communion's engagement with its social and economic role. Although distinctions of emphasis and

[64] Mrs Ashley Carus-Wilson in *Report of the Women's Meetings held in connection with the Pan-Anglican Congress of 1908* (London, 1908), p. 19.

[65] *Pan-Anglican Papers*, I; *Pan-Anglican Congress*, V, pp. 103–10.

[66] L. Creighton, 'The Ministry of Women. Its Relation at the Present Time to Work Done by Men', *Pan-Anglican Congress*, IV, Part II (Papers), SC 3(a), pp. 1–7; Creighton, 'Women's Work for the Church and for the State', *Papers for Consideration*, no. 7; *Report of the Women's Meetings*, pp. 98–108.

allegiance were apparent in its debates, it could still draw on a propitious ideological fluidity around the turn of the century. From the 1880s to around 1900 socialism constituted a wide ethical field within which Christians could claim a critical and constructive voice. The languages of anarchism, socialism, feminism, liberalism, individualism, and collectivism could all intersect and dovetail with Christian theological frameworks.[67] Rigidities were increasingly to develop, however, in particular forms in different countries, over whether the Church should align itself with particular political parties or standpoints on the role of the state. Tensions over these concerns, especially provoked by Temple,[68] split the CSU in Britain from 1908 and contributed to its post-war decision, in a transformed international and ideological context, to merge with the more evangelical and overtly collectivist Industrial Christian Fellowship. But whilst the organizational forms changed, the impetus to organize to debate Christian social and economic ethics did not. The discipline of economics was to develop through most of the twentieth century on a secular and increasingly technical basis, limiting formal scope for the sorts of creative methodological holism aspired to by so many nineteenth- and early twentieth-century Anglicans. But in a wider intellectual history of the interstices between theory and practice, many Anglicans, as individuals, groups, and institutional Churches, continued to concur with the conviction that 'it was mere muddle-headedness to talk about confusing economics with ethics ... economics could never give practical advice without making assumptions which fell within the region of the Christian religion'.[69]

SELECT BIBLIOGRAPHY

Bateman, Bradley and H. Spencer Bauzhaf, 'Keeping Faith, Losing Faith: An Introduction', *History of Political Economy*, 40 (2008): 1–20.

Boylan, Thomas A. and Timothy P. Foley, *Political Economy and Colonial Ireland: The Propagation and Ideological Function of Economic Discourse in the Nineteenth Century* (London, 1992).

Bradizza, Luigi, *Richard T. Ely's Critique of Capitalism* (New York, 2013).

Dixon, Thomas, *The Invention of Altruism: Making Moral Meanings in Victorian Britain* (Oxford, 2008).

Eckbert, A. A., 'The Social Thought of the Christian Social Union, 1889–1914', MLitt thesis, Oxford University, 1990.

67 Susan Hinely, 'Charlotte Wilson, the "Woman Question", and the Meanings of Anarchist Socialism in Late-Victorian Radicalism', *International Review of Social History*, 57 (2012): 3–36.

68 William Temple, 'The Church and the Labour Party', *Economic Review*, 18 (1908): 190–201; Garnett, 'Hastings Rashdall and the Renewal of Christian Social Ethics', pp. 310–11.

69 William Temple, *Pan-Anglican Congress*, II, p. 100.

Garnett, Jane, 'Aspects of the Relationship between Protestant Ethics and Economic Activity in mid-Victorian England', PhD thesis, Oxford University, 1986.

Garnett, Jane, 'Commercial Ethics: A Victorian Perspective on the Practice of Theory', in Christopher Cowton and Roger Crisp (eds.), *Business Ethics: The Practice of Theory* (Oxford, 1998), pp. 117–38.

Garnett, Jane, 'Evangelicalism and Business in Mid-Victorian Britain', in John Wolffe (ed.), *Evangelical Faith and Public Zeal: Evangelicals and Society in Britain 1780–1980* (London, 1995), pp. 59–80.

Hilton, Boyd, *The Age of Atonement: The Influence of Evangelicalism on Social and Economic Thought, 1795–1865* (Oxford, 1988).

Phillips, Paul T., *A Kingdom on Earth: Anglo-American Social Christianity, 1880–1940* (University Park, PA, 1996).

Searle, G. R., *Morality and the Market in Victorian Britain* (Oxford, 1998).

Skinner, S. A., *Tractarians and the 'Condition of England': The Social and Political Thought of the Oxford Movement* (Oxford, 2004).

Thompson, David M., 'The Christian Socialist Revival in Britain: A Reappraisal', in Jane Garnett and Colin Matthew (eds.), *Revival and Religion since 1700* (London, 1993), pp. 273–95.

Index

Printed and bound by CPI Group (UK) Ltd, Croydon, CR0 4YY